Also by Bruce Allen Murphy

Fortas: The Rise and Ruin of a Supreme Court Justice

The Brandeis/Frankfurter Connection:
The Secret Political Activities of Two Supreme Court Justices

Approaching Democracy (with Larry Berman)

Portraits of American Politics (editor)

WILD BILL

WILD BILL

THE LEGEND AND LIFE OF
WILLIAM O. DOUGLAS

Bruce Allen Murphy

Random House
New York

RANDOM HOUSE and colophon are registered trademarks of
Random House, Inc.

Grateful acknowledgment is made to the following for
permission to reprint previously published material:
Newsweek: response to a reader letter entitled "Douglas' 6 Cents," from the
April 10, 1939, issue of *Newsweek.* Copyright © 1939 by Newsweek, Inc.
All rights reserved. Reprinted by permission.
Yakima Herald: editorial from the August 9, 1937, issue of the
Yakima Daily Republic. Reprinted by permission of the *Yakima Herald,*
successor in interest to the *Yakima Daily Republic.*

Library of Congress Cataloging-in-Publication Data
Murphy, Bruce Allen.
Wild Bill : the legend and life of William O. Douglas / Bruce Allen Murphy.
p.   cm.
Includes bibliographical references and index.
ISBN 0-394-57628-4 (alk. paper)
1. Douglas, William O. (William Orville).   2. Judges—United States—Biography.
I. Title.
KF8745.D6 M87 2003
347.73'2634—dc21
[B]   2003023114

Printed in the United States of America on acid-free paper
Random House website address: www.atrandom.com

2   4   6   8   9   7   5   3

First Edition

BOOK DESIGN BY MERCEDES EVERETT

For Carol, Emily, and Geoff

"The Greatest Journey I Have Made Has Been with You."
— William O. Douglas, 1975

and

For My Mother and Mother-In-Law

Mrs. Jean H. Coe and Mrs. Patricia G. Wright

And the Memory of

Alfred E. Coe and Harold M. Wright

William O. Douglas was the oddest duck to ever serve
on the United States Supreme Court.

—*Raoul Berger*

CONTENTS

PROLOGUE

THE LEGEND OF GOOSE PRAIRIE

He sure didn't look like a Supreme Court Justice. Standing just over six feet tall, rail thin, topped with a shock of long white hair, he possessed penetratingly crystal-clear blue eyes that could, depending on his mood, either twinkle impishly in amusement or chill your blood with an unblinking stare, William O. Douglas had traded in his black judicial gown for the rugged mountain outfit he much preferred: a crushed sheepherder's hat with a cigarette hole burned in one side, a fraying flannel shirt, his favorite red-and-black-checked lumberman's jacket, and an old pair of Levi's 505 jeans with the zipper so worn that it no longer held. As he rode, his horse weighed down by two saddlebags filled with liquor bottles, one pant leg was stuffed inside one of his scuffed cowboy boots, while the other hung outside.

Douglas was dressed this way in August 1970 for one of his favorite adventures: a ten-day pack trip deep into the Hindoo region of the breathtaking Cascade Mountains. He and his young wife, Cathy, and ten of their friends from around the country were being led on the trip by Kay Kershaw and Isabelle Lynn, the proprietors of the Double K dude ranch in tiny Goose Prairie, Washington. With its total population of eight people, and the nearest phones being two dilapidated public booths in the parking lot of the Whistlin' Jack's Motel, some seventeen miles away, Goose Prairie was one of the last true frontiers in America. But even it was well behind the group now. And, with the crisp smell of the cool pine-scented air, not to mention the glorious changing of the leaves, the mountain trail on which they were riding was so lovely and so quiet in its total natural isolation that it literally took their breath away.

On such pack trips continual motion is the order of the day, yet from time to time Douglas, without warning, simply dismounted and stopped the procession of horses and riders. Moving to the side of the narrow trail, he would pick a flower, ask its name of his guides, stuff it into a plastic bag taken from his pocket, and scribble a few words into the little spiral notebook that he carried in his back pocket on such occasions. Everyone forgave Douglas this practice because of their love and admiration for him.

For hours they had ridden on the switchback paths that were carved in zigzagging patterns up the mountains. Less than a yard in width and often dropping off in sheer cliffs below, they were the only paths in the region. Finally, with dusk about to fall the group stopped by a gently rolling stream to camp for the night. It would be, past experience indicated, another night of good talk, delicious campfire food, and more of the old jurist's captivating autobiographical stories.

But soon they would all understand that this night was not like the others. For when Dagmar Hamilton, Douglas's literary assistant, peered off to enjoy the sun dipping behind the nearby peaks, she could not believe her eyes. Across the deep, green valley, on the mountain where they had just been riding, she saw three figures walking in a row along the path. Actually, they seemed to her to be marching, much as if they were in a parade. It was so rare to see other human beings so many miles into the hills that she felt compelled to watch as the three men stepped perfectly in unison, back and forth along the trails.

As the figures got closer and closer, Hamilton noticed something very unusual about them. They all were dressed not in the old blue jeans and comfortable hiking boots favored by mountain travelers but rather in fancy business suits and leather dress shoes. To be able to navigate the gravel- and rock-strewn trails in such footwear was a feat worthy of attention. As Hamilton studied the three moving figures further, though, she noticed something even more unusual about them. Each of the men was holding a briefcase!

When she pointed out the astonishing sight to the other members of the party, all but one of them turned to watch in astonishment—all of them, that is, except for William O. Douglas. His blue eyes turned instantaneously from glittering merriment to cold fury. He knew who the men were—didn't know them personally, but he knew why they were coming and whom they were seeking. So he slowly pulled up the collar on his jacket, tugged his cap down over his eyes, and started walking away from the group. "Don't tell 'em I'm here," he growled to the Double K gals as he passed them. "Tell 'em I'm the wrangler, and don't give 'em anything to drink. And whatever you do, don't let 'em sleep here."

"I'm not going to give them anything to drink," responded Kay Kershaw sharply. "And unless you give them your sleeping bag, I'm not going to give them any place to sleep either."

Satisfied with the response, the old man silently nodded, retreated across the small creek, and hid behind a large pine tree.

Unaware of this exchange, the other campers sat down and began preparing their cocktail hour while they waited for the visitors to arrive and the curious drama to unfold. When the three men in suits approached the camp, Kay Kershaw at first made like she did not even see them. When that did not work, she finally grunted in their direction.

"We are looking for Justice William O. Douglas of the United States Supreme Court," announced the lead figure in a stentorian tone.

The tiny but still fiercely imposing Kershaw ceremoniously folded her arms across her chest, glared at the man, and said sharply that there was no Justice Douglas in her party.

"We are attorneys here to deliver an emergency appeal," the man continued, acting as though he had not noticed her. They had tried to find the Justice in Goose Prairie, he added, but they were told by the folks at the small general store there that he was on this pack trip. So they bought a trail map, got directions, and began hiking. When they heard this, the campers in the pack trip glanced at the horses that had brought them this far and tried not entirely successfully to keep from laughing out loud.

Finally, when the visiting attorneys made very clear that they were not leaving, the white-haired old man in the lumberman's jacket sauntered across the creek, raised his cap above his eyes with his index finger, and said simply, "I'm Douglas. What can I do for you?"

The three lawyers who had brushed off Kershaw immediately froze in awe when they saw that he was telling the truth. Here *he* was before them, appearing bigger than life: Justice William O. Douglas, the living legend on the Supreme Court. Here was the last of the New Dealers, the man who had cleaned up Wall Street during the New Deal, had played poker with Franklin D. Roosevelt, and had served on the Supreme Court since the age of forty. Here, too, was the man who had tried to save the Rosenbergs, created a constitutional right of privacy, protected the environment, and even single-handedly tried to stop men from being shipped to the Vietnam War from his seat on the Bench. Even more than the legendary Oliver Wendell Holmes, Douglas had become the true "Great Dissenter," often representing the last vestige of hope for the poor, the oppressed, and the downtrodden.

William O. Douglas, the lawyers knew, was by then well on his way to setting the Supreme Court record for most years served, most opinions issued, most dissents, and most solo dissents. These men cared little at this moment for Douglas's other, less distinguished, records: while serving in an institution of which no members had ever been divorced, he had ended three marriages, taken four wives (the last two of whom were several decades younger than he), and was now facing impeachment charges for a record fourth time.

Without any further preliminaries, the lawyers got down to business: handing a sheaf of papers to Douglas, taking out a legal-sized file folder, and appropriating a tree stump for a podium. While Douglas sat down on a large rock to read the documents, the campers realized in amazement that they were about to see, in these isolated woods, an official appeal to the U.S. Supreme Court.

They were representing a group of Vietnam War protesters, the three attorneys explained. Their clients had picketed the national convention of the Veterans of Foreign Wars in Portland, Oregon, in defiance of a local judge's injunction, and summarily been arrested, though it was a peaceful protest, and no laws had been violated. The lawyers then explained that they had sought a temporary restraining order to keep the protesters out of jail, had been blocked by the lower federal courts, and were now making an emergency appeal to the Supreme Court. Since the Court was not in session for the summer, they were making an individual appeal to Douglas because he was the supervisory Justice of the Ninth Judicial Circuit. And even if fortune had not thus smiled on them, Douglas would have been their first choice.

While the lawyers argued their case, the campers began cooking their steaks and refilling their glasses. As they did, the hungry and thirsty men in dusty and crumpled suits began looking longingly at the food and drink.

Upon finishing their argument, the three men waited for the ruling, which they expected would take the Justice about a minute to formulate. It was well known that he hated the Vietnam War only slightly more than he hated President Richard Nixon, who was then personally trying to remove him from the Bench.

But what the men did not understand was that Douglas hated one thing even more than the war: being interrupted in his natural sanctuary.

For the first time since the argument had begun, Douglas raised his eyes from the petition and peered icily at the three men for an overly long moment before saying firmly, "I will take your petition and consider it overnight."

"Overnight!" cried the panicked lawyers in unison. With no bedrolls in their briefcases, this meant that they were going to have to hike back out of the mountains by the light of the moon, find their car, and drive back to Whistlin' Jack's, only to have to retrace their steps the next day.

"Yes," explained Douglas, "I'm going to have to think about it. If you want an answer you will have to come back in the morning. Then you will have your answer. That's the best I can do."

Appearing "sadder than you can imagine any three human beings looking," recalled Dag Hamilton, the three men in suits knew that there was no way to change William O. Douglas's mind. So they slowly picked up their briefcases. But before leaving, one of them decided to make one final appeal. "Do you suppose we could have something to drink?" he asked Kay Kershaw, coveting the rows of liquor bottles and canteens strewn around the roaring campfire.

In making the request, the tenderfoots failed to understand that in the mountains one ate and drank only what he or she personally carried. Peering at the three men without cracking a smile, the mountain lady handed one of the men a small tin cup, pointed in the direction of the creek, and said, "Help yourself." With that, the three lawyers had their branch water, without bourbon.

The next morning, after Douglas had packed up his saddlebags, he took out his small spiral notebook and pencil, scribbled something, tore the page out, and placed it under a rock on the tree stump where the three men had argued their case. That done, everyone packed up their gear and mounted their horses to ride off to the next campsite.

Hours later, the three lawyers returned to the same spot, somewhat more appropriately dressed and fully expecting to see the group and hear Douglas's pronouncement in their favor. When they arrived, though, all they found was the piece of lined paper fluttering in the breeze. It read, simply, "DENIED. WM. O. DOUGLAS, AJ."

When the residents of Goose Prairie and the legal community in Yakima heard this tale, knowing how much the Justice loved his privacy in the mountains, they decided that the intruders had gotten off easy. But while this appeal was not successful, and word of his ill treatment of the attorneys spread, desperate and adventurous attorneys kept on coming to the Cascades in search of help because over the years William O. Douglas had proved to be the one person who could and did make a real difference in the American judicial system.

PART ONE

YOUNG MAN DOUGLAS

JULIA'S "TREASURE"

With a good education, you can always be free.

—*Julia Bickford Fisk Douglas*

He arrived at Columbia Law School smelling of sheep, carrying nothing but a battered suitcase and the burden of his mother's ambition that he should become president of the United States. With his unruly sandy-blond hair and dirty, rumpled clothes, Orville Douglas felt in mid-September 1922 a lot less like the valedictorian of North Yakima High School and a Phi Beta Kappa graduate from Whitman College and a lot more like one of the sheep he had tended on a train part of the way cross-country.

Now, outside of the Beta Theta Pi fraternity house, Douglas knew that he would have to change everything about himself—even his name—to put all of the ghosts of Yakima, Washington, behind him. But Julia Fisk Douglas had raised her eldest son to meet such challenges.

Julia had named her son William Orville to bring honor to the two men whom she most admired: Orville Fisk, the father she adored, and the Reverend William Douglas, the husband she deified. Raised on his mother's stories about these patriarchs, young Orville grew up believing that his very name destined him for greatness. His grandfather, he believed, had served with distinction as a member of the Union forces in the Civil War. He thought that his father had been a devoted family man. Only Julia knew that the truth was far different—and that Orville's life thus far, filled with obstacles and disappointments, had closely mirrored the lives of the men whose names he bore.

A New England farmer, like his father before him, Orville Fisk had stood five feet nine inches tall, with an unruly tuft of light hair, a very pale complexion, and compellingly clear blue eyes. In 1861, at the age of twenty-four, he married Salome Bickford Richardson, a widowed mother of two who was six years his senior, and fully expected that the rest of his days would be spent tilling the earth. Like so many of his peers, though, when the government called for assistance in quelling the rebellion in the South, Orville enlisted for three years. On October 4, 1861, he became a private in Company D of the Sixth Regiment of the Vermont Volunteers and was mustered into the army in Montpelier eleven days later.

But while his regiment trained, Orville quickly discovered that military life did not suit him. By February of the following year he chose to follow his own path, checking himself in and out of a series of military hospitals over the next several months without his commander's permission, all the while complaining of diarrhea and stomach pains. The precise nature of Orville's ailment was never fully diagnosed. Only when his exhausted unit returned on August 9 from the front for a leave at Fort Monroe, Virginia, did he feel well enough to rejoin them. Just under a month later, however, as the men of the Sixth Vermont marched off toward South Mountain in Maryland, Orville Fisk disappeared once again. And so, with his comrades on the verge of fighting in the bloody battles at Crampton's Gap and Antietam, on September 7, 1862, Private Fisk was listed on the company muster rolls first as being "absent without leave" and a month later as a deserter—charged also with stealing his gun and equipment.

Orville convalesced for two months in the General Hospital in Steuart's Mansion in Baltimore before moving to the Army General Hospital in York, Pennsylvania, where he was eventually taken into custody on February 7, 1863, and relieved of his gun and equipment. Orville was then put on a train to Brattleboro, Vermont, to face a court-martial. While all of the military's records indicated that he had been a deserter since September 7, 1862, and little more than a wandering hospital patient prior to that, Orville was somehow able to persuade the military authorities to send him to a convalescent hospital at Fort Wood on Bedloe's Island in New York. There he remained until May 25, 1863.

Finally, in June 1863, the itinerant private, now listed on the muster rolls as being "gained from desertion," rejoined his regiment for active military service. But his time with the regiment near and at Gettysburg, at Funkstown, Maryland, and in various locations in Virginia did not change his mind about the desirability of military service. In March 1864, after reenlisting for another three years as a "veteran volunteer"— entitling him to receive a month's pay in advance, be promised a bounty of $402 (sixty dollars of which would be paid immediately), and get a month's furlough home—Orville left for Glover, Vermont, and was never seen by his regiment again.

Knowing that the Union bounty hunters would be looking for him, Orville and his wife packed up all their belongings and traveled thirty miles, past the Canadian border to the tiny township of Bolton Centre in Brome County, Quebec. There, Orville used his reenlistment money and Salome's savings to pay one hundred dollars for forty acres of land from Elbridge L. Loyal on June 27, 1864. While his old army comrades were fighting in such places as Ream's Station, Virginia, Charles Town, West Virginia, and Opequon, Virginia, Orville and Salome built a new home and began farming in Canada. And six months later, in December 1864, with the men of the Sixth Vermont welcoming a respite from the shooting in their winter camp south of Petersburg, Virginia, the Fisks were welcoming their first child, Alice. Over the next four years, they would be blessed with two other children, May and Walter.

After nearly eight years of life in Canada, in the spring of 1872 Orville and the again-pregnant Salome decided that it would be safe to return to the United States, but only if they moved to the frontier state of Minnesota. Salome's nephew, E. A. Bickford of Glover, Vermont, had already been lured to the area by the promise under the Homestead Act of 1862 of eighty acres of free land to anyone who would live on and "improve" it for at least five years. Ten years later, the Fisks obtained full ownership of their land in the tiny community of Maine, Minnesota, just eighteen miles northeast of the growing city of Fergus Falls.

Soon after their arrival, tiny twin girls, Julia and Jennie, were born to the Fisk family on June 24, 1872. Julia came to be nicknamed Mite because she was so small that she had to be carried around for months on a pillow and was not able to walk until after her third birthday. Only through exercise and sheer force of will was she eventually able to overcome her physical inadequacy and run "like a deer."

While Salome raised the children, including her youngest son, Milo, who was born in 1874, and supported the family by tilling the wheat fields, milking the cows, tending the vegetables, and cutting the firewood, the perpetually sickly Orville went into politics, winning election year after year as the town clerk. Besides keeping the small town's modest records, Orville spent his time sitting on a rocking chair on the porch of the town hall, telling harrowing stories of his "distinguished" military service during the war. But even this limited amount of activity proved to be too rigorous for Orville, as he came down with pneumonia and died at age forty-eight on May 15, 1885. The local

paper hailed Orville in its obituary as one of the town's "most prominent citizens" who "took an active and brave part" in the Civil War.

Despite the undistinguished nature of her husband's military service,
Salome came to believe that as a veteran's widow she had a government
pension coming to her. So she hired Washington attorney P. J. Lockwood to file for one on May 18, 1888. Despite Salome's diligent two-
year effort gathering supportive affidavits, her petition was denied
when the Pension Board discovered that her husband had deserted the
army not once but twice.

Not satisfied with this response, in December 1888 Salome instructed her attorney to seek a removal of the desertion charge from
her husband's record in order to reestablish her eligibility for a pension. She argued that her husband had left his post because he "had
been sick a great deal, was in several hospitals, the last one was Brattleboro, Vt. Was sick after he came home his mother was sick and on
account of his own health and his mother's he never went back he was
the only child of a widowed mother whose mind was not right" [sic].
Not only did Salome fail to mention their move to Canada during the
war, she also failed to mention that Orville's sister Emma had been
able to care for their mother. Even without these facts, though, the
two-man appellate panel in the army adjutant general's office denied
her petition.

While for most people this would have been the end of the issue,
such was not the case for the determined Salome Fisk. She commissioned the building of a grand new farmhouse. By the time the masons
had finished what was described as "one of the best houses in town,"
all the neighbors marveled at what a large pension Orville must have
received, providing so well for his family even after his death.

But that did not mean success would be enjoyed by all their children. The oldest son, Walter, would one day inherit the family homestead, so Julia and her sisters each began to chart different courses for
their lives. All of them decided to pursue one of the few options open
to them: a teaching career. Twenty-one Maine residents, including all
the Fisk girls, took the state teacher's exam on March 7, 1889, in order
to gain admission to the state-run institute for teachers. A passing
grade there would result in the issuance of a teacher's certificate and
eventually a job.

But on October 24, when the *Fergus Falls Weekly Journal* proudly
listed the dozens of people who had passed the exam, Julia's was the
only Fisk name not among them. She did not then realize that her life
had taken a fateful turn.

While her sisters had promising futures, unless she married, Julia's life was now tied to the family farm. Years later, Julia would repeatedly tell her children, "With a good education you can always be free." But her children never learned of her own personal experience. While she felt trapped by circumstances beyond her control, the same, she vowed, would not be true for her children.

Just three days after her sisters left for the institute, their younger brother, Milo, then just fifteen years old, began complaining of acute stomach pain accompanied by a high fever and nausea. In a matter of days, the young lad died of peritonitis, a severe inflammation of the abdominal lining.

The loss of her adored little brother deeply affected the devoutly religious Julia. This was God's will, she said, and Milo was dead because either he or someone close to him had sinned. As a result of this experience, and perhaps also her father's history, Julia developed an intense fear of stomach troubles. By the middle of April 1890, when her three sisters had finished their training and left for new teaching jobs in the townships of Gorman, Leaf Lake, and Friberg, Julia seemed destined to live out the remainder of her life supported by the charity of her mother and elder brother.

Julia decided she would develop a life of her own by teaching herself to play the organ. While this did not lead to a paying job, late in the fall of 1894 it brought her to the attention of the most eligible bachelor in town: the new Presbyterian home missionary, William Douglas.

Standing more than six feet tall, this slender, auburn-haired, handsome man possessed startlingly clear blue eyes, like Julia's father's, and a soothing baritone voice. A well-groomed full mustache made William look older and more serious than his thirty-seven years. In time, Julia would learn that thus far his life had been no more successful than her father's military career. He had already pursued several professions in his native Nova Scotia: shoe merchant, traveling evangelical choir member, and, when his throat became inflamed from overuse, dry-goods salesman and part-time minister. After hearing about the great financial opportunities available in California, in early 1894 William had traveled across the continent and invested all his life savings in a retail business opportunity in the tiny town of Shandon, some two hundred miles south of San Francisco. In a matter of weeks, however, the new business failed, leaving him with only enough money for a train trip back home.

Taking this as a signal from God that retail trade was not his calling, William decided to turn permanently to the business of saving souls. He had heard of a newly established divinity school in Chicago, the Bible

Institute of the Chicago Evangelization Society (later the Moody Bible Institute), which had been founded by evangelist Dwight L. Moody, a former shoe salesman like himself. This school was designed to train "gapmen," lay evangelists who filled the gap between the lay world and the ministry, aiding those who had studied in seminary.

Despite his lack of training and financial resources, William successfully made his application and began his studies in the spring of 1894. Just one month later, though, he was forced to leave the school abruptly because of a lack of funds. What remained of Douglas's financial stake now allowed him only to complete the journey back to Nova Scotia.

To their surprise and delight, when members of the First Presbyterian Church in Maine, Minnesota, acting on the advice of a nearby minister who had met Douglas in Nova Scotia, contacted him in early September asking if he would like to replace their departing minister and serve other churches in the region as well, with no other job prospects in hand, Douglas said that he could come immediately. So for the fourth time that year, William Douglas packed his meager belongings and boarded a train, seeking his new destiny.

When Douglas arrived in Maine, he began his service as the "stated supply" local evangelist, meaning that he could preach but not serve communion. However, his frail health would not even permit him to do that much. As soon as William arrived in Fergus Falls, he was laid up until late October while his throat recovered from the trip. And after he was able to begin his new job, William became so debilitated after just two weeks of work that he was forced to return to Dr. McLean's in Fergus Falls for more treatment. Not until the end of November did the doctor pronounce Douglas fit enough to return to work, but he warned that Douglas's throat was so weak that he should preach only once a day. For a minister whose duties now extended over several congregations, Douglas knew that this would be impossible.

When he finally began his full-time preaching duties, the pleasant new minister began to take an interest in the church's organist. By this time, Julia Fisk had developed into an attractive woman, standing about five feet four inches, with reddish-brown hair framing her schoolmarm-like face. When William eventually proposed marriage, Julia quickly accepted, unconcerned by the fifteen years that separated them in age. Shortly after Julia and William quietly eloped on April 13, 1896, William's health began to fail him again, and it was now his wife's duty to care for him.

Since for William his far-flung church duties always came first, with each passing week Julia found herself more and more abandoned. A typical Sunday began with an early service in Maine followed by a long buggy ride, often through blizzards so bad that passing buggy-riders could not see each other, torrential rains, or scorching heat, to the other nearby towns for other services. Should there be a marriage, a funeral, a counseling session, or some other function on the week-days in between, regardless of the challenges faced by buggy-riders in bad weather, William's presence was required there as well.

Beyond dealing with this sense of abandonment, Julia, like her mother, was required to be strong. In late 1896, when Julia was preg-nant and bedridden, William, rather than ministering to his wife's needs, left that task to his parishioners as he continued on his ministe-rial rounds. Likewise, on April 17, 1897, after the ordeal of the delivery of their first child, a tiny girl whom they named Martha, the incapaci-tated minister's wife was once more left to the care of her friends. Only when the reverend himself became quite ill five weeks later, with his eyes so weak that he was unable to read, did he pause in his duties. Needing what the local newspaper reported as "a perfect rest from study," he and Julia's cousin, E. A. Bickford, immediately left on vaca-tion to join James Richardson, Salome's son from her first marriage, in North Yakima, Washington. While the three men went "into the mountains to rest, hunt, and have a good time" for ten weeks, the still bedridden Julia and their newborn daughter were left in the care of a midwife at the parsonage.

For Julia, the period was not a pleasant one. Three weeks after Wil-liam left, a thunderstorm swept through Maine, and a powerful light-ning bolt struck the steeple of the church. The electrical surge raced the length of the church roof, tearing away the wainscoting and wall plaster and starting a small fire in a corner of the building. With her husband half a continent away, the impact on the frightened, lonely woman with a baby daughter was considerable. Then, a month later, illness struck the Douglas household as both Martha and Julia caught the measles. With the manse now quarantined and no one able to come to help her, the townspeople were reassured by the local news-paper report that the reverend would return home in a few days to care for his ailing family. Only later did they learn that instead he had chosen to extend his trip to attend a religious convention in San Fran-cisco and returned only after both his wife and daughter were fully re-covered.

Life for the Douglas family seemed to turn a corner in 1898 when the townspeople decided to reward Reverend Douglas for his faithful service by installing him as the permanent minister for their church and the one in nearby Maplewood. For Julia, though, her husband's new status meant no change in her own. Just as she was giving birth to their first son, William Orville, on Sunday, October 16, 1898, William left to preach in Maplewood.

The sandy-haired infant with the clear blue eyes would be called Orville to distinguish him from his father. Once more, the trauma of the birth sent Julia to her bed, where she was unable even to sit up for six weeks. Relays of neighbors came in to help her while Reverend Douglas split his time between continuing his church duties and visiting a battery of local doctors while complaining of a variety of his own assorted ailments. Only when Julia had to fill her husband's Christmas church duties because he had become so sickly that he was completely bedridden with what the paper described as "some kind of stomach trouble" did she finally leave the house. Thereafter, for the Douglases, the first twenty-one months of their new son's life were filled with illness, especially eye problems and undiagnosable stomach ailments, for the reverend and hard work for his dutiful wife, who was saddled with raising both their family and helping to lead their church.

By mid-July 1900, Reverend Douglas was so "broken down in health" that, after stomach surgery, he was ordered by the doctor to his bed for several weeks. In early August, with the temperature soaring to 104 degrees in the shade and sickness of all types spreading throughout the county, the reverend departed by himself on another month-long vacation. Abandoned once again, Julia immediately relocated her family to Salome's farm. This time, though, a wave of the deadly typhoid fever struck Maine during the week of August 26, terrifying the woman who knew that it could result in peritonitis, which had killed her brother Milo.

Soon the papers reported that little Orville Douglas was "very ill." While the precise nature of Orville's illness was not described, readers were reassured that Reverend Douglas was being summoned to return to help his wife. In fact, just as in the previous year, Reverend Douglas decided not to return until his planned vacation had concluded.

For a time, the twenty-two-month-old infant rallied, but any early optimism was misplaced. By the time Reverend Douglas finally returned, Orville had suffered such a severe relapse, running a high fever, that he had not spoken a word for several days. Despite his son's critical condition, the reverend immediately departed again to preach at the Maplewood church, leaving family friend Mettie Jenne to help Julia, who remained at her mother's farm. "Reverend Douglas's son Orvil [sic] is still very sick," reported *Wheelock's Weekly* on September 13. "He has not spoken for ten days. The doctor has hopes of his recovery." The doctor from nearby Battle Lake, H. C. Leonard, prescribed that food be given only by the teaspoon and that warm saltwater massages be given for fifteen minutes every two hours. He was likely hoping to get the blood flowing to the limbs to help prevent atrophy. "[Mother] told me 'I only had my clothes off to change them. For six weeks I rubbed his arms and his legs in salt water day and night,'" recalled Douglas's sister, Martha, years later.

It seemed to Julia that she was the only person in the world interested in saving her little boy. Salome Fisk journeyed to Minneapolis with her son Walter to bring home Elmer Richardson, another son from her first marriage, who visited for a month. After they returned, relatives and neighbors came to the house to meet the distant visitor in the front parlor. Meanwhile, a sleepless and frazzled Julia labored mightily in the back bedroom, massaging her son's limbs vigorously and praying fervently for his recovery.

But nothing she did had any effect. By the end of September, little Orville had become so ill that Reverend Douglas, for the first time in his married life, interrupted his religious duties to tend to his family. Martha later told her brother: "I remember Father walking the floor with you and you were so hungry, you'd chew your fists. And they would feed you only a few teaspoons full at a time." But despite these efforts, on September 27 *Wheelock's Weekly* reported ominously, "A doctor spent three nights last week with Reverend Douglas, working for the life of his boy. The task seems nearly hopeless."

By early October, the *Fergus Falls Weekly Journal* prepared the Maine religious community for the worst: "Orvill[e], the little son of Reverend Douglass [*sic*], who has been very ill, is no better and his recovery is doubtful." *Wheelock's Weekly* added somber news indeed for those who knew of their minister's devotion to duty: "Reverend Douglas will not preach again until his little boy is better."

Then, without warning, just a week later, the newspapers reported that while waves of typhoid fever ravaged all of the communities in the Otter Tail County region, a miracle had occurred in the Douglas household. "Reverend Douglas's boy is very much better and is now considered out of danger," reported *Wheelock's Weekly*. The *Fergus Falls Weekly Journal* added that the little boy had "sufficiently recovered from his long illness to be removed from Mrs. Fisk's to his home at the parsonage." For the little boy's first meal following his recovery, Julia made a huge pot of baked beans, which he ate with great relish. Just one week after his recovery, little Orville was well enough to celebrate his second birthday with a party in his own home.

Having already lost her father and a brother to intestinal ailments, not to mention the unrelenting stomach difficulties of her husband, the sudden recovery of her little "Treasure," as the family now called him, had a profound impact on Julia Fisk Douglas. Only *her* constant massages and *her* prayers, she told her children over and over, had saved the young boy. God had spared her tiny Orville for some noble purpose, she decided, and now it was her job to help him fulfill that heavenly destiny: He was to become president of the United States. Julia vowed that she would make that possible by protecting him from harm for the rest of her life.

As a result, nothing was ever really the same in the Douglas household after little Orville's sickness. Orville now occupied all of Julia's waking thoughts, while her three-year-old daughter, Martha, was left to the care of the preoccupied reverend, who taught her to read and prepared her meals. The reason, Martha was told, was that her younger brother was special and deserved more attention from their mother.

After more than a year of seeing their church expand in size, in mid-April 1902 the Maine congregation was shocked when Reverend Douglas, exhausted from his increasing duties at the larger parish, his efforts to start churches in other towns, and his frequent attempts to recover from various illnesses, submitted his resignation. He had received three calls to take charge of a church in Estrella, California, they were told. But the townspeople never learned that in going to the town just miles from Shandon, Douglas was actually returning to the same California area from which he had come by way of Chicago and Nova Scotia nearly eight years earlier.

Even more oddly, no one in Estrella knew that he was coming either. "He just *arrived* one day is all anyone in the area knew," recalled Ross McMillan, whose family lived near Estrella in the early 1900s. After visiting friends in Yakima, Washington, and attending a religious meeting in San Francisco, the Douglases eventually settled in nearby Shandon, where they lived by a small church that was shared by the area's Methodists and Presbyterians. But the reverend quickly discovered that he could not have come to a worse place for his health. Having been in the region during the late winter and early spring in 1894, when the weather was more temperate, he found in the summer of 1902 that the area's dust-filled air, searing hot winds, and unrelenting sunlight were about the worst combination of conditions for his health. His throat was now so bad that on occasion he could barely speak. And the reverend's eyes hurt so badly that he was forced to write his sermons in the darkness of the church manse's dank basement.

But as bad as the move was for him, it was that much and worse for Julia. Seven months into her third difficult pregnancy, immediately upon arriving in the arid town in mid-August she took to her bed. No one in town knew just what ailed the new reverend's wife, with some even voicing the suspicion that it was more psychological than physical. And just as he had done in Maine, the reverend could not take time away from his duties for her care.

Entrusting Martha to the care of his bedridden wife, the reverend took little Orville and rode up to McMillan Canyon, named for the huge wheat and barley farm and cattle ranch established and run by Canadian émigrés Alex McMillan and his wife. His wife was terribly sick, the minister explained to the McMillans, the area's most visible Presbyterians; would they mind taking care of his three-year-old son? The McMillans were not thrilled with the idea, but since Douglas was now seen as their minister, they agreed.

Alex McMillan drove the little Douglas boy in his wagon out to the home of his spinster sisters, Kate and Helen McMillan, to be cared for along with his youngest son, Donnie. In no time at all the two women began complaining that they had never seen anything like the new preacher's little boy. "He was such a mischievous and hard-to-handle kid," recalled another of Alex's sons, Eben McMillan. "Even as a young boy he was very determined and extremely competitive. Douglas was a problem. He had his own ideas about what he wanted."

As word spread throughout the region about what their new minister had done, people grew downright angry. "The community didn't like the fact that he was never around his family," recalled Eben McMillan. "He relied on others to take care of his own responsibilities." And as the caretaking duties continued for several weeks, the community grew still angrier. "Reverend Douglas was not thrifty at all," explained Eben McMillan. "He lived off the goodwill of the farmers, and so he didn't command any respect at all." As a result, the town soon lost interest in anything that Reverend Douglas had to offer. When the Douglases' second son, Arthur, was born in October 1902, leading the community to believe that there would be a need for more child care, the self-sufficient people of Shandon and Estrella turned against him. "In the end," remember both Ross and Eben McMillan, "the judgment on Reverend Douglas was that he was just too eccentric for us."

So, in April 1904, less than two years after their arrival, Douglas announced that he was leaving to accept a call from central Washington State. "Frankly, no one in the community was too sorry to see him— or them—go," recalled Eben McMillan. "He was a rather itinerant in- dividual, and he didn't seem satisfied to stay in one place for too long." Just as two years before, though, there had actually been no call from central Washington. But since many of Julia's family and old friends had followed E. A. Bickford and now lived in the North Yakima, Wash- ington, area, the Douglases knew that they could provide them with support.

Though he had no job in hand after the move, providence was with the reverend. Just one month later, Reverend J. G. Hodges, then serv- ing the small communities of Cleveland, Bickleton, and Dot, a little more than fifty miles south of North Yakima, unexpectedly resigned. When the $450 per year job was offered to Douglas, he quickly ac- cepted and moved his family to his new post.

But despite the more agreeable cool mountain climate, the rever- end's health began to fail once again. By early July, Douglas was so stricken by what the doctors now diagnosed as stomach ulcers that he was totally bedridden. Since no medical remedy seemed to work, after leaving her children with family members in North Yakima, on August 1 Julia and her brother-in-law, Samuel C. Pettit, took William by train to the Northern Pacific Sanitarium in Portland, Oregon, in the hopes that cutting out a portion of the stomach (the prevailing medi- cal treatment for ulcers) would help.

While the operation itself was a success, the end result was not. Gastritis soon set in, to the point that Douglas could not take any food, making a slow death by starvation inevitable. By August 10 his bereaved wife was by his bedside, pleading, "Do you know me? Do you know who I am?" The fast-fading reverend, though, seemed as uncon- cerned facing death as he had with his own earthly fate. "If I live it will be grace," he said, "if not, it will be glory." On Thursday, August 11, 1904, he passed into glory.

Three days later, the thirty-two-year-old widow, now bearing deep, dark circles under her eyes and still unable to shed tears because of the depth of her grief, donned a black dress to accompany her husband's coffin on the train to North Yakima. When she arrived at her sister May's Yakima house, Julia locked herself in a room, to keep her grief from her children.

Days later, five-year-old Orville, dressed in his Sunday suit, trailed behind the dust raised by the horses carrying his father's coffin up the hill to its plot in Tahoma Cemetery. His mother looked terribly small and thin in her black dress and veil as she stood solemnly over her husband's open grave. Reverend F. L. Hayden, the local minister, said a few words and turned to young Orville to say, "You must now be a man, sonny." But rather than staring into the new gaping hole in the earth or dealing with the new burden placed upon him, Orville shifted his eyes elsewhere:

> As I stood by the edge of the grave a wave of lonesomeness swept over me. Then I became afraid—afraid of being left alone, afraid because the grave held my defender and protector. . . . My throat choked up and I started to cry. . . . I tried to steel myself and control my emotions.
>
> Then I happened to see Mount Adams towering over us on the west. It was dark purple and white in the August day and its shoulders of basalt were heavy with glacial snow. It was a giant whose head touched the sky.
>
> As I looked, I stopped sobbing. My eyes dried. Adams stood cool and calm, unperturbed by the event that had stirred us so deeply. Suddenly the mountain seemed to be a friend, a force for me to tie to, a symbol of stability and strength.

For the young boy who had known so much uncertainty, the mountains would come to symbolize permanence and peace.

But there was no peace for Julia. For days after the funeral she kept to herself, remaining unable to cry. For the rest of her life "Mumsey," as her children called her, held her dead husband up to them as the smartest, gentlest, and most handsome man she had ever known. Nothing they would ever do, she told them repeatedly, no success that they achieved, would ever approach his greatness in her eyes. Julia did this out of love for her husband, seemingly unaware that by holding him up as an icon, she was sowing the seeds of their belief that they would never achieve any real success in life when measured against their ancestors.

After a while, Julia came to accept that though she was now a widow, there were three little children who needed her help, and it was her destiny to take care of them. Given the choice of returning home to her mother's Maine, Minnesota, farm or returning to Cleveland to get their things and then moving to North Yakima, where most of the rest of her extended family now lived, Julia decided to stay in the west. It was the first real decision she had made for the family, and it was one that had a profound impact on the life of her elder son.

Now, eighteen years later, that son, Orville Douglas, was perched on a similarly decisive precipice, contemplating how to take the next step toward fulfilling his destiny in New York City. As the blue bloods of Columbia's Beta Theta Pi fraternity, all clad in tweed jackets, inspected the man who had just come through the door claiming to be one of them, his future appeared to be in their hands.

ORVILLE AND THE "POOR WIDOW LADY"

Douglas was a screwball, and it was his mother who
made him that way.

—*Mercedes Davidson Douglas Eicholz*

Just how Orville Douglas came to be standing at the doorstep of the
Beta house in New York City was a story in itself. But the true story
was not necessarily one that he wanted anyone to find out. "All I remember of my childhood is pain and poverty," he later told his close
associates. His pains, though they were nothing compared to those
faced by his mother, had been, ironically, often caused by her.

As the members of the Douglas family stood on the platform of the
Northern Pacific Railroad depot in North Yakima on that hot August
day in 1904, after their trip from their old home in Cleveland, they
knew that they would be moving as close to the Wild West as existed
in the United States at that time. They walked into town along the
hundred-foot-wide, tree-lined, unpaved Yakima Avenue, engulfed by
what seemed like a parade of people, and passed by the Switzer Opera
House, which served as a combined brewery and city office building. It
looked to them as if two cities, one very up-to-date and the other two
decades older, had somehow been unnaturally joined together. On one
side of the road were a string of newly built two- and three-story brick
office buildings, each with its own fancy awning and fronted by a
newly poured narrow cement sidewalk. But across the street were
twenty-year-old one- and two-story ramshackle wooden-frame structures fronted only by wide wooden boardwalks.

The reason for this appearance was that North Yakima (pronounced YA-ki-maw by the locals) had been shaped by the railroad
that built it and the irrigation canals that nourished it. The community
lay in a barren, semi-arid area near the center of Washington State that

was dotted with sagebrush, bunchgrass, and populations of jack-rabbits and rattlesnakes. The topography of the region looked much like a saucepan, the town being ringed by mountains—the mighty Cascades to the west, which blocked the moist Pacific air and kept the average rainfall to seven inches a year, and a series of much smaller foothills linked in a circle adjoining them. As a result, residents could feel cut off from the rest of the world, not caring much about what happened elsewhere.

The secret to the future of the region, settlers realized in the mid-nineteenth century, was in finding water. Farmers discovered that the rich, flourlike soil of disintegrated lava, volcanic ash, and windblown loess could be combined with just a little bit of water to yield extraordinary crops in the sun-drenched region. The passage of the 1902 National Reclamation Act, under which irrigation projects could be financed with federal funds, made it possible to construct irrigation canals sufficient to support more than four hundred thousand acres of land. Soon thereafter, one marked the seasons in the Yakima Valley not by the calendar but by the change in harvests from strawberries to cherries to apricots to peaches, with several varieties of apples in between.

But in fact finding the water had been only half the battle, as farmers soon discovered that their highly perishable farm goods were worthless unless some way could be found to bring them quickly to larger markets. Thus it was that the Northern Pacific Railroad became the true shaper of the region. The company had been authorized by Congress in 1864 to construct a new rail line from Duluth, Minnesota, to Spokane, in the Washington Territory, and then south to Walla Walla before going to Puget Sound. Railroad executives now literally had the power to reshape the west by their construction decisions.

In the early 1880s, the people of Yakima City pressed the railroad company to build the Cascade Branch of its line right through the town. But for the railroad executives, many of whom were using these decisions to fill their own pockets, this was not the most lucrative direction. Instead, the Northern Pacific secretly decided to locate the line, and its companion depot, on the cheaper desert land several miles to the north. When people complained that there was no town there, Robert Harris, the president of the railroad, promised that a new city called North Yakima would be built there and become the crown jewel of the region. This would certainly be an accomplishment, everyone agreed, since at that time the area not only lacked water and trees but was populated only by gamblers, outlaws, and prostitutes. Harris was undeterred, enlisting Colonel Henry D. Cock to plant two thousand trees in the region and hiring a crew to divert water to the area using an existing canal from the Naches River. Then he hired H. K. Owens from Seattle to design the town from scratch. Owens modeled the new town on the layout of the main streets of his hometown of Baden-Baden, in southern Germany, with eighty-foot-wide streets, save for Yakima Avenue, which would have a width of one hundred feet, and Naches Avenue, the "centerpiece of the city," which would have a width of 140 feet. Since the new city needed people, the railroad executives then offered the residents of Yakima City one simple choice: Either move to the new city or be passed by. After the railroad company agreed to pay the expenses of moving both the residents and their buildings four miles north to the new town, the choice was easy.

Thus began, in the spring and summer of 1885, one of the strangest migrations in the history of the Pacific Northwest, as the buildings of Yakima City were physically dragged to their new locations. David Guilland, the proprietor of Yakima City's "leading hotel since 1876," agreed to become the first to move his building in January 1885. His two-story structure was lifted on jackscrews and placed on a complex platform of huge timbers that could be rolled over a rotating set of giant logs. Four-inch-wide wooden planks were then laid in straight rows along the roadway, and thick ropes connecting the levitated building to teams of waiting horses were wound around heavy capstans anchored to the ground. This unique pulley structure made it possible to move the hotel to its new location using only ten men and four horses. Unwilling to lose any business, Guilland continued to operate his hotel, sitting beneath the wooden awning in the front, smoking his pipe, and greeting his ever-moving guests as they came and went. Horses were tied to hitching posts along the building's side and walked along as it moved. Guests who left their rooms in the morning would simply come back at the end of the day to find their beds and belongings several hundred yards farther up the road. Three weeks later, the Guilland Hotel stood four miles away, on the corner of First Street and Chestnut Street in the new city of North Yakima. Seeing this success, other homes and businesses soon followed, resulting in a line of moving structures that resembled a series of wooden floats in a parade.

While the new buildings arrived, laborers in North Yakima feverishly built two-story brick structures along one side of Yakima Avenue and on every vacant lot they could find on Naches Avenue. One resident described the chaotic scene in vivid detail: "The streets were all new and ground into powder by the freighting and the moving of houses from the old town. . . . The way the dust would fly was a caution. . . . Add to this . . . the din made by hundreds of carpenters, the banging of pianos and the tooting or twanging of wind and stringed instruments in the numerous saloons, the rolling of the rondo and roulette balls and the betting cries, and you have a medley of sounds that is difficult to describe." With Yakima City rapidly becoming a ghost town, North Yakima began to take on the trappings of industrial-age life, with fifteen lawyers, five real-estate agencies, 126 houses, three blacksmith shops, a telegraph office, a post office, a government land office, and three weekly newspapers.

By the time that Julia Douglas and her young children arrived in their new home, North Yakima had grown to a population of six thousand. The telephone and the Stanley Steamer automobile had arrived, but it was still common to see groups of Native Americans leading long strings of packhorses through the streets. Dusty miners and sheepherders arrived by foot seeking the season's supplies and a visit to the town's highly active "red light" district with its many teeming brothels and busy opium dens. The more law-abiding residents had decided that something needed to be done about the new city's unsavory reputation. So, they again hired Colonel Henry D. Cock, this time to serve as their new marshal and fill up the abandoned boxcar that the Northern Pacific had generously donated for use as the town's new jail.

Such a place was destined to leave a mark on five-year-old Orville Douglas. The unfenced libertarian spirit in this recently created Wild West town, together with its ever-changing and diverse population, instilled in the residents a sense of endless possibilities for the future. Years later, Douglas would look back on these childhood years in Yakima, as it was renamed in 1918, and see the origins of his independent, anti-Establishment, nonconformist public identity. Indeed, his love of the American spirit, his egalitarianism, his love of democratic rights, his respect for the rights of privacy, and his desire never to be chained in by anyone or anything, were also created and nurtured by his early years in this thrillingly adventurous frontier city. However, these childhood experiences were also the source for another powerful impulse: his fear of poverty.

As she surveyed her new surroundings, Julia Douglas realized that after meeting the challenges presented by eight years of her husband's illness, three difficult pregnancies, and three major family relocations, she now faced the biggest challenge of her life: raising and supporting her three children by herself. She looked, one longtime Yakima resident recalled, like "a poor young widow who was woefully unprepared to make a life for her three little children." Fortunately for Julia, all Presbyterian ministers were covered by life-insurance policies that provided their survivors with between $1,200 and $2,200. Because

Julia's brother-in-law Samuel C. Pettit was then serving as an elder and a deacon in the First Presbyterian Church of Yakima, her benefit package was placed at the high end of the scale. Also, since Reverend Douglas had remained a member in good standing of the Order of the Modern Woodmen in Maine, she received another $1,000 from that organization's life-insurance policy. After the burial costs, Julia Douglas had around $3,000 to rebuild her family's life. Finally, the local Presbyterian Board granted Julia an annual pension from the national Presbyterian Church's Widows' Fund of $150 for a few years. By supplementing this money with laundry that she took in from neighbors, Julia figured that she would be able to keep her family afloat.

The question now was how to secure their future. First, with no rent-free church manse available to occupy, Julia used $960 of her insurance money to buy from carpenter George Wise and his wife, Sadie, a newly built five-room ranch house at 111 North Moxee Avenue (renamed North Fifth Avenue in 1908). Since the house was located right behind the Columbia Grade School, the children could easily attend classes. And if problems should arise, just one block over, on North Rainier Avenue, lived a former Maine resident, family friend Barney L. Bull. Should she have any troubles with the house, its builder lived right down the street. Three years later, Julia's sister and brother-in-law, May and Sam Pettit, moved right across the street from her, while her half brother James Richardson and his family moved into a house a short walk away on South Eighth Avenue. For Julia, it was as if the Maine community had been rebuilt around her.

The Douglas home was located in one of North Yakima's many middle-class communities, containing such residents as two salesmen, a teacher, a grocer, a lawyer, a dentist, and a civil engineer. "[We] never thought of the Douglases as poor," said Al Egley, who lived just a block away from them and ran in the same childhood gang as Orville. "The general level of income wasn't all that high in those days." John Gavin, a Yakima attorney and prominent local historian, explained sociologically why that was true:

> The train divided the town and the "wrong side" was the east side, toward the river, where the really poor people lived. . . . If you were poor you lived in these suburbs of town. The richer folks lived on the west side of the train tracks, toward the middle of town. *That's* where the Douglases lived—on North Fifth Avenue. They weren't rich, mind you—the rich folks in this agricultural community were the farm owners who lived in the western hills overlooking the town. But they weren't poor either.

Indeed, until 1909 Julia was paying taxes on a reported $300 of annual taxable personal property, which placed her around the middle of the city's property-tax structure.

But disaster loomed on the horizon. When Julia's church pension ran out, in 1910, her reported taxable personal property was more than cut in half, with another sharp drop to $115 the following year. In just two years her financial position had dropped her into the bottom 20 percent of city residents. Rather than depleting the remaining $2,100 of the insurance money for their weekly living expenses, Julia decided in 1911 to take the bold step of investing it in the hopes of developing interest payments on which they could live for many years to come. Since she lacked experience in such matters, Julia put her faith in a local attorney, James Oliver Cull.

Had she consulted other investors or attorneys in the area before making this decision, it is quite certain that Cull would not have been her first choice. "Cull didn't attempt to be a good lawyer, and he wasn't," said Chalmer Walter, a Yakima attorney in the 1920s. Fred Velikanje, another longtime attorney in town, concurred: "Jim did mostly mining stock work. We don't have any mines here; so that ought to tell you all you need to know about his legal skills." Normally for Cull, having a widow like Julia Douglas place all of her worldly funds in his hands was a dream come true. This time, however, quite contrary to his reputation in town, Cull treated Julia much better than he treated his average clients, or even himself. He actually helped her make money.

Rather than offering her one of his soon-to-be-worthless stock deals, as an officer in several mortgage companies James O. Cull decided to arrange a couple of mortgage investments for Julia. Cull first recommended purchasing the mortgage on a fine four-and-one-third-acre piece of farm property in the Terrace Heights area, on a small bluff just northeast of the city. The location of this property, which was then held by his Central Washington Investment and Power Company, was especially choice because the area abutted the Selah-Moxee Canal. With every parcel of land came shares in the water rights of both the Selah and Moxee Canal Company and the Terrace Heights Water Company, thus making it possible to farm there. This particular parcel had been bought from Cull in June 1911 by A. A. Nicol and Ruby and Nina Poole, who intended to build a new farm. In a matter of three months, though, the investment group ran into financial trouble, still owing $870 on the mortgage to Cull's company. So Julia Douglas bought the note, acting, according to the deed filed in the Yakima County Courthouse, in her capacity "as guardian of the persons and estates of Martha Bickford Douglass, William Orville Douglass, and Arthur Free-born Douglass [sic], minors." The 8 percent interest on this note guaranteed her nearly seventy dollars a year, an excellent start.

But Julia may not have known what she actually held title to. R. A. Poole and Company raised and sold hops. Thus, the Presbyterian minister's widow, who was so devoted to the temperance tenets of her faith that she constantly preached to her children about "demon rum" and refused to help drifters who had alcohol on their breath, now held a note on farmland that would help to provide beer for the many saloons in the area. However, investing in hops farming in an area where oceans of beer were sold daily was about the safest bet one could make.

For the remainder of Julia's money, Cull suggested an excellent piece of business property in the Nob Hill section of downtown Yakima, at the corner of Chicago and West Yakima avenues. Not only was this plot of land the perfect place for a small business or a small apartment building, the mortgage seemed even safer because the borrowers were James Thomas and his wife, Lucy, two of the most successful real-estate tycoons in the region. Julia quickly invested the rest of her money, some $1,200, again at 8 percent interest, in buying up this mortgage in November 1911. When she added up the numbers, she found that the interest generated by these two investments provided her with sixteen dollars more per year than her now expired church pension had.

However, investors in real estate are always quick to say that while the land is forever, deals on it frequently are not. And, indeed, the Poole investment group ran into trouble almost immediately, missing one mortgage payment after another. After a year of nonpayment, Julia filed suit against the group in Yakima County Court. Rather than risk losing everything through a foreclosure judgment, the investment partnership split up, and the Pooles separately renegotiated their loan in January 1913, promising to pay Julia all of the money and accrued back interest, plus 8 percent interest on the entire debt, over the next three years.

To Julia's dismay, at the very same time that the Pooles were having troubles, the Thomases also became overextended and began reneging on their interest payments. When James Thomas died suddenly on May 27, 1915, Julia became understandably concerned about her investment. She immediately filed suit against Lucy Thomas, successfully recovering all of the back interest owed to her. At that point, though, the executor of the Thomas estate deemed that the property had little value and satisfied the mortgage by simply transferring the land to Julia in June 1916. Upon learning that the property still retained a great deal of value in the rapidly expanding downtown community, Julia wisely held on to it while its worth increased.

The dramatic impact of these investments on Julia's finances was evident. By 1914, as her investments began to mature, Julia's tax base had rebounded to $345, meaning that she had moved up to a position 15 percent higher than the one she had enjoyed with the church pension. Her financial position was now so good, in fact, that Barney L. Bull, Samuel C. Pettit, and James Richardson, all with full-time jobs, reported substantially less of a tax base. Just two years later, as Orville was graduating from high school, Julia's $300 in taxable personal property placed her higher than three fifths of the other taxpayers in the city. Five years of successful investments, then, had enabled Julia Douglas to raise her family from a distinctly lower-class status to one solidly within the middle class.

Just a few months after Orville graduated from high school in August 1916, Julia owned both her own house and her downtown property free and clear. And by 1919, when the Terrace Heights mortgage was fully satisfied, her original investment there of $870 had yielded payments amounting to $1,296. By this time, Julia had increased her original investments by nearly one thousand dollars.

But having endured insecurity all of her married life, Julia never felt financially secure. Around town she began referring to herself as "a poor widow lady." "She was seen as being kind of meek, mild, small, [and] inclined to be a little bit of a whiner," said Yakima historian George Martin. And she could not help visiting those fears upon her children. "Well, we've only got fifty dollars left; it's all the money we have in the world. I don't know what's gonna happen," Julia would tell Orville, Martha, and Arthur as they ate their dinners. As a result, the children grew up believing themselves to be destitute.

Young Orville resolved to do whatever he could to find the money to put food on the table. Every day after school and all day on Saturdays, Orville and his brother and sister took every moneymaking job they could find and helped with the family garden. Orville pushed an ice wagon from house to house, did yard work, washed store windows, picked fruit at the local orchards, swept the floors of local businesses, and gathered junk for scrap iron. As Orville got older, more lucrative jobs were available to him. He delivered newspapers, worked as a pin boy in the local bowling alley, manned the assembly line in the local ice-cream factory, and picked up whatever other odd jobs he could find.

Some of these jobs were odd indeed. Once, he was hired by town authorities to deliver some legal documents to the residents of the local brothels. He told his friends that when he tried to complete his task, one of the women made him a better offer. So Douglas took on a new job. "He was an errand boy for some of the brothels," explained longtime friend Ira Ford.

As a young lad, Orville Douglas knew that if he was going to succeed, it would have to be on his own talents. Fortunately, his talents abounded. However, so did the obstacles confronting him.

Having already lost a brother and a husband to illness, Julia Douglas was determined that the same would not happen to her "Treasure." She overprotected him, constantly reminding his siblings, "He's not as strong as other boys. He has to be careful what he does." In time, Orville came to think of himself as "puny" and a "weakling," even believing that one of his legs was skinnier than the other, despite the fact that none of his friends could see such a difference. Along with this low self-esteem came certain physical symptoms. On some days he felt faint, getting sick to his stomach, and at other times he suffered for days from severe migraines. Throughout his life, whenever he heard the name his mother had given him, it reminded him of all of these negative emotions. "Orville? Oh, he did hate that name. But it was the one his mother insisted on," recalled an old friend, Frances Penrose Owen.

To build up the young boy's self-esteem, Julia used a very special technique. Time and again, she called Orville to her side and recited a presidential nomination speech that she had composed for him. The address always began with the same poetic lines from Sir Walter Scott:

> *And dar'st thou then*
> *To beard the lion in his den,*
> *The Douglas in his hall?*

Then she would "nominate" William Orville Douglas for president of the United States. She would always end this inspiring political call to arms the same way she began, with the poetry hailing the Douglas name.

So dare he surely would, Orville promised both his mother and himself each time he heard this speech. Dare he would as no one on either side of his family had dared before.

Despite Julia's overprotectiveness and ambitious dreams for Orville, his friends thought he was just like them. "Although he was no athlete, Bill joined in the neighborhood sports on an equal basis and held his own in duck-on-the-rock and other games," recalled Al Egley. All that

was really "wrong" with Orville, they agreed, was that he was terribly
skinny, and it certainly showed more than anywhere else in his legs.

Every time Orville gathered with his buddy Tommy Pickering and
a group of older teenagers around North Fifth Avenue called "the
Gang," he would be reminded of his skinny physique. Since all the
gang members were dubbed with nicknames, when they looked at
Orville they knew immediately what he should be called. At that time
he was a full six inches shorter than the older boys, and with his skinny
legs in his short knickers he looked for all the world like a little
peanut. So "Peanuts" is what they called him. It was a nickname he
came to hate and vowed to get rid of as soon as possible.

Embarrassed by his physique, Orville began to wonder if his legs
could be built up through some form of the same hard work that
helped him on a daily basis try to overcome what he saw as his family's
poverty. On the advice of a friend whose lungs and legs had suffered
from the aftereffects of tuberculosis, Orville sought to build himself
up by marching toward the yellow-brown sagebrush-filled foothills
that rose some five or six hundred feet near the town of Selah Gap, a
couple of miles north of his house. Whenever he could, he would
climb to the top, and then hike back home as fast as he could. By high
school, he was Peanuts no longer, as a growth spurt had made Orville
so tall and gangly that he became the center for North Yakima High
School's basketball team, for which he earned a varsity letter.

Prior to this, however, lacking both financial and physical security,
Orville decided that he could prove his superiority elsewhere: in the
classroom. "I can get good grades, if I work. . . . I can get 100 in every
course," he told his family. Julia encouraged academic competition in
her children, reviewing school assignments and playing games of "Authors" with them, as they tried to match famous writers and their
works. Blessed with a photographic memory, Orville learned that all
he needed to do to outperform his classmates was just glance at a page
before turning to the next one. His grades consistently ranged in the
low to middle 90s.

When her children weren't working either for extra money or on
their schoolwork, Julia raised them spiritually, as she knew her husband would have wished. Each week, she would direct her children to
read the notes she had written out from her husband's sermons. On
Sundays, all of them attended a series of area church services. They attended Sunday school at 9:00 A.M. and church service at 11:00; after a
prayerful lunch, the Douglases were back at 5:00 for the Christian Endeavor religious-group meeting, only to be followed by the 8:00 P.M.
church service. Julia also mandated attendance at the Thursday prayer

meeting. In time, this routine turned Orville away from the Presbyterian Church, and he began attending services in the more relaxed Congregational Church, before abandoning religion almost entirely.

Orville also joined as many extracurricular activities as time would allow. After reaching the finals of an "oral English" contest as a sophomore, he earned a letter in oratory the next year and participated in the Discussion Club for two years. Orville became something of a local hero as a senior by leading his school's Debate Club to victory in three of their four debates on the topic, "Resolved, that the Monroe Doctrine should be discontinued." In time, because of his oratorical accomplishments, Orville was called "the deacon" by his admiring classmates.

Hampered by a combination of painful shyness (making his oratorical work especially difficult), embarrassment over his physique, and an overprotective mother and sister, Orville faced many challenges when it came to relating to members of the opposite sex. Schoolmate Eddie Thompson later remembered how Orville would always try to drag him off to church service. But it was more than the word of the Lord that he was now seeking. "When we reached the door," Thompson explained, "he copped a gander inside, and made a bee-line for a bench where a very pretty little girl happened to be sitting. Evidently the songbook was heavy, as it took two to hold it. . . . She was a lovely little thing."

One of Douglas's childhood friends from North Fifth Avenue, Paul L. Marble, revealed the lengths that the attention-starved Orville Douglas went to in high school to attract the attention of a pretty female classmate:

> Orville bought [a brand-new checkered suit] just about the time he began to take a deep interest in a fair classmate. The rest of the school believed his sartorial elegance was the direct result of his budding romance. So he had to take a lot of teasing. Then, to make matters worse, a visiting teacher, Mrs. Reed, who taught student guidance or something like that, addressed an assembly. She asserted that any boy who wore flashy clothes was not of the serious-minded type and that he wouldn't get anywhere in life. And there was Orville right up in a front seat, squirming in his checkered suit and blushing furiously. But he kept right on wearing the suit. He had to. He didn't have any other and he couldn't afford to buy a new one.

Seeing this, Orville's high school classmates tagged him with a new name: "Checkers."

Just so everyone would remember their class intellectual leader's nickname for all eternity, Marble drew a cartoon for their yearbook showing a long-legged but still peanut-shaped lad, both hands stuffed in the pockets of his hideous checkered suit. It bore the inscription: "Who Is It? Why It's the Valedictorian Of Course!"

Burdened by his many pressures, Orville searched for a place where he could find some peace. After years of seeing the magnificent mountains off at the distant horizon from his home on North Fifth Avenue, Orville decided to visit the lushly forested Cascades. Whenever they could, as teenagers Orville and his buddies would hop on the Sagebrush Annie, a train that went the dozen or so miles up to the town of Naches, sometimes paying the dime fare and sometimes just hopping on illegally to "ride the rods" like the hoboes they had met around town. On occasion, if Orville's buddy Elon Gilbert went along, they rode his father's horses to make the journey.

Then the fun would begin. Days were filled with hiking and fishing in the crystal-clear streams and lakes, and the nights were filled by baking sourdough bread and beans that they carried in their horseshoe-pack bedrolls. Having easily conquered the foothills around Yakima, Orville now loved long marches in the mountains with his brother, Arthur, and their friends. They hiked dozens of miles a day on the narrow, steeply inclined, and rocky trails as they journeyed toward the mountains' summits. But getting to the top was not as important as what he saw along the way. As opposed to the drudgery in Yakima, there was always a new adventure in the mountains. For the overprotective Julia, a woman of untold numbers of phobias, including snakes, lightning, and bears, these unchaperoned forays into the wild woods became exercises in sheer terror. Every night that Orville and Arthur were gone, Julia would wake her daughter in the middle of the night and say, "Do you think the boys are all right?" Then Martha would rub her mother's leg, which constantly ached, until Julia could fall back asleep. Martha later recalled why her mother allowed these trips: "She was so afraid you boys growing up without a father would be sissies, she wanted you to do all the masculine things you could do."

Despite his mother's misgivings, Orville Douglas loved his trips into the mountains very much. Here alone he found refuge from the pain and privation of life in Yakima. Here he found peace, total equality, and absolute beauty. For the rest of his life, the mountains were where he always really wanted to be, but the city was where he would have to be.

3

MANHOOD'S GATE

We lay claim to Orville only for the Whitman era. . . . When he was gone, he was gone. He was no longer Orville Douglas. . . . Oh, we crossed paths over the years, but by then he was slowly becoming someone else. Someone none of us recognized.

—*Frances Penrose Owen*

It was money, or rather the lack of it, that dictated Orville Douglas's choices of college in 1916. Orville knew where he wanted to go, but he didn't know how to get there. The University of Washington in Seattle had everything that he wanted in a school: a large and diverse enrollment of five thousand, a big-city location, national prestige, and, most important, a mountain range between it and life on North Fifth Avenue. However, with Martha about to begin her second year of studies at Whitman College, a tiny liberal-arts school in the sleepy eastern Washington town of Walla Walla, and Arthur too young to make any real money, Orville's mother told him that only if he earned all of his tuition and living expenses and sent home twenty dollars a month could they afford for him to leave. He would have to have some substantial scholarship help, which was not available at the state university.

To his great relief, though, Orville discovered that Whitman College offered a scholarship for the first year's two-hundred-dollar tuition to the valedictorians of a small number of high schools in the state. Since North Yakima was on the list, off to Whitman College he would go.

There was just the matter of finding additional money to pay for books and room and board, as well as to send back to his family. Fortunately, during his senior year of high school Orville had gotten to know three Walla Walla boys—Philo Rounds, Jerry Cundiff, and J. Howard Shubert—at the annual Yakima–Walla Walla football game. Rounds and Shubert were already in the Beta Theta Pi house at Whitman, with Cundiff making plans to pledge there in the fall. Seeing an opportunity to increase their fraternity's academic average, the three of them talked with North Yakima High School's newest valedictorian about the merits of pledging with their house if he attended Whitman. Since these boys had also mentioned their jobs with Walla Walla's "jeweler of quality"—Falkenberg's—Orville kept up their acquaintance. In the summer of 1916, he rode the train to Walla Walla to see if his new friends would help him get a job in Falkenberg's. In no time at all, Orville had an offer of a dime an hour for washing windows, sweeping up, and serving as a delivery boy during the school year, with the promise that in time he would become a sales assistant at a whopping fifty cents an hour.

But even this fine job would not provide enough money. If he arranged all of his classes in the morning, thus allowing him to work all afternoon in order to make fifty cents a day, the three dollars a week would not even meet his living expenses, let alone give him any money to send home. So Orville knocked on every door in town and very quickly lined up a slate of additional jobs. He would work as a janitor from 5:30 to 7:30 in the morning at a combined office building and candy store downtown and also wait tables for both lunch and dinner at a boardinghouse, thus saving himself the expenses for his meals. During the summers he would find odd jobs, picking fruit, making fruit boxes, logging trees, and even helping on occasion to fight forest fires. For Orville, this schedule meant that life in Walla Walla would be just as it had been in Yakima: a constant struggle to avoid poverty. The good news was that between gulps of food and dashes from job to job he would be getting the education that he hoped would take him to a better life.

And what an education Orville and his classmates got at Whitman in those days. The school, under the guidance of its legendary president, Stephen B. L. Penrose, was modeled after the rigorous liberal-arts programs of colleges in the northeast, with everything geared toward comprehensive exams in one's major field. Students took very few electives in their first two years, with compulsory attendance in nearly every class. "Fussers"—those who spent time in social endeavors and avoided the steady diet of daily essays and homework assignments— were informed that more than one unexcused absence from class meant a zero for the course.

A semester of living in a ramshackle dorm was all that it took to persuade Orville to accept his Falkenberg chums' offer to join the Beta Theta Pi fraternity. In those days, classmate Wesley ("Jack") Mendenhall recalled, the decision as to which fraternity to join made a great deal of difference: "If you were a member of one fraternity, you simply did not socialize with anyone else from another fraternity."

Once he had pledged the fraternity on February 6, 1917, Orville started eating at the house three days later and moved in by the end of the month. He and the other pledges were initiated on March 30–31, in a banquet at the Grand Hotel in Walla Walla, where toast after toast was given, extolling the virtues of "The Beta of Old," "The Ideal Chapter," "The Fraternity and the College," "The Beta Pin," and "Beta, My Choice, and Why." With that, the evening closed with a round of singing the fraternity's songs. The ceremony had a profound effect on the young man. "The night I walked home after my initiation," Douglas told an audience of Betas in Washington, D.C., in 1939, "I experienced a sense of elation which one does not frequently have. It was a rare spiritual experience. . . . Beta Theta Pi . . . made such a lasting contribution to my own education in the American ideals of Democracy."

Now free from Julia's watchful eye, studying during that second semester made way for Orville's busy social life. His time now revolved around the activities of his fraternity chapter. "[Beta Theta Pi] Ah me!" he jotted happily in his diary on February 14. "The clock strikes twelve & I am still awake for [Beta Theta Pi]." He also went to the movies a couple of times a week (sometimes after "lights out" in the dorms), attended several fraternity functions, went dancing, saw various girls, attended the college basketball games and debates, and joined whatever parties he could find. Orville knew that all of this was taking its toll on his studies. "Guess I'm too strong on fussing," he wrote on February 21. Finally, the effect of his playing became evident as he fell further and further behind in his classes. "A week behind in math," he admitted a couple of days later.

For the first time in his life, Orville got involved in a serious relationship, with the attractive daughter of a local minister. Fraternity brother and roommate Bill Wilson later remembered that the affair caused some aggravation for the house members who thought Orville was paying her too much attention. The two had grown so serious about each other that Orville even bought her a ring, causing great financial anxiety for his family. When the family of his young love moved away, however, the relationship ended, to Orville's great sadness. It was not until the following year that he recovered from his heartbreak to begin dating one of the girls in the new freshman class: Frances Penrose, the president's youngest daughter.

All of this socializing, on top of the time required by his several jobs, soon caused his grades to suffer. His grades were averaging only about an 80 at the end of February. And a week later he flunked a math exam. Toward the end of March, his grades were an A for French, an 85 in Latin, and B's in both math and English. For the Yakima valedictorian, who got nothing but solid A's throughout his grade school and high school years, these were poor grades indeed. But it was something of a common tale for a young man testing his first bit of independence and freedom.

International events touched Douglas's life during the second half of his freshman year when war fever swept the Whitman campus after the United States' entry into World War I in April 1917. With his older classmates facing the prospect of fighting and dying in Europe, and his high school buddies from Yakima volunteering to help, Orville felt the pressure to join up. But it was not possible for him to do so. Federal law required anyone younger than twenty-one to have parental permission to join the military. And Orville knew that there was no way that his mother would allow him to risk his life in this fashion. Age did not prevent other young men from involving themselves in the war effort. "I was not old enough to join the military," recalled Jack Mendenhall, who was a year ahead of his friend Orville Douglas at Whitman College. "When I heard they were organizing an ambulance corps over in Spokane, I rushed over to join. There were a bunch of doctors and nurses and a bunch of drivers, and we were all sent to the front. We ended up driving Model T Fords over in France." Others also served in this way, even though they were younger than Douglas.

Instead, in the fall of 1918, Douglas joined the Whitman College regiment of the Students' Army Training Corps, the World War I version of ROTC. In this setting, Orville did impress his peers both with his leadership ability and his physical conditioning as a result of all of those years of tramping in the Yakima foothills and the Cascade Mountains. Fellow SATC member Blaine Hallock later recalled, "[Douglas] didn't say much but he thought a lot. I shall never forget those pre-dawn scampers across the frosted grass when Bill would get out in front of us, blow his whistle, shout 'follow me,' and lead us on a wild run toward a theoretical enemy. I shall always remember the charley horses which would settle in my aching legs as I panted along, gradually dropping to the rear and gasping for breath."

But beyond these runs and marching drills, the nature of the "service" here was quite minimal indeed. The corps was supposed to be trained as an infantry unit, President Penrose later explained in a magazine piece he titled "S.A.T.C.—A Comedy," but his students only received "fourteen hours a week of outdoor drill, and never laid hands on a gun." The reason was quite simple: The supply of guns, ammunition, and bayonets for the Whitman training unit never arrived. Indeed, Penrose explains, it took countless letters, telegrams, and finally even senatorial intervention for the unit to get their uniforms, which did not happen until a full three weeks after the war ended on November 11, 1918.

Equipment problems were not the only obstacles facing the unit. As the young men drilled in their street clothes and without weapons, many of them succumbed to the deadly ravages of the influenza epidemic that was sweeping the globe in 1918. As they did, they were quarantined in a temporary infirmary that was set up in both Reynolds Hall and the Beta house. There the sick students were cared for by Mrs. Ethel Moore, a local registered nurse. In time, Orville Douglas fell victim to the epidemic. Years later, Mrs. Moore was fond of telling residents in her boardinghouse on East Isaacs Street that of all those students, he still stuck in her mind as being the "worst patient she had ever seen."

Despite the limited nature of his military service, Orville was determined that it not go unnoticed. As soon as his SATC uniform arrived, he had his picture taken, even though the war had ended. One classmate believed that Douglas hoped it would appear in the school newspaper, so that everyone could see that the secretary of the Associated Student Organization, the man just elected president for the coming year, had served his country. And in the 1919 Yakima City Directory, a small flag emblem was placed next to his name, like those of the city's war veterans.

As his college years went by, Orville Douglas participated in as many student activities as he could find. He spoke in oratory contests, joined the student political club, was elected to student government, worked in the local YMCA, wrote for the literary magazine, appeared in school plays for the Dramatic Club, worked in the Economics Club, and played in the school tennis contest. In all of these activities Orville was always second place to the real "big man on campus" in his class, Robert Porterfield. It was Porterfield who defeated him in the campus tennis tournament, beat him out for the William Thomas Dovell Oratory Prize in 1919, became the school newspaper's managing editor while Douglas became a reporter, and got the leads in the Dramatic Club plays while Douglas played only supporting roles.

But at Whitman only one extracurricular activity really mattered. The tiny school, given to boasting that in a 120–6 football loss to the mighty University of Washington they had at least been able to score six points, was determined to demonstrate its intellectual superiority. The only playing field available to it that was level against much larger schools was the annual debate series. Here all you needed for success was a couple of talented debaters and access to a library. From the moment that each new freshman class arrived on campus, the search was on to find the school's next pair of skilled competitors. And from the opening days of the appearance of the new class of 1920, the boy whose star rose the fastest was Orville Douglas of Yakima, Washington.

Just three weeks after "Deacon" Douglas arrived on campus, he was debating in the Political Club's quadrennial presidential-election review before an audience that included both candidates for Washington's contested senatorial seat. Knowing that participation in such an event was almost unprecedented for a freshman, Douglas was encouraged to try out for the campus debate team. Schools would arrange months in advance for a pair of debates, one to be held on each campus. Weeks would then be spent negotiating the topic, and months more would be spent researching its nuances. When two schools debated, each would send their less experienced team to the other school, where they would debate in front of the entire student body in the main auditorium. Normally, each member of both two-person teams would give a five-minute main speech, to be answered by three-minute rebuttals. For the winning school, it was a chance to claim superiority in intellect and education, while for the losing school it meant twelve long months before getting a chance to exact revenge.

The search at Whitman for students who could withstand this pressure and uphold the honor of the entire school was a careful one. Orville joined thirteen classmates in the trials for the annual debate with the University of Washington, which were judged by President Penrose himself, aided by various faculty members. To no one's surprise, the experienced upperclassmen took all four top spots. The following year, though, sophomores Orville Douglas and Robert Porterfield were chosen as alternates for the team. For Porterfield, an award-winning debater for Lewis and Clark High School in Spokane and winner of the John Brining Prize in freshman extemporaneous speaking, this was to be expected. But Douglas accomplished the same thing with no formal training other than a single year on the North Yakima High School debate team. Try as he might, in the spring of 1918 Douglas lost both the "away" debates—the first with Porterfield at the University of Washington and the other with Marion Dickey at the University of Idaho, where, according to the college newspaper, the two spent much of their time drinking and chasing young women.

Having amassed this less than stellar record, what happened next could not have been predicted. When the school's star debater, Robert

Porterfield, decided not to debate the following year, Orville was tapped in March 1919 to appear for the first time on his home campus in the annual struggle with the University of Washington. Eight hundred students and faculty filled Memorial Hall to see Douglas and his new partner, freshman Harold Eugene McGahey, debate two Washington visitors before a local reverend and two state judges on the question of whether "a federal board of arbitration with compulsory powers should be established to settle industrial disputes between capital and labor." As the more experienced member of the team, Orville Douglas bore the primary responsibility for Whitman's performance.

In the hopes of exploiting what they saw as their oratorical superiority over the Whitman debaters, the Washington team had arranged for a much longer debate: twenty-minute opening speeches with five-minute rebuttals. For an hour and thirty-five minutes, the strategy worked to perfection, as the contest was all Washington's. By the time Douglas stood up for his final affirmative rebuttal to end the debate, everyone agreed that it was seemingly hopeless for the home team. With the fate of his proud, tiny school in his hands, what was there left for Orville to say to crystallize the judges' opinions? his classmates now wondered. And how could he say it in just five minutes? One eyewitness to the debate recalled that students in the audience literally held their breath and prayed that he would be equal to the task. "I'm counting on Orville's rebuttal," Frances Penrose wrote on her program that day. It seemed as if Douglas held all of their intellectual self-esteem in his hands.

And to their relief, he did not let them down. In fact, what he did that day was so remarkable that few who were present ever forgot it. Rather than, as expected, covering all of the arguments in the debate, Douglas intentionally dropped all of the major issues that he believed to be either settled or irrelevant to the final decision, focused on the single biggest weakness in the negative attack, offered a few passionately persuasive sentences on that issue appealing to the sensibilities of the judges, and then, with almost all of his speaking time still remaining, sat down, to the audience's stunned silence. "Orville gives the most remarkable rebuttal I ever heard a student give," Frances Penrose wrote in her journal after she had watched in admiration. "He was not just debating. He was pleading a cause. And it was magnificent." On the basis of this compelling performance, the underdog Whitman team won the debate, to the delight of the cheering students.

It was an act of consummate ability and supreme confidence. Out of nowhere he had hatched the "Douglas style" of being able to get to the absolute heart of an issue without any excess verbiage. With one dramatic performance, Orville Douglas had transformed himself into the campus hero. In anticipation of next year's debating success, Douglas was elected president of the Debate Society and the faculty chose him in the spring of 1919 to be the class marshal for the annual commencement. Everyone on campus expected that with all that debate experience, Orville would lead Whitman to victory once more.

But soon thereafter something threatened to change Orville's plans. Despite all his work to raise funds upon first entering Whitman, money had become so tight that his sister, Martha, had dropped out of school after her second year in order to support Orville's college education. Even with Martha's help, each new letter to Orville from home carried with it the potential of some new problem and brought back all the unhappy memories of Yakima.

Then one day, a terrible letter came telling Orville that for some reason the family's finances were now so bad that he would have to come home. All Orville could do was say good-bye to the place he had come to love so dearly. Whitman College had represented his one chance to escape from poverty, and now it was on the verge of slipping from his grasp.

But fate intervened on Orville's behalf. Desperate for money, Julia decided to liquidate her real-estate holding in the Nob Hill section of downtown Yakima. The $1,500 that Ruby M. Holler paid her for the property in June 1919 (a 25 percent increase over the value of Julia's original investment), together with Julia's fully paid-off house and the proceeds from her other successful investments, would support her, she believed, for the rest of her life. Julia now felt, after leaving the investment proceeds with James O. Cull to reinvest, secure enough to tell both her son and her daughter that they could complete their studies at Whitman.

.   .   .

Going into his senior year, not even the fact that Kalamazoo College had hired away Whitman's debate coach could dampen the college's enthusiasm about Orville Douglas's contribution to the team. But Orville had another plan: He simply quit debate. Why had he done it? No one really knew for sure. Was it the financial crisis, which told him that more time needed to be spent earning money? Had he decided to give up on some of his activities and devote more time to raising his class average to make up for the low grades from his first year? Having already reached the pinnacle of his debating career, and knowing that there was no way he could surpass his remarkable performance, had the restless young man simply decided that it was time to move on?

Whatever the reason, Orville was gone, and a somber Whitman student body watched as their compatriots lost both their debates to the University of Washington in 1920.

If Orville had quit debate to help raise his grade-point average, then it proved to be a wise move. Orville's college career, which had begun so inauspiciously, ended with great success. He became one of seven members of his graduating class of forty to be inducted in Whitman's newly established Phi Beta Kappa chapter. Even more significantly, the faculty asked him to give a commencement speech.

But once he graduated, Orville was determined to put all of his experiences at Whitman College, and Yakima before that, behind him. What he most wanted was to get over the mountains and become a professor of English at some college or university. When he learned that a Rhodes scholarship could allow him to pursue both goals by financing graduate training at Oxford University, that became his life's wish.

Orville did not fully understand that as a graduate of Whitman, he faced an uphill battle. Competition was always keen for a scholarship, especially for students in the Pacific Northwest region, where the much larger University of Washington had so many good candidates. Over the years, the state school's graduates nearly always won that region's award. And so it happened that year when Orville lost out in his region to Washington's Kenneth Cole.

Douglas was crushed. If his family had had more money, he believed, he would have attended the state university, and he would now be a Rhodes scholar. Despite the fact that Orville had proved in his debates that he could compete with, and best, the University of Washington students, he was being left behind.

For Orville, this disappointment meant that he now faced a bleak return to the dead-end life in Yakima. With a fine education as a liberal-arts major, a stepuncle, James Richardson, who had just retired as the superintendent of the Yakima schools, and a sister who had been working in that system for two years, his most likely job prospect seemed to be teaching.

Despite her son's dismay, nothing could have made Julia Douglas any happier than having her "Treasure" back home living with her. Now he could begin building a solid career teaching English and coaching the debate team at the high school. He was earning a living wage of one hundred dollars per month, and, she told him, if he worked hard enough, one day he too could become the superintendent of Yakima schools.

Orville hated the job. Teaching was hardly enough to keep his active mind occupied. So he canvassed the town for more challenging pursuits. Sauntering into the office of *The Yakima Daily Republic,* for which he had once worked as a delivery boy, Orville parlayed his English degree into a job as a part-time reporter and copy editor.

In his spare time he also began writing fictional cowboy stories for pulp magazines and even a couple of dime novels, adopting the pen name William Fraser, the name of a long-ago minister and writer hailing from Reverend William Douglas's native Nova Scotia. As soon as he saved some money, Orville tried his hand at investing to make a quick score that would make escape possible. However, after losing nearly all of the five hundred dollars he had invested in his friend O. E. Bailey's "sure-fire" life-insurance proposal, he became soured on all such speculative schemes.

Teaching high school in Yakima was the loneliest of jobs for Orville Douglas. He always had an eye for a pretty girl, and students in his classes began noticing that he moved all the pretty girls to the rows right in front of him, while consigning the boys to the back of the room.

The truth was that the social situation for him was horrible. Most of the young ladies that Douglas had met in high school had gotten married while he was away at college. The same was true with the female teachers with whom he now worked. Living at home with his mother did not help his chances to meet people.

Everything changed, though, in the fall of 1921, when Mildred Riddle arrived from La Grande, Oregon, to take over the Latin classes. Blessed with long blond hair and blue eyes, this quietly reflective woman immediately won Orville's heart. Few realized that Mildred, the daughter of an apple rancher, was actually returning to her educational roots. Eleven years earlier she had left her home in La Grande to spend her senior year at North Yakima High School, little realizing that fifteen months after she graduated the man of her dreams would enter the same school. "She is always the same—quiet and happy," her classmates wrote of Mildred, whom they nicknamed "Chubby," in their yearbook. When she attended the University of Oregon, she was held in similarly high esteem.

Mildred had a natural gift for teaching. She brought to the school four years of experience teaching Latin and mathematics at La Grande High School. In addition to being one of the most popular teachers in the school, she was soon recognized as one of the true intellects on the faculty. And in no time at all, Mildred made the dead Latin language come to life for the sons and daughters of farmers and poor northwest city folk.

When Mildred and Orville met in the fall of 1921, the attraction was immediate. Living in the same general neighborhood, these two shy, attractive, and brilliant people soon discovered that intellectually they had much in common. Personally, though, one potential obstacle lay in their path. As soon as she learned Orville's age, Mildred strove mightily to keep hers from him and everyone else. Not even her own children would learn that Mildred was born on September 4, 1892, making her more than six years older than Orville. She had the kind of ageless beauty that made keeping this secret possible.

Mildred became the subject of constant and tireless attention from the lanky, sandy-haired English teacher. He invited her for long picnics, driving with her into the hills in his beat-up car. There seemed to be a perfect balance between the quiet, contemplative, bookish woman who loved to listen and the brilliant, likable young man who loved to talk about himself. As their relationship deepened, though, Mildred sensed her beau's deep emotional needs, and she sought to provide for them in any way that she could. In time, Mildred's communications with Orville took on an almost childishly innocent and loving tone. He became her "lovingest boy," while she referred to herself only as "girl."

Orville began to cast about for a new career by sitting in the courtroom of a local judge named Frank H. Rudkin and dreaming of the day when he, too, might preside over his own court. Knowing that such a job required a law degree, Orville recalled that an attorney in Walla Walla named Grant Bond had offered him money for law school if he would agree to come back and join his law practice. And then there was the recommendation of O. E. Bailey, who, after helping him lose the money on the insurance scheme, suggested that a law practice was the ticket to real riches for a young man with his intellect. Seeking advice on this issue, Douglas went to the one man he trusted: his mother's attorney, James O. Cull. Practicing law is a good living, said Cull, and when you have your degree you can come back to Yakima and practice law with me. Since that prospect seemed a lot better than a lifetime of correcting grammar papers, Orville began making plans to become a lawyer.

After several dates, Mildred took Orville home to meet her parents in La Grande. As pleased as he was, given his favorite daughter's advancing age, to see any young man at his doorstep, Charles Riddle sensed that young Douglas would not be teaching high school in Yakima forever. "That young man will not only be a good lawyer," he predicted, "he will be a judge someday."

Now all Orville needed was a law school to attend. To the young man who had twice failed to attend some of the best institutions—the University of Washington and Oxford—the answer seemed obvious. Since the best law school at that time was Harvard Law School, Orville applied. He was admitted, only to realize once again that he had no money to attend. At a chance meeting, a local Yakima attorney named James T. Donald, who had worked his way through Columbia Law School, suggested to Orville that with the wealth of job prospects in New York City he could do the same. After his application to Columbia was accepted, Orville arranged to leave Yakima once again.

When Orville told Mildred about his plans, he pulled out a small diamond engagement ring and asked her to marry him. She agreed immediately. But since they did not have enough money to get married before his departure, Mildred agreed to remain in Yakima, teaching Latin, while Orville attended law school.

He had a career direction and a fiancée, but Orville still had to figure out how to get to New York. The answer, he decided, was to follow the lead of many of his Whitman classmates who paid for their train trips east by sheepherding a couple of thousand sheep on freight trains that went from Wenatchee, Washington, to the East Coast by way of Chicago. "Lord, that was luxurious stuff in those days. You rode in the caboose," recalled Chester Maxey, a longtime Douglas friend from Whitman College. "You had to help water and feed the sheep on the way east, but you lived on the fat of the land and got free transportation to and from. All the boys were competing for those jobs."

When the arrangements were made and the time came to leave for school in mid-September, the Douglas family gathered around the organ to sing together one last time. As Orville sat on the stool gazing at them, the inevitable doubts began to creep into his mind. How would he deal with being so far away from these people, who had been his life for so long? Would he succeed in this new career? Would he ever see them again? But he knew that he just had to go.

The next morning, Orville gathered all of his belongings—his checkered suit and a change of clothes—in a battered suitcase and stuffed what remained of his savings, less than one hundred dollars, into his pocket. Julia and he walked to the alley, where he would take a shortcut to the Yakima freight yards. Julia cupped the head of her "Treasure" in her hands, tears rolling down her cheeks, and kissed him. "Go to it, son," she said bravely. "You have the strength of ten because your heart is pure." And as she watched him walk out of sight, Julia had every confidence that finally, unlike her, Orville would be free—free of the limitations of Yakima.

Plan as young man Douglas might, nothing ever went routinely for him. When his sheep train reached Chicago, it stopped dead because of a nationwide railroad shopmen's strike that made it difficult for freight trains to get crews. Day after day, Orville remained stranded, growing increasingly fearful that he would miss the opening day of classes. With his funds now almost entirely depleted by what had turned into a ten-day delay, Orville was told by a hobo from the sheep train that if he planned on arriving at Columbia on time, he'd better find a way to get going soon. So he found a passenger train going east that was still operating and wired his brother, Arthur, then in Yakima preparing for his own return to Whitman College, for fifteen dollars to cover the cost of a coach ticket to New York.

When he arrived at the bustling Grand Central Terminal, Douglas did not even have enough money left to eat. So he found a nearby restaurant that would allow him to pay for his first meal in the city by washing dishes. Now all he needed was a place to stay and some money to register for law school.

"You have the strength of ten because your heart is pure," his mother had told him at the beginning of his journey. But now he found that he had the luck of ten.

Like all members of Beta Theta Pi, Douglas knew that with the taking of his fraternity pledge came the promise that a bed was waiting for him at other chapters around the country, including Columbia's. Douglas hiked over to the elegant fraternity house at 40 East Fortieth Street, not far from the school's original location, that all the nattily dressed Ivy League Betas called home. But when the boys in tweed jackets cast their eyes on the dusty, rumpled, sheep-smelling foreigner with several days' growth of beard in their entryway, they wanted no part of him.

Just as Douglas was about to be tossed out, he glanced up the fancy staircase to the second floor only to see, to his amazement, his old Whitman College roommate Bill Wilson coming down. A shouted greeting and the few quick words that followed told him that Wilson was on his way to Baltimore to begin his medical studies at Johns Hopkins University, having just spent the night at this Beta house himself. Three thousand miles and more than two years since the friends had said their good-byes at graduation in Walla Walla, here they were meeting with the type of coincidental timing that Hollywood invented. Wilson surveyed the scene and later told Whitman College classmate Frances Penrose that he didn't know who was more surprised—him, the relieved Douglas, or the puzzled New York Betas, who began to wonder if Wilson had fooled them as well. After the explanations were made and the laughter and hearty handshakes with the eastern Betas finally subsided, Douglas was offered a room and his meals for as long as he cared to stay. But Wilson's service to his old classmate was not done just yet, as Douglas tapped him for the seventy-five dollars necessary to register.

Now "Bill," as he preferred to be called once he arrived in New York, was faced with the chance to put all of the ghosts of his past life behind him. After what seemed to be a lifetime of overcoming financial obstacles, the wheel of fortune seemed to have turned. Bill Douglas would now become a law student.

THE YAKIMA APPLE KNOCKER

> Bill used to write that he put himself through law
> school by hard work, and that it hurt his perfor-
> mance.... But I always thought that he actually had
> a financial *advantage* over most of us at the time.
>
> —*Simon Rifkind*

Nothing in Bill Douglas's life had prepared him for what he faced at
Columbia. The impersonal urban life of New York City was totally unlike that of rural Yakima. There were no more friendly neighbors; instead, people trudged by in faceless droves. There were no more
home-cooked meals from his mother or Martha; instead, his food now
came from the coin-operated machines at Horn and Hardart, or the
Exchange Buffet, so named because you paid for your food according to the honor system. There were no more gorgeous natural vistas;
instead, there was just row after row of tall buildings. For the boy
from the mountains, this was hell on earth. To ease his homesickness,
Douglas decided to leave the Beta house and found a classmate from
"home"—Carrol Mateer Shanks, a 1921 graduate of the University of
Washington—to room with on campus in Furnald Hall.

By now, Douglas was heavily engaged in what had become all too
routine throughout his young life: the pursuit of money to survive and
remain in school. Tuition and fees amounted to $212, the cost of the
room in Furnald Hall would be at least $145, and board was an addi-
tional $300. To get through the first semester, Douglas's savings and
various loans from his family and others had to be supplemented by
doing, Shanks recalls, "considerable tutoring, particularly in Latin."
But the truth was that Bill Douglas still did not have enough money
for a full year of law school.

By Christmastime, Douglas had nearly run out of money, and he was
on the verge of being evicted from his dorm room for nonpayment of
rent. In desperation, he turned to the school employment office. When

nothing turned up and no prospects presented themselves nearby, he began to look into teaching jobs in Bernardsville, New Jersey, expecting that he would be forced to drop out of school. Then, Shanks remembers, "by a stroke of luck" early in the spring semester, a job opened up to revise "a set of [business] law books used by a correspondence school." For this effort, Douglas was told that he would get a two-hundred-dollar advance to keep him in school and an additional four hundred upon completion, which together with more tutoring would pay for his second term. He accepted the job. While updating the books was difficult for a second-semester law student, according to Shanks, "Douglas pitched in and found out enough about the various subjects involved to turn out a workmanlike job."

As his classmates got to know Douglas, they became aware that he was different from them. "The thing that really set him apart from the rest of us," remembered classmate Herman Benjamin, "was not his brilliance—we were all pretty smart—and it was not his poverty— we were all pretty poor. . . . No, what set him apart from the rest of us was his age. He was a full two years older than the rest of us." Indeed, in an entering class of 264 people, nearly all twenty-one or twenty-two years old, Douglas was one of only two who were about to turn twenty-four. Embarrassed by this difference, Douglas made up a story to explain it. "He got a late start in law school, he said, because he had served in the army in Europe for a couple of years during the war," recalled Benjamin. Douglas conveniently overlooked the highly limited nature of his actual military service at Whitman. The story had the added benefit of hiding his two lost years teaching English at North Yakima High School because he had failed to get the Rhodes scholarship. With no reason to doubt the story, his classmates viewed Douglas as a distinguished war veteran. Douglas soon discovered that this gave him an extra amount of prestige because they all felt guilty about having been too young to fight. And after Douglas saw their reaction, it became a story that he told throughout his life.

To show their respect and their acceptance of him, his classmates searched for a nickname that described their Bill Douglas. The answer came in one of the stories he enjoyed telling about his home. In a class in which nearly all of the students came from the New York City area, Douglas stood out, being from "Yokima," as it was listed in the Columbia University Bulletin of Information for the law school. He loved to tell them all how his family had been so poor that as a child he had earned money to help feed them by using a stick to knock ripe apples from the trees. So for his classmates he became "The Yakima Apple Knocker." "The nickname had a double meaning," explained a classmate. "It was meant to tell everyone that this fellow was not like the rest of us, being from the far west. It told people he was something of a hayseed. But those closest to Bill knew that it was a private joke. If there was anyone who was just the *opposite* of a hayseed it was Douglas. You see, he was older than the rest of us, had been in the army, and as such was more sophisticated than the rest of us."

Douglas liked the nickname but knew that, though his classmates believed that they had him wrong, they had him exactly right. He *was* a hayseed. He still lit his cigarette matches either on his pants leg or on the soles of his shoes. He alone knew how to camp in the mountains with nothing in his pockets. And, like all good "Yokima" boys, he could drink the eastern law students under the table.

Now all this hayseed needed to do to make the joke complete was to outperform them all in the classroom. This time, though, the task proved to be more difficult than he expected. Surrounded by some of the best young legal minds in the country, for the first time in his life the high school valedictorian and collegiate Phi Beta Kappa member faced stiff competition in the classroom.

Beyond the high caliber of his classmates, Douglas initially found it difficult to satisfy the school's highly distinguished faculty. Gathered at Columbia at that time were some of the brightest legal minds in the nation. Nearly all of the faculty members had written books that defined their fields of study—contracts with Herman Oliphant, personal property with Harlan Fiske Stone, real property with Richard Powell, torts with Young B. Smith, pleading and practice with Edwin W. Patterson, and criminal law with Ralph W. Gifford. The lineup was enough to intimidate any student, let alone the product of the isolated North Yakima High School and tiny Whitman College.

This combination of intellectual challenges took its toll on Bill Douglas's scholarly performance. At the end of the first year's exams, when the top several students were acknowledged by being named James Kent Scholars, Douglas was not among them. Douglas's friends believed that his lack of academic success was due to causes beyond any intellectual weakness on his part. "Douglas was not well-off in law school," explained Herman Benjamin. "He was the only one of our class who absolutely had to work. . . . The rest of us worked to get spare money, but Douglas *had* to work to live. I think it's quite possible that his financial straits may have affected his scholarship."

As disappointed as Douglas was, there was still a chance to signify his intellectual superiority by being selected for the Columbia Law Review. While he knew that membership on the elite legal publication was based exclusively on grades, with more slots available than in the

Kent Scholar selection process, he thought he had a chance to be chosen here. But, once again, when that initial group of seven nominees was announced in August 1923, he was not among them. One of the coveted spots went to his close friend Herman Benjamin. A month later, Douglas was passed over again as another four members of his class, including another of his close friends, Al McCormack, were chosen for the Review. Two months later, yet another name—Eugene Raphael—was added to the list, making it at least a dozen classmates who were now ranked higher in the class than Douglas. In the Darwinian world of law school, where senior Law Review members serve as editors, and those editors generally receive the best job offers, Bill Douglas knew that he was already way behind in the race for postgraduation employment.

For the first time in his life, Bill Douglas had failed to excel in school, and it was a bitter pill to swallow. Fatalistically, Douglas could already envision how this story would end: Because of a lack of funds, there would be no Law Review for him, no academic honors, and no career-accelerating judicial clerkships thereafter. After struggling to make ends meet, once more he feared that he would see the entire effort wasted as others got the good jobs, the successful careers, and the happy lives. Unless he made some drastic change in his life, all that his years at law school would produce would be a train ticket home to Yakima. Suddenly, he realized, the two lost years of teaching in Yakima were not wasted ones after all.

In the summer of 1923, Douglas boarded a train and rode back to La Grande, Oregon. There, on August 16, he and Mildred were married in the presence of her family and his brother, Arthur. After a brief honeymoon camping in the Wallowa Mountains, the two of them got back on a train to New York City. While law-school classes would not begin until September 27, they needed the extra time for Mildred to find a teaching job in the city's public schools.

For Bill Douglas this marriage was the best of all possible worlds. Deeply romantic, he loved the feeling of being in love. Homesick as he still felt for the Pacific Northwest, Mildred also would represent a piece of his home in New York City. Accustomed as he was to women caring for him in times of distress, here was someone who would look after him. Finally, and most important, strapped as he was financially, Mildred would now be available to support him, enabling Douglas to use his time to compete for the highest possible grades in the classroom.

The marriage was just as appealing for Mildred. Now just three weeks from her thirty-first birthday, such a union was all that she had ever wanted. Just two years before, she was a spinster in Yakima with no prospects of marriage at all. A year later, she was thousands of miles from her fiancé with only a few letters, an engagement ring, and a promise of marriage to hold on to. Now only Bill's graduation from law school in two years separated her from the chance to raise the family she so craved.

But strangely, in the foxholelike world of law-school education, where few secrets are kept from fellow students, none of Douglas's classmates knew about Mildred or the recent marriage. The way that Douglas hid his new marriage from his colleagues illustrated both his desperation to succeed while also making it look like he alone was responsible, and Mildred's gentle willingness to aid him.

With married students not permitted to live in the law-school dorms, the Douglases took up residence a few blocks from the law school, at 525 West 124th Street. Try as she might to find a job, Mildred found that there was no call for a Latin teacher, especially one who was arriving from way out west without a local teaching certificate. The Douglases got a break when Edna Hummer, the Latin teacher at Bernards High School in Bernardsville, New Jersey, ironically precisely where Bill had looked for a job the year before, unexpectedly announced that she would be retiring on October 18. Suddenly, the pleasant, talented, and newly available western lady became a very attractive candidate. Mildred interviewed for the job and signed a contract for a yearly salary of $1,900 on the same day that Hummer retired.

The problem with the job for the Douglases was its location. Situated some thirty-five miles from New York City near the Watchung Mountains, Bernardsville was hardly the first choice for daily commuters. Rather, the town was a resort called "the Mountain," serving the area's millionaires. The only passenger train going into the city at the time was nicknamed the Millionaires' Express because the rich people in the area would simply hook up their private railroad cars to the trains that ran to Hoboken. From Hoboken, it would still be a long and convoluted journey up to Columbia Law School.

Faced with the prospect of her husband commuting long hours to class each day, Mildred agreed to live by herself in New Jersey and support him while he went to school in New York City. She found a boardinghouse where single teachers in Bernardsville lived, the Dayton House on Olcott Avenue, and spent the school year there while Bill remained in their new apartment. Never telling the law-school administration that he was married, he saved a little money in his third year by moving back into a Livingston Hall dorm room to live with his first-year roommate Carrol Shanks. Accustomed as Mildred was to living a continent apart from her "lovingest boy," she now found being only part of a state away to be an improvement.

In an era in which single schoolteachers were always placed under a microscope, residents of Bernardsville gossiped about Mildred actually being married and putting a husband through law school. The only reason that they overlooked her unconventional lifestyle was because, as her principal Harry G. Stuart remembered, "She was a lovely woman, one of the finest people I ever met. And the kids loved her."

Thanks to his wife's efforts, Bill Douglas now had all the time he needed to study, improving his ability to compete in the classroom. In time, Douglas found an intellectual mentor in a legal legend named Underhill Moore. The brilliant and eccentric Moore believed that no important legal principle should be taught without first pounding on his desk to get students' attention. Only when the class began responding by pounding on their own desks in response, he believed, could the teacher-student relationship evolve. Moore's approach to the law, called legal realism, was to focus his considerable intellect on a simple real-world problem and, using a combination of legal and social-science research techniques, expose every relevant fact involved in it. That fall, Douglas took two of Moore's classes—Agency, an examination of the relationship between principal and agent, and Sales of Personal Property—and in the spring he enrolled in his Bills and Notes course, which examined the legal principles of bills of exchange and promissory notes.

The first professor at Columbia to take great interest in the boy from Yakima, Underhill Moore had a significant influence on young Bill Douglas. His sociological and intensively fact-oriented approach to the study of law fit perfectly with Douglas's iconoclastic training. Beyond that, Moore's idiosyncratic and irreverent intellectual temperament led Douglas to abandon the old style of memorizing legal cases and principles used by the other members of the faculty and take up Moore's technique of searching for the real-world implications of these legal doctrines.

As time went on, the relationship between the two men deepened. Since the professor was in the process of revising his casebooks, Douglas was hired as his research assistant for the year. The following semester, Moore was so impressed with Douglas's performance that he asked the young law student to help revise his casebook for Bills and Notes, despite the fact that he was taking the class at the time. Later, Douglas accompanied Moore on an inspection tour of the Portland Cement firm, for a Supreme Court case that was being prepared.

Bolstered by Mildred's financial help, Douglas performed well enough in the fall classes of his second year to enjoy a dramatic jump in his class rank and win at last a coveted seat on the Law Review. Years later, when Douglas's classmates learned that he had been hiding his marriage, they understood how he had improved his class standing.

While for some, membership on the Law Review was a dream come true, for Bill Douglas it was ultimately just a means to an end. Like others on the Review, Douglas was expected to research and write his own law note to be published, edit articles from professors and students on esoteric facets of law, and print digests of all cases of interest to the readership. It was like another full-time job, one more draw on Douglas's precious time. "Class work was sort of pushed aside," Herman Benjamin recalled. "We worked day and night in the Law Review dungeon trying to get our issues out. And we were always behind. Friday nights, Saturdays, Sundays . . . it didn't matter . . . we were always there."

Since membership rather than the work was his goal, however, Douglas dealt with it accordingly. Colleagues noted that Douglas did his work with great efficiency and without their passion. "He didn't have the same interest in spending all hours of the day and night in the Law Review office," remembered Benjamin. "Most of us had a passion, almost an obsession, for the law. We loved it. We would follow up exotic points of law. . . . We did it because it interested us—it became a part of us. But Douglas wasn't like that at all. He just did what was required . . . and nothing more. He didn't have the same passion for the law. It was as if he were just putting his time in to get the credential."

Why was Douglas in such a hurry? they wondered to one another. Part of the answer lay in the secret wife, who expected him to visit her at least occasionally on the weekends. Part of it was also the multitasking style that Douglas had developed since college. The major reason, though, lay in the task that Douglas had set for himself. He had to catch up to the academic performance of his friends, many of whom were Kent Scholars, and all of whom were on the Law Review a full six months before him. Indeed, even the announcement of his election to the Law Review staff bore evidence of the challenge in front of Douglas. On the opposite page was the announcement that several of his classmates had just been elected to the Review's editorial board for the following year. Alfred McCormack was elected editor-in-chief, William Gilbert secretary, Eugene Raphael business editor, Herman Benjamin associate decisions editor, Bernard Sobol note editor, Arthur Kramer decisions editor, and H. Struve Hensel book-review editor. To Douglas and his classmates, here was the list of Columbia Law

School's future legal superstars. Somehow, some way, he would just
have to catch them.

But as Bill Douglas was poised for his academic assault in the latter
part of the spring semester of his second year, he got very, very sick.
Whatever the sickness was, nobody other than he and Mildred knew,
but it went on for weeks. Deeply concerned about her husband's well-
being, Mildred moved out of the rooming house, where she could have
no extended visitors, and took a room in a family residence in order to
care for him. Douglas's normally competitive classmates became so
concerned by his prolonged absence from classes that several of them
began putting carbon paper in their notebooks and taking notes for
him. At the end of the semester, Douglas was too sick to take his
exams. So while everyone else was off making money in the summer of
1924, Douglas remained behind to study for a special set of makeup
exams.

Knowing that a great performance was needed to ensure good job
recommendations, Douglas was stunned when he glanced at the exam
prepared by his own mentor, Underhill Moore, for Bills and Notes. Instead of seeing what he thought would be routine questions based on
the casebook he had been revising, Douglas found a single question
that made absolutely no sense to him. After laboring over the exam
book for hours, he turned in his work, certain that he had failed.

Only later did Moore confess that, having already made up his
mind about Douglas's grade based on his earlier work but still being
required by the school to administer an exam, he decided to play a little joke on his young assistant. Moore asked him a question that was
so complicated that even he could not answer it. In fact, he later explained to Douglas, the question had become a topic for discussion
that year among members of the Columbia faculty, and *no one* had
been able to answer it. So, Moore assured him, a second-year law-
school student should not have been concerned that his contribution
did little to advance the cause.

In playing his joke, though, Moore discovered that he did not
know his protégé well enough. Even the honors grade that he received
for the class did not give Douglas any satisfaction. Rather than see the
joke as a sign of respect by a senior professor, the thin-skinned Douglas spent several weeks during his final year of law school researching
and writing a long and esoteric Law Review note, never published,
that attempted to solve the unanswerable question.

Despite all of his labors in the second year, Douglas still failed to
crack the top ranks of his class. The James Kent Scholars for that year

were his close friends Carrol Shanks and Alfred McCormack, along with Solomon Sklar and Arthur Kramer. Since Kramer had been a Kent Scholar both years, and the other three had been in the first cut for the Law Review, it was now clear that they were at the top of the class of '25.

Douglas was still behind, but there was one more year to catch up. With so many credits already under their belts, though, he knew it would require an overwhelmingly superior performance in the third year to make up any ground.

Unfortunately, it wasn't to be—for in his way stood Professor Thomas Reed Powell.

Powell loved two things in life: shredding the Supreme Court's latest decisions and doing the same to students in his constitutional-law class. Bill Douglas was no exception, getting a C, his lowest grade in three years at the school, in the subject that would one day make him a legend. As the spring term came to a close, and students' thoughts turned to jobs, Bill Douglas did not know how or where he wished to practice law. Despite the offer of a partnership in Walla Walla with Grant Bond, the man who had offered to help him through law school, the thought of returning to his old college town to work was unacceptable. The same was true of returning to Yakima to work with James O. Cull.

Then a more prestigious option presented itself when former Columbia Law dean Harlan Fiske Stone was named to the Supreme Court and asked his old school to send him a candidate for the coveted clerkship in his new office. Douglas now convinced himself that he was that candidate. Once more, however, Douglas's reach exceeded his grasp.

Most everyone at Columbia knew all the time who the nominee would be—the editor in chief of the Law Review. As class of '26 and Columbia Law Review member Milton Handler recalled the process: "The outstanding member of [Bill Douglas's] class . . . was Alfred McCormack. It was a foregone conclusion and expected by students and faculty that Stone would select Al McCormack as his law clerk." So he did.

The effect on Bill Douglas was devastating. "The news reached the Law School in April, and I was so unhappy that for two weeks the sun never came out for me. The world was black and I was unspeakably depressed that for all those years and all that work, I had so little to show," he remembered later.

Unlike the Rhodes competition five years earlier, though, this time Douglas did not come away from his years of study empty-handed. He and Carrol Shanks were judged by the faculty to be so outstanding from the class of '25 that they were chosen for the exclusive lecturer-in-law positions, enabling them to teach two courses in the law school the following year. Douglas now had the opportunity to explore a career that he had never really considered: law-school teaching.

5

THE CRISIS

Something's crooked someplace.

—Julia Bickford Fisk Douglas

Commencement Day, June 3, 1925, promised to mark the turning point for Bill and Mildred Douglas. With his law degree and part-time teaching position now safely in hand, and facing the New York bar exam in just a few days, Bill was ready to find the full-time legal job that would support them both. Like all Law Review graduates at Columbia, this now seemed to him to be a routine quest because, still shy of his twenty-seventh birthday, time was his ally.

For Mildred, though, the biological clock ticked loudly. Then facing her thirty-third birthday, all that she had to show for her decade of labor in school systems around the country was a husband with a sheepskin. Since they had been unable to save any money, she knew that it would take at least a couple more years to get on a firm enough financial footing for them to start a family. So, for her, it was going to be at least a couple more years of full-time teaching.

Reasoning that Bill's job would be in New York City, the two of them searched for a suburb where they could live on the commuter-train line. While it would require Mildred to give up her tenured teaching job at Bernardsville, she had the necessary experience now to get another one. In July they settled on Pelham, just northeast of New York, where the frequent trains would better accommodate Bill's likely around-the-clock work schedule. And, making it all seem so perfect, Mildred immediately landed a teaching job at Pelham Memorial High School. The only problem was that since they were not able to move into the apartment until early September, Mildred would have to supervise the move after her new job had started.

Once Bill began searching for his job, however, it was not long before he realized that being a member of the Columbia Law Review did not guarantee him the job of his choice. He had decided to interview with the elite Wall Street law firms, where, he fully expected, the practice of high-level corporate law meant that he would never be poor again. For the young man who had struggled throughout his life with low social self-esteem, a Wall Street position would finally give him the status he had long craved.

But Douglas quickly learned that on Wall Street as elsewhere, it was who you know rather than just what you know that governed the job-search process. He interviewed with John Foster Dulles at the elite Sullivan and Cromwell firm, only to see the job go to James Gifford, Jr., the son of the influential professor of evidence at Columbia. After being passed over as well by the great trial lawyer Emory Buckner, Douglas visited the powerful Wall Street firm of Cravath, Henderson & de Gersdorff, where he was interviewed by a young associate named John J. McCloy. As McCloy listened to the young man's tale of overcoming financial obstacles, he was intrigued that the story was so much like his own. McCloy persuaded his firm to take a chance on Douglas, offering him a position beginning on September 15, starting at an $1,800 salary. In order to give him time to adjust to the new job, Douglas arranged to teach both his Columbia courses in the spring term, as well as an evening business-law course in the university's extension school to further supplement his income.

Like all new Cravath associates, Douglas quickly learned that the practice of law on Wall Street was a great deal less glamorous than he had imagined. New associates were crammed two to an office no bigger than a large closet and expected to bill three hundred hours per month. Since not every hour in the office can be billed to a client, this meant that each junior attorney was expected to be working in the office for eighty to ninety hours a week. For Douglas, this meant arriving at the office before 9:00 A.M. in order to be available for the first summons from his supervising partner, which always occurred between 9:30 and 10:00. Then for the next fourteen to sixteen hours he labored at a breakneck pace over a blizzard of legal papers. It was not unusual for his workday to last until two, three, or even four o'clock in the morning, whatever it took to prepare the papers for the next day. Then, he rode the train home to Pelham for a couple of hours of sleep, a shower, a fresh set of clothes, and a quick cup of coffee with Mildred before racing back to start the same cycle all over again. There were no weekends for Wall Street legal associates, only the hope that the reduced number of phone calls on Saturday and Sunday would give them a chance to catch up on the paperwork.

With each passing day, Bill Douglas realized that life on Wall Street was not for him. Just as in law school, the grinding, high-pressure work was exacting its toll on his health. Periodically, he had terrible migraine headaches, often accompanied by long periods of fever. Other times, he would get stomach pains so severe that he was literally doubled over in pain. Thinking back to his father's stomach ailments and early demise, Douglas soon feared that he, too, would need an operation for ulcers.

Day after day, he told Mildred about his unhappiness. The work was too hard, the pressure was too great, and he was just a small cog in a very large legal machine. Each time, they ended the conversation the same way: Perhaps they could go back home to the west, and he could begin a small-town law practice. But with no savings, they knew, it would take a couple of years on Wall Street to build enough of a nest egg to do so.

When the physical pains recurred, Douglas called Dr. Bill Wilson, the Whitman classmate who had saved him at the Columbia Beta house and who was now a resident at the Women's Hospital in Baltimore, for advice. After conducting a series of diagnostic tests, Wilson concluded that the symptoms were more psychological than physical. The solution, he told Douglas, was to reduce the stress in his life. Since that stress was apparently being caused by working at Cravath, offered the doctor, maybe a different job, such as teaching full-time, was the answer.

Any changes were put on hold, however, as Douglas's personal life began to fall apart. On December 27, 1925, Mildred's beloved oldest sister, Sara, who had been ill for nearly three months, died. Mildred packed as quickly as she could, got a leave of absence from her school, and took the train home for what would turn out to be a several-week stay. For Douglas, ever the loner unwilling and unable to confide in others besides his wife, this meant that his entire psychological support system was now far away.

With pressure on him building, the situation suddenly got worse. Douglas now found his mailbox filled with letters from his mother containing terrible news about her financial situation. Julia had moved to Minneapolis in 1924 to live with Martha, who moved there after her brother Arthur's graduation from Whitman College. Now she needed her eldest son's help for the legal fight of her life. Her business partner, James O. Cull, she wrote, had stolen all of her life savings.

In a series of letters, Julia poured out the sordid details of a story that had been previously unknown to Bill. Sometime after her husband's pension had run out in 1910, Julia wrote her son, she had "loaned" the law firm of Cull and Rankin $2,100, to be repaid at 10 percent interest. She failed to mention that this happened, in fact, several years after 1910 and after she had made some successful investments through Cull. Julia explained that while the new investment paid her money for a couple of years, after Cull's law firm went "nearly bankrupt" no additional money was forthcoming for a four-year period. The effect of this loss on her finances became evident in her 1921 city tax records, which indicated that her personal property tax base had been cut to $300, down from $480 the year before. Then, in November 1921, Cull drew up a new trust agreement with the local Valley Bank, under which Julia was promised 4 percent on her total investment, which at that time amounted to $3,010, with the expectation of being repaid in November 1928. But no money came from this new agreement either. As a result, Julia figured that in late 1925 and early 1926, after several more years of nonpayment, her investment had accumulated on paper to about $3,500. But there was still no cash, nor was there any evidence that it would be forthcoming from either Cull or the bank.

The problem, she explained to her son, was that she had had such faith in Cull that she had signed these documents after he had read them to her and had not been given a copy. Julia wanted action and she wanted it now: "Well if they keep the law to the letter I would have rec[eive]d my money before this & I *intend* to get it. I want you to write . . . & ask . . . why I am not getting it & why he hasn't informed me in regard to it." Her son, the prominent Wall Street lawyer, she believed, would make it all right.

On top of all this, she added, the rest of her financial world had collapsed. In 1923, with no money to live on and Arthur then in college, Julia was forced because of Cull's nonpayment to take out a $1,200 mortgage on her house with the Yakima Savings and Loan Association to meet her living expenses. After spending years free of house payments, this meant that with no incoming funds and no job she was in danger of losing her home. When she decided to leave Yakima a year later, she tried to sell the house to cover the mortgage, but the market was so depressed that it did not attract any buyers. Finally, on December 22, 1925, as Bill had advised, she transferred the deed to her house to a janitor from the Columbia Grade School named Charley Cooper and his wife, Elizabeth, who agreed to assume the remainder of the mortgage, $885.62. In addition, the Coopers had also agreed to pay rent on the furniture she had left in the house and reimburse her for "50 feet of brand new hose."

But now, Julia said, the Coopers were turning out to be deadbeats as well. No rental payments for the furniture and the new hose had been received, and she had been notified that they had not paid the house's insurance as agreed. All of this, Julia wrote her son, was great cause for worry to her, since she was still legally responsible for the house payments. "You can see that this is what they have planned to do right along, get it for nothing," she wrote. "That's the reason they never replyed [*sic*] to my letters. They are dead beats; it looks like it to me."

Julia's lifetime of financial hardship made it impossible for her to realize that things were not as bad as she feared. Even if the Coopers defaulted on their agreement, she would, just as had happened before with her other failed land investments, have the option of getting the house back for resale. And as for the missing investment money, even if it was completely lost, Julia, now being supported by Martha, was guaranteed to be taken care of for the rest of her life.

But that was not how she saw it. This was the only money that she had for the rest of her life, and it was her beloved husband's legacy to her, no less. Wasn't there something that Orville could do? Desperate for help, she wrote: "Hope you get the money from Coopers for Furniture & Insurance on house. *They have* to pay it. Lots of love from Mumsey." No longer thinking of herself as the totally powerless, poor widow lady, Julia sought vengeance.

But this time she was wrong. Douglas quickly realized that there was absolutely nothing he could do. His years of legal training, not to mention his work in the Cravath firm, told him that Cull hadn't stolen the money. Instead, this was just another failed investment, one that confirmed all the rumors that had long been swirling around Yakima about Cull. His mother, Douglas could see, had gambled her money foolishly and lost. As for the problem with the sale of her house, he could see that the Coopers would have to be evicted. Since the family lawyer with whom he would normally work was now the man that his mother was accusing of theft, Douglas decided that he would have to leave this effort to others.

Without realizing that she had done so, Julia had told her son in these letters a great deal more about his life than he had ever known before. The hard labor as a child to support his family, the inability to attend the University of Washington, having to work his way through Whitman College and his early time at Columbia Law School, had all come from a feeling that his mother could give him no financial support. Most people who had survived such an experience to practice law on Wall Street would see a life that was successful. Douglas, however, tended to focus on the negative. For him there was no Rhodes scholarship, two years lost from his life teaching English in Yakima, and no graduation at the top of his law-school class. Consequently, now it was classmate Alfred McCormack who was sitting at the right hand of Justice Harlan Fiske Stone, while Douglas's stomach churned painfully at Cravath. In reviewing his life, all Bill Douglas saw was missed opportunities and failed chances, all due, he had always believed, to a lack of family funds. And now Douglas knew that money had not been nearly as tight at 111 North Fifth Avenue as he had been told. The now lost $2,100 could have made all the difference in his life, if only Julia had invested it in his education. But instead of investing in his future, he now knew, she took a foolish chance on a speculative deal.

All of these events had a profound impact on Douglas's increasingly fragile psychological state. In a matter of days, it became more than he could handle. Seeking to resolve the psychological pain, even though his wife was still a continent away, he quit his job at Cravath on January 28, 1926, after just four and one half months of work.

Where should he go and what should he do? the out-of-work attorney now wondered. With no other full-time job in hand, Douglas's means of support now was, as it had been during law school, his wife's full-time job, to be supplemented by his part-time teaching in the spring term. Just what was left of his once promising legal career was no longer certain.

When Mildred returned from her family visit, only to discover that she was once again the family's sole full-time breadwinner, the gentle woman was happy to support her husband until he found his niche. So she returned to Pelham Memorial High School to fulfill the remainder of her contract teaching Latin. Meanwhile, Douglas tried to patch some jobs together to reduce the impact of his rash decision on the family's finances. His Columbia courses would provide them with $1,600. Even with his course in the extension school, which would pay an additional $300, how could they save money for their escape to the west? The answer, he decided, was to get a raise from Columbia. After making the request, in early February, he was notified that another $700 would be coming his way for the spring term, meaning that he would be making $100 more in salary during that four-month period than if he were still working at Cravath while teaching at Columbia. And all of this would come to him for teaching just a handful of hours a week.

But the question remained as to what would happen to the Douglases after the spring term. With no guarantee that his lectureship could be extended to the fall, Bill Douglas had to decide quickly what he was going to do. And his options were more limited than they had been when he graduated from law school. By quitting the Cravath firm so abruptly, in the middle of one of their most important cases, the reorganization of the nearly bankrupt Chicago, Milwaukee, and St. Paul Railroad, Douglas had put his legal career into great jeopardy. And things got no better in the summer months, when all he could find was a few legal-research jobs for friends such as Carrol Shanks and other members of the Columbia faculty.

By the middle of August 1926, after nearly eight months of underemployment, Bill Douglas was a very unhappy young man indeed. And with finances for the Douglas household very tight, when Mildred went in August for her yearly visit to her family in La Grande, there was no money for Bill to accompany her. The thought of his wife relaxing in their beloved pine-cooled Pacific Northwest while he pounded the pavement in search of work, with only an occasional visit to Rye Beach, was more than Douglas cared to consider. Self-pity took over as he wrote his wife a long, whining letter about his plight. It just wasn't fair, he wrote her. He was sick again, and, to make matters worse, his mother was now in New York visiting him. With the dinnertable conversation devoted to the question of how to recover her lost money, Douglas needed to do something to change his life.

And he had. Douglas wrote his wife that, on his own initiative, he had found a new way to balance their books by leasing a smaller, furnished apartment in Pelham, thus saving them $180 a month. And, best of all, Douglas told his wife, he had already figured out how to spend the newly found money: He was coming to visit her in the Pacific Northwest. More than that, he added, the time had come for them to move west permanently.

Like most people in Douglas's life, Mildred generally found it difficult to refuse him. But she decided to try to do so now. "Lovingest boy," she began in her letter to him, "As to your coming west right now, I don't just know what to say. . . . As you say it would take at least $200. . . . Boy has worked hard for 4 years and girl for 3 and we haven't a single cent to show for it."

But for Mildred, there was another consideration now: "If we have a little Billie, I want to [have] the money . . . all ready for him. [But] anything boy wants is all right with girl, isn't it, boy."

When Douglas reluctantly agreed, it appeared that all was well. He would devote the next month to moving their belongings to the new apartment because, given her experience the previous year, Mildred did not want to have to move them again after her classes had begun. But the situation continued to work on Douglas as he thought about it. If he was lucky, another year of part-time teaching at the law school would only keep them out of the poorhouse while he considered his career options. And for another year he would have to listen to Mildred's concerns about starting a family while she worked full-time to support them.

To Bill Douglas this seemed to be the most agonizing point in his life. But he was wrong. Things were about to get worse.

"LAWYER, AGED 37"

People will say you are nuts. But remember, no one
is nuts if he can find a responsible person who agrees
with him.

— *Dr. George Draper to Douglas*

It all started so innocuously.

On August 24, 1926, Bill Douglas read the front-page headline of
The New York Times that blared: VALENTINO PASSES WITH NO KIN AT SIDE;
THRONGS IN STREET. In a riveting newspaper account, he learned how
Rudolph Valentino, the thirty-one-year-old sex symbol of the silent
screen, had undergone a double operation for acute appendicitis and
gastric ulcers on August 15, before succumbing days later to peritonitis. The effect on the country was unprecedented. Thousands of fans,
many of them clothed in black shirts, who had blocked the street in
front of the hospital waiting for medical-update bulletins, went into
mourning.

But the strangest reaction of all may have been by the young New
York lawyer who hailed from Yakima, Washington. From the first news
that he had seen about Valentino's declining health, Bill Douglas had
felt compellingly drawn to the story. Then, within hours of reading
about the movie star's demise, Douglas was doubled over with the
worst stomach pains of his life. As he was completely prostrate, his
stomach wall became absolutely rigid, and he vomited more violently
and frequently than ever before. Finally, just as had happened several
times during his work at the Cravath firm, without any warning the
pain suddenly disappeared and Douglas was immediately overcome
by a powerful craving for baked beans.

This most recent painful attack caused Douglas to assess his career
options once more. He decided that since the pains were not linked to
the pressures of his legal work, he might as well return to his old job

at Cravath and earn some additional money. Fortunately for him, the firm was happy to have another experienced person on hand to help with the still ongoing Chicago, Milwaukee, and St. Paul Railroad reorganization case. So, on October 1, Douglas agreed to return, even getting an increase in salary to $2,400, with a promise of an additional six hundred dollars three months later. Since he had agreed to teach a course on partnership at Columbia, Douglas had it scheduled for 8:00 A.M., thus making it possible to put in his sixteen-hour stint at the law office. Then he arranged to pick up an extra four hundred dollars by teaching a business-law course during his dinner hour.

For the first time in nearly a year, the Douglases enjoyed a more normal lifestyle. Mildred's classes were going well, and Bill's around-the-clock work was very much appreciated at both Cravath and Columbia. Bill and Mildred found that they enjoyed their new apartment, which was just a five-minute walk from the train station.

The only troubling issue now was Bill's health. Deeply concerned about his stomach, even though the symptoms did not return after the Valentino incident, he began visiting one doctor after another, seeking a proper diagnosis and treatment. Each one had a different diagnosis, it seemed, but the recommended cure was always the same. It's a duodenal ulcer, one told him, and we have to operate. No, it's gallstones, said another, and, yes, we do have to operate. For the young man who remembered seeing his father go off to Portland for a stomach operation and never return, the prospect of such surgery was terrifying. In October, he consulted yet another doctor, who diagnosed the problem only as "faulty digestion" and put him on a regimen of diet and exercise. The disciplined but rail-thin young man who once drank everyone under the table in law school now dutifully cut out liquor entirely, watched his diet, and played handball twice a week. When his weight increased and the stomach pains failed to return, Douglas was relieved.

But by early 1927, the strain of having every minute of his life taken up by Cravath and classes started to show. "Sometimes I fear a tight and ever tightening web is being cast about me here," he wrote to his friend and fraternity brother A. Howard Meneely, then a professor at Amherst College, as he assessed his career options in a series of diary-like letters.

Despite his earlier misgivings about the practice of law on Wall Street, Douglas now confessed to Meneely: "I like the work at the firm immensely. I like the men. I like the office spirit and morale. I like the work at Columbia too. In fact I have many likes. Ain't it hell?" Each day seemed to him to bring a new challenge of using legal loopholes to protect the firm's corporate clients. Because of his fine work, promises were being made of an eventual partnership, the surefire ticket to a much higher salary, not to mention a substantial boost to his ego.

But Douglas's interests now lay in more than just the practice of law. His natural teaching and research skills in the academic world were also beginning to display themselves, leading the faculty at Columbia Law School to offer him a full-time position as an associate professor. Carrying an initial salary of five thousand dollars per year, with a promise of an additional $1,400 annually in outside teaching and research, the position would likely lead in five or six years to a full professorship with tenure at double the salary. The promise of tenure meant much to the man who had been unemployed for most of the previous year. "The faculty is all for me, for some reason or other," he wrote to Meneely. "They argue hard and sincerely and are quite subtle in the pressure they are putting on me." The only drawback, it seemed, was that if he took the job he would have to give up his law practice.

One aspect that enticed Douglas to work at Columbia was the chance to make a difference to the legal profession. Douglas believed that in the ongoing era of reform in legal education toward the legal-realist views of professors such as Underhill Moore, a young, innovative professor could make his mark in a hurry. "There is a big piece of work to be done at Columbia in legal education," he explained to Meneely. "And mark my words—the old school is going to set the pace for legal education in the next 15 years. So I must admit their offer to me has manifold possibilities. The chances are more than just ordinary. The time is auspicious. There is a re-shuffling of all the cards. The old order changeth. A young fellow like myself will be given every opportunity to spark."

The choice for Bill Douglas was not an easy one, and it weighed heavily upon him. "Ye Gods, why was I ever put together in such fashion that I can be worked on and influenced and swayed," he moaned to Meneely. "Oh for a non-macaroni spine and an inflexible, fixed, determined, solid purpose and aim in life."

There could be no better appraisal of Bill Douglas at age twenty-eight. For the truth was that, as attractive as both of these offers were, neither of them appealed to him more than the other. It was not the choice of the direction of his career that haunted him the most but its location. Douglas confessed to Meneely that he just wanted to go home to "the golden west, where men can walk to work & mow the lawn in the evenings." He and Carrol Shanks had become so enchanted with the idea of practicing law thousands of miles from the pressure of New York City that they had talked seriously about leaving that year.

But, they had finally agreed, the timing was not right. "We have decided that the seasoning process we are undergoing now is too valuable to miss & that another year spent here will be well spent." Still, he concluded, "the old western urge still burns."

After much reflection, Douglas decided in early February to accept Columbia's offer. But he was not at all certain that he had made the right choice, telling Meneely that he had left himself an escape hatch by "reserv[ing] the privilege to leave at the end of next year."

And it was good that he had, for without any warning Douglas had already received another indication that his life was still not in order. Once more, he had found himself doubled over with another terrible stomach attack. This impelled him to consult his old Whitman friend Bill Wilson again to determine whether Columbia was his best option. Return home to the west where "the environment is more restful," the doctor advised him, and his "whole nervous system would vastly improve." It was advice that Douglas now seemed quite prepared to accept. "I have been seriously considering returning to Yakima where life is peaceful & quiet," he wrote Meneely. "I am sure I could have a good business [in Yakima] in a few years with the nearby mountains & streams so readily available. I am confident I could keep in much better health than I can here. Besides that, a big city like N.Y. takes a lot out of a fellow by just living in it even tho[ugh] the work is not hard. That you well know. The Columbia offer is very attractive & appeals to me of course. But at its best it is just a N.Y. job. While I like N.Y. in many ways & would no doubt miss it, I hate it in so many ways that I would not long for it eagerly."

Thinking that the time had come to back out of his agreement with Columbia, Douglas made plans to see the dean and "re-hash the whole thing over," telling Meneely that "I think he will release me from my promise."

Douglas also consulted yet another doctor in mid-April. "At last I have found a wonderful Dr.," he wrote Meneely on April 20. "He has been taking all sorts of pictures of my insides & knows more about me than any living being. This Dr. is A1. I have some interesting dope to tell you." Because of a sheer coincidence of location, Meneely later learned, Bill Douglas had found the one doctor in the country with the unique set of credentials to help him: George Draper.

To some, Columbia medical professor George Draper was a pioneering genius, while others saw him as a total quack. But Draper was no quack; rather, he was years ahead of his time. A 1906 graduate of Columbia University's College of Physicians and Surgeons, Draper made his reputation in epidemiology. After four years of research in

Germany and a stint in France during World War I, Draper became an internationally acknowledged expert on infantile paralysis, scarlet fever, and various cardiac diseases. His 1917 volume *Acute Poliomyelitis* led him to become a protégé of Dr. Robert M. Lovett, the nation's leading authority on poliomyelitis, and subsequently to treat an old prep-school chum, former assistant secretary of the navy Franklin Delano Roosevelt, when he was stricken with the illness in 1921.

Despite these accomplishments in epidemiology, in the 1920s Draper pioneered what he called "scientific constitutional medicine"—the relationship of the mind to physical ailments. Convinced by his earlier studies that certain psychological traits in patients made them more susceptible to various serious illnesses, Draper studied patients' susceptibility to peptic ulcers, gall-bladder ailments, diabetes, and rheumatic fever. When he published these analyses in 1924 as *Human Constitution: A Consideration of Its Relationship to Disease,* Draper was on his way to becoming known as the "father of psychosomatic medicine."

George Draper was thus uniquely qualified to deal with Bill Douglas's stomach pains, for which no clear physical cause could be found. In early May, Douglas suffered another crippling stomach attack immediately after learning of the death of a three-year-old neighbor boy from peritonitis. Draper believed, linking it with the Rudolph Valentino attack, that he now had all he needed to resolve the young lawyer's stomach pains.

While normally any doctor-patient relationship is privileged, Draper and Douglas's sessions became the basis for one of Draper's pivotal publications. In 1930, in his seminal volume on psychosomatic illness, *Disease and the Man,* he documented his treatment of Douglas, whose case study he labeled only as "Lawyer, Aged 37" in order to protect Douglas's confidentiality. This fascinating case, Draper wrote, involved a man who "complained of attacks of violent gastric pain associated with vomiting and great prostration. . . . But the patient's clinical history revealed that ingestion of food did not bear any chronological relationship to the pain."

Draper wrote that two things made these attacks especially unusual and easily diagnosable as linked to neurotic tendencies. First, there was the matter of what triggered two of the attacks: the sudden deaths of Rudolph Valentino and later of a neighbor's son, from peritonitis. Then Draper took particular notice of the consistent pattern in the denouement of the symptoms: "When the pain was over a ravenous hunger supervened. Associated in every instance with this hunger was a clearly defined craving for baked beans."

Draper searched for the earliest origins of links to these stomach ailments and the unique craving that signaled their disappearance. The patient recalled that "at the age of 10 he had listened with secret terror and dismay to the accounts of the agonising death from peritonitis of an old family friend; indeed, he still remembered keenly the fear sensations associated with that experience." But beyond that, the patient added, "At an even earlier age, possibly 3 or 4, he himself had been the subject of a severe and prolonged intestinal colic which nearly caused his death." Draper further reported: "An interesting detail of his recovery from this illness, which had often been told him by his mother, was the enormous appetite he had at once developed, and that his first real meal had been made of baked beans."

Draper reasoned that the patient's "colic-like attacks, followed by hunger and a well-defined craving for a specific food, were directly related to an emotional reaction set up by the prospect of an acute fatal peritonitis." On that basis, the doctor set out to prove to the patient that his problem was not physical but psychosomatic. Seeking to educate his patient, Draper gave the lawyer the same bismuth meal-test treatment that the other doctors had used in seeking to detect an ulcer or other stomach problem. The patient was instructed to ingest a metallic and fluorescent substance, which would register on a fluoroscope, thus allowing a view of the gastric and muscular action of his stomach. The radiologist then massaged the patient's stomach to demonstrate the "gastric peristalsis," or muscular contractions of the stomach in response to the touch. Whenever the massages were interrupted, the stomach again became calm on the fluoroscope. After two or three minutes of rest, Draper simply whispered in the patient's ear, "Rudolph Valentino died of peritonitis." The result, the doctor reported, was amazing: "After a delay of a few seconds, clearly visible, active, almost violent increase in gastric peristalsis began to appear. Synchronously with these, the patient complained of rumbling feelings in his stomach." The patient could see for himself on the fluoroscope that his mind stirred the reaction in his stomach. After several repetitions of this exercise, the ailing lawyer became convinced that his problem was nothing physical. As a result, Draper reported, "with a growing insight into the mechanisms of these attacks, the patient was greatly relieved."

Having worked on the the psychological problems of his patient, Draper then turned his attention to the bodily functions that might be contributing to the problems. Douglas was told to stop smoking and "reduc[e] the volume of his work activities."

This Douglas did on May 1, quitting the Cravath firm for the second time, after just seven months back on the job. "I hate to sever connections here in many ways as I am in a favorable footing & to start all over again is a task," he wrote Meneely at the time. "But I deem it best." And rather than continue his teaching at Columbia, Douglas told Meneely that he was planning to take a summer vacation with a very specific purpose attached to it. On May 22, after his classes on Bankruptcy and Insolvency and Damages were completed, Douglas intended to travel back to the Pacific Northwest to seek a job in a law firm. Since family finances were still tight, Douglas would be going without Mildred.

By the end of May, he was on his way west on the very Chicago, Milwaukee, and St. Paul Railroad that had been occupying his professional attention because of its bankruptcy reorganization. "I hated like hell to finally say farewell to my east coast friends & to pull out. But no doubt a year from now I will be cussing myself for staying as long as I did in N.Y.C.," wrote Douglas to his friend. "Golly, I hated to leave Mildred behind for so long. The actual going pulls the old heart strings. But the summer will no doubt move along quite fast." So certain was he of finding different employment, in fact, that Douglas had already secured an agreement from Carrol Shanks to join him in a year. With the pressure of Cravath behind him now and the comfort afforded him by George Draper's psychological explanation supported by his new lifestyle changes, his stomach attacks never again returned. But nothing was ever certain in Bill Douglas's life, as he added in his letter to Meneely: "Of course if I do not like it I will double back." As Douglas knew, Columbia Law was still expecting him in the fall.

Had Meneely known more about his friend's family background, however, this letter would certainly have made him wonder about Bill Douglas's actual state of mind in making this journey. "My address for the time being will be c/o J.O. Cull, Miller Bldg," in Yakima, Douglas wrote him. Of all the places that he could have gone in the Pacific Northwest, he was returning to the hometown that had once made him so unhappy and from which he had once been so desperate to escape. And of the nearly seventy attorneys that he could have worked with there, Bill Douglas was going to work for the very man who, while having offered to employ him years before, just one year earlier had been accused by Julia Fisk Douglas of cheating her out of her life savings.

MR. DOUGLAS GOES TO YAKIMA

Get the hell out of here. You'll go to seed my boy.

—*O. E. Bailey to Douglas, June 1927*

Bill Douglas found that he very much liked the man his mother reviled. "Cull was full of enthusiasm & pep & had grand ideas as to what he could & would do for me in the way of building up a practice for me," he wrote A. Howard Meneely. "His intentions were very good & I appreciated his spirit & attitude very much." The truth was that he needed Cull's help a great deal if he was going to make a go of practicing law in Yakima. He possessed absolutely no knowledge of small-town legal practice and lacked a Washington State license. For his part, Cull thought that by combining his knowledge of the area with Douglas's obvious ability in the law, they might be able to build the finest firm in town.

But Douglas's appreciation for Cull could not overcome another feeling that quickly overtook him. As soon as he arrived in Yakima, Douglas realized that he had made a big mistake by coming. "The old town got me," he wrote his friend. "I never felt more depressed in my life. All the old memories of days of privation and hard toil came back on me in ever increasing waves. I simply did not have an ounce of energy to tackle the big job ahead. I was in utter despair—a peculiar, but altogether rational, psychological condition." With his personal support system—Mildred and also George Draper—a continent away in New York, Bill Douglas was in psychological turmoil once again.

Douglas's paralyzed mental state soon became evident to complete strangers. He went to the Yakima bar association's law library, to begin studying for the state bar exam in June. There Douglas found another recent law-school graduate, Joe Cheney, doing the same. The two men agreed to begin studying together. Douglas, however, soon turned the conversation away from the exam and toward his doubts about his future. He was not so sure now that he wanted to take the exam at all, he told Cheney. For hour after hour, Douglas reviewed his personal history and asked this stranger what he should do. Should he go back to Columbia or should he stay? He just didn't know. To Cheney, it seemed that Douglas was filled with so much self-doubt that studying for the bar exam was not going to be possible—for either of them.

The truth was that practicing small-town law in the west turned out not to be as golden as Douglas had expected. Cull's legal practice, he quickly learned, had dwindled to the point that there wasn't enough business to support two men. And with thirteen other lawyers by sheer coincidence coming to town and looking for work the same week that he did, Douglas could see that the competition for business would soon be even keener. Beyond that, he learned at the Yakima bar's yearly picnic that the nature of the small-town legal community was not what he had expected. "They were a backslapping 'You no [sic] me, Al' gang," a shocked Douglas complained to A. Howard Meneely. "Booze was their strongest fort [sic] & everyone from the judge down was hailed by his first name or nickname. There was more rah-rah stuff in five minutes being thrown around than I had heard in 5 years. And on top of it all they all seemed to be sops intellectually but were so damn conceited & egotistical that they were just common bores. I couldn't endure it. I hadn't a thing in common with them."

Then there was the unseemly nature of the legal work itself. Unlike the more sanitary practice of corporate law on Wall Street, where rich corporate clients lined up for the chance to be served by the Cravath firm, Douglas learned how small-town private attorneys made their livings. Evenings were spent getting to know the judges and searching for new clients in meetings of the various community clubs—the Lions, the Rotarians, the Elks, the Kiwanis—while the noon hour was spent cruising the luncheon-club circuit. Douglas discovered that the legal community was in something of a turmoil, since a new luncheon club had just been formed—meaning that there were now seven such clubs and only six workdays on which to attend them. People were "at each other's throats" deciding which club would have to be inconvenienced to accommodate the new organization.

What time was not spent by lawyers eating and boozing was devoted to doing charitable work in search of other future clients. "I was opportuned [sic] to immediately get into civic work to boom up the old [business]," Douglas explained. "I was even told that it was the most interesting of all work. One young chap told me the week I was there he had spent but 2 hours in his law office—the rest of the time being given to the Comm[ercia]l Club. Good contacts—meet the big men—get to know them at sight—call them by their first names." When Douglas complained to his senior partner, Cull told him that this was his "duty," and he "would have to do it whether [he] wanted to or not." Douglas really didn't want to. When the hot topic that week turned into a free-for-all over who would have the honor of dedicating the city's newly constructed railway station, he had seen enough. "Get the hell out of here. You'll go to seed my boy," said his old insurance buddy, O. E. Bailey. "I talked to Cull—frankly & freely," Douglas later wrote Meneely. "We talked for hours & finally Cull advised me not to stay. He was very nice & sympathetic & saw the thing thru [sic] my eyes. So we shaked hands [sic] & I hit [the road]."

For his part, Cull later recalled it a bit differently. He told anyone who would listen that when Douglas announced that he was leaving, he was "happy not to stand in the way." "Douglas just wasn't any good at the practice of law," Cull explained to the locals. "He couldn't seem to make any money at it." Coming from a man who regularly ran his law practice into near bankruptcy, this was a harsh assessment indeed.

So Bill Douglas left Yakima—after only four days. And, he later confessed, "I could not have stayed a day longer." His old hometown was just not a place where this reformed teetotaler wanted to live. As he described it: "Yakima is in a whirl of bridge & booze. . . . They play 4 days a week 10 mo[nths] in the year & wind up in a drunken orgy. I could not see Mildred & Martha & Carrol & I hitting that pace. You can't turn down a drink there. If you do, you're a sissy or snob & there is no such thing as appreciating your point of view."

But it was more than just the shock of seeing the practice of small-town law that drove him away. Psychologically, he just had to leave. "As soon as I crossed the Cascade Mts.," he explained to A. Howard Meneely, "the feeling of depression left me & once again was I free & full of pep & spirit. What a whale of a difference a few miles make!"

Still, Douglas was not ready to give up on practicing law in the "golden West" entirely—perhaps Seattle would be better. For two days he banged on the doors of the city's law firms and found that the news was both good and bad. Several firms had open positions, but none of them carried more than a $3,600 salary. For the man who had a five-thousand-dollar full-time law-school teaching job waiting for him, that was just not enough. Even if he was willing to accept the lower salary in return for the change in location, Douglas also discovered that new associates in Seattle were expected to pay their own way until they had both passed the bar and been fully trained by a member of the firm. So he did not have the financial means to take the job. "I would have stayed in Seattle to practice. But I thought a larger stake would be needed. So I decided to return for at least another year before going," he wrote Meneely.

With his savings nearly depleted, and after spending less time "practicing law" and job hunting in the Pacific Northwest than he had on the train traveling to it, his options were now limited to one. "I have accepted my professorship at Columbia @ $5000 plus $400 for my extension course," he announced to Meneely. "So, I am doomed to N.Y. rattle & bang for another year. But I am so highly pleased the way things have turned out! I have seen the light. I know now what last spring I only dreamed. I know I would *never, never* be happy in Yakima. It was worth $300 to find it out before I got settled there & was broke." This "trial and error method" of searching for a new career direction, as he was now labeling it, had given him a new plan. When they had built up enough of a financial stake to do so, Douglas announced, he and Carrol Shanks would go west. "I am confident Seattle is the place for me," he wrote Meneely. "I went into conditions there quite thoroughly & they convinced me it was *the* place. I'm going west, Howard. But I'm glad I didn't go last month & stay."

With this new course charted, Douglas rode the train back to New York and convinced Mildred to spend the money he had "saved" by shortening the trip on rent for a cottage in Wolfeboro, New Hampshire, on Lake Winnipesaukee. To help them enjoy the rest of the summer before the daily grind of their classes resumed, Douglas invited his old college buddy Bill Wilson to join them. "We fished all day," Wilson said later. "I had brought a bottle of rum and brought it out one evening. I offered some to Bill but he wouldn't take it. Finally he drank some and got very sick. Mildred got very mad at us. She didn't like it at all." But Douglas, who on George Draper's advice had not had a drop to drink in months, did not learn his lesson. When his stomach problems did not return, Douglas took it as a sign that he could resume drinking and smoking.

Douglas looked forward to the peaceful life of an ivory-tower professor of law. "The future seems clearer & more certain & my mind is at greater rest," Douglas wrote Meneely. "I now *know* my goal. Before I didn't quite know—at least not with my present assurance. It makes a lot of difference once the objective stands definite & clear before one."

But Douglas was about to discover that he had traded the cutthroat business of practicing law for the equally cutthroat world of academia.

COWBOY ON A HORSE

The old school here is on the skids—much as I regret it. I fear for its future.

—*Douglas to A. Howard Meneely*

From the opening bell of the fall 1927 law-school classes, Columbia's newest junior professor made an indelible impression on his students. "The first time I slapped eyes on him I knew the electricity of the Roaring Twenties was running through him," recalled Ernie Cuneo, one of the students. "Douglas literally charged in.... [He] blew in like a cowboy on a horse.... He was bursting with energy. He sat down, but he couldn't sit still. He weaved. Then he jumped up and he walked; strode would be more accurate. He had a long first stride. I noted that he was both quick and fast."

After this dramatic entrance, Douglas would proceed to conduct his class unlike anyone else in the school. "He was all over the room, cracking out his precedents and questions as fast as we could write, driving, driving, driving, driving us as he drove himself. 'Get along little doggies, get along,' I thought," recalled Cuneo. Then, as each class came to a close, Douglas would pose a long list of questions that was the research assignment for the next class. "I didn't know what road Douglas was walking, but I knew he wasn't walking the road of the ancient common law," concluded Cuneo.

Accustomed to working at a whirlwind pace, when he was not in class Douglas threw himself into the task of building an academic career. He was often in the Kent Hall library preparing his lecture notes for his two courses, Security I and Security II. Lunch was the only break in the schedule for the junior professors, so day after day Douglas ate with colleague Milton Handler, who had graduated from Columbia Law the year after him. Handler quickly learned that for

Douglas life revolved around work, as he found his colleague to be "very taciturn and secretive" about his personal life.

For their senior colleagues, however, that year was all about academic warfare. Columbia was in the middle of the "legal realist" revolution, as some of their ranks joined the growing national movement to search the economic, political, sociological, and psychological fields for help in understanding judges. For this group, law was not found but made, meaning that the function of law in society preoccupied them. Only by studying the forces that influenced judges, using social-science lines of inquiry, could their decisions be fully understood.

Columbia's foray into this field was led by Professor Herman Oliphant, who sought to reorganize the entire curriculum of the school according to the functions that each legal subject performed for society. Oliphant himself had already organized a course called Illegal Contracts and Combinations (later titled Trade Regulation), which analyzed the consequences of illegal business transactions for commerce and industry.

This new movement had appealed to Douglas when he decided to teach at Columbia. Now, in his few spare hours, he hurried downtown to find lecturer in law Adolf A. Berle, Jr., then also practicing corporate law, so they could work on combining three existing courses—Agency, Partnership, and Corporations—into one legal-realist course called Business Organizations. Douglas knew that once this task was completed he could write a casebook for the new course and launch his publishing career, on which his future promotions would be largely based, should he choose to stay at Columbia.

Like most academic debates, though, this one was fueled as much by politics as by intellectual theory. The legal realists at Columbia were also seeking to reduce their teaching loads by transforming the school into a research institute that produced legal theorists as well as practicing lawyers. For an institution funded largely by tuition and staffed by senior faculty members still devoted to teaching, this was a recipe for academic infighting between the liberal, research-oriented legal realists and the conservative, teaching-oriented old guard.

The reform forces were united under Herman Oliphant, while the old guard looked to Professor Young B. Smith for leadership. Encouraged by Columbia University president Nicholas Murray Butler to "go hammer and tongs" at reform, in 1924 Oliphant had expected to replace Dean Harlan Fiske Stone when he left to become attorney general of the United States. Instead, though, President Butler chose the more moderate Huger W. Jervey to fill the post, and for a time it seemed to be an inspired choice. Holding no brief for either side, Jervey tempered his sympathy for the old guard with a display of considerable respect for the reformers.

Under Jervey's direction, in the spring of 1926 various members of the faculty met weekly to discuss curriculum revision with Professor Leon C. Marshall, an economist who had directed the legal-realism course revision at the University of Chicago. After months of meetings, the faculty produced one hundred reports, amounting to more than eight hundred pages, that argued that Columbia could begin preparing lawyers for public service by concentrating on new areas of legal research. When the faculty appeared satisfied with the direction of the debate, it seemed as if Jervey would be able to contain the intellectual forces that threatened to rip the school apart.

In the end, though, this mediation took too much of a personal toll on the dean's health. When a possibly cancerous gastrointestinal problem struck him in the spring of 1926, Jervey departed for the Mayo Clinic in Minnesota, leaving the school in the hands of one member of each camp, Herman Oliphant and Thomas Reed Powell. After Jervey took an indefinite leave of absence in the summer of 1927, President Butler angered the school's publishing faculty by selecting Young B. Smith as the acting dean for the coming academic year. Only the hope that Jervey would eventually reclaim his position kept the school from immediately exploding. But when Jervey's illness compelled him to resign in February 1928, effective upon the appointment of his successor, his old colleagues began to inventory their intellectual arsenal for the war that would surely follow.

While all of this was happening, Bill Douglas, like other first-year faculty, was much too busy laboring on his lecture notes and future publications to be actively involved in this battle. In a year of lunches together, Milton Handler recalled, the two men never once discussed the problems on the faculty until the very end of the dispute.

But Douglas's effort to distance himself from the fighting was fueled by another impulse: He was fully engaged in planning his permanent move to the Pacific Northwest. Still lacking the funds for the start-up costs to practice law in Seattle, Douglas had begun negotiating with Jim Donald, the old Yakima friend who had once advised him to attend Columbia Law School, and Blaine Hallock, one of his SATC buddies from Whitman College, to join their small law firm in tiny Baker City, Oregon, near Mildred's home, La Grande. By late April 1928, they had hammered out the rough outlines of a deal, but to Douglas's regret, and for reasons that were never made clear to him, the offer fell apart.

In a fortnight, Douglas would have good reason to regret the loss of that job prospect. As President Butler considered the choices for a new, permanent dean, he could see that it came down to either Young B. Smith or Herman Oliphant. On Wednesday, May 2, without consulting the faculty and knowing that three members of the reform group were out of town, Butler announced that he would recommend to the trustees Young B. Smith's appointment as dean the following Monday unless he could be persuaded to the contrary by the faculty. A "thunderstruck" Bill Douglas wrote A. Howard Meneely: "If the appointment is made, my resignation goes in on Tuesday. It's the most high handed piece of politics ever seen. It's a damnable outrage. . . . Every good man will leave. The school will disintegrate. All that in [the] face of the promising new project which would blaze the trail for legal education in the future."

After the faculty was unable to fashion a united response to the president, Douglas decided to move on his own. "Your decision to nominate Professor Smith as Dean of the Law School disturbs me greatly," he wrote President Butler on May 5. "If the office of Dean required nothing but routine, secretarial, intra-University duties, the choice would be admirable. But the office is not thus delimited." Having observed him at close range as a student and a faculty member, Douglas made it clear that he had absolutely no confidence in Smith: "His lack of general culture and his uncouthness are patent. Even students in his classes are open in their comment on it." More than that, Douglas argued, Smith would be unable to deal with the high-powered and intellectually volatile legal-realist faculty. "His almost total lack of imagination and his decidedly deficient intellectual equipment make it not only unlikely but impossible that he can bind together and lead and direct that group of unusually promising young men who are well launched on the new project and on whose efforts the success for the new law school depends." After reviewing all these flaws, Douglas concluded that "the appointment presages for legal education at Columbia mediocrity rather than excellence; recession instead of progress; disintegration rather than new life." For the man who had lamented his own "macaroni spine" the year before, Bill Douglas was now showing for the first time that he was more ready to take charge of his career.

But Douglas had also learned from his abortive trip west the year before the value of hedging his employment bets while he charted a new course of action. So after the trustees appointed Young B. Smith on May 7, Douglas chose to delay sending his letter of resignation.

Instead, Douglas decided on the cool spring evening of May 8 that the best course of action was to go drinking. For residents of Pelham who wished to drink during the Prohibition years, that meant going to the fashionable Pelham Country Club, where bootleg whiskey was served among the wooden benches in the club's locker room. With the local chief of police and fire chief frequently found drinking nearby, one could be certain that an untimely raid was not likely.

Douglas had been invited there that night to the annual dinner of the Pelham Men's Club as a guest of its incoming president, Richard Walsh, who was also the president of John Day Publishing Company and the husband of novelist Pearl Buck. The speaker for the evening was someone Walsh believed would appeal to his friend: the "Boy Wonder," Robert Maynard Hutchins, who had the year before startled the academic legal community by being named dean of the Yale Law School at the tender age of twenty-eight.

True to his reputation, the legal-realist-oriented Hutchins gave the club members a full taste of his iconoclastic style that night in a speech that lambasted the state of American education. "Most American boys go to College because it is the thing to do — to get to know the fellows, to thus qualify for the charmed circle of college-bred men, and not because of any great desire for intellectual development," he argued. And the conditions were unlikely to improve, Hutchins added, because when "full-fledged professors received salaries on a level with those of a well-paid janitor there could be no expectancy of greater intellectual ability and exertion being engaged in our colleges than commensurate with the salary involved."

To Bill Douglas, it seemed as though Hutchins had been speaking directly to him. As soon as he had the opportunity, he sidled over to Hutchins to impress him with the story of his life and the tale of his troubles now at Columbia. As the two men talked, it seemed as if they had more in common with each other than they did with their own brothers. Both were the sons of ministers who never quite fit in with their own church's doctrine. Both had been gifted orators in college, relying on intellectual powers far beyond that of their age cohorts. Both had exceedingly quick wits, enjoying the verbal repartee of topping each other's stories, and each had an extremely clever sense of humor. Also, both had graduated with distinction from their respective law schools in the class of '25.

However, Hutchins was not able to see on their first meeting the differences that defined why one of them had risen to the top of his profession while the other, three months older, was on the verge of looking for a new job. Unlike the itinerant Douglas, Hutchins had lived a charmed academic life, graduating first in his class at Yale Law School, teaching full-time immediately thereafter, and already having made his reputation working in the field of evidence. More than that, he had scorched the tenure track, been named a full professor before his time, headed Yale's Institute of Human Relations, and been appointed the acting dean in just two years, before getting his present post. While Bill Douglas's Business Organization work was promising, and his teaching skills were evident, Robert Maynard Hutchins was, in 1928, already earmarked as the most remarkable legal educator of the age.

Part of what made Hutchins great as an administrator, though, was his ability to spot future academic talent, especially potential geniuses who did not quite fit into the stodgy academic community. By the time Douglas drove him to the train station that evening, Hutchins sensed that here was a man who could make Yale Law School better by his presence.

Mornings are tough for those who have drunk too much the night before. "Did I wake you?" the cheery voice on the telephone asked Douglas at 6:00 the next morning. Still trying to place the voice through his mental fog, Douglas heard a male voice say that in three hours the Yale law faculty was going to offer him a position as professor of law at Yale. Best of all, he was told, the contract would be for three years at six thousand dollars a year, more than Douglas had earned thus far on Wall Street or at Columbia. Douglas was so stunned that all he could do was jokingly mumble, "Where is Yale?"

"I'll be in Pelham in two days," Hutchins laughed, "and I'll bring a map."

Douglas realized that with this offer he finally had the security that he had been craving for so long. But still he delayed resigning from Columbia until the deal was finalized. And it was good that he did, because he had no idea just how tenuous his move to Yale was on May 9. Before Bill Douglas could be appointed, the faculty would have to approve him and the contract would have to be supported by the university president, the financial prudential committee, and the supervising Yale Corporation. Once the latest shock waves of Columbia's revolution reached New Haven, with the school labeling its disaffected faculty "the mutineers," these approvals were far from automatic.

Making the move even more dangerous was the fact that, without telling anybody, Hutchins had temporarily shelved his plans to get Douglas in favor of an even bolder scheme for raiding Columbia Law School. If this junior untenured professor was ready to walk out the door, he thought, perhaps other, more prominent scholars might be willing to do the same.

Two days after meeting Douglas at the Pelham Country Club,

Hutchins met with his faculty and laid out his plan for stripping Columbia of its finest scholars. As a result, the Boy Wonder was "empowered to negotiate" with Douglas, legal theorist Hessel Yntema, and banking expert Underhill Moore. By the next day, though, Hutchins had secured Yale president James Rowland Angell's permission for a full-fledged raid of as many Columbia faculty as he could get. He headed to New York to enlist an unwitting Bill Douglas as his scout for the assault.

Hutchins's discussions with Douglas in New York on May 11 convinced him that nearly one third of Columbia's regular faculty might be up for grabs. Hutchins decided also to pursue tax expert Roswell Magill; the reformers' leader, Herman Oliphant; Underhill Moore's research assistant, Theodore S. Hope, Jr.; and Fred Hicks, who had made Columbia's law library one of the finest in the world. Hutchins reported to his faculty that these men were "the best of the Columbia group," citing as an example Bill Douglas, who was, "unquestionably, with [James] Landis of Harvard, the best man of his age in any eastern law school." By securing all of these additions, Hutchins believed, Yale's reputation would be propelled past Columbia's. Now all that he and President Angell had to do was convince the fiscally conservative members of the prudential committee that this "extraordinary opportunity" was worth the twenty-nine thousand dollars it would add to Yale's annual salary outlays.

While these negotiations were under way, Douglas began to inform his friends that he would soon be on the move again. "Well the jig is up," he wrote A. Howard Meneely on May 12. "Out of the clear sky comes an offer from Yale to go up there as a member of their law faculty. It's a peach of an offer." Always ready to find the dark cloud near a silver lining, however, Douglas added, likely thinking of the Baker City firm's offer: "I am considerably perturbed for I had decided to go back into practice. I must admit New Haven offers a life more nearly that of your present environment [at Amherst College]. And the life of the law school is marvelous, I hear. They have as promising a group as any law school—more so than any but Columbia."

He even began to announce his plans to some of his junior colleagues in Kent Hall. "Subsequent to the announcement of the Smith appointment," Milton Handler recalled, "[Douglas] walked into my office and told me about the heated discussions that had gone on all year, of which I had no inkling. He then proceeded to inform me that many of the faculty members were resigning and that he [had] decided to accept an invitation to join the Yale faculty." Douglas "then embarked upon a vehement personal attack on Smith." But still, just to be safe, the resignation letter remained in his typewriter.

Meanwhile, Hutchins's bold plans were threatened when Walter Wheeler Cook, who was looking to build a legal-research institute at Johns Hopkins University, where he then served as the school's only professor of jurisprudence, decided to raid the same disaffected Columbia faculty. Fortunately for Cook, Johns Hopkins's lack of bureaucracy made it possible for him to move much faster than Hutchins. After enlisting the chairman of the board of trustees to join him in visiting Moore and Oliphant, they were ready to offer fifteen thousand dollars to each man, more than either scholar could imagine earning from Columbia. And with no existing law school at Johns Hopkins, neither man would have to burden his researching with the teaching that Hutchins would require of them. Moore and Oliphant leaned toward accepting this package immediately.

For his part, Hutchins was concentrating on recruiting Moore. Once he secured his acceptance, the Yale dean was prepared to offer contracts to Oliphant, Magill, and Yntema. Only if there was money left in the kitty, he had decided, would an offer go to Douglas.

Douglas seemed totally unaware of how close his deal was to collapsing. "The Yale proposition is hanging fire," he wrote A. Howard Meneely on May 26. "I am going if we can get together on terms. I think we can, though of course the money has not been appropriated or voted yet. I look for no hitch there—but then again it is not a certainty. So I am sitting tight for awhile. I ought to hear in a few days." The one thing that he did know was that he would be leaving Columbia: "The old school here is on the skids—much as I regret it. I fear for its future. I am afraid it will fast fill up with second rate men—and for a school to be thus constipated means death & stagnation."

During all of Hutchins's wheeling and dealing, President Angell's enthusiasm for the expensive project began to wane, leading him to suggest that some of the hiring be delayed until the following academic year. But Hutchins was determined to make something happen. Since the senior people were still hedging on their decisions, Hutchins decided to reorder his recruitment proposal, reporting to his faculty on May 31 the "probability" that Douglas, Hicks, Moore, and Yntema would accept appointments for the coming year, while Oliphant and Magill would be coming the following year. Of course, everyone realized, the prudential committee and the Yale Corporation would have to vote on the offers at their next meeting.

Before that meeting, most of the potential appointees removed themselves from consideration. Moore and Oliphant decided to accept Johns Hopkins's standing offer, leading Walter Wheeler Cook to then successfully recruit Hessel Yntema. (Moore would eventually back out of the deal and remain at Columbia, speaking to no one as he considered his future options.) When Hope and Magill decided to remain at Columbia, the only men left available for Yale were the junior professor of business law, William O. Douglas, and the law librarian, Fred Hicks. And with fears now being openly expressed in New Haven that they might be hiring, in their words, the "neighbor's cook," thus opening themselves up to the problems already faced by Columbia, Hutchins would be lucky to get them through the process.

Finally, on June 8, Douglas got word that the Yale Corporation would vote the next day to extend him an offer. The delighted young man crowed to A. Howard Meneely: "I have accepted the Yale offer. It has not been officially confirmed yet but I expect it to be in a day or two. I am confident it is the best decision."

Three days later, after being informed that the offer letter was on its way, Douglas finally typed and then hand-delivered his three-sentence letter of resignation from Columbia, explaining in part: "The reason for this action is your nomination to the Trustees of Professor Y. B. Smith to be Dean of the Faculty of Law, without consultation with the members of said faculty. Such action makes it impossible for me to continue to serve this institution at this time."

Bill Douglas was on his way to New Haven. Together with Bob Hutchins, he now believed, they would mold a law school that would make history and suit them both.

PROFESSOR DOUGLAS

It never occurred to us that Douglas was a country boy.

—*Thomas I. Emerson*

Nobody could have been happier about Bill Douglas's move to Yale
Law School than his wife, Mildred. After so many years in the suburbs
of New York City, the Douglases discovered that they enjoyed the
comparatively bucolic life in New Haven. They found a house at 284
Orange Street, in a quiet, tree-filled neighborhood near Yale, where
Douglas could work in peace. Even though they could well afford to
buy the house, given his salary, Bill reflected on his youth and the im-
permanence of wealth and chose instead to rent. The choice turned
out to be a wise one when, after discovering that Bill's delightful
teaching colleague Thurman Arnold and his wife, Frances, lived on
Willow Street, an easy two-mile walk from campus, they decided to
move to the same block.

For the first time in her life, Mildred was able to stop teaching and
begin planning for their family. Now thirty-six years old, she was acknowledged as one of the most attractive faculty wives on campus
with her long, fluffy blond hair, peaches-and-cream complexion, and
round, clear blue eyes. This dainty, gentle, unassuming woman impressed everyone with her sincere, natural personality and quietly reflective intelligence. Her days were occupied now with keeping the
house in order, playing badminton with friends, swimming and playing tennis, reading current biographies or classic works in the original
Latin, preparing meals for Bill when he returned from his labors at all
hours, and planning intimate dinner parties for their new friends at
Yale.

With Bill consumed by his work at school, Mildred devoted her energies to the needs of her husband while she hoped for news that she had become pregnant. A family, a pleasant home, and, most of all, a husband who loved her—it was all that she had ever wanted out of life.

But it was not all that her husband wanted. As pleased as he was with his new job, Douglas was still not one to commit himself whole-heartedly to any single career path. No sooner did he arrive on campus than he resumed his now perennial debate over how soon to leave for the west. "The Baker Boys," as he now called them, were at it again, as Jim Donald tried to recruit Douglas to his Baker City, Oregon, law firm. Their annual business had increased by now to one hundred thousand dollars, and since they had just lost their law clerk, the part-ners had decided to look for a new junior associate. They all agreed the only choice for them was Bill Douglas.

Though they could offer only half his present faculty salary, $250 a month, with it came the promise of an eventual full partnership that would allow him to share in the firm's profits. When Douglas ex-pressed an interest, Donald said that he was so anxious to have him on board that he wanted him to start on January 1. Douglas once more turned to A. Howard Meneely. "The prospects for business expansion are great, they say," wrote Douglas. "I believe them. They have the biggest & best practice in eastern Oregon & Idaho. . . . So that makes a possible entry for our C[arrol]. M. S[hanks]." While the money was not quite right and he had grown to enjoy teaching, what still ap-pealed to him was the lifestyle: "Life in eastern Oregon has many attractions. Of course Mildred will be near her folks. The town is small. It nestles close to some beautiful mountains. The elevation promises delightful weather. The only thing lacking among the values I have will be the scholastic air. In its place will be a rough & ready atmosphere—comparable a bit to the old west they say."

But now, for the first time, there was something more. As he con-sidered his options, there was one other career prospect that appealed to him. "The thing that strikes me about it all," he confessed, "is that a man in that country in the legal profession can go a long way & spend his last years on the bench in an honorable, interesting way." For the man whose stomach would not allow him to compete in Wall Street legal circles, and who had never been fully in control of his own work-ing environment, the gentle world of a small-town judge presiding over his own courtroom now seemed to be just about the best possi-ble career option. So Douglas now convinced himself that what he had seen in Yakima as the grubby business of small-town rainmaking for legal clients—and the quest to "call everyone by their first name" to get ahead—would not be as true in small-town Oregon.

Upon deciding by the first of the year that he was ready to accept the job if the money could be worked out, Douglas pressed the firm for a "more definite commitment." After delaying for six weeks, though, the Baker City firm offered more arguments rather than more money. The lower salary is acceptable, they argued to Douglas, because of the incredibly cheap living expenses in eastern Oregon. Besides, they added, this was the amount *they* had each started at when launching the firm. But if he still wanted more money, they promised to raise the salary after six months to three hundred dollars a month; later, it would be adjusted according to Douglas's " 'worth' to the firm."

Douglas was unpersuaded, explaining that it would actually cost him more to move. His earlier health problems had driven his insurance costs up to seventy dollars per month, and the interest on the debts he now carried were costing him another twenty-five to fifty dollars per month. He said financial survival required at least $311 a month. The Baker boys decided, however, that Bill Douglas just wasn't worth that initially.

Meanwhile, Douglas had presented the Oregon offer to Hutchins, expecting that it would improve his financial standing at Yale. The dean did not disappoint him, increasing his salary immediately to seven thousand dollars. Douglas leaned toward staying. On top of that, Carrol Shanks was offered a job at Yale to administer the faculty's field research. For Douglas, this meant that he would have a coauthor close at hand to work on the casebooks for his new business-organization courses. But what really got his attention was that Hutchins had just secured a $7.5 million endowment, mainly from the Rockefeller Foundation, for the Institute of Human Relations, which would operate just like the interdisciplinary legal-research institute that Walter Wheeler Cook was developing at Johns Hopkins University.

Since an additional five million dollars had been secured to erect a new law-school building, Douglas was positively enthused. "The conventional law school is disappearing," he gushed to his friend A. Howard Meneely. "Law as a social science is appearing. It and psychology, sociology, economics et al will be inseparably intermingled in the Institute of Human Relations. Things are booming here." Moreover, when Hutchins asked him to remain and help build up the law school as a personal favor to him, Douglas told his friend that he found the request hard to deny: "The chances are I'll stay here [at Yale], tho the decision's a very, very close one."

Just then, though, Douglas's world fell apart. In a move that stunned the academic community, on April 26, 1929, the University of Chicago named the thirty-year-old Hutchins as its new president. "I meant to get a letter off to you last night," he wrote A. Howard Meneely, "But Bob being made Pres. of U. of Chicago demoralized & depressed me beyond words. So I could do nothing but walk around. . . . It throws my plans all ajar." For him, now, there was only one thing to do: "I have renewed dickerings with Baker [City], Ore."

But he also decided to provoke a bidding war by shopping his services around. "Columbia wants me back," he proudly announced to his friend four days later. In truth, Douglas was now so desperate to leave that he was willing to work for the same dean for whom just a year earlier he held "no respect . . . either as a person or as a scholar." After meeting for four hours with Young B. Smith and several of his old colleagues, Douglas decided that if Columbia wanted him back, they would have to make him immune from administrative whims that could further disrupt his life. "The conditions under which I would go — I mean, consider it — are a full prof. & $10,000. Nothing less," he wrote at the time. "I doubt if I get it. But that amount & status would be necessary to eliminate the administrative risks. I could not go back & put my head in the noose. I know only too well those campus politicians. I am not at all sure I would go at that offer." For the man who had many writing projects under way but had yet to publish his first article, let alone complete his second full year of teaching, it was a bold play indeed.

As he thought about it, Douglas realized that Yale without Bob Hutchins held no attraction for him. "The challenge to my imagination here has gone pretty much," he said. In his opinion, the appointment of Charles Clark as the new dean was not a good sign for the future. "He is not Bob — far from it," Douglas complained to a friend. "I hardly know my mind," he kept repeating these days in his letters, as if it had become his mantra. Still, in the crazy world of academic politics, where only those who are thinking of leaving are deemed by the administration as worthy of retaining, Douglas knew the likely result: "Yale of course will bid up for me, I am told. So the budget will be improved no matter what the decision."

By this time, though, Douglas's career decisions were being made like they were restricted railroad tickets, good for one day and train only. Even now, Douglas confessed in a letter, "here is the secret of all. Bob [Hutchins] wants to take me to Chicago. . . . The possibilities there are great. The law school is punk. Bob must recreate it. And he will. I hate to be a gypsy. But the call is strong. I hardly know what weight to give the personal friendship. It looms large. I suppose I should think of my work first. But that seems second."

After ten more days of intense negotiations with Columbia, all of Douglas's doubts about a Hutchins-less Yale were papered over by dollar bills. "Yale it is," he proclaimed proudly only two weeks after Hutchins's departure was announced. "Columbia made a good offer. But it didn't quite match Yale's. And the environment at Columbia didn't seem the best for genuine work." While Yale's counteroffer wasn't the ten-thousand-dollar full professorship that he had been seeking, it did agree to raise his salary to eight thousand, with the promise of a five-hundred-dollar raise the following year. With Carrol Shanks's acceptance of Yale's offer, the working environment became an even more hospitable place. "Together we plan a series of monumental publications," Douglas wrote A. Howard Meneely. "So that's that." Bill Douglas had managed to increase his salary by 33 percent in a matter of only three and a half months.

Knowing that Bob Hutchins would pay whatever it took to get him to Chicago, and with Mildred now pregnant with their first child, a daughter they would name Millie when she was born in November 1929, Douglas settled down in New Haven to build the kind of résumé that would convince others to back him. Douglas dropped all of his interest in teaching as he focused his energies on research and publications. For many in his classes, it showed. "[Douglas was] considered at the time to be a somewhat dull teacher and not in a class with a number of other performers," recalled Thomas I. Emerson, Yale '33. "He was not considered in any sense among the outstanding teachers, or among the more stimulating ones." A former teaching colleague, Myres McDougal, thought he saw the reason why: "In large classes he didn't seem to be putting out. He asked a few questions, but let students do the rest. . . . In terms of structure, I have never seen a better set of notes. . . . He just couldn't communicate well; he seemed to freeze before a large audience because he was shy."

Seeking both to bolster his credentials on campus, and increase his psychological distance from his students, many of whom were not much younger than he, Douglas began telling stories in and out of class about the success of his early legal career. "Douglas came to Yale with the reputation of a very expensive star," recalled Thomas I. Emerson. "He gave the impression of somebody from New York who had been bought away from Columbia at a high price by Hutchins. Money was thought to be significant. It never occurred to us that Douglas was a country boy." Tales of his stomach ailments at Cravath, the misery of underemployment, failing to make a go of it with James O. Cull and the Yakima bar, and the inability to be influential at Columbia Law were never heard now. Instead, now the legend of "William O. Douglas, Wall Street lawyer," began to grow.

Those students and faculty, though, who were allowed to peek behind this developing facade discovered a very different kind of person. Gerhard Gesell, Yale '35, recalled: "In those days he was full of energy and enthusiasm. We might go out to dinner with him and play poker half the night, and then go back and sit in his class in the morning."

One time, Douglas and some of his students and colleagues got so drunk on Prohibition applejack that they staggered late into a dinner honoring English political theorist Harold Laski, a noted friend of Harvard law professor Felix Frankfurter. Seeking to show their disdain for the socialist intellectual, Douglas and his students, though wearing the required tuxedos, had painted their shirt collars red. This might have been forgiven had the men not begun throwing biscuits at one another in front of the puritanical James Angell and his wife. "Who are those objectionable people down there?" President Angell barked at Dean Clark. "If they are in any way connected with the Law School, I want them dismissed from the University immediately."

"Well," replied the dean, "starting at your left is Howard Marshall, who will be Assistant Dean of the Law School next fall; then Gerry Wallace who will be law clerk to Judge Tom Swan of the Second Circuit, a former dean of the Law School, as you know; then comes Fred Rodell who will be legal adviser to that great old Yale man, Governor Gifford Pinchot of Pennsylvania; next is Bill Gaud, whose appointment as assistant professor at the School, starting in September, you and the Corporation have authorized; and then comes—surely you know him—William O. Douglas."

"Hrrumph," replied the president. "Very well then. Very well. But I insist that you secure apologies from all of them for this discourteous display."

On Monday morning, the dean commanded that each of the offending parties present himself in his office to be personally informed of the president's ire. Each new paragraph in his litany of their offenses, though, brought forth more gales of laughter. Whereupon, Clark ended the session with a sly grin, saying, "Thank you, gentlemen, I shall report to the President that you have apologized."

In time, even students critical of Douglas's lecture style began to appreciate his approach to the legal-realism movement. "His contribution was somewhat different," explained Thomas I. Emerson, "in the sense that he was one of the few that were not engaged primarily in destructive operations. Rather he tended to assume that we had training in breaking down orthodox legal ideas. So he devoted his efforts more toward an affirmative rebuilding of the legal system, working primarily in the field of corporate law. He reorganized those courses and taught them from a more functional point of view." What was interesting, the better students soon discovered, was Douglas's unique ability to bring the outside world into the classroom. Recalled Gerhard Gesell, "He had a way of bringing into the seminar an account of what he had been doing the day before or the week before. . . . He would tell us, first of all, what was going on—what the malefactors of great wealth were doing with other people's money and then we started asking questions around the table." It was precisely this approach, serving as a corrective to those on the faculty who buried themselves in teaching arcane legal philosophy, that was Douglas's contribution to the curriculum.

Having found his profession for the moment, Bill Douglas was intent on rising to the top of it. And Yale Law School could not have been a better place in which to do so. To many, the atmosphere in the school became palpably electric. Frank R. Strong, Yale '34, recalled of his student days there: "Evening use of the Law Library, magnificent in physical beauty and rapidly expanding in the availability of materials beyond the strictly legal, revealed to us the hectic pace at which many faculty were working. . . . This heavy time investment was symptomatic of the almost messianic atmosphere that pervaded the whole enterprise." Just to keep up, faculty worked into the wee hours of the morning, with some even sleeping on cots in their offices. At least one junior faculty member "cheated" by napping for two hours after dinner and then returning to the school around 10:00 P.M. for the remainder of the night. Through all of this bustle, Professor Douglas became a familiar figure to students as he dashed down the hall, usually with a pencil over his right ear and a trail of cigarette smoke wafting behind him. After balancing his time at Cravath between teaching and the practice of law, this job, which required a presence in class for only a handful of hours a week and allowed him to choose his own writing projects, was like a vacation for him.

For the first time, Douglas felt that he was a full partner in a team effort as he labored to revamp the law school's offerings in business law. He began to reorganize the corporate-law offerings along legal-realist lines. Douglas's idea was to offer an entire curriculum organized not on business theory but on the "life cycle" of corporations. Thus, new courses on the incorporation and financing of a business would be followed by others dealing with various real-world corporate problems, such as labor management and marketing. In time, Douglas teamed up with Harvard Business School professor George Bates in an effort to launch a joint degree program between the two schools. When the stock-market crash in October 1929 launched the Great Depression, thus making the field of business bankruptcy even more relevant, Douglas drew on his firsthand experiences in the reorganization of the Chicago, Milwaukee, and St. Paul Railroad, not to mention his memories of his mother's business failures.

Since these courses would require entirely new casebooks, Douglas began to assemble the materials that were to make him the leading national expert on the subjects. In just five years, Douglas would publish five major corporate-law casebooks—four written with Carrol Shanks and one with Charles Clark—dealing with "reorganization," "financing," "management," "losses, liabilities, and assets," and "partnership, joint stock associations, and business trusts." In time, all of this pedagogical activity dealing with the greatest economic failure in the nation's history placed Douglas in the center of his profession on this issue.

Outside of the classroom, the workaholic Douglas simultaneously launched many different research projects. After carefully choosing a subject, evaluating among other aspects its potential for high visibility, he would delegate the initial researching and drafting duties to groups of hired assistants or volunteer law students; later, he would rewrite the work to give it the "Douglas flair." Before the research was even under way on the first project, Douglas was already absorbed in developing the next one, with a different group of assistants. Years later, social scientists would develop this method for use in research; for the time being, Douglas was one of the few legal academics to use this technique.

Meanwhile, Douglas would tout all of his new projects to various administrators who could provide him with grant money and other necessary resources. That way, even if some of the projects did not work out, they had been fully milked for their publicity value without any loss of research time.

In researching the bankruptcy field, Douglas had not only chosen the hottest area in legal studies but decided to pursue it with the most fashionable technique of the era: empirical social-science research. Seeking to demonstrate the cutting edge of his "hard science" research, Douglas focused initially on the question of whether businesses failed because of the maladministration of bankruptcy laws. Originally, Douglas planned to use teams of lawyers and economists to examine survey data and personal interviews regarding the bankruptcy practices uncovered in the Southern District of New York.

When the sixty thousand dollars in research funds that this project would have required did not materialize, however, he was forced to scale back the investigation to a study of thirty-five failed retail grocers in Philadelphia.

Teams of unpaid Yale law students acting under Douglas's supervision had examined court records and interviewed bankrupt businessmen to discover that company failures were due more to bad business practices rather than to any failure of the nation's credit system. Moreover, they found that bankruptcies usually enriched attorneys rather than compensated creditors. While the study's sample was too small for reliable conclusions to be drawn, Douglas now had a proven technique for conducting future bankruptcy investigations in other fields.

Douglas's choice of research topic proved to be fortuitous when a legal scandal broke out in the Southern District of New York, with several lawyers and district-court personnel being indicted for engaging in fraudulent practices during bankruptcy hearings. After a grand jury was convened to conduct an investigation of the entire bankruptcy system, District Court Judge Thomas D. Thacher and future bar-association counsel Colonel William J. Donovan were charged with supervising the study. They turned to Douglas to do a comparative study of the bankruptcy systems in the United States, England, Canada, France, and Germany. So delighted was Thacher with Douglas's report, which lambasted both speculative American business practices and the nation's inefficient bankruptcy procedures, that he read it directly into the judicial record.

This effort brought Douglas to the attention of yet another district-court judge, William Clark of New Jersey, who was interested in studying bankruptcy reform for his region. Clark, too, engaged Douglas, this time to supervise a Department of Commerce–backed study of business failures in Newark, New Jersey. The judge planned to order all of the bankruptcy petitioners in his court to submit to a written and oral examination administered by a newly created "bankruptcy clinic" run by Douglas. Douglas would thus be generating research data for additional articles on the causes of all bankruptcies, including those of individual wage earners, with the full investigative power of the federal judicial branch and the U.S. Commerce Department behind him.

Never one to waste time, though, Douglas launched yet a third study, designed to examine the efficiency of the bankruptcy procedure for liquidating or saving a business. Enlisting another set of assistants to investigate court records of the federal district of Connecticut, Douglas supervised the study of forty-four equity receiverships, which were designed to avoid the liquidation of failing businesses. While the study failed to yield significant results, Douglas was able to determine that the high legal fees paid to various court officials did nothing to prevent the eventual liquidation of the businesses. In reaching this judgment, he became one of the handful of scholars well versed in this vital policy area.

The combination of his three new research projects gained Douglas what he desired most professionally: permanent research funding for his work from the Institute of Human Relations. Having accomplished this task, Douglas quickly abandoned the relatively low-profile equity-receivership study and concentrated his energy on the Newark study, which held promise for even greater national visibility. After securing the help of a fine statistician named Dorothy Thomas and enlisting input from judges, lawyers, economists, psychologists, sociologists, and doctors in the Newark area, Douglas and his team designed the questionnaire for Judge Clark's bankruptcy clinic. After just fifty-eight failed businessmen had been given the intelligence and psychiatric tests, though, political problems developed because of the controversial nature of the program, and the bankruptcy clinics were closed. With a data sample too small for verifiable results, Douglas sought to develop some findings by sending his questionnaire to other recently bankrupted businessmen and interviewing a third group on his own.

Since he relied on so many different types of research instruments to fill in gaps in the study, Douglas was not able to draw any reliable conclusions from his data. But even lacking reportable research findings here, he nevertheless published two articles that analyzed the theory behind how his questionnaire could be refined for future investigations. After only two years of work, even his failures became successes.

In the fall of 1930, Judge Thacher left the federal bench to become Herbert Hoover's solicitor general. Now determined to investigate bankruptcies on a nationwide scale, Thacher called on Douglas once again. Using the questionnaire from his Newark study, Douglas directed a Department of Justice examination of bankruptcies in Boston. Here, Douglas gleaned enough material to produce two more articles.

Realizing that the search for bankruptcy causation was likely a futile one, Douglas now went beyond the simple reporting of data to begin editorializing on the need for bankruptcy-law reform, using as a model the English laws he had researched earlier. These articles exhibited what become Douglas's literary trademark in those years, as he picked a hot topic, positioned himself in front of the issue by posing the right questions for future study, and then left that often tedious work for others. As a result of this work, the attorney general issued a report to Congress suggesting a bankruptcy-reform bill and thanked Yale Law School, in particular William O. Douglas, for its assistance in drafting it. Once again, having achieved this success, Douglas immediately dropped this subject of study and moved on to more promising avenues of research.

·　　　·　　　·

It was not all work and no play for Bill Douglas and the legal realists at Yale. Professor Walton Hamilton's wife, Irene, recalls that the entire operation was "something of a men's club." Every now and again, the faculty would meet at one of their houses, get rip-roaring drunk, and play games such as Murder, in which a participant was blindfolded and others were given the opportunity to hit him over the head with a newspaper.

It was during these years that the social side of Bill Douglas began to emerge. By now, his stomach had improved to the point that he no longer worried about the effect of liquor or tobacco on his health.

When exercise was required at these gatherings, the group called a meeting of their infamous Hunt Club, an elaborate game of hide-and-seek played late at night in East Rock Park. The task here was for the drunken participants to trap the elusive snipe, a bird that has eluded generations of tenderfoot Boy Scouts at summer camp. As the Mattress Bearer, Bill Douglas carried whatever was handy to make some noise, and Thurman Arnold provided the light as the Flashlight Bearer. Young protégés such as Abe Fortas, a Yale '33 graduate then teaching there, were made apprentices in the hopes of becoming "Beaters," who rustled through the bushes. While no snipe was ever found, the fact that none of the searchers was ever permanently lost gave the gatherings an air of success.

At other times, the legends of Sterling Law Building played jokes on one another, with Douglas's unique sense of humor always giving him an edge. When the dean got too drunk one day to get himself to the railway station in order to travel to a speech he had to give that night in one city, Douglas kindly took him and put him on a train heading for a different city. Thurman Arnold tried to make contact with the mysterious "Yvonne," an admirer who had sent him a lovely note offering her number and suggesting that they meet for cocktails, only to find out that he was phoning the local morgue. And then there was the "publicity game," in which Arnold, Douglas, and a third law-school colleague, Wesley Sturges, gave one another points for any mention or picture in a newspaper—one point for a speech, five points in the New Haven *Register,* ten points for *The New York Times,* twenty-five points in a national magazine, fifty points for *The New York Times Sunday Magazine,* and one hundred points for a *Times* editorial. Once, when he was about to give a speech in New Haven, Arnold was puzzled to get a telegram from Sturges asking to be mentioned in his address, which would have meant another point for him. Upon returning to the office the next day, Arnold confronted his colleague about the breach of the game's rules of etiquette, only to find out that Sturges had gotten a similar telegram from "Arnold" asking for the same favor in *his* speech that same evening in Bridgeport. The grinning rail-thin imp with the uncontrollable shock of hair, they realized with a laugh, had struck again.

For many of these men, taking up with women other than their wives also became a way of life. Fred Rodell, a brilliant but eccentric scholar, would get so drunk during parties that he would occasionally marry whomever he met. Once he sobered up to find out he had married a telephone operator. After that marriage ended in a costly divorce, Rodell married another woman, who got tuberculosis; he then took up with her nurse in the sanatorium.

Bill Douglas was no exception to this rule. With his wife pregnant and later fully absorbed in raising her children, his eyes soon began to roam. "Bill was a free spirit with the women, and Mildred knew about it," recalled Irene Hamilton. "But she liked to play the 'injured party' in talking to the other wives about it. She and Bill had begun to grow more distant, and all of the other wives would sympathize with her, fearing that it would happen to them." On such occasions, Hamilton said, Mildred would repay her husband by telling the most hurtful story that she could: "how she had worked to put Bill through law school."

.   .   .

But while the faculty played hard, they worked even harder. And none of them worked harder than Bill Douglas.

Having abandoned the bankruptcy field, Douglas found a way to curry favor with those who could help him as he now turned to a brand-new, even more promising research topic. Dean Charles Clark had begun a study of inefficiencies in the judicial system by compiling a census of criminal and civil cases in Connecticut and then determining the eventual disposition of those cases. Since the dean's research methods—

investigating case studies gleaned from court records—mirrored his own, Douglas joined the research team. A fifty-five-thousand-dollar grant then made it possible for them to expand the study to other states.

This relationship with Clark expanded when President Hoover called for a national study of the state of criminal justice, most especially the lack of enforcement of Prohibition. When former Attorney General George W. Wickersham was put in charge of the National Commission on Law Observance and Enforcement, known soon thereafter as the Wickersham Commission, he began searching for suitable scholarly investigators. A proposal from Robert Hutchins and Charles Clark for a national study of criminal justice along the lines of the Connecticut study convinced Wickersham to ask both men in January 1930 to join the work. They in turn adopted the research techniques of their mutual friend Bill Douglas by enlisting him to supervise the research while they directed their respective academic institutions.

For Bill Douglas, the opportunity both to increase his national visibility in a new field and to work with two such prominent college administrators was welcome. The only drawback was the sheer volume of work to be done, so he found a way to delegate the duties. He quickly hired as his assistant Charles Samenow, a recent Yale graduate, who was assigned the task of designing the questionnaire for collecting the data. Law-student volunteers from various schools were then enlisted to search criminal-court files around the nation, hand-punch each of the thousands of responses onto data cards, and process them using a Hollerith tabulating machine.

Such calculation was tedious and seemingly endless work. Originally, the plan was to gather data over a five-year period, but after a year of arduous work, internecine warfare broke out between the schools enlisted to do the research and the members of the commission waiting to interpret it. By May 1, 1931, the Yale group was working night and day just to process the Connecticut data for a progress report. Already worried that his group was completely "used up," and with an ocean of data yet to be collected and processed, Clark despaired that the task might never be completed.

Despite these problems, the preliminary research results were quite extraordinary. Clark and Douglas had expected, based on the legal literature at the time, that many sources of delay and inefficiency in the criminal-justice system would be found. Instead, their research indicated that the system was working perhaps too efficiently. According to their preliminary findings, 70 percent of the defendants pleaded guilty on the day they were charged, while eventually 90 percent of the defendants pleaded guilty before their trial. They found that in more than 85 percent of the cases, defendants reached their final judicial disposition in only two months. Despite the logistical, statistical, and technological handicaps in this initial study, Douglas and Clark not only delved into earliest stages of the field of modern criminology but also reached findings that have never been challenged.

However, since nonreformist research findings, no matter how accurate, are of no use to politicians seeking to make points with the public, when the study's funding ran out in July 1931, the commission shut it down and refused to release any of its findings.

Despite this setback, with so many of his research projects still progressing at various stages of completion, Douglas was fashioning an academic career for himself with unprecedented speed. All he needed now was for someone who was in a position to advance his career further to notice. But he need not have worried.

THE PRINCE OF NEW HAVEN

I never understood why [Bill] didn't come to Chicago. He just said he couldn't come. I don't remember his giving any reasons.

—*Robert Maynard Hutchins*

When Robert Maynard Hutchins announced his move to the University of Chicago on April 26, 1929, everyone in his New Haven retinue
became a free agent. Determined to be targeted for raiding, Douglas
was careful to keep in very close contact with Hutchins and kept him
fully informed of his progress. Work was going on around the clock,
he proudly proclaimed, and a vast body of literature was being published.

Thicker and thicker the Douglas file grew, as he sent Hutchins
copies of everything he was publishing and reports of the new projects
that were under way. Finally, Douglas began raising hints about a move
to Chicago. In accepting an invitation in mid-May 1930 to stay in the
president's quarters during a Chicago speech-making visit, Douglas
warned that he could not stay longer than two days "unless you decide
to employ [me]." A week later, Douglas suggested that Hutchins could
hire him as an assistant while also providing "enough income to keep
me from starving."

Never one to miss an opportunity, by the end of that month Hutchins offered Douglas a full professorship. But having just been blessed
in November of the previous year with his first child and now fully engaged in supervising all of his new research projects, Douglas responded that the time was not right for him to accept. Such a move
would embarrass Dean Clark, he fretted in a two-page handwritten letter to Hutchins, and it would set his research agenda back a year. Since
Hutchins had offered to delay the transfer for a year to overcome these
concerns, Douglas added that such a move would render him a lame

duck in his New Haven work. Only toward the end of the letter did Douglas confess what really seemed to be bothering him about the move. He had been warned by others that the dean of the Chicago Law School, Harry Bigelow, was totally overmatched by his job. Still, Douglas was careful to leave the door open, adding, "New Haven is quite dull."

What Douglas failed to mention was that, just as he had with the earlier Oregon law-firm offer, he had simply marched Hutchins's offer into Dean Clark and gotten him to match it. Now his salary would be raised another $2,000 to $11,000, with promised future jumps to $13,000, $14,000, and the school maximum of $15,000. On top of that, the school agreed to promote him immediately to associate professor, with a promise to recommend him for a full professorship the following year.

But Robert Maynard Hutchins was never one to give up.

"You are, of course, an idiot but I knew that before," he wrote to Douglas by return mail. "Tell Charley to keep his shirt on. He can't expect us to lay off you indefinitely." He also wrote Bigelow: "I have a letter from Douglas saying that because of his commitments at New Haven he cannot get away at once. I think we can get him another year." By the end of 1930, angered that Yale had just stolen his eminent anthropologist, Edward Sapir, Hutchins decided it was time to repay his old school by stealing Bill Douglas.

When they met in New York on Tuesday, December 9, Hutchins asked Douglas what it would take. Since the intellectual opportunities were not as good at Chicago, Douglas explained, it would take a huge salary to make the sacrifice. Pulling a number out of the air, he said he would come for twenty thousand dollars, which he knew was outrageous in the academic world, where the average salary was six thousand dollars. But Douglas had underestimated Hutchins's boldness; without a moment's hesitation, Hutchins agreed.

Two days later, Hutchins explained to his board of trustees that Douglas was worth a dean's salary because he was "the most outstanding law professor in the nation." The trustees' committee on instruction and equipment empowered Hutchins to negotiate. When Douglas got the offer, he phoned various members of the profession for advice. One of those calls went to the renowned Felix Frankfurter of Harvard Law School, who advised against accepting the offer. "Think of the jealousy of your colleagues when they hear about your salary," he warned. "And, how tough do you think it will be for Mildred, when the other professors' wives hear the same?" What Frankfurter left unsaid, of course, was his own jealousy over this offer when compared to what he was being paid in Cambridge.

Nevertheless, recognizing the offer for what it was—a chance to leapfrog ahead of all of his colleagues at Yale, not to mention everyone else in the legal academic world—Douglas accepted. But in doing so, he played the bet-hedging game he had perfected over the years. Even for this amount of money, he told Hutchins, he refused to leave Yale unless two conditions were met. First, he would not come on board until July 1, 1931, thus giving him time to complete his current research. Then, his time would be divided among the law school, the school of commerce and administration, and the social-sciences division, thus placing him beyond the control of the law-school dean. These Hutchins granted immediately, expecting that the negotiations were now concluded.

But unknown to him, Douglas had secretly added his own third condition. Since Chicago was not nearly as prestigious as Yale, he decided to leave only if Yale refused to match the offer.

· · ·

"The most outstanding law professor in the nation." In a single phrase, Hutchins had coronated Bill Douglas. The truth was, though, that when compared to top scholars such as Underhill Moore, who had a lifetime of scholarly achievements, Douglas was not even the most outstanding law professor in New Haven. Just thirty months into his Yale career, he had by this time published only four law-review articles, two of which appeared in his home law journal, which was predisposed to print the works of its own professors. Such a body of work showed great promise, but little more.

This made little difference to the men who would determine his fate in New Haven. By becoming the golden boy of the upstart president of the University of Chicago, Bill Douglas automatically became the golden boy of Yale's blue-blooded president, James Rowland Angell. Angell was suddenly prepared to keep his new star at all costs. But the Yale administration very quickly found itself at a disadvantage in fashioning a counteroffer. Since Douglas was already slotted to earn the school's maximum salary of fifteen thousand dollars three years hence, Dean Clark had to find a way to immediately raise his compensation to that amount, hoping that the difference between Chicago's offer and Yale's could be papered over by making extra research money available. But even with this increase, the dean warned his superiors, "This difference is so large that I am convinced it will overcome Mr.

Douglas's desire to stay here and that he is pretty sure to accept." Clark pleaded with the upper administration for help: "It would be most distressing to us to lose Mr. Douglas, for his position in the School is important and he can hardly be replaced." President Angell agreed to talk with Douglas on the telephone, and he extended the offer to raise his salary to the maximum the following year. While Douglas told him that this offer would make his "decision even more difficult," he stalled for time by worrying that being paid more than the dean would cause some embarrassment. To Dean Clark, though, this was beginning to look like "a rationalization on his part of an approaching decision to go to Chicago."

Indeed, it was. Ten days later, Douglas decided to accept Hutchins's offer. Unable to face Dean Clark with the news, he simply left a note on his desk informing him that he was leaving.

Seeking to both seal the bargain and tweak his old colleagues at Yale, Hutchins announced the new appointment in the January 2, 1931, edition of the *Chicago Tribune*. NEW PROFESSOR TO AID FINANCE STUDY AT U. OF C., the piece began, explaining: "A program of cooperative research in problems of finance is planned for the University of Chicago. This was revealed yesterday by President Robert Maynard Hutchins in the appointment to the university staff of William C. Douglas [*sic*] of the Yale law school. Prof. Douglas, an expert in finance, will be a member of the law school, the school of commerce and administration, and the division of social sciences." Hutchins sent a copy of the article to Douglas, saying, "I send you herewith a statement that appeared in the Chicago Tribune this morning. All of it is untrue, including your name, but it must be regarded as binding on you, nevertheless." With that, Hutchins waited in Chicago for his newest academic star to arrive. He was destined to wait for a very long time.

When the announcement appeared in the newspaper, Dean Clark had no choice but to inform his president that the war had been lost. "Mr. Douglas has finally decided to go to Chicago and Mr. Hutchins has already made the announcement through the newspapers," Clark wrote Angell, adding that "[Hutchins] says that he considers Douglas only a fair exchange for Sapir." Angell decided that this was not the end of the war but only the end of the first battle.

Seemingly unaffected by the forces swirling around him, Douglas settled down in early 1931 to run the University of Chicago from his office in New Haven. Breaching etiquette if not academic ethics, Douglas wrote to Hutchins that he stood ready to go after a potential

Yale donor who had just visited the school and had not yet pledged his money. Then, in letter after letter, Douglas offered Hutchins his suggestions for running the law school. Why not bolster the faculty by hiring a lawyer from Chicago named Miller, a fellow in the Department of Commerce named Plummer, a Harvard law professor named Warner, and a Columbia law graduate named Doskow? And Douglas crowed that he had "nowhere near reached [his] limit of ideas."

But Hutchins, with a university to run, had about reached his limit for receiving them. In typical tongue-in-cheek fashion, he responded, using the name that Douglas so abhorred: "Dear Orville: The stack of mail that I have received from you in the past two weeks makes me regret my precipitant [sic] action in appointing you a professor at my University. I should like to have you take the copies of these brilliantly-illiterate communications and go down to New York to talk with [social-science dean Beardsley] Ruml about them. They are all in his field and my purpose in appointing him Dean was to relieve me of the burden of listening to the childish expressions of your ideas." Besides, he added, there was no money to hire anyone else.

This typically irreverent letter did not appeal to the thin-skinned Douglas. Given "your desires," he wrote Hutchins, "I will cease thinking." The more he thought about it, though, the less Douglas liked it. So, four days later, he wrote Hutchins a letter resigning from the mythical committee on finance that the two men had playfully used to discuss how to fund various projects they envisioned for the university. Instead, he said, he was now prepared to play "Follow the Leader."

Hutchins failed to see the significance of this "resignation." The truth was that Douglas still wanted to be the leader somewhere, and since he apparently would not be running the university side by side with his friend, Douglas decided that perhaps it was not the place for him after all. After meeting with Hutchins in Washington on April 19, Douglas announced that so much new work had been placed on him, and the time needed to dismantle his research projects was so great, that he wondered if he could delay his arrival in Chicago for another year, to 1932.

With Douglas's arrival in Chicago anticipated in less than two months, the question presented by this request was how to list the University of Chicago's newest faculty member in its 1931–1932 catalog. Hutchins wired Douglas: AM REGRETFULLY WILLING TO RECOMMEND TO BOARD OF TRUSTEES LEAVE OF ABSENCE FOR ONE YEAR LISTING YOU IN OUR CATALOGUE AS PROFESSOR STOP SUGGEST LISTING AT YALE AS VISITING PROFESSOR STOP WHAT I THINK OF YOU CAN ONLY BE EXPRESSED

ORALLY[.] But then, hoping that Douglas would change his mind, the Chicago president delayed making the announcement.

Unknown to Hutchins, though, Douglas had already decided to reopen the negotiations to remain in New Haven. Upon being told that this new deferral represented "the beginning of the end so far as [his] transfer to Chicago is concerned," Yale's Dean Clark hatched a new plan to keep Douglas on his faculty. Since a pile of money alone was not the answer, perhaps a promotion to the coveted position of Sterling Professor of Law would do the trick. With this professorship, Douglas would have the one thing that Hutchins had failed to see that he needed: total academic independence and prestige. No one, not even the law-school dean, would come between Douglas and the president of the university. In short, it would make him a prince in the feudal academic world of New Haven.

Clark well knew that there were a few bureaucratic obstacles in the path toward offering Douglas the university's "highest honor." The Sterling Chair required that one be a full professor, have an advanced law degree, have a significant level of publications, and get the president's approval. At the time, Douglas had none of these things. Furthermore, Douglas's long-promised three business-law casebooks would not be published until the following year. But all things are possible in a university aggressive enough, and interested enough, in retaining its own faculty. By putting off Chicago, Douglas was really giving Yale the time it needed to finesse his elevation to the Sterling Chair, while also giving himself time both to consider what to do and to bring out the casebooks that would allow him to do it.

When the faculty agreed unanimously to promote Douglas at the end of the academic year to full professor, Clark set out to enlist the upper administration in fulfilling the rest of his plan. Now determined not to be bested in this contest by Hutchins, President Angell agreed to award Douglas both an honorary degree and the Sterling Chair. This would be, everyone knew, the best that Yale could offer. "In this Douglas matter," Provost Seymour wrote Dean Clark in June 1931, "everyone concerned has been racking his brains to discover a way by which your desire to keep Douglas might be fulfilled; and the arrangement approved by the President gives to him the most prized of all our academic appointments." And so the offer was made.

But when Douglas did not immediately accept, seeking to force his hand the Yale administration decided that he would have to take the offer of the Sterling Chair before the bureaucratic wheels would begin to spin toward tendering him the final appointment. So Clark insisted that they be allowed to drop the "Visiting Professor from the University of Chicago" designation for Douglas in their catalog and list him once again as one of their own faculty members. Since Hutchins already intended to list him in the Chicago catalog, Douglas could see that his waiting game was in danger of being tripped up by the most mundane of bureaucratic requirements.

But Clark had underestimated Douglas's skill at delaying such decisions. Why should he give up the sure thing at Chicago, when he had only promises of a Sterling Chair at Yale in the future? So, in telegraphing to Hutchins his thanks for the additional year's leave, Douglas had already given his assent to CARRY ME [in the catalog] AT CHICAGO ANYWAY YOU DESIRE[.] Yale was going to raise him to full professor, he added, and it wanted to omit the title of "visiting professor," but the decision was now with Hutchins. For his part, Douglas was now entirely willing to be listed as a full professor at *two* schools. Still, he kept the discussion of a possible Sterling Chair hidden from his friend in Chicago.

Stock in Western Union must have risen considerably on May 21 as Hutchins and Clark launched telegraphic broadsides at each other over the the right to Douglas's name in their catalogs. Caught in the middle, Douglas tried to preserve his relationship with Hutchins by distancing himself as much as possible from Yale's action. After explaining that he had not resigned from Chicago but was only on leave from the school until July 1932 and that he had no knowledge of how Yale would list him, Douglas kidded that he would be "grieve[d] sorely" to be listed in the Chicago catalog as "W. O. Douglas, Prof. of Law, S.O.B." Still unaware of the Sterling Chair offer discussions, Hutchins finally informed the Committee on Instruction and Equipment for the Board of Trustees that Douglas would remain on a leave of absence without salary for another year.

But Clark was not done yet. The dean played his trump card by granting Douglas an additional year as a visiting professor at Yale and also naming him the first ever visiting professor of law on the Sterling Foundation. Then, taking a page from Hutchins's playbook, he proudly announced this appointment in the local newspaper, knowing that word would reach the Chicago president. Douglas could see that with the attachment of Sterling's name to his, Hutchins would sense the direction of the negotiations in New Haven. So the time had come for him to confess his arrangement. Trying to pass off the significance of this new appointment, Douglas wrote that it was "a lousy title . . . befitting the job." Knowing from his years at Yale the prized nature of anything with the name Sterling attached to it, Hutchins signaled that he knew now what the future held: "You should be flattered to have the name Sterling attached to yours, even if it is only the name of a crooked old lawyer in New York and not an indication of high quality as in silver." Try as he might to assure Hutchins that the next year would be spent "liquidating" all of his projects at Yale, Douglas's hand was now tipped.

But Hutchins wasn't ready to give up yet; after all, Douglas was still technically on his faculty, even if nobody at Chicago Law School had seen him teach a class. When he met with Douglas in Chicago in November, ostensibly to begin arranging for his arrival on campus, Hutchins arranged for his friend to confer with his future colleagues at the law school. Those discussions with Dean Bigelow and various faculty members went so well that when Douglas returned to New Haven, he wired Hutchins that he would resign from Yale by January 17, Hutchins's birthday. A delighted Hutchins responded, HAVE TOLD OUR BOARD AND FACULTY YOU ARE COMING JULY 1 AS PER YOUR FIRST TELEGRAM STOP ANNOUNCEMENT MAY BE MADE ANY TIME STOP SHOULD LIKE TO HAVE IT ON BIRTHDAY OF AMERICA'S GREATEST EDUCATOR[.]

Believing that he was still a dean running his law school, Chicago's Harry Bigelow wrote Douglas about his duties for the upcoming year. Douglas, he said, would be expected to reorganize and teach the courses in mortgages, suretyship, bankruptcy, and pledges; the reorganization of the rest of the courses would be left until the following year. These assignments fed into Douglas's fears that Bigelow would grant him no more control over his teaching duties than Young B. Smith had at Columbia. So he fired off a telegram to the Chicago dean, saying that he was not coming because, as they had discussed earlier, "those subjects are not within my province."

Now convinced that Bigelow didn't really want him, and realizing that as the Sterling Chair at Yale he would be beyond all of these kinds of academic political decisions, Douglas wired Hutchins to see just how much power he had. Complaining that he was being regarded by the dean as little more than an academic "utility outfielder," Douglas expressed doubt about the wisdom of "tying up with those babies." To Douglas's way of thinking, by threatening to resign after having wired that he was coming, Hutchins would have to choose between him or the dean.

Now, a mere five years after describing himself as having a "macaroni spine," Bill Douglas was no longer a lost soul, buffeted about by events beyond his control. Instead, he was charting his own destiny. And the lessons that he was learning about changing his relationships with friends depending on their value to his career, just as he had done with his research projects, would shape the rest of his career.

Hutchins called Douglas on the phone immediately, with good results. DELAYED RESIGNING UNTIL I COULD SEE YOU, Douglas telegraphed Hutchins on December 28, promising to meet in the next few days. Once more, the personal meeting mollified Douglas, as he promised to arrive in June, and began suggesting a new batch of people to steal from Yale and other law schools. But if Douglas was hoping for a resignation from Dean Bigelow to pave the way for his arrival, he would be disappointed.

While various members of the Yale law faculty visited Douglas in his office to try to convince him to stay, Clark planned his endgame. Cutting through the bureaucratic red tape, he set about to secure Douglas's immediate promotion to the Sterling Chair. Rather than waiting until the end of the fiscal year on June 30, Yale promoted Douglas to full professor in April 1932. Then, even though Douglas had not yet agreed in advance to accept the Sterling Chair, Clark arranged for him to receive his honorary master's in law, simultaneously with the promotion to Sterling Professor of Law in June 1932. No one seemed concerned any longer with the length of Douglas's publication list.

With all of the obstacles cleared, Clark was prepared to formally make the offer of the Sterling Chair. But the problem now seemed to be money again. Faced with increasing financial pressures during the Depression, Yale could offer Douglas only fourteen thousand dollars, which was only one thousand more than he had already been promised for the year, with the rest of his promised fifteen-thousand-dollar salary to be made up by research grants. The difference between what was in effect a "dry promotion" and Chicago's munificent offer seemed too great.

But the fates were with Clark now.

Still assuming that Douglas was coming in the fall, Hutchins called him in early April 1932 with the bad news that with the university's finances collapsing, his offer now had to be reduced to fifteen thousand dollars, thus making it only one thousand dollars more than Yale was willing to pay. And with administrative deadlines once again approaching at Chicago, the dean needed to know Douglas's answer in the next two weeks. Hutchins tried to pass off his deal-closing move by joking that the dean "has a very unadministrative feeling that he should not misrepresent the situation in his catalog. I cannot account for this attitude in a member of my group of deans."

Faced with the hint of financial insecurity, the poor boy from

Yakima's decision was now irrevocably made: He was remaining at Yale. But still Douglas wanted to hedge his career bets. So he telegraphed Hutchins for yet another year's leave from Chicago.

When Clark learned of this action, he knew he had his man. There would be no more years of visiting-professor status for Bill Douglas in his course catalog, he decided. If Douglas wanted the Sterling Chair, he was going to have to make the final decision to stay in New Haven permanently.

Realizing that he had no choice now but to accept, all that remained for Douglas to do was to resign from the place where he had been employed for seventeen months but had never taught a class. So the next day, Douglas sent a tortured, five-page, handwritten letter, trying to explain to Hutchins why he would not be coming to Chicago Law School after all. One by one, he offered the many reasons for this "bitter and genuine disappointment." Yale was pressuring him to stay, even though his wife really wanted to go to Chicago, he claimed. (In truth, Mildred, who that year was to deliver their second child, William O. Douglas, Jr., had never wanted to leave New Haven.) While Chicago offered to him the best academic prospects in the nation, Douglas explained that the worsening economy made him reluctant to move. Everyone at Yale Law School was so frightened by the financial crisis that Douglas decided to "ride out" the bad economic times, or at least one more year, in New Haven.

Even still, at the end of his letter Douglas could not bring himself to close the door totally on his old friend. While he still wanted to come to Chicago, Douglas tipped off what had kept him at Yale and what it would take to get him there, explaining that he would come for the Wilson Chair, a different academic position, even if it was not fully funded. Before he agreed to move, Douglas was saying, he would have to be made a prince of Chicago — one who was totally independent of the lower administration.

Chicago was not yet prepared to give up the fight, as Bigelow wrote to Hutchins: "A good letter. I think that despite the [second paragraph] of his letter we can keep him on the faculty list and give him a leave of absence for another year." But Hutchins knew different. In June, he announced to the board of trustees that Douglas had resigned from the university effective July 1, 1932.

Having won the academic chess game, Dean Clark proudly proclaimed in his 1931–1932 yearly report, "Professor William O. Douglas becomes Sterling Professor of Law and will remain on permanent appointment at Yale."

For Douglas's part, he had gotten what he always wanted: complete academic independence.

But Robert Maynard Hutchins need not have lamented long the loss of his friend. For having reached the pinnacle of academia, Douglas now decided that it was time to leave it to follow his true destiny—the one initially imprinted on him by his mother.

THE PROFESSOR WHO
JUMPED FROM NOWHERE

No one in Washington or the nation had heard of
Bill.

—Irene Hamilton

Having conquered the academic world, Bill Douglas decided that, with the election of Franklin Delano Roosevelt to the White House in 1932, the time had come to venture into the political world of Washington, D.C. Like many of his faculty friends, he wanted to join FDR's New Deal. "He was terribly ambitious," recalled Irene Hamilton. "He had an almost desperate need to become entrenched in the political system."

By the summer of 1933, it seemed to Douglas that everyone from Yale had a position in the new administration except him. Thurman Arnold, Wesley Sturges, and Douglas's protégé Abe Fortas were all laboring in the Agricultural Adjustment Administration (AAA). So many members of the Yale Law School faculty had been drafted for temporary duty in Washington that the Yale administration began to worry whether its fall courses could be staffed.

Since who he knew did not seem to be getting him to Washington, Douglas turned to what he knew. After deciding to abandon the field of bankruptcy regulation he now sought to become the nation's expert on the new Securities Act of 1933, which had been passed in reaction to the 1929 stock-market crash. Beginning in November 1933, he and his staff generated seven major articles on the law in just eight months. This pace in a field that had not previously been his major area of interest was a remarkable accomplishment. The explanation for this increased output, however, lay not just in Douglas's ability to delegate work but also in the type of pieces he was now writing. Unlike the earlier work in which he presented new and original data,

Douglas's articles now offered a series of theoretical analyses, leaving the empirical research for others to perform. And since his early support of FDR's securities law had gotten him nowhere, in time all of his articles became highly critical of the measure, arguing that it did not go far enough to protect investors.

For all his careful career planning and posturing, though, Douglas's initial opportunity in Washington came almost by accident. When the Securities Exchange Act of 1934 was signed into law, creating the Securities and Exchange Commission (SEC) to regulate Wall Street, Douglas pressed friends, such as General Counsel for the AAA Jerome Frank and Representative Francis T. Maloney of Connecticut, for whom he was then campaigning for the Senate, for help in securing an appointment to the new body. But once again the appointments went elsewhere, with the chairmanship going to Wall Street financier Joseph P. Kennedy and one commission seat to Felix Frankfurter's frequent coauthor, James Landis. Fortunately for Douglas, though, section 211 of the act instructed the SEC to investigate the practices of the so-called protective committees, which in theory protected investors during bankruptcy or receivership-reorganization proceedings but were suspected of being used to safeguard moneyed interests. For that investigation, a director still needed to be appointed.

As it happened, Bill Douglas had just published an article entitled "Protective Committees in Railroad Reorganization," which dealt with this very subject. Relying on both his bankruptcy research and his legal experience at Cravath on railroad reorganization, Douglas laid out the case for governmental reform here. So impressed was James Landis by this piece that he persuaded the commission in July 1934 to appoint Douglas as the director of the protective-committee study.

Despite working so hard for this opportunity, Douglas now seemed anxious to leave himself a safety net for his career. He explained to Landis that he "could give [the new post] substantially half of my time," while continuing to teach at Yale. Even with his chair-level professor's salary, the Douglases' past debts were so great that they had to borrow against Bill's life-insurance policies to remain afloat financially. By commuting part-time to Washington, he would receive forty dollars a day, plus expenses. The day-to-day administrative and research work would be delegated to the staff he would hire. Though he had been looking for a full-time director, Landis approved this unusual relationship.

To Douglas, this new appointment signaled the beginning of his rise to the top. "Bill began telling us he would be the chairman of the SEC," recalled Irene Hamilton. His analysis was very simple. Everyone knew that Joe Kennedy would not stay on the commission for the long haul. After he left, the chairmen of the SEC's various subordinate investigative groups, including Douglas, would be in the best position to move onto the commission itself. That new commissioner would eventually be in a prime position to compete for the chairmanship of the agency when Kennedy's successor departed. But his friends at Yale snickered when they heard such predictions. "None of us took it very seriously, and we tended to discount it. No one in Washington or the nation had heard of Bill," recalled Irene Hamilton, "so this idea caught everyone at Yale by surprise." Indeed, when Douglas's appointment to the protective-committee study was first announced, some newspapers did not even know how to spell his last name, adding an extra *s*.

But Douglas's friends and colleagues misjudged how enterprising he could be once he focused his sights on the next rung on the career ladder. Lacking a large budget, Douglas searched for cheap but highly competent help to do the necessary investigative work. Since the cheapest and best lawyers available were now graduating from law school, Douglas looked to his own. Realizing that he would need a chief of staff, someone in whom he had absolute trust, to direct the day-to-day tasks in Washington while he continued to teach at Yale, only one name occurred to him: Abe Fortas. The problem was that Fortas already had a job working in Jerome Frank's legal division in the AAA, and it was one that he liked very much. But despite the president's decree that one should not raid other agencies for talent, Douglas was never one to let such details get in his way. After a series of arm-twisting letters to both Fortas and Jerome Frank, promising better career prospects for his former student, Douglas succeeded in getting Fortas as his right-hand man.

Fortas would handle the hiring, firing, and managing of the personnel, run the day-to-day operations, supervise the production of the financial surveys sent out by the committee, conduct the behind-the-scenes negotiations with the bankers and law firms under investigation, and lead the background hearings. And he would constantly keep Douglas apprised, through stacks of daily letters. The Yale professor was then able to use the information in teaching his classes and writing his law-review pieces while waiting to be called down to conduct the public hearings.

With the subsequent hiring of a staff, it was left to Douglas to give them specific instructions as to how to proceed. Others write long memos and hold extended meetings in such situations, but Douglas, in his pithy western manner, chose to capture his philosophy in just three words, which he uttered whenever his aides asked for guidance: "Piss on 'Em."

And piss on 'em they sought to do through hard work, as the staff took its cues from their leader. "Douglas would sit and listen to a long meeting with his staff with all kinds of views being expressed, and then it would come around to him, and he would say just a couple of sentences, nothing more, and go right to the heart of the issue," recalled Abe Fortas. "The matter would be discovered, and the issue would be laid open." The same was true when they worked in public sessions. Former SEC assistant C. David Ginsburg recalls that when Douglas "was interviewing . . . [there] was the same total commitment. The energy of the things. Douglas would work on through dinner, midnight, two o'clock in the morning then. This was a major effort, and . . . some of [his staff] hated him." But the results were worth it. "Bill was a great man, an utter genius at the SEC," recalled Fortas, years later. "He had the most remarkable ability, better than any lawyer I have ever seen before or since, to go to the jugular of the issue."

For all his efforts to position himself in a more prominent governmental position, Bill Douglas soon realized that he had landed in the best possible place for a man of his talents. Corruption in bankruptcy proceedings, he would soon discover, was far more vast than anyone realized. In time, his staff would be investigating well over two hundred thousand protective committees, which controlled more than thirty-six billion dollars in assets. After sending out investigative questionnaires to a sample of over 1,600 protective committees nationwide, Abe Fortas and his staff personally interviewed, and later subpoenaed the files of, members of many of these protective committees. To their surprise, the corrupt practices of these groups were so commonplace that many of the respondents openly admitted their unethical and illegal practices. Douglas realized that his problem would not be in finding examples of corruption but in selecting the clearest ones to illustrate to the general public the need for vast financial reform.

After six months of investigation, Douglas decided to open the hearings on February 5, 1935, with an examination of the reorganization of the Celotex Corporation, which had gone into receivership in 1930. At the two-day public hearing, the witnesses from Celotex revealed time and again, in response to Douglas's probing questions, all of the secrets of their financial agreements: the committees that did not have to register with the SEC because of loopholes in the law; the total control of the reorganization process by a corporate elite, often divorced from any responsibility; the means of dominating the process through various financial agents; and the shifting of resources from investors to reorganizers during the process. Douglas even uncovered that during the reorganization of Celotex, the failed businessmen created new companies through which they could control the new board of directors and buy up more stock. At one stage in the effort, the company's new board of directors even announced that it was considering whether to delist themselves from the stock exchange, thus causing the company's stock to drop eight points and allowing the committee to make a financial killing by buying up the devalued shares to sell later at a profit.

When Douglas confronted Wallace Groves, the president of the reorganized company, with this charge, Groves saw no problem, saying: "It is a very constructive way to employ capital for an investment trust to do underwriting and hold the securities in the portfolio until conditions get better and then sell." What about the expenses charged for this unproductive reorganization? Douglas asked Bror Dahlberg, the ex-president of Celotex. "I have no problem with this," Dahlberg responded: Celotex was busted, and "frankly I was busted too." Upon the completion of the hearings, *Barron's, the National Financial Weekly,* proclaimed that Douglas's investigation was "obviously a complete victory for the commission . . . [with] all salient points of the investigation [being] disclosed."

Thanks to a tip by Tommy Corcoran, FDR's legislative draftsman, Douglas's work came to the attention of a young newspaperman named Robert Kintner, the financial columnist for the influential and conservative New York *Herald Tribune.* Always looking for highly placed government sources to supply him with off-the-record information for his subsequently influential columns, Kintner very quickly settled on Bill Douglas as a rising player in the financial-reform game. Douglas's pithy, brutally honest, and frequently salty western way of speaking, together with his cogent analyses, always made good copy. Kintner's pieces did wonders for Douglas's public visibility. Within a year, he was being featured in at least one article each week, often accompanied by his picture, on the first page of the financial section.

More publicity came Douglas's way when he returned to Washington on April 16, 1935, for a hearing on the reorganization of the St. Louis–San Francisco Railway. Adding to the drama was the fact that he would be grilling his own former boss, Robert T. Swaine of the Cravath firm, who had served as general counsel for the so-called Frisco Railway. Once on the stand, Swaine detailed the problems that the company faced in 1932 as it tried to get an agreement among the bankers, the insurance companies, and various other interested parties in drafting a reorganization plan that would avoid receivership. Why were the bankers, and not representatives from the affected insurance companies, consulted first? Douglas asked. Early consultation with the bankers was "a natural step," the Wall Street attorney replied, adding with a grim smile that bankers "felt that theirs was a highly honorable profession." That must be why the early reorganization drafts had been changed to reflect the bankers' interests, Douglas pressed. Swaine responded sharply, "The implication that something was taken out in order to put something else in, to put something over on somebody else, is unwarranted." All of this had been done under a mandate from the Reconstruction Finance Corporation, the lawyer insisted, and he had made every effort to reflect the concerns of all interested parties.

Why then, Douglas asked, had Swaine's own law firm been voted their regular salaries as well as a "special fee for services rendered" of twenty-five thousand dollars about two weeks prior to the creation of the receivership that froze the company's assets? Swaine argued that his company had always recognized the "possibility of receivership," even as it worked on its reorganization plan, so it earned the money. How can you "reconcile this thought with statements in [the company's] advertisements emphasizing that bondholders must deposit in order to avoid receivership?" asked Douglas. This led Swaine into a complicated description of how $188 million in securities were eventually deposited in the reorganization plan for the Frisco Railway after it went into receivership on November 1, 1932. After all of these efforts, though, the reorganization plan was abandoned in December 1932, and the railroad filed for bankruptcy in May 1933 under section 77 of the Federal Bankruptcy Act.

When Douglas discovered that Swaine had helped to write the central paragraph in section 77 that dealt with railroad reorganization, he moved in for the kill. Didn't the wording of this law give a "stranglehold" to the moneyed interests by providing "gifts" for them? he asked. Swaine admitted that he had indeed worked on the law but denied that it was written in a way that would protect his clients. But wasn't it true, Douglas asked, that he was working with the Frisco Railway at the very same time that he was helping to draft the law? Yes, responded Swaine. And, pressed Douglas, wasn't he at the very same time working for other railroads? Yes, Swaine agreed. Had he disclosed this dual relationship to the bar association of New York, which had appointed him to a committee to study bankruptcy legislation? "Not that I know of," replied Swaine. It was now clear that a Wall Street legal icon had been playing a game using rules that he himself had designed for his and his clients' own benefit.

Despite this success, Douglas was disappointed when there was no general outcry from either the public or government officials for corrective legislation. Hoping to increase the ripple effect of his work, Douglas focused all of his non-Yale attention on the June 18 investigation of the reorganization of the film company Paramount Publix Corporation into Paramount Pictures, Inc. Abe Fortas had already uncovered that the banking house Kuhn, Loeb and Company had realized $1,316,684 in profits from underwriting seven issues of stock in the company over an eleven-year period. By demonstrating through this new hearing how the moneyed interests had actually found a way to *expand* the size of the failing company to their benefit during a bankruptcy reorganization, Douglas and Fortas hoped to reach a turning point in their investigation.

But from the very start, Douglas's inquiry ran into trouble. His plan was to show how Kuhn, Loeb had tried to keep control of Paramount during the reorganization and how they had eventually lost control in a fight with other improper participants. Try as he might, though, Douglas could not get these officials to admit their misdeeds. He began questioning Frank A. Vanderlip, the chairman of the protective committee for Paramount Publix debentures, who freely admitted that all of the members of the protective committee had been suggested by Kuhn, Loeb. When Douglas pointed out that none of those members held any stock in the company—meaning that they did not represent the stockholders—Vanderlip expressed his "complete surprise." Douglas then noted that none of the banking houses represented on the protective committee held any of the corporation's securities at the time either, which only caused Vanderlip to argue strenuously that the membership of a protective committee should also include the bankers who sold the stock issue. When Douglas revealed that even Kuhn, Loeb held no stock in the company, Vanderlip expressed his "surprise" once again. Only when Douglas showed that these banking houses traded "substantially" in Paramount Pictures securities *after* the formation of the protective committee, leading one member to make a personal profit of nineteen thousand dollars, did Vanderlip concede his knowledge that Kuhn, Loeb had indeed sold such stock in 1934. With that admission entered into the record, Douglas then demonstrated that Vanderlip himself had bought several hundred thousand dollars' worth of Paramount stock and then resold it at a profit after he became chairman of the protective committee. However, the banker responded that this was a "commendable" action on his part, since in his view it was his "duty" as a member of the committee to buy Paramount stock. The truth was, he insisted, that all of his work here stemmed not from a desire for profits but from his budding "educational interest" in the motion-picture industry.

As a result of Vanderlip's skill at evasion, Douglas feared that his whole investigation would be derailed. If he could not show how the banks and financiers benefited here, then none of his planned hearings on other bankruptcies would have any impact. Depressed by the whole turn of events, Douglas consoled himself by going to a local bar to drink in solitude, only to run into an old friend, Columbia classmate Herman Benjamin, who happened to be in town doing some legal work. "Bill was very, very low in spirits at the time," recalled Benjamin. "He knew that the guy who ran the committee was a 'corner-cutter,' but no matter what he tried he couldn't get him to admit it. He couldn't find the chink in the armor. 'I'm at the end of my rope. I'm going to give this one more day,' Bill told me, 'and if it doesn't work then I'm giving it all up and going back to New Haven.' "

But as it turned out, one more day was all that Douglas needed. His next witness, Sir William Wiseman, a British partner in Kuhn, Loeb, was far less skilled in the art of avoiding government questioning. Under Douglas's withering interrogation, which lasted the entire morning of June 20, Sir William admitted that the banking firm had carried on a "stabilization" operation in the market for Paramount Publix stock. By creating an "orderly market" during the period in which Kuhn, Loeb was buying and selling the company's stock, substantial profits could be made by those who knew what was going on. Sir William was quick to add, though, that the company had done all of this not for business reasons but because of a "moral obligation." Few observers in the room agreed with this choice or the reasons for it. By now, the arguments in the hearing room over who was to blame for this fiasco became so heated among representatives from the various sides in the reorganization that, after a recess was declared, there was a near fistfight in the hall outside.

Douglas was jubilant the next day when *The New York Times* reported that his investigation had proved that the collapse of Paramount "resulted largely from poor financiering, [and] the payment of excessive salaries to officials." Herman Benjamin recalled, "Once he broke that fellow down on the stand, Douglas was off and running. He knew that it would make his career in the SEC, and it did."

In his subsequent examination of the reorganization of the powerful Swedish match manufacturer Krueger-Toll, Douglas saw an opportunity to even the score with one of his old nemeses: John Foster

Dulles, who had once refused to hire him. Following the suicide of Krueger-Toll's owner, Ivar Krueger, two different committees were set up with a mandate to safeguard the interests of stockholders. One group represented the bankers in the house of Lee, Higginson and Company, which had supervised the reorganization and had retained Dulles as its counsel, while the other, representing the buyers who were alleging fraud, had retained another legendary lawyer, Samuel Untermeyer. Though the two lawyers should have been at each other's throats, Abe Fortas had discovered that Dulles and Untermeyer had privately agreed to split their fees while also safeguarding each other's clients' interests.

When Douglas raised this fee-splitting arrangement with Dulles in his questioning, the Wall Street legend insisted that there was no financially lucrative "deal" in the arrangement. Rather, he argued, Untermeyer was "better qualified" than he was to make recommendations.

Wasn't this instead "a consideration which Mr. Untermeyer was to receive for stilling his big guns that he had been firing at your committee?" asked Douglas.

"No," responded Dulles, "there was no deal of that sort at all." Rather, all of this was done by the bankers, Dulles assured Douglas, out of a "strong sense of moral obligation to the stockholders who through their negligence lost a large amount of money." There is "a great deal of honor in Wall Street," he added helpfully.

Suspecting otherwise, Douglas called Samuel Untermeyer to testify, only to be informed that he was now too sick to appear. So Douglas said that he would conduct his examination personally at the attorney's summer home at Hastings-on-Hudson, New York. Fearing that Untermeyer might feign illness to avoid questioning, Douglas brought along his old psychoanalyst George Draper as his "medical advisor." It was good that he did. As soon as Douglas read the transcript of the Dulles testimony on the fee-splitting arrangement, Untermeyer passed out. Draper examined the rotund attorney and winked to Douglas, indicating that Untermeyer was in much better health than it appeared. As soon as Untermeyer "recovered," Douglas resumed his questioning by pressing directly on the nature of the fee-splitting arrangement, only to have the hapless witness "pass out" once more. After another examination from Draper and a sufficient period for "recovery," the grilling resumed. Throughout the afternoon, this process of questioning, fainting, recovery and more questioning was repeated until Untermeyer finally acknowledged the deal under which Dulles would receive $540,000 and his firm would get $272,500. The admission represented another significant victory for Bill Douglas.

Other members of the financial community who had made killings in various company reorganizations soon trooped before the committee, confessing their misdeeds after being subjected to Douglas's skilled questioning. In August, Douglas uncovered the mechanics of the transformation of the Cuba Cane Sugar Products Company into Cuban Cane Products Company, at a cost of more than one million dollars to the shareholders. Soon thereafter, the committee exposed the unethical reorganization of the McLellan Stores Company, a chain of "five cent to one dollar" stores located throughout the eastern half of the United States.

Despite these successes, with the new school year approaching Douglas could see that he was not going to meet Congress's January 3, 1936, deadline for submitting his investigative reports. So reporter Robert Kintner was offered some early indications of the committee's eventual recommendations. On the basis of this information, Kintner confidently forecast in a column on August 25 that Douglas's committee would recommend that "members of protective committees should be allowed to serve only if they hold securities involved; members of protective committees should be limited in their trading of issues of the company during the reorganizations [sic] period; officials of banks, which are creditors of the company, should not be permitted on protective committees; each committee's personnel should be separate, as far as business interests go; and a limitation should be placed on reorganizations [sic] costs." The final study, Kintner predicted with confidence, "will not be mild. The investigation has been comprehensive and the commission officials are not pleased with some of the revelations."

The timing of this leak was not accidental. Joe Kennedy had just announced that he would be leaving the SEC, and, just as Douglas had predicted, rumors began to swirl that he would be replaced by Commissioner Landis, thus leaving a seat open on the commission. Douglas began marshaling his forces to promote himself into Landis's seat. Senator Francis T. Maloney of Connecticut, who had last year been elected in part because of Professor Douglas's campaign help, sent a letter of recommendation on his behalf to the president. Douglas also asked his new friend Tommy Corcoran to put in a good word in the Oval Office. When Landis was indeed elevated to chairman, the formal race to fill the vacancy he created was on.

Seeking to catch the president's eye, Douglas decided to unleash another attack. For quite some time he had been training his investigatory sights on two U.S. senators, Gerald P. Nye and Burton K. Wheeler. Both men, he believed, had taken undue advantage of the

1933 change in the Cuban government by forcing the repayment of forty million dollars in defaulted Cuban public-works bonds held in the United States. In preparing for this attack, Douglas had leaked to *The Wall Street Journal* that Senators Nye and Wheeler had been "negotiating" with the new government while also serving as chairman and associate counsel for the Cuban Bondholders Protective Committee for the outstanding Republic of Cuba bonds. By acting in this dual capacity, the paper charged, the senators may have improperly threatened officials of another country with American government action if the bonds were not repaid. If he could prove that the two senators, one from each political party, had not fairly protected American financial interests in Cuba, as FDR had intended, then Douglas would be displaying both the nonpartisan independence and fairness required of an SEC commissioner.

But, in fact, Douglas paid a political price for his great copy. In what the New York *Herald Tribune* described as "the first criticism ever made by a member of Congress of the Securities and Exchange Commission," junior congressman Emanuel Celler of Brooklyn sent a letter of protest to Chairman Landis about the unfairness of this attack. Why, Celler asked, could the investigation not have been timed when the two senators, who were then in the Philippines on official business, were present to defend themselves? Might not these attacks result in the discrediting of Nye's upcoming Senate Committee on Foreign Relations investigation into war financing by investment houses such as J. P. Morgan? And, why, if the committee was now so concerned over the default of foreign bonds, had it not yet examined the equally questionable and harmful default of German bonds? For the first time, the New York *Herald Tribune* also turned a critical eye toward Douglas's investigation: "There are some distinctly unfortunate aspects to the long series of Washington hearings on foreign-bond defaults and the protective endeavors that followed." While the commission announced in response that "there would be no change" in the nature of the foreign-bond default investigations, in actuality these hearings were abruptly terminated.

By the time Douglas's committee had turned its attention to the study of bankruptcy reorganizations in the real-estate field, and of the Baldwin Locomotive Works, everyone could see that the director's attention was diverted. Rather than grilling these witnesses himself, Douglas turned the conduct of the public hearings largely over to Abe Fortas and the rest of the staff. Douglas was preoccupied by his lobbying to fill Landis's vacant seat. After the leading candidate to fill the vacancy, SEC general counsel John Burns, announced that he would be leaving government in order to make more money to support his large family, Landis, too, favored Douglas for the post. When FDR heard the suggestion on December 20, 1935, Landis later recalled, "he picked up the phone from his desk and called Douglas right then. . . . Douglas accepted right at that time." In doing this, Franklin Delano Roosevelt had succeeded where all others in Bill Douglas's early professional life had failed: He got him to accept a job immediately and then actually fill it.

The selection did little to capture the imagination of the press or the American people. The real news that week was the resignation of the undersecretary of the treasury, T. Jefferson Coolidge. To the press, Bill Douglas's new appointment meant little more than a few filler paragraphs. *The New York Times* labeled the appointment "somewhat as a surprise" because Douglas was "relatively unknown" and "his only appearance since he joined the S.E.C. [had] been in connection with a series of protective committees and these were inconspicuous." To which *Business Week* added, "No policy significance is attached to the appointment."

Regardless of what the East Coast press thought, the appointment thrilled the city of Yakima, Washington. "It is not every day that a Yakima boy can make the first page of the *Wall Street Journal* . . . , but W. O. Douglas made it," crowed the Yakima *Daily Republic* in an editorial entitled "Wall Street Takes Notice." "He is traveling in pretty big company," the hometown paper added. "Whether he reforms the world of finance and makes Wall Street a safe place for the lambs is not predictable, but he'll do it if anybody can, and Yakima will always be proud to say he lived here as a boy and started work here as a man, and above all, that he married a Yakima girl."

With this promotion, Douglas had now received everything that he had been seeking from his work on the protective committees, so he left to Fortas and his beleaguered staff the tasks that were now long overdue: finishing up the hearings, assembling their findings, and drafting the recommended corrective pieces of legislation along with their accompanying reports.

Bill Douglas would soon come to be known in the press as "the Professor Who Jumped from Nowhere." But to move any farther up the government career ladder, Douglas knew, he needed to find a way to move his name from the financial pages to the front pages of the newspapers.

And, relying on an old skill, he found a way to do just that.

BIRTH OF A LEGEND

In matters of grave importance, style, not sincerity is
the vital thing.

—*Oscar Wilde,* The Importance of Being Earnest

Once the Douglases moved to Washington, D.C., family life was quite a
bit different from the "loving-husband-and-caring-father" public image
of Commissioner Douglas fostered by admiring press accounts. Like
many of the New Dealers who worked night and day seven days a
week, for Bill Douglas there was no time for family life. Young Millie
and her little brother, Bill Jr., or "Bumble" as he was called because of
his clumsiness as a child, would only hear their father's breathing and
chewing from behind the newspaper at the breakfast table and never
dare to bother him, for fear of being scolded. Mildred was left to raise
the children and was expected to have dinner ready at whatever hour
Bill returned from work. The only time that Douglas seemed to pay
any real attention to his family was when the press photographers
wanted a picture.

But there was one occasion when the other Douglases could count
on seeing him. The commissioner now occasionally liked to gather his
two children and his wife in the living room of their rented pink-brick
house in Silver Spring, Maryland, where he would pace back and forth
in front of the fireplace, telling them one of his stories. As he spoke, always in a halting western twang, with each phrase punctuated by a
loud "harrumphf," which made it sound like he was clearing his throat,
his hands moved jerkily in uncontrollable twitches. Sometimes he
would paw at his face, appearing either to wipe away his facial features
or to catch his own words and stuff them back in his mouth. At other
times, he would nervously and vigorously tussle the top of his graying

hair, leaving it in complete disarray. To his family on these occasions he was "the Storyteller."

In spinning a new yarn, Douglas would begin by recounting some recent event as accurately as he could, seeking to make the occurrence into some kind of parable of general importance. Then, over and over, his family would sit and listen as Douglas tried out one version of the tale after another, as if he were practicing it. Each time he retold it, he would change a detail or two, accepting or rejecting the changes depending on whether they helped the tale. Slowly the story would be honed and shaped. And as it came to have that casual but dramatic western Douglas flair, they could all see that it got further and further from the truth. Finally, Douglas would indicate his satisfaction with the result simply by leaving the room without further comment. Their job finished for the moment, the rest of the family then went about their lives.

Bill Douglas had learned his storytelling craft during his early mountain hikes while sitting as an enthralled teenager at roaring campfires in the Cascades of northern Washington and listening to the tales of Scottish sheepherder Billy McGuffie, or Bumping Lake reservoir superintendent Jack Nelson. He learned from them that tales told at the campfire were judged by the heartiness of the laughter or the look of genuine admiration at the end, rather than the veracity of a random fact or two in the middle. If the truth had to be altered somewhat to fit the purpose or the pacing of the tale, then so be it. This was how the oral tradition of the Pacific Northwest was shaped.

And this, he now decided, was how the oral tradition of "Commissioner Bill Douglas" would be created as well. Later, Millie and Bumble would sit on the stairs in their house and overhear their father at a party tell his friends a story that had seemingly occurred to him on the spur of the moment, but which they had already heard many times before. And their father's tale was always exactly like the final, fictionalized version of the story rather than the original one. Whenever Millie later questioned these stories by saying, "Dad, you know it didn't happen," Douglas's crystal-blue eyes would twinkle as he uttered just two words in response: "literary license."

His strategy worked. With each new performance on the Washington cocktail circuit, Bill Douglas's reputation grew as one of the finest storytellers in a town full of them. His tales went unchallenged and were retold over and over again by his admiring listeners. As some of these tales found their way into the newspapers, they defined the Douglas persona that the general public came to know.

In this manner, the William Orville Douglas born on October 16, 1898, was reborn as "William O. Douglas," the developing public legend, in the *Time* magazine of January 27, 1936. An article entitled "Walla Walla to Washington" offered the first full biographical portrait of the new young bureaucrat who now symbolized the New Deal by promising to clean up Wall Street. This image was straight out of the Horatio Alger tales of poverty to riches:

> This remarkable young man turned up in the East in 1922 on the brake rods of a transcontinental freight train. Son of a poverty-plagued Presbyterian minister, he odd-jobbed his way through Whitman College, Walla Walla, Wash., washing his own clothes, living at times in a tent. Burning for a big university degree he arrived at Columbia Law School with 6 cents in his pocket. Before he graduated high in his Class of 1925 he had written a legal textbook for a correspondence course. In his last year he taught three courses on the side.

Oh, how this first incarnation of Douglas's tale resonated with a nation hungering for saviors to deliver them from the effects of the Depression! Here was the new political hero for the general public—the poor boy from Yakima who would bring those robber barons on Wall Street to heel. Little did they realize, or even care, that so much of it was untrue or incomplete. Nothing was said here about his widowed mother's efforts to raise the family through her real-estate deals with James O. Cull. Nothing was said about his brother's, sister's, and wife's financial aid to get him to and put him through college and law school. And nothing was said about the personal insecurities that had once threatened his legal career.

While his family remained silent about the inaccuracies in this account, the story of impoverished Bill Douglas "riding the rods" east to attend Columbia Law School puzzled some of his friends. Whitman College classmate Silas Gaiser, then the superintendent of the Salem, Oregon, school system, ventured in 1939 that "there has been some exaggeration, I think about his beating his way East." Whitman College president Chester Maxey later explained that eastern writers "couldn't imagine anybody being so poor that he would have to ride on the sheep train. Well those were nice jobs and very much prized, if you could get a sheep train to Chicago." Said Maxey, "The kids would beg for an opportunity to travel on the sheep train."

Indeed, even Bill Douglas himself knew at the time that the story was a gross exaggeration. Only the closest readers of *Newsweek* learned this, however, when one of its readers complained three years later in a letter to the editors about the inaccuracy of a similar version in that magazine of the Douglas biographical story:

"Douglas' 6 Cents"

Somewhere along the way from Whitman College, at Walla Walla Wash., to Columbia University, in New York, Mr. Justice William O. Douglas appears to have lost 30 cents. In your article "Douglas, Jurist," you say he arrived with 6 cents in his pockets. Previous reports have said 36 cents. Perhaps the 30 was what he looked like when he crawled out of that more or less mythical box-car.

Don't be that way. I read your paper every week and I want to believe that your stories are truthful accounts of facts, not "hopped" up to make 'em lively. There is a man out here who says he loaned Douglas some cash from his own slender funds about that time and that [he] did not have as tough a time as is being made out.

Silvanus Kingsley
Portland, Ore.

To which the editors responded in part:

Douglas himself is the source for the "myth" that he landed in New York with 6 cents. As he has repeatedly described the incident to the chief of NEWSWEEK's Washington bureau [Ernest K. Lindley], [he] rode in a car loaded with sheep as far as Chicago, where he was held up ten days by a railroad strike. Although he was not worried by the delay, a hobo traveling in the same car suggested that, if he was going to arrive at Columbia University in time for the opening session, he ought to get going. So Douglas wired his brother for $15, all of which, with the exception of 6 cents, went for his day-coach fare to New York.

Despite the lack of accuracy, Douglas was not inclined to deny any of it. "If the darn fools want to write that stuff, who am I to contradict them?" he would laugh to his friend Chester Maxey.

With each new telling, the story of Douglas's life became embellished a little bit more. Three months later, reporter George Creel offered a more elaborate portrait of Douglas in *Collier's*. Titled "The

Young Man Went East," the article tapped even further the sentiments
of Depression-era readers:

> Doubtless due to his Scotch strain, Bill had a raging thirst for edu-
> cation. . . . [So] in his eighteenth year he pedaled to Whitman Col-
> lege in Walla Walla, his sole possession, other than an extra shirt,
> being a secondhand bicycle. The first term's tuition was free, due to
> the fact that he had been honor man in his high school class, but
> there remained the problem of eating, and sending money home.
> He solved it by getting a janitor's job . . . his pay being fifteen cents
> an hour. As for housing, a tent overcame all difficulties. . . . Ex-
> pressing a trunk to New York with his meager belongings, he com-
> mitted his skinny frame to an open boxcar, and headed East.
>
> September 1922, was the date of his arrival in New York. He
> had exactly six cents in his jeans.

As compelling and thrilling as the tale of childhood poverty was
for the nation, it was bewildering for those few around Douglas who
knew the truth. "Dear Comrade," teased Douglas's brother, Arthur, in
a letter when he first saw these tales in print, "Can't you stop this 'living in a tent' and 'washing clothes in a stream' business? Think of your
children."

Chester Maxey viewed this behavior more critically. The real origins
of Douglas's "living in a tent while at college" story, Maxey explained,
were quite different from his story: "The truth is that Bill Douglas
lived in the Beta House. And the Beta House was as nice as any of the
houses on campus at that time. . . . In the spring, there was a lot of
warm weather at that time. The Betas pitched a big tent in the back of
the yard. . . . On warm nights the boys would go out and sleep in that
tent. Bill, along with the rest of the gang was out there sleeping in the
tent. . . . Frank Howard owned the tent." Even more interesting, Maxey
recalled that Frank Howard "always claimed that Bill Douglas stole
[the tent] from him." Maxey understood why the stories, accurate or
not, were being endlessly repeated in the growing legend of Douglas:
"About people like Bill Douglas, myths grow up, and the people pre-
fer to believe the myths. They are much easier to believe than the
truth."

These three pillars of Douglas's Horatio Alger legend—his childhood poverty, sleeping in a tent in college, and riding the rods to law
school—became the foundation for his public image for the rest of
his life and beyond. For decades at Democratic party assemblies, reporter Hugh Sidey later recalled, "the caustic, rumpled Supreme Court

Justice William O. Douglas would stomp through such gatherings reminding people that he rode the rods out of Yakima, Wash., to go to Columbia Law School in 1922." In time, as layer upon layer of biographical stories were added, two men would come to exist: "William O. Douglas," whom the public knew from these published accounts and the subject's own interviews, and the private "Bill Douglas," whom only a handful of real friends and family members were permitted to see. Based on his several-decade friendship with the Justice, Chester Maxey said: "I knew Bill Douglas, the public figure, and Bill Douglas, the private person. And I liked the private person much better than the public person. And I think everybody would if they knew him."

But it was the public Douglas who would be dealing with Wall Street.

THE BOGEYMAN OF
WALL STREET

The story of Bill Douglas's accomplishments at the
SEC has not been told, certainly not adequately. It
was a great achievement, which in some respects
rivals those of his subsequent career.

—*Abe Fortas*

Now that he was on the SEC, Bill Douglas set his sights on the next step
in his career. He realized that if he could shape his public image as a reformer, then perhaps fate would smile on him when the chairmanship
opened up again. With the first of his protective-committee reports in
May 1936, Douglas began carving out his place on the commission.
This report criticized the minimal restrictions on municipal-debt re-
adjustments and recommended suitable reforms.

The report was immediately praised by the New York *Herald Tribune* as "a bitter indictment" that "caustically commented upon the
arbitrary fees, the lack of proper accounting and the highhanded control of those who are classed as fiduciaries for the depositing bond-
holder." All in all, the press observed, the report "aroused a good deal
of concern" among municipal-bond specialists, who argued that it was
pervaded by a "highly accusative spirit" and contained "instances of
bias." While such controversy unsettled new SEC chair James Landis,
the entire experience pleased Douglas immensely.

Early in June, Douglas's study of protective committees was once
again the focus of national press attention when his second report, on
real-estate protective committees, was released. In Douglas's own
words, his committee had uncovered "one of the greatest tragedies in
the history of finance at this time." An admiring *New York Times* reported that the study contained "sharp criticism of past and present
procedure in connection with defaults on real estate bonds, reorganization committees and voting and liquidating trusts." Two weeks later,
Douglas presented another report on trustees under indenture, criti-

cizing prominent banks such as Chase National Bank, Guaranty Trust Company, and Manufacturers Trust Company. Douglas now told reporters that "by and large, the corporate trustee had been sitting idly by while bondholders had been exploited." He left no doubt about his targets: "When I speak of the corporate trustees, I am speaking about some of the leading banks of the country, some of which served their proprietary interests in an issuing company before fiduciary interests were served." A front-page article in *The New York Times* praised the latest report as being "sharply critical," while the New York *Herald Tribune* added that "the tenor of the corporate trustee survey, like those on municipal and real estate protective committees, is caustic."

These reports made Douglas the focus of the financial community's attention. The New York *Herald Tribune* reported that bankers found the reports "far from being to their liking," describing the proposals in them as "revolutionary." The recommended reforms, *Herald Tribune* reporter W. S. Lyon predicted, would "upheave the banking world" as banks found "themselves differing with much of the theory running through the commission's corporate trustee recommendations." Robert Kintner, now serving as Douglas's informal publicity agent, devoted an entire *Herald Tribune* financial column to proclaiming that "Mr. Douglas, while the newest of the S.E.C. commissioners, appears to be doing much to set the tone of the commission." Now convinced that the president would be impressed by his new image as a strong reformer, Douglas looked for opportunities to convey that image.

With his new visibility came a great rise in the number and importance of his public-speaking offers. Douglas had been invited by the New York Stock Exchange to speak on July 11 at a roundtable at the University of Virginia on financial affairs. There, Douglas attacked the manner in which many in the audience made their living by praising the SEC's effort to segregate the broker and dealer functions, so that well-informed exchange traders would not benefit from selling stocks to customers who were less informed. While the audience shifted nervously in their seats, Douglas promised that the SEC was "committed to a continuing and increasingly intensive study of the whole problem with a view of moving progressively forward toward the objective of high standards of conduct in our security markets."

In setting himself apart from the business accommodationist Landis and his colleagues, Douglas could see in the next day's press accounts that he had found his voice. *The New York Times* reported that "floor traders, as well as many other members of the Exchange were nettled by the remarks of William O. Douglas." Why were these people so upset by the comments of a lone commissioner? Because, the paper explained, it had been rumored for months on Wall Street that Douglas was "being groomed to succeed James M. Landis as chairman of the SEC if and when Mr. Landis returns to his professional post at Harvard."

Seeking to solidify his future career prospects, Douglas had already requested a meeting with the president so that he "could have the privilege of thanking you in person for the opportunity for public service which you have afforded me." He wanted, he wrote to FDR, to note his "deep appreciation of this opportunity to serve you and the nation in your great constructive reform program." Douglas closed by saying, "I want you to know that I am ever at your service in the high cause which you are serving."

The day after delivering his University of Virginia address, Douglas sent a copy to Roosevelt's press secretary, Stephen Early, with a short cover note describing the pages as "campaign materials" for FDR's reelection bid that year. Roosevelt was so impressed that he instructed his appointments secretary, Marvin McIntyre, to call Douglas "and say [that] I was delighted to have his letter and I hope very much that he will come in and see me sometime in August on my return [from vacation]."

Having learned how to gain attention in the Oval Office, Douglas journeyed to Boston on August 25 to deliver another speech, this one expanding upon his committee's findings about municipal bankruptcies to the Municipal Law Section of the American Bar Association. This time, Douglas's harshly critical comments resulted in the great consternation of the bond community. Finally, Douglas met for the first time with the president in the White House on September 16.

Three days later, Douglas's allies kicked his campaign for SEC chairman into high gear. Robert Kintner noted in an article on the anticipated resignation of SEC Commissioner J. D. Ross: "Mr. Landis is also expected to quit. Mr. Douglas would then be a strong contender for the chairmanship." Kintner also trumpeted Douglas's protective-committee successes in a column on October 4, 1936, while also promoting the commissioner's upcoming reorganization reports. Even though Congress would not act for another two years on these proposals, which were still being produced by Abe Fortas and his staff, Kintner provided Douglas with all the publicity that he needed from the effort.

Knowing that the financial community was still capable of playing a role in preventing his elevation to the chairmanship, Douglas began working both sides of the street. Privately, in meetings with journalists he expressed admiration for Landis's moderate position on Wall Street regulation and remained, according to press accounts, "on good terms with the N.Y.S.E. [New York Stock Exchange] leaders." Seeking to reinforce that view, he carefully choreographed a series of personal contacts with key leaders on Wall Street.

Publicly, though, Douglas continued his one-man war on moneyed interests. At Robert Maynard Hutchins's invitation, Douglas delivered the Moody Lecture at the University of Chicago on October 27, where, for the benefit of the trustees of the university founded by wealthy industrialist John D. Rockefeller, Douglas titled his speech "Termites of High Finance." A "financial termite," Douglas explained, was one who fed off the efforts of others, making money by market manipulation rather than by manufacturing anything of substance. As a result, like the termite who lives by destroying wood, this "exploitation and dissipation of capital" by those "who practice the art of predatory or high finance" eats away at the structure of the financial system. Thus, Douglas charged, using Justice Louis D. Brandeis's favorite term, these financiers were feeding on "other people's money." But what was to be done? "Irresponsible, laissez-faire democracy is dead everywhere," Douglas proclaimed, warning that "there is no alternative; either we run the risks of sacrificing liberty, or we set ourselves earnestly and steadfastly to build a structure of democracy based on security and stability." Once more, Douglas sent a copy of his speech to the White House.

Two weeks later, Douglas delivered yet another "two fisted address," choosing as his forum the Stock Exchange Institute, a school run by the New York Stock Exchange for member firms' employees. The future brokers, he said, would face "subtle and subversive influences at work to corrupt the high functions which business, finance and the other professions perform." Douglas's call for greater fiduciary standards on Wall Street found few takers in the audience, whose members bristled instead at what they told the press was the "cynical attitude of the speaker and his failure to credit the Exchanges with efforts in the last five years to elevate customers' men's standards." But the reaction did not bother Douglas, who was focused on only one reaction: President Roosevelt's.

Early in January 1937, it began to appear as if Douglas's careful political efforts were about to pay off, as rumors circulated that Landis would be resigning. "It is thought likely that, unless the President disapproves, Mr. Douglas would get the votes of the Democratic majority of the S.E.C.," reported Robert Kintner. When Landis, after meeting with FDR, told reporters that he was "contemplating leaving government service some time late this summer," and Harvard Law School an-

nounced less than a week later that he would be its next dean, the race
for the chairmanship was formally on. For its part, the liberal magazine
The Nation had already selected its nominee: "President Roosevelt
would do well to appoint . . . William O. Douglas, who has shown
firmness and realism in his conduct of hearings."

While the White House mulled over its choice, Douglas had to deal
with the extremely controversial issue that had become the litmus test
of every New Dealer's loyalty to the president. In February 1937, President Roosevelt, frustrated by the Supreme Court's declarations that
many of his economic reforms were unconstitutional, had proposed a
plan for the reorganization of the federal judiciary that became popularly known as the Court-packing bill. This measure would allow the
president to add one new member to the Supreme Court for every
member over the age of seventy, up to a maximum of fifteen total
members. The stated reason was to enable the "nine old men" to keep
up with their work, though few would dispute that the most efficient
worker on the Court at the time was eighty-year-old liberal Justice
Louis D. Brandeis. The real reason for the proposal was to change the
political balance, and thus the direction, of the Court as quickly as
possible.

Such an open attack on a branch of government, especially the
"nonpartisan" Supreme Court, placed all of the president's men in a
quandary. How should they respond to the constitutionally suspect
plan while remaining loyal to their patron? The man who knew the
most about the Supreme Court and who was widely expected to provide intellectual cover for the plan, Felix Frankfurter of Harvard, so
distanced himself from the White House by his public silence that
journalists believed a feud was under way. On the other hand, Assistant Attorney General Robert H. Jackson lobbied hard in favor of the
proposal, despite the fact that it did not completely enthrall him either.

For his part, Bill Douglas claimed privately to have very strong
views about the plan. Writing to his old confidant, A. Howard Meneely, he said: "The President's Court proposal has Wash D.C. (like the
nation) stirred. Feelings run very high. I am for it. I am working behind
the lines long hours on it. It will pass—the only thing being 'when'
and 'at what price.' " But as had become his custom, in matters affecting his career, Douglas played it safe publicly, making no statements to
the press. Instead, he privately directed others to defend the program.
SEC assistant Milton Katz later recalled: "Douglas . . . took on one of
the main jobs of organizing the political battle in favor of the Court
plan. He summoned a group of us to his office and assigned responsi-

bility for writing speeches for different phases of the legislative battle."
To supplement this effort, Douglas leaned on his old Yale colleagues
for help. As a result, the Yale law faculty voted eleven to eight in favor
of a resolution supporting the plan, and Dean Charles Clark became
the only law-school administrator in the nation to testify in favor of
the plan before the Senate Judiciary Committee. Douglas himself
never had to say a word.

In time, his academic colleagues caught on to what was happening.
"Dean Charley Clark was enraged at Douglas at the time," recalled
Irene Hamilton. " 'Douglas convinced me and all of us to come out for
FDR's Court-packing plan but never said a word about it himself publicly,' he would say. He was too politically astute to say anything." By
trimming his own political sails, Douglas had maintained his career
prospects, Clark later told his friends, while his own testimony had so
offended opponents of the Roosevelt administration that it delayed
his own appointment to the federal court.

Despite all these careful efforts, Douglas's promotion plans threatened to go awry on March 11, when the New York *Herald Tribune*
reported that Robert H. Jackson had "been prominently mentioned recently in influential Administration circles as the successor to James M.
Landis on the Securities and Exchange Commission." Knowing FDR's
predilection for rewarding leading advocates of his plans and for staff-
ing New Deal agencies with "outsiders" loyal to him, Douglas took the
Jackson threat seriously. Douglas searched for a chance to prove his
value to FDR once again. Unwittingly, the Bond Club of New York
offered him just such an opportunity by inviting him to speak on
March 24 at the opulent Bankers Club in Manhattan. Douglas knew
to expect a capacity luncheon crowd including, *The Wall Street Journal* reported, "nearly every investment banker of importance in New
York." He decided to deliver a speech that, though titled, innocuously
enough, "Democracy in Industry Finance," none of them would ever
forget.

As he stood to speak, the bankers rose to greet him "with a sponta-
neous round of applause." Then, peering through the haze of cigar and
cigarette smoke rising from this assemblage of men in fancy suits,
Douglas lit into them with a ferocious fourteen-page diatribe delivered with what *Time* later called "savage candor." "Today, as you well
know," he told the bankers, "we have a practical usurpation of the
rights of the great body of investors which can only be described as financial royalism." These "oppressive plans, . . . selfish endeavors, . . .
and vicious and unsound labor policies" were being practiced, he said,
by investment bankers as they served on the boards of industrial cor-

porations. The solution, Douglas argued in a stentorian voice, was to establish "democratization in industrial management," through several proposed reforms:

1. Creation of a permanent national organization to which grievances of investors could be carried.
2. Segregation of the underwriting and selling functions of investment bankers.
3. Competitive bidding for security offerings.
4. Independent directors to represent public interest.
5. A practical basis for director compensation. . . .
6. Elimination of non-voting stock.
7. Elimination of voting trusts.

As he explained each item in great detail, Douglas might just as well have simplified things by telling his audience that they should empty out their pockets, resign from their jobs, and turn to gardening for a living.

These words, delivered on hostile turf, "fell upon an astounded audience." "I understand he used to ride your trains blind baggage," one shocked banker whispered to his neighbor, a director of the Northern Pacific Railroad. "Do you suppose he really is God?" said another in a stage whisper.

When the speech ended, *The New York Times* reported, "the spattering of clapping was far from cordial, and the members broke up into little groups of outspoken critics." All around the room phrases such as "inconsistent meddler," "impractical reformer," and "theoretical logician" rang out. In time, the New York *Herald Tribune* reported, the stunned investment bankers staggered back to their offices as "a grumpy lot" and feeling "rather gloomy." All agreed that these recommendations amounted to "nothing less than a complete remaking of the country's investment business," which "left bankers gasping."

Following this speech, Douglas became known as "the Bogeyman of Wall Street," striking fear into the hearts of men in fancy suits. If *he* became the chairman, they knew, his "impractical" theories would become their nightmarish reality.

Wall Street was now very concerned about Douglas's prospects for the chairmanship, with several "influential brokerage interests" actively opposing his elevation after the Bond Club speech. Some brokers even went to Landis personally to argue against Douglas. But when word seeped out that fellow SEC commissioners George Mathews, Robert Healy, and J. D. Ross did not want the position, it became clear that if the choice came from inside the commission it would be Douglas. Opponents tried to shift the attention to an outside prospect, suggesting that even "someone of the experience, perhaps, of Joseph P. Kennedy" should get the nod.

While the debate raged over his future, Douglas filled his calendar in the summer of 1937 with efforts to get his protective-committee reform bills through Congress. However, after weeks of testifying at hearings, negotiating with critics, and aiding his supporters, it was apparent by early August that none of the bills was likely to pass during the current congressional session.

The commission's agenda changed, however, when Charles R. Gay, president of the New York Stock Exchange, issued a report on August 17, 1937, blaming the SEC for negatively affecting the market by issuing "excessive regulation [that] stifles individual initiative, intimidate[s] and confuses honest men so that they are unable to determine how to act." The vituperative nature of this attack surprised even Gay's allies. The New York *Herald Tribune* reminded him in an editorial "that things are not quite as bad yet for the business man in Wall Street as they are for the business man in Nazi Germany." The commission deliberated over its response to the attack, but the moderate Landis persuaded the other members to ignore the charges for the time being.

While the decision turned out to be a bad one for the nascent agency's public image, it did wonders for Bill Douglas's promotion prospects. The SEC's failure to respond to Gay led many in the Roosevelt administration to publicly criticize the agency for its lack of "aggressive leadership." By September, whispers were being heard that perhaps the aggressive reformer Bill Douglas, who was then vacationing with his family on Cape Cod, would bring a stark contrast in style to Landis's coolly moderating policy of silence.

Frustration built as Landis took a full month before responding to Gay's attack. Finally, following his announcement on September 14 that he had tendered his formal resignation to the president, Landis spoke on the matter, but only in his capacity as a "private citizen." The only source of stability in the economy, he argued, was the "small man" who was the "backbone" of the nation, while Wall Street, in being far too "jittery," was threatening to cause another Depression. "It would be difficult to imagine a more feeble valedictory than that which James M. Landis delivered," wrote the *Herald Tribune*.

Landis's resignation now drove the press into a frenzy over the issue of who would be his replacement. While formally the commissioners possessed the power to name Landis's successor, they refused to do so, thinking that the president might wish to name an agency outsider to the post. The betting in the press was still that Douglas would get the position, but with new candidates for the post being mentioned daily the odds were no longer prohibitively in his favor. Journalists now began to assess, among others, the chances of J.M.B. Hoxey of the New York Stock Exchange's stock-list committee and Frank Shaughnessy, president of the San Francisco Stock Exchange. Meanwhile, Landis was reported to be privately supporting David Saperstein, director of the SEC's trading division, who had resigned from his post at the same time as the chairman. Behind the scenes, Wall Street had stepped up its own "Anyone but Douglas" campaign. W. A. Harriman, head of the Business Advisory Council for the Department of Commerce, reminded Commerce Secretary Daniel C. Roper that the appointment of a new chair would have a vital impact on businessmen throughout the entire financial community. Roper passed this letter on to FDR, saying that the financial community's model chairman would be an industrialist like Sears and Roebuck's president, General Robert E. Wood.

Knowing that any further appointment delay would only hurt his chances, Douglas enlisted his media and administration allies in an effort to gain some momentum. "Supporters of Commissioner Douglas were somewhat disturbed by the failure of the commission to elevate him to the chairmanship," wrote the *Herald Tribune* in an unattributed story that had Tommy Corcoran's fingerprints all over it. "Friends of Mr. Douglas argue that there is no reason to believe that the President is opposed to Mr. Douglas's promotion. In fact, on the basis of his 'liberal' record, there is every reason to believe he will receive White House approval, they said."

Douglas decided to force the wheel of fortune in his direction. Leaving his vacationing family on Cape Cod, Douglas traveled to Washington to attend Landis's final meeting at the SEC. As soon as he arrived in his room at the Cosmos Club on Friday evening, September 17, Douglas phoned his old boss, Joseph Kennedy, who was then serving on the Maritime Commission. A delegation from the Yale Law School had offered him its deanship several months earlier, Douglas explained to Kennedy, and while he had tentatively accepted the job, he did so only on the condition that the chairmanship of the commission did not come his way. Now, explained Douglas, since no appointment had been forthcoming and the matter seemed hopelessly delayed, he had a train ticket back north at 10:00 A.M. the following morning to take the post. Known to play fast and loose with the truth himself, Kennedy would have appreciated the fact that the only people who would have been more surprised than he by Douglas's story would have been the Yale law faculty, which had made no such offer, and Charles Clark, who had expressed no desire to leave his deanship. The story was not entirely untrue; Douglas did indeed have a train ticket north, back to his vacation on Cape Cod. Upon hearing this tale, Kennedy told his old friend to wait awhile and he would see what he could do.

One phone call later, the popularly anointed "Irish Mafia"—Joe Kennedy and Tommy Corcoran—formed, in the words of one news account, an "unholy alliance" in intensively lobbying the president to get Douglas "the big job." And it worked. On the morning of Saturday, September 18, Douglas packed his bags, ate his breakfast, and was leaving his room when the phone rang. "You will not be leaving town," Kennedy promised, adding that he had been to see the president and that Douglas should wait by the phone for a call from the White House. Shortly thereafter, the phone rang again, and the president, in his cheery patrician voice, invited him over to 1600 Pennsylvania Avenue for a chat at 11:00 A.M. As soon as Douglas arrived, he was offered the job. He accepted without hesitation. With the offer firmly in hand, rather than remaining in town for the formal coronation vote by the commissioners, Douglas picked up his bags and journeyed back to Cape Cod.

Despite the fact that, by one press account, every "powerful broker and banker interest sought to put every obstacle in the way of his selection," on September 21, 1937, Bill Douglas was unanimously elected by his colleagues on the SEC to be their chairman. Unlike the largely invisible response to his earlier appointment to the SEC, the reaction in the national press to this new appointment was significant and supportive. The New York *Herald Tribune* hailed the elevation of this "liberal" and "radical," saying that it ensured "a vigorous regulation policy by the S.E.C." *Business Week* noted that change was quite likely: "Landis likes to be liked. Douglas is not so apt to try and please . . . [as he is] tougher than Landis."

Only one group was far less optimistic about the appointment. YAKIMA NOT AT FAULT, blared the editorial headline of the Yakima *Daily Republic*. The same paper that had praised him so heartily just twenty-one months earlier now sought to disown him in a piece personally approved by its conservative publisher, W. W. Robertson:

> The Yakima school system should not be held responsible for the career of the infant prodigy who seems destined to become chairman of the security and exchange commission [sic]. It is true that William O. Douglas—known in the I-knew-him-when club as Orville—

acquired the rudiments of his education in the public schools of this city, but that does not account for the vagaries of his later life.

Certainly when he sat at the feet of Prof. Davis and his faculty young Douglas was not subjected to any germ which could later have developed into a hate-the-rich attitude of mind; nor did he in his sojourn at Whitman College learn anything that would have inspired him to make the life of a man with a dollar as hectic as possible.

No, it must have been in the halls of Yale and Columbia that he acquired the idea of becoming a crusader and an irritant to all dealers in stocks and bonds. It was there he developed the propensity for tearing all balance sheets to shreds and for revealing the secret plots of those who conspire to sell public securities at a profit to the public.

There is much to be said to Douglas's credit; he is as intellectually keen as any New Dealer in the pack; he knows his corporations as well as Jim Farley knows his Tammany politics; he is one of the ablest men of the present administration. He doubtless acquired the foundation for his splendid scholastic record in the public schools of Yakima. For that this community takes credit but beyond that it need not assume responsibility.

While most people would be embarrassed by such an attack, it tickled Bill Douglas. For decades thereafter, he carried a copy of this editorial in his wallet and proudly pulled it out to show his friends. When the tattered clipping finally fell apart, he contacted the newspaper and asked for another copy, but the paper claimed to be unable to find it.

The truth was that it made little difference to Douglas what his conservative old hometown thought of his work now. After a decade spent meandering through one indecisive career move after another, followed by his successful efforts to secure advancement to the top of two professions, Bill Douglas had finally reached center stage, and he knew exactly what he had to do. Former Columbia law student Ernie Cuneo saw the change in his old professor almost immediately: "So far as I could see, Bill Douglas was not a Happy Warrior, he was a deadly one. Of all the gunslingers I've ever seen, there are only two I ever counted who were dead shots and shot to kill. One was Douglas, the other was [Fiorello] La Guardia. . . . The land and its people were being despoiled by a bunch of bastards, and Douglas and La Guardia were out to gun them down."

And Douglas wasted no time in getting that message across. "Under Joe [Kennedy] the gains made toward protecting the rights of investors through President Roosevelt's legislative program were consolidated. Under Jim [Landis] we were taught how to get things done. And we're now going to go ahead and get them done," he told *Time*. Wall Street was about to find out just what a totally focused Bill Douglas, armed with the full financial regulatory machinery of the SEC at his disposal, was capable of doing.

SHOWDOWN ON WALL STREET

A Smith and Wesson beats four aces.

—*Murphy's Law axiom*

As he looked around him on September 22, 1937, Bill Douglas could see that his career had reached a crossroads. With the all-male press corps gathered around his new office desk, overlooked by a picture of Louis D. Brandeis, whom he constantly referred to as his good friend and mentor, Douglas knew that if he ever was to make a run for the presidency, he would have to begin by making his mark here. Though he was ready for the challenge, his attire did not impress the members of the press, who were accustomed to covering the well-dressed aristocrats on Wall Street. His rumpled suit looked like it had been stored in a pile on the floor of his closet rather than on a hanger. His tie, usually adorned with various food stains and ashes from his ever-present cigarette, was gathered very loosely around his neck in a balled-up knot. The shoes he liked to rest on his desk to demonstrate his casual lack of concern, revealed a hole in one of their soles. And on the top of a file cabinet lay the ten-gallon cowboy hat that he wore to tell everyone that things were going to be different.

Now, with the camera bulbs flashing all around him, Douglas took control. Rather than take questions, he posed three of his own to answer: "What is the proper role of the SEC in relation to finance and investment? The second is: What kind of bird am I? The third is: What is my own attitude toward a number of specific, live problems that we have before us and that we have been thinking about?"

Dealing with his first question, Douglas said that the SEC "should be, and I think we will continue to be, what I might call 'the investors' advocate.' We have got brokers' advocates; we have got exchange advocates; we have got investment banker advocates, and we are the investors' advocate." While the agency could not "provide any substitute for investors' judgment," it could "demand full disclosure of the facts . . . insist upon a market free of manipulation . . . [and] fight fraud." All the agency sought to do, he added, was to "maintain a free market, not a fixed market."

That said, Douglas then turned to his second question: "What type of bird am I?" His answer was straightforward:

> To tell you the truth, I think that I am really a pretty conservative sort of fellow from the old school, perhaps a school too old to be remembered. I think that, from the point of view of investors, the one safe, controlling and guiding stand should be conservative standards of finance, no monkey business. I am the kind of a conservative who can't get away from the idea that simple honesty ought to prevail in the financial world. I am the kind of a fellow who can't see why stockholders shouldn't get the same kind of fair treatment they would get if they were big partners instead of little partners in industry.

As to the question about specific changes in policy, Douglas said that while he was reluctant to expand on this question because he was "catching a train in a few minutes to go back and finish getting acquainted with [his] family and, secondly, to mull over some of the major problems that lie ahead," he would offer a few hints. The SEC, he said, needed to become "the pace setter in the accounting field," to be bolstered by its companion role initiating "direct, aggressive prosecution" of those involved in investment pools and manipulations.

That said, the press conference quickly concluded, with the consensus that Douglas sounded more like a potential friend of the financial community than its nemesis. The "statement to the press . . . was certainly not calculated to create the jitters, on the contrary, it was decidedly reassuring," raved the New York *Herald Tribune.*

Privately, though, the new chairman was presenting a very different image. "[Douglas] acted as if he were a brooding U.S. Marshal, who took meticulous care of his guns, because it was coming in to High Noon, and he was going to walk down Wall Street for the shootout, hell, high water or snow, and he was going to get his man and he did," recalled a friend. And the man he wanted to gun down, the chairman's allies knew, was the leader of the New York Stock Exchange, Richard Whitney.

By 1937, the forty-nine-year-old Whitney was a legend among legends on Wall Street. With a father who had served as the president of a Boston bank, and an uncle and later an older brother, George, who both had become partners in the esteemed House of Morgan, Richard Whitney seemed bred to become a Wall Street baron. He had attended the exclusive Groton preparatory school, where one of his school-mates had been Franklin Delano Roosevelt, and later enrolled at Harvard. After serving a brief apprenticeship on Wall Street, in 1916 Whitney purchased a seat on the New York Stock Exchange. Although he was only twenty-eight, his family connections gained him immediate acceptance into Wall Street's inner circle. By 1920, he had founded Richard Whitney and Company, which thrived on business funneled to it by the Morgan Guaranty Trust Company.

Whitney's base of power on Wall Street lay with a group of prominent brokers known as the old guard. This group considered themselves to be the direct descendants of "the beaver-hatted brokers" who "swapped stocks under the old Wall Street buttonwood tree." These men traded in person, dealing directly with others on the same social scale, thus allowing them to control the exchange despite the fact that the general public had begun trading on the market during the 1920s.

Whitney's Wall Street legend began the week after Black Thursday, the stock-market crash of October 24, 1929. With financial panic surrounding him, the tall and handsome Whitney, impeccably dressed as always in his stylish fedora, fancy suit, and polished imported shoes, and sporting a pocket watch attached to a gold chain with a charm from his Harvard Porcellian Club, marched with deliberate assurance across the exchange floor to the post for U.S. Steel. "What is the current price of the stock?" he asked in his usual condescending manner. The price had only briefly stopped at 205 on its plummet to the basement, he was told, and was surely now worth much less. Upon hearing that, Whitney brought the floor to a hushed silence as he placed an order for ten thousand shares at 205. Then, he calmly went around the floor placing similar above–market value orders for several other nose-diving stocks. In one fell swoop, Richard Whitney had briefly put his financial finger in the bursting exchange dam.

A week later, acting in his capacity as vice president of the NYSE (the president of which, E.H.H. Simmons, was out of the country, getting married), Whitney closed the exchange temporarily, thus enforcing calmness on the market. For these actions, Whitney was immediately crowned by the press "the 'White Knight' of Wall Street." Just three months later, he was elected president of the exchange.

By the mid-1930s, however, a group of traders consisting mostly of members of the commission houses that dealt directly with the general public arose to challenge Whitney and the old guard. Cleverly calling themselves the "new guard," these brokers depended for their living upon the public's perception of the fairness of the market, so they were very much concerned with maintaining that image of the stock exchange. Two leaders of this group, E. A. Pierce—later a founder of the Merrill, Lynch, Pierce, Fenner, and Smith brokerage firm—and Paul V. Shields, who worked as Wall Street's representative with the Senate Banking and Currency Committee's investigative Pecora Hearing, which studied stock-exchange practices and led to the SEC's formation, considered taking action by going to see the then SEC chairman, Joseph P. Kennedy.

In the hopes of instigating a power struggle between the old and new guards, on January 25, 1935, Joe Kennedy submitted an eleven-point program to Congress that was designed to increase the power of the new guard in the exchange's government. Then he pressured the group to back him, saying: "You association people say you're friends of mine. Now I want you to endorse the program and let Whitney and his ——— ——— crowd go fry." And fry they would. While the governors of the exchange pronounced the Kennedy plan "heresy," they were forced to create eight new exchange governorships appointed from the brokerage houses.

Finally, in the spring of 1935, Whitney was forced to step aside, and Charles Gay was selected as the next president of the exchange. Derided by journalists as "a mediocre man, blundering but well-intentioned," Gay appealed to the exchange because he was the diametric opposite of Whitney. A graduate of Brooklyn's public schools and the Polytechnic Institute, Gay had climbed up the Wall Street ladder all the way from the post of office boy. Gay was "an obvious compromise choice" because he associated with neither the reformers nor the old guard.

However, this election hardly constituted the reform of Wall Street that Kennedy had sought, as indicated when Gay immediately appointed E.H.H. Simmons as his vice president. Moreover, when Richard Whitney garnered more votes for an exchange governorship than Gay received, he was given a seat on the powerful Law Committee and the even more influential Governing Committee, already dominated by the old guard. Seeing all of this, Paul Shields confronted Gay about his support for the old guard. "What else can I do?" Gay pleaded. "My hands are tied." Upon hearing this, Bill Douglas began referring to the president as "Charlie 'McCarthy' Gay," after ventriloquist Edgar Bergen's dummy.

Whitney, Gay, and the old guard were not the kind of men to worry about William O. Douglas as chairman of the SEC. That would cost them dearly.

.   .   .

Shortly after the chairman took office, he got his first break when Shields and Pierce arrived in Washington for an informal chat with him.

"We think the management is pretty damned bad. What would the S.E.C. think of reorganization of the Stock Exchange?" said one of the visitors.

"Would you mind saying that again?" Douglas asked.

"Why, we believe the Exchange ought to be reorganized. You can't get anywhere so long as the Exchange is a sort of private club. We wonder whether the S.E.C. would back us in a fight for reorganization?"

"Why, damn it," Douglas responded gleefully, "that's exactly what I want."

Within minutes, it had become clear to Douglas that his Wall Street opponents did not have a united front. When pressed by his visitors as to what sort of reorganization he had in mind, Douglas responded: "That is primarily a matter of internal management of the exchange. I will not attempt to submit a blue-print on that. You know your business better than I do."

Despite this encouragement, the old guard was still in control. On Tuesday, October 19, 1937, however, the bottom fell out of the stock market once again. Publicly, the Roosevelt administration presented a picture of calmness. "[I am] not convinced there is any need at this time for government intervention to halt the bewildering break in the stock market," FDR told a group of reporters. Privately, though, the president dispatched his son James to Wall Street to observe it first-hand and make some recommendations. While the younger Roosevelt suggested closing the market immediately, Paul Shields proposed instead a series of talks about reorganizing the exchange. On October 20, a meeting was arranged between Shields and Joe Kennedy.

In turning such delicate negotiations over to the past chairman of the SEC, the president was able to distance his administration from any untoward results. And well that he did because Kennedy was not in a mood to be diplomatic when the meeting took place. "[I am] —— —— —— —— sick and tired" of the exchange's "warfare" with the government, Kennedy shouted at Shields. When he demanded movement toward exchange reorganization, Shields repeated his earlier promise to fight for such a goal.

But Shields had promised more than he could deliver. As soon as he returned to New York, he was summoned to Charlie Gay's office, where he was confronted by a group of the most powerful men on Wall Street: one of the counsels for the exchange, Roland Redmond; E.H.H. Simmons; exchange governor Gayer Dominick; and, unsurprisingly, Richard Whitney. After rebuking Shields for acting behind their backs, the old guard nevertheless realized that the government's increasing pressure could be mitigated only by some kind of reorganization. So they began to craft a memorandum for the president that outlined their proposed reforms. After hours of wrangling, though, all they could agree on was a one-paragraph promise of cooperating in talks with the government in order to establish some kind of new management for the exchange.

Shields was designated to present the memo to the president in a meeting at Hyde Park on October 26 at which both Kennedy and Douglas were present. When the president expressed his disappointment with the new memo, Shields promised that if the exchange leaders did not cooperate further, he would prevail on his own by using his allies in other brokerage firms. The decision was made that the government's peace talks with the exchange would continue.

On October 29, a delegation of five of the stock exchange's most powerful officials, including Paul Shields, journeyed to the SEC offices in Washington for what they thought would be their first formal head-to-head meeting with the new chairman. Their reception was not a pleasant one. Unbeknownst to the visitors, Douglas had invited as his personal guest Joe Kennedy, who was still anxious to make his points with his old investment colleagues. Shields was not even able to outline his group's initial proposal before Kennedy began blasting the visitors for Charles Gay's memo ten weeks earlier that had blamed the SEC for causing the recent market crash. When the inevitable congressional investigation comes this time, Kennedy promised, it will be the SEC that blames the exchange for market conditions.

Douglas, however, was not willing to leave the threats solely to others. "The job of regulation's got to be done," he shouted vehemently. "It isn't being done now and, damn it, you're going to do it or we are. All you've been doing is give us the run-around. The Exchange calls it co-operation, but the S.E.C. calls it the run-around. If you'll produce a program of reorganization, I'll let you run the Exchange. But if you just go on horse-trading, I'll step in and run it myself." It was no bluff, the traders knew, for through Kennedy the threat would quickly find its way back to the Oval Office.

As if to demonstrate that power, Douglas then ordered the exchange to write him a letter promising to reorganize, whereupon he would write an approving reply. Wall Street was fully on notice now that Bill Douglas was no Jim Landis.

The reaction surprised Charlie Gay, who, just three weeks earlier, had taken the highly symbolic step of leaving his regal, old-fashioned office in New York with its oversized desk ornamented with a bronze bear and bull flanking the inkwell on top, to visit the "ratty," "third-class quarters," of Bill Douglas on the corner of Seventeenth and Pennsylvania in Washington. There, expecting to meet the devil himself ranting and raving about the need for reform, instead Gay had encountered a genial man who behaved like a good ol' boy from Yakima, cracking open his well-stocked liquor cabinet so that the two of them could enjoy an evening of serious drinking and smoking, all the while thoroughly charming his guest. At the end of the evening, the exchange president believed that Bill Douglas was a man with whom he could deal.

But when they met a third time, at the Yale Club on the Saturday of the Yale-Princeton football game, Gay and his two fellow negotiators—Paul Shields and exchange counsel William H. Jackson—unexpectedly encountered a very different Bill Douglas. Now the tall tales were replaced by some very real threats and hard-nosed negotiating tactics as they labored to frame the reform letters, with the result that in no time at all the peace conference degenerated into a shouting match. By late afternoon, with the football game long since forgotten, Douglas announced that he would write the exchange's letter for them and then draft his response. With that, he called in an SEC stenographer to help him with the task. As soon as his draft was finished, Douglas turned it over to the three men, who proceeded immediately to strike out the only provision that really mattered to Douglas: the creation of an outside paid presidency to run the exchange.

A good deal more shouting ensued before Gay finally tossed down his pencil and pleaded: "Is this necessary? We have a fine organization. We're willing to co-operate. I can't understand all this." When Douglas indicated that he was unwilling to budge, the talks broke down.

Gay returned to his office only to find the old guard waiting for him. When they heard what had ensued, George Whitney and his partner Thomas W. Lamont reminded Gay that the SEC's silence in the face of his attack that summer had made the agency so weak that there was no reason to let them "off the spot" by agreeing to anything with

Douglas. Perhaps, they all decided, it might still be possible to out-flank the chairman. Since the president apparently still retained confidence in Joe Kennedy, perhaps a split could be created between the old and new SEC chairmen that would derail the reorganization effort. William H. Jackson was dispatched to meet with Kennedy in Washington. In no time at all, Jackson discovered that Kennedy's personal agenda was indeed far different from Douglas's. The ex-chairman was far more concerned with the political ramifications for the SEC of Gay's report in August, which placed blame on it for the weakness in the market, than with Douglas's notion of a new outside paid president for the exchange. Jackson quickly offered to add a paragraph to the exchange's proposed letter to Douglas that would exonerate the SEC of any responsibility for the market crash. When Kennedy expressed his approval, the Wall Street representative thought that a deal had been reached.

Little did they know that Douglas had appointed his executive assistant, Milton Katz, as his negotiator on the letter and instructed him to agree to no changes from the draft that had been rejected by the Wall Street leaders. For three days and nights, exchange counsels Jackson and Roland Redmond met with each other, with Katz sitting in the waiting room outside, laboring continuously, through lunches, dinners, and even a Sunday, in an effort to draft the new communiqué. Periodically, one of the men would come out to ask Katz whether the SEC would accept a particular provision, but each time Katz's answer was the same: "I'm sorry. Douglas simply isn't going to accept this unless you do the whole thing."

After nearly twenty drafts, the deed was done. Katz proudly called Douglas to tell him the good news: "Bill, they've adopted every single thing we want without even a change of a comma or semicolon." Wall Street had totally capitulated to Douglas.

"Good. Call Joe Kennedy," said the chairman.

Kennedy could not have been more pleased when the letter was read to him over the phone. "Good, good," he said. "You know, Milt, when you deal with those fellows you know what you've gotta do? You've got to force their mouths open and go in with a pair of pincers and just take all the gold out of their teeth."

But total victory was no longer enough for Bill Douglas. After thinking about the arrangement overnight, Douglas called Katz the next morning to dictate a whole series of new demands. Knowing that he had gotten everything he could from the exchange leaders and seeing now that his assignment was "fruitless," Katz refused to convey Douglas's demands and instead asked his permission to resign. The task of "negotiating" for the agency now returned to Douglas himself.

While no one really knew why Douglas had suddenly had a change of heart, the reaction from Wall Street was predictable. "The whole business is off," Gay told the chairman in a phone call on November 19. But Douglas demanded that Gay reassemble the negotiation team for one final round of talks. Gay agreed to do so, but only on the condition that John W. Davis, the counsel to J. P. Morgan, serve as an outside adviser to the process.

When the group reconvened, Davis proved to be even less willing to negotiate than Douglas. He tempered the language of the exchange's letter to such an extent that even the paragraph exonerating the SEC was watered down. By the time Jackson arrived at the SEC offices to deliver the revised letter in person, Douglas had already organized the commissioners' response.

"Have you read the last draft of our proposed statement?" Jackson asked Douglas.

"The S.E.C. has read it," the chairman responded coldly, "and it is not satisfactory. The negotiations are off."

"Well, I suppose you'll go ahead with your own program?"

"You're damned right I will," Douglas barked.

"When you take over the Exchange, I hope you'll remember that we've been in business 150 years. There may be some things you will like to ask us."

"There is one thing I'd like to ask," responded Douglas.

"What is it?"

"Where do you keep the paper and pencils?"

For the old guard the questions were suddenly many indeed. Was Douglas serious? Did his agency really have the resources to carry out the threat? Didn't he realize that the shaky public image of the SEC made the success of such an action questionable at best? After twice rejecting the results of his own negotiations, the exchange leaders no longer believed that they understood Douglas's motivations and intentions. So while he assessed his options, they waited for the inevitable counterattack by the government regulation–hating "White Knight," Richard Whitney.

But they were destined to be disappointed.

·   ·   ·

Unknown to nearly everyone, Richard Whitney was in deep, deep trouble. Addicted to both the excitement of market speculation and the extravagant life that it provided for him, Whitney had for years been risking everything by illegally making deals using securities from his wife's trust fund as collateral for personal loans from friends. Unfortunately, his efforts to market an applejack drink called Jersey Lightning and other such surefire losing ventures, put him in even greater financial jeopardy. In a matter of a few years, Whitney's personal loans from thirty-one different Wall Street sources amounted to a total of $8,284,000.

When this massive indebtedness failed to provide for a man of Whitney's lifestyle, the man who had stolen from his wife and friends decided to steal from widows and orphans. Since Whitney was a trustee of the stock exchange's Gratuity Fund, created to give money to the families of deceased exchange members, his firm acted as the fund's broker. When the trustees had decided in March 1937 to sell some of the fund's bonds, Whitney instead used them as collateral for one of his personal loans. And since no one appeared to notice, as the Gratuity Fund's trustees continued to shift their assets, he converted each one of them in the same way. By the end of November 1937, Whitney had loaned himself more than one million dollars in this manner. For the common man, this would be called embezzlement, but Whitney saw it as just a temporary loan that would be repaid with interest in due course. The process might have continued for several more years had Whitney not failed to take account of a lowly stock-exchange clerk named George Lutes, whose weekly salary of $37.50 could not even support Whitney's monthly shoe-shine bill. So meager was Lutes's pay that he fed his family with an extra twenty-four dollars per month he received as the clerk for the Gratuity Fund. Since one of his responsibilities was to note when the fund's assets were returned to its vault, Lutes alone knew that Whitney had not deposited any funds from the sale of the bonds.

On five occasions, he "reminded" Whitney that the bond assets had not been returned, only to hear each time that the broker was too busy to do so now. While Lutes knew that this was not the "orderly and proper way" to conduct business, he later told SEC investigators that "never at any time" had he suspected any impropriety on Whitney's part. The truth was that with a wife and child to support in Roselle, New Jersey, even if he had had such suspicions Lutes would have been too intimidated to confront Whitney directly.

On November 22, 1937, though, the same day that Douglas was threatening W. H. Jackson about taking over the exchange, Lutes saw his opportunity to place the matter before the trustees of the Gratuity Fund. With Whitney absent from a meeting of the group, Lutes told the trustees about the missing assets.

The trustees were initially more upset with the clerk than the embezzler. *Why had they not been informed of this irregularity earlier?* barked fund chairman E.H.H. Simmons. Following the meeting, Simmons called Whitney's office and directed that the missing cash and securities be returned immediately. The next day, Whitney paid a visit to Simmons and asked for a day's delay because his office was "shorthanded."

"As a friend I would not hesitate," Simmons responded, "but as a Gratuity Fund trustee the money must be returned by 3 p.m. [today]." Whitney promised to do what he could. The White Knight had less than a handful of hours to find millions he no longer had.

Events were spiraling out of his control. That same day, an article appeared on the front page of the New York *Herald Tribune* under the byline of financial editor C. Norman Stabler, offering a behind-the-scenes account of the recently failed negotiations between the exchange and the SEC. Citing "an exclusive interview" with a "source close to William O. Douglas," Stabler claimed that the SEC was about to reverse its policy of allowing the securities exchanges to write their own rules concerning trading practices of members. To members of the New York Stock Exchange, this "notice to the Exchange to do what the S.E.C. wishes, or bear the consequences" was seen as nothing more than a bluff. "We'll not do anything now which might be misunderstood as being prompted by a shotgun," vowed one Wall Street source.

When the Dow Jones news ticker in Bill Douglas's office spewed out at noon that day that Stabler's story had been confirmed by "a source generally considered reliable," the chairman decided that he had taken all that he was going to take. Now "enraged," Douglas began drafting a six-page "bombshell" letter, which constituted his formal declaration of war on Wall Street. While it "would be desirable to have all national securities exchanges so organized and so imbued with the public interest that it would be possible and even desirable to entrust to them a great deal of the actual regulation and enforcement within their own field," Douglas scrawled, "at the present time . . . I have doubts as to the desirability, from the standpoint of the public interest, of assigning to exchanges such a vital role in the Nation's economic affairs." After citing examples of the exchange behaving much like a "private club," Douglas argued that these problems needed to be met with "progressive action." Exactly what constituted "progressive action" was left unclear, but everyone involved knew that Douglas's threat to take over the exchange was still on the table.

The chairman was so impatient to get his answer out that he called members of the press into his office before the ink could dry on the mimeographs of his statement. As they entered, the reporters found Douglas seated calmly back in his chair, with his left hand resting on the back of his head and his right hand nestling a cigarette. While he watched them read the new statement, it did not take long to notice that it failed to even mention Stabler's critical story. When one of the reporters asked the chairman what he thought of the account, Douglas suddenly jumped up, his hair flying in the air, and swung his arm down sharply on the tabletop, shouting, "Bullshit!"

But Richard Whitney was not cowed. While the press was meeting with Douglas, he was visiting his brother George seeking to borrow a spare million or two to cover the missing money from the Gratuity Fund. George Whitney was "aghast" and "thunderstruck," as his brother had already borrowed more than three million dollars of his money, with more than two million of it still outstanding. *How could you do such a thing?* he demanded over and over. There was no answer. But family was family, so Richard would get his money. Since George Whitney did not have the money, he turned to his partner Thomas W. Lamont for help. As surprised as Lamont was that Richard could do such a thing, both men agreed to make the loan without informing the rest of the partners. In covering up this illegality through more unethical conduct, Wall Street was operating just like the private club that Bill Douglas had described.

Later that day, Richard Whitney called E.H.H. Simmons to say that the funds would be delivered the next day. Assuming that Whitney had simply been pressed for cash, Simmons was now willing to let the matter drop. But others were not so willing to do so. Two days later, over Thanksgiving dinner, George Whitney ordered his brother to liquidate his business. The following week, another of the Gratuity Fund trustees, Blair Williams, had become so concerned about the Whitney situation that he considered bringing the whole incident to the attention of the exchange's Committee on Business Conduct. But upon hearing that George Whitney had "fixed the whole situation up," he agreed that "there was no necessity of doing anything."

Incredibly, through all of this, exchange president Charlie Gay remained totally unaware of Whitney's difficulties. Instead, he was concentrating on dealing with Douglas's takeover threat. He requested that the exchange's Governing Committee appoint an impartial group to make recommendations for changing the exchange's management. With Whitney busy dealing with his own problems, his allies were unwilling to fight the move, and the decision was approved.

With this authorization in hand on November 29, Gay was ready to respond publicly to Douglas's critical diatribe. His manner, though, was destined to disappoint those who were hoping for a return of fire by the exchange.

> My experience has convinced me that the Exchange is fully alive to its public functions; that it is constantly improving its methods; that it stands ready to cooperate with public authorities in every way for the better performance of those functions, and that in the long run the public interest can best be served by leaving to the exchanges, under the supervision of the commission, much of the regulation of their own business, rather than by an immediate and more pervasive administration of all phases of Exchange business coming within the purview of the Securities Exchange Act of 1934.

After a point by point rebuttal of the facts and figures presented by Douglas, Gay then announced that he was going to appoint a special committee to study reforming the exchange management.

As shocking as this conciliatory statement was to some members of the exchange, it was even more so to Douglas. Why was the exchange being so magnanimous? The answer must be, he concluded, that the real response would come from the "unquestioned general of the stock exchange old guard," Richard Whitney. But to his surprise, the White Knight remained inexplicably silent. Clearly, the decision point for the SEC was fast approaching.

Fortunately for the chairman, Charlie Gay continued to backpedal as quickly as he could. In December, Gay made good on his promise to appoint the Organization Study Committee, headed by exchange governor Carle C. Conway, chairman of the Continental Can Company. In many respects, it was the perfect compromise group, with the reformers disparaging it as the "Gay Protective Committee" while the old guard complained that it was unrepresented as well. The committee worked at a feverish pace, while Conway kept Douglas apprised of its progress. By the end of 1937, the committee publicly announced that it was expediting its schedule in an effort to have its report ready in two months.

While this period was shaping up as a turning point in the public career of William O. Douglas, the same was true for Richard Whitney—but the futures of the two men were proceeding in opposite directions.

.   .   .

Whitney's opponents now began to smell blood in the water. Bernard E. Smith, a successful speculator, member of the exchange, and Whitney opponent, decided to make his move when Charlie Gay invited him to lunch. When the discussion turned to what could be done to improve the image of the exchange, Smith said that nothing could be done "as long as he had the old guard in there." What did he mean by that? asked Gay. Smith responded that he was referring to the "clique that had run the Exchange and brought it into discredit." Be more specific, pressed Gay, whereupon Smith blurted out, "Richard Whitney," adding that "the quicker [you get] rid of him the better off the Exchange [will] be . . . [because he is] in a large measure responsible for the discredit in which the Exchange stood."

Deciding that he had heard enough, Gay asked Smith if he had any concrete evidence for his charges. "He['s] broke and owe[s] money all over the Street," claimed Smith. It was the first time that Gay had heard a thing about the charges, but he quickly dismissed them because of Smith's bitterness and the fact that rumors about a firm's insolvency were commonplace on the Street.

Still totally unaware of the problems confronting Whitney, Bill Douglas did what he could to support the work of the reform-oriented Conway committee. In late December, the SEC issued its annual report, charging that the "national securities exchanges have not as yet demonstrated the capacity themselves to police their markets effectively against manipulative and deceptive practices." This report, proclaimed *Time,* represented the SEC's "latest bomb in its recent attack on the New York stock exchange," and indicated that the commission was ready to do what the exchange could not.

Then on January 7, 1938, Douglas sprang another attack while speaking at the Bond Club of Hartford. For some time, he told them, he had been thinking about the dangers to the market presented by the practice of "selling short." In such transactions, an investor who believes that the market price of a stock will drop sells shares that he does not actually own, borrowing the stock from a broker to deliver to the purchaser, and then buys shares of the stock the next day, with luck at a lower trading price, to reimburse the broker for the borrowed stocks. If successfully executed in a falling market, it is possible to realize an immediate and sizable profit by purchasing stocks at much lower prices than those at which they were sold. The problem for the market is that such transactions create an artificial increase in the number of sellers of a stock, generally forcing that stock's price to drop. Large financial operators known as "bear raiders" were making huge profits by selling short to deliberately manipulate market prices. By creating falling prices in an already declining market, these traders could change a simple downturn into a crash.

For Bill Douglas, the prospect of issuing a regulation on selling short was tailor-made to demonstrate the commission's seriousness about instituting reform. So, just over two weeks later, the SEC issued a surprise regulation requiring that any short sale of a stock be made at a higher price than its most recent sale price. By thus arresting the forced decline of a stock's price, this rule, the New York *Herald Tribune* predicted, would "in effect spell the death knell of bear raiding." For the first time in its young history, the SEC had unilaterally imposed a trading rule on the stock exchange.

The regulation accomplished its intended effect. On January 26, the Chicago Stock Exchange adopted a plan to reorganize itself that mirrored the provisions Douglas was now seeking from the New York exchange, including the imposition of outside paid officers. The following day, the Conway committee issued its report, endorsing the Douglas reform plan in its entirety: a salaried independent president and treasurer, public representation on the board of governors, a reduction in the number of exchange committees (including the elimination of the Whitney-dominated Law Committee), and a series of rule changes that would incorporate the reformers into the exchange leadership.

Bill Douglas hailed the report as "a great step forward in the direction of sound Stock Exchange organization along the lines on which the commission has been thinking." Meanwhile, an exuberant SEC staff was gloating that the report was "a complete victory for Douglas." Douglas, however, knew that the report was useless if its recommendations were not adopted by the rest of the exchanges, including Richard Whitney and his cronies of the old guard.

But just as the time came for Whitney to fight, it seemed as if the Fates had totally turned their backs on him. In mid-January 1938, John B. Shethar, a specialist broker in the Greyhound Company, noticed an unusual sale of three thousand of the company's shares by Whitney's firm. Having heard the rumors about Whitney's troubles, Shethar suspected that this was a case of the White Knight trying to save himself by dumping stock. Since this affected his own financial position, Shethar decided to pass his suspicions on to Herbert G. Wellington, a member of the exchange's Governing Committee.

Wellington in turn relayed these suspicions to Howland S. Davis, the chairman of the Business Conduct Committee of the exchange, failing to mention that Whitney also owed him a great deal of money. Before Wellington could even leave the spot where he and Davis had been talking, Whitney approached him for yet another loan. This time, though, Wellington refused.

Davis knew that the truth of the rumor could easily be checked by consulting the Whitney firm's latest responses to the extensive financial questionnaire required by the exchange. But Davis discovered that, because of the prominence of the owner, the firm had never been compelled to fill out a questionnaire.

Now Davis's curiosity was aroused even further. Knowing that a new round of questionnaires was scheduled to be sent to all of the exchange companies over the next several months, Davis placed Whitney's firm at the front of the line. So, rather than getting his form in late May, which might have given him some time to borrow more money to cover his debts, Whitney got his form in late January, with instructions to reply by February 15.

With disaster staring him in the face, an ordinary man would find a way to recede into the background. But Richard Whitney was no ordinary man. Rather than absent himself from the next meeting of the Governing Committee on Monday, January 31, where the highly charged issue of the Conway committee reorganization proposals would be discussed, Whitney chose to attend and continue to lead the opposition. The report should be accepted only "in principle," he argued strenuously, and, despite all of Gay's work in the preceeding days to garner support for the report, Whitney's appeal began to take effect. Sensing the change in sentiment, for the first time Gay stepped down from his rostrum and went to the well of the chamber to argue for the proposals. The governors were so startled by this act that all of them immediately voted with their president, with only Richard Whitney abstaining.

Then, in an event that close observers found to be terribly odd, E.H.H. Simmons agreed to head the newly formed committee investigating changes in the exchange's constitution. To Wall Street pundits, Simmons had just gone "over the fence to the reformers so fast he left his pants hanging on the barbed wire." But just why he had done so was still not clear to any but a few insiders.

·   ·   ·

When Whitney's financial questionnaire came due on February 15, 1938, he asked for and received a one-week extension on the pretense that an outside auditor was still working on the figures. But Whitney was only delaying the inevitable. As soon as the questionnaire came in on February 22, New York Stock Exchange officials immediately discovered the firm's massive and improper deficiency in working capital. The next day, the Business Conduct Committee ordered a complete audit of the books and records of Richard Whitney and Company. By February 28, the auditor found evidence of even greater financial misappropriations.

Four days later, a meeting was set up with Whitney, his attorney, and several exchange officials to discuss the findings. How much money would be required "to put him square in the world?" asked the committee's counsel. Whitney solemnly pulled out a small notebook, consulted it briefly, and said that another $282,000 would settle everything. The embarrassed silence in the room told everyone that they knew he was lying. After asking for a short recess, Whitney's lawyer insisted that he stop lying and change his statement. But all the White Knight would say was, "I insist that $282,000 is all that is needed to straighten out my situation." Richard Whitney, everyone now realized, was beyond their help.

But he was not beyond their reach. After three days of negotiations, the exchange drafted formal charges. Whitney decided to try one last ploy, going to see Charlie Gay and asking for more time to pay off his "debts." The request so stunned the exchange president that he fell over and literally knocked himself out on the hard floor. After he was revived, Gay explained to his visitor that there was nothing that could save him now. But Whitney thought differently. "After all," he said, "I'm Richard Whitney. I mean the Stock Exchange to millions of people. The Exchange can't afford to let me go under." Gay, however, knew better. If *he* did not go under, then Bill Douglas would surely see to it that they would *all* go under. The exchange, he responded calmly, would proceed with its charges. So, the Governing Committee voted on the afternoon of March 7 to present its formal charges against the partners of Richard Whitney and Company, and it changed life on Wall Street forever.

Charlie Gay knew that the time had come to concede defeat. Picking up the phone, he asked Bill Douglas if they could meet later that night in Washington to discuss something that could not be put over the telephone.

.   .   .

A somber Charles Gay and Howland Davis met with Douglas at 8:00 P.M. at the Carleton Hotel and explained why the exchange had just voted to press charges against one of its most prominent members. Both of them knew that Bill Douglas held all the cards necessary to guarantee an SEC victory over the Street. Immediately, he called Commissioner John Hanes at his house and asked him to join them two hours later, whereupon he heard another rendition of the news.

Douglas then dispatched Hanes on the 2:00 A.M. train to New York to determine the potential loss of public funds. As soon as he arrived, Hanes enlisted the services of the SEC's crack investigator in New York, Pat Dowd. Despite their efforts the next morning, so much confusion reigned at the Whitney firm that no one could determine the extent of the loss, let alone whether any of the money had come from the general public. Douglas became so concerned about keeping the matter away from New York's aggressive district attorney, his Columbia Law School classmate Thomas E. Dewey, who might derail their efforts with early indictments, that he issued subpoenas for the relevant files.

It was left to Douglas to brief the remaining commissioners before going to see the president, who as usual was conducting his early-morning meetings from his bed in the White House. When FDR learned of the impending charges against his Groton schoolmate, all he could say was "Not Dick Whitney!"

"Yes," Douglas replied, "Dick Whitney."

"Dick Whitney—Dick Whitney," FDR kept repeating. "I can't believe it."

And neither could anyone else on Wall Street.

At a hearing before the Business Conduct Committee that morning, Richard Whitney and Company admitted that it would not be able to meet its financial obligations. A letter from the firm was then sent to the exchange secretary, which read: "We regret to advise you of our inability to meet our engagements." As a result, the company's trading privileges were immediately suspended.

Rumors of Whitney's insolvency spread like wildfire around Wall Street. Charlie Gay spent the early morning preparing a statement to read to the exchange, hoping to do so before the opening bell, but the 10:00 A.M. gong had already sounded when he reached the floor. So at 10:05 the gong sounded again, and all trading ceased. In a voice cracking with emotion, Gay announced the suspension of Richard Whitney and Company for "conduct inconsistent with just and equitable principles of trade." The rumors about the legendary White Knight were true.

The news of Whitney's corporate demise paralyzed the financial district. As one Wall Street observer put it, "The sense of shock was indescribable." In the words of another, there was a "gloom that pervaded Wall Street as the revelations continued in the Whitney affair." A "sense of defeat" that "was personal to every leader in the financial district" spread throughout the community.

Bill Douglas now governed Wall Street. On March 10, Whitney was indicted by Thomas E. Dewey. A week later, the brokers voted 1,013 to 22 to expel Whitney from the exchange and agreed by the same margin to adopt the reorganization measures proposed by the SEC. On March 22, Douglas cabled the prosecutors in charge of the Whitney case asking for a delay in sentencing to enable the commission to finish "an investigation of all phases of the circumstances which resulted in the insolvency of Richard Whitney & Company and the indictment of Richard Whitney." One by one, members of the leadership of the New York Stock Exchange and the old guard were called in to testify. In time it became clear to the press and the public that Whitney's situation had been more or less an open secret on the Street for a long time.

Seeing that Wall Street had been brought under government control, the American public had found a new hero. Though he was not yet forty years old, Bill Douglas had accomplished so much that in just a handful of years of service on the SEC, he had become to the press " 'Mr. Trouble,' in person."

But Douglas took none of this for granted, for this was not the final stop on the career ladder he had constructed for himself. The time had come, he knew, to institutionalize the government's powers over the financial world.

THE PRACTICAL ADMINISTRATOR

[Bill Douglas] found the New York Stock Exchange
a private club and he left it a public institution.

—*Robert W. Kenny, 1944*

Douglas's "total victory" over Richard Whitney had made him one of
the rising stars in the New Deal. "Bring me another victim so that I can
disembowel him," Franklin D. Roosevelt would tease him with a smile
in the months that followed. Douglas's challenge now, though, was to
institutionalize a series of Wall Street reforms in order to ensure that
the Richard Whitneys of the future would not rise from the ashes of
the SEC battle.

Douglas had launched this effort while still battling Whitney when
he turned to the question of regulating the over-the-counter (OTC)
market—those businesses off of Wall Street where securities were also
traded. So little was known about the totally unregulated OTC market,
which handled nearly eight times the business done in the markets on
Wall Street and all of the other financial districts put together, that
Douglas began calling it the "under-the-counter" market. Anyone with
a phone and a basic knowledge of the market could open an office, buy
or sell stocks by quoting customers any price they wanted, and charge
them any commission they chose for the service. The result, *Time* reported, was that OTC firms ranged in size "from one man behind a dirty
glass partition to frenzied establishments with 175 telephones. . . .
[with] customers [possessing] little means of telling whether they are
quoted a fair price or charged a fair commission." Despite these irregularities, few exchange members wanted the government to corral the
cash cow that was bringing new investors into the market.

Consistent with his overall regulatory philosophy, Douglas now intended to force the OTC to form voluntary regulatory associations

that would in turn be supervised by the SEC. So confident was Douglas in the soundness of this plan that, even before announcing it to the public, he had already handed a draft of the corrective legislation to his good friend Senator Francis T. Maloney of Connecticut for introduction in the Senate. The bill, journalists predicted, would have "nothing but the plainest sailing" through Congress. But that did not make everyone happy; even the once supportive, business-oriented New York *Herald Tribune* now protested against "this attempt at Nazification of the private finances of the country."

Douglas turned his attention, meanwhile, to shepherding three other pieces of legislation through Congress dealing with bankruptcy. The first bill, proposed by Clarence Lea of California, sought to bar all interested parties from serving on bankruptcy reorganizations and to set the fees paid to those officials. In addition, the bill stated that if a court requested, the SEC could intervene to determine the fairness of a reorganization plan. Douglas's chances for legislative success here were complicated by the simultaneous efforts of Congressman Adolph Sabath of Illinois, who as a result of his own committee investigation into the issue had drafted a different corrective bill on bankruptcy reorganization. Rather than joining forces with this congressional insider, thus improving the prospects of passage of a compromise measure, Douglas decided to go his own way. But without coalition support for his bill, Douglas could only watch as it was "tossed about" for a year until the SEC decided to abandon it.

This lesson was not lost on Douglas as he turned his attention to the remaining two pieces of legislation. One bill sought to rewrite the federal bankruptcy code in a way that would allow the SEC to ensure that employees, creditors, and all stockholders would have a say in bankruptcy proceedings. Under the new chapter 10 of the bankruptcy code, a judge could ask the SEC to become an active participant in every phase of a bankruptcy reorganization, no matter how large or small. So effectively did Douglas bargain over the provisions of the bill with the National Bankruptcy Conference and members of Congress that it was passed.

The third bill was introduced by Senate Majority Leader Alben Barkley to regulate so-called trust indentures, which specified the terms of a debt arrangement. Formerly, no safeguards existed for the investor except those that the issuers and the underwriters of an indenture were voluntarily willing to incorporate. This bill would protect investors' interests in the issuance of corporate bonds and other securities by guaranteeing that at least one disinterested trustee would be included in the negotiations. After skillfully splitting the bill's ad-

versaries so that they worked at cross-purposes, Douglas helped ensure the bill's enactment. The result was the Trust Indenture Act of
1939.

Lobbying on behalf of the three bankruptcy-reorganization bills,
while also dealing with the administrative rubble left by the collapse
of Richard Whitney's Wall Street firm and directing the upcoming
OTC regulation, would have been enough to keep a small army of ordinary men occupied. But admiring observers in the press could now
sense that Bill Douglas was no ordinary man. "One way or another,"
wrote columnists Joseph Alsop and Robert Kintner in February 1938,
"the SEC pot is always boiling, and usually with toil and trouble."

And now "boiling" in the SEC's pot was the issue of the constitutionality of the Public Utility Holding Company Act of 1935, which
addressed the regulation of giant corporate utilities. As the technology
of supplying electricity developed in the early twentieth century, allowing power to be distributed over hundreds of miles, the size of the
utility companies that supplied it grew accordingly. Local businesses
were slowly linked into large, complex interstate holding companies
that soon exercised a death grip on the industry. As a result of this
pyramidlike corporate structure, the management level was removed
from the actual operating companies dealing with customers, sometimes by thousands of miles. And as the costs for providing utilities
rose, along with the corporations' exorbitant management fees, smaller
local operators were forced to raise their prices substantially.

Having already focused on this issue during his governorship in
New York, FDR proposed a bill in 1935 that required public utilities to
register with the SEC, thus making them subject to strict governmental
regulation. Under section 11 of this bill, the so-called death-sentence
provision, after five years many of the holding companies most distant
from the final product were to be abolished in order to achieve geographic integration of the industry. As Bill Douglas later explained to
Congress in his homespun manner, this meant that "a holding company may have some children, and it may have some grandchildren,
but it may not have great-grandchildren."

No sooner did Roosevelt sign the Public Utility Holding Company
Act into law in August 1935 than corporate counsels began lining up
to challenge its constitutionality. Knowing that it would soon have to
defend the law in court, the SEC decided to create a favorable test case
by compelling one holding company located in the district of a likely
sympathetic federal judge to register under the law. The agency picked
as its target the Electric Bond and Share Company, organized by General Electric in 1905 to hold the securities of small utility companies

around the nation. Since the headquarters of this holding company was located in the Southern District of New York, the case would be heard by reform-oriented Judge Julian Mack, a close friend of leading antimonopolist Justice Louis D. Brandeis.

To no one's surprise, Judge Mack ruled that the companies were required to register with the SEC. In subsequently hailing Mack's ruling as a "great milestone in constitutional law," Chairman Douglas promised that the SEC was not "out looking for scalps." Since nearly 35 percent of the industry was already registered, he explained, the court's opinion "affords a new opportunity in my judgment for the realists in the utilities industry to move up into the driver's seat." This "welcome conciliatory attitude" won the chairman much praise from the New York *Herald Tribune*.

But inside this velvet glove lay an iron fist. Without warning, in early February 1938, Douglas once again went on the attack in a speech at the Commonwealth Club in Chicago: "I am shocked by the farflung cry of 'wolf, wolf' from the mouths of management over the grave dangers of the misnamed 'death sentence.'" It was "the whiphand of New York finance," he said, that was "paralyz[ing] into inaction" those utility companies who should be cooperating with the SEC for their own good and that of their investors. The New York *Herald Tribune* worried whether "a man in the prominent position of Mr. Douglas must feel constrained to make such political speeches."

But these speeches were all part of Douglas's master plan. Once "the least admired of all New Dealers" on Wall Street, Douglas's personal stock by this time had noticeably improved as a result of a series of unpublicized private dinners arranged by reformer Paul Shields with leaders on the Street. Even powerful financier Harrison Williams was heard to say after one such occasion, "Mr. Douglas does not have horns and is indeed a practical administrator." And all of this lobbying paid off as, after several more months of negotiations, the Maloney OTC regulation bill became law in June 1938, leading *The Wall Street Journal* to pay "tribute" to the chairman for his "common sense and moderation" in handling the measure.

When the Supreme Court finally upheld the registration requirement of the Public Utility Holding Company Act by a six-to-one margin, Douglas set out to fully implement this decree. Several large holding companies immediately took steps to register with the SEC, but not all were so cooperative. C. E. Groesbeck, the head of Electric Bond and Share, claimed that because of the need for "diversity of investment" in his industry, the "death sentence" provision should be overturned altogether. Upon hearing this, Douglas quickly fired off a letter to the industrialist disabusing him of any notion that the SEC would back down from the provision.

Before declaring another full-fledged war, though, Douglas proposed a series of roundtable negotiations with utilities executives to discuss compliance with the law. A two-hour conference between industry representatives and the SEC on May 31 resulted in the appointment of a consulting group to study the anticipated impact of the law. While the SEC expressed its "gratification at the progress which had been made toward the establishment of a harmonious relationship between the industry and the commission," the more Douglas thought about it, the angrier he got at the utilities executives' claim that his agency was threatening their "diversity of investment."

Having learned from the battle with Richard Whitney and the old guard that "cooperation" was often enhanced at the end of a legal gun, the chairman decided that the time had come for another test of wills. On July 19, the SEC announced that the powerful Utilities Power and Light Corporation would become the target for the agency's first enforcement of the "death sentence." In early August, Douglas also directed sixty-six holding companies to present their reorganization plans to the SEC by December 1. "I wish to emphasize again that we are not departing from our program for cooperative endeavor," Douglas announced, "but are seeking rather to implement the round-table technique with a concrete proposal to those who want to get on with the job." In short, either comply or face the consequences.

Just as Douglas was about to give an "off-the-record" talk at the Harvard Club on October 10, word reached him that another utility firm, the North American and United Light and Power Company, had agreed to submit a reorganization plan. It's "the best news we've had in a long time," an exultant chairman told the press. A few days later, C. E. Groesbeck announced that Electric Bond and Share as well was conceding defeat and would offer their reorganization plan by the December 1 deadline. Thereafter, in rapid succession, all of the other major utilities fell into line. Bill Douglas had conquered the utilities industry.

None of these activities, however, diverted Douglas's attention for long from his effort to reorganize the New York Stock Exchange in the wake of the Whitney battle. Completing Douglas's victory over the old guard, on April 11, thirty-one-year-old liberal Wall Street reformer William McChesney Martin had been unanimously elected the exchange's new chairman and empowered to serve as the group's spokesperson until a paid president was chosen. Douglas and his team considered the new chairman to be "a straight arrow," and even Wall Street's perpetual critic, John Flynn, agreed that McC. Martin was "a thoroughgoing reformer, who is honest and who . . . knows what it is all about." Upon taking office on May 16, McC. Martin promised to "do everything in our power to provide as safe and as efficient a market for the nation's securities as can be devised," leading Douglas to announce that he was now willing to reappraise all of the government's financial regulations. Six weeks later, McC. Martin was unanimously selected as the new paid president of the New York Stock Exchange. Douglas promised the SEC's "fullest cooperation and our unqualified support in working out the solutions to the items for unfinished business which are before us." For *The New Republic*'s John Flynn this represented "an armistice . . . between the SEC and the New York Stock Exchange . . . as well as a very large-sized victory [for Chairman Douglas]."

While McC. Martin's selection was still under way, in the interest of encouraging this self-regulatory process Douglas initiated another series of roundtable negotiations, but this time between representatives from his agency and the New York Stock Exchange. For the first time in the history of stock exchanges, the government and financial communities would sit down together and negotiate the nature of their relationship. Since the only condition that Douglas had placed on the discussions was that they not take place in the commission's New York office, the group met a block away, at the Metropolitan Club. As the discussions began, their importance was underscored by a personal visit from Douglas.

Douglas had signaled his hope that these talks would launch a new era of cooperation in a speech before the Association of Stock Exchange Firms. Sermonizing on his now familiar theme of democracy and finance, the chairman offered his own spirit of cooperation:

> Some will always look with longing back to the gay days of 1929. But you and we know that as a nation we cannot and should not turn back. You and we know if we work together rather than apart, if we expend our energies on the problem rather than on each other, that we can make this segment of capitalism work. . . . So as the green light flashes, I bid you safe riding down this broad and open highway that lies ahead. I do more than that—I offer you a police escort.

Just how much of a "police escort" the chairman was now willing to offer was not clear even to members of his own staff.

Once the roundtable discussions were under way, Douglas, through his negotiators, began pushing McC. Martin and reformer Paul Shields for more than just the establishment of total broker-dealer segregation. Now he also proposed the creation of a central brokers' bank to accomplish this result. But the notion of a central bank to protect customers from losses in stock transfers by bankrupt firms caught no one else's fancy.

Seeking to spur the reform effort, Bill Douglas decided to release his full report of the Whitney investigation, complete with recommendations for a harsh set of corrective legislation, which included the creation of his proposed bank. Douglas also convinced McC. Martin to add his old friend Robert Maynard Hutchins as a public member to the New York Stock Exchange's reformed governing board in September 1938, to help Douglas keep an eye on Wall Street.

With the release of the Whitney reports, Douglas was able to stir up more reform pressure on Wall Street. In the first of the reports, released on October 27, all of the events leading up to Whitney's demise and the exchange's reaction to them were detailed. Four days later, the next report was released, containing all of the agency's reform recommendations, which had already been worked out after months of negotiations with Wall Street. To ensure the support of the board of governors, the exchange firms agreed to segregate in new companies their stock and bond underwriting business from their brokerage selling business. This agreement led Douglas to crow that the commission and the exchange were "going to town," showing "what a live-wire progressive group of business people can do when they sit down at the good old round table." To encourage that trend, Douglas released on November 30 the last of the Whitney reports, which had been watered down to be much more conciliatory in arguing that the old exchange administration was "lax, archaic, and unbusinesslike," while adding that "happily, a new management has taken control." Douglas believed that he had finally won the war with the New York Stock Exchange.

But sometimes maintaining the peace is harder than winning the war. Everyone now expected government action against the Wall Street officials who had covered up Richard Whitney's unethical conduct. When neither the Justice Department nor the State of New York took any action, Douglas sent copies of the reports to the exchange's board of governors, fully expecting that they would conduct their own investigation and disciplinary procedure. Robert Maynard Hutchins made a motion at the governors' meeting on December 14, 1938, calling for an investigation by the exchange itself. The other governors, however, rejected such a move, arguing that the old rules were vague, especially in a situation such as this, where one Whitney brother was helping another. When Hutchins could not persuade a single governor to back him, he resigned in protest.

Hutchins's withdrawal stunned New York financiers, who now feared that his sponsor, Douglas, would resume his assault on them. And their fear was not without justification, as the chairman began preparing a memo on December 18 that left little doubt where he stood. The SEC, he threatened, might reopen the Whitney hearing to consider the true state of exchange members' knowledge of Richard Whitney's conduct in November 1937 and might propose new laws and regulations "to prevent a repetition of such a white-wash." After finishing this memo, though, Chairman Douglas held his fire, choosing not to release such a hostile statement in the interest of promoting further negotiations with the Street. While such restraint won favor on the Street, it caused the liberal community to raise a skeptical eye.

.   .   .

No New Dealer had achieved more during this sixteen-month period, and by the end of 1938 the rewards were now all Bill Douglas's. He and C. E. Groesbeck were honored for their utilities-industry negotiating efforts in *Fortune* magazine's "Faces of the Month" for December 1938, and then again in its "Faces of 1938" the following month. Douglas's photograph spoke volumes about the effect of such a sustained, around-the-clock reform effort: He peered dully at the camera through puffy eyes, looking as if the weight of the cigarette in his hand could be supported only by resting his elbow on the desk. Month after month of eighteen-hour days without a break, the unrelenting sniping from his opponents, and the work required to supervise so many simultaneous battles for New Deal reform had clearly left him utterly exhausted.

But physical exhaustion was not the only problem faced by Douglas now. His increasingly conciliatory actions toward the stock exchange had begun to erode his support in the liberal media. Long the darling of the financial scribes, now for the first time in his Washington career he had begun to take some serious hits from the reform-oriented press.

More problems began on December 29 when, after failing to discipline anyone in the Whitney affair, the exchange decided to demonstrate its "seriousness" about reform by announcing that J. A. Sisto, a small-time commission broker, had been expelled because he was found "guilty of conduct or proceeding inconsistent with just and equitable principles of trade." While Sisto was a very small fish, and one speared seemingly at random in rancid waters, Douglas took the opportunity to praise the decision effusively: "In my own personal opinion this Sisto case is an excellent illustration of what a bang-up job the Exchange can do in most cases and of the adequacy of the present rules of the Exchange to cover such cases."

Speaking just days before to Arthur Krock, Washington bureau chief of *The New York Times,* Douglas sounded as if his job was now done: "Mr. McC. Martin and I have worked closely together and we are going to continue to do so. For the SEC as for the Exchange the Whitney case is closed. From it we both have learned something." The liberal press disagreed, arguing that the chairman had sold out the public interest. "The latest reform era in the New York Stock Exchange has, like its predecessors, gone up in smoke," warned *The New Republic* at the end of December. To which *The Nation* added two weeks later, "the readiness of Chairman Douglas of the SEC to declare the Whitney case closed . . . warrants inquiry at Washington. Is the SEC so anxious to fraternize with President 'Bill' Martin of the Exchange that it is willing to shut its eyes to fact which disturbs the carefully built-up picture of a 'reformed' Stock Exchange?" By February, *The New Republic* was charging that under Douglas the SEC "came close to whitewashing the New York Stock Exchange for the future" by instituting actions that represented an "ultra-red warning signal." Even *The New York Times* was now saying that Douglas "had lost his liberalism."

Douglas tried to rebuild his reform credentials by launching yet another investigation, this one of the thirty-billion-dollar insurance industry as part of his work on the Temporary National Economic Committee (TNEC), a joint executive-legislative enterprise studying business monopolies. Throughout February 1939, Douglas and his assistant Gerhard Gesell grilled one witness after another in the stately, marble-pillared Senate caucus room. Despite the eventual success of this investigation, though, close observers of Bill Douglas could see that his zest for the job had now changed. No longer was he speaking of pressing future attacks on big business but instead seemed to be reflecting on more philosophical issues. Speaking in New York City's Hotel Commodore on February 9, Douglas sounded much like the anti-monopolistic Louis D. Brandeis in arguing that "the disappearance of free enterprise has led to a submergence of the individual in the impersonal corporation. . . . That has been especially true with the growth of bigness."

To those around him, Bill Douglas seemed like a man preparing to leave office. And the truth was, he was thinking about it. But just where he was headed now, not even he seemed to know.

THE WESTERNER
FROM CONNECTICUT

I had never had any idea of being a judge. It never
entered into any of my calculations. I never even
thought of it as a remote possibility, either being on
that Court or any other court.

— *William O. Douglas*

Bill Douglas had a lot on his mind on Monday, February 13, 1939. With
his term of office ending in June, his political enemies multiplying by
the day, his own sense of exhaustion growing, and his benefactor in
the White House entering what everyone expected to be his last two
years of office, Douglas had decided that the time would soon be right
to leave office.

But where could he go now? More to the point, where could he afford to go? Long-term financial security was now uppermost in his
mind. His living expenses in Washington, together with the loans that
he was still paying off from his law-school years, now far exceeded his
income of about ten thousand dollars a year. The answer to this problem, Douglas had decided, was very simple: Having never formally resigned from his Sterling Chair at Yale Law School, a tenured position
still awaited him in New Haven. And, as luck would have it, the law
school's deanship had just opened up on January 5, when Charles
Clark was appointed to the Court of Appeals for the Second Circuit.
Perhaps the post that Douglas had once used to bluff Joe Kennedy
could now be his for the asking.

After being informally approached about the deanship, Douglas
began telling his Washington inner circle that he was going to take it.
While Douglas had decided on Yale, though, not all of Yale had decided on him. No longer the bastion of revolutionary legal realism
where Douglas had once worked, Yale Law School was now split between the reformers, many of whom had served in the New Deal, and

a group of old-line conservatives. While Douglas was Clark's personal nominee to succeed him, a number of other people—including Dean Acheson and Yale law professor Harry Shulman—also had substantial faculty backing. Beyond this, several members of the university's ultra-conservative governing board had seen enough of this radical's war against Wall Street to begin promising that his nomination would bring "a fight in the [Yale] Corporation." So while the *Yale Daily News* was circulating the rumor that Douglas would become the next law-school dean, the matter was still very much in doubt.

It was in this state of mind—with his bank account nearly empty and his employment options under active consideration—that Bill Douglas decided to go drinking that night at Edmund Pavenstadt's party. A minor functionary in the SEC, Pavenstadt would occasionally open the bar at his house, lay out some soggy, stale sandwiches, and see which members of the New Deal came to visit for one of his fa-mous "bull sessions." It was on just such occasions that Arthur Krock, of *The New York Times,* liked to gather information.

Having heard the rumor that Douglas was leaving for New Haven, Krock wanted to confirm it. When he finally spotted Douglas, the re-porter sidled over and said, "Bill, what is it about this law faculty at Yale that has drawn you back to it despite all your promise of ad-vancement in public life and political affairs?"

"Security," Douglas answered simply.

"Is it more secure than any other position you think would be open to you?" pressed Krock.

"Yes, the only way you could lose your job would be to rape the wife of the President of Yale University. But even then it would proba-bly have to be on the campus at high noon," laughed Douglas.

But, Krock said, you are uniquely qualified for "the vacancy on the Supreme Court."

"What vacancy?" responded Douglas, who explained that he had been working so hard in the office that day that he had neither seen a paper nor heard any news.

"Brandeis retired today," explained Krock. While the news hardly came as a complete shock, since the frail eighty-two-year-old jurist had only recently returned to his duties on the Bench after spending a month in bed with the grippe, Douglas was taken by surprise.

"He did?"

"Yes, and I think it's within your range."

"Well, that hadn't occurred to me, but then I didn't know about the retirement."

That said, Douglas made Krock understand in a circumspect manner that he *could* see himself as the successor to the "People's Attorney" on the Supreme Court.

Would you mind if our conversation was repeated to Attorney General Frank Murphy? the reporter asked. With nothing to lose, and knowing that any appointment to the Supreme Court begins in the Justice Department, Douglas responded that he had no objections at all.

No sooner did Krock return home than he dialed the attorney general's number and made his suggestion. "That's a natural, that's a natural," Murphy kept repeating in his soft, reflective manner, as he listened to the proposal. "I'm going to submit that name to the president," he promised as they rang off.

But it's a long way from the Justice Department to the Oval Office when Supreme Court vacancies are being filled.

One look at the next morning's paper made that point very clear as, other than Solicitor General Robert Jackson, the list of prospective candidates for the position consisted substantially of men living in the western half of the United States. After the recent retirements of the only representatives from that region—Justices Willis Van Devanter of Wyoming and George Sutherland of Utah—western senators had been demanding that the geographical balance of the panel be rectified. And the appointment just four weeks before of Professor Felix Frankfurter from Massachusetts to replace Benjamin Cardozo of New York only increased their concern. Senator Alva B. Adams of Colorado told *The New York Times* that he would personally lead a delegation of western senators to the White House to ensure that their region got some attention this time. The westerners' wish list for filling the Brandeis vacancy consisted of Federal Circuit Court Judge Harold M. Stephens from Nebraska, Judge Sam G. Bratton of New Mexico, Judge William Denman of California, and Dean Wiley Rutledge of the University of Iowa College of Law. But, seeking to guarantee success this time, they had united on a man they believed to be an unimpeachably confirmable candidate—Senator Lewis Schwellenbach from Washington—whose only failing appeared to be that Attorney General Frank Murphy did not like him. In all of the speculation, Connecticut's William O. Douglas appeared nowhere on anybody's list.

Fully understanding his status, Douglas decided to use a long-standing appointment with the president at 4:15 on February 14 to announce his impending departure for New Haven. The work at the SEC was largely done, he told FDR, and in June it would be time to return to private life. "We'll see," the president teased.

While they spoke, Arthur Krock was putting the finishing touches on his private scheme to affect the course of legal history. In a box insert that would appear the next day on the bottom of page one of *The New York Times,* Krock described the president's recovery from his own recent bout with the grippe, outlined his plans for an upcoming Caribbean cruise, and suddenly switched gears to add, regarding the Supreme Court vacancy, "prominent among those mentioned in capital discussion of those on whom the President's choice might fall is William O. Douglas, chairman of the Securities and Exchange Commission." After all, the journalist explained, why else would Douglas have just visited with the president for half an hour? "In view of the prevailing belief that the President desires to name a jurist from the West," Krock continued, "the fact that Mr. Douglas was born and educated in the State of Washington is now having weight in the discussions." While the report was unsubstantiated, Krock was not going to let the truth stand in the way of a good story.

Douglas saw the story and got the message: It was time to drum up western support for his nomination, despite having worked out there only a total of four days since 1922. His brother, Arthur, then working in New York as treasurer and general counsel for the Statler Hotels, volunteered to round up letters from Yakima attorneys and old Beta buddies from Whitman College to verify the candidate's "westernness." Meanwhile, Carrol Shanks organized the bar associations of Chehalis, Everett, Bellingham, and Seattle, Washington, as well as some lawyers from San Francisco, to join the Douglas lobbying effort. In short order, a flood of letters from the west began appearing on the attorney general's desk.

Then, the Douglas brothers hit upon a new scheme. Perhaps the members of the Yakima County Bar Association, despite their difficulty in agreeing on anything that did not involve liquor, might unite on a resolution endorsing their hometown boy for the Court. Evidently, the Douglases had either forgotten about the critical YAKIMA NOT TO BLAME editorial nearly two years before, or perhaps they just dismissed the influence of the paper's publisher. Knowing that they needed a local point man to plead their cause throughout town, they settled on James O. Cull. But try as Cull might, only fifteen of the more than one hundred attorneys in the Yakima County Bar Association agreed to sign the petition, with many others complaining that, at just over forty years old, Douglas was much too young for the High Court.

In any event, stacks of letters from nobodies in the West could not equal the impact of a few whispers in the right places from somebodies in the nation's capital. So Douglas asked for help from his new political acquaintances, Secretary of the Interior Harold Ickes and presidential adviser Tommy Corcoran. By the end of February, Corcoran reported that their entreaties to the White House had created "a good chance" that Douglas would get the appointment.

While the two men pressed Douglas's case, the western senators did the same for Schwellenbach, and the impact of their work was evident. Roosevelt told Ickes at a lunch on March 8 that the senator would likely be his nominee. Here was a true westerner, said FDR, whom he both liked and owed for his political support of the New Deal. If the appointment did not go to Schwellenbach, Ickes concluded from the president's comments, then it would probably go to a different westerner, dean of the University of Iowa College of Law Wiley Rutledge.

As soon as the lunch ended, Ickes paid a visit to Tommy Corcoran, who was in the hospital recovering from emergency surgery. Haven't we misled Douglas into thinking that he has a better chance than he really does? he asked. Absolutely not, responded the perpetually confident aide. Not even a hospital stay could prevent Corcoran from making the case for Douglas in a phone call to Frank Murphy. Once more the will of "Tommy the Cork" prevailed; a day later, when Murphy was informed by the president that he had chosen Schwellenbach for the seat, he responded: "Would you mind waiting awhile, Mr. President? Is there any big rush about this?" Given some more time, the attorney general added, he might have some other suggestions to make. Conceding that he was in no hurry, FDR agreed to put the announcement off until after his upcoming Caribbean cruise.

With a new lease on life, Corcoran continued to perform his lobbying magic. By now, he had developed a distinct modus operandi for placing candidates in the administration. First, he would propose three names for a post: One was the candidate he desired, and the others were ones who could be easily knocked out in some way, thus leaving his candidate as the only viable option. In this case, knowing that FDR was proposing Schwellenbach and Wiley Rutledge, Tommy the Cork designed an opposition strategy for each of them while also proposing Douglas. First, he convinced the president that since Rutledge was just a law-school dean, perhaps it would be best to prepare him for the Supreme Court by appointing him to the Court of Appeals for the District of Columbia, where there also was a vacancy. This the president agreed to do. Then, knowing of Schwellenbach's numerous political disputes with fellow Washington senator Homer Bone, Corcoran simply fanned the flames of growing political discontent in that region, knowing that once word of a partisan uprising reached the

Oval Office, it would negate the "western" advantage of that candidate. In this way, despite Justice Hugo Black's prediction that it was all "sewed up" for Schwellenbach, Corcoran succeeded in knocking him out of the race as well. After one more weekend of lobbying the president, Corcoran proudly reported to Ickes on March 14 that FDR was finally inclined to appoint Douglas.

When Douglas learned about Tommy the Cork's claim of victory, he knew it was not yet time for celebration. Douglas had been in Washington long enough, and seen the president work at close enough range, to know that nothing was ever certain until the announcement was made. Following old job-search habits, Douglas had already notified Yale that he would definitely be returning regardless of whether he was appointed dean or not. He was under consideration for the Supreme Court, he further explained, and would understandably take the job if offered, but he did not expect to get the post.

With his safety net firmly in place, Douglas had been focusing his attention on improving his chances for appointment to the Court. After enduring months of withering attacks by the liberal press, Douglas now feared that FDR might yet suspect his liberal credentials for the Court. Just within the previous week, *The Nation* had questioned whether Douglas should be appointed, saying that while he was "generally considered a liberal, certain reservations have to be made." After reviewing the "disturbing" recent actions by the SEC and recounting the apparently pro–Wall Street nature of some of Douglas's early law-journal articles, the editors questioned just "how hardy Mr. Douglas's liberalism would prove to be in the cold isolation of the Supreme Court."

As luck would have it, Douglas saw a perfect opportunity to renew his liberal credentials. After a year of meetings with the SEC to discuss changes in governmental regulations, the representatives from the nation's seventeen stock exchanges had descended on Washington's Shoreham Hotel for a final summit meeting with Douglas's lieutenants. One of the agency's negotiators, Milton Freeman, later recalled: "All of the fat cats from Wall Street showed up and talked and talked, . . . but all they really were there for was to repeal the insider-trading regulations." Indeed, the exchanges desperately wanted to repeal section 16(b) of the 1934 act, which prohibited insider trading by officers, directors, and principal stockholders of the companies under regulation. To them, the SEC's recent announcement that it would welcome any "reasonably constructive" proposals from their roundtable discussions indicated that success was imminent.

But on the eve of the summit, it became clear that someone in the agency had a much different agenda. Citing their ever-knowledgeable confidential SEC sources, Joseph Alsop and Robert Kintner had reported that an "exquisitely embarrassing incident" was likely to happen if the head of the exchanges' negotiating team, John Hancock of Lehman Brothers, decided to present a relaxed "insider trading" recommendation to the SEC:

> Unhappily, there is every indication that what the exchange representatives will ask is very different from what the SEC is ready to give. "Clarification" of the SEC's restrictions on market manipulation, relaxation of the rules against trading by insiders—these are two of the things the exchanges want. And these are precisely the policies that the SEC regards as the very heart and soul of effective regulation. Repeal or modification, the SEC will probably say, means return to 1929.

To close readers of the financial press, both the forum and the wording of the piece indicated that Chairman William O. Douglas was putting the Wall Street leaders on notice one final time.

The fireworks came on March 15, when Hancock presented to Douglas the policy proposals resulting from the two days of meetings. As soon as he received the recommendations seeking to loosen the insider-trading regulations, Douglas released a statement carrying the unanimous backing of the commission. "Stripped of its legal phraseology," the agency proclaimed, "[the Hancock committee's proposals would] bring the pool operator back into the market. This strikes at the very heart of stock market regulation. The Securities and Exchange Commission is unalterably opposed to any attempt to legalize manipulation in the stock market." Then, mirroring Alsop and Kintner's language, the statement added that these proposals would "redound only to the benefit of the market rigger," destroy "investor confidence," and induce investors into the market "on a 1929 basis."

Never one to leave any doubt with the press as to where he actually stood, Douglas was determined not to leave his post stamped as "the tool of Wall Street." Speaking at a press conference, Douglas shouted that "the [Hancock] report is a phoney. Opening things up so that the boys in the street can have another party isn't going to help recovery." When reporters asked if he could be quoted directly, he replied, "Yes, you spell phoney, p-h-o-n-e-y."

Wall Streeters were livid. "Everybody in the financial district seemed to be willing to talk—and to talk at length, with a wealth of imagery, but nobody wanted to be quoted," reported *The New York*

Times. These proposals were no different from the ones already implicitly agreed to by Douglas, complained William Martin; he requested a meeting with Douglas to clarify certain "misunderstandings." To Wall Street, this represented one final and totally unpredictable left-hand turn by Chairman Douglas, much like his reversal on the negotiations over the New York Stock Exchange reform letter. With the pot now sufficiently stirred, Douglas professed surprise at this reaction, confidently predicting that there would be no serious breakdown in the relationship between the exchange and the commission.

To those laboring to put Douglas on the Supreme Court, however, the timing of this outburst made perfect political sense. With the president now only days away from making the appointment, they realized, this liberal, pro–New Deal regulatory blast could only help Douglas's prospects.

Douglas's allies, too, labored to put his name over the top. Jerome Frank thought he knew just how to do it. For a long time he had been looking for a way to repay Douglas for rescuing his career from oblivion by guiding him to the SEC a couple of years after he was railroaded out of the Agricultural Adjustment Administration. Now Frank appealed to his close friend on the Temporary National Economic Committee, Idaho senator William Borah, who was both the acknowledged leader of the western senators and the ranking minority member on the Judiciary Committee. In a personal meeting, Frank talked to Borah about the poor boy from Yakima who still lit his matches on the soles of his shoes while he burned eastern moneymen alive. Was Borah going to sit by idly while those same fancy bankers got even by denying Douglas a seat on the Court, where he could continue to fight for the common man? Intrigued by the argument, Borah asked how could he be sure about Douglas's western qualities. With that, Frank promised to provide the necessary evidence.

Having discovered that western journalist Bill Hutchinson was also a close friend of the senator, Frank and Tommy Corcoran invited him to meet with the SEC chairman in his office. When the journalist arrived, instead of finding yet another boring bureaucrat or the ogre who had crushed Richard Whitney, he encountered the same good ol' boy that Charles Gay had once met, sitting with his feet up on the desk. As Douglas set out the glasses and liquor bottles, Hutchinson took note of the ten-gallon hat in the office. After just a few hours of consuming vast quantities of scotch and engaging in salty cracker-barrel talk, Hutchinson decided to mobilize his pal Borah for the purpose of putting their "fellow westerner" on the Court. And so he did.

As soon as Douglas's allies got word that the senator was now on board, they arranged a press conference for him, telling the press that the agenda was foreign policy. At the end of the conference, though, someone "unexpectedly" asked a series of very different questions tapping Borah's expertise from the Judiciary Committee.

Did the Senator know William O. Douglas?

Only slightly, responded Borah.

What did he think of Douglas's qualifications for the Court?

He is "eminently qualified," responded the senator.

Then came the question that was the real reason for the press conference.

Did the Senator think that Douglas was "a true westerner"?

Borah's response came without hesitation: Douglas is "our native son"; he represents not only the great state of Washington, but also Oregon, Montana, and Idaho as well. When fellow senator George Norris, of Nebraska, heard this, and agreed to lend his support to the cause, this development was immediately passed on to FDR by Tommy Corcoran.

A short while later, Douglas was working in his office at the SEC with assistant Gerhard Gesell when the phone rang. "I'd like to drink to the newest member of the Supreme Court," said Arthur Krock, patting himself on the back after hearing the early word for what he saw as his successful bit of governmental matchmaking.

When he hung up the phone, Douglas looked at Gesell and said quietly, "I'm going to the Supreme Court."

"Goddamn it, Bill, what are you doing that for?" asked the disappointed assistant, thinking about the battles yet to be fought with Wall Street.

"I need the money," Douglas responded. (The Justices earned twenty thousand dollars annually.)

The news came as no small disappointment to Gesell: "A lot of us felt that he had the potential to become an important political leader in the country . . . a successor to many of the things that Roosevelt stood for. . . . [And] a lot of us felt he was awful young to go on the Court."

But Douglas had other plans, so he waited for the summons from the president.

.   .   .

Bill Douglas's life changed forever when he got home on Sunday, March 19, from his round of golf to find that a message was waiting that the White House had been trying to reach him all day. Could he

come down to see the president right away? he was asked when he returned the call. Would 4:30 be soon enough? Douglas responded. Assured that it was, because on Sundays the president's schedule was
highly flexible, Douglas dressed as fast as he could and headed toward
1600 Pennsylvania Avenue.

Upon his arrival, Douglas was immediately ushered into the president's study, where FDR greeted him warmly. "I have a new job for
you," the president began. "It's a mean job, a dirty job, a thankless
job." Douglas feared what might be coming next, as the president's
comments might indicate a post at the Federal Communications Commission, which was setting new records for ineptness and mismanage-
ment.

Trying to leave himself an escape hatch, Douglas began to protest
that, as the president knew, he was planning to leave the administration. Only if the job was a really "tough" one and if FDR personally
was "drafting" him for the post would he even think now about staying in Washington.

But the president acted as if he didn't hear him. "It's a job you'll
detest. This job is something like being in jail," said FDR, smiling. "Tomorrow I am sending your name to the Senate as Louis Brandeis' successor."

Too dazed and overcome to speak for the moment, despite all his
preparation, Douglas finally composed himself enough to thank Roosevelt. For the next hour the two friends spoke about the problems of
the nation, thinking that it was the last time they would be able to do
so unfettered by the norms of separation of powers.

At noon the following day, the president's press secretary, Stephen
Early, gathered the White House press corps to inform them that FDR
had just sent the name of the next Supreme Court nominee to the Senate. "It's William O. Douglas," he said, adding, with a wry smile for
these insiders who had confidently predicted a "western" selection, "of
Connecticut."

Congratulatory messages flooded in from the press and people all
over the country. "Never before . . . has any man young or old been
named to the highest tribunal who has had so much of America in his
past," gushed Marquis Childs of the *St. Louis Post-Dispatch*. Demonstrating the public-relations success of Douglas's recent anti–Wall
Street outburst, *The New Republic* now hailed him as "an admirable
choice" for the position and a "worthy successor to Brandeis." Even
the Yakima *Morning Herald* now forgave him for his work on the SEC,
praising Douglas as the "Apostle of Financial Honesty," but warning,

too, that he "is one of the most colorful men ever named to the high court." Of all the accolades, though, the one that touched Douglas most was the banner that the members of the Whitman College Beta chapter draped in front of their house reading, "Brother Douglas, We Are Proud."

Still, the unpredictable Senate confirmation process lay ahead. When Senator Carl Hatch of New Mexico gaveled the confirmation hearings to order just five days later, at 2:00 P.M. on March 24, 1939, Attorney General Frank Murphy appeared alongside the nominee in the Judiciary Committee room. While Douglas, his wife, Mildred, and Murphy watched in silence, each senator was polled in turn by Hatch to learn whether they had heard of any witnesses who wanted to testify on this nomination, thus making a hearing necessary. When two of the senators said that they had received only a handful of letters on the matter, and even then no one wished to testify, Hatch ruled that there was no need for a hearing. That done, the nominee was thanked for his appearance and the proceeding was moved to an executive session a mere five minutes after it had begun.

But even after Douglas cleared the Judiciary Committee, a couple of old enemies lay in wait for him on the Senate floor. Senator Burton K. Wheeler of Montana had not forgotten how Douglas had excoriated him in the SEC's protective-committee study for his work on the Cuban Bondholders Protective Committee. Wheeler's assistant, Max Lowenthal, had not forgiven Douglas for once brutally investigating a friend whom he had recommended for a vacancy on the protective committee.

Nowadays, a spark like this can cause a senatorial conflagration; in 1939, though, all it did was get the attention of Senator Lynn J. Frazier of North Dakota. For two days, Frazier held the Senate hostage with a meandering diatribe against Douglas, supplied, the nominee was convinced, by Lowenthal and Wheeler's staff. Citing every recent critical news account of Douglas's March 15 attack on the stock exchange, the senator claimed that he saw evil motives in the policy reversal. Could there be any doubt, he argued, that Douglas was, in fact, just a pandering opportunist trying to bolster his liberal credentials in seeking this appointment? Even if this was true, just why it disqualified anyone for the Supreme Court in the city of unlimited ambition was not clear. Frazier also examined Douglas's early law-review articles and asked whether he would become "the tool of Wall Street" once he was safely on the Court. Only three other senators—Republicans Henry Cabot Lodge, Jr., Clyde Martin Reed, and Gerald P. Nye (who had also been attacked by Douglas over the Cuban Bondholders Protective

Committee)—were bothered enough by these charges to join Frazier in voting against Douglas on April 4, making the final vote sixty-two to four in favor of the nomination.

.   .   .

On April 17, 1939, William Orville Douglas was joined by his wife, Mildred, his brother, Arthur, his sister, Martha, and his two children, Millie and Bill Jr., to be sworn into his seat on the Supreme Court. As the other robed jurists were filing into the Court chamber, his old law dean, Justice Harlan Fiske Stone, welcomed him with a smile to "the chain gang." Too feeble after a yearlong illness to attend the ceremony, Julia Douglas sent her own unique kind of blessing. Tell him, she instructed her daughter, "he's as smart as his father, but not as handsome."

Julia Fisk Douglas raised her eldest son to be president of the United States. Now, it appeared to her, he was well on his way.

PART TWO

MR. JUSTICE DOUGLAS

PART TWO

YOUNG MAN
IN AN OLD MAN'S JOB

It seemed to me that I had barely reached the Court
when people were trying to get me off.

—*William O. Douglas*

For many, the only issue when Bill Douglas came to the Supreme
Court was how long he would be there. Congressman John Elliott
Rankin of Mississippi told the press that Douglas's appointment, on
the heels of his successful SEC work, would "probably mean his nomination for President on the Democratic ticket in 1940." *American*
magazine agreed, reporting that the "Lincolnesque" Douglas was now
being "frequently mentioned in Washington as a future possibility for
the presidency."

Douglas protested to friends that the White House was not his
goal. "I hope this talk of me for President in 1940 or 1944 dies down,"
he wrote A. Howard Meneely, "I have no desire or ambition for it
whatsoever. Among other things, I have been too close to the Boss to
fail to see what a terrific toll it takes." But privately, Douglas's family
knew different. In a Mother's Day card to Julia, he enclosed a press account speculating on his prospects for the vice presidency. "Mumsey
says to thank you for your Mother's Day letter which came early Sunday morning," his sister, Martha, responded. "The part about your
being a candidate for Vice-President was very exciting, but Gaga says,
she always knew you would be PRESIDENT some day."

Meanwhile, Douglas tried to settle into the Supreme Court's recently built "Marble Palace." He moved into the office previously assigned to Louis Brandeis, a fact that Douglas underscored by putting
on the wall the same etching of "The People's Attorney" that had hung
in his SEC office. But he was not happy there. Within days he began
complaining that his phone had just stopped ringing, and he was feel-

ing isolated. "I'm too young to go on the Court," he complained to his former SEC assistant Gerhard Gesell.

Others weren't sure he belonged on the Court either. As the youngest of the Justices by more than a dozen years, Douglas looked entirely out of place. "Who's the young one?" confused tourists would ask the Court marshals. With his perpetual cowlick, unkempt manner of dress, love of smoking and heavy drinking, lack of respect for tradition, and manner of speech laced with, in the words of one journalist, "a man's vocabulary found in no dictionary," Justice Bill Douglas seemed more like a westerner than a member of Washington's high society. "He looks and acts a hell of a lot more like my fireman than a Supreme Court judge," said an engineer on the Pacific Limited train in La Grande, Oregon. "Why, I saw him strike a match for his cigarette on the seat of his trousers at lunch in the Hay-Adams House," complained one well-connected socialite.

Knowing that his first job was to pick a clerk to help him with his duties, Douglas brought along for his first partial term an assistant from the SEC, C. David Ginsburg. Thereafter, since nearly all of the other jurists picked their clerks from among the graduates of three eastern law schools—Harvard, Yale, and Columbia—Douglas decided that his clerks would come from far-western law schools, with the first three coming from the University of Washington.

The job was demanding indeed. As Ginsburg recalled: "When [Douglas] was in the office and in the room, he worked. . . . He got at it. And did it. He put pencil to paper. And he started writing right away, just as soon as he had finished [reading] the record of the case. Or he called me and said, 'I want a memo on this subject.' He didn't tell you enough to [figure it out]. You would have to guess at it. . . . And he had his yellow tablets and sent it [*sic*] to [his secretary] Edith [Waters] to get it typed. I always had the feeling of 'get it done.' . . . Any undone job was just hovering at him. He had to get it finished." And Douglas's tasks for his assistants were very specific. "He didn't really discuss very many things with me," recalled his first full-term clerk, Stanley Soderland. "What I was doing was organizing things for him. I would get notes from him, [he would say] 'Find me a case on such and such,' and I would get over to the library and look. He wrote his own opinions in longhand. . . . My job was to read it over and make a suggestion here or there, [and] make sure all [the] citations were right, . . . and that is just mechanical."

Douglas's formal introduction to his new job came on Saturday, April 22, 1939, at his first judicial conference, a meeting in which the full Court meets in private to discuss cases heard in oral argument that week and to decide which cases to hear in the future. By tradition, as the most junior Justice, Douglas took over from Felix Frankfurter the duty of being the "doorkeeper" to the conference room, relaying messages to and from a page outside the door.

Arrayed around the huge rectangular mahogany conference table was a Court clearly in transition. Four of them had battled FDR over New Deal legislation: James C. McReynolds, 77, appointed by Woodrow Wilson; Pierce Butler, 73, appointed by Warren G. Harding; Harlan Fiske Stone, 66, appointed by Calvin Coolidge; and Owen Roberts, 63, appointed by Herbert Hoover. Joining them were four FDR appointees: former Alabama senator Hugo Black, 53, former solicitor general Stanley Reed, 54; the peripatetic Harvard law professor Felix Frankfurter, 56; and Douglas, 40. Presiding over all of them was the austere, full-bearded, 77-year-old disciplinary taskmaster, Chief Justice Charles Evans Hughes. Having resigned from the Court to accept a draft presidential nomination to oppose Woodrow Wilson in 1916, he had been reappointed to the Court as its chief in 1930 by Herbert Hoover. Among those members, Frankfurter was the one Douglas knew and liked the best, saying of him: "I had thought of him as a great progressive liberal professor and student and advocate. I had held him in very high esteem."

Only a handful of cases remained to be decided in the 1938–1939 term. Two of those cases, *Coleman v. Miller* and *Chandler v. Wise*, examined the legality of the ratification procedure used in Kansas and Kentucky for a proposed anti-child-labor amendment to the U.S. Constitution. As the chief, Charles Evans Hughes's duty was to summarize the facts of the cases argued before them that week, explain his analysis of the possible judgment, and turn the discussion over to each of his colleagues in descending order of seniority for their analyses. Then, to preserve the independence of the most junior Justices, the voting on the case would proceed in reverse order back up to the chief. Douglas found Hughes to be much too political in directing the Brethren, seeming to leave no doubt as to how he thought they should vote. When the Justices split four to four on the issue of whether the Coleman litigants had proper legal standing to bring the suit to Court, Hughes assigned the opinion to himself, saying that he would find a compromise position. Douglas suspected that he knew what that meant, telling Felix Frankfurter that they would all be forced to follow Hughes's lead in holding that the Court had no power, with Congress being silent, to set the time limit for an amendment's ratification.

When the conference ended, there was still the matter of assigning the newest Justice his "maiden opinion." Traditionally, a new Justice is given his or her choice of a relatively minor case in which there is a unanimous decision. Of the three such cases that had been argued that week—*United States v. Morgan,* which dealt with a matter of administrative law, *Newark Fire Ins. Co. v. State Board of Tax Appeals,* which dealt with New Jersey state tax procedures on companies whose executive offices are in New York, and *United States v. Powers,* which dealt with interstate commerce regulations on petroleum products—the first two excited Douglas most, seeming to best fit his regulatory experience. Hughes, however, saw it differently: "I think that the best thing for you to do is to take a little case you may think is a nondescript case." So Douglas was told to "cut his teeth" on the *Powers* case. "In effect, I did not have a choice," he said, years later.

Douglas labored on his draft. After all his years working on the commuter train to New York City, he found that in drafting his opinions he liked to dash off his thoughts longhand by using pencil or a green-ink pen on a yellow lined pad balanced on his knees. So, like Oliver Wendell Holmes, who wrote while standing at his writing desk and would close when he got tired, Douglas many times seemed to write short opinions. For a man of Douglas's genius, who saw the entire case with all of its companion issues as one total whole, these opinions could frequently be dashed down in one burst of creative energy. Then thinking them perfect, he very often saw little reason to revise them significantly. In time, Douglas developed the reputation of being "the quickest opinion writer since Holmes."

With his lack of regard for legal jargon in his work, Douglas soon came to see a different audience for his decisions. Rather than writing for the legal community using complicated Latin terms and judicial doctrines, he wrote in plain English for the general public. It was almost as if, rather than writing a judicial opinion, he were drafting a sermon on an issue, much like his father once did, and preparing it for delivery from his high pulpit on decision day.

Douglas's draft opinion in the *Powers* case immediately won the assent of all but one of his colleagues. Deciding to teach his new colleague the importance of seniority, James McReynolds objected to Douglas's use of the word *dictum,* a term covering language that was not part of the actual holding of a case and thus did not have the force of law, to describe a decision by the great Chief Justice John Marshall. Using this term, McReynolds lectured, would "downgrade" Marshall. It made little difference to the senior jurist that the work was in fact dictum, since the point of having Douglas change his description to "statement" was to teach him the value of respecting his elders. Whereupon, McReynolds quickly signed on. Having acceded this first time, Douglas immediately resolved to ignore all of McReynolds's views for the remainder of his tenure on the Court.

But the old curmudgeon made one additional impression on Douglas when he informed the rest of his colleagues that since he had already made plans to leave town on May 27, the rest of the Court could finish the term without him. The lesson was not lost on young Justice Douglas, who still lamented the loss of the three-month break in the academic year that he had given up by joining the SEC. After several summers of being chained to Washington, he made plans at the term's end to spend the summer in the Pacific Northwest, which became an annual tradition.

One of the first cases in which Douglas participated in during the final weeks of the term was *O'Malley v. Woodrough,* dealing with whether the exemption from federal income tax for federal judges should be continued. Since the Constitution bars a reduction in the salaries of Supreme Court Justices, an earlier court had upheld the exemption, arguing that any increase in their tax burden would constitute a violation of this provision. In the April 29 conference, Douglas, who had discovered that his heroes, Brandeis and Holmes, had voted against the exemption, now cast his vote to make the Justices' salaries taxable. Years later, he told journalist Eric Sevareid in an interview, "As I made the little entry into the docket sheet I said to myself, 'Young man, you've just voted yourself first-class citizenship.' I decided that, if we were going to pay taxes like everybody else, that you should be a citizen like everybody else, except that unless the thing that you are doing interferes with the work on the Court." And from that day forward, he did not hesitate to exercise his First Amendment rights as a citizen.

In the term's final conference on June 3, Douglas began to learn about the nature of his future alliances. With the Court now depleted by the loss of the Chief Justice, who was bothered by the flu and an ulcer, and the vacationing McReynolds, Pierce Butler was left in charge. When the Brethren discussed *American Toll Bridge Co. v. Railroad Commission,* which dealt with the power of a California railroad commission to reduce the tolls charged on bridges, Butler argued for the majority that the state had properly observed "due process." Douglas, however, was inclined to write a concurring opinion arguing that it was still the Court's duty to examine in "businesses affected with a public interest," such as bridges, the "fairness" of the action as well as the procedure itself. In so writing, Douglas anticipated being able to pick up the votes of his fellow New Deal appointees Hugo Black and Felix Frankfurter. However, after some early promising negotiations, Frankfurter inexplicably reversed field and argued that the three of them should just concur without writing an opinion. Only after Douglas agreed with the suggestion did he discover that Frankfurter's change of heart had been spurred by a request by the ailing Chief Justice to reduce the number of separate opinions from the increasingly divided Court. Within six weeks of coming to the Bench, Douglas decided that Felix Frankfurter's role as a covert operative for the Chief Justice now made him worthy of great suspicion.

With the term finished, Douglas piled his family into their car and drove to the Pacific Northwest for their three-month vacation. For the family that saw him only rarely, the annual trips west became the highlight of their year. "My earliest memories, I think of the family as a unit, was traveling," William Douglas, Jr., said later. "[Dad] loved to drive. He was a good driver. Drove his cars as if they were race cars. . . . We would go along the highways lickedysplit." As his family drove west for the cross-country trip the day after Court recessed, Douglas "had never seen [his] father so happy. He was out of the building, he was on his own, traveling through space." Eventually for Douglas, nothing— *nothing*—stood in the way of his mentally refreshing summer break from the "dreariness" of Court life from October to June.

                    .   .   .

As he thought about his first two months on the job, Douglas wondered if he had made the right career move. "I found the Court . . . a very unhappy existence," Douglas later explained. "I had been very, very active in the Executive Branch. I was now doing things that . . . [were] like having a professorship without any classes to teach. It was a research job in fields that were very remote from any past experience or knowledge." C. David Ginsburg understood the reason for his boss's dislike of the job: "He was not fulfilled by the Court. . . . He didn't have trouble understanding the records that came before the Court. These are things with which he was familiar, and he could move through them fast. . . . It wasn't a question with him of speed-reading, it was simply quick comprehension." It was not long before Douglas's friends could see the difficulty he was having in making the adjustment to what he now called "the monastery." Arthur Krock of *The New York Times* observed: "Having been so suddenly lifted from the bullring to the stratosphere of public service, the smell of blood and sand . . . [was] still strong in his nostrils."

Knowing this, the same group that had helped to get him the Court appointment now sought to arrange his next move up the Washington ladder. By this time, the pro-Douglas group was an eclectic alliance of old-line New Deal liberals seeking to maintain that philosophical direction for the Democratic party, bureaucrats seeking to remain in government, deposed officials seeking to return to power, junior officials seeking to shortcut their rise through the ranks, and an assortment of journalists ready to add to the growing Douglas publicity bank. This constant, quiet campaign by such men as Secretary of the Interior Harold Ickes, New Deal bureaucrats James H. Rowe, Jr., Benjamin V. Cohen, and Abe Fortas, Congressman Lyndon Baines Johnson, former student and now attorney Ernest Cuneo, and journalists Robert Kintner, Richard Neuberger, and Eliot Janeway allowed Douglas to play the part of the reluctant political candidate, forever denying that he had any interest in higher office.

But always at their head was one man: Tommy Corcoran. Once the most powerful man in the New Deal as half of a legendary legislative drafting team with Benjamin V. Cohen, Corcoran had been denied the only position he wanted in the government—solicitor general—because of the betrayal of his former mentor, Felix Frankfurter. When he was finally forced from the government by his tendency, in his own words, to "break a few eggs in order to make an omelet," Corcoran saw Bill Douglas as his ticket back into power. Douglas considered no career moves in politics without seeking Corcoran's advice, and the redheaded power broker was happy to give it.

With everyone's political future now controlled by FDR's decision as to when to leave the White House, the Supreme Court served as a sort of bullpen for frustrated presidential hopefuls. Trying to boost Douglas's prospects, Harold Ickes suggested that the westerner be invited to the president's regular poker party. On these occasions, all talk of work and politics was banned as the most powerful men in the country tried to bluff their colleagues out of two dollars per hand. Douglas sat at the table with Secretary of the Treasury Henry Morgenthau, Solicitor General Robert Jackson, Press Secretary Stephen Early, and presidential intimate Colonel Edwin M. "Pa" Watson. In honor of the new guest, the president used his "dealer's choice" rights for the evening's final hand to play a game called "Mr. Justice McReynolds," in which there were too many wild cards to make sense of one's own hand.

"Bill was a terrible poker player," his friend Clark Clifford recalled. But blessed with what FDR called "his fund of good dirty stories," his quirky sense of humor, and his ability to drink with the best of them, Douglas quickly became a favorite at FDR's own table.

Such closeness to the president never went unnoticed. In October 1939, the New York *Herald Tribune* cited "a report which [was gaining]

credence" that FDR was about to designat[e] Douglas as his preferred
successor. With Douglas also rumored to be called "the Crown Prince"
by FDR himself, close observers of the White House came to believe
the veracity of this view. Who better to follow up the revolutionary
New Deal president than the courageous man who had cleaned up
Wall Street? So seriously was this report being taken that even Douglas's judicial campaign manager, Arthur Krock, was moved to complain in his column: "This will damage him and hamper the Supreme
Court." Later he added: "Justice Douglas's boomlet appears and reap-
pears without his consent. . . . It would seem therefore he should hang
a brick around the neck of this black cat and drown it as soon and as
deep as he can." But the truth was that Douglas liked swimming in
these waters very much. So, rather than put an end to the rumors by
making an unequivocal statement disavowing his presidential ambitions, he remained silent, thus fueling them further.

                    .   .   .

With the opening of the new term in the fall of 1939, Bill Douglas decided it was time to become a full-fledged member of the club. For
him, this meant finding his place amid the newly developing alliances
on the Court. Unlike the SEC, where initial agreements were done on
a more personal and political basis, Douglas found that on the Court
"blocs" or "wings" tended to align on philosophical grounds. He felt
his best prospect for an ally was the man he knew the least: Hugo
Black. The two men seemed to have more in common than they at first
realized. Both came from political backgrounds, both were libertarian
populists by nature, and both had been dyed-in-the-wool New Dealers.

    Douglas assumed that just as on the SEC, where allies frequently
threw votes to each other in anticipation of future favors, the same
would be true on the Court. So he developed a strategy to win Black's
favor in the *Board of Commissioners of the County of Jackson, Kansas v.
United States* case, which was argued before the Court on October 16,
1939. Here an Indian tribe was seeking a refund of county taxes, arguing that lands held in trust under federal treaties were not subject to
taxation. When Felix Frankfurter was assigned the opinion, he circulated a Solomonic draft that would return the tax payments to the
petitioner while exempting the county from paying interest on the
money. Douglas gave every indication that he would sign the opinion,
writing on his copy of the draft, "I agree. This is very deftly done."
When Black decided to write his own concurrence, arguing that Congress had *intended* to exempt communities from having to pay interest

in such situations, a point which changed nothing in Frankfurter's decision, Douglas had a sudden change of heart. The same day that the opinion was to be announced, he told Frankfurter as they were changing into their judicial robes, "I think you were right on this, but I concurred with Hugo." When asked why he had switched his vote, Douglas said simply that he "didn't want Hugo to be alone." Frankfurter, who viewed himself as the leader of the New Dealers on the Court, "was just furious," according to his law clerk at the time, Edward F. Prichard, Jr., that Douglas would vote for political rather than philosophical reasons. A still embittered Frankfurter wrote two years later that "Douglas *never* thereafter referred to this case, nor to his shift, nor to his reasons for going 'with Hugo.' " As a result of this dispute, Prichard later recalled, "Frankfurter never had any more use for Douglas."

The Court began to change when conservative Pierce Butler died on November 16, 1939. By this time, FDR had come to rely so much on Robert Jackson that he wanted to put him in the Cabinet. To accommodate that, the president decided that the highly political attorney general, Frank Murphy, would be put on the Court. When the double appointment was made on January 4, 1940, Roosevelt had appointed more than half of the Justices, creating a group that would eventually average a full sixteen years younger than the group that had earlier plagued him. And when the judicially inexperienced Murphy immediately joined with the New Deal liberals, a powerful bloc of Justices on the left cohered.

This change was evident in one of the major civil-liberties cases in that 1939–1940 term, *Minersville School Dist. v. Gobitis,* which concerned the rights of Jehovah's Witnesses. The State of West Virginia had compelled all schoolchildren to salute the flag, despite Walter Gobitis's contention that such a law forced his children, Lillian and William, to worship a "false icon," contrary to the family's religious beliefs. When the issue came to conference, Hughes told his colleagues that he "approached that problem like a skittish horse approaches a band." To him, this was just like the secular regulation against polygamy that had been upheld in the face of the Mormon religious adherence to the practice in 1878. When no one else saw any freedom of religion problems with upholding the state law here, it was left to the Chief Justice to assign the case.

Desperate to assert his leadership, Felix Frankfurter concocted a plan for landing the task. "Knowing of my close relationship to Hughes, [Frankfurter] called me into his office and asked if I would go to Hughes and have Hughes assign the flag-salute case to him to write," recalled Douglas. Now hypersensitive to being manipulated by Frankfurter, Douglas "told him that [he] couldn't be any such errand boy and [he] wouldn't do it." He added, "Frankfurter, I think, was very upset."

Nevertheless, Hughes assigned the opinion to Frankfurter. For the Court's only Jewish member—an Austrian immigrant who had landed on Ellis Island as a boy, unable to speak a word of English, and who just eleven years later graduated from Harvard Law School at the head of his class—the chance to express his love for America in this opinion was a dream come true. In exalting patriotism even over the rights of religious minorities, while also exercising the judicial self-restraint of his mentors Oliver Wendell Holmes and Louis D. Brandeis, Frankfurter ruled in favor of the state's flag-salute law. When the opinion was circulated among the rest of the Court, all but Harlan Fiske Stone quickly signed on. Douglas personally praised the draft as "historic" and "truly statesmanlike." Stone, however, circulated a solo dissent capturing all that was wrong with the majority's view: "The Constitution expresses more than the conviction of the people that democratic processes must be preserved at all costs. It is also an expression of faith and a command that freedom of mind and spirit must be preserved, which government must obey, if it is to adhere to that justice and moderation without which no free government can exist." Immediately after the opinion was announced, an avalanche of journalistic and scholarly support for Stone's dissent descended on the Court, including complaints from Eleanor Roosevelt that it was not in the interest of American democracy to force little children to salute the flag.

After discussing this reaction, Bill Douglas, Frank Murphy, and Hugo Black decided that they had "made a mistake" in following Frankfurter's "leadership." "We were concerned about our joining the Frankfurter opinion," recalled Douglas. "We thought we had been taken in and we mentioned this several times.... We wished we hadn't ... gone along. We wished we had had a reargument." So the three of them began to plot to arrange for one.

·   ·   ·

By now, though, it was clear to Douglas that he cared much more about politics than about his work on the Court. But not all of his allies supported this view. In late June 1940, when the president's final decision to run for a third term was accompanied by calls to balance the ticket with a westerner, even Tommy Corcoran expressed doubts to FDR as to whether Douglas had the campaign skills at this stage in his career to switch from the Court. Nevertheless, a month later, with Democrats considering removing FDR's running mate, John Nance Garner, a "Douglas for vice president" boomlet began to swell, with presidential adviser Harry Hopkins acknowledging that Secretary of State Cordell Hull, Secretary of Agriculture Henry Wallace, and Douglas were the leading contenders. When FDR announced to his staff that his choice was coming down to either Wallace or Douglas, Democratic party leader Jim Farley, himself interested in the Oval Office if Roosevelt had decided not to run again, argued that Douglas's selection would be "asinine" because he lacked the necessary public visibility to be nominated.

Douglas had been continuing to take pains to deny to others any political ambition on his part. "In spite of my persistent and emphatic objection, at least a few of my intimate friends have from time to time expressed the thought that if the President decides not to run again this year, I must (or can) be the Democratic candidate. . . . But I do desire to have an end of all those rumors," he wrote to his friend A. Howard Meneely in early 1940. He added, "In the first place, I have no political ambitions. My sole desire is to give a life time of service here in an endeavor to fill the shoes of my illustrious predecessor." But C. David Ginsburg thought otherwise: "I'm convinced that he wanted to be president. Whether he wanted to do good for the country or whether he wanted to achieve the highest rung, I'm inclined to think it's probably the latter."

But the Justice's promoters had not given up yet. With Douglas out of touch on a pack trip in Oregon's Wallowa Mountains during the nominating convention of 1940, Tommy Corcoran looked for someone who would put his name forward. Thinking that Hugo Black might help, Corcoran approached him only to discover that the Justice had already offered to leave the Court to work on Roosevelt's campaign, in the hopes of receiving the vice-presidential post himself. With no political support, Douglas's name was dead, and in time Henry Wallace was tapped.

The passing of this opportunity was of little consequence, however, to the not quite forty-two-year-old Justice, who had so much time left on his political clock. "It will be an interesting campaign to watch from the sidelines," he later wrote A. Howard Meneely. "I am delighted that I was passed by. I feared for a period of two weeks that pressure might be put on me to go on the ticket. So far as I personally am concerned the result was most gratifying." Far from disappointed, when he returned in the fall Douglas bragged to Harold Ickes that he had "spent the whole summer having a glorious vacation fishing and camping, etc." and "hadn't done more than one week's work." The Supreme Court, the young man added forcefully, "is an old man's job."

But unknown to his friend in the Cabinet, Douglas had not given up on his chances for the White House just yet. Just one day after FDR's renomination, Douglas had become concerned about the purchase by a Pittsburgh newspaper of a bizarre set of campaign documents known as the "Guru" letters. In the letters, between Henry Wallace and a Russian mystic named Nicholas Roerich, the vice-presidential hopeful had seemed to endanger the ticket's electoral chances by his descriptions of his political colleagues. While the information had been kept out of the race for a while as part of a trade by which the Democrats did not reveal that the Republican candidate, Wendell Willkie, had a mistress, now it was in the hands of the press.

Knowing that if Wallace was removed from the ticket his name might resurface, Douglas now surreptitiously took a leading role in trying to unseat him. In a discussion with *Time* journalist Eliot Janeway, who had helped pursue the story, Douglas suggested, "Let's do it through Harold [Ickes]." At lunches over the next several weeks, Douglas traded political gossip with the secretary of the interior, trying to convince Ickes that he should tell the president that Wallace should resign. When Ickes wondered whether the letters were authentic, Douglas insisted, "If the President sees them, he will be so angry that he will be willing to force a resignation from Wallace."

Normally a man who loved to inject himself everywhere, Ickes seemed ready to let the matter drop. So Douglas arranged a dinner at journalist Robert Kintner's house, so that Ickes could meet with someone who was familiar with the letters. Later, Douglas instructed Janeway to bring copies of the letters to Ickes's office, where Robert Jackson, Tommy Corcoran, and Ben Cohen brought Henry Wallace to defend himself.

Wallace was nonetheless retained on the ticket. Ickes had seen, however, Douglas's continued interest in politics, so he began lobbying the president to find him another job off the Court in the hopes of building him up as a possible successor in 1944.

.   .   .

Meanwhile, politics on the Court continued. Justice James C. McReynolds retired in January 1941, and then five months later Chief Justice Hughes called the Brethren together to announce that he, too, would be resigning from his position.

With the main question now being who would replace Hughes, Douglas began to lobby for the elevation of Hugo Black. Believing that

Harlan Fiske Stone had fed a negative story about Black to journalist Marquis Childs, thus posing a danger to Court relations, Douglas's biggest fear was that Stone would get the appointment. This, however, was the fondest hope of others. Hughes himself "strongly recommended" Stone to the president, suggesting also that FDR consult Felix Frankfurter about the issue. Frankfurter also recommended Stone to the president at a White House lunch. That done, the egotistical Justice from Harvard told Stone the next day, "Be prepared to be C.J."

While the president told Harold Ickes that Attorney General Robert Jackson would be perfect for the Chief Justiceship, he was persuaded by the argument that, with war seemingly on the horizon, he should appear nonpartisan and appoint a Republican. He told Jackson that while Stone would get the Chief Justiceship, Jackson would fill the Court vacancy created by the elevation. But then FDR held out an olive branch to the man who had served him so well, telling Jackson that when Stone retired, which the president expected to be in a couple of years, the seat would be his. When Jackson informed Stone of the arrangement, Stone confirmed that he would not remain on the Court much longer, and the deal was done. On June 12, 1941, the same day that Harlan Fiske Stone was elevated, with Robert Jackson filling his old seat, presidential ally Senator James F. Byrnes of South Carolina was appointed to replace McReynolds. Seeking to solidify his relations with Hugo Black, Douglas wrote him that with Stone as chief, "it will not be a particularly happy or congenial atmosphere in which to work—at least so far as I am concerned."

The Stone appointment renewed Douglas's willingness to consider leaving the Court for a new career in politics. With the darkening war clouds in Europe, he became interested in the defense-mobilization effort, in which the same fat cats whom he had battled on Wall Street were positioning themselves to make a financial killing. These men, Douglas was convinced, cared little for the boys on the battlefield and much more for how to make an immediate profit. "They have their straws in the punch bowl sucking away," he wrote a friend. What was needed, Douglas believed, was another regulatory campaign, just like he had headed on the SEC, that would bring all of these interests to heel. After unsuccessfully trying to interest Harold Ickes in this matter, Douglas decided to personally contact the president. But with America not yet at war, the issue was dropped.

By the middle of 1941, even Douglas's judicial colleagues could sense his restlessness. "Bill does not have a passion for the court," Felix Frankfurter told Harold Ickes, "and [he] has not fallen in with the notion that he is wedded to his present job for life." To Frankfurter, whose sole ambition in life had been to serve on this august body, and whose foreign birth rendered him constitutionally ineligible for the White House, this was inexcusable. But Ickes, who by now had become Bill Douglas's personal placement director for government positions, was working hard to grant his wish for a new challenge. As soon as he heard from Douglas's protégé Abe Fortas that the Justice might be willing to head up a new defense-mobilization agency that the president was thinking of forming, he sprung into action. In a matter of days, he and financier Bernard Baruch had launched the "Douglas for Defense Head" effort, arguing in a letter to the president that the Justice was the only one innovative enough, strong enough, and liberal enough to carry out the difficult tasks. Meanwhile, Douglas himself made plans to speak with Harry Hopkins about his ideas for defense reorganization.

As was true whenever he contemplated leaving the Court for politics, Douglas felt the need to deny any such interest to his fraternity brother A. Howard Meneely: "The talk about me leaving the Court to head the Defense Commission is all talk. There is nothing in it—at least so far as I know. I would not want to do it. It is the furthest thing from my thought." But, the Justice revealed, during a courtesy call that he had paid on the president before the end of the Court term, FDR had said, "Bill, I was talking to the Director of the Budget this morning. The topic of economic warfare came up. I said to him—'Let's get Bill Douglas for that.'" Then the president roared.

To which Douglas responded: "Mr. President, you have overlooked one thing."

He said, "What's that?"

Douglas answered: "Economic warfare—why that's the job the Court is doing." And with that the two men laughed, and the matter was dropped.

"Actually," he claimed to Meneely, "I think he was casting a fly on the pool to see if there were any trout in it. I don't think he found any." The truth, though, was that this trout was being more selective about the type of fly he was seeking.

With the end of another term, Douglas again piled his family into their inexpensive sedan for the drive to the Pacific Northwest for his summer break. En route, he gave a speech in Nashville for the Tennessee Bar Association to pay for the trip and stopped in Chicago to visit with his sister, who had moved there to take a new job, and his mother, whose health had been declining. Once in the Wallowa Mountains, he put on his favorite faded gray Stetson, old blue jeans, and beat-up work shirt. These three months free from the pressures of Washington were all that made life tolerable for him. When the mail sacks filled with appeals petitions arrived from the Court in the Lostine, Oregon, post office, it was not uncommon for Douglas to immediately take them into the woods, turn a wooden crate on its side for a desk, and sit on a stump under a fir tree to do his work. Other than that, he spent his days fishing for huge trout in the roaring Lostine River, hiking and riding horseback deep into the mountains, attending the rodeo at Pendleton, and sitting around the cracker barrel in Crow's Mercantile Store to chew the fat with the locals. Nothing interrupted his solitude—not even when word arrived in early July 1941 that his mother had suffered a fatal heart attack. Rather than traveling to Chicago to console his sister and accompany his mother's coffin to Yakima, Douglas simply waited for her body to be shipped west for burial.

But there was one exception to this rule in those first years on the Court. On a hot summer day in late July, a man ran up to Douglas while he was shopping in the tiny Pendleton grocery store and breathlessly whispered that the president of the United States was on the phone for him. By the time the Justice arrived to pick up the antique hand-cranked phone receiver, a crowd of gawking townspeople had surrounded him, making it impossible to say anything in response to FDR other than a simple yes or no. The president told him that everyone seemed to think that Bill Douglas was the only man who knew how to run the defense effort. "Yes," Douglas said noncommittally. The nation needed him in a "more active" job, the president continued. "Yes" came the response. Would he be willing to come to Washington as soon as possible, resign from the Court, and head up the new defense effort? Douglas responded that he could come to Washington on August 4. Agreeing that the president would be back in touch, the two men hung up. "I didn't say yes or no but asked for more time to think it over," Douglas later wrote a friend.

But as soon as he hung up the phone, Douglas seemed to return to the indecisiveness of his early career as he began to have second thoughts. He fired off a letter explaining his dilemma to Hugo Black, a man known for his sense of judicial propriety. This offer had come to him without any personal encouragement, said Douglas. Would Black see him after the White House meeting on August 4? Repeatedly, Douglas insisted that he was reluctant "even to consider the prospect of leaving." Only if the nation was in chaos would he feel the need to leave the Court to help, Douglas insisted.

Douglas bought his railway tickets and waited in the mountains for the second phone call from the president, summoning him for the meeting. But week after week passed, and it did not come.

By the first week of September, Bernard Baruch decided to speak with the president about the need to appoint a defense czar. To his way of thinking, only Douglas or Undersecretary of War Robert Patterson could handle the job. As he frequently did when he received advice that confirmed his inclinations, FDR finally called Douglas, saying that while the decision had been deferred until the Justice returned to Washington, he was still planning to put him in as his "alter ego" on defense at that time. This new call was nothing less than a presidential draft, Douglas explained to Hugo Black in a letter, adding that to him there was "nothing less attractive—except practicing law in New York City." But despite these reservations, Douglas added that, with war on the horizon, "there comes a time when all bets are off & every man has to shoulder a musket or do some chore for his country."

While Douglas believed that Felix Frankfurter had inspired this potential offer to remove him from the Court, nothing could have been further from the truth. At that very moment Frankfurter and Harry Hopkins were laboring feverishly to *stop* Douglas's appointment as the defense czar. Following the old political axiom "You can't replace somebody with nobody," they frantically scoured the political horizon for anyone who might be an acceptable alternative to Douglas.

By the time of his departure for Washington on September 12, Douglas's "macaroni spine" seemed to have returned as he appeared to be having sincere doubts about his future course of action. "God, how I hate to return. I hate to do so because immediately on my return I will be faced with a momentous decision," he wrote A. Howard Meneely. Should he leave, or should he stay? Could he afford not to leave if he wanted to have any hope for higher office? And if he left, when the job was done what would he do to feed his family? Beset with these old doubts, Douglas poured out his soul to the man who had held his hand through all of those earlier career crises. "That job has absolutely no attraction for me," he wrote his old college friend. "I am content and want to remain just where I am. But the President is a hard man to turn down. And there is a job in the defense program for someone to do. I dislike even to think of running into these aegea [*sic*] stables. I would rather join the army." Douglas, though, was trying to steel himself for the response he had settled upon. "I am going to try to get out of it. I am not sure I can. That job is nothing but a heartache & a headache—at least as it has been run. And too much water has run over the dam for one to start all over. So I return to Wash. D.C.

with no enthusiasm or joy. There are a lot of ambitious boys who would jump at the chance. And there are quite a few who could do it well. But as for me—I have no ambition or capacity for that task. I hope I can convince the President."

Despite these denials, as soon as he arrived in the capital Douglas telephoned Missy LeHand, the president's secretary, to say that he was ready to leave the Court and report to work as he had agreed. But once again the call from the White House never came.

When he saw in the newspaper in late September that Roosevelt was going to create a seven-member board to supervise the defense buildup, with Vice President Henry Wallace at its head, Douglas told his friends that he had been passed over for reasons that were not clear to him. Max Lowenthal, former senator Burton Wheeler's assistant and one of Felix Frankfurter's followers, began spreading the rumor that "throughout the affair D[ouglas] was angling for an offer or a statement from FDR that he would want D[ouglas] for vice-president the next year, but he, FDR, wasn't going to pay that price." Seeking to cushion the blow, Douglas wrote a friend: "He definitely has in mind drafting me in case that [the] Board does not do the job. I hope for everyone's sake that it will succeed."

But it didn't, and by late October Douglas learned that a presidential draft for the job might still be coming. But this prospect still held no appeal for him, as he wrote to A. Howard Meneely: "Once it had been decided to put the whole productive capacity of the country to work (a decision really not made up to last month) the rest is an engineering job — at least basically. Furthermore, the present organization is honey-combed with big shots who have private interest to serve first. One who has depended on them for his technical data would be thrown out at first base. The alternative would be to start from scratch & build a new organization. That however is, or may not be, feasible. So, however I look at it, I am convinced I should not do it." But he said that he would continue to wait for a call with "an uneasy frame of mind."

Not until the morning of December 6, 1941, did Douglas finally have an opportunity to speak face-to-face with the president in a forty-five-minute appointment. Whether or not the two men spoke about any new job, what happened the next day at Pearl Harbor changed Douglas's mind about leaving the Court. "Now that we are in a life or death struggle (and it is not less serious than that) I have been turning over in my mind possibilities for a more active participation on my part," Douglas now wrote A. Howard Meneely. "If the President should ask me to take over the Defense program, I would of course not hesitate. . . . It's hard to keep one's mind in the work with the violent issues joined. Yet I suppose it is as important as anything else to keep important and essential domestic functions operating. I felt like joining the Marines, however, and taking a personal swat."

Only with the appointment of Donald Nelson as the new War Production Board head in January 1942 did Douglas realize that this "opportunity" had passed him by. Years later, he would claim to an interviewer that the president had actually done him a favor: "It was Harry Hopkins who had his way and relieved me from the embarrassment of resigning from the Court to undertake such a relatively minor job." But close students of Douglas's career could see the truth. "You know WOD was serious about the offer," explained his former law clerk Lucas A. "Scot" Powe, "because . . . he was willing to come back from his summer vacation in the west to Washington [to take it]."

CHOOSING SIDES

[Bill Douglas] was the prodigy thrown at an early
age into a world of big shots, of doers. And so, he
grew up and came of age and reached his attain-
ments pinching himself like a country boy and saying, "How the hell did I get here among these
giants."

—*Eliot Janeway*

With the Court's annual recess fast approaching in June 1942, speculation about Douglas's political ambitions began yet again. Over the
course of several talks, FDR asked Douglas to become a roving assistant
to him during the summer, working on a variety of assignments. The
beauty of this idea was that Douglas would not have to give up his
Court seat. It was not an assignment that he relished, however. "I would
be in a terrific row with some dunderhead within 24 hours & would be
a veritable duck in a shooting gallery. I disliked very much to turn him
down because God knows he needed help. But I still think my decision
was a wise one. I think the Court as an institution and I as a judge
would have suffered injury," he told A. Howard Meneely after the fact.
Just as central to this decision was Douglas's desire for his annual un-
interrupted three-month vacation. But still, seeing a possible spring-
board to political advancement from the post, Douglas kept the door
open by remaining ready to answer a presidential call. "Bill Douglas
called me this afternoon and said that he was still ready to report. He
said he had talked the matter over with [Justices] Black and Roberts,
and both questioned the wisdom. He said you would understand, and
so on," presidential secretary Marvin McIntyre wrote FDR. Once again,
Douglas was not tapped for the position.

By the end of November 1942, Harold Ickes had become convinced
that there was no post on the political horizon worthy of Douglas giving up his seat on the Court. However, with Douglas's name now beginning to appear on the Gallup poll of potential presidential candidates,
speculation about his political career continued. When A. Howard Me-

neely and Abe Fortas began talking about collecting information for a flattering biography of him to appear in the spring of 1943, Douglas begged them to reconsider. "What with me still showing up now & then in the Gallup poll, it would surely be taken as political activity. I am more wed to the Court than ever. I would not want to leave it for anything. So I want to discourage any activity which might be taken as implying something different," he wrote to Meneely.

.   .   .

Douglas's private life was no more settled than his public one. The experimentations in marital infidelity that had begun at Yale now had expanded into a full-fledged lifestyle. Once in Washington in a tenured job, Douglas decided that he was beyond the rules. All of his close friends now either had mistresses, had divorced their wives and remarried younger women, or both, talking freely all the while about their conquests. Douglas's protégé Abe Fortas and his friend Congressman Lyndon Baines Johnson pursued women relentlessly while also engaging in serious affairs outside of their marriages. Tommy Corcoran liked to play the swashbuckling bachelor around town before and after his marriage in 1940. Harold Ickes had a finely developed eye for women and a legendary reputation for conquering them. When his first wife died in 1936, he married Jane Dahlman, who was nearly forty years his junior. Seeing all of this womanizing going on around him, Douglas began to express an open preference for young blondes. As journalist Eliot Janeway recalled of that period, "Douglas was a tomcat. He would go after anything that would wear a skirt—or wasn't wearing a skirt."

Douglas's wandering eye and new relationships had an impact on his family life. It was life in the fast lane for the once cloistered academic, recalled his daughter, Millie: "That whole crowd did a lot of drinking. And I can remember that even as a child some Fridays when we lived out in Silver Spring that everyone in our house was really over the top, as far as drinking is concerned. . . . And he was just joining in, and everybody looked up to him, a new Supreme Court Justice. He had done all these things on the SEC, great man, great Justice, and he enjoyed it."

But there was a price to be paid for this behavior, and it was paid by those closest to him. Douglas had always treated his family badly, but now it became much worse. "He was there in body but certainly not in spirit," his daughter continued. "You would speak to him [and only get a] 'Hunh? What?' Just wasn't there. And he never talked to us like people." To both children, he was "scary." Whenever they sought to speak to him, Douglas would just stare at them for minutes on end "as if he had never seen them before," with his blue eyes turning to a cold unblinking glare. "Dad could look at us like that, . . . [and] we wanted to avoid him. And when he got angry at us, which was often over the slightest things, he would simply not speak to us for days on end. . . . [For him,] the children should be seen and not heard. . . . So he backed off and refused to have anything to do with us. And it was my mother's job to bring us up," said Millie Douglas Read.

But he was no easier to be married to. The Douglases' daughter saw the relationship begin to deteriorate in those years: "I admired him, I loved him. But I didn't like him very much because of the way he treated my mother. . . . My mother was one of the most charming women that I've ever met. . . . She was loving. . . . She radiated a warmth, and her friends realized it. And her children realized it." But her husband did not. "He was very cutting to her. And he could cut her in public without ever opening his mouth—just by the looks." The reasons for this harsh treatment were never clear to his daughter. "I think he was afraid of being hurt. . . . I think Dad cut her off . . . because he was afraid of it . . . the ties that it would make. . . . He would never apologize for anything, even if it was quite obvious that he was wrong. . . . He would make some joke out of it. . . . No, he wasn't very easy to like," she concluded.

From the time they arrived in Washington, Mildred and her children came to understand their role: Be ready to do whatever was necessary to further William O. Douglas's career. Sometimes this meant putting on a happy face for the photographers. And sometimes it meant being ready to be put on parade for the parties of important people in their Silver Spring home. "At these parties that Mom and Dad had, every once in a while my brother and I were brought down," explained Millie Douglas Read. "Think about it. . . . I realize that the more Dad had to drink, the more likely we were to be brought down to the parties, then we would be shown off and patted on the head, which I don't remember having any emotions about whatsoever. Afterwards I resented it, but at the time, you just went cold. I smiled when people said things, and I laughed, but other than that, this was Dad. This was the way he did things. . . . I felt totally frustrated at him as a father."

Even life for the Douglases on vacation in the summer was little different once they disembarked from the car in Oregon. Sacks of mail containing appeal petitions to review and fan mail to be answered would be stacked for Douglas in the local post office. Upon retrieving them, Douglas would ignore his family, lock himself up in a cabin to get through his work, and then later go off by himself on riding or fishing expeditions. The only break in his routine came when friends would arrive to join him on pack trips into the mountains. Every now and again, Douglas would just get in the car and disappear on trips to Yakima or Pendleton, engaging in activities undisclosed to his family.

Those precious few months in the Wallowas helped him to spiritually and physically renew himself enough to be able to deal with his public life in Washington. For a sum of one dollar, Douglas "purchased" the right to build on a choice parcel of forest land at their now traditional family camping ground, high in the Wallowa Mountains near Lapover, Oregon, from a friend named Roy Schaeffer, who owned a dude ranch nearby. The land was eighteen miles from civilization and lay within a corridor of the Wallowa-Whitman National Forest, which Douglas could lease for ninety-nine years at an annual charge of fifteen dollars.

For Douglas, a vacation camp in the Wallowas was Eden. Situated at an elevation of 5,200 feet, in a narrow tamarack pine–filled canyon between two mountain ranges that are no more than a mile apart, the parcel of land has the raging, trout-filled Lostine River running through it, with one of the finest fishing pools nearby. In the summer of 1942, the Douglases began building three log cabins near the spot where they had honeymooned. Over the front door of one of the cabins, built specifically for doing his work, Douglas jokingly put a brass plate bearing a quotation from Genesis 1:3: "Let there be light."

·   ·   ·

Life on the Supreme Court during the war years was tense at best. Like the other politically inclined men who were now ensconced on the Court—Hugo Black (who never wanted anyone to know his presidential ambitions), Frank Murphy (who would have been just as happy to become secretary of war), Robert Jackson (who had once been proposed for the presidency), and James F. Byrnes (who so believed that he belonged in the White House that he left the Court in October 1942 to become "assistant president" for domestic affairs)—Douglas could see that this position had become the place where presidential hopefuls went to cool their heels while waiting to see if Franklin D. Roosevelt would ever leave the White House. Throw this bunch of sidetracked but still ambitious political careerists in with the scheming Felix Frankfurter and the pliable Owen Roberts and Stanley Reed, to be headed now by the weak leadership skills of Chief Justice Harlan Fiske Stone, and you had a recipe for institutional disaster.

By now Douglas had developed enough confidence in his position that his relationship with his law clerks was changing. Newly hired clerk Vern Countryman discovered this while working on a Douglas opinion in a federal robbery case. "I didn't think very much of his opinion, and I rewrote the whole damn thing and took it in to him," recalled Countryman, who served from 1942 to 1943. "He just thanked me and took it. When the final version of the opinion came down, there was one sentence [of mine] as a footnote. So that's the only effect I had on that opinion."

Unlike other Justices, who socialized with their clerks, Douglas was now all about one thing: work. "He worked me like a goddamned dog," recalled Countryman. "But that seemed fair. I only had to do it for a year. He was doing it for life. So I never had any trouble with it at all." Lucile Lomen, the first woman to serve as a law clerk for the Supreme Court, worked for Douglas during the 1944–1945 term. She recalled her own observations of Douglas's work ethic and brilliance: "You worked till you dropped, and then you picked yourself up, and you worked some more. . . . He himself was the fastest, most accurate researcher I've ever seen. He could pull a case out just like that. I'd be researching for three or four days to get what he'd get in three minutes. I don't know how. But he had a very retentive memory. Of course, he'd only been on the Court for five years. And he could remember every line of cases and every opinion he'd written, as far as I could tell."

But much as they admired his work, his law clerks could not say the same about his personality. "He was not a warm man," recalled Vern Countryman. "I usually got to the office just a few minutes before he did. He would come through my office to go to his own. . . . He never stopped to chat. He would say hello and keep on going. But that didn't bother me any. It bothered other people, I know. The only thing he ever talked to me about at the time I was clerking were the cases we had to decide. . . . But that was it. . . . There were no extraneous social gestures whatsoever." And from Countryman's perspective, his attitude by this time was the same toward other members of the Court: "He was a lone ranger. . . . In the year I was there, I don't recall — and everybody would come through my office to go to his — [Hugo] Black ever going to his office or to my knowledge Douglas ever going to Black's. Chief Justice Stone used to drop in once in a while. . . . But that's the only Justice that I can ever remember going into Douglas's office."

In anticipation of the day when he would leave the Court, Douglas showed little interest in learning the craft of a career jurist. He had no interest in developing a long-term jurisprudential philosophy. Instead, he behaved in each case just like he had as a commissioner on the SEC: determining which issues were in his own best interests, battling with his enemies, and taking positions with an eye to his political future.

Just such a process occurred when Court opened in the fall of 1942, when Douglas, Hugo Black, and Frank Murphy sought to reverse their decision supporting Felix Frankfurter's opinion compelling the children of Jehovah's Witnesses to salute the flag in public schools. For Douglas, this was a personal as much as a philosophical decision. "Frankfurter had lost the respect of Black and myself and Murphy, just generally speaking," he later told an interviewer. "We learned that he was utterly dishonest intellectually, that he was very, very devious. . . . None of us had known him very well, but he spent his time going up and down the halls putting poison in everybody's spring . . . trying to set one Justice against another."

Douglas took great pleasure in informing Frankfurter of their changed view on this issue. "Hugo would now not go with you in the Flag Salute case," he told Frankfurter.

"Why?" responded the Harvard jurist. "Has he re-read the Constitution during the summer?"

To which Douglas replied, "No, but he has read the papers."

The opportunity to signal this shift came when the Court accepted an appeal by the Jehovah's Witnesses in another case, *Jones v. Opelika*, which tested whether local communities could impose a license tax on the sale of all printed material. In effect, it was argued, these laws created a barrier against those seeking to propagate their faith by distributing religious materials. While the Court's majority stated that a "reasonable and nondiscriminatory license fee" could be exacted from religious adherents whose activities were seen as sufficiently commercial, Murphy, Black, and Douglas argued in dissent that this represented a violation of the First Amendment's freedoms of speech, religion, and press. Then, in a separate opinion for the three men, Hugo Black added: "The opinion . . . is but another step in the direction which *Minersville School District v. Gobitis* . . . took against the same religious minority and is a logical extension of the principles upon which that decision rested. Since we joined in the opinion in the *Gobitis* case, we think this is an appropriate occasion to state that we now believe that it was also wrongly decided." In short, the three Justices were sending a message to the legal community that they were prepared to reconsider their flag-salute vote. As this group began to act in concert, Frankfurter now labeled them "the Axis," an especially pejorative term in wartime, and began to search for allies to oppose them.

Meanwhile, Douglas took the opportunity to begin to explore his views on personal autonomy in the case of *Skinner v. Oklahoma,* which involved the compulsory sterilization of so-called habitual criminals. Relying on a 1927 case, *Buck v. Bell,* in which Virginia had been allowed to sterilize "feebleminded" residents of state institutions, Oklahoma now sterilized convicted defendants who were involved in two or more crimes "amounting to felonies involving moral turpitude." While Oklahoma thought that it was acting consistently with the constitutional rulings, the Court unanimously overturned this law.

Speaking for the Court, Douglas demonstrated his willingness to rule expansively on behalf of human rights: "Marriage and procreation are fundamental to the very existence and survival of the race. Thus anyone who is subjected to this law is forever deprived of a basic liberty." This language would one day be credited as a cornerstone for the "fundamental rights" line of cases, by which any legislation dealing with these areas would be subjected to a higher level of judicial scrutiny than the prevailing standard, which afforded great deference toward legislatures. Here Douglas hinted at what would one day become his libertarian skepticism toward the government: "The power to sterilize, if exercised, may have subtle, far-reaching, and devastating effects. In evil or reckless hands it can cause races or types that are inimical to the dominant group to wither and disappear. There is no redemption for the individual whom the law touches. Any experiment which the State conducts is to his irreparable injury." Despite this hint of what was to come, Douglas had yet to concern himself with the development of an overall judicial philosophy.

When the Court—altered in February 1943 by the addition of liberal Court of Appeals Judge Wiley Rutledge in place of Jimmy Byrnes—decided to revisit the issue of license taxes on the literature of the proselytizing Jehovah's Witnesses, Douglas had a chance to further explore his views on the First Amendment's free exercise of religion clause. A majority of the Court now voted to reverse the *Jones v. Opelika* case after just one year, ruling that such a regulation in the town of Jeannette, Pennsylvania, would constitute a burden on the freedom of religion. Given the opportunity to write the majority opinion overturning this regulation, Douglas did so in a way that left little doubt that he saw the issue as the son of an evangelistic preacher would: "The hand distribution of religious tracts is an age-old form of missionary evangelism—as old as the history of printing presses. . . . It is more than preaching; it is more than distribution of religious literature. It is a combination of both. Its purpose is as evangelical as the revival meeting." Faced with an extended dissent by Robert Jackson complaining about the alleged aggressiveness of such practices, Douglas gave them his ringing endorsement: "This form of religious activity occupies the same high estate under the First Amendment as do worship in the churches and preaching from the pulpits. It has the same claim to protection as the more orthodox and conventional exercises of religion. It also has the same claim as the others to the guarantees of freedom of speech and freedom of the press." Plainly, for him, the work of the Jehovah's Witnesses, like the work of his home-missionary father, was no different from priests, ministers, and rabbis with places of worship of their own.

In thus overturning the *Jones v. Opelika* precedent, Douglas restored "to their high, constitutional position the liberties of itinerant evangelists who disseminate their religious beliefs and the tenets of their faith through distribution of literature." And, he made clear, he was prepared to do so in absolutist fashion when confronted with other liberties restrictions, as he proclaimed: "Freedom of press, freedom of speech, freedom of religion are in a preferred position."

This case, however, was the beginning of the end of Douglas's relationship with Robert Jackson. In an early version of his dissent, Jackson mentioned that the arrest of the Jehovah's Witnesses in this case occurred on a Catholic holiday. "Check with Jackson's clerk," Douglas told his clerk when he saw it. "This is wrong." When Vern Countryman got hold of the clerk, his response was, "Hell, I know it. I already told Jackson, and he sent it around anyway." When Jackson resisted making the change, Douglas became so angry that he amended his majority-opinion draft to point out that the minority was "falsifying the records." As Countryman later explained, "Then and only then did Jackson take out that statement. . . . But Black and Douglas were so mad at Jackson [as a result] . . . that they couldn't stand him. . . . He wasn't so much a Frankfurter ally as he was just a disagreeable son of a bitch." After a while, Countryman recalled, a proxy war was being waged among the clerks as well:

> The clerk for Frankfurter . . . was about as likable as Jackson. He would come snooping around my office trying to find out what the hell Douglas was going to do on a particular case. And then I finally told Douglas, "We've got to watch this guy." So Douglas prepared a fake opinion, and I very carefully left it on my desk, went away, and came back, and [the Frankfurter law clerk] was sitting in my office. And I know he read that goddamned opinion. It was a complete fake. It never was the opinion in the case. But we kind of set him up on that. . . . Frankfurter must have thought for a while

that he knew how Douglas was going to come out of it, and he went to the other side.

Several other religion cases that term and the next illustrated what five votes solidly in favor of religious freedom could do on the Court. With Douglas's help, the Court invalidated a town ordinance that forbade the knocking on doors or the ringing of doorbells by those who sought to propagate their religion. And, fulfilling the promise of the dissent to *Jones v. Opelika,* when the Court once again accepted for review a compulsory flag-salute case for schoolchildren, this time in West Virginia, that statute was overturned as well. Douglas joined Black's concurrence laying out their reasons for changing their opinions from the *Minersville v. Gobitis* case issued just two years before: "Words uttered under coercion are proof of loyalty to nothing but self-interest. . . . Neither our domestic tranquility in peace nor our martial effort in war depend on compelling little children to participate in a ceremony which ends in nothing for them but a fear of spiritual condemnation."

The real test for Douglas and the Court in this era, though, came in the form of a challenge to the government's program of establishing a curfew for, and later interning, 112,000 Japanese-American citizens. The dispute began after the bombing of Pearl Harbor in December 1941, when fears arose on the West Coast that some of the American citizens of Japanese heritage might pose security threats to the rest of the community. While no such risk could be proved, on the advice of the military authorities President Roosevelt issued Executive Order 9066 on February 19, 1942, authorizing the creation of a military zone from which persons deemed a threat to the armed forces could be excluded. A month later, General J. L. DeWitt designated an area all the way up the Pacific Coast and inland about forty miles as Military Area Number 1, and a curfew was placed on all citizens of Japanese heritage found in that region.

The Court accepted for review the appeal of Gordon Kiyoshi Hirabayashi, a senior at the University of Washington who had been convicted for knowingly violating the curfew and for failing to comply with military orders to report to assembly centers for processing. This decision provided Douglas with the opportunity to express his concerns about this program. While he had thus far supported Roosevelt and tended to defer to the military in wartime, the entire lack of due process for the affected citizens bothered Douglas a great deal.

And others were prepared to help. Douglas's law clerk Vern Countryman was a graduate of the University of Washington Law School and had been deeply troubled by the problems faced in the spring of 1942 by his Japanese-American classmates in law school. "It outraged me a lot," Countryman said, years later. "I knew that the [military explanation for the exclusion] was a bunch of bullshit. The main purpose was to get the Japanese out so that they could seize their property." By the time the case got to conference it became clear that a majority led by Felix Frankfurter, Hugo Black, and Chief Justice Harlan Fiske Stone were prepared to let the military have its way. Douglas did not like the fact that his colleagues had discounted the notion of individualized suspicion of guilt, raising instead the prospect that such decisions could be made on the basis of race rather than a lack of loyalty. So when he saw the first draft of Stone's opinion ratifying the military's decision, he offered some suggestions for revision to avoid even the hint of racial discrimination. To him, the 90 percent of the people who were free of guilt should have the opportunity to prove their loyalty rather than evacuating them for the duration of the war in order to keep the 10 percent who were suspect out of harm's way. At some stage in the classification proceedings, Douglas wrote Stone, people should have the chance to "prove that they are as loyal to the United States as the members of this Court."

The issue here was complicated for Douglas, however, since he had thus far been very devoted to the policies of the man who had appointed him to the Court, Franklin Delano Roosevelt. He was tempering his views not only out of love for FDR, but also on account of the fact that he personally knew and liked General DeWitt. Later that summer, after having dinner with the general and his wife on a trip west, Douglas wrote Hugo Black, "They are really grand people. We enjoyed them immensely."

When Countryman saw Stone's opinion, he tried to convince his Justice of the folly here: "You used to be in the army, and you never thought much of the generals then, I'm sure. What makes them so goddamned reliable now?" he asked. While failing to correct his clerk's misperception of the true nature of his military service, Douglas remained unpersuaded: "Well, the generals think that it's necessary." What Douglas was not saying, however, was that the chief's mind could not be changed on this issue. "When Stone made up his mind," he told an interviewer years later, "he's like a horse that knew that the oats were in a certain stall. And that was where he was going and there was no turning back. He was very solid in his position once he took his position."

When Stone, at the urging of Felix Frankfurter, refused to adopt any of Douglas's suggestions, the man from Yakima put pen to paper, turning out a sharp four-page concurrence. "We are engaged in a bitter war for survival against enemies who have placed a premium on barbarity and ruthlessness," Douglas began. But he continued by arguing that the Constitution provided due-process safeguards for everyone, even in wartime. Besides the lack of due process here, Douglas was also troubled by the apparent *reason* for the military action. "Loyalty is a matter of mind and of heart not of race. That is indeed the history of America," Douglas wrote, adding that "guilt is personal under our constitutional system." So he was prepared to grant each affected person "at some stage an opportunity to show that being loyal he was improperly classified." Then, reaching beyond the agreed parameters of the decision in this curfew and evacuation case, Douglas appeared ready to rule on the issue of confinement, arguing against "detention for accidents of birth."

This opinion landed right on the fault line of a fracturing Court. Felix Frankfurter belittled Douglas's opinion as being nothing more than a patriotic "spread eagle speech," appealing to the baser instincts of the electorate as he continued to campaign from the Bench for higher office. Frank Murphy, who was himself planning to write a dissent on the inherent racism of the policy, called Douglas's draft "the most shocking thing that has ever been written by a member of this Court." To Murphy, this was "a regular soap-box speech," which was "addressed to the mob." Hugo Black complained that this opinion would lead to "a thousand *habeas corpus* suits in federal district courts" by people seeking to remedy their rights. And Robert Jackson called the draft "a hoax," promising more than could be delivered by the Court.

When Stone refused to alter his opinion in accordance with this draft concurrence, he wrote Douglas on June 9 that if he accepted these new suggestions "very little of the structure of my opinion would be left," and he would lose his majority. Frankfurter then persuaded Murphy to change his draft dissent into a much narrower concurring opinion arguing that there was "a rational basis for a discriminatory curfew," even though it went "to the brink of constitutional power." With no one left to support his "lack of due process" position, Douglas issued a much watered-down concurring opinion that no longer supported the use of habeas corpus suits to determine whether individuals were, in fact, loyal. Despite the fact that five members of the Court had at some point expressed reservations about this case, Felix Frankfurter's lobbying had helped to gain the unanimous decision in favor of the government's program.

When the case was over, Vern Countryman made a bet with his

boss that he would one day realize that he had made a mistake by joining Stone's opinion. When Douglas did, the clerk would be owed a
fancy bottle of scotch. Years later, Douglas admitted to an interviewer
that he had "had grave doubts" about his concurrence here. He also
wrote of this case, "I have always regretted that I bowed to my elders
and withdrew my opinion." But when he refused to admit the same to
Countryman, another of Douglas's clerks, Montana Podva, took it
upon himself to present him with the bottle of scotch for the Justice *in
absentia.*

It was another case that term, involving political leader Enoch
"Nucky" Johnson, however, that revealed how frayed the personal relations had become on the Court. Johnson was a Republican party political boss in Atlantic City, New Jersey, who had been convicted for
federal income-tax evasion. He was now appealing because of the state
attorney's comments to the jury that his exercise of his Fifth Amendment right not to testify and possibly incriminate himself constituted
an indication of his guilt. Johnson believed that his arrest had stemmed
from a misunderstanding of the nature of his duties as a political boss.
While he admitted to having taken, from 1935 to 1937, cash "donations" from a numbers syndicate in return for arranging for police protection and converting the funds to his own use without paying any
income tax on them, Johnson argued that this money should be considered tax-free reimbursements for his unspecified political-party
"expenses." When Johnson admitted on the stand that he had also received $1,200 a week from gamblers in 1938, also in his view tax-free,
he was accused of voluntarily admitting a new crime rather than being
protected by his earlier Fifth Amendment claim. The question for the
Court was whether a defendant's assertion of his constitutional privilege on one charge could fairly be used to test his credibility on another one.

In conference, Felix Frankfurter, to the annoyance of his colleagues,
availed himself of the opportunity to lecture them, using the full history of British and American jurisprudence, on his view that this defendant had not been unfairly prejudiced. The opinion was assigned to
Douglas, who was willing to hold against Johnson despite being troubled by the judge's willingness to allow a comment on the exercise of
Fifth Amendment privilege. For Frankfurter this was no problem, because "for fifty years, so far as I know, no criminal conviction has been
reversed by this Court for such an error as we are now discussing when
no exception had been made at the trial." But Douglas was unconvinced. Owen Roberts showed up at Frankfurter's office door saying

that "Douglas has been buzzing around me both yesterday and today with questions about the Nucky Johnson case." Douglas, Roberts had learned from Hugo Black, had also been assigned an opinion that term dealing with a similar income-tax-evasion case against the Missouri Democratic party boss, Thomas Pendergast, this time overturning the charges on the basis that the statute of limitations on his crime had expired before any prosecution was begun. As Roberts explained to Frankfurter: "Black [clearly speaking also for his colleague] thought it was rather unfair of the Chief to assign the Pendergast opinion to Douglas. . . . If we are to sustain Johnson's conviction, having reversed that of Pendergast, it wasn't fair to make Douglas write that opinion whereby it would appear that he let the Dem[ocratic] boss out but kept a Rep[ublican] boss in prison."

Frankfurter believed that Douglas and Black were using the highly naive Roberts as their stalking-horse here. He was "shocked and outraged." For him, "the only possible ground for any thought of unfairness in any criticism that might come to Douglas for being the organ of the Court could only derive because it might be unfair to [the] political ambitions of Douglas." When he heard that Douglas was prepared to write "either way" in the case, he was further shocked.

Frankfurter told Roberts that if he wished to bring this matter to the chief for reassignment, he would be glad to write the judgment. Seeking to stir the pot, Frankfurter immediately conveyed all of this to his ally, Robert Jackson, who responded: "Roberts is just beyond me. He's a complete sap so far as understanding men is concerned and those two fellows are just systematically playing on his innocence. . . . I suppose the thing to do is to let out all bosses who commit crimes to show our impartiality."

After deciding to fight a proxy war on this minor case, the following day Frankfurter brought the entire matter before Stanley Reed, who professed not to be shocked by any of it. "Black always was a politician and he didn't and can't cease to be one by becoming a judge. . . . He is one of those people who is sensitive to every current that might affect public feelings," Reed explained.

But what about Douglas? responded Frankfurter. "He's never been a politician, he was a professor."

"But he is a politician now," responded Reed, "though this episode about Nucky Johnson is a revelation to me. For I had assumed he had put all thoughts of the Presidential nomination in '44 out of his head, but plainly not." In the end, Douglas wrote both of the opinions, upholding Johnson's conviction on the grounds that he had waived his objection and overturning Pendergast's conviction. But the notion of his colleague now running for the White House from the Court became an obsession for Felix Frankfurter.

As the Court's term dragged on to Saturday, June 12, 1943, Douglas told Frank Murphy that he just wanted him to get a final opinion out on another minor case, so that he could leave on his annual pilgrimage to the Pacific Northwest. When Murphy refused to go along, citing a need to polish his work, Douglas, to the dismay of his colleagues, simply drafted a concurring opinion without telling anyone, gave it to his secretary to release at the appropriate time, and left town.

In time, relations among the members of the Court became so frayed that conflicts spilled into the media. Washington political investigative reporter Drew Pearson, who was known to have close connections to Bill Douglas, correctly predicted in advance the Court's decision in a case dealing with the Hope natural-gas company. Since Douglas had written the opinion, Justices Roberts, Jackson, and Frankfurter became convinced that he had leaked it. The truth was that Douglas could not have known for sure how the final vote would come out. But that made little difference to Justice Roberts, who by now had convinced Frankfurter that Douglas had broken the Court's tradition of maintaining absolute silence about forthcoming decisions.

When Pearson made another correct prediction three months later in a case dealing with the Southeastern Underwriters Insurance Company, Roberts was certain that Douglas was prematurely releasing opinions. A full conference was held to discuss the issue, but when Douglas was unable to attend because he was home sick with the flu, this provided even more evidence to his opponents that he was the guilty party. Such an argument ensued among the Brethren about this case that they deliberately withheld the release of the final opinion to make it appear as though Pearson was wrong. But Roberts was not ready to let the matter drop. He went to Hugo Black and repeated his accusation, only to have Black defend his colleague vigorously as being incapable of such an ethical transgression. As a result, Roberts became so bitter that he stopped talking to all of the other Justices. Despite their earlier relationship, in which they all had been invited to his Pennsylvania farm, he now refused even to shake their hands in conference. As a result, Douglas later recalled, his own previously warm friendship with Roberts now "became a very, very ugly relationship around the Court."

With so many frustrated presidential prospects on the Court, it had now become much like Abraham Lincoln's cabinet—a boiling pot of politically ambitious men who would turn on one another at the drop of a hat. For Bill Douglas, with FDR deciding to run for an unprecedented fourth term, the only escape from this cauldron now would be in angling himself ahead of all of his colleagues, not to mention such political figures as James F. Byrnes, Harold Ickes, Sam Rayburn, and John Nance Garner, should Henry Wallace's vice-presidential seat open up.

THE ALMOST PRESIDENT

I had two classmates who wanted to be President
in that class—one [Thomas Dewey] who ran for the
office, and one [William O. Douglas] who didn't.
[Douglas] just wanted the office handed to him, but
he wanted it just as much as the other.

—*Simon Rifkind*

The phone rang in Teddy Hayes's apartment in the Mayflower Hotel on
the evening of Tuesday, July 4, 1944, and changed Bill Douglas's life.

On the line was Hayes's good friend and sometimes apartment
mate Ed "Boss" Flynn. They were the unlikeliest of friends. Flynn, a
muscular, imposingly tall man with an Irish appearance, was the fifty-
three-year-old political boss of the Bronx, New York, who served as
one of that state's power brokers in the New Deal. Hayes, on the other
hand, had a smallish frame and the fine delicate features of an accoun-
tant, belying his profession as an ex-prizefighter who now trained
other boxers. The two men became fast friends one day when Flynn
and New York mayor Jimmy Walker required an expert to revive them
for an important meeting after an all-night bout of drinking.

Flynn was calling that night from the White House, where he was
sharing a private dinner with FDR. "I need to speak with you later
tonight," he told Hayes. "I have some important news to tell you." It
was just like Flynn, who was too secretive even to put anything on
paper, to be this evasive on the phone. Always anxious to get the latest
political gossip, Hayes found it hard to wait the rest of the evening for
his friend's return.

With the 1944 Democratic National Convention set to begin in
two weeks, what concerned the Democratic party's leaders most, given
the president's obviously grave health, was the selection of a vice
president for the ticket. "[We] are not nominating a Vice President of
the United States, but a President," said Edwin Pauley, a California oil-
man then serving as the party's treasurer. For many Democrats, that

meant getting rid of the ultraliberal and increasingly unpredictable Henry Wallace.

The topic had preoccupied both Hayes and Flynn for several weeks. Flynn had a strong preference for Senator Harry S Truman of Missouri, whose work heading a Senate committee exposing price gouging by war industries had received favorable notice. For his part, Hayes had been pushing the man who had gunned down Wall Street, Justice Bill Douglas. "I kept telling Flynn what a great fellow he was, strictly a westerner," Hayes later recalled, "rugged, tough, direct, no pretensions. A powerful mind and a working man's hands."

Just before eleven o'clock, Flynn blew into their bachelor pad with a huge grin on his face. "Teddy," he said, "I think your man is in." He and the president had been discussing the vice presidency, he explained, and FDR had "tossed out" Douglas's name. As soon as he learned the president's wishes, Flynn said that he abandoned any thought of pressing for Truman.

Since the Democratic National Party chairman, Robert Hannegan, lived in an apartment on one of the hotel's upper floors, Hayes and Flynn decided to call him first with the news. "Busyman Bob," as he was called, was a tall, black-haired, square-jawed Irishman, who had distinguished his career as the chairman of the City Central Committee in Saint Louis by "finding" the spare eight thousand votes that provided Harry Truman with the exact margin of victory in his 1940 Senate primary race. For this favor, Hannegan became collector of internal revenue in the Eastern District of Missouri and later, thanks to his new patron, commissioner of internal revenue in Washington, D.C. In January 1944, Truman had helped install him in his current post. In that capacity, Hannegan told friends, his only mission besides reelecting FDR was to be able to put on his gravestone that he was the man who kept Henry Wallace from becoming president of the United States.

Within minutes of their call, Hannegan appeared at their apartment door dressed only in his pajamas, bathrobe, and house slippers. FDR will "go along" with Bill Douglas for vice president, Flynn said breathlessly, adding, "The President wants to have a dinner a week from tonight with the executive committee. You're the chairman, Bob. You call and tell them." Hannegan quietly thanked Flynn for the word and bid both men good-night without revealing his plans. The truth, he now knew, was that there was a lot of work to do, and not much time to get it done.

Early the next morning, Bill Douglas picked up his phone to hear the voice of an excited Teddy Hayes, who had been so charged up by

his news that he had not been able to sleep that night. Don't say anything because you will have to hear this directly from the president,
Hayes told the Justice, but FDR wants you to run on the ticket with
him. Douglas was only one phone call away from all but fulfilling the
destiny his mother had laid out for him, though after the War Production Board disappointment he knew better than to make any new
plans just yet. Two days later, when Hayes called to see whether the
offer had come and Douglas replied in the negative, he said, "Don't
worry about it. You're the choice."

But while Douglas's phone remained quiet, the same could not be
said of the phones of Busyman Bob and the party bosses who were
plotting and scheming about the next election. To them, Bill Douglas's
lack of political experience made him almost as unpredictable and uncontrollable a candidate as Wallace. After several days of phone conversations followed by a group luncheon, they devised a plan of attack
for bypassing him.

On July 11, Hayes accompanied Hannegan and Flynn as they
walked from the Mayflower to the White House for the president's
dinner. Along the way, Hannegan turned to Flynn and said, "What
about Truman?"

"I leaned toward Truman myself," Flynn responded sharply. "Why
didn't you say something a week ago when I told you the President
wanted Douglas?"

Teddy Hayes's heart began to sink as Hannegan responded, "Do
you think it is too late to raise the issue one more time?" After saying
that he wasn't sure, Flynn asked whether this matter had been mentioned to the other executive committee members. It has, said Hannegan, adding that everyone seemed ready to get behind Truman.

"Okay," Flynn said, "I'll reopen the subject after dinner. You tell the
President your thoughts. You can carry the ball. You're the chairman."

A sickened Hayes left the two men at the White House gate and
walked slowly back to the Mayflower for what he knew would be an
unpleasant duty. After dialing up Bill Douglas at home, he explained
what Flynn and Hannegan were about to do. "To this day I believe that
[Douglas] felt Ed Flynn double-crossed him," Hayes wrote later.

But Hayes did not understand Douglas's temperament when he
was this close to something he really wanted.

While Hayes was making his call, the party bosses, all dressed in
dark summer-weight business suits, sauntered into the White House.
One by one, FDR greeted each member of the party executive committee as he entered the private, second-floor family dining room,
inviting each to remove his coat and accept a martini as a defense

against the hot, sticky evening air. Joining Hannegan, Postmaster General Frank C. Walker, and Flynn at the dinner table were Democratic National Committee secretary George Allen, Chicago mayor and machine boss Ed Kelly, and Edwin Pauley.

After dinner, the party retired down the hall to the oval Blue Room, which served as the president's study, where they were joined by the president's son-in-law, John Boettiger. The highly superstitious FDR purposely took his place next to Hannegan on the same settee that he had occupied four years earlier when the party leaders had come to press him to run for an unprecedented third term. Within minutes of the opening of the discussion on the vice presidency, nearly all of the candidates were eliminated. Everyone agreed without much debate that James F. Byrnes and former majority leader Alben Barkley were too southern; Speaker Sam Rayburn of Texas was too unknown; and Henry Wallace's instability was the reason why this conversation was now taking place.

At this point, to the amazement of many in the room, the president raised the names of two other prospects: Ambassador to Great Britain John G. Winant and Supreme Court Justice William O. Douglas. Douglas, said Roosevelt, has "the following of the liberal left wing of the American people; the same kind of people whom Wallace had." On top of that, Douglas has "practical experience from the backwoods of the North West as a logger," and he "look[s] and act[s] on occasions like a Boy Scout." All of this, the president said, would have "appeal at the polls." "And besides," FDR added, Douglas "play[s] an interesting game of poker."

When someone raised Harry Truman's name in response, the president said that while "he had not known him too well," the senator "had done a good job" as the head of the War Investigating Committee. This work "demonstrated his ability and loyalty, and that he had been trained in politics." His one concern, though, was with Truman's advanced age.

"Does anyone know how old Truman really is?" asked Bob Hannegan innocently, knowing full well that at sixty (to Douglas's forty-five), his candidate was a mere two years younger than the ailing president himself.

When no one spoke up, John Boettiger offered to search for the Congressional Directory. By the time he returned, the conversation had moved on; he handed the volume to Edwin Pauley, who simply buried it in his lap with his finger marking the appropriate page.

After a few more minutes of taking the political temperature of the group, FDR put his hand on Hannegan's knee and said, "Bob, I think you and everyone else want Truman. . . . If that is the case, it is Truman."

The group was so relieved and delighted by this news that they took the first opportunity to get up and leave before the president could change his mind. As they all trooped downstairs, Hannegan remained behind with Roosevelt. Knowing the president's propensities, Frank C. Walker had advised the party chairman to seal the president's choice by having him write it down. As soon as Hannegan put the request to him, Roosevelt readily agreed and, grabbing a piece of light tan notepaper from a small pad on his desk, he began scribbling. The note, he explained, would be postdated July 19, thus making it look like it was being sent during the opening of the convention.

Once the letter was safely in his hand, Hannegan turned to leave without even reading it, only to see Edwin Pauley walking back into the room, saying that in all the confusion he had put on Hannegan's coat by mistake. Having the two party leaders there now gave the president a chance to say what was really on his mind: "I know that this makes you boys happy, and you are the ones I am counting on to win this election. [But] I still think that Douglas would have the greater public appeal." (Later, FDR's son, James Roosevelt, who himself had crossed swords with Douglas during his SEC days, would say of the president's desires: "Although Father did not commit himself, I came away with the distinct impression that he really preferred Justice William O. Douglas as the vice-presidential nominee.") Both party leaders assured FDR that "what Truman might lack in this regard [they] would make up in [their] enthusiasm [for the ticket]." That said, they all shook hands, and the visitors departed.

"I've got it," Hannegan told Walker downstairs as he patted his suit-coat pocket containing FDR's letter.

But Hannegan's mood would change later when he pulled out the note and read it for the first time and learned that the president had also endorsed Douglas.

·   ·   ·

Without knowing what had happened at the White House, Tommy Corcoran picked up his phone, dialed a series of numbers, and each time he made a connection said simply, "Buffalo tails together." Tommy the Cork liked to use this term in calls to his political operatives for his "number-one alerts," taking it from the way a herd of buffalo facing a pack of wolves will put their tails together so as to point a defending ring of horns outward.

Everyone who got such a call now knew just how desperate Corcoran was to advance Bill Douglas's career. Having placed Douglas on the SEC and later on the Supreme Court, Corcoran was now determined to get his friend to the Oval Office, in order to return himself to power. For the last five years, Corcoran had used his contacts in the business and political worlds to arrange lucrative lecturing invitations for the ever financially strapped Justice. With each speech, Corcoran advised Douglas how to appeal to various political constituencies, wrote many of the speeches himself, told him which prominent personages to court, and even arranged for various honorary awards to be presented him in order to garner even more press attention. In addition, Corcoran arranged intimate political dinners for Douglas with prominent political figures. Now the time had come to use all those contacts to build a campaign organization.

By this time, Corcoran had also built a small but impressive force of political operatives. There was Jerome Frank at the SEC and Leon Henderson at the Reconstruction Finance Corporation, both of whose appointments Corcoran had arranged. Then there was Abe Fortas, now undersecretary for the Interior Department, who had in turn recruited Lyndon Baines Johnson, who himself used the Douglas crowd as a means for securing influence. And, from time to time, Corcoran could also count on James H. Rowe, Jr., one of FDR's "anonymous assistants." From behind the scenes in his law office, Corcoran also used his web of contacts throughout the government to ignite people such as Speaker of the House Sam Rayburn, Attorney General Francis Biddle, Secretary of the Navy James Forrestal, and various members of the Senate. It was these men who had been spreading his story that Vice President Wallace was becoming even more erratic, even to the point, they said, of quite possibly being insane.

As Corcoran reviewed his political troops in July 1944, he began to add to their numbers in anticipation of the party convention. First, he approached Secretary of the Interior Harold Ickes, who agreed to back Douglas at the convention if Wallace's chances in fact became doomed. Corcoran then tapped Ernie Cuneo, an attorney (trained in part by Douglas at Columbia) and former professional football player who now worked as an associate general counsel for the party, as his legman and advance man. A classically educated three-hundred-pound good ol' boy, Cuneo had a unique ability to contact the key political players in the Roosevelt administration who were beyond Corcoran's reach. Finally, he tapped Eliot Janeway, the business editor of *Time,* to serve as Douglas's publicity agent.

That mission accomplished, Corcoran summoned Janeway and Douglas to his office to handicap the opposing field of possible candidates for the vice presidency. "What about [House Speaker Sam] Ray-burn?" began Corcoran.

To which Janeway responded, "Possibly, but what about [Secretary of State Cordell] Hull?" While Douglas watched in silence, the two men reviewed a series of governors and senators whom they believed had a chance of being chosen. Having never gotten the word about the July 11 meeting, in all of the names on their list they never once mentioned Harry S Truman.

When the list was completed, Douglas's only response was: "Jimmy Byrnes will be the man to beat, and he will be tough. As a South Carolinian, he can deliver a powerful coalition of southern states, every one of which FDR needs to be re-elected."

Much later, Janeway explained: "Douglas had a great respect, almost a fear, for those who either were elected to their posts or worked competently in an administration post."

Then Douglas detailed why, unlike the other candidates, his campaign was tougher. As a sitting Supreme Court Justice, he was bound by the stricture established by Charles Evans Hughes in 1916 that one does not run for political office from the Court without first resigning from the Bench. Moreover, Douglas made clear that his wife was very opposed to his entrance into politics. Eliot Janeway knew this to be true: "[Mildred] was going around bleating and whining about how if her husband got off the Court they would never be able to make a living. They never had enough money, 'What would they do?' she would say. [She was] petrified that the political fellows would talk him into leaving the Court, and they wouldn't know how to survive. He couldn't get a job. . . . She was even petrified when he left the payroll at Yale." So Douglas dared not resign from the Court without having a backup job in hand.

Despite these problems, both men knew how desperately Douglas wanted to be president. Bill Douglas, Tommy Corcoran penned in his unpublished memoir, "wanted the Presidency worse than Don Quixote wanted Dulcinea."

"He really wanted it [in 1944]," recalled Eliot Janeway, "because he knew the situation with Roosevelt's health. Everyone did." And they knew that he had a chance, with Harold Ickes reporting after a lunch in mid-July with FDR that the president "believed Bill Douglas would be the strongest candidate."

Given all these challenges, the three of them agreed that they would have to engineer a draft. "The secret was to create a situation where Douglas was the beneficiary without getting caught reaching for it," explained Janeway. It was decided that Corcoran would direct the campaign from Washington, with Ickes hopefully serving as a power broker in the hotel suites of Chicago's luxurious Blackstone Hotel, while Janeway and Cuneo worked the convention scene. Since Douglas was from the west, they quickly agreed on enlisting Robert Walker Kenny, the attorney general and Democratic leader of California, to deliver the support of the Pacific states as a way of countering the likely negative impact of the big-city party machines.

Kenny had only one slight problem when Corcoran called him for help. While he had committed his vote for Henry Wallace on the first ballot, he had also promised the Truman people to vote for their man on subsequent ballots. But, always ready as a good politician to plan for all contingencies, Kenny told Corcoran that he would write a nomination speech for Douglas and carry it into the convention. Should the convention become deadlocked, Kenny promised to try to start a delegate stampede for the Justice by making it look as though his name was coming out of nowhere.

With all this activity under way, Cuneo was summoned by his own "buffalo tails together" alert to Corcoran's office. When the lawyer arrived, he found, as always, the sounds of ringing telephones and shouting voices echoing around him. It "gave the impression of the Stock Exchange, which, in a sense it was," Cuneo later wrote. *The president is certain to run for a fourth term,* shouted Corcoran over the din, *and I am absolutely sure that he will ask Bill Douglas to be his vice-presidential running mate.* This came as a great surprise to Cuneo, who remembered the War Production Board fiasco and wondered whether the White House power broker, Harry Hopkins, who was quietly backing Byrnes, would ever allow such an appointment. Corcoran then got Cuneo set up to go to the Chicago convention.

As soon as Cuneo arrived in Chicago on Friday, July 14, he began hearing rumors that Harry Truman would get the vice-presidential nomination. When informed of this by phone, Tommy Corcoran confessed that he, too, had just heard the same rumor, but the twist was that Bob Hannegan had some kind of letter from the president naming his choices for the vice presidency. The good news, Tommy the Cork added, was that while Truman's name was on the document, it was listed second to that of William O. Douglas. Corcoran had conveyed this same rumor to Douglas, bragging falsely that he had engineered the letter's production. You have made "a ten strike," the excited Justice had exclaimed when he heard the news.

Duly reassured, Cuneo returned to his suite, only to realize that things were not looking good for Douglas's chances. "Victory has a thousand friends," Cuneo later wrote, "but no 'friends' crowded to my suite." On top of that, while Bob Hannegan had at his disposal the entire political machinery of the Democratic party, Corcoran had provided Cuneo with only one confidential legman, who turned out to be so drunk that he was immediately dismissed. "I now had a following equal to my delegate vote, zero in both cases," wrote Cuneo.

Seeking some psychological reinforcement, Cuneo hurried up to the suites occupied by Harold Ickes and Francis Biddle, only to find that neither man had gotten the word that Douglas was the certain nominee for vice president. If these two Cabinet officers did not know, then who did? Cuneo began making the rounds, searching for someone, anyone, who had heard that Douglas was the president's first choice for a running mate. One by one, the political bosses acted as though it was news to them. Tammany Hall's George McLaughlin was angry that any candidate had been selected and he had not been told. Jake Arvey of Illinois was also in the dark, as was Frank Hague of New Jersey. Instead, they told Cuneo they had all heard a different version of the rumor that Corcoran was spreading. Bob Hannegan had a letter from the president endorsing his choice for a running mate, they insisted, but the names were ordered Truman before Douglas.

Whatever the letter said, Cuneo knew, if it was in the control of Bob Hannegan it was certain to be of little worth to any candidate who was not connected to the Pendergast machine in Missouri. So as soon as word spread that the chairman had arrived in town, Cuneo searched him out, demanding to see the letter. "What letter?" replied Hannegan innocently.

The truth was that even if Hannegan had wanted to show him the letter, something he had no intention of doing until it was in his own candidate's best interest, he could not do so now. All that he really had in his possession was a handwritten note from the president on a piece of scrap paper, without any permission to release it. But the chairman planned to remedy both of those matters when he met in secret with the president in the Chicago rail yards the following afternoon.

Somewhat rattled by Hannegan's response, Cuneo found a safe phone and told Corcoran just how little he or anyone else now knew about what was really going on. "Tom was absolutely certain the letter was in existence, absolutely certain," Cuneo later recalled. "It was clear that we were being flanked, but where was not discernable [sic]." With Corcoran's approval, Cuneo went to the press box and accused Hannegan of lying about the very existence of a presidential letter. But nobody in the press corps was paying any attention.

Hoping that the party bosses could smoke the letter out, Cuneo took George McLaughlin aside and brazenly accused *him* of holding out on the president by helping to hide the letter from the rest of them. "You know who the President really wants," Cuneo shouted.

But this accusation only made McLaughlin even madder. "I give you my word that when I do [learn anything], I'll call you," he yelled back.

Meanwhile, back in Washington, D.C., Tommy Corcoran decided that it was time to phone the president directly at the White House. His call was not put through, however, leading him to conclude that Harry Hopkins was now blocking him. So he began to wonder if perhaps a call should be placed to Bill Douglas, who was now vacationing in Oregon.

While Corcoran and others were laboring mightily to engineer Douglas's draft for the vice presidency, the Justice was laboring just as hard to preserve his appearance of not wanting it. With rumors swirling in the press about his vice-presidential prospects (fueled in no small part by his own political lieutenants), Douglas wrote to the Chief Justice on July 12 from Lostine, Oregon, that he was not a candidate because of his firm belief that the Court should not "be used as a stepping stone to any political office."

Two days later, Douglas finished another six-page handwritten letter to Senator Francis T. Maloney of Connecticut, disavowing any interest in politics. After claiming that he had just come down from his mountain retreat to discover to his surprise that he was being mentioned as a candidate for vice president, Douglas said that he had "done all that is possible to discourage" the use of his name for political office. Knowing that Maloney would be at the convention, Douglas asked the senator to pass the word that he would not accept a nomination even if it were offered to him. That done, the Justice said that he would be returning to his cabin for a ten-day horseback trip into the "high mountains" and thus be totally out of communication.

While the handwritten nature of the letter made it look to Maloney as though the Justice had just dashed it off from his heart, in fact it was the result of an extraordinarily careful effort. After typing out one version and making extensive revisions on that draft, only then did he copy by hand his final version on the fourteenth. Then he delayed sending it for a day so that it would arrive on the eve of the convention.

Somewhat disconcerted by the communication, before releasing it to the press Maloney decided to call the one man who always had the inside skinny on the Justice's real moves: Eliot Janeway. "What do we do now?" he wailed on the phone, reading Janeway the entire letter. "Should I release it to the press as Bill says?" he asked.

"Aw hell," said the reporter, who had no taste for the Justice's disavowal efforts, "just put the thing in your pocket and disregard it. Bill doesn't mean it. Douglas wrote this letter as a cover for what was really going on. So, just forget about it, and join forces with us in Chicago." To that, Maloney happily agreed.

Unbeknownst to Douglas, while he was mailing his letter to Maloney on July 15, his political fate was being determined in FDR's private train car, the *Ferdinand Magellan,* which was some 1,500 miles away, rolling into the maze of tracks at the Fifty-first Street rail yard in Chicago. The president was on his way to observe troop maneuvers at Camp Pendleton, near San Diego, before traveling to Hawaii to discuss Pacific war strategy with General Douglas MacArthur and Admiral Chester W. Nimitz. For all intents and purposes, the president was now cut off from the rest of the world, living in a heavily armored Pullman car that was reinforced with more than a half inch of extra steel plate and with three-inch-thick windows that were totally blacked out. But the party bosses were not the rest of the world. At around 1:30 P.M., Bob Hannegan, Edwin Pauley, and Mayor Ed Kelly entered for a prearranged meeting to speak with the president. Reporters following the three men and, viewing the scene from a discreet distance, recorded that the meeting lasted only fifty-two minutes, but it was more than enough time to change the course of history.

Hannegan was there at the president's request to fill him in on convention details, but, with just four days remaining until the opening gavel, the chairman also had an agenda of his own. He wanted to get FDR's handwritten note from July 11 typed on White House stationery and secure permission to release it during the convention. *How is the convention going?* the president asked as soon as they were alone. All of the other candidates are refusing to get out of the race for vice president, Hannegan complained, explaining the need for a public endorsement note. When the president agreed, secretaries Grace Tully and Dorothy Brady made quick work of the task. The timing was so tight, though, that just as Hannegan snatched up the newly typed letter and its original version, the train started to move, forcing the three visitors to jump to the ground.

"What does the letter say?" Pauley asked Hannegan as soon as they righted themselves.

The time had come for the chairman to admit what he had already known for several days. He pulled the typed White House envelope addressed to "Honorable Robert E. Hannegan, Blackstone Hotel, Chicago, Illinois" from his pocket with great flair. Pauley grabbed the green White House stationery from his hand and saw that it read:

July 19, 1944.

Dear Bob:—

You have written me about Harry Truman and Bill Douglas. I should, of course, be very glad to run with either of them and believe that either one of them would bring real strength to the ticket.

Always sincerely,
Franklin D. Roosevelt (signed)

Honorable Robert E. Hannegan
Blackstone Hotel,
Chicago, Illinois.

By phrasing the endorsement this way, Pauley realized, FDR was not only giving the delegates the impression that he was leaving it up to them but signaling that he had not given up on his choice of Douglas. "Here we were, then, with a letter we could not use," Pauley later recalled, "with Roosevelt on his way to the West Coast—and with that man, Douglas, confronting us again."

In the taxi back to the Democratic campaign headquarters, Hannegan and Pauley agreed that the only thing to do was to continue to leak word that the president had written a letter offering his choice for a running mate but to withhold the document from public view until it was too late for the Douglas team to adjust. Once the letter was released, they could only hope that the delegates would interpret Truman's name being first as a sign that he was indeed the president's choice.

It was a foolproof plan, but only if they could continue to dodge a three-hundred-pound former NFL lineman.

Totally unaware of the events at the rail yard, after three more days of fruitless digging for information Ernie Cuneo became rattled on the morning of July 18 when he learned that the powerful labor leader Sidney Hillman, of the Amalgamated Clothing Workers of America (ACWA), was having breakfast with Harry Truman. Having heard that FDR had told his aides regarding any choice for a running mate to "clear it with Sidney," this was certainly not good news at all. Indeed,

Senator Joe Guffey of Pennsylvania was now telling Harold Ickes that he could not possibly release his state's delegation for Douglas until the labor leader cleared him.

Corcoran's advance man decided to give up on organized labor's support for the moment and seek help by picking off some individual state delegations. After several talks with the delegation from Michigan, where he had worked on labor problems with then-governor Frank Murphy in 1938, Cuneo now counted them in his corner. And with Robert Walker Kenny carrying around the Douglas nomination speech, he counted on about half of the California delegates. Figuring that the long list of favorite-son candidates would make a first-ballot victory by Wallace impossible, Cuneo then went to the Wallace forces hoping to trade his state and a half of support for their votes after their man was out of the race. By this time, though, he found the Wallace forces in such a state of panic that not even his friend and former graduate teacher, investigative political columnist Drew Pearson, was willing to unite them for Douglas down the road.

The only chance, Cuneo reported back to Corcoran, was either to force Hannegan to release the letter from FDR, if it in fact existed, or to attack the chairman personally for not doing so. For the first time, though, Cuneo noticed that the normally superconfident Tommy the Cork was sounding a bit worried.

And nothing that Cuneo had seen would have reassured the Washington lawyer. "I hadn't had one nod of understanding from one state chief, not one assurance, not one knowing handshake," Cuneo later wrote. Since "the silence was ominous," Cuneo said, "I knew we were in some trouble, how much I did not know." By this time, Cuneo was so desperate that he decided to create a rumor of his own. There is a letter from the president endorsing his running mate, he insisted to members of the press and party bosses, and it names Douglas and Truman in that order. In doing this, Cuneo knew that he was putting his reputation on the line, but this was the way Tommy Corcoran had told him it was, and Tommy had never misled him before. As a result, some of the more adventurous reporters ran with the tip.

When Cuneo learned that Hannegan, who professed to be unbiased about the choice of a vice president, was about to hold a secret meeting on the matter with the Missouri delegation, he decided to crash the party. Upon arriving at the Hotel Morrison, Cuneo saw several pot-bellied party-machine operatives blocking the ballroom doorway. Flashing back to his days in the NFL, he lumbered toward them as if he were bursting through the old Portsmouth Spartan defensive line. The double doorway banged open as the pile of humanity fell through it, and when Cuneo looked up he saw a red-faced and breathless Bob Hannegan, neck muscles bulging from the exertion of shouting, gesturing wildly and screaming at the delegates, "Truman means everything to Missouri." No sooner were the words uttered than the chairman froze, one clenched fist pointing off in the distance like a military statue gesturing to some unseen enemy line, mouth still open as he spotted the Douglas lieutenant now sprawled in their midst. "Bob," Cuneo said as he rose and spun for the door, "you *are* a son-of-a-bitch." Finally, Cuneo knew something of use to the Douglas forces: Busyman Bob was apparently so unsure of victory for Truman that he still felt it necessary to harangue his own state's delegation.

What he did not know was that after days of denying the endorsement letter's existence, seeking to build maximum publicity for its eventual release, Hannegan was now ready to begin the buildup for its announcement. With several of the party leaders, including senators Claude Pepper and Joe Guffey, seated around a dinner table on the evening of the eighteenth to celebrate the opening of the convention the following day, Hannegan and Ed Kelly told everyone that the president had written a letter endorsing Truman for the vice presidency. William O. Douglas's name on the same letter was never mentioned.

With the convention only hours from opening and Douglas's delegate count remaining at zero, Cuneo decided to try making a deal with the Wallace forces one more time. He approached Congress of Industrial Organizations president Phil Murray and made his pitch for labor-union support: Your man is going down—can't you see your way to backing Douglas when he does? "I can't, Airnee," Murray said, revealing his Scottish brogue. "Wallace is in trouble and if I admit I have a second choice it would break his line. If I commit for a second choice, I lose my first one. Further, I'm not certain the second has any better chance than the first."

So back the portly attorney went to the New Deal palace guard's suites at the Blackstone Hotel, where he found Harold Ickes more concerned with scribbling notes for his diary than in working to line up votes. For all his efforts on Douglas's behalf, Cuneo reported, in the ever-changing world of convention politics, the Michigan vote that he once thought was theirs was now committed elsewhere, and California was still offering only to split their vote for Wallace and Douglas on the first vote and then go unanimously for Douglas on any later ballots. So the only problem was how to create the conditions for such a deadlock.

When the convention opened on Wednesday, July 19, with the vice-presidential nominations scheduled to be made the next day, Cuneo ran into one of the Tammany Hall leaders. *How could it be that you don't know who the president's choice for vice president is?* he asked. "I give you my word, Ernie," the man said, as he neared tears, "they haven't told me a thing. I don't know from nothing." The hurt look in the man's eyes told Cuneo that even in the president's home state they knew that the choice was being dictated by Bob Hannegan.

That night, Cuneo and the other Douglas supporters were squir-reled away in the Ickes suite when the door flew open to reveal Post-master General Frank C. Walker. "Hello, fellows," the big man said as he leaned against the door, "I just dropped by to tell you it's Truman."

Upon hearing that, Harold Ickes jumped up and "erupted like Vesuvius," shouting in a voice quivering with rage, "Goddamn it. I'm a member of this cabinet and they haven't told me yet."

"Well," Walker responded with a wan smile, "I'm telling you now. It's Truman." Then, trying to beat his retreat while Ickes sputtered and fumed, Walker added quietly, "Remember, Harold, we're all members of a team."

"Goddamn it," yelped the secretary, "so was Pontius Pilate."

After Walker left, only one question remained in the minds of the Douglas forces: What would Hannegan do with the letter now?

But Hannegan knew exactly what he would do. After the president was overwhelmingly renominated on Thursday, July 20, and the con-vention had placed the names of his potential running mates into nomination, the party leader called the press together. The young lady over there, he said, motioning in her direction, has copies for all of you of the president's letter endorsing his choice for the vice presidency. Without waiting to hear what else Hannegan might have to say, the journalists mobbed the poor woman, knocked the pile of mimeo-graphed sheets from her hands, and piled on top of one another in a mad scramble to grab their copies from the floor.

There it was for all to see: FDR endorsing Truman or Douglas. The timing of the letter's release was perfect for Truman's chances. "By that time," recalls Edwin Pauley, "it was too late for any Douglas forces to organize." Once they had a chance to read the letter, though, the press had a few obvious questions.

How did the letter come to be produced?

"Sometime ago," responded the chairman, "I received requests from Missouri delegates on how President Roosevelt looked upon the possible candidacy of Senator Truman and I also was asked about how he felt about the nomination of Justice Douglas."

But this was thoroughly unsatisfactory to anyone who could read. How could FDR date the letter July 19 when he was not even in town and Hannegan had been talking about this letter since before the convention began? Not even Busyman Bob, they knew, was capable of receiving a letter before it had been sent.

"When did you get it?" one of the journalists asked.

"It is dated July 19," said Hannegan, making it clear that he would amplify on this matter no further.

"May I ask why your letter of inquiry to the President was limited to two men when other candidates for the nomination were known to be in the field?"

"I had on other occasions discussed in general with the President a number of other possible candidates," he responded. "A number of persons, some of them in Washington, had asked me about Justice Douglas."

Despite the irregularities, the letter was to be duly printed in the next day's papers.

As soon as he saw that Truman's name was listed first, Cuneo knew that his cause was dead. "Our throats were slit. The battle was over; you can't be deader than dead," Cuneo wrote. But how was it that Corcoran's information about the order of the names on the letter had turned out to be so wrong? The answer, Cuneo decided, was simple: "At long last, Hannegan produced *a* letter, not the letter, but *a* letter. The names had been switched."

After decades of reflection, Eliot Janeway would recall with an expression of regret on his face, "The truth is that we goofed. I don't know why none of us asked to see the original note. We just didn't. You have to understand it wouldn't look good for us to be challenging the Democratic Party Chairman at the Convention on behalf of a Supreme Court Justice."

By Thursday night, with the vice-presidential nomination to be considered, so many Wallace supporters jammed into the stadium, using counterfeit and misdated tickets, that Mayor Kelly designated himself the city's acting fire chief and declared that the packed stadium now constituted a fire hazard. Then Hannegan bullied the convention's permanent chairman, Senator Samuel D. Jackson, a Wallace supporter who was charged with running the gathering, into gaveling the proceedings to a close. As the increasingly morose Douglas men reviewed the day's events, they could all sense success slipping away. "Fuck 'em," said Harold Ickes to Eliot Janeway. "What are they going to do if we just go on the floor and start voting for Bill?"

But realizing that even with that plan they were about 575 votes short of the 589 needed for nomination, Frank Maloney suggested that maybe Joe Kennedy could help them. When they reached him in Palm

Beach and explained the problem, Kennedy said, "If I send you enough money to keep the floor fight on the Convention floor going for a week, can you turn around enough votes to get it for Bill?"

But Douglas's men knew that wasn't the answer. "By the end of the week," Maloney answered, "the nomination wouldn't be worth having." Indeed, the president would be open to charges that his party was out of his control. Moreover, by exposing the Justice's political desires, Douglas would either have to pull out of the race entirely or leave the Court immediately (which they all knew the financially insecure Justice would never do).

With the final vote coming on Friday, there was only one card left to play. Hoping that Douglas was still the president's personal choice, the men decided to try to reach FDR in the hopes of getting him to override the party leaders. But just who should place the call? Over and over they debated this issue, until finally they decided that only Douglas himself could make such a call. Repeatedly, Corcoran and Janeway begged Douglas, but he said that he was not inclined to do it. It would expose to the president his interest in the post, he said. And besides, he told them, FBI director J. Edgar Hoover might be tapping FDR's phones, and they all knew that he would not hesitate to leak this tidbit to gossip columnist Walter Winchell. Douglas's men were willing to take that chance, but they had failed to understand the Justice's unwillingness to expose himself to another rejection like the one in 1942.

Douglas's forces finally decided to make the call themselves. But, not knowing how to reach the president on his train west, they went to the only man who could help them: Bob Hannegan. Hannegan told them that the reported train trip west was actually a publicity ruse by the White House to cover the fact that the president was in such poor health from prostate difficulties. He isn't going to the West Coast to see army bases, Hannegan lied; rather, he is sedated into unconsciousness and getting an operation out of sight of the Washington press corps. With no way to confirm or deny the report, they gave up the attempt. Only later, after the president kept all of his appointments out west, did the Douglas team discover that in fact Hannegan and Edwin Pauley had remained in direct communication with FDR throughout the convention by using a direct line from a phone in a small office under the speakers' platform in the convention hall. But by then it was too late.

Not even the passage of five decades could keep Eliot Janeway from shaking his head sadly at this memory, saying: "Never before has the course of American history been changed because the intelligence on the status of the president and the White House was so important." His lament still stung deeply: "We brought Douglas to within a nickel's phone call of the vice presidency. . . . But Hannegan was the only one who knew about Roosevelt's condition. Once the president left the station in Chicago, Hannegan was operating as the de facto acting president on election matters. What he said went because Roosevelt was totally out of touch."

For this reason, Ernie Cuneo was still apologizing to Douglas decades after the fact: "Clausewitz (in his book *Rules of War* [*sic*]) warned that at all costs, communication lines must not run parallel to the battle line. In the 1944 Convention we just couldn't help it. [They] had the line of communications to the President. We didn't."

On Friday morning, Hannegan began waving the president's letter in front of one delegation after another, seeking to strong-arm them into switching their votes to Truman after the initial ballot. Cuneo saw Hannegan, flushed with impending victory, take the podium along with Edwin Pauley and Hannegan's lieutenant Paul Porter to read the letter. "The guillotine dropped on the two heads of Wallace and Douglas and, subsequently, the Palace Guard of the New Deal," he later wrote. Without even waiting for the final vote, he returned to the Blackstone Hotel to pack and phone Douglas with the bad news. But his calls to Douglas now, for some reason, went unanswered.

Once the voting began, Hannegan's plan worked to perfection as the siphoning effect of the 428 votes in combined favorite-son support produced a first ballot of 429½ for Wallace and 319½ for Truman, well short of the 589 needed. Then, even before Edwin Pauley could choreograph the votes for the second ballot, the roll call had already started. Maryland switched to Truman, followed shortly by Oklahoma, and the bandwagon was well under way. In a matter of moments, delegation chairmen everywhere clamored for attention. Harold Ickes yelled to Robert Kenny to get in front of the steamroller by moving for an immediate adjournment until the following day. Kenny, however, possessing a keen sense of political health, not to mention his own physical well-being, remained silent. "It would have been impossible to gain recognition from the chair at this hectic moment," Kenny wrote later. In no time at all, it was 1,031 votes for Truman to 105 for Wallace.

After all of Hayes's, Cuneo's, Corcoran's, Janeway's, and Ickes's efforts, Justice William O. Douglas was never formally nominated for the vice presidency and received only two votes from the Oregon delegation. For the man who just seventeen days before had been the president's personal choice for a running mate, it was a long, precipitous drop indeed.

As he was leaving the hotel later that night, Ernie Cuneo saw Bob Hannegan marching triumphantly across the lobby in the opposite direction. The two men just stared at each other for a moment, and then, like the old pols that they were, just laughed as hard as they could. "Bob," said Cuneo, "I understand you cut my throat, very appropriately, in the Chicago stockyards. Thank you very much, believe me, I'd have done as much for you." With that, the two men shook hands and parted ways. "There was no rancor," Cuneo later recalled. "It was part of the game."

But one thing still puzzled him: Why had he not been able to reach Douglas by phone at his summer place? The Justice later told him and others that he had been on a ten-day horseback trip. But that wasn't exactly true.

Always acting with one eye on the public-relations aspect of any event, Douglas had in fact been making plans to receive the phone call that would change his life. Believing that the nomination call should unexpectedly come to him at a place of great meaning for the press, Douglas drove from Lostine, Oregon, to Walla Walla, Washington, in order to attend a commencement party at Whitman College, having told only Eliot Janeway to reach him at President Chester Maxey's house. Striding confidently into Maxey's mansion, the Justice took his old friend aside and informed him that he was waiting for a historic phone call from the Democratic convention in Chicago. Maxey, he said, was looking at the next vice president of the United States. Would he mind that his phone number had been left with a person at the convention? Hardly surprised to be so honored, Maxey was fully prepared for such occasions. A brilliant man, but given to delusions of grandeur, the president of this tiny college had actually installed a phone booth in his house for all of his important calls.

After the final vote, Eliot Janeway dialed the Walla Walla exchange, all the while trying to form the best way to break the bad news to his temperamental friend. When the phone rang and Maxey heard that it was indeed for his distinguished visitor, he motioned for Douglas, who marched proudly into the booth. "He talked for quite awhile in the booth and the party went on," recalled Maxey later, "and nobody else knew what was going on." As it turned out, neither did Douglas.

"You didn't get it," Janeway said simply. "It went to Truman."

"How the hell did Truman get the nod?" Douglas asked. "Didn't anyone know that Roosevelt wanted *me*? Teddy Hayes assured me of that. Didn't anyone know that Tommy Corcoran had seen my name first on the letter from the president?"

"The names on the president's note were switched," responded Janeway. "Truman's name was first, and yours was second. They just stampeded for Truman."

"And what about Byrnes?" continued the Justice. "What happened to him?"

"Byrnes was shoved aside, too," came the answer.

As bad as he felt, Douglas's pain was eased knowing that. "And they did it to Jimmy Byrnes—the master pro!" he said. With that, there was nothing left to add.

Seeing Maxey's expectant face when he came out of the phone booth, all Douglas could manage was a thumbs-down gesture. "He got the word," Maxey recalled. "Truman had received the nomination because the city votes have turned their thumbs down on him."

With the battle now over, Douglas publicly moved to cover his tracks on July 27 by writing the president that while others had been putting his name forward, he was so uninterested in the vice presidency that he had instead been in "the high Wallowa Mountains of Oregon on a pack trip" while the convention was under way. Three weeks later, Douglas sent a similar letter to Chief Justice Stone, insisting that he was so removed from the political process that he had been fishing with his old friend, lawyer Jim Donald, in "spots where not even the Lone Ranger could find me." Neither man would ever learn that the horseback trip, on which Fred Rodell also went, had concluded more than a week before the opening of the convention, thus making possible the much more modern trip to Walla Walla for the nomination call that never came.

But privately, Douglas's reaction was much different. "All I needed to do to win was to get two cases of scotch and some girls and get a suite of rooms in the convention city and operate," he bitterly spat out to Eliot Janeway. "But I have to get off of the Court to do it." Having heard too many times about his financial problems, Janeway now believed that if the Justice was ever going to the White House, it would have to be because it had been "handed to him like a top hat."

·   ·   ·

Bill Douglas never got over this defeat. For a full week he had *known* that he had been FDR's personal choice for vice president. As Clark Clifford, who saw firsthand the effect of this stunted presidential ambition in a number of men, observed: "It certainly would take a lot of the luster out of your life, I would think. . . . When a man knows that—that he was that close to the top — well, it sort of takes some of the shine, I think, off the rest of your life." And, even worse, Douglas was now convinced that he had been cheated out of his rightful place by Hannegan and the party bosses. For this reason, friends such as Teddy Hayes now with great sadness referred to Douglas as "the Almost President."

Still three months shy of his forty-sixth birthday, Douglas believed that there would be many more chances in the future to get to the White House. Until then, Douglas developed his own peculiar way of dealing with this disappointment. Over and over again, he told others the "true" story of how he had been cheated out of the vice presidency. Robert Lucas, a close friend of Douglas and a former editor of the *Yakima Herald-Republic* recalled: "He told me once that in 1944 . . . he had it on information he considered to be absolutely solid that his name was on top of the list, but the national Democratic party chairman switched the order of the list putting Truman's name on top." Never would Douglas learn that in fact the "switched names" story was not true; rather, it was a tale invented by his own lieutenants to explain their unsuccessful support for him at the convention. Truman's name had appeared first in the handwritten note.

That a Douglas administration would have been far different from a Truman administration is beyond question; whether, however, it would have been better, or any more successful, is open to serious debate. Whatever the determination, Robert Hannegan and the party bosses had changed the course of history—and William O. Douglas's life—forever.

And both men knew it. Sometime after the convention, Douglas was at a cocktail party in Washington when he saw Bob Hannegan approaching him. "Bill, we really did you in," Hannegan laughed as he stuck his hand out.

"Bob," responded the Justice as he put his arm around Hannegan, "if I ever did run for anything, I'd want you as my manager."

What Hannegan said next caught Douglas's attention. "We are beginning to think of some vice-presidential possibilities the next time around. Your name keeps coming up. We hope that you will be available." With that, Hannegan smiled and disappeared, no doubt expecting that he knew how this play would end. But Douglas, in his mind, was already writing his own script.

JUSTICES AT WAR

The Supreme Court is like nine scorpions trapped in a bottle.

—*Alexander Bickel*

Having missed out on the vice presidency, Bill Douglas returned to his life on the Supreme Court. In the months following the Democratic National Convention, cases were brought to the Court by Japanese-American citizens named Fred Korematsu and Mitsuye Endo, each challenging the wartime internment policy. Korematsu's and Endo's cases raised the issues that Douglas had been forced to put aside in the earlier *Hirabayashi v. United States*. *Korematsu v. United States* presented the issue of the constitutionality of the exclusion policy, whereby Japanese Americans were forced to report to an assembly center and then evacuated to a so-called relocation camp. Korematsu argued that this incarceration violated his Fifth Amendment rights by discriminating against him on account of race and denying him his due-process right of appeal.

Endo took the argument further. Incarcerated in a relocation camp near Tule Lake in California, she had filed a writ of habeas corpus seeking to be released on the basis of her provable loyalty to the government. When that petition was denied, she was transferred instead to another relocation center in Topaz, Utah. Even though she was adjudged to be loyal by the local administrator and given a permit to leave the camp, she had not been released because of "resettlement problems." Endo was now asking for her unconditional release.

By the time the Court considered both these cases in its conference on October 16, 1944, it was clear that the fragile unanimity from the *Hirabayashi* case no longer held. Five members of the Court—Stone, Frankfurter, Black, Rutledge, and Reed—remained steadfast in their support of military policies during time of war. However, four Justices—Murphy, Douglas, Roberts, and Jackson—now objected strenuously to the notion that American citizens were being incarcerated based on race and without being formally charged with a crime.

In *Ex Parte Endo,* though, the Justices all agreed that when "loyalty is shown, the basis for the military decision disappears," making a release mandatory. Thus Endo and seventy thousand others in similar situations were a finished judicial opinion away from being released.

With his frequent ally Black drafting a majority opinion for *Korematsu* that was designed to defer to the military, Douglas began writing a stirring dissent. Still conceding the existence of the grave emergency that had justified the *Hirabayashi* holding, Douglas now was troubled by the fact that Korematsu had not had the option of voluntarily leaving the military zone, as had Gordon Hirabayashi. Instead, his "choice was to go to jail or to submit" to what amounted to an indefinite detention. In short, to Douglas, this was an efficient means for excluding and incarcerating a class of citizens based on their racial heritage, without probable cause. To him, this was unconstitutional.

Douglas, however, signaled to Black that he was willing to drop this dissent and join the majority opinion if a short paragraph was added ruling that the evacuation to, and detention in, an assembly center "were inseparable." Since the curfew policy was lawful under *Hirabayashi,* this would allow Douglas to concede that the evacuation and detention policy was legal as well. Black agreed. Only Justices Murphy, Jackson, and Roberts dissented. For Murphy, "This exclusion of 'all persons of Japanese ancestry, both alien and non-alien,' from the Pacific Coast area on a plea of military necessity . . . [went] over 'the very brink of constitutional power' and falls into the ugly abyss of racism."

Douglas, a man who rarely second-guessed himself, came to regret his decision to go with the majority in this case. "My vote to affirm was one of my mistakes," he later wrote, adding, "The evacuation case, like the flag salute case, was ever on my conscience."

When Douglas was assigned to write the opinion in the *Endo* case, he finally expressed publicly his opposition to the internment policy. "Whatever power the War Relocation authority may have to detain other classes of citizens, it has no authority to subject citizens who are concededly loyal to its leave procedure," he wrote for the Court. Since this was now a civilian agency acting under a congressional statute, Public Law 503, rather than military policy, no questions of military law prevented the Court from holding in favor of Endo's rights. Even here, Douglas later expressed regret that the Court did not go beyond this narrow finding to consider the larger constitutional question of whether the entire program was permissible. "It seemed to me to be a much more wholesome thing from the point of view of the Court as an educating influence just to say what you can and can't do," Douglas told an interviewer. Not until later did Douglas learn that Stone and Felix Frankfurter held up the opinion for another three weeks in order to work with government administrators to get the internment policy changed so as to lessen the political damage to Roosevelt. Thus, just one day before the *Korematsu* and *Endo* opinions were released on December 18, 1944, the War Department announced that all Japanese-American citizens who had been adjudged loyal would be freed.

Douglas's generally pro-government stance was evident eighteen months later when the Court ruled in the case of a man named Jack Davis, who was convicted for having in his possession 168 gasoline ration coupons, which he had used in running a black market. Government agents had searched Davis's gas station in New York City without a warrant and compelled him to open a locked filing cabinet so that they could retrieve the coupons that were eventually used to convict him. The issue for the Court was whether federal agents had more latitude to search and seize evidence without a warrant when it consists of public papers.

Speaking for the majority in *Davis v. United States,* Douglas argued that since the ration coupons were public property and the place being searched was a business rather than a private residence, the Fourth Amendment's protection against unreasonable searches and seizures did not have the same force. "The distinction is between property to which the government is entitled to possession and property to which it is not," wrote Douglas. While the agents could not break the law in conducting their search, Douglas ruled that they did not exceed the permissible limits of investigation in this case: "Whatever may be the limits of inspection under the regulations, law enforcement is not so impotent as to require officers, who have the right to inspect a place of business, to stand mute when such clear evidence of criminal activity is known to them."

Here, Felix Frankfurter, who was normally deferential to the government, argued in dissent that this search was "a travesty" of the Fourth Amendment, adding that Douglas's ruling constituted "a sudden and drastic break with the whole history of the Fourth Amendment and its applications by this Court." After an exhaustive review of the applicable precedents, Frankfurter saw real danger here: "The approval given today to what was done by arresting officers in this case indicates that we are in danger of forgetting that the Bill of Rights reflects experience with police excesses. It is not only under Nazi rule that police excesses are inimical to freedom." Finally, Frankfurter took a personal shot at Douglas: "I am constrained to believe that today's decision flows from a view of the Fourth Amendment that is unmindful of the history that begot it and of the purpose for which it was included in the Bill of Rights." Wiley Rutledge added in a dissent of his own that "the search was justified neither by consent nor by the doctrine of reasonable search as incident to lawful arrest."

To them, Douglas was no civil libertarian. That impression was confirmed in another decision announced that day, *Zap v. United States*. Edward Zap, a man who was accused of stealing a payroll check while doing some contract work on airplane wings for the Department of the Navy, challenged the government's power under a congressional statute to audit his business's books without him being present. Over Zap's protests, the FBI had recovered the disputed check from an employee, without a proper search warrant, and used it as the basis for the federal prosecution. Speaking for a five-person majority, Douglas ruled that the evidence was admissible. For him, Zap and other federal contractors automatically waived their Fourth and Fifth Amendment rights when they entered into a contract with the government: "When petitioner, in order to obtain the government's business, specifically agreed to permit inspection of his accounts and records, he voluntarily waived such claim to privacy which he otherwise might have had as respects business documents related to those contracts." It made no difference that while consent had been given to make the search, no consent had been given to seize the check. "To require reversal here would be to exalt a technicality to constitutional levels," wrote Douglas in offering incredibly broad support of the government's search power. For him, this was just "the means of insuring the production in court of the primary source of evidence otherwise admissible." Once more, Frankfurter, Rutledge, and Murphy dissented strongly to such deference to the government's power. "The legality of a search does not automatically legalize every accompanying seizure," wrote Frankfurter.

·   ·   ·

With the death of FDR in April 1945, President Harry Truman had to deal with the fallout from the personal animosity that had been bubbling on the Court. Justice Owen Roberts was becoming so concerned about the political inclinations of three of his judicial colleagues— Hugo Black, Frank Murphy, and Bill Douglas—that he began complaining about it to outsiders. To him, Douglas had also become "tricky" in his professional dealings.

But such complaints were now common on this Court. Black and Jackson plainly did not like each other. In conferences, Black would argue against Jackson's positions so forcefully that the offended New Yorker would pound the conference table during their arguments, once even yelling that the Alabaman had "attempted to bully him and that he would not submit to it any longer." And Felix Frankfurter was driving everyone to distraction, disposed as he was toward giving fifty-minute dissertations on a case in conference because, his colleagues said, that must have been the length of the classes at Harvard Law School. Such expositions were interrupted from time to time by his tendency to jump up to recite case passages and citations from memory and to grab volumes of Court cases off the shelf to prove his brilliance. Sometimes during these performances, Douglas would retire to a seat in the corner of the conference room, appear to ignore the monologue, and then reappear at the conference table when it was his turn to speak, only to say that while he had previously been inclined the other way he had now been persuaded to change his vote and rule against everything that Frankfurter just said. After one lecture, Douglas said: "Well, Chief, it seems to me that if Felix is right, he's the only member qualified to sit on this Court, and all the rest of us ought to disqualify ourselves." Law clerk Vern Countryman explained, "Douglas just did it to make him squirm. He couldn't resist sticking the needle into him whenever he could." Through it all, Chief Justice Stone compounded the problem by his inability to keep his charges under control, instead extending the conferences into two-day marathons.

By this time, the gentlemanly Owen Roberts had endured enough of his colleagues' bickering on the Court. Now seventy years old, and entitled to a lifetime pension of twenty thousand dollars per year, Roberts told Harry Truman that for him life would be more peaceful in retirement. But even his departure at the end of July 1945 from the legal battleground became an occasion for dispute to the members of the Court. When Chief Justice Stone circulated the traditional letter commemorating their colleague's long years of service to the nation among the Brethren, it contained the sentence, "The announcement of your resignation as a Justice of this Court brings to us a profound sense of regret, that our association with you in the daily work of the Court must now come to an end." To Hugo Black, the senior associate Justice who was asked to sign the letter first and who had endured Roberts's unwillingness to shake his hand or talk to him for years after siding with Douglas in the battle with Felix Frankfurter, this was more than he was willing to accept. So he refused to sign the letter unless everything after "sense of regret" in the sentence was struck. Moreover, he wanted Stone to strike another sentence that read, "You have made fidelity to principle your guide to decision." It was a position that had great appeal to Douglas, who argued that "the truth of the matter was that Roberts, who was a very highly principled man, a man of great character, was so bitter, a bitterness that he carried month after month, that he would just be emotionally against anything that either Black or Murphy or Rutledge or I were for. He was . . . a pitiful, pitiful character in those days and the sadness was accentuated by the fact that once we had all been so very close."

Rather than signing the letter, Black circulated his own much less generous draft. However, when he failed to include Stone's original draft in the communication with the other Justices, it only became an occasion for more wrangling. "This strained relationship [with Roberts] was so pronounced and was so prolonged that Black being a very honest man intellectually just couldn't put his name to something that wasn't true," explained Douglas years later. Unable to secure unanimity on his own draft, in the end Stone announced the retirement using the language suggested by Black. Said Stone's distinguished biographer, Alpheus Thomas Mason, "Silence would have been more charitable." When Roberts was replaced by Republican Ohio senator Harold Hitz Burton, a Truman crony, the two blocs of combatants on the Court immediately sought to enlist him to their side of the cause.

By late 1945, with World War II over, Douglas's political brain trust began to worry about his future in government. Seeking to ensure that he would get his chance to leave the Court, the Justice initiated a series of long talks with Bob Hannegan, now the president's adviser. The conversations seemed to have some positive effect, with Truman even asking Douglas to visit from time to time to discuss matters.

Douglas was now ready to consider even a relatively unappealing job in the Truman administration. The reason, he explained to friends without any knowledge of the Chief Justice's understanding with Jackson, was that in the future, when Harlan Fiske Stone decided to resign, his successor would be dictated by Felix Frankfurter. And Douglas had no intention of staying on a Court that not only bored him but was being run from behind the scenes by Frankfurter.

Ironically, it was Secretary of the Interior Harold Ickes who unwittingly provided Douglas with his best chance of leaving the Court for a Cabinet seat. When Edwin Pauley, former treasurer of the Demo-

cratic party, was nominated to be secretary of the Navy, Ickes announced that he would testify against him at the confirmation proceeding. He claimed that Pauley had pressured him before the last
election not to press a departmental claim for offshore oil leases in
California in the hopes that the party would receive greater contributions from the industry. The political uproar directed toward the Truman administration was so great that Ickes, as had long been his
practice whenever he disagreed with FDR, symbolically offered his resignation on February 12, 1946, in a letter that Douglas helped to draft.
This time, though, the strategy backfired as the president quickly accepted.

Within days, Truman decided that Bill Douglas was the man to replace Ickes. Knowing that with so many of the Interior Department's
issues originating in the west, Douglas was in the best position to serve
the administration's interests with distinction, Truman told his special
counsel, Clark Clifford, to tender the offer. Clifford was a tall, handsome man who dressed with impeccable style and spoke in such a
serious, almost aristocratic manner that he commanded people's attention. While he did not know Douglas personally, in no time at all
the two men discovered that they shared many common interests, including a friendship with Clifford's legal mentor from Saint Louis, attorney James Counselman, and an interest in country music. The men
would delight each other with funny song titles they had discovered
such as "Songs I Learned at My Mother's Knee and at Other Low
Joints" and "My Wife Ran Off with My Best Friend, and I Sure Miss
Him." Over time, Clifford found Douglas so engaging that he invited
him occasionally to the president's poker game. Once Douglas even returned the favor by holding the game at his home, only to have the Secret Service clean out the refrigerator, leaving the Douglas children
with nothing to eat for breakfast the next morning.

Having heard from Douglas that his early lifetime goal had been to
become chief of the Forest Service, like his boyhood hero Gifford Pinchot, Clifford fully expected that Douglas would accept the offer of interior secretary. "Every now and then Bill would get restless," recalled
Clifford of the conversation. "He was a restless man. With some men,
when you get to the Court, and you keep saying, 'My God, this is everything I wanted in my life. I'm the happiest man on earth.' But that
wasn't Bill Douglas. Bill never quite knew where fate was going to lead
him, you see. . . . So he would get some restlessness, which I would
sense from time to time."

Clifford drove over to the Court building and invited Douglas to "go for a drive," his code for wanting to talk about important political matters without risking being overheard by anyone. Once they were safely on the road, Clifford presented the offer "as attractively as possible." But, as was always the case in deciding about career moves, Douglas said that he wanted "to think it over" for a while.

Clifford reported back to the president that while Douglas needed a few days to decide, the prospects were very good that he would join the administration. "All right," said the president, "but stay with him. I think he's just the right man."

As he did on such occasions, Douglas canvassed his political allies for advice. When Harold Ickes learned that his old job was Douglas's for the asking, he immediately went to see him. "Whether [you] consider taking Interior depend[s] altogether upon what [you] wan[t] to do with [your]self in life," the outgoing secretary told him. To which Douglas replied simply that "he should not leave the Court except for a higher office, and that only the Presidency was higher." And the Justice did not see how taking such a job would get him to the White House, nor did he see why he should give up his lifetime security on the Court. He told his friends that he had to discuss the matter with Chief Justice Stone, which to them meant that he would not leave.

But Ickes was not satisfied with this argument. Like Tommy Corcoran, he could see that his only entrée to the White House lay with Douglas. So the two men searched for a way to get him off the Court and onto the political treadmill. The secretary proposed to Tommy the Cork that the job might be more appealing if the department's responsibilities were expanded to include rural electrification, national forests, naval oil reserves, and all river authority except for the Tennessee Valley Authority. Such an increased jurisdiction would require the addition of several new assistant secretaries, who would be located in the west, and make it arguably the most powerful agency in the government. From this political base, Douglas would have an easy time establishing his credentials for a future run for the White House. Corcoran was so impressed by the plan that he promised to present it to Douglas.

What Douglas and his friends did not know was that while they discussed these matters on the phone, President Truman was being made completely aware of all their deliberations. Six weeks after taking office, in June 1945 Truman had instructed his top aide and close friend, Edward McKim, to ask FBI director J. Edgar Hoover to place a wiretap on the office and home phones of Tommy Corcoran. The FBI never bothered to get court permission or even the approval of Attorney General Tom Clark. While the stated reason for this unlawful invasion of privacy was to protect national security and uncover any possible illegalities, Hoover suspected that the president just wanted to keep tabs on one of his main political adversaries. Three times per week, a special courier from the FBI would bring a "Personal and Confidential" report containing summaries and several days of annotated phone transcripts to Truman's military aide, General Harry Vaughan, who in turn would show them to the president.

Corcoran always suspected that he was under electronic phone surveillance, one day even tapping the phone repeatedly with a pencil while talking to Douglas, telling him to their mutual delight, "I'm doing my own tapping now." So he thrilled in using code names such as "Big Bob" for Robert Hannegan and "Little Bob" for Robert Jackson in spinning his conspiratorial tales on the phone with friends and journalists. He even went to the trouble of filling his pockets with nickels, for which he took a deduction on his income tax, to use at the pay phone in a Connecticut Avenue drugstore, which he used for really important calls. But sometimes more information slipped out from Corcoran than he had intended, and the Douglas team's reaction to the Interior Department offer was one of those times.

The truth, Truman learned, was that the Justice's political team was in a tizzy. All of them could see that the Interior Department position represented a chance for Douglas to become a major political player. Even Congressman Lyndon Johnson and House Speaker Sam Rayburn were pressing Douglas to take it. "I had about three or four hours last night with SAM and LYNDON and the heat is really on," Douglas complained on the phone to Corcoran on Friday, February 15. When Corcoran said that he "wanted to come down and talk to you if I could," the two men arranged to meet at a friend's cabin that Sunday afternoon. "I thought you might want to talk to him and LYNDON," Douglas pleaded, ". . . because the heat is really on."

Early that evening, Corcoran called Democratic National Committee treasurer George Killion, who had labored for Douglas in 1944, only to discover that the Justice had already called him to say that "he, Tom, and Sam should get together right away as the lid was blowing off." When asked for an update, Corcoran said "that he knew 'our boyfriend' [Douglas] had been asked to take the place that has been vacated and that is what he meant by 'the heat's on.' " Corcoran promised to arrange a breakfast meeting with Rayburn to plot strategy.

Not even three hours later, when Lyndon Johnson called for a Douglas update, Corcoran told him, "Well, I'm for you, boy. I'm going to step in and try to get this guy to say yes."

But when Corcoran added that he was having breakfast with Rayburn the next morning, Johnson got very nervous about his involvement in the plot: "Be careful now how much background you give Sam. Don't cut my head off, because if he thinks I discussed it with a human he'll cut it off. You make him tell you. . . . Tell him about Bill [Douglas] calling you . . . because he's awfully ticklish." Only when Corcoran promised to keep his services private did Johnson feel secure in ending the conversation.

After more reflection, Douglas called Clark Clifford to request that they again "go for a drive." The two men spent a great deal of time in the car discussing the future of the department and all of the political ramifications of the offer. Finally, Douglas decided that he had heard enough and, shaking his head, said, "I am gratified and flattered by the offer, but I can't do it. I have a great responsibility on the Court, and I haven't been on it too long. With the balance [of political power] that we have here [on the Court], I've got to meet that obligation." But Clifford was not about to give up, suggesting that the Justice should speak to Truman directly about it. Privately, Clifford hoped that Douglas's mind could still be changed by direct presidential pressure.

By February 17, it was Ernie Cuneo's chance to synchronize marching orders with Tommy the Cork. "I had a long talk last night with Bill and [gossip columnist] Walter [Winchell] and [journalist] Leonard [Lyons] were there and so forth," the lawyer/journalist reported to Corcoran on the phone. "He [Douglas] is being called to the White House tomorrow morning and they are going to ask him what he thinks he should do, you know, and he asked me. There is some little talk of somebody in State [Department] going to Interior [Department] you know and Bill going to State. It isn't the stakes even then, Tom. Either you get control of the machinery or you don't and the other things are just plums on the end of the branch you see."

"What did you advise him to do?" asked Corcoran.

Cuneo responded, "I just told him. I said, for Christ's sake, there is a rudimentary thing, Bill, in warfare. You don't go after territory you go after the enemy's forces you see and for Christ's sake don't shell them out of existence when you capture them. . . . [F]or Christ's sake make an effort to get the machinery and not the position. . . . Who the hell cares about the position." After a prolonged discussion over the latest public dispute between the president and Ickes, Cuneo once more tried to drill his point home: "I told Bill, I said, Bill, for Christ's sake don't take the responsibility without the command."

Despite all of this discussion, when the Justice visited the White House for lunch with the president, his mind was not completely made up. "When President Roosevelt appointed me to the Court I was at first not too happy, but after a year I had gotten to like it and it seemed to fit me and my temperament, and I had decided to make it my career for life," he told Truman. Even after making this argument, Douglas said in a half-joking and half-serious manner that he might consider leaving the Court to become secretary of state, but not for the Interior position. Seeking to change Douglas's mind, Truman said that he had been looking at the world and concluded that Alaska would one day become the crossroads for international air transportation; so he wanted the next secretary of the interior to develop the region. But even with this expanded vision, the prospect still seemed to hold little appeal for Douglas.

Not yet having discussed the matter with the Chief Justice, Douglas asked for time now to do so. After he did, Stone—who had objected to the extrajudicial jobs of Robert Jackson as the American prosecutor at the Nuremberg war-crimes trials in 1945–1946 and, three years earlier, Owen Roberts as the head of the commission inquiring into Pearl Harbor—immediately went to see the president and asked him to "please quit disturbing my court."

"You ought to let Bill make that decision," responded Truman. But Truman knew how it would turn out, telling assistant Eben A. Ayers that Stone was unwilling to lose Douglas because "he was one of the hardest workers on [the Court] and was needed there." Finally, a week later, Douglas visited the president once more, this time to say that "after talking it over with the Chief Justice he had decided to remain on the Court."

It would not be long before Douglas would have reason to regret the decision.

．　　　．　　　．

War was formally declared on the U.S. Supreme Court at 1:45 P.M. on April 22, 1946. Chief Justice Harlan Fiske Stone began mumbling so incoherently as he tried to deliver an opinion in open court that he had to be helped from the bench by his colleagues. A short time later, he fell into unconsciousness because of the effects of a cerebral hemorrhage. Stone's death five hours after that left a vacancy in the center seat of one of the most volatile and talented Courts in U.S. history. With Robert Jackson thinking that he had been promised the Chief Justiceship, Hugo Black hoping that the seat would come to him, Frank Murphy knowing that he could run the group, Felix Frankfurter expecting that he could dictate the choice, and Bill Douglas fearing all of the above, a major dispute was brewing on the Court.

Just before 8:00 P.M., Douglas phoned Tommy Corcoran with the news. "Oh Lord, does the world know that?" asked Tommy the Cork.

"You're the first one," said Douglas. "I just got a flash from his house. His secretary just called me. . . ."

"Well the lightning is striking isn't it?" said Corcoran. What he was not telling Douglas was that he had just told a mutual friend, "If there is a Chief Justiceship, [Truman] ought to make Douglas the Chief in order to make Douglas a captive for political purposes. . . . [It] would keep him out of the political arena." But since this would have destroyed Corcoran's own plans, he now had mixed feelings about this new opportunity.

"Washington adores a funeral—especially if it ushers in a vacancy," wrote Robert Jackson. Even before Harlan Fiske Stone could be interred, prominent columnists set about attempting to bury the chances for the succession of Robert Jackson, who was still serving in Germany as chief prosecutor at Nuremberg. Drew Pearson, known to have close contacts with both Douglas and Black, wrote on April 24 that two members of the Court had already told the president that they would resign if Jackson was appointed. Columnist Doris Fleeson predicted, based on her sources, that the seat would go to former Justice and now Secretary of State James F. Byrnes, with Jackson moving to the State Department.

For his part, Tommy the Cork set out to stir the pot in a way that might keep Douglas from being made chief. (Truman, of course, remained fully informed on Corcoran's moves thanks to the wiretaps.) On April 28, Corcoran told Ernie Cuneo, whom he knew was likely to spread the rumor in his capacity as president of the North American Newspaper Alliance, "What's going on down here is . . . a real struggle for the Chief Justiceship in which it's Jackson against Black, with the chances out of it will emerge Jimmy Byrnes."

"Jimmy may emerge huh?" responded Cuneo.

"[I] don't think either man [Jackson or Black] frankly, will accept the appointment of the other. I think either of them will resign and quit if the other man went in, but that isn't because of Jackson. . . . It's the old, old struggle, [Frankfurter] can't keep out of it. It's Frankfurter against Black. That's what it is. . . . And Bob Jackson is being hurt enormously by that factor." Both men expressed the hope that Black would get the job.

The next evening, Corcoran was spreading reports about various judicial delegations visiting the White House on the issue. Charles Evans Hughes had been in to see the president that day, but Corcoran did not know what message had been conveyed. Justice Reed, he said, was "pulling strong for Bill." On May 2, Owen Roberts, no fan of either Black or Douglas, visited the White House to offer his recommendation of Secretary of the Treasury Fred Vinson. After a few days of observing the fighting on the Court, Corcoran put aside his own aspirations to begin lobbying for Douglas's appointment as a compromise. Drew Pearson called on May 4 to learn the details of the appointment battle, saying, "Tom, I've been trying to check into a story on our Supreme Court to [the] effect that Bill Douglas was in [the] lead then Frankfurter threw his weight as hard as he could against him and is now leaning toward Jackson. Wonder if you've heard anything on it."

Corcoran was happy to fill him in by creating a rumor of his own. "Well, I don't know. I think that was true. I know that Truman wanted to appoint Bill and then Felix threw in behind Jackson hard, as hard as he could throw. . . . Then this is just between us the thing was settled for Jackson two days ago and then the left wing of the Court who heard about that let it be known how they felt about it. . . . Now I think it is likely to be Fred Vinson or Jimmy Byrnes." While there is no evidence that Douglas and Black had ever in fact "let it be known how they felt," and both Truman and Douglas denied it vehemently, just by asserting this fact Corcoran had given it the ring of truth.

"Is it lost for Bill?" Pearson asked Corcoran. While neither could say for sure, Tommy the Cork never gave up lobbying for him. Over the next six weeks, this issue became the subject of twenty-eight conversations by Corcoran on his phone, ten of which involved Douglas himself.

On May 16, all of this internecine warfare became public knowledge when Doris Fleeson published a column in the Washington *Star* about a "feud" between Justices Jackson and Black. Three days later, Corcoran's lieutenants were using the piece as ammunition in their lobbying for Douglas. Leo Crowley, former administrator of the office of Lend-Lease Administration, told Tommy the Cork that upon discovering that Jimmy Byrnes was "not sympathetic to . . . Black . . . I asked him to put in a plug for Bill. . . . He's very friendly to Bill now."

By May 19, Douglas told Harold Ickes in a private lunch that the president had been inclined to appoint Jackson until the blowup with Black occurred. The contest, he added, came down to him and Black, and that he had been slightly in the lead until the conservative Justices, led by Felix Frankfurter, lobbied against him. Now it appeared that the appointment would be from the outside.

Since choosing any member of this fractious Court was a recipe for disaster, Truman decided instead to reward an old friend. Fred Vinson, a former congressman and U.S. Court of Appeals judge who was both a poker buddy of the president's and now his secretary of the treasury, needed something to sustain him should the administration end in two years. So, after six weeks of deliberation, Truman asked Vinson during a lunch on June 6 whether he would like to go to the Court. "Any man who had been in the law would jump at such an offer and of course [I'd] take it if [I] had the chance," responded the visitor. Before the afternoon was out, Truman had granted his wish.

As soon as Douglas heard about the appointment, he, Sam Rayburn, and Lyndon Johnson journeyed to the treasury secretary's apartment to offer their congratulations. When they arrived, though, they were greeted by a tearful Roberta Vinson, who had learned about the appointment in her beauty parlor and now feared that the new post would prevent her husband from making enough money in private industry to support her after his death.

And as Vinson himself would soon learn, the nomination did not sit well with all of his new colleagues. Two days later, Jackson sent a cable to the president complaining that his chances for the center seat had been spoiled by Black, a man whose ethics he claimed were in question because he had refused to recuse himself from a recent case that was being argued by a former law partner. When Jackson sent a similar cable to the congressional judiciary committees, the resulting public firestorm made it very clear that even a man of Vinson's diplomatic and political skill would have trouble managing his new colleagues.

·   ·   ·

In November 1946, in the early days of the Vinson Court, William O. Douglas was given the opportunity to display his continued progovernment conservatism. First, he did so in developing his views on the free exercise of religion clause in the case of Heber Kimball Cleveland, a Fundamentalist Mormon and a practicing polygamist who had been arrested by federal authorities for transporting his wives outside of the state. The litigants in the case, who were simply observing their religious beliefs, were arrested for violating the federal Mann Act, the so-called White Slave Traffic Act, which bans the transportation of women across state lines "for the purpose of prostitution or debauchery, or for any other immoral purpose." When Douglas ignored the religious issues here to vote to sustain the conviction, he was tapped to write the majority opinion. In it, Douglas dismissed the free exercise of religion implications and had no trouble upholding the federal statute's application here: "The establishment or maintenance of polygamous households is a notorious example of promiscuity. The permanent advertisement of their existence is an example of the sharp repercussions which they have in the community." For him, this religious practice was no different from banned "debauchery" across state lines, upholding a precedent issued some thirty years earlier. And Douglas was unwilling to give any credence to the religious justification for this activity: "It is also urged that the requisite criminal intent was lacking since petitioners were motivated by a religious belief. That defense claims too much. If upheld, it would place beyond the law any act done under claim of religious sanction." In indicating both his deferential conservatism and his inability to appreciate the subtleties of the civil-liberties arguments, Douglas indicated that for him the government's interests, existing statutes, and prevailing precedents were to be upheld against an individual's religious beliefs if at all possible. Once more, it was Douglas's liberal colleague Frank Murphy who argued the clear distinction between criminal behavior and what to him was the highly religious justification for this lifestyle. For Murphy, this case "results in the imprisonment of individuals whose actions have none of the earmarks of white slavery, whatever else may be said of their conduct."

Douglas's continued lack of sensitivity toward other civil liberties in this period was evident in a treason case. Douglas had little trouble upholding the conviction of Hans Max Haupt, who was convicted of treason for providing shelter for his son, one of several German saboteurs who had landed by boat in the United States during the war. But he went even further, suggesting that the conviction should be upheld despite the fact that the constitutional requirement of proof from two witnesses to such a crime had not been met. On the other side, Frank Murphy along with Wiley Rutledge argued that the sheltering of one's own son should not be held a treasonable act without substantial proof. Years later, a much changed Justice Douglas wrote of these years: "Though [Murphy] and I did not always agree, I thought that he was a great Justice. In retrospect I realize I made more mistakes in not following him."

In the spring of 1947, Douglas began for the first time to display some hope of fulfilling on the Court the liberal promise of his New Deal background. These initial steps came in a First Amendment freedom-of-the-press case, *Craig v. Harney,* that involved a publisher, an editorial writer, and a news reporter working for newspapers in Corpus Christi, Texas, all of whom had been found in contempt by a judge for their critical treatment of his erratic handling of a property case. When the judge three times refused to accept the verdict of a properly impaneled jury, these newsmen reported that he was "high handed" and a "layman" who was not a "competent attorney." Having already faced criticism himself by the media, Douglas believed that such news stories should be allowed under the First Amendment. "A trial is a public event," wrote Douglas for a six-person majority. "What transpires in the court room is public property. . . . Those who see and hear what transpired can report it with impunity." Douglas even argued: "The vehemence of the language used is not alone the measure of the power to punish for contempt. The fires which it kindles must constitute an imminent, not merely a likely, threat to the administration of justice. The danger must not be remote or even probable; it must immediately imperil." Rather than offering a lengthy, ponderous, jargon-filled opinion, weighed down by a drawn-out history of case law or legal philosophical discussions as was commonly found in the opinions of his colleagues, Douglas now appealed to people in short, clearly written opinions presented in layman's language.

Even with this protective stretching of the old "clear and present danger" test, by which speech can be restricted only if it leads to an immediate danger, Frank Murphy still outflanked Douglas on the liberal side. Murphy argued that there must instead be an "actual impediment" to the administration of justice in order to permit judges to restrict the press. In adopting his protective legal standard, though, Douglas had shown for the first time that he was willing to consider placing his vote squarely on the side of individual rights as opposed to an autocratic judge.

A closer reading of the arguments in this case indicated that the Justices were still feeling the effects of the fallout from the battle over the Chief Justiceship. In his dissent, Robert Jackson seemed to be swinging at Douglas personally:

> With due respect to those who think otherwise, to me this is an ill-founded opinion, and to inform the press that it may be irresponsible in attacking judges because they have so much fortitude is ill-advised, or worse. . . . From our sheltered position, fortified by life tenure and other defenses to judicial independence it is easy to say that this local judge ought to have shown more fortitude in the face of criticism. . . . I am not so confident that we would be indifferent if a news monopoly in our entire jurisdiction should perpetrate this kind of attack on us.

Any time Robert Jackson showed independence from the rest of the Court, Felix Frankfurter labored hard to forge greater bonds with him for the future. Based on his personal friendship with Oliver Wendell Holmes, the inventor of the clear-and-present-danger test, Frankfurter also lashed out in his dissent at Douglas: "Is it conceivable that even the most doctrinaire libertarian would think it consonant with the impartiality which adjudication presupposes to publish a poll regarding the outcome desired by a community in a pending case?" The ever widening gulf between liberals Murphy and Rutledge and conservatives Frankfurter, Jackson, and Vinson would now be bridged by the key swing votes between them: Douglas and Black.

By the spring of 1948, perhaps not uncoincidentally with the Democratic presidential convention approaching, Douglas indicated that his views had now changed to the point that he was ready to support free exercise of religion rights. Samuel Saia was a Jehovah's Witnesses minister who had secured permission from the chief of police of Lockport, New York, to use sound equipment mounted on the top of his car to amplify his sermons on designated Sundays in a local park. When the permit was not renewed because of the townspeople's complaints, and Saia continued to speak, using his amplifier, he was arrested and convicted for violating a public sound ordinance. He argued that this decision violated his freedoms of religion, speech, and assembly. Writing for the five-person majority, Douglas had little trouble disposing of the vaguely implemented statute. Though the ordinance "was dressed in the garb of the control of a 'nuisance,'" he argued, by leaving the issuance of the permits up to the chief of police it gave that official "uncontrolled discretion" to limit speech. Thus, "he stands athwart the channels of communication as an obstruction which can be removed only after criminal trial and conviction and lengthy appeal. A more effective restraint of speech is difficult to imagine."

While a younger Justice Douglas might have offered some circumstances—say a repeated, amplified offering of abusive language—to justify the government's regulation, now his position was that "the power of censorship inherent in this type of ordinance reveals its vice. Courts must balance the various community interests in passing on the constitutionality of local regulations of the character involved here. But in that process they should be mindful to keep the freedoms of the First Amendment in a preferred position."

The more absolutist Douglas became in protecting religion, the more vigorously his former New Deal colleagues—Robert Jackson and Felix Frankfurter—protested. In a dissent that evidenced no pretense of traditional judicial courtesy, Jackson argued that Douglas's opinion was "neither judicious nor sound" in making free speech "ridiculous and obnoxious" and thus to him represented "a startling perversion of the Constitution."

Despite these criticisms, time and again in these years Douglas was signaling that he was slowly moving in a new philosophical direction. And with Wiley Rutledge, Frank Murphy, and Hugo Black now congratulating him for moving to the left by frequently joining his opinions, the liberal bloc of four jurists appeared to be ready in mid-1948 to work together in changing American jurisprudence.

21

SECOND CHANCE

> I never was a-runnin'.
> I ain't a-runnin' and I
> ain't goin' tuh.
>
> —*William O. Douglas*

While the Court labored on, in early 1948 Bill Douglas had decided that it was now indeed time to leave. The world was moving too fast, there were too many issues that would not reach him on the Court for several years, if at all, the personal animosities on the Court were wearing on him, and the truth was that he was just plain bored as a Justice. Seeking to develop some employment options, Douglas began asking various associates in the private legal community—among them his Columbia Law School classmate Simon Rifkind and Abe Fortas—whether they would join him in creating a law firm if he resigned from the Court. But by now these old friends knew better than to take his inquiry seriously.

Knowing that private legal practice was the last place that Douglas truly wanted to be, Tommy Corcoran went into high gear campaigning for his man to secure the presidential nomination in place of Truman. Seeking to get the south behind Douglas, Tommy the Cork worked on two old friends, Sam Rayburn and Alabama senator Lister Hill, reminding them of past political favors and asking for their help now. In time, Hill issued a public statement that if Dwight Eisenhower was not willing to run on the Democratic ticket, he would back William O. Douglas. It was not long before Corcoran's efforts with many members of the Cabinet and the Democratic administration, as well as various labor leaders, had the same effect. In time, Corcoran tried to enlist on his side the same political bosses who had done his candidate in during the 1944 campaign. Pretty soon, all of the tumblers seemed to fall into place.

"To err is Truman" had by this time become the watchword among critical Democrats and Republicans alike. And enough former New Deal liberals were distressed about the direction of the Truman administration to begin using the newly formed Americans for Democratic Action (ADA) to do something about it. Only two years in existence, this group of twenty to twenty-five thousand members, many of them old New Dealers, including both Eleanor Roosevelt and Franklin D. Roosevelt, Jr., wanted to make two thrusts: They wanted to establish their position as the rightful heirs of the New Deal and to shape the political landscape to match it.

By the time the ADA held a convention in Philadelphia in February 1948, the hostility toward Truman from the left, because of his perceived divergence from FDR's New Deal as well as the charges of cronyism in his appointments, had grown to such a point that they were contemplating a complete break from the administration. For weeks prior to the meeting, the organization had heaped abuse on the president in one critical resolution after another, but no one yet dared to propose that a sitting president from their own party be replaced.

It took Franklin D. Roosevelt, Jr.'s expression of opposition to the administration to break the dam holding back the flood. Leon Henderson, then chairman of the ADA, and a longtime political ally of both Tommy Corcoran and William O. Douglas, began demanding that an open Democratic convention be held, in which any candidate could be nominated. But who should become the party's candidate in such an event? asked the press. Well, General Eisenhower would be fine, Henderson said, or perhaps William O. Douglas. With each of the local chapters of the ADA now clamoring for a national board meeting to discuss the organization's position, Henderson and Franklin D. Roosevelt, Jr., both began touting Eisenhower for the Democratic nomination because his hero status in post–World War II America made him extremely electable.

The board meeting of chapter representatives was finally held in April in Pittsburgh, with everyone fully expecting that action would be taken against Truman. Trying to stem the negative tide was Washington attorney Paul Porter, the vice chairman of the organization, with close ties to the White House. He called up Joseph L. Rauh, another Washington attorney who was then chairman of the ADA's executive committee and said, "Joe, I have a message for you from the president of the United States."

"Well, what is it?" responded Rauh.

"He says to tell you that any shithead behind this desk can get renominated, so you guys are crazy."

If Porter thought that this message would intimidate the liberals, he was wrong. The board meeting that followed was, according to Rauh, "a madhouse . . . with everyone clamoring for recognition." Porter desperately tried to defend Truman's policies, while the rest of the liberals in attendance were instead arguing over who would be the better nominee, Eisenhower or Douglas. Most of those present were for Douglas just on the issues, but the feeling was that he didn't have the kind of voter support that Eisenhower could command. *Douglas is the only true liberal,* someone said. To which another shouted, *But he won't leave the Supreme Court. Eisenhower can get elected easily,* argued several of the general's backers. *What makes you think that Eisenhower is even a Democrat?* came a call from across the room.

Finally, as the clamor grew and the group began to fragment, labor leader Walter Reuther gained the floor and delivered a major address on the Justice's behalf. It was a magnificent speech, everyone agreed. And well it should have been, Joseph Rauh knew, since he, Reuther, and several other ADA leaders had spent many hours over the past month drafting this address side by side with Douglas himself. "There is not the slightest doubt in my mind that Douglas wanted to be president," recalled Rauh, years later.

With his philosophical foundation now laid, Rauh rose and proposed a compromise that he said could bring all of the liberals in the room together. Just as Robert Walker Kenny was prepared to do in the 1944 Democratic convention, Rauh was now reading from a script which Douglas himself had written, edited, and approved. "Since no one knows whether either Eisenhower or Douglas is willing to run," he argued, "why quibble over the details just now? Why not draft a resolution that makes it possible for everyone to join hands under the same tent? Since we all agree that Douglas has impeccable liberal credentials and Eisenhower has an impeccable public standing, why not get the best of both worlds, and endorse them both?" The problem, Rauh knew, would be how to leave open the question of which man would be on top of the ticket if they both consented. So Rauh's and Douglas's resolution language left that issue for a later time in stating: "The A.D.A. feels that an open Democratic convention will serve the best interests of the country. At this stage of world crisis, the American people must have a free choice of the best leadership the country can produce. No person qualified for democratic leadership can enjoy the privilege of declaring himself unavailable in this hour of the Nation's need. We feel strongly that this Nation has a right to call upon men like Dwight D. Eisenhower and William O. Douglas if the people so choose." Recalled Rauh of the reaction: "No one quite knew what this meant, but they liked it." Minutes later, the wording was adopted unanimously.

The Eisenhower and/or Douglas draft was on. In a matter of days, a nickel-sized red, white, and blue campaign button appeared, reading "Draft Eisenhower/Douglas/A.D.A." Soon thereafter, red, white, and blue lithographed buttons appeared reading "Justice DOUGLAS for President," "Wm. O. Douglas for President," and "We Want DOUGLAS for President."

The ADA also produced and distributed a twenty-three-page pamphlet entitled "William O. Douglas: The Man, His Life, His Views." Using as its basis pieces of the Douglas legend that had appeared in the popular press, the pamphlet argued:

> Those who know Washington know Douglas. They know the role he has played in national affairs since 1936. In the scarcely New Dealish pages of the *Saturday Evening Post,* back in 1942, Douglas was acclaimed as "one of the most brilliant minds enlisted by the New Deal, and perhaps the most deadly and efficient administrator it has produced." He possesses a genius for accurate diagnosis, an unerring instinct for feeling out the adversary's soft spot, and a natural sense for timing the payoff punch. He is an excellent justice and a contented one, but some observers feel that at least half of his talents are lying idle. His political attractiveness has been heightened by a distaste for the pushing tactics which other men of his age have exhibited in reaching for the juicier gifts of the voters.

After offering selections from a litany of his liberal judicial opinions and speeches, the pamphlet concluded by reminding people: "William O. Douglas is a tested liberal who stood shoulder to shoulder with Franklin D. Roosevelt in the forging of the New Deal. His concept of a democratic foreign policy has been clearly stated. Under his leadership we could expect the cause of liberty and economic justice to be secure in America and to be championed throughout the world."

The only problem for the ADA was that, at least publicly, neither of their candidates wanted any part of this effort. Over and over Eisenhower said that he was not interested in any nomination, let alone the Democratic one, and Douglas refused to commit himself.

On top of that, Truman had no intention of leaving the White House. So speculation began that, with the current vacancy in the vice presidency, Douglas would be offered the position, thus balancing the electoral ticket with a liberal New Dealer. Tommy Corcoran heard this rumor and told Douglas simply, "Bill, you don't want to play second fiddle to a second fiddle." Douglas liked the phrase so much he began repeating it around town to people such as former senator Burton K. Wheeler, who was once one of his enemies but by now had become a friend.

As so often happens in Washington, after being repeated so many times the comment came to the attention of certain members of the press. So Jack Beale of *Time* phoned Tommy Corcoran, explaining that he wanted to write "a very readable little light story about this theory that you're master-minding this thing, and I'd like to quote you on what you said."

Skilled in the art of dodging the press, Corcoran laughed and responded, "I'm sorry, for Douglas's sake as well as my own—I don't want to be quoted. I don't want to involve him in any of this sort of publicity."

After fencing for a bit about whether this conversation was on or off the record, Beale pressed: "Well, tell me. Is it correct? . . . There's something I heard elsewhere to the effect that when Douglas was approached about being Vice President, he said, 'I don't want to play second fiddle to a second fiddle.' "

"No. Yeah, I've heard that quotation too, and I'll tell you where I got it from," responded Corcoran. "I got that from Wheeler, who quoted Douglas to me as saying that. But I don't— But I asked Douglas flatly whether that was true, and he said, 'No.' He said, 'I wouldn't say anything that undignified or that indiscreet.' " In deciding not to write the story, the reporter could not have known that Corcoran was now covering his *own* tracks.

When Tommy the Cork hung up the phone, thinking that he had dodged a public-relations fiasco, he did not realize that in fact he had created another one, for still listening in on his phone conversations was a team of FBI agents. Within days, the transcript was sent to the White House for the president's reading pleasure. While Corcoran went on phoning and meeting delegates and moneymen on behalf of Douglas, and while Harold Ickes did his part by writing favorable columns, the president made his plans with full knowledge of their view of him and Douglas's political intentions.

Douglas got the chance to make his own political statement when Eleanor Roosevelt asked him to deliver two Memorial Day speeches at her husband's grave site in Hyde Park, New York. The Justice took the opportunity to allude to connections between his own work and that of the great president:

The men and women who come here will recapture for a moment the precious sense of belonging that Roosevelt gave them. The sense of belonging is important to man. The feeling that he is accepted and a part of the community or the nation is as important as the feeling that he is a member of a family. He does not belong, if he has a second-class citizenship. When he feels he does not belong, he is not eager to assume responsibilities of citizenship. Being unanchored, he is easy prey to divisive influences that are designed to tear a nation apart or to woo it to a foreign ideology.

Close observers viewed these speeches as the opening of Douglas's political campaign for the White House. Taking this as a sign that Douglas was ready to leave the Court, Tommy Corcoran went to Harold Ickes's home and for his future writing reminded him of the Douglas public legend—poor childhood in Yakima, son of a minister, former schoolteacher, great lawyer, great law-school teacher, married to a schoolteacher—and "the Curmudgeon," as Ickes was now known, was duly impressed. But Corcoran held back one item that he alone knew, outside of Douglas's family. Through Mildred Douglas, he had learned that she and her husband were barely communicating, and only the children seemed to be holding the marriage together.

Seemingly oblivious to the information leaking out of his camp, Douglas resumed playing his now familiar role of reluctant candidate. Calling up an old friend, *St. Louis Post-Dispatch* reporter Irving Dilliard, Douglas gave permission to release to the public yet another of his political disavowal letters. Later, when a group of supporters from the western states visited him in the Supreme Court to volunteer to back him and line up more delegates at the convention, all Douglas did was look out the window in stony silence.

On July 9, Eisenhower left no doubt as to his political intentions, issuing an unequivocal William Sherman–style withdrawal from the race, saying that he was not running for office and would not serve even if he was elected. This did not deter Leon Henderson, who said that the ADA was prepared to throw all of its support behind Douglas, if he was available. Upon hearing that, the press searched out the Justice for his response. But when they caught up with Douglas, he sent out mixed signals. *Did he plan to be a candidate?* the Justice was asked. *Not at this time. Would he accept a draft?* came the follow-up. "I have no comment at this time," he replied. The press and his supporters took this answer from the normally loquacious jurist to be a qualified yes.

By July, Harry Truman had come to believe that, given his diminishing liberal support, he had no other choice but to choose an avowed New Dealer for the ticket. Without a liberal running mate, he might not have any chance to win. His likely opponent, Thomas Dewey, would take all of the Republicans, the conservative southern Democrats could not be counted on for help because of the party's civil-rights position, and the rank-and-file New Deal Democrats had concluded that Truman was no Roosevelt. In order to win, the president now had to reenergize the same powerful liberal coalition that had elected Roosevelt four times. And, Truman was being told by everyone around him, only William O. Douglas could deliver the needed liberal voters to his column.

The party bosses who had once opposed Douglas were now desperate to have him on the ticket. But Douglas was giving them no satisfaction. Assistant Secretary of the Treasury Ed Foley barged into Corcoran's office and accused him of preventing Douglas from considering the vice presidency. No, answered Corcoran, you know that Douglas does what he wants to do. And besides, he had left for the Wallowa Mountains and wasn't in touch with anyone. But, the attorney added, if Douglas does ask me I will tell him what I have told him all along—that he should not run with Truman on any ticket. To do so, he said, would be a mistake.

Foley, who had worked with Bob Hannegan and the party bosses to prevent Douglas from getting the vice presidency four years before, didn't know that he had been duped. Corcoran actually knew that Douglas was just a phone call away, but for now he kept the number that the Justice had left with him safely in his pocket. Unlike four years before, Corcoran detected from Foley's visit that they were now dealing from a position of strength.

.　　.　　.

The answer came shortly. In the week before the Democratic convention in Philadelphia in mid-July, the president called his old ally Bob Hannegan and asked him to offer the Justice the second spot on the ticket. The choice of emissary here was an interesting one. If the president thought that Hannegan and Douglas had some special bond, or that Hannegan had some special persuasive powers, he was sadly mistaken. By picking the man who had personally short-circuited Douglas's chance for the vice presidency in 1944, the president had ensured that his entreaty would receive a short hearing.

Hannegan decided to approach Douglas first through his political lieutenants. "Hannegan was all over me to get Douglas on the ticket," Eliot Janeway remembered. "He worked two ways, through me and through Abe Fortas to try to get us to pressure Douglas into taking the post. He used us both to make sure with the overlapping effort that the message would get through."

But the Douglas camp had a different agenda. All of them vividly remembered the past and, even more important, they were now worried that the Justice would be sacrificing his political career by running with Truman. Four years before, Douglas and his allies had needed Busyman Bob, and where had he been then? Now he needed them, to make himself look like the big political operator with the president, and they all wanted to pay him back.

When Janeway reached Douglas by phone and told him the news, the Justice started laughing. "How do you think we can string this one out?" he said. "I'd take the job only if they could guarantee me that the ticket would lose." The game, he explained, would be to have Truman out of the way, not have to serve as his second in command, and position himself as the future standard-bearer for the Democratic party.

"Exactly," said Janeway.

"The problem is," Douglas continued, "you and I both know [Republican nominee] Tom [Dewey]. He'll screw it up, and Truman will win."

With that in hand, Janeway reported back that Douglas had no interest in the position and preferred to serve the nation with distinction from his position on the Supreme Court.

When Hannegan revealed his lack of success to the president, rather than search for a new running mate Truman decided to change intermediaries. Maybe Douglas could still be persuaded to join the ticket if he were approached directly by Clark Clifford, who had no connection to the events of 1944. During several conversations in the Oval Office, Clifford could see just how desperate his boss was to get Douglas on the ticket. Truman had lost the ADA, was losing the south, and his Missouri homespun wisdom was not playing very well with the poor and the immigrants in the cities either. As the two men reviewed all of the possible running mates who might correct this slide, Douglas's name continued to head the list. Truman asked his aide to call Douglas. Make sure, the president added, that Douglas understands that I need his help and that I am certain I can win the election. Clifford suspected that the latter part was not true, but as a skilled advocate he thought that he might be able to persuade Douglas otherwise.

Getting in touch with Douglas at that time was no easy matter. By then, he was in fact vacationing with his family at their cabin deep in Oregon's Wallowa Mountains. The only outside telephone line in the area came into Huckleberry Look-Out, the forest-ranger station west of the cabin. To reach Douglas, the call would then have to be rerouted to a neighbor's cabin, where there was an old-fashioned crank phone. Finally, someone would have to be dispatched to find the Justice and bring him to the neighbor's house. Through it all, everyone would have to pray that the connection would hold up long enough for a crackly conversation.

When Clifford finally mastered the communications logistics and reached Douglas to extend his offer, the Justice acted completely surprised, even though his operatives had long before warned him that it was coming. The president had thought it over very carefully, Clifford began, and gotten a great deal of advice, and everyone believed that Douglas was the best man to serve the nation in the capacity of vice president. Douglas responded that he was honored and flattered, but since it required that he leave the Supreme Court, this was a very important decision. He asked for a little time to think it over. Fine, Clifford responded, but with the convention upon them, the president will need your answer in three days. But Douglas already knew how he would likely respond, for he had been waiting for this chance for the last four years.

Despite Douglas's casual air on the phone, Clifford sensed where his friend would end up. And he knew the president would not like it.

"How did he sound about it?" Truman asked.

"Dubious," said the attorney. The more the two men discussed it, the more they came to the conclusion that Douglas would refuse. That option was unacceptable for Harry Truman. "Well, he respects Mrs. Roosevelt," the president told Clifford, "so why don't you call her and ask if she will try and persuade Douglas to take the offer." When Clifford put the request to her, she responded that she would be happy to make the effort. Douglas, she added, would make a splendid running mate for Truman. But the pitch worked no better for FDR's widow than it did for Truman's assistant.

Desperate, Truman decided to call Douglas himself. As soon as Tommy Corcoran got word from his administration spies that the president would be calling Douglas personally, he became worried. Having been warned by Harold Ickes that Douglas seemed in a recent conversation with him to be leaning a bit toward taking the job, Corcoran flew cross-country to talk him out of it. The ticket would lose, he was certain, and Douglas would become the scapegoat in what would be seen as the biggest mistake of his political career.

"Don't be a number two man to a number two man," Corcoran reminded his friend when they finally met. Since Douglas had nodded in agreement, Corcoran returned home thinking that he had accomplished his mission.

Now caught between the president and his top political ally, Douglas did the only thing he could think of: He drove to Yakima and hid. "I remember sitting in my office at the old [Yakima] Herald-Republic building back in 1948," recalled Robert Lucas, former editor of the newspaper, "and who should walk through the door and sit down but Justice Douglas. I asked him what the hell he was doing out here, and he told me he was trying to stay away from the phone. He said Harry Truman wanted him on the ticket with him as vice president, and he was trying to avoid the call. He said he didn't want to be on the ticket with Truman."

When Douglas finally had to give his answer, he chose to call one of the men who had extended the offer. "I just can't do it," Douglas told Clark Clifford by phone. "My work on the Court is just too important. I've talked it over with my family and several close friends, and they are all in agreement that I should not leave the Court just now. This is the place that I can render the greatest service." When Clifford relayed the message to the president, both of them suspected that this was the end of the matter. But neither man realized the real reason for Douglas's refusal.

The truth was that he had not yet given up on his chances for getting Truman's job. As the convention approached, Bill Douglas had been egging on Walter Reuther, Joseph L. Rauh, and Leon Henderson to keep his name afloat in the hopes that Truman's political support for the nomination would evaporate. Word of Douglas's continued interest in the presidency reached the press as the weekend before the July 12 opening of the convention approached. An enterprising reporter for *The Philadelphia Inquirer* located Douglas, who by this time had returned to the Wallowas, but when he put the rumor to him the Justice said firmly: "I am not a candidate, have never been a candidate and I don't plan to be a candidate."

"Would you accept the nomination if drafted?" pressed the reporter.

"I have no comment at this time," responded Douglas.

It was all that the liberals in Philadelphia needed to hear. Tan paper fans with Douglas's picture on them were printed for the hot convention, reading, "I'm a DOUGLAS Fan!!!" West Coast–based publicist Jimmy Allen tried to keep the boomlet going by generating stories of Truman's political weakness among the liberals and Douglas's growing support in that quarter. But without the electoral drawing power of Eisenhower, a Douglas ticket had limited appeal among the general public. "I think the only thing that caught fire was Eisenhower. . . . Douglas was sort of the tail of that kite," recalled Joe Rauh, years later.

"It was the only way to make the thing fly, because we were really trying to get rid of Truman. . . . But without Eisenhower there wasn't enough strength." Realizing this, the ADA leaders urged Douglas to make an unequivocal statement that he was either in or out of the race, like Eisenhower had done, in order to prevent the embarrassment of appearing to have been passed over. But Douglas was unwilling to do it.

Meanwhile, back at the White House, with all of his advisers still telling Truman that his political life depended on the Justice's help, the president decided to place his call to Douglas. The pitch Truman intended to make was a good one, saying to Douglas, "I'm doing what FDR did to me. [You owe] it to the country to accept." In doing so, the president knew, he would be putting himself in the embarrassing position of being refused to his face.

By the time the president's call from the White House was placed through Huckleberry Look-Out to the neighbor's cabin, quite a crowd of locals had gathered, clucking about what a president had to do to reach Douglas in these mountains. One of those gathered by the phone was his daughter, Millie, who recalled the moment well: "The president asked Dad to run for vice president, and Dad said no, right then and there." But Truman didn't stop talking, and in a few minutes he had managed to turn the no into a "well, I'll think about it." So it was left that Douglas would think it over for the next forty-eight hours, but an answer had to be given by then, for the convention would be beginning.

But the president could not wait for an answer, as he called a second time, and it seemed to the Justice as though he was now "begging" him to take the position. After saying that he could not give a definitive answer while pleading for more time to think it over, Douglas hung up the phone and told his daughter, "I'm not going to do it."

"Why not?" Millie Douglas asked.

"Because," he said, laughing, "they don't pay me enough money." Later, Millie would explain that she understood this to mean that "his standard of living had increased, his bills had increased, and he just didn't think he could do it." While this may have been true, he also was not willing to risk giving up his tenured position.

Beyond that, Millie saw that her father's personal life was a factor as her parents continued drifting apart. "Dad had to have . . . excitement and something adventurous happening," explained Millie. "Probably even Washington became too conservative for him from that point of view." But her mother was not like that at all and would never change from who she had been in New Haven. "Mother let the world come to her. . . . She just kind of did her own thing," said her daughter. "She didn't try to become like lots of the other women did in Washington—politically minded [and] politically oriented. She just tried to keep her political thoughts to herself and was the perfect lady, you know. Trying to encourage him and help him by supporting him. And that's what she felt her role was. . . . Some people think she was a shy little mouse of a woman, but she only accepted [life] on her terms."

With both of them on such divergent paths, by the summer of 1948 their marriage existed in name only. Millie and Bill Jr. knew that divorce was in the offing, but "they were waiting for us to get through school." In stringing Truman along, she reasoned, perhaps Douglas was also peering into his own marital future: "You know, in those days, the question of a divorced president or a divorced vice president had never arisen." But, she added, the declination may have been simpler than that. "I think he felt if he was going to be something, he would rather be president than just a vice president, or stay where he was. But it would have to be offered on his terms."

When the president called a third time on Saturday night, all the Justice would say was that he would call with an answer the next day from Portland, where he would be visiting on business. But when Douglas did call the next day from the Benson Hotel, he asked for twenty-four more hours to make a final decision. This time, though, Douglas gave Truman hope for success by saying, "I would like to do it, though I had made up my mind, as I said two years ago, to remain on the Supreme Court."

While he debated the issue, Douglas's friends weighed in with their advice. Tommy Corcoran urged Harold Ickes to bolster the Justice's resolve to stay off the ticket. When the two men connected on Sunday afternoon, July 11, Douglas confessed that he was indeed having serious second thoughts about staying out of the race. I "just cannot bear the thought of Dewey winning," he told Ickes. Doubtless part of Douglas's concern was that a victory would make Dewey the unquestioned success story of the Columbia Law School class of '25.

Seeing clearly that the political bug had bitten Douglas hard, Ickes played his two trump cards. First there was Douglas's insecurity about finances. What if you run, Dewey wins anyway, and you're out of a job? he argued.

True enough, Douglas responded, but Truman had just called him for the third time and was "put[ting] a lot of urging" into these calls.

Then there was Douglas's thin skin. Did he really want to help Truman? Ickes asked. Weren't these the same men who had cheated him out of his rightful spot on the ticket four years before? With that, Douglas got the message, telling Ickes that he thought now he would not run on the ticket.

But no career decision was ever final for Bill Douglas. He decided that what he needed was a financial fallback position, should he run and the ticket be defeated. Perhaps his old friend Joe Kennedy could help. Hadn't he been in sympathy with the Douglas forces four years before? Since that time, hadn't they become so close that occasionally he had been invited to vacation at Kennedy's home in Palm Beach, Florida? Yes, Douglas decided, maybe Joe Kennedy would be willing to make a White House run financially possible.

So while Truman and his men were pressing for an answer, Douglas phoned the Wall Street financier and laid out his situation, concluding by saying that he was now inclined to run with Truman. Kennedy's answer was a simple one: "If you ran for vice-president, and got licked, as you will, who will provide for your wife and children?" Douglas was devastated. He thought Kennedy would understand what he was asking. But apparently Kennedy's political agenda had changed dramatically. So the tycoon acted to keep Douglas off the ticket, thus seemingly ensuring its loss. While the choice for Douglas now seemed clear—remain where he was—Douglas still hoped for good news from the ADA convention.

But good news did not come for him, as on that same Sunday before the convention, the ADA liberals voted to endorse Truman. Joe Rauh and Leon Henderson went back to their suite and placed a call to Douglas in the Wallowas to let him know about the vote before the news reports reached him. To these old political pros it was a routine call; they knew all along that the chances of unseating an incumbent president were extremely slim. But, reminiscent of the call to Walla Walla four years before, the Justice who had been avoiding all other calls from the east now appeared to be anxious to take this one. *We've had to endorse Truman,* Henderson said, with Rauh on an extension line. *If you have anything you want to say to the press you'd better do it now.* The long silence that came from the other end of the line made it clear to both men that Douglas was very reluctant to get out of the race.

"Isn't there something else that can be done?" he responded. "Can't labor help us?"

But Henderson and Rauh made him understand that it was just too late. The fight was over. So, on Monday, July 12, Douglas picked up the phone in his hotel room and called Truman. "I am very sorry, but I have decided not to get into politics," he said, adding, "I do not think I should use the Court as a stepping stone."

All that an embittered Truman could say in response was, "I am disappointed. That's too bad."

Then Douglas gathered the press at the Benson Hotel lobby, took a typed statement from his suit-coat pocket, and read:

> Four years ago, at the time of the Democratic Convention, when President Roosevelt found me, among others, acceptable as his running mate, I said that I was not a candidate for public office.
>
> I thought then, as I think now, that no person while a member of the Supreme Court should seek political preferment. And so in this year of 1948, I likewise have not been a candidate, and am not now a candidate for any public office.

What the press did not know, though, was that once more it was money and security, not to mention a bit of political payback toward Truman, that dictated his decision to remain on the Court.

For Harry Truman, this was a very, very personal rebuke. "I stuck my neck all the way out for Douglas and he cut the limb out from under me," the president told his staff. In a private memo, Truman complained: "[Douglas] belongs to that crowd of Tommy Corcoran, Harold Ickes, Claude Pepper crackpots whose word is worth less than [ADA leader] Jimmy Roosevelt's. . . . No professional liberal is intellectually honest." By the time he reviewed these events in his private diary, Truman had reflected on the FBI wiretap transcripts he had seen: "I'm inclined to give some credence to Tommy Corcoran's crack to Burt Wheeler that Douglas had said he could [not] be a number two man to a number two man."

Two weeks later, Douglas tried to mend fences with the president, writing that he would have enjoyed "stand[ing] shoulder to shoulder with you in the fray." The letter sounded a lot like one he had written sixteen years earlier to Robert Maynard Hutchins to explain why he finally wasn't coming to teach at the University of Chicago Law School. And Truman's response sounded no more comprehending than Hutchins: "I was very sorry that you couldn't go along on the Vice-Presidency. Senator [Alben] Barkley, however, will make a good campaign, I am sure."

When the story began circulating around Washington, spread in large part by Douglas's lieutenants, about how he had strung the president along, the Justice immediately called the White House to deny it. "Unfair and vicious reports were circulated that I kept you, Mr. President, dangling for an answer," Douglas told Truman by phone. "That was not true. I had a devil of a decision to make. All my sentimental intentions were to do it. My only reason for refusing was my desire to stay on the Court, as I had decided at the time when you asked me to join your Cabinet as Secretary of the Interior."

Neither man believed it, but Douglas did not care. "Truman isn't going to win anyway," he told Eliot Janeway. "And even if he does, by 1952 anyone will be able to beat him. Maybe I'll make a run then." It was the kind of plan that a nearly forty-nine-year-old man could still make.

TROUBLE IN THE MOUNTAINS

You make your own happiness, but Bill made his own unhappiness in his private life.

—*Kay Kershaw*

With Harry Truman's unexpected victory in 1948, Bill Douglas's surprised political lieutenants set their sights on securing a prominent post for the Justice in the new administration. As gossip began to focus on which Cabinet members would be replaced, Douglas settled on where he wanted to end up. With George C. Marshall retiring as secretary of state, Douglas told Tommy Corcoran that he was "willing to go after" the position. Believing that he "was on good terms again with President," Douglas was looking to his allies to help him get the offer. Corcoran suggested to Ickes, who was about to interview the president for an article he was writing, that he raise Douglas's name during his meeting by mentioning the Justice's support from the teachers' unions. Corcoran's hope was that Truman would see the political value in offering Douglas the secretary of state vacancy, thus perhaps signaling his own concern for education worldwide.

So, in the course of a very pleasant interview, Ickes turned the discussion toward the topic of federal aid to public schools and suggested: "Bill Douglas is useful to you because of his close connection with the teachers. He used to be a teacher himself and he is regarded more or less as a symbol." The mood of the conversation changed instantly as Truman responded sharply, "I used to like Bill Douglas, but I am through with him. I offered to make him Secretary of the Interior when you left."

"I know that," said Ickes, "and I advised him to take it."

Then the president continued, "I called him from Philadelphia to ask him to run for the Vice President. But he was afraid that I was not going to win and he declined to run. In politics a man has to take some chances and he would not take any."

It was clear to Ickes that Truman was not going to offer Douglas any administration position. And when the president picked Dean Acheson to become secretary of state, Douglas knew that his fate once more lay with the Supreme Court.

·   ·   ·

The long-simmering behind-the-scenes feud among the members of the Vinson Court erupted into open conflict on May 16, 1949, with the announcement of the decision in a major free-speech case called *Terminiello v. Chicago*. Arthur Terminiello, a defrocked Catholic priest, had been convicted of disorderly conduct because of a speech he gave to the Christian Veterans of America in a Chicago auditorium. With more than eight hundred people in attendance and another thousand outside the hall protesting the occasion, Terminiello had called people of Jewish faith "scums," referred to Eleanor Roosevelt as "one of the world's Communists," and declared that Generalissimo Francisco Franco of Spain was "the savior of what was left of Europe." While there was only minimal hostility to the speech from those inside the hall, the "angry and turbulent crowd" outside threw stones, ice picks, and bottles through the windows and the doors of the hall. When a phalanx of policemen found themselves unable to keep this incident from getting out of control, Terminiello was arrested and later convicted for breach of the peace. This in turn led to an appeal alleging that this conviction violated his First Amendment right of free speech.

After Douglas's announcement in the Court's conference on February 5, 1949, that he was prepared to affirm the conviction, making him the fifth and thus the swing vote in the decision, Chief Justice Vinson assigned him the opinion, seeking to keep him in the majority. However, when he realized that he was voting this time with Frankfurter, Jackson, and the conservatives rather than with the group including his liberal allies (Black, Murphy, and Rutledge), Douglas changed his vote, shifting the majority against the conviction. As was the Court's practice, with the Chief Justice now in dissent the senior Justice in the majority, Hugo Black, had the power to assign the opinion. This he did—to Douglas. Now charged with reversing his earlier direction, the matter for Douglas became one of deciding whether the defendant *might* have been convicted for exercising constitutionally protected speech. The trial record showed that the judge had instructed the jury that behavior represents "a breach of the peace if it stirs the public to anger, invites dispute, brings about a condition of unrest, or creates a disturbance, or it molests the inhabitants in the enjoyment of peace and quiet by arousing alarm." By this construction, asking whether there had been merely "unrest" rather than immediate injury to the state, as First Amendment law required, it appeared to some that the judge was telling the jury to convict Terminiello for the exercise of protected speech.

For those who sought to protect freedom of speech because it was in a "preferred position"—as did Douglas, Black, Rutledge, and Murphy, along with Stanley Reed in this case—overturning this conviction on the basis of the unconstitutionality of the statute was now easy. As Douglas argued: "A function of free speech under our system of government is to invite dispute. It may indeed best serve its high purpose when it induces a condition of unrest, creates dissatisfaction with conditions as they are, or even stirs people to anger. Speech is often provocative and challenging. . . . There is no room under our Constitution for a more restrictive view. For the alternative would lead to standardization of ideas either by legislatures, courts, or dominant political or community groups." Terminiello had certainly invited dispute, but had he gone beyond the bounds of protected speech? Douglas made very clear that he was not even reaching that issue. Instead, he argued that the law should be overturned because, "as construed by the trial court, . . . it permitted conviction of petitioner if his speech stirred people to anger, invited public dispute, or brought about a condition of unrest."

In a long and bitter dissent that showed the psychological effects of his searing experience as the chief prosecutor at Nuremberg, Robert Jackson accused Douglas of creating a threat to democracy, as this speech "was the local manifestation of a world-wide and standing conflict between two organized groups of revolutionary fanatics [fascists and communists], each of which has imported to this country the strong-arm techniques developed in the struggle by which their kind has devastated Europe." For Jackson, the results of Douglas's ruling were apparent: "This Court has gone too far toward accepting the doctrine that civil liberty means the removal of all restraints from these crowds and that all local attempts to maintain order are impairments of the liberty of the citizen. The choice is not between order and liberty. It is between liberty with order and anarchy without either. There is danger that, if the Court does not temper its doctrinaire logic with a little practical wisdom, it will convert the constitutional Bill of Rights into a suicide pact." The battle between the activist liberals—Black, Douglas, Murphy, and Rutledge—and the self-restraint conservatives—Frankfurter and Jackson—was now fully joined.

.   .   .

After the contentious Court term that he had just endured, Douglas would normally be in desperate need of a trip west. But none of that bothered Douglas in the summer of 1949. After several years of increasing marital distance from Mildred, he had fallen in love with a gorgeous, blond socialite from near Washington, D.C., who was both two decades his junior and married to a journalist. ("She was the most beautiful woman I've ever seen," recalled mutual friend Isabelle Lynn, who saw the affair firsthand, "and Bill was really in love with her.") So he devoted his summer to pursuing her.

The courtship had actually begun the year before. Douglas had told her that he was writing a nature book on the Pacific Northwest and asked her to come along in June 1948 on a research trip to the place where he had hiked as a teenager in the northern Cascades, in Goose Prairie, Washington.

Goose Prairie had experienced a virtual population explosion from the three people that Douglas had met there as a young man—the town prospector and founder, "Uncle" Tom Fife; Jack Nelson, the superintendent for the federal irrigation reservoir at Bumping Lake; and Nelson's devoted wife, Kitty—to nearly a dozen. The first wave of new residents consisted of Yakima barber Ira Ford and his family. Ford had moved to the region in 1927 for the fresh air that his doctor said would ease his pain while waiting for his inevitable death within six months. As Ford put it in an interview nearly sixty-five years later, "that was over 8 doctors ago."

By the 1940s the population grew again with the arrival of Albert and Claudine Botsford, who owned the small general store, Ed and "Zeddy" Bedford, and two recent arrivals, Kay Kershaw and her partner, Pat Kane. Kershaw was a special breed of adventurous person even for this region. She flew the old biplanes that were used to deliver mail and had even been a wing walker in local air shows. She quit, however, on a windy day when her partner ignored her warning to wear a parachute and fell off the plane to his death.

Kershaw and Kane, who was a former social worker from Seattle, had built by hand a two-story log cabin in Goose Prairie in 1945 and 1946 and decided to support themselves by attracting guests to their new Double K ranch, from which visitors would take extended horseback pack trips into the mountains. They opened in January 1948, but, with several feet of snow on the ground, clients were hard to find. With business remaining slow into the summer, Kershaw decided they needed to do something to advertise the Double K's hospitality. She had heard that Justice William O. Douglas and his party were staying at a dude ranch run by a local doctor in Nile, farther down State Highway 410, toward Yakima. Seeking to create good word of mouth for the ranch, Kershaw offered her rival's most famous client free room and board at her place for him and all of his guests for as long as he wanted to stay.

On June 19, 1948, Douglas brought his Washington girlfriend and several members of his childhood friend Elon Gilbert's family to inspect the place. In a matter of moments, it quickly became clear that the Double K had everything that the Justice was looking for in a summer hideaway. Since it was located a full seventeen miles from the nearest phone, and fifty-seven miles from Yakima, Douglas knew that no one in Goose Prairie—or, more important, no one in his own family in the Wallowas—would be concerned about his personal life there. "It's the Secret Valley," said Jack Nelson. And so it was. And that was just the way Douglas wanted it. He immediately accepted the offer and relocated his entire party to the ranch, thereby beginning a relationship that would last for the rest of his life.

The Double K was just what the Justice needed for total rest. While Pat Kane prepared dinner, the rest of the group gathered in the kitchen to drink, and Douglas began the practice of sitting in an old chair next to the refrigerator with a cold beer or a mixed drink in his hand. From there, he would lead the festivities, sometimes telling his stories, other times singing old cowboy ballads, accompanied by the howls of his hostesses' dog, Lucky. Over the years, Douglas spent his time there hiking and riding in the mountains, courting various women, and chatting with the proprietors of the Double K. "Even with all of our rules, Bill never gave us a lick of trouble," recalled the crusty Kay Kershaw, who tolerated no infractions. "He did exactly what we told him. He liked the life here—the way we did it—and wanted to be a part of it. Besides, if he'd given us any trouble we'd have thrown him out."

"We never knew what Dad did in Goose Prairie," recalled his daughter, Millie. "He would just be gone for long periods of time [during the summer]." And he took advantage of this privacy, especially in his relationships with women. "Bill was the biggest whorer around," recalled Isabelle Lynn, an early guest and later Kershaw's partner at the Double K, "but we still loved him, though." Kay Kershaw had built a one-room, tin-roofed outbuilding, complete with a fireplace and a half bath, where a guest could live in total seclusion even from the main ranch. This very quickly became Douglas's home away from home. "Bill came here when he had a girlfriend, or when he didn't have a girlfriend and was writing one of his books," recalled Kershaw, adding with a knowing smile, "and he was here *a lot*." His female guests were arranged by an old friend. "Douglas would just see what he liked in Yakima, and Elon Gilbert would ask the girl up," explained Kershaw. "I was always seeing girls come by saying, 'Is Bill around?' There were all types and all ages, and they came all the time. . . . Poor Bill," Kershaw concluded, "he was no family man. His personal life was all fouled up."

.   .   .

The summer of 1949 was a time of great transition for Douglas and the Court. He spent seven weeks traveling through Iran, climbing the nearly nineteen-thousand-foot Mount Devamend, and other parts of the Middle East, as well as Europe, with Bill Jr. While he was away the balance of power on the fractured Court changed horrifyingly and dramatically. After two years of battling various illnesses, on July 19, Frank Murphy died of a coronary occlusion at the age of fifty-nine. Just seven weeks later, on September 10, 1949, Wiley Rutledge died suddenly at fifty-five. This removal from the Court of two of Douglas's liberal allies left him with an enormously changed work environment.

But that was not all that was changing. By now, he had become so enamored with his Washington mistress that he asked her to marry him as soon as he could divorce Mildred. Sensing what he would be like as a husband, not to mention already being married herself, the woman refused and broke off the affair completely.

Heartbroken over this turn of events, Douglas immediately sought new female companionship and developed a powerful crush on an even younger woman, a secretary in Clark Clifford's office. The hope of a new love interest made him giddy once more with puppy love.

With Mildred by now driving to Lawrenceville, New Jersey, to return Bill Jr. to prep school, and then to vacation separately in Cumberland, Maryland, Douglas decided that he wanted to take one last horse trip into the mountains before returning to the Court. Usually Kay Kershaw supervised the Justice's rides, since he always worried her. She prided herself on the fact that she never lost a guest, something not everyone in the treacherous area could claim. She drilled two rules into her "dudes" before taking them on a horseback trip. First, never turn a horse's head in toward the mountain. Preventing your horse from seeing the outside of the ledge on which it was walking may cause it to misstep or panic. And second, never pull back on the reins, forcing the horse's head up in the air. This can make the horse rear up and land on its back, on top of its rider.

The problem with Bill Douglas, she knew, was that despite his self-

constructed legend as a skilled rider, there were very few horses he was
capable of handling safely on the mountain trails. "He was a terrible
rider," Kershaw explained. "Bill didn't know how to saddle a horse or
how to bridle it. He would finish riding a horse hard and not cool it
down, just leaving it saddled there for someone else to tend to. The
only reason he survived was he did what we told him to do. 'Bring 'em
back alive,' that was my motto. But it wasn't always easy keeping him
alive." Douglas's daughter, Millie, herself an accomplished rider, confirms that "the truth was that he had no horse skills."

So when Douglas announced to the Double K gals on September 29 that he was going to take a final ride with Elon Gilbert, rather
than them, they became concerned. Douglas explained that he wanted
to check one last time on a trail that Elon's brother Curtiss and his
friend Clarence Truitt used to travel, for his ongoing nature-book project. Kershaw tried to dissuade him. "You know about Elon's horses,"
she counseled gravely. "They are all knotheads, high-headed, and they
are not safe." But Douglas was unconcerned. When a pea-soup fog
rolled in that day, however, postponing any travel, the matter was
dropped for the moment.

It took three days for the fog to clear, but when it did, on the morning of Sunday, October 2, Douglas figured that if he changed his plane
reservations to the red-eye out of Seattle, he could arrive the next day
in Washington, a bit bleary to be sure, just before Court was scheduled
to open the term at 10:00 A.M. Come hell or high water, he decided, he
was going into the mountains one last time. So, at first light, Douglas
put on his favorite old olive-green jacket, blue denim pants, cowboy
boots, and battered gray hat before dashing down to Whistlin' Jack's
Motel. There, he phoned Gilbert, and persuaded him to drop everything so that they could ride up to Chinook Pass toward Crystal Peak.
Gilbert quickly agreed, as he always did for his old friend, and generously offered to loan him his prize thoroughbred, Kendall. Having
never laid eyes on the horse before, the Justice had no reason to know
about the stallion's high-spirited nature. Four hours later, after hauling
their mounts up Highway 410 to Chinook Pass, he and Gilbert were
laughing together as they rode into the mountains along the gentle
trail that is now called the Sourdough Gap hike. Shortly before 11:00,
they reached the lovely, deep-blue Tipsoo Lake, which was just a couple of miles from their destination, the Cascade Crest Trail. To their
delight, they happened upon the legendary mountain storyteller, Scottish sheepherder Billy McGuffie and his son-in-law, Carl Bishop, Jr., as
they were enjoying an impromptu breakfast picnic with their families.
Want to join us? Douglas called out as they dismounted and ambled

over to say hello. After a few minutes of discussion, the picnickers decided not to go. So, Douglas and Gilbert remounted.

They rode up the Cascade Crest Trail, which was a narrow but relatively flat and gentle grade carved along the side of the mountain, paralleling the state highway some 100 to 150 feet below. After a couple of miles, though, the two men decided that the fastest way to Crystal Peak might be to turn their horses west off the marked trail and head straight up the mountain, which was roughly a sixty-degree incline. Douglas dismounted to tighten the cinch on his saddle before beginning. Gilbert, the more skilled rider, immediately turned his horse, roused it with a kick of his heels into its side, and disappeared up the hill. After remounting, Douglas likewise turned his animal uphill onto the steep, slate-strewn wild-game trail.

Several hundred yards up the path, though, disaster struck as the horse suddenly reared back until it was standing straight up on only its hind legs. Fearing that his mount was about to come over on top of him, Douglas did the only thing that made sense under the circumstance: He slid back in the saddle and then rocked off the horse's back to jump over its tail to the ground. But as soon as he touched the ground, Douglas lost his balance and began to roll uncontrollably down the steep mountainside. As he did so, Douglas heard a fearsome sound above him and realized to his horror that the sixteen-hundred-pound animal was also rolling down the mountain and bearing down on him at an even faster rate of speed. With no time to react, all Douglas could think to do when the animal reached him was duck. Incredibly, though, at that very moment he was nestled for a split second in a hollow created by the rocks. So the horse passed directly over his body without harming him at all.

But the crisis was not over. Both man and animal continued to slide down the mountainside, until the animal kicked out its legs in an effort to right itself and slowed up just long enough for the tumbling rider to slide in front of it once again. A few yards later, Douglas's body got hung up on a small ledge. He picked up his head and saw that the huge animal was about to pass over him *a second time*. This time, he was not so lucky. "He rolled over me and I could hear all the bones break," Douglas later wrote. "Then he was gone and I was paralyzed with pain and unable to move." The horse ended up on its feet on the main trail below, with nary a scratch on it. But the crushed rider was left motionless and near death on the mountainside.

Farther up the mountain, Elon Gilbert realized that the terrain would not allow him to continue, so he turned back to save his friend the unnecessary trip. But as he rode down the mountainside, he became increasingly concerned. Douglas was nowhere to be seen, and Gilbert feared the worst. Frantically, he began shouting and looking all around him, until he finally heard a faint "Elie" coming from a bushy area. Only by peering closely into the scrub bushes below could Gilbert see Douglas's broken body crumpled against the rocks.

By the time he had dismounted and slid down to him, it was clear that the Justice was in mortal danger. Normally, any injury in the isolated mountains is cause for concern, but this one was potentially devastating; Douglas's back might be broken. Gilbert put his first-aid knowledge to use. Deeply concerned about Douglas going into shock, Gilbert gave him some tea from his thermos to keep him warm and covered his body in blankets from his saddlebag. Then he tied his horse to some scrub brush on the trail and scrambled on hands and feet the seven hundred feet down the mountain to the highway below. Remembering that McGuffie and Bishop were less than a mile down the mountain range, Gilbert frantically flagged down the first car he saw. The driver, Ray Ulbrickson from Bellevue, Washington, agreed to go fetch the two men.

Only a little more than an hour had passed since Douglas and Gilbert had disappeared up the trail when the McGuffies saw a stranger frantically waving his hands and running toward them, shouting that a Supreme Court Justice had just been critically hurt on the mountain. Without a moment's loss, the mountain folk knew exactly what to do. McGuffie and Carl Bishop, Jr., grabbed a first-aid kit and went running up the rough trail in the direction they had last seen their friends riding. At the same time, Carl Bishop, Sr., jumped into his own car and sped around the treacherous mountain-highway curves, looking for a state patrolman.

By the time McGuffie and Bishop, Jr., had scrambled up the rugged terrain to reach their friend, twenty minutes had passed since the accident. What they found scared them to death. The normally ruddy-faced and twinkle-eyed man was now ashen with shock, and his glazed eyes made it clear that he was only semiconscious. Douglas's labored breathing in the high mountain air told them that he had probably broken several ribs, and might have internal bleeding and even a broken back.

Fearing that they were witnessing Douglas's last minutes, all the men could do was to make him as comfortable as possible in the hope that Bishop, Sr., could bring help. McGuffie pulled out an ammonia pack and broke it under his friend's nose, while everyone added their coats to a green marine blanket now wrapped around him, thanks to a passerby named Warren Gundry. Then the men tried to raise his head

a bit to take more of the tea from Elon Gilbert's thermos, while one
of them took off Douglas's boots and started rubbing his feet and
hands to keep the circulation going in them. "How do you feel, Bill?"
McGuffie said. Hearing that old familiar voice seemed to rouse Douglas, as he opened his eyes, gritted his teeth, and said with a puckish,
crooked grin, "Not too bad, thanks, Bill."

Bishop, Sr., meanwhile, had located a patrolman named Wayne
Hinkleman near the entrance of nearby Sunrise Park. Knowing that direct radio contact with Yakima for medical assistance was not possible
given their remote location, Hinkleman initiated a radio relay through
the Wenatchee police. Word was relayed back that Shaw and Sons
Emergency Service was dispatching their ambulance, along with Dr.
Joseph Low of Yakima. But, they warned the officer, because of the distance and the nature of the roads, it would be well over an hour before
they could reach the injured man.

That done, Bishop, Sr., and Hinkleman sped up the highway toward
the accident site. They grabbed the stretcher from the trunk of the patrol car and scrambled uphill to join the cluster of men on the mountainside. The men could see the difficulty of the rescue facing them:
How do you take a nearly unconscious man with a possible broken
back down a steep mountainside on a stretcher without painfully jar-
ring his unanesthetized body or even having him roll off to the ground
below? Relying on his twenty-two years as a scoutmaster, Carl Bishop,
Sr., took charge. He told the men to clear away the rocks next to Douglas and carefully lift him onto the stretcher, and he then tied him to the
stretcher with bandages. While one man forged a trail for the rest of
the party by clearing rocks ahead of them with his feet and hands, another man held the bottom of the stretcher as high as he could, while
a third man bent over and carried the top of the stretcher as low as he
could, thus keeping the patient as level as possible. Meanwhile, five
other men gripped the sides of the stretcher, trying to act as shock ab-
sorbers for the delicate ride. To keep themselves from tumbling over,
the men moved only a few feet at a time, skidding their feet in a zigzag
direction down the mountainside, while another man stood below
them with his arms outstretched to catch anyone who slipped.

Remarkably, it took them only about twenty minutes to reach the
road, without any additional harm to Douglas. But as there was no
ambulance in sight, all they could do was place Douglas gently by the
side of the pavement while they debated what to do next. By this time,
Douglas was so dazed that it all seemed to him like a dream as he
stared at the puffy clouds against the blue sky. All of a sudden, the face
of a man he did not recognize appeared, whispering questions about

what had happened. Thinking that he had just witnessed the aftermath of a routine mountain accident, the man said that he was amazed to learn that the victim was a member of the Supreme Court.

"Who are you?" Douglas croaked. "Why all these questions?"

"I represent the Associated Press," said Leroy M. Hittle.

With that, the Justice managed a weak smile and asked, "How in the world did the Associated Press get here?"

"Well," said the reporter, "my wife and I were up here from Seattle on an outing, and we were about to walk into Dewey Lake when this happened." Even in his searing agony, the always publicity-conscious Douglas tried to conduct a press conference. Moments later, the interview ended as the rescue party announced that they had concocted a plan. Seeking to shorten the time required to reach the ambulance, they decided that they should put the stretcher lengthwise in the backseat of the patrol car and begin driving toward Yakima. Since the litter was too long for the seat, Elon Gilbert would ride in the front seat facing backward on his knees and keep the back passenger door open with an extended arm while they drove. Even though they knew that every jostle would be sheer agony for the Justice, at least they could start the journey toward the hospital. "A prayerful, 'Oh God' " was all Douglas could utter as the men carefully lifted him to his makeshift ambulance.

As they drove along, the police siren wailed away, causing Douglas in his shock to turn his head and ask, "Who's that for?" Seeing the look of confusion on Elon Gilbert's face, Douglas realized what kind of trouble he was in and mumbled, "Oh, it's for me."

As they got down to the American River turnoff near Goose Prairie, a distance of some twenty miles, the ambulance from Yakima was approaching them. Once the vehicles stopped, Dr. Low jumped out and immediately administered a shot of morphine. By the time the ambulance arrived at Saint Elizabeth's Hospital in Yakima, at least four hours had passed since the accident, and Douglas had slipped into unconsciousness. Only when the doctors read Douglas's medical records did they realize to their horror that their famous patient was allergic to morphine. They tried to counteract the effects of the sedative while they took a series of X rays to assess the damage. The first radiograph indicated that Douglas had broken thirteen ribs. However, the cloudiness of the image caused by the collapsed right lung, which had been punctured by one of the broken ribs, prevented the doctors from realizing that in fact he had broken all his ribs but one, a total of twenty-three.

Word of the accident spread quickly. When the dire news reached the Supreme Court, an excited law clerk blurted out to his colleagues, "Douglas fell off a cliff!"

"Where was Frankfurter?" shouted another without even pausing to think.

The Double K gals and Douglas's daughter, Millie, heard about the accident on the radio, which began blaring special reports almost before he arrived at the hospital. This was somehow a better fate than that of Mildred Douglas, who got an anonymous call in the east saying only: "Your husband is slightly hurt. His back is broken." When she arrived the next day after a cross-country flight, she found that Douglas did not even recognize her or Millie. In time, when he became more coherent, Douglas was more interested in talking to his old friends rather than his relatives.

Goodwill messages flooded into the hospital. "I want you to know that I am thinking of you as you suffer this painful ordeal. Keep your courage up and we'll all hope for better days soon," wired Harry Truman.

"I regret that [a] mere horse finally did what most troublesome problems and politicians of 20th century have been unable to do for 30 years," wired Senator Lyndon B. Johnson.

Even common folks sent their condolences. One of them, Harry Mock of Indiana, wrote that based on the pain he had suffered from his own three broken ribs, "thirteen must be horrible."

Douglas replied to Mock, "When you have fourteen broken ribs, a hiccup is a crisis, a cough a disaster, and a sneeze, a calamity. And the most unfriendly act in the world would be a pat on the head."

DOUGLAS RALLIES FROM INJURIES, the inch-high headline blared in the local newspaper the next day. The doctors determined that there was no need for surgery because, incredibly, the broken ribs had punctured none of his vital organs beyond the one lung; in time, they would mend themselves. After determining that there was also no need for a blood transfusion and no threat of pneumonia, the hospital elevated Douglas's condition to "very satisfactory." But the truth was that Douglas's life hung in the balance for seventy-two hours. Unable to take any sedatives, for fear of another allergic reaction, the Justice had to ride out the excruciating pain in a semiconscious state. In the end, his doctors all agreed, it was due only to his extraordinary physical condition for a man his age and his will to live that Douglas survived an accident that would have killed eight out of ten other people.

While Douglas recuperated, his friends puzzled over what had really happened on that mountain. In full storyteller mode three weeks later, Douglas reframed his account of the accident from the *Yakima*

Daily Republic interviews, writing Yale law professor Fred Rodell: "Suddenly the horse reared. Probably a hornet bit him. As he reared he wheeled and put his front feet on the side of the mountain. That put him practically straight up and down. I dismounted by sliding off his tail." When Rodell included this account, blaming the horse, in a Law-Review article, later to be repeated by Douglas in his memoirs, it became the official version.

Kay Kershaw of the Double K, who knew Douglas's riding skills better than nearly everyone else, believed that he was simply covering for his own stupidity. "Douglas rode on Elie's horses on that ridge when he knew he shouldn't have," she said. "He was really afraid of horses, but he was also quite a risk taker. . . . He pulled the horse over on himself." Whatever the real cause, everyone agrees that Douglas could have died on that mountain.

But since he did not, the accident became a turning point for him. As he lay in the hospital bed, thinking not only of his own near death and the sudden deaths of his two liberal colleagues on the Court but also of the recent abrupt demise of his political enemy Robert Hannegan, a man nearly five years his junior, the Justice decided that all of this was a sign that he should live life to the fullest.

.   .   .

In mid-November, six weeks after Douglas had entered the hospital, the doctors were ready to discharge him, but they told him that returning to work was out of the question. Thinking that his punctured lung would improve faster in the dry heat of Arizona, the doctors told Douglas he should go there until at least February. Tommy Corcoran found him a place to stay called the Rancho Tranquilo, near Tucson, so Douglas told his wife to drive his car down there while he took the train. But when he arrived to find that the rancho was anything but *tranquilo,* Douglas was almost instantly ready to leave. When a real-estate agent told him about a vacancy at the El Mirador ranch in Sasabe, southwest of Tucson and right on the U.S.-Mexico border, Douglas moved in immediately.

Meanwhile, the thought of Douglas's broken body softened Harry Truman's resolve never to have anything to do with him again politically. When Secretary of the Interior Julius Krug resigned in late November after nearly a year of battling various ethics allegations, the president decided to personally offer Douglas one more chance at the post for which he seemed so perfectly suited. It was the fifth time in nine years that Douglas had been offered a legitimate chance to leave the Court, as he said he wanted, but his handling of this new offer was no different from the rest. "Again he hemmed and hawed," recorded Truman, so the president quickly elevated Undersecretary of the Interior Oscar Chapman to the position instead. Truman had learned his lesson. After Chapman's tenure was cut short by a fatal heart attack twenty-five months later, Bill Douglas did not even make the list of possible replacements.

While Douglas recovered enough to begin thinking about returning to work, though, the thought of rejoining a Supreme Court without Frank Murphy and Wiley Rutledge held little appeal for him. "The bones are mending O.K.," he wrote Hugo Black, then laboring on a Court in a transition period, in late December. "But it takes a long time to get the full reserve of strength back. . . . I had been thinking that if I couldn't get back on the job in a month, I should resign. I do not want to cripple the work of the Court by my absence."

The truth was that Douglas had been toying with the idea of resigning from the Court to return to the private practice of law. In the end, though, after discussing separately with Abe Fortas, Clark Clifford, and Simon Rifkind the possibility of going into practice with them, Douglas was unwilling to make the change.

In early March 1950, Douglas, putting aside the cold shoulder he had received during the 1948 presidential convention, accepted an invitation to visit his old friend Joe Kennedy at his Palm Beach estate. His daily regimen of riding and walking changed to a steady diet of drinking, seeing beautiful women, eating lobsters, and enjoying rides on the Kennedy yacht, despite his tendency to get sunstroke and seasick. When he returned to Arizona, the doctors finally pronounced Douglas fit to return to work.

But the Justice was unwilling to pronounce himself fully fit until he proved to himself that he was ready. Day after day during his months of convalescence Douglas had stared off into the distance at the 7,300-foot Mount Baboquivari. Like Mount Adams at the time of Douglas's father's burial, the Yakima foothills when he suffered from skinny legs, and the Cascade Mountain trails as a shy teenager, Mount Baboquivari became to Bill Douglas the symbol of his ability to transcend a crisis. If I can just get well enough to climb to the peak of that mountain, he told friends, I will be able to move on.

In late March, Douglas drove toward the mountain, bringing along his canteen, a camera, some mountain-climbing gear, and, most important to him, a copper capsule with a screw top. The trip was not an easy one, requiring that he start driving from the ranch before daybreak, find a bumpy dirt road to the south of the mountain, park his car by a clump of live oak, and hike along a five-mile trail just to get to the base of the mountain. At dawn, Douglas began climbing on his own on the southern and eastern faces, but once he was within sight of the peak he had to make the final ascent on the western face, where a sixty-foot cliff could only be scaled by using pitons, a hammer, and a piece of rope. It was almost as if Douglas had to risk his life once again on a mountain to assure himself that he was still alive. When he finally reached the summit, he pulled out the little notebook he always carried in his back pocket for his nature walks, signed his name and the date to it, and placed both it and the pencil into the copper capsule, which he deposited next to a scrub oak on the summit.

More than any other climb, this one had particular significance for Douglas. Now he was ready to return to Washington, D.C. But before doing so, he decided, the time had come to reintroduce himself to the American public.

23

OF MEN AND MYTHS

Autobiographers with a histrionic flair . . . can make
enthusiastic use even of their neurotic suffering,
matching selected memories with the clues given to
them by their avid public to create their own official
identities.

—*Erik H. Erikson*

George Draper's most famous patient again needed his help — only
the patient did not know it. Having once helped Bill Douglas conquer
the stomach pains that threatened his career and later beat his fears of
swimming and of lightning, Draper was now being called on by the
Justice to second-guess all of his other doctors.

But it was the Justice's psychological state that continued to interest the doctor. Douglas, he knew, was struggling with the idea of at-
taining the presidency. Over and over, Draper inserted in his letters a
reminder that being a Supreme Court Justice "is quite good enough
for a life time." "I always told you to keep out of politics," Draper reminded him.

Knowing that Douglas had nevertheless not given up on his political dreams, the psychiatrist was excited to hear that he had been hard
at work on a nature book and memoir tentatively entitled "Men vs.
Mountains." Would Draper like to review it? asked the Justice. "Very
excited about 'Men v. Mountains,' " Draper responded. "Didn't know
you were doing it. Delighted to read it & comment. Send it at once."

This was a continuation of the literary relationship that the two
men had recently been enjoying. Draper had drafted his new manuscript, "Polio, F.D.R. and Other People," a memoir of his lifelong study
and treatment of the disease, and sent it a few years earlier to Douglas
for publication suggestions.

Having helped to treat Franklin D. Roosevelt and published three
highly regarded books on the disease, Draper was determined to persuade the scientific community and the general public that the mind

could be made more resistant to polio germs, and that future epidemics might be limited by improving mental health rather than pursuing the highly competitive search for a vaccine.

When no publisher was willing even to review his new manuscript, Draper asked Douglas if there was anything he could do to help. The Justice told him to send a copy of the manuscript along. Upon receiving it he persuaded a friend, publisher Stanley Young of Farrar, Straus and Company, to examine it. But Young believed, as did Douglas, that the volume was much too short for public consumption and urged the undertaking of a major revision. Instead, Draper gave up, and the book was never published.

Now in reviewing Douglas's new manuscript after he received it in November 1948, Draper found no new insights into the Justice's state of mind. Far from being a strong autobiography, the draft was nothing more than a rambling narrative of his observations and adventures in the Cascade Mountains. The manuscript was filled with seemingly randomly assembled accounts of trips Douglas and his brother, Arthur, had taken, characters they had met, and stories they had heard. To fill out the pages of the book, Douglas followed the path of his great-great-uncle, Daniel Pierce Thompson, who wrote *The Green Mountain Boys,* a book that purported to be a novel about life in early Vermont settlements but was in fact based on oral accounts that the author had copied down while talking to older Vermont residents. Similarly, Douglas drew on the fishing and camping stories of people around Goose Prairie, such as Jack Nelson, to fill his book.

When Douglas sent an early draft off to publisher Stanley Young, the same man who had rejected Draper's manuscript, the initial reaction was not promising. The book was too long and too repetitious, the publisher wrote Douglas, and it lacked anything that would capture the attention of the reader. But perhaps if he put more of himself in the manuscript there would be more interest for the general reader and for the publisher.

Spurred by the publisher's criticism, Douglas undertook two major revisions of the manuscript. In time, he decided just how to spice up his manuscript. He completely revised what was then chapter 4 and opened it with a new dramatic sentence: "There was a driving force that took me first to the foothills and then to the mountains, though I myself did not recognize it for what it was until years later." And what was that driving force? With one sentence, Douglas changed his public image forever: "It was . . . infantile paralysis that drove me to the outdoors."

The chapter, now entitled "Infantile Paralysis," was Douglas at his most dramatic.

> I had it when I was a small child. I ran a high fever for several weeks. All but the country doctor despaired of my life. . . . He finally confided in Mother and gave her his candid opinion: There was a good chance that I would lose the use of my legs; even if I did not, I would not live long—probably not beyond forty. He had no remedy for the short life. He did, however, have a prescription for the legs—a prescription that the medical profession forty years later had hardly improved upon. His prescription was frequent massage in salt water, a fifteen-minute massage every two hours every day for weeks.
>
> Mother kept a vigil. She soaked my legs in warm salt water and rubbed it into my pores, massaging each leg muscle every two hours, day after day, night after night. She did not go to bed for six weeks. The fever passed; but the massages continued for weeks thereafter.
>
> I vaguely recall the ordeal. I lay in bed too weak to move. My legs felt like pipestems; they seemed almost detached, the property of someone else. They were so small and thin that Mother's hands could go clear around them. She would knead them like bread; she would push her hands up them and then down, up and down, up and down, until my skin was red and raw.
>
> Each day I tried to walk a bit. The weakness in my legs gradually disappeared. . . . Before many months I relearned to walk, and the frailty which the disease had caused seemed to pass. Someone said that the salt water and massages had effected wonders. Mother was silent awhile and then said, "So did my prayers."

Readers of the memoir could not help being struck by the intensely vivid and chilling imagery of this dramatic account. With near-photographic and phonographic precision, Douglas recounts for his readers every detail of the crisis.

No one ever challenged or investigated this story. Had readers and reviewers of the book checked his account against the contemporaneous story of his illness in Maine, Minnesota's three area newspapers at the time—the *Fergus Falls Daily Journal*, the *Fergus Falls Weekly Journal*, and *Wheelock's Weekly*—they would have discovered that tiny Orville Douglas had indeed been struck down by a severe, but unspecified, illness as an infant of twenty-two months. Such vivid recollections that he had of those days likely came not from his own memory but from the constant retelling of the story by his mother and older sister and, of course, from his own literary license.

Douglas added to this story. In order to combat the effects of this illness as a young boy, he said, he had hiked to the foothills of Selah Gap, near Yakima, and climbed to their summits before hiking as fast as he could back home. In time, his leg muscles grew and grew to the point that he could conquer the mighty Cascades. The lesson in this account was unmistakable for the reading public. Only by hard work, such as walking up mountains, both physically and spiritually, might we be able to overcome the obstacles in our lives.

In explaining the origins of his love of the mountains, Douglas did far more than spice up his nature-book manuscript. He had created the core of an entirely new public image for himself. Once the book was published, in the spring of 1950, many journalistic portraits of him would begin with words like: "Justice William O. Douglas, who overcame a near fatal bout with polio as an infant." Few could miss the implied lesson that, while he had suffered from the same disease as the nation's beloved president, unlike FDR he had been able to overcome its effects through sheer willpower and exercise. In so writing, Douglas was staking his claim as FDR's heir.

And the public loved it. *Of Men and Mountains,* billed by the publisher as "A Book of Adventure—Physical and Spiritual—in the Mountains of the Pacific Northwest," received glowing reviews. The stunning polio tale and its courageous aftermath captured the imaginations of the nation's top book reviewers. Victor P. Hass wrote in the *Chicago Tribune:* "In more than a decade of book reviewing I have read many hundreds of books, but I have never read a book whose author I envied and respected more than William O. Douglas." To which Daniel Polling of the *Christian Herald* added: "[This is] a book of heroic proportions with spiritual mountains higher than the rugged Cascades the author knows and loves."

The polio story had all the more impact because this new account came as a complete surprise to the press and public. Never once, in all of the dozens of interviews that Douglas had given about his life over the years, had he or anyone else mentioned his battle with this dread disease. Even the laudatory pamphlet printed just two years earlier by the Americans for Democratic Action, hungry for an FDR clone, had not mentioned this illness. With one bold stroke, Douglas had recrafted his public image so dramatically that even the encyclopedia *Current Biography* revised its lengthy 1941 article on him and published what it termed a "supersed[ing]" version in 1950.

Of Men and Mountains quickly became a national bestseller. In doing so, it did far more for Douglas than increase his already substantial public visibility; it also provided an extra $32,900 to the man who had become so financially strapped that he had been borrowing money from his brother. Beyond the money, it did wonders for his state of mind. Now it no longer mattered that his marriage was in a shambles, that his girlfriend had left him, that he had missed a second chance for the White House, and that two of his judicial allies were now dead. With five and one half pages in his first published book, William O. Douglas had obviated all of those problems.

He had touched a central nerve in the reading public, as the stacks of fan letters that poured into Douglas's Supreme Court office attested. But among the two full boxes of adulatory letters, one was curiously neutral. "I am about half way though [your book] now and am impressed with your easy style and fine selection of illustrated material," Dr. George Draper wrote his patient. "It surely should become a best seller and perhaps may have valuable political influence, but I can't imagine anybody wanting to have Mr. Truman's job nowadays." Draper, of course, knew from his diagnosis of Douglas in 1927 that this childhood illness was in reality a "severe and prolonged intestinal colic," followed by young Orville's memorable meal of baked beans after his near miraculous recovery. However, this new story served both the Justice's and the doctor's goals. For Douglas, it made him a legend. For Draper, it served as vivid and dramatic evidence that his theory was correct: A determined mind was all that was needed to conquer the effects of polio. What better evidence could one hope to find of this lesson than the polio-stricken infant who was now the healthy, world-traveling, mountain-hiking, physical-fitness guru sitting on the Supreme Court of the United States?

But Draper was not the only one who knew that Douglas's polio story was untrue. Douglas intimate Chester Maxey related: "Arthur [Douglas] told me that Bill never had polio. He said, 'He never had anything that was diagnosed as polio.' Well I said, 'How come?' Well, Arthur said, 'Bill made that up.' He said, 'He made up a lot of things.'" To Maxey, this made perfect sense. "Bill had so much interest in the disease that he decided that he had polio," he explained. "And so he had polio the rest of his life, and that's the story he told." Many others close to Douglas did not believe that he had polio, and the known facts seem to bear them out.

One by one, the old-timers in Yakima who had known Douglas as a boy also began to ask one another about this new polio story. Did anyone remember Bill Douglas, or anyone close to him, ever mentioning that he had had polio as a youth? The conclusion that everyone drew was pretty much, in the words of longtime resident George Martin, "most probably not."

Yakima natives also noticed that many of the stories of life in the mountains sounded just like the fabulous tales that mountain man Jack Nelson had told for years. Helen Williams, whose family owned Whistlin' Jack's Motel, asked Nelson after the publication of the book why he didn't now write his own memoirs. He responded, "Why should I write my memoirs? Douglas already did that!"

But to Bill Douglas the hometown opinion made little difference, because after the publication of *Of Men and Mountains* his readers believed that it was truly the story of a great man's life. And with the transformation thus afforded him, Douglas now had what he had always wanted: He was finally number one in the public's heart.

THE CORK'S REVENGE

The smallest worm will turn being trodden on.

—*William Shakespeare*, King Henry VI

Bill Douglas was named Father of the Year in 1950 by the National Father's Day Committee in New York, but surely not because any member of his family was polled. "My brother and I had a good laugh about that," said Millie Douglas Read some years later. "You just shake your head and have a giggle because what else can you do?"

And Douglas was no better a husband than he was a father. By this time he was taking an even greater interest in other women—especially young blondes. Yakima native Fred Redmon learned this fact firsthand when he went to the nation's capital as a twenty-one-year-old marine on furlough. As he moved through the bar of the old Willard Hotel, feeling somewhat homesick, he stopped in disbelief when he spotted an old family friend seated in a poorly lit back booth. It was Bill Douglas, with his arm around a beautiful blonde who, Redmon said, was "too young even for me." But when he went up to say hello to Douglas, the Justice acted like the two of them had never even met and refused to speak to him. "He was a chaser," recalled New York editor and Douglas friend Ken McCormick. "He would lay anyone anywhere. He just couldn't keep his hands off the women. It was kind of pathetic." Even Douglas's first literary agent, Helen M. Strauss, could see the effect of women on him: "Douglas's greatest weakness was his naiveté with women and his almost fatal susceptibility to their flattery. How often I watched him being taken in by pretty speeches and the flutter of feathered eyelashes."

In time, Douglas's urges began to get him into trouble at the publishing house for *Of Men and Mountains*. "He worked his way through the female editorial corps [at Harper]," recalled Ken McCormick. "Then he got a real fix on a girl, and she went to Harper's chairman of the board, Cass Canfield, and said, 'If you want me to stay, he has to go.'" Canfield reluctantly told Douglas to look elsewhere for future publication.

Despite his publishing success, Douglas's personal life was in nearly complete disarray. First, he faced continual financial problems. Fearing that he might need an operation to repair some damage from the horse accident, Douglas had asked his brother, Arthur, who was by then president of Statler Hotels, for a loan. Art Douglas immediately sent his brother a check for $2,500, and would not allow him to repay it.

Then there was the state of his love life. To Douglas's great dismay, his relationship with Clark Clifford's secretary, begun just before the horse accident, had fizzled out while he was in the hospital recovering. Puzzled, Douglas wrote: "I sure descended fast. Maybe I'm too old or something." This jilting had a devastating effect on the Justice. Having just turned fifty-one and been dropped once more by a younger woman, Douglas became afflicted with what the Germans call *Tor-schlusspanik,* or "panic at the approach of the closing door." Neither his father nor his grandfather, Douglas realized, had lived to his current age.

With all of this and his recent catastrophe swirling in his head, Douglas decided to make some radical changes in his life. As soon as he returned to Washington from his convalescence in Arizona, he told Mildred that he was moving out of the house. The announcement came as no surprise to his son and daughter, who that year would turn eighteen and twenty-one. "There was no particular moment that I felt that their marriage was falling apart," explained Millie Douglas Read. "It was a very gradual process. It started, I believe, maybe when he was appointed to the Court; maybe slightly before, and they just drifted further apart. . . . So it was a gradual falling apart." But it did come as a shock to Mildred, who was still confident that her marriage would hang together, since she and Bill had agreed to try to make things work out until the children were through college.

Possessing no money for another place to live, Douglas moved into the only facility he could afford: his Supreme Court office. With a shower off of the main office and with the building cafeteria down-stairs, it seemed to have what he needed for now. But it made for a strange scene to visitors. "We visited him in Washington, D.C., and he was just between his first and second wives," recalled Elon Gilbert's son Cragg. "And at that time, he had everything all duffel-bagged out, on chairs and on the floor of the office." When he got a little money, Douglas found an inexpensive apartment at 2029 Connecticut Avenue, NW.

Now freed of family obligations, Douglas wanted to go abroad. Having already traveled abroad the year before with Bill Jr., Douglas decided to spend part of the 1950 summer recess overseas as well. The only problem was that he had no money to do so. So, relying on the success of *Of Men and Mountains,* Douglas convinced a publisher to underwrite his research for a book called *Strange Lands and Friendly People,* an account of his trips to the Middle East, Greece, Cyprus, and India. When the firm agreed, Douglas realized the secret to financing his foreign travel for the rest of his life. On the basis of just a short prospectus and his reputation, he could get an advance from a book publisher or *National Geographic* for a literary and photographic "research" trip abroad, at their expense, return to make a small fortune in lecture fees presenting slide shows, and write a largely forgettable travel book with the help of his office staff and sometimes even his law clerks. Even if one book did not sell well, other publishers were always willing to give him another advance to support a new trip, in the hopes that the next one would succeed.

In the summer of 1950 Douglas took Bill Jr. and Elon Gilbert for two months to Iran, Iraq, and India. But his health was a concern. By this time, the scar tissue in his lungs made it impossible to fully inflate them. Two severe bouts with dysentery during the journey caused him to lose so much weight that his clothes now hung limply on him. Still, the trip became a public sensation when Douglas cut his return trip to Court a bit too close and, because of delayed plane connections, arrived two minutes before the conclusion of the eleven-minute opening session. The press now dubbed him the "globe-trotting justice." Douglas liked the term, believing that his conversations with common folk abroad now made him a foreign-policy expert.

Now back on the Court, Douglas was on the lookout for a new girlfriend, and he thought he had a prospect. Mercedes Davidson, a blond, vivacious Louisianan and the wife of former Assistant Secretary of the Interior C. Girard (Jebby) Davidson, was then working in Representative Helen Gahagan Douglas's office. She had written the Justice a brief get-well card after his horse accident. Such a letter from a beautiful woman eighteen years his junior seemed to him to be an invitation for something more, so Douglas now showered her with letters, phone calls, and unexpected attention. "It was almost a frightening thing to have a man like Douglas start pursuing you," she recalled years later.

"This went on for several months. I passed [on] them all. . . . And one day his secretary called and . . . something made me give up and I went."

All of Douglas's friends could sense his excitement over his developing relationship with Davidson. "She was a sexy bombshell back then," recalled Charles Reich, a former law clerk to Hugo Black. "Boy, she was attractive then. And that's what he liked was the blond bombshell who was smart and who is savvy. And she was savvy. . . . She was smart about everything. She was the most capable person that I think I ever knew." To which former Supreme Court law clerk Robert Hamilton added: "Mercedes is one of the most organized and sharpest women I have ever met. She is so capable that you could give her anything—say, your broken tape recorder—and she would instantly know how to fix it."

By the spring of 1951, the still married Douglas seemed ready to leave his wife on the spot in order to marry this beautiful younger woman. After Mercedes had returned with her husband to his native Portland, Oregon, where he would be practicing law after leaving government service, Douglas somewhat frantically began to search for a way to get her back to Washington. Deciding that he now required a research assistant for his new travel book, Douglas contacted Jebby Davidson to ask if his wife might like to review the page proofs of *Strange Lands and Friendly People*. While her husband never suspected anything, Merci Davidson could see that there was more at work here than the literary enterprise. As she would later tell an interviewer: "[Douglas] had a ploy. I see it as a ploy now, but nevertheless, this went on for over a year or so and I resisted, and the pursuer was so hot and heavy that he wore me down." "It was like walking into a trap," she wrote later to Douglas's daughter.

By late summer 1951, Douglas decided that it was time to end his marriage. When he returned from his summer-recess trip abroad with a stop in San Francisco, he sent word to Mildred to meet him at their Oregon cabin. As soon as she arrived, Douglas simply announced that their marriage was over and then left without saying another word. Douglas believed that he could keep the matter secret by telling only three people: Clark Clifford, whom he tapped as his lawyer in the upcoming divorce proceedings, and Tommy Corcoran and Eliot Janeway, who could handle his public-relations problems. The Justice imagined that the Washington superlawyer would beat up on any small-time attorney his wife chose to represent her, while Janeway and Tommy the Cork would figure out how to smooth over the impact of the divorce on his national political image.

But not everyone was willing to follow the game plan. When Corcoran heard about Douglas's action, he was incensed. "You don't have to marry 'em, just sleep with 'em," he shouted at the Justice, knowing the impact that this decision would have on his own dreams of returning to the White House. "I told Bill that 'in politics you don't get a divorce,'" Corcoran explained later. "Sure you have women. But you don't get a divorce. He would have been President if it hadn't been for this divorce business." Hoping to contain the damage, both Corcoran and Janeway begged their candidate to hold off on any public announcement of the breakup, if not actually reconcile with his wife, until after the 1952 presidential-election season.

But Douglas was determined to move ahead. When her husband's decision finally sank in, Mildred Douglas was heartbroken. "You are the only man I've ever loved, do, and ever will," she wrote to her departing husband, ". . . I am hoping you will find that something that has been lacking in our relationship." Still, she was not ready to admit that the marriage was over. Hoping that her husband would change his mind, she decided to drag the divorce process out by demanding that it take place in her home state of Oregon, where there was a two-year legal waiting period before the action was made final.

Unable to wait, Douglas settled back into his ninety-dollar-a-month apartment on Connecticut Avenue, and continued his courtship of Mercedes Davidson, who by this time had divorced her husband. Clark Clifford was left with the task of negotiating the most favorable terms for the Douglases' divorce. And when Mildred hired as her attorney his old friend from Whitman College Blaine Hallock, one of the "Baker boys," everything seemed on the verge of working out in his favor financially.

But once more the risk-taking side of his nature got Douglas into trouble. One of his love letters to Mercedes was returned to his old home address due to insufficient postage, and when Mildred inadvertently read it, she learned for the first time that there was another woman. Word of this faux pas got to the media, and though friends were able to kill the "adulterous Justice" story, the chance for him to take the high road in the divorce proceedings was gone. Convinced of the hopelessness of her cause, in March 1952 a distraught Mildred picked up her pen and conceded defeat:

I hope it is possible for you to be patient with me. I have been packing, lifting, and carrying until I've reached the end of my physical strength. What is the net result? The breaking up of a family—a fine family—one week—then thirty or fifteen minutes be-

fore a judge—it's all over—it never was—or one is supposed to believe it never was—I can't forget 28 years of devotion, loyalty and
hard service that quickly and easily. I am physically and emotionally played out. . . . So will you please be patient? You are a famous
and brilliant man. May God help you find it in your heart to forgive
yourself, as our children and I do. With all good wishes, Mildred.

By the following month, unseemly and sensational rumors about
the failed Douglas marriage began appearing in the press. A headline
appeared in the New York *Daily News* reading JUSTICE DOUGLAS WANTS
DIVORCE TO WED; SHE'S 30ISH. Another piece painted an even more
tawdry picture: "Supreme Court Justice William O. Douglas, 53, is
begging his wife for a divorce so he can wed blonde Mercedes Davidson, divorced wife of C. Girard (Jebbie) [*sic*] Davidson. . . . The Douglases and Davidsons formed a popular and happy foursome in
Washington until Cupid intervened. . . . This personal scandal has
touched the highest court of the land." Indeed, this would be the first
divorce in the Supreme Court's long history.

As they read these accounts, the Douglas family members agreed
that it was not Mercedes who had broken up the marriage but the Justice. "I think many people, especially friends of my mother, have
blamed Mercedes for breaking up their marriage, but I think it would
have been any woman," said Millie Douglas Read. "Mercedes happened to be the one who was there at the time."

As the months of separation went by, the effect on the Douglas
family's financial well-being was severe. "My father was very tight-
fisted," recalled Millie. "My mother never had enough money even to
clothe the kids. He would keep her on a very strict budget because he
had other things to do with his money. . . . Even though all my friends
thought we were rich because my father was a Supreme Court Justice,
we never saw the money." Douglas even claimed that he didn't have
enough money to send Bill Jr. to college for his final year, so his sister,
Martha, ended up giving her nephew half of the money for his fall semester at school.

Douglas was so anxious to shed his wife and family in order to get
on with his next marriage that he told Clark Clifford he would pay any
price to do so. "When my father decided to get rid of a woman, he
would do anything to get rid of her," said Millie Douglas Read. It was
good that Douglas had reached that decision, because unknown to
him Mildred had gained a powerful ally who was willing to make him
do exactly that.

Operating from both his affection for Mildred Douglas and his eye-for-an-eye mentality in politics, Tommy "the Cork" Corcoran agreed to represent Mildred in the divorce negotiations at no charge from behind the scenes. "Mr. Corcoran cared very deeply for my mother," explained Millie Douglas Read, "and he thought she had gotten a very raw deal. So he vowed to Mother that he would help her take Douglas for a ride." Given the impact of Douglas's divorce on Corcoran's own political chances, Eliot Janeway was unsurprised by this action: "For [Tommy], there were two ways to get into a house. One is to take your time and ring the doorbell; the other is to blow the wall down with a flamethrower and never mind about the door. Tommy was a flamethrower. And with Tommy, you were either with him or you were against him. There was no in between." To him, this divorce made Bill Douglas one of his enemies who needed to be destroyed. The fact that his legal adversary was Clark Clifford, his old political opponent from the Truman administration, made the process even more pleasurable for Corcoran.

So while the general public was led to believe that this was an amicable divorce proceeding being steered by two small-time general practitioners in the Pacific Northwest—Blaine Hallock of Baker, Oregon, for Mildred and Moe Tonkon of Portland, Oregon, for Bill—they were only the front men who swapped property-division proposals and filed the legal papers for the real heavyweights in Washington, D.C., who were privately calling the shots.

Corcoran knew just how many political and financial cards Mildred actually held against her publicity-conscious husband. Early on, Tommy the Cork instructed Hallock to remind Douglas not so subtly of his own responsibility for the breakup, as evidenced by the wayward love letter, and make clear that good publicity in the face of these adulterous circumstances now depended on the nature of the settlement for his poor wife. In no time at all, the Justice agreed that the financial terms had to be as "generous" as possible.

Then there was the matter of fairly splitting up the joint property. The problem was that the Douglases did not own a house of their own in Washington, D.C., having chosen to rent. Since Mildred now had to establish a legal domicile in Oregon for the divorce to take place there, and the only property they owned jointly were the three cabins that Douglas loved so much in the Wallowas, they now had to be transferred to her. And since no respectable ex-wife of a sitting Supreme Court Justice (who still harbored hopes of reaching the White House) could be left without a home in the nation's capital, on January 16, 1953, Douglas bought her a house there at 124 Third Street, NE, taking out a $17,500 mortgage on the property and agreeing to pay the yearly real-estate taxes. He left it to Mildred to divide the belongings in their apartment on Dupont Circle. Douglas reserved to himself only the right to take a second mortgage on the Third Street house for up to ten thousand dollars in order to buy a house of his own, agreeing to repay the money "as fast as he possibly can." Effectively, Douglas had confined himself for the time being to his Connecticut Avenue apartment.

But Corcoran was not finished yet. Since Mildred had no other means of support, Douglas agreed to pay her $650 a month, or $7,800 a year in support, based on his current salary of $25,000. Douglas also agreed to pay all of the "support and maintenance and educational expenses" of his two children. With Millie now married, that meant that he was now responsible for Bill Jr.'s final semester at Whitman College and his later graduate education at the University of Washington. And since Mildred had no retirement plan and had been unable to work while raising the children, she was given the rights to all of the Justice's life-insurance policies and guaranteed half of his net estate over one hundred thousand dollars, should she survive him. In addition, all of the lawyers' fees for both parties became Douglas's responsibility.

It was in the next provision of this agreement, though, that Tommy Corcoran truly began to tighten the financial screws on his old political ally. After the initial agreement had been negotiated, Corcoran persuaded Mildred not to sign it but instead to ask for a side agreement that would automatically increase her support payment proportionately with any increase in Douglas's Court salary. Corcoran's instinct that the Court was due for a pay raise proved to be correct as two years later the Justices' salary was raised to thirty-five thousand dollars, thus increasing Mildred's monthly payments to $910.

Noting that the Justice's extrajudicial yearly income had unlimited potential, Corcoran exacted his full measure of revenge through an ingenious legal device. He had an escalator clause inserted into the final agreement, under which Douglas would have to pay additional money, in increasing installments, for all of the income that he earned over and above his regular salary. Beginning in 1961, for every dollar of net income that he earned over his $25,000 salary up to $40,000 (to be adjusted if the Court's salaries increased), 15 percent would go to Mildred. She would get an additional 25 percent of everything he earned between $40,000 and $60,000. And whatever Douglas earned over $60,000, 35 percent would go to Mildred. Corcoran knew that this clause, likely involving tens of thousands of dollars, was like a financial noose.

With the two-year Oregon waiting period in the process of expiring, Douglas ignored the final pleas from his friends to remain with his wife. Unwilling to deal with the details, Douglas left them all to Clark Clifford, saying that Mildred should file the papers during the Court's recess so that he could sign the final decree just before he departed on another foreign trip in the summer. "Without you I would be a lost man," he wrote Clifford.

Douglas was left with no property assets, two small life-insurance policies intended for his two children, and more than eighty thousand dollars of debt. By mid-April of 1953, still months from his final divorce decree, Douglas was so strapped for funds that he borrowed another twelve thousand dollars from Arthur (nearly half of Bill's yearly income but a pittance for the well-to-do hotel executive). But no matter how steep the price, in his eyes he had gotten the only thing that he really wanted: his freedom. Finally, he was free to marry Mercedes Davidson.

The divorce took its toll on Douglas, who was always a heavy drinker, as he now began drinking to even greater excess. Now allergic to the gin he once preferred, Douglas consumed massive quantities of vodka gimlets (always with an onion rather than an olive). The evidence of his deteriorating lifestyle became a matter for gossip in the capital. Congressman Frank Boykin of Alabama reported to J. Edgar Hoover that Douglas was now so drunk by the end of "practically every evening" that someone had to "put [him] to bed." A short time later, the FBI learned that it was not uncommon for him to simply drink his lunch of three or four gimlets, making it very difficult for those informing the bureau about "dining" with him to recall the precise nature of the conversation. All of this was duly added to the FBI director's growing "official and confidential" file on Douglas.

With his divorce arrangements settled, Douglas left in the summer of 1953 for the Far East to research his next book, now for Doubleday since his problems with the editorial corps at Harper had caught up with him. Then he returned to hide out at Elon Gilbert's place in Yakima while Mildred dealt with the final details. Seeking to avoid the press and save Bill Jr. from disgrace, she arranged to meet Hallock in a remote location in Oregon, change to his car, and be driven without notice to Baker, where she could personally file papers before Judge Forrest L. Hubbard on July 20. In yet another act of compassion for her famous husband, rather than charging him with "cruel and inhuman treatment" and adultery as she could have done, her complaint simply charged Douglas with "desertion," making it appear as though he had chosen his devotion to work over her. After thirty years of marriage, the decree was granted in just twenty-five minutes.

Now a single man, Douglas tried to repair the damage to his public image by leading the public to believe that he was living an ascetic bachelor existence following his failed marriage. But friends knew that this was not the case. By mid-1954, Mercedes was living at 2300 Connecticut Avenue, NW, while Douglas rented a new place down the street at 3701 Connecticut. Charles Reich, who now lived a few doors away from Douglas, was often called upon to keep an eye on Davidson's two teenage children. He recalls the lovers' living arrangement as being different than the public image: "For a long time, Mercedes lived at one place, and he lived somewhere else, but they really were living together. . . . It was basically a tiny apartment. No separate dining room, so the dining room was a part of the living room. And yet they were trying to live there."

Despite the cramped quarters, Douglas insisted on presenting the image that nothing had really changed for him by entertaining all of his political buddies in Davidson's apartment. "I was invited to a dinner in which they had Sam Rayburn and Lyndon Johnson—all in this little tiny place," explained Reich. "Everybody was scrunched in together. Unbelievable. About eight or ten luminaries like that." While they all passed around bottles of liquor while seated on the floor of the little living room, Merci cooked Louisiana specialties for them. But the food did not matter at all—they were there to talk politics and gossip.

Douglas was no more successful helping to raise the children of his prospective family than he was in dealing with his natural offspring. The unusual stepfamily arrangement greatly bothered Merci's thirteen-year-old son, Michael, as Charles Reich recalled:

> I found out that Mike bitterly resented his new "stepfather." . . . He was afraid to invite his teenaged friends home to dinner because you just never knew when the judge could just blow up. . . . It was no fun to be one of Douglas's stepkids, any more than it was fun to be one of his real kids. He just could be awesome as far as ignoring people and not be[ing] sensitive to their needs. He's just inexcusable. . . . That's Bill Douglas the bastard, there is no way to get away from it.

The announcement of Douglas's new relationship came at Christmastime, when friends got Christmas cards from Mildred signed "Bill and Mildred" and also cards directly from Bill, which was most unusual, signed "Merci and Bill."

Before he could get married again, Douglas realized, he would have to find a way to replenish his funds. So he embarked on a search for outside income. With Davidson's assistance, Douglas found that he could begin to publish on a lucrative book-a-year schedule. *Beyond the High Himalayas* was published in 1952, with *North from Malaya* to come in 1953 and *An Almanac of Liberty* a year later.

When these efforts proved to be insufficient to balance his finances, Douglas began playing a monetary shell game. Tipped off by Arthur that Statler Hotels was about to change hands because of the divorce and remarriage of the company's board chairman, Douglas used some of the money loaned him by his brother and the money he had gotten from refinancing Mildred's new Third Street house, a total of more than twenty-two thousand dollars, to buy 650 shares of stock in Statler Hotels at thirty-four dollars a share. Then Arthur himself bought additional shares of stock in both Bill's and Martha's names. Just two months later, when the company did change hands, ironically causing Arthur to lose all of his power as president, Douglas made a quick profit of eight thousand dollars. Fifteen years earlier, as the chairman of the Securities and Exchange Commission, Douglas might well have railed against such a transaction as illegal insider trading. But now he was simply too strapped for funds to worry about such legal niceties.

By now, Douglas was borrowing from everyone he knew who had money in anticipation of buying a suitable property in Washington, D.C., for his future bride. He had already turned to a close friend, Mrs. Florence Smith, from whom two years before he had borrowed and quickly repaid one thousand dollars, to get another twelve thousand dollars from her, without any interest terms being discussed. Douglas sought to avoid any ethical problems by arranging with Clark Clifford to repay the money through one of his law partners, William H. Dorsey, Jr. When problems arose over the years in repaying this note, Douglas left it to Clifford to make the excuses and arrange future terms.

When this loan, along with his lucrative stock deal, was less than he needed to buy another property, in late 1954 Douglas borrowed several thousand dollars from Clifford himself. "I cannot put into words my full gratitude," wrote Douglas to his old friend after receiving the money. For an attorney who would one day appear before the Supreme Court to serve as a Justice's banker certainly posed some potentially sticky ethical questions. But since Clifford had always acted as Douglas's personal attorney, even arranging to pay bills for the Justice when he was on vacation, neither man saw any problems here.

After what he deemed to be a respectable nearly five-month wait-

ing period following his divorce, Douglas married Mercedes on December 14, 1954, in her parents' home in Tallulah, Louisiana. Knowing
that his brother still needed money for the fashionable home they had
chosen on Hutchins Place in northwest Washington, Arthur Douglas
was still willing to help. He tried to cancel his brother's outstanding
loan notes as a wedding present. But the Justice would not accept that,
insisting that he would repay them even if the money came from his
estate. But he never got the chance. When Arthur Douglas died in
March 1956 due to complications from his heavy drinking (though
some would say that it was caused by a broken heart from the loss of
his job with Statler Hotels), no loan notes surfaced in his financial papers. Distraught at the thought of the unpaid debt, Douglas learned
from his sister that Arthur had simply destroyed the notes before his
death to free him of the obligation.

Douglas's mounting debts became a constant problem for him.
When he was having trouble in 1957 finding the money to repay the
remaining $1,500 on the loan by Smith, he wrote Clifford about the
difficulty, saying that he hated to discuss personal issues "on the telephone because I am sure it is tapped." Douglas failed to tell his good
friend that the real reason he could not pay off the loan was that he
needed the extra money to buy the summer cottage that he and Merci
had been renting in Glenwood, Oregon (to replace the ones he lost in
the divorce decree). While Douglas asked Clifford to rearrange the
terms for the final payment, Clifford did more than that. He soon returned the promissory note to the Justice, having paid the rest of it out
of his own funds.

Once the escalator clause in his divorce agreement was triggered,
Douglas would come to understand how bad his finances really were.
The financially punitive divorce terms ensured that he would always
be scrambling for money. Thus, the man who was so unwilling to risk
his financial security by giving up his tenured position on the Court to
seek the presidency that he so coveted now had done exactly that in
giving up his first wife.

But beyond the monetary consequences, the divorce from Mildred
cost Bill Douglas far more than he would ever admit. It cost him his
friendship with Tommy Corcoran. "They broke completely," recalled
Eliot Janeway, "and they did not speak again after the divorce for decades thereafter."

Douglas's public reputation continued to suffer, and his mailbags
filled up with letters of criticism from former admirers sickened by his
behavior. The divorce also hurt his relationship with Hugo Black.
"Black loved Douglas," said Charles Reich. "But when this business

with all these women [came about], Black was very disapproving of that. He wished he'd stayed married. . . . To Black, it was nothing but tomcatting around. . . . It's just what men do if they don't have any discipline or character or something."

But for Bill Douglas, the man who so loved the mountains and wrote about them with such affection, perhaps the biggest loss was being cast out of his personal Eden: the cabins in the Wallowas. "Mother knew that he loved it up here at the cabin," Millie Douglas Read recalled. Family friend Dagmar Hamilton explained it somewhat differently: "Taking the cabins was clearly Mildred's revenge. She was very, very bitter about the divorce and wanted to make Douglas pay for that." And so, she spent the rest of her days alone in the cabins she and her husband had built together.

BLACK AND DOUGLAS DISSENTING

Douglas inspires fanatical loyalty in some people
and absolute mistrust in others.

—*Arthur M. Schlesinger, Jr.*

When Court opened on the first Monday in October 1950, Douglas returned to his first full term after the horseback-riding accident to find
a very different group than the one he had left. Truman had replaced
the liberal Frank Murphy and Wiley Rutledge with two conservative
friends, Attorney General Tom Clark and Court of Appeals Judge
Sherman Minton. As a result, the vast majority of the Court was now
conservative, with Douglas and Hugo Black largely in dissent. For
Court followers, the phrase "Black and Douglas dissenting" became
the shorthand way of counting votes in civil-rights and liberties cases.

It was also perfectly evident to Court observers that there was a serious conflict between Black and Douglas and the more conservative
Robert Jackson and Felix Frankfurter. "The bitter, really frightful feud
within the [Vinson] Court" became so bad, political journalist Marquis Childs later revealed, that Jackson began accusing Douglas of fak-
ing footnotes in his judicial opinions. "[Jackson] had his law clerk go
back, and on at least three occasions those citations were not there,"
recalled Childs.

Douglas's relations with Frankfurter were no better, as the two men
had ceased communicating except to lob verbal grenades at each
other. Frankfurter wrote Harold Laski that Douglas had become "more
and more of a *momser* [bastard] as the years went on." Having already
described Douglas in his diary as "malignant," in just a few years
Frankfurter was to call him "the most cynical, shamelessly amoral
character I've ever known. . . . He is just too unscrupulous for any
avoidable entanglements." The feelings were mutual, as Douglas on

various occasions referred to his diminutive colleague as "the Little Giant," the "little bastard," or simply "Der Fuehrer." Douglas had even suggested to the rest of the Court that Frankfurter was delaying the release of decisions, making it impossible to assign him other opinions, so as to give him time to engage in all of his extrajudicial political efforts to lobby political figures for policy changes. When the two men did communicate in the Court's conference, it was to yell at each other loud enough for the staff to hear them down the hall.

The two men also began attacking each other by using scholarly proxies who published critical articles on their judicial opinions. Douglas, who relied on Yale Law School's Fred Rodell for his defense, accused Frankfurter of working "practically full time" through former law clerks, ex-students, and journalistic contacts at getting derogatory articles written about him and the other liberals on the Court because of his unwillingness to have the "mantle of liberalism go to other shoulders." One Frankfurter technique became evident to Douglas when early in the week editorials in *The Washington Post* used the exact words that Frankfurter had offered in the Court's secret conference the previous Saturday.

By this time, even Chief Justice Vinson had had enough of Frankfurter's pontificating style in conference. One time, the normally placid and gentlemanly Vinson was so angered by Frankfurter's patronizing remarks that he clenched his fist, rose from his place at the end of the oval table, and began to rush at his colleague with the intention of beating him. As the Chief Justice moved to the left of the table, Justice Tom Clark pushed out his chair, trying to cut him off. Seeing that Clark's move would be unsuccessful, Sherman Minton tried to do the same, but his phlebitis prevented him from moving his chair fast enough. Only when Frankfurter stopped his lecture and sat down was a disastrous scene finally averted.

. . .

The first of the cases argued just after the opening of the new term illustrated to Douglas just how much the direction of the Court had changed because of the new Truman appointments. A college student named Irving Feiner was convicted of disorderly conduct in Syracuse, New York, for giving a public speech on behalf of the Young Progressives of America. Though he had been denied a permit for a meeting, Feiner stood on a box in a small shopping area and, using a loudspeaker, delivered a vituperative speech in a "loud, high-pitched voice" attacking the American Legion as "a Nazi Gestapo" and labeling President Truman and the mayors of Syracuse and New York City as "bums." When Feiner began trying to arouse blacks against whites, one member of the audience told the police that "if you don't get that son of a bitch off, I will go over and get him off there myself." As the increasingly restless crowd began pushing and shoving, the police asked Feiner three or four times to get down off of his box. When he refused to do so, the police "stepped in to prevent it from resulting in a fight" by arresting Feiner.

Given the holding two years before in *Terminiello,* Feiner had a right to expect that his ability to speak, no matter how objectionable, could not be limited by the "heckler's veto" of an angry crowd. However, on January 15, 1951, a six-person majority upheld the arrest because the officers were not trying to control the content of Feiner's speech. "Rather," the Court argued, "it was the reaction which [the speech] actually engendered" that moved the police to try to keep the peace.

Without Murphy and Rutledge to stake out the liberal position, Black and Douglas, joined this time by Minton, could see that it was time to pick up the mantle. Black argued in dissent that it was "far-fetched" to believe that there was an imminent threat to the speaker, noting that the man who had threatened Feiner was accompanied by his wife and child and not close enough to Feiner to do him any harm. It appeared to Black that the police arrested Feiner not because of the commotion but rather because of the content of his speech, which would violate the First Amendment. Douglas joined him in dissent, arguing that "public assemblies and public speech occupy an important role in American life." Then he considered whether the arrest was permitted by the doctrine of "fighting words," which had been created by the Court in 1942 to justify the restriction of speech that consisted of especially provocative words. Here, he argued that the doctrine did not apply to mere "exaggeration, . . . vilification of ideas and men, [and] the making of false charges." In concluding that the police should have tried to protect the speaker, Douglas exhibited his increasing skepticism of the power of government: "If they do not receive [constitutional protection] and instead the police throw their weight on the side of those who would break up the meetings, the police become the new censors of speech. Police censorship has all the vices of censorship from city halls which we have repeatedly struck down."

A week after *Feiner v. New York,* in two cases dealing with suspected membership in allegedly subversive organizations, *Joint Anti-Fascist Refugee Committee v. McGrath* and *Bailey v. Richardson,* Douglas signaled that he was fully prepared to assume the Murphy/Rutledge position on the liberal side of the Court. In 1947, President Truman had issued an executive order establishing a procedure for removing from federal employment any person whose loyalty was suspect, as indicated by "membership in, affiliation with or sympathetic association with" any organization deemed by the attorney general to be "totalitarian, fascist, communist, or subversive." Without any notice to, or hearing for, the affected organizations, then Attorney General Tom Clark had drafted such a list of allegedly "subversive groups" and released it to the press, while also sending it to the various "loyalty boards" making these determinations. Dorothy Bailey was removed from her federal job as a training officer for the U.S. Employment Service on the basis of testimony from unidentified informants that she had been a member of one of these organizations. She had no opportunity to cross-examine these witnesses, and indeed the loyalty board itself did not know the accusers' names or have the means to investigate these charges. Yet she was still fired. Subsequently, Bailey's attorney, Abe Fortas, now of the Arnold, Fortas, and Porter law firm in Washington, D.C., challenged this procedure as being a violation of "due process of law." Because Tom Clark recused himself, due to his involvement in the dispute as attorney general, the action was affirmed by a four-to-four vote, and no opinion was issued.

Unable to express his views in *Bailey,* Douglas went on the record in *Joint Anti-Fascist Refugee Committee v. McGrath.* In this case, the Joint Anti-Fascist Refugee Committee, primarily a charitable organization, had sued along with two other organizations to have their names removed from the attorney general's subversive-groups list because they said they were not a threat to the nation. The Court limited itself to the highly technical question of whether these groups had standing to sue in federal court. A majority ruled that they did because harm was done to them by this designation. Douglas, however, went far beyond this ruling to write a powerful concurring opinion on what he termed "one of the gravest issues of this generation": the constitutionality of the entire investigative process. His opinion opened with a call to arms:

> There is no doubt in my mind of the need for the Chief Executive and the Congress to take strong measures against any Fifth Column [traitorous subversives] worming its way into government—a Fifth Column that has access to vital information and the purpose to paralyze and confuse. The problems for security are real. So are the problems of freedom. The paramount issue of the age is to reconcile the two. In days of great tension when feelings run high, it is

a temptation to take short-cuts by borrowing from the totalitarian techniques of our opponent. But when we do, we set in motion a subversive influence of our own design that destroys us from within.

When Douglas examined the fairness of the process of being labeled as subversive, he found lacking the due-process requirements of knowing the charge against oneself, facing one's accusers, receiving notice of the upcoming legal proceedings, and being afforded the opportunity to be heard.

In further challenging the investigative power against individuals for disloyalty just on account of organization membership, Douglas tried to tweak Robert Jackson, the former chief prosecutor at Nuremberg: "The technique is one of guilt by association—one of the most odious institutions of history. The fact that the technique of guilt by association was used in the prosecutions at Nuremberg does not make it congenial to our constitutional scheme. Guilt under our system of government is personal. When we make guilt vicarious we borrow from systems alien to ours and ape our enemies." Rather than writing as a Justice, it was as if he was preaching a sermon on politics to the general public, in plain, clear, passionate language.

Douglas continued to be critical of the government's investigative powers the following term in the case of Eugene Dennis and ten other members of the national leadership of the American Communist Party who were charged with violating the 1940 Smith Act. The Smith Act criminalized those who "knowingly and willfully advocate, abet, advise, or teach the duty, necessity, desirability, or propriety of overthrowing or destroying any government in the United States by force or violence," and organize or help to organize any group that would do the same. The Court limited its consideration of the case to the theoretical question of whether the Smith Act was a constitutional violation of the freedom of speech. The Court knew that the test of such an issue, the so-called "clear and present danger" test dating back to Oliver Wendell Holmes and Louis Brandeis, required that it judge the immediacy of the link between usually protected speech and the constitutionally regulable action that might result from it. But by narrowing the scope of its inquiry, the Court did not explore the question of the *actual* nature of the threat posed by the speech.

In a decision announced on June 4, 1951, Chief Justice Vinson led a seven-person majority in altering the definition of "clear and present danger" to uphold the convictions. They did so by adopting a sliding-scale version of this test, called the "gravity of the evil" test, under which the government would have to prove much less if the potential nature of the threat was greater. Since the allegation here was that the American Communist Party was connected to the world communist movement with an ultimate goal of overthrowing democratic governments, this would lessen the burden of proof needed for successful prosecutions. As the Court majority put it, the words of the "clear and present danger" test "cannot mean that before the Government may act, it must wait until the *putsch* is about to be executed, the plans have been laid and the signal is awaited. If Government is aware that a group aiming at its overthrow is attempting to indoctrinate its members and to commit them to a course whereby they will strike when the leaders feel the circumstances permit, action by the Government is required." Under this standard, all the government would have to show was that the men were preaching communism, not that they were actually undertaking a revolution at that time.

Never one to be bound by his colleagues' rules, Bill Douglas in dissent expounded on the issues that the Court majority had ducked. Both he and Hugo Black could see that, in the words of one constitutional-law scholar, "the defendants were not convicted of *attempting* to overthrow the government, or even of *conspiring* to overthrow the government, but of conspiring to *advocate* the overthrow of the government." This should have been protected speech, they said.

Now he had to justify that conclusion in a dissent. Douglas assigned to his law clerk, Hans Linde, the task of reviewing the massive transcript of the trial, saying: "What I want to know from these twenty-three volumes is this: Is there any evidence in here that the Communists have advocated or privately agreed among themselves to advocate the actual use of violence against the government?" As Linde quickly worked through the volumes, he could clearly see that it was "a terrible trial. . . . The government planted evidence of what it wanted to prove, which was very little." All that had been proved, the young clerk discovered, was that the men on trial were somehow linked to a French Communist on his way to San Francisco for the meeting of the United Nations, and all of them had tried at some point to organize the teaching of four books on the theory of communism, which could then be found in any bookstore: Stalin's *Foundations of Leninism,* Marx and Engels's *Manifesto of the Communist Party,* Lenin's *The State and Revolution,* and the *History of the Communist Party of the Soviet Union.*

Assured by Linde's memo that there had been no real threat, Douglas carefully handwrote an opinion draft that viciously attacked the persecution of the group. Linde admired the way that his boss now sought to protect civil liberties: "Douglas chose [to argue] that the

constitutionality of applying a statute depended upon a clear and present danger in the classic sense. . . . You know, they weren't teaching
anybody to do anything dangerous at this point."

Douglas's attention to detail in this case illustrated to his clerk how
concerned he was at this point in his career with the technical duties
of being a judge. "People don't think of Douglas as a 'lawyer,'" Linde
argued. "They think about him as if he was nothing more than a pro-
pagandist. . . . Douglas had demonstrated that he was perfectly capable of writing the kind of properly documented, legal-precedent-filled
judicial opinions. . . . But Douglas never wasted his time doing that."

Douglas's final draft became a model of a vigorous free-speech argument. "The freedom to speak is not absolute; the teaching of methods of terror and other seditious conduct should be beyond the pale
along with obscenity and immorality," he began, adding that "this case
was argued as if those were the facts. . . . But the fact is that no such
evidence was introduced at the trial." Then Douglas got to the heart of
what outraged him about the government's prosecution case: "The
present case is not one of treason. But the analogy is close when the illegality is made to turn on intent, not on the nature of the act. We then
start probing men's minds for motive and purpose; they become en-
tangled in the law not for what they did but *for what they thought;* they
get convicted not for what they said but for the purpose with which
they said it." It was freedom of belief, which in turn energized their
freedom of speech, that Douglas was trying to protect here, even for a
group that was, in his view, "the best known, the most beset, and the
least thriving of any fifth column in history." With these words, Justice
William O. Douglas had established himself as one of only two members of the Court who were willing to extend the blessings and protections of America's Constitution even to the Communists.

·   ·   ·

As part of the research for another book, Douglas spent a good part
of the summer of 1951 hiking and exploring the Himalayas, along
the southern frontiers of Russia and China, crossing into Little Tibet
and Turkestan. When he learned that rumors were circulating in the
United States that he might be interested in running against Truman in
1952, Douglas quickly fired off a note from New Delhi to the president, denying any political ambition on his part and suggesting that
the president rely on this fact using as his "authority the best there is,
viz. the horse's mouth."

But try as he might to avoid politics, it would not avoid him. As
soon as he arrived at the San Francisco airport on August 31, on his

way to see his wife in Oregon to end their marriage, news reporters stuck microphones in his face and quizzed the "globe-trotting justice" as to what U.S. foreign policy should be toward Red China. Having just published a piece in *Look* magazine saying that the United States should make a political settlement with China as a means of breaking its apparent alliance with Communist Russia, Douglas simply repeated the argument.

"Does that mean recognition of Red China?" shouted a reporter.

If such a settlement could be worked out, explained Douglas, then recognition would be inevitable and would constitute "a real political victory" for the democratic world. Such a diplomatic coup would capitalize on the prevailing struggle between Chinese nationalism and the Russians' effort to solidify the Far East, he added. This, the Justice said, was "the greatest source of friction between any two nations in the world today." But, Douglas added, the challenges here were great: "Recognition will require straightforward and courageous thinking by all Americans, but it is the only logical course." Failing to sense the explosive nature of his jet-lag-induced, off-the-cuff comments, Douglas called in some reporters a few hours later and explained in detail how a "political settlement" with Red China would "swing the whole pendulum of Asiatic politics away from the Russians and back toward the western world."

The effect of these statements was like tossing a bomb into the Capitol. Republican senator Herman Welker called Douglas "a high Administration spokesman" and tried to secure unanimous consent to insert a newspaper account of the interview into the *Congressional Record*. Whereupon the Democratic chairman of the Senate Foreign Relations Committee, Tom Connally, stood up and shouted: "We do not intend to recognize Red China. Justice Douglas is not Secretary of State. Douglas is not President of the United States. He never will be. I don't agree with Mr. Douglas. I think he ought to stay home instead of roaming all around the world and Asia making fool statements. We're really at war—in a sense—with Red China now." When a chastened Welker protested that perhaps Douglas said these things because he was considered by many a candidate for president in 1948, Connally barked back: "[He] may have considered himself a candidate for President, but nobody else did. It's outrageous. It's ridiculous." Not a single member of the Senate rose to support Douglas's position, and some, such as Connecticut's Brien McMahon, simply disavowed him as "a private citizen without influence on the course of American foreign policy."

While members of the State Department privately expressed concern that Douglas's statement would have a negative impact on foreign policy, plain-speaking Harry Truman decided to deal with the free-agent diplomat personally. Using a letter that he had just received from Douglas reporting on his meeting with President Soekarno of Indonesia as a pretext, Truman responded:

> I was somewhat embarrassed by your statement on Communist China. As long as I am President, if I can prevent it, that cut throat organization will never be recognized by us as the Government of China and I am sorry that a Justice of the Supreme Court has been willing to champion the interest of a bunch of murderers by a public statement.
>
> I am being very frank with you Bill because fundamentally I am very fond of you but you have missed the boat on three different occasions if you really wanted to get into politics. Since you are on the highest Court in the land it seems to me that the best thing you can possibly do would be to give your best effort to that Court and let the President of the United States run the political end of foreign and domestic affairs.

Douglas tried to make amends, writing the president that he regretted any embarrassment or offense that he might have caused him. Then, after explaining the nature of the press conference, Douglas spent the rest of a four-page typed letter explaining his views with respect to Red China. To him, the greatest danger in foreign policy was an alliance between China and Russia. But, Douglas was careful to add, Truman should not listen to those who saw red-tinged motives in this liberal's views: "I hate Communism . . . [because of] the impact of its venal, godless system." For Douglas, the weakness of the Soviet dictatorship lay in the passionate nationalism of its satellite nations. In the years to follow, Douglas's views would prove to be absolutely correct.

This apologetic letter did the trick, as the president wrote on October 2 that there was no lasting damage from the incident. To which Douglas responded the next day that there was "nothing to dilute the abiding affection I have for you." This explanation did not satisfy all the members of the Senate, with some talk still being heard of a possible impeachment of Douglas. Although no one took it seriously, and no hearings were ever held on the matter, by accident Bill Douglas had set himself up as a member of a shadow government on foreign affairs.

.   .   .

The 1951–1952 Court term provided the occasion for Douglas to expand his free-speech vision from the Bench. Just after New Year's Day, the Court heard a challenge by several schoolteachers, headed by Irving Adler, to New York's so-called Feinberg law, which provided that anyone who taught or advocated the overthrow of the government by force or violence or who was knowingly a member of an organization that did these things would be automatically disqualified from employment in public schools.

Writing for a six-person majority on March 3, 1952, Justice Minton dismissed the notion that this law violated the employees' rights of free speech and assembly. To the Court, "the school authorities have the right and the duty to screen the officials, teachers, and employees as to their fitness to maintain the integrity of the schools as part of ordered society." The majority was untroubled by the notion that someone could be barred from employment just for being on a membership list, regardless of their actual views.

Neither Douglas nor Hugo Black, joined this time by Felix Frankfurter, who dissented on separate jurisdictional grounds, was prepared to withdraw civil-rights protections from public-sector employees. The man who knew how public schools operated from his days teaching English in Yakima now argued that "the law inevitably turns the school system into a spying project. Regular loyalty reports on the teachers must be made out. The principals become detectives; the students, the parents, the community become informers. Ears are cocked for telltale signs of disloyalty. . . . This is not the usual type of supervision which checks a teacher's competency; it is a system which searches for hidden meanings in a teacher's utterances." Such investigatory procedures, Douglas added, would ultimately destroy the teaching process: "There can be no real academic freedom in that environment. . . . Fear stalks the classroom. The teacher is no longer a stimulant to adventurous thinking; she becomes instead a pipeline for safe and sound information. A deadening dogma takes the place of free inquiry. Instruction tends to become sterile; pursuit of knowledge is discouraged; discussion often leaves off where it should begin." In arguing now that even in public employment "the guilt of the teacher should turn on overt acts," Douglas showed how far he had come since the *Zap* case in 1946, where he had ruled that just by entering into a contract with the government one waived Fourth and Fifth Amendment rights.

Douglas's changing posture on civil liberties also became evident when the Court was asked to review its position on the establishment of religion in the public schools. A New York City program that permitted public schools to release students early, with parental permission, in order to take religious instruction was challenged by a man named Tessim Zorach. Essentially, this was the same program as the one in Illinois that, just four years before, the Court, including Justice Douglas, had declared to be an unconstitutional violation of the First Amendment's establishment of religion clause because it was "beyond any question a utilization of the tax-established and tax-supported public school system to aid religious groups." While the religious instruction was now taking place outside of the school instead of on the school grounds, as in the earlier case, it was still true that those students who were not taking instruction were compelled to remain in class.

This time, though, Douglas baffled experts by reversing himself and writing an opinion for a six-person majority upholding the program in *Zorach v. Clauson*. To him, the two plans were easily distinguishable because "this 'released time' program involves neither religious instruction in public school classrooms nor the expenditure of public funds." Douglas argued that "we are a religious people whose institutions presuppose a Supreme Being. We guarantee the freedom to worship as one chooses. We make room for as wide a variety of beliefs and creeds as the spiritual needs of man deem necessary. . . . When the state encourages religious instruction or cooperates with religious authorities by adjusting the schedule of public events to sectarian needs, it follows the best of our traditions."

This posture perplexed those in dissent. Hugo Black argued that the "statement that Americans are 'a religious people whose institutions presuppose a Supreme Being' . . . was at least as true when the First Amendment was adopted; and it was just as true when eight justices of this Court invalidated the released time system in McCollum." To Robert Jackson's way of thinking, the problem with the program was the compulsion felt by those students who did not want to participate in the program: "My evangelistic brethren confuse an objection to compulsion with an objection to religion. . . . The day that this country ceases to be free for irreligion it will cease to be free for religion—except for the sect that can win political power."

Why had Douglas ruled in this way? While others speculated about the possible changing of his views toward religion, Justice Jackson thought he saw another, more cynical motive relating to the timing of this decision. After commenting on the lack of difference that he viewed between this case and the one from Illinois, *McCollum v. Board of Education*, yet with two different results from Douglas, he wrote: "Today's judgment will be more interesting to students of psychology and of the judicial processes than to students of constitutional law." For Jackson, his colleague appeared to be taking this proreligion position because of his thoughts about the need to win the support of a Catholic constituency for a possible run for the presidency later that year.

That same term, Douglas examined whether a state could restrict the free-speech rights of critics of government in a case involving a man named Joseph Beauharnais. Beauharnais had been convicted for defaming minorities by circulating petitions seeking to persuade the city council and the mayor of Chicago to pass segregation laws. The Court upheld a conviction under the Illinois "group" libel law, which punished someone for falsely portraying "depravity, criminality, unchastity, or lack of virtue of a class of citizens, of any race, color, creed or religion." Douglas, however, argued in dissent that this was the exercise of pure unregulable speech: "The First Amendment is couched in absolute terms — freedom of speech shall not be abridged. Speech has therefore a preferred position as contrasted to some other civil rights." Once more, Douglas saw clearly the folly of the Brethren's decision for future disputes: "Today a white man stands convicted for protesting in unseemly language against our decisions invalidating restrictive covenants. Tomorrow a Negro will be hailed [sic] before a court for denouncing lynch laws in heated terms." For Douglas, precisely this situation had been foreseen: "The Framers of the Constitution knew human nature as well as we do. They too had lived in dangerous days; they too knew the suffocating influence of orthodoxy and standardized thought. They weighed the compulsions for restrained speech and thought against the abuses of liberty. They chose liberty. That should be our choice today, no matter how distasteful to us the pamphlet of Beauharnais should be."

In another portion of the opinion, Douglas showed signs of being willing to consider the extension of constitutional protection for other civil liberties, most notably the "right of privacy": "For example, privacy, equally sacred to some, is protected by the Fourth Amendment only against unreasonable searches and seizures. There is room for regulation of the ways and means of invading privacy."

After opening this door, Justice Douglas used two other cases that spring to explain how he might go beyond even the most expansive rulings of Hugo Black in this area. The first case involved a District of Columbia streetcar company that played radio programs on loudspeakers for its riders. This policy was challenged by some riders who did not wish to be forced to listen to it, although a survey indicated that 92 percent of the travelers liked the music. Not surprisingly, the conservative majority of the Court could not find a constitutional right to listening on a streetcar only to what one wants to hear, or perhaps even to silence, in either the First or the Fifth Amendments.

When the opinion was handed down on May 26, 1952, Justice Harold Burton argued for a seven-man majority that any perceived right of privacy of a rider would be "substantially limited" by the rights of others as a result of the decision to travel on the streetcar. Even Hugo Black agreed that only if the streetcars started broadcasting "news, public speeches, views, or propaganda of any kind and by any means would [they] violate the First Amendment."

Once again, though, William O. Douglas saw an issue that no one else saw and argued it vigorously in a solo dissent. For him, this was a case of what he termed "the right to be let alone," his description of the right of privacy: "This is a case of first impression. There are no precedents to construe; no principles previously expounded to apply. We write on a clean slate. The case comes down to the meaning of 'liberty' as used in the First Amendment. Liberty in the constitutional sense must mean more than freedom from unlawful governmental restraint; it must include privacy as well, if it is to be a repository of freedom. The right to be let alone is indeed the beginning of all freedom."

For Douglas, even riders on a streetcar still had this right: "The streetcar audience is a captive audience. It is there as a matter of necessity, not of choice. . . . One who tunes in on an offensive program at home can turn it off or tune in another station, as he wishes. . . . But the man on the streetcar has no choice but to sit and listen, or perhaps to sit and try *not* to listen." In a single catchphrase—"The right to be let alone"—William O. Douglas not only had summarized his constitutional philosophy as to the relationship of the individual to the state but also had joined Justice Louis D. Brandeis in arguing that the Constitution protected a right of privacy from incursions by others. But here, Douglas seemed to be arguing that the Constitution also safeguarded a right of personal autonomy.

Having made this argument, Douglas amplified his view, during what scholars came to label his "privacy spring," in *On Lee v. United States.* The case involved the Court's approval of the use of evidence gained by an undercover narcotics agent who, in conversing with the defendant, was wired with a hidden microphone. Although in 1942 Douglas had voted with the majority in *Goldman v. United States,* to allow the use of covert electronic surveillance, ratifying the Court's earlier allowance of telephone wiretapping in the landmark 1928 case *Olmstead v. United States,* now his position was much different: "I now more fully appreciate the vice of the practice spawned by *Olmstead* and

Goldman. I now feel that I was wrong in the *Goldman* case. Mr. Justice Brandeis in his dissent in *Olmstead* espoused the cause of privacy—the right to be let alone. . . . The nature of the instrument that science or engineering develops is not important. The controlling, the decisive factor is the invasion of privacy against the command of the Fourth and Fifth Amendments." Coming as this did from the man who, just six years earlier, in *Davis v. United States,* had upheld the warrantless seizure of evidence by federal agents, it indicated the dramatic evolution in Douglas's thinking.

.   .   .

Having had some time to reconsider their wartime action in the Japanese internment cases, Douglas and the other Justices revisited the issue of presidential power when President Truman seized U.S. steel mills on April 8, 1952, to prevent the United Steelworkers of America from stopping Korean War production with a crippling strike. In citing the inherent powers of the executive office during wartime to justify the action, Truman had every reason to believe that the Supreme Court, on which were serving four of his appointees, would support him.

But the Court did not. Six Justices, led by Hugo Black, voted to overturn the seizure, arguing that Congress had expressly chosen not to give the president this power by passing the Taft-Hartley Act of 1947, which dealt with labor strikes during emergencies. However, six Justices made clear that if Congress *had* granted the power to the president to seize private businesses in order to stop a strike prior to his doing so, they would have upheld Truman's action.

Douglas wrote a passionate concurrence: "Today a kindly President uses the seizure power to effect a wage increase and to keep the steel furnaces in production. Yet tomorrow another President might use the same power to prevent a wage increase, to curb trade-unionists, to regiment labor as oppressively as industry thinks it has been regimented by this seizure." When he saw this opinion, Truman expressed his reservations to an aide about Douglas, who "really surprised me. He is looking to the future."

Realizing the president's anger over this decision, in the middle of the summer of 1952 Douglas wrote from his West Coast vacation spot, trying as best he could to soothe Truman by expressing his hope that the president would reverse his March 29 announcement not to run for reelection—if so, he "would gladly leave the Court and stump for you."

But Truman was not placated. A week later, he drafted a response:

"I am writing a monograph on just what makes Justices of the Supreme Court tick. . . . I don't see how a Court made up of so-called 'Liberals' could do what that Court did to me. I am going to find out just why before I quit this office." After reviewing the letter, though, the president decided not to mail it. Instead, four years later, a still angry Harry Truman wrote in his memoirs: "A little reading of history would have shown that there was nothing unusual about [the steel seizure]. . . . I would, of course, never conceal the fact that the Supreme Court's decision . . . was a deep disappointment to me."

What Douglas did not tell Truman was that he was exploring yet another try for the White House. Various members of the administration had already been approaching Eliot Janeway and Abe Fortas, seeking to offer the Justice the slot. But thinking about it some more, Douglas realized the horrible accuracy of Tommy Corcoran's prediction about the political impact of his divorce. "I think he felt he had lost the possibility," Douglas's second wife, Mercedes, recalled years later. "The definitive decision not to run for president, or to try to run for president was a very difficult one for him to make." But since he was still only fifty-three years old, Douglas believed that he still had time to run for the White House.

APPEALING TO THE
CONSCIENCE OF THE NATION

[This] stunning decision . . . touched off, within the
next 24 hours, one of the most dramatic and novel
episodes in all the august annals of the U.S. Supreme
Court.

—*Time,* June 29, 1953

The personal hostilities on the Vinson Court culminated in June 1953
in one final, violent explosion, with Justice William O. Douglas at
ground zero. After dissenting thirty-five times that term, more than he
had in the previous two terms put together, the issue that precipitated
Douglas's most visible action to this point was one of the most contentious ones in twentieth-century American legal history: Should
Julius and Ethel Rosenberg be put to death?

After being convicted and given the death sentence under section 34
of the Espionage Act for leaking atomic-bomb secrets to the Russians,
the Rosenbergs appealed to the Supreme Court. On October 7, 1952,
the Court met in conference to consider whether to accept the appeal
for review. Some Justices argued that since the Rosenbergs had been
convicted of treason without two witnesses testifying to the same
overt act, as was required in Article 3, Section 3 of the Constitution,
there was indeed a serious federal question worthy of review. By the
Court's rules, the support of only four Justices was necessary for it to
hear the case. Both Black and Frankfurter argued that as a matter of
policy the Court should review any death sentence imposed by the
federal government in times of peace. When the issue came around to
Douglas, whose denials to such appeals were "usually curt and unac-
companied by argument," he now voted no, in the words of Felix
Frankfurter, "with startling vehemence." All of the votes were counted,
and after Frankfurter backed off, the petition was denied by an eight-
to-one margin on October 13, with Justice Black taking the unusual
step of writing a dissent to the Court's denial.

Usually, this would be the end of the matter for the petitioners, but a case of this importance was not destined to end so quietly. Two weeks later, another petition for rehearing was filed. With the public calling for blood, the Court took up the matter once again on November 8. As they went around the table, it became clear that no one on the Court had changed his mind, and once more Frankfurter noted that Douglas's "deny" vote was offered "with unwonted vehemence." But the Rosenbergs seemed to be making progress. When the negative ruling was made public on November 17, Felix Frankfurter issued a statement that while he still adhered to his view that dissents should not be issued to denials of appeals, the matter of clemency for the death sentence, which in his opinion was beyond the review of the Court, was now in the hands of the president.

Some months later, a separate case came to the Court on behalf of the Rosenbergs, this one alleging the existence of prejudicial conduct by the U.S. attorney in his release of information to the press during the trial. When the matter was discussed on April 11, 1953, Felix Frankfurter warned his colleagues about the dangers of failing to satisfy public questions about the fairness of the trial. "I charge your conscience," he told them. "You have a duty to consider how this sentence, and this Court, will stand in the light of history if you leave the cloud of these allegations hanging over the trial." Just as before, however, the passion of Frankfurter's arguments was not accompanied by his vote. And, he noticed, once more "Douglas said, DENY, in the same harsh tone." When the votes were tallied, it was still eight to one against hearing the Rosenbergs' case.

Upon seeing this, Frankfurter asked his colleagues for time to consider whether he wished to change his vote, join Black, and file a dissent to this denial. Week after week he wrestled with the problem, until just before the Court's conference on Saturday, May 16, when he wrote a note to Chief Justice Vinson asking for one final week to decide whether to make his reservations public. During the conference, though, the Chief urged that the denial be made public the following Monday; Frankfurter could issue his dissent later. As they went around the table, it was clear that Justices Black, Douglas, Jackson, and Burton were ready to grant Frankfurter the extra week. However, Douglas and Jackson expressed their unhappiness that the proceedings had been delayed for so long. With the Court's term only a month or so from being concluded, it seemed clear to all of them that the Rosenbergs' time was running out.

The next day, however, Robert Jackson informed Frankfurter that if the proposed dissent would just comment on the "misconduct" of the

U.S. Attorney, he was prepared to join him. "I cannot imagine," Jackson told Frankfurter, "that you can be too severe on him to suit me." Each of them knew that, with Black's dissenting vote, this action would put them just one vote short of hearing the case. When Frankfurter finally decided on May 20 not to dissent in the case and Jackson also withheld comment, the Court's public posture was to remain unchanged, with another eight-to-one vote to be recorded against the Rosenbergs.

By this time, though, Bill Douglas had changed his mind. At lunchtime on Friday, May 22, with the ruling scheduled to come down the following Monday and with many of the Court's members then attending a luncheon for the National Conference of Judicial Councils, Douglas circulated a memo that read:

I have done further work on these cases and given the problems more study. I do not believe the conduct of the prosecutor can be as easily disposed of as the Court of Appeals thinks. I therefore have reluctantly concluded that *certiorari* should be granted.

Accordingly, I will ask that the order of denial carry the following notation:

"Mr. Justice Douglas, agreeing with the Court of Appeals that some of the conduct of the United States Attorney was 'wholly reprehensible' but believing, in disagreement with the Court of Appeals, that it probably prejudiced the defendants seriously, votes to grant *certiorari*."

This meant that if Frankfurter and Jackson followed through with their earlier plan to join Black's vote, the Rosenbergs had the necessary four votes to stay their execution and have their appeal heard.

While the Rosenbergs waited in their cells, the Supreme Court went to war once again. Douglas's action did not sit well with Jackson's law clerk at the time, William Rehnquist. "[To grant *certiorari* now] would be allowing one justice—WOD—to force the hand of the court and get the result which he now so belatedly wants," he wrote Jackson. It also infuriated Frankfurter, who told Robert Jackson that after all of his deliberation and final tortured resolution not to write, now he would have to make a public statement. "Don't worry," an equally angry Jackson told Frankfurter, "Douglas' memorandum isn't going down Monday. . . . Douglas' memorandum is the dirtiest, most shameful, most cynical performance that I think I have ever heard of in matters pertaining to law."

With Hugo Black sick at home, the Justices' conference on this case began on Saturday, May 23. When the discussion came around to Douglas, he explained that Frankfurter's long memo of May 20 had "alerted" him to the argument about the prejudicial prosecutorial conduct in the case. He added that he "had previously concentrated on the merits of the case only, but now realized there were other issues which he had overlooked." Years later, Douglas would explain to a scholar that until this time he had not considered the case to be "*cert.* worthy," and while he still believed that the Rosenbergs "were probably very guilty," the fact was that "even though an accused is clearly guilty he deserves, under our regime, a fair trial. By the time No. 687 [the May 1953 petition] reached us I was doubtful if the Rosenbergs had had one."

Jackson then announced that he, too, would grant the appeal, partly because of his fear that the public would become aware that a total of four members of the Court had at some point in the process been willing to grant the review, and partly because the Rosenbergs should not be put to death with one member of the Court on record as saying that their trial had been unfair. "Well it is granted," said Chief Justice Vinson, knowing that Frankfurter, Black, and Douglas would do the same, thus making the fourth vote, and with that they began to consider when the appeal could be heard. For quite a while, the Brethren debated how to speed the appeal along while still giving the matter full consideration. Should they issue the ruling before the death sentence was scheduled to be carried out on June 19 and write opinions justifying their decision later? Could Harold Burton cancel his planned summer cruise abroad? After remaining silent for quite a while as his colleagues debated the plans, Douglas got their attention. Frankfurter recorded Douglas as saying that "he ought to say something [and] . . . what he had written was badly drawn, he guessed . . . he hadn't realized it would embarrass anyone." So Douglas said that "he would just withdraw his memorandum if that would help matters." Jackson responded that if the memo was withdrawn then the Court was back where it had been before, with only two others voting to accept, and he would leave his vote against accepting the appeal, thus leaving the Rosenbergs' conviction intact.

"That S.O.B.'s bluff was called," Jackson crowed to Frankfurter after the conference. Still, when the announcement of the denial of *certiorari* was made, Douglas registered a dissent to the denial, though without issuing the offending statement.

In reporting on the entire proceedings to the still bedridden Hugo Black, Douglas said that he had withdrawn his memorandum because "it was becoming evident from the discussion that the hearing the

Court was proposing to give the Rosenbergs was to be on the issue of whether their petition for *certiorari* should be granted rather than a hearing on the merits of the petition, subsequent to an outright grant. It did not seem worthwhile . . . to have such a hearing and then deny *certiorari* anyway." To which Robert Jackson said when he heard this explanation, "Of course that is wholly false. . . . It wasn't that at all. We voted to grant until Douglas withdrew his memorandum." Whether Douglas was saying that while *he* would grant the appeal because of the misconduct but had no intention of later voting for the Rosenbergs on the merits of their case, or whether he had not completely thought through this game of judicial chess, was unclear for the moment. But whatever his real view, the Court was nowhere near finished with this issue.

In sitting for its final session that term, on June 15, the Court considered the last desperate appeals from the Rosenbergs' attorneys. Days earlier, an application had been made to Robert Jackson in his chambers, seeking an oral argument before the entire Court on whether a permanent stay of execution would be issued and also asking for a temporary stay of execution to be imposed until that hearing could take place. Jackson had referred both of these questions to the full Court in their June 13 conference, where a majority vote of the Justices was necessary to grant a stay of execution. When the issue came up for discussion, it was clear that Justice Harold Burton was now prepared to vote to hear oral argument on the question but would *not* vote for the stay of execution prior to that presentation before the Court. Because of the lineup of the votes, the matter now rested in Douglas's hands. But Douglas voted exactly the reverse of Burton, saying that he was *not* willing to hear oral argument on the stay but *was* willing to grant the stay without oral argument, which had the effect of denying both petitions by five-to-four votes. Douglas notified his colleagues by memo that he wished to add to the end of the order that while he thought that the "petition presents substantial questions . . . since the Court votes not to hear it and since no new substantial question is presented, I vote to deny the motion for a stay." To a puzzled Felix Frankfurter, it seemed as though whatever the Rosenbergs' attorneys tried, Douglas was voting to ensure their loss.

After Chief Justice Vinson announced this judgment on June 15, one Rosenberg attorney, John Finerty, jumped up and interrupted the Court's proceedings to move for a writ of habeas corpus seeking to release his clients. This petition, which can bring jailed defendants back into court for another hearing, would be used to seek yet another hearing to deal with allegations that the U.S. attorney had knowingly used perjured testimony. The Court agreed to consider the matter in a special conference that afternoon and then convene a special session to issue its ruling. Once more, the Court was unwilling to rule in favor of the petition, with Felix Frankfurter dissenting. But this time, it was Bill Douglas who argued most vigorously against the petition, saying that in such a petition it is necessary to prove that the government manufactured evidence rather than alleging that it had just used perjured testimony.

The full Court turned them down, but the lawyers knew that with the Court's adjournment a single Justice could now grant a temporary stay of execution. So they decided to canvass them individually, starting with William O. Douglas. Late that afternoon, counsel for the Rosenbergs appeared before Douglas alone and argued for an hour and a half. It was the sixth time they had made such an effort, and there was no reason to believe that the result would be any different. While their appeal should have been made before Jackson, who was the supervisory Justice over the Second Circuit, in which the case had been heard, they told Douglas, "We know that we won't have time to present it to Jackson and then present it to you because we understand that you are leaving town [and] driving West." Indeed, Douglas was planning to leave town the next morning by car for an engagement with an old friend, journalist Irving Dilliard of the *St. Louis Post-Dispatch,* at his home in Collinsville, Illinois. And besides, the lawyers suspected from Jackson's earlier denial that they already knew the result of any appeal to him.

Their argument, Clerk of the Court Harold B. Willey later reported to Felix Frankfurter, "ran along rather broad lines. There was emphasis, in view of Douglas's deep understanding of the Asiatic world, on the effect of letting the Rosenbergs go to their deaths upon Asia public opinion. The likelihood was alluded to that such action would win about 20,000,000 Asians to the Communist cause." When the presentation concluded, Douglas told them that unless they could bring him a new argument, he was not willing to change his position on their last appeal. But, he added, although he had been planning to leave the next morning at seven o'clock, he was willing to hear any new arguments the next morning at ten o'clock. In the meantime, Douglas told Willey that perhaps Felix Frankfurter would be willing to hear the appeal while he considered his own course of action.

That evening, so as to prevent any additional delay in his departure, Douglas sat down with a tablet of yellow legal-sized paper and scrawled out his judgment in advance of the argument. "It is to me questionable whether the Rosenbergs have had the kind of trial

American justice demands," Douglas wrote. While to him "the record makes a strong—indeed a powerful—case of prejudice of the prosecutor in the trial . . . my Brethren—all high-minded and conscientious judges—have another view of the case. A majority of them have concluded over and again that the point is not one of substance and that the cause of justice would not be served by review of the case. I feel strongly the other way. But since the Court has spoken, I bow to its decision." After reviewing the arguments involving possibly perjured testimony in the trial, Douglas argued that he was not "writ[ing] on a clean slate" as "the case has been before the Court in all its aspects." After pointing out that as a judge he could find no "new and different evidence that would put the case in a different posture than it was when the Court considered it," Douglas still made a political appeal on behalf of the Rosenbergs:

> The case of the Rosenbergs is a *cause celebre*. But it must be governed by the rules applicable to any criminal trial in the federal courts, no matter how inconspicuous. Judged by that standard I have thought and still think that substantial questions are presented which call for our review. But once the Court has spoken one who is in the minority should not undo what has been done except on a new and convincing showing. That showing has not been made. Hence the voice of a dissenter in this case can appeal only to the conscience of the Nation. *Stay denied.*

But after all of this work by Douglas, the opinion was never to be issued. When Frankfurter was informed on the morning of June 16 that Douglas had directed the lawyers his way, he wanted no part of them. The case was in his colleague's hands until he had finally disposed of the matter, he said. Frankfurter then relayed the whole sequence of events to Robert Jackson.

While the two Justices were trying to puzzle out their interpretation of Douglas's action, he was hearing additional arguments. The pleas came from two sets of attorneys for the Rosenbergs: their regular counsel, Emanuel Bloch, and two newcomers named Fyke Farmer and Daniel Marshall, each of whom had led legal crusades in other areas.

While District Court Judge Irving Kaufman had rejected Bloch and Farmer's right to bring the appeal, labeling them as "intruders . . . [and] interlopers," to Douglas these men were the first ones to present an entirely new argument on this case. The conspiracy for which the Rosenbergs had been charged under the Espionage Act of 1917 had in fact taken place over a four-year period, they began. Prior to the issuance of their indictment, the federal law governing this type of conspiracy had been changed by the passage of section 10 of the 1946 Atomic Energy Act, which made the death penalty no longer mandatory and requiring issuance by a judge but optional, and then only after a jury so recommended it. Moreover, the sentence could be issued only if it had been proved that "the offense was committed with an intent to in-jure the United States." None of this, the lawyers argued, had been done in the Rosenbergs' case.

This new position appeared to Douglas to have some merit. His planned departure west for the summer recess would have to wait. So, the man who never sought anyone's advice now sought counsel that afternoon from his Court adversary, Felix Frankfurter. After being given some encouragement by his colleague, several times over the next few hours Douglas contacted Frankfurter to suggest that perhaps Jackson, as the supervisory Justice, should be the one to hear this new matter. Did Frankfurter know Jackson's views on the matter? he asked. Should he refer the matter back to Jackson? Would Frankfurter like to review the ruling that he was preparing? The answer, Douglas was told each time, was no. Try as he might to reach Jackson, not until the next morning did Douglas receive a memorandum from him stating that "the thing is in a situation where you are practically compelled to make a decision."

Since Douglas's law clerk had already left for the summer, he bor-rowed one of Hugo Black's clerks to help him with the research. Hour after hour they labored, checking all of the lower-court records until they concluded that not only was this an entirely new issue that had never been presented before but indeed it seemed to have merit. Most of the acts for which the Rosenbergs had been convicted and sentenced to death—indeed, the most incriminating ones, Douglas discovered— had occurred after the law had been amended. Since the required jury instruction on the death-penalty decision was missing, in his view they could not be put to death on the basis of this trial.

So he prepared a memorandum granting the stay of execution until this new argument could be heard by the full Court. After extensively quoting from the relevant provisions of the Atomic Energy Act, Doug-las argued that "this point has never been raised or presented to this Court in any of the earlier petitions or applications. . . . This question is presented to me for the first time on the eve of the execution of the Rosenbergs without the benefit of briefs or any extended research. I cannot agree that it is a frivolous point or without substance." After conceding that some of the acts of conspiracy took place after the Atomic Energy Act had been passed, Douglas argued that his course of action was clear: "I do not decide that the death penalty could have been imposed on the Rosenbergs only if the provisions of [section] 10 of the Atomic Energy Act of 1946 were satisfied. I merely decide that the question is a substantial one which should be decided after full argument and deliberation."

By 11:00 P.M., the opinion was done, but before releasing it Douglas decided to place the matter before Chief Justice Vinson. Washington was afire as Douglas journeyed to Vinson's apartment. A large crowd of newsmen was milling around the Court, waiting for Douglas's ruling, thus making it necessary to slip out the back way, through the garage to Second Street NE. None of the reporters noticed the man in the cowboy hat who now held the Rosenbergs' fate in his hands, and neither did the protesters on Capitol Hill, who carried signs with such slogans as "Kill the Dirty Spies."

After Vinson and Douglas sat down, the Chief Justice said he found the new issue frivolous, and besides, in his opinion, the new attorney for the Rosenbergs had no standing before the Court. Nevertheless, he felt this new issue should be placed before the full conference. Attorney General Herbert Brownell, he added, had urged the same course of action. Douglas failed to hear alarm bells when he learned that the attorney general was apparently in contact with Vinson during the Court's deliberations. "The more that he talked the more convinced that I became that the point had some substance," Douglas later recalled. After two more hours of argument, Douglas decided that the time had come to get some sleep.

By the next morning, June 17, Douglas knew what he would do. He was prepared to grant the stay of execution on his own authority, but there was too little time before the planned execution two days later to properly draft and present the necessary legal arguments to the full Court.

Before taking any steps, though, Douglas sought reassurance even from his Court opponents. "What do you think?" he asked Felix Frankfurter after reciting all of the arguments with Vinson from the night before.

"Do what your conscience tells you, not what the Chief Justice tells you," said Frankfurter. "Further, I cannot advise you. Tête-à-tête conversation cannot settle this matter." Beyond that, Frankfurter added, "The point raised did not appear to be frivolous."

Douglas then showed his printed opinion to Hugo Black, who penciled on the back of it: "Bill: I think this opinion is sound. . . . This point is very substantial & I certainly do not recall having heard it suggested before."

That was all that Bill Douglas needed to hear, and by noon he released the stay of execution. Then, without another word, Douglas took off his judicial gown, marched down to the garage below the Court building, got in his car, and drove west. As soon as Douglas left the building, one of his secretaries, Fay Aull, and the others in his office raided his lower desk drawer and broke out the liquor bottles and glasses to toast the peace that they expected would reign for the summer. But peace would not be theirs just yet.

Fred Vinson and Robert Jackson had already planned their response to their colleague's lone-wolf action. They met privately with Herbert Brownell, who in turn immediately "instruc[ted] the Justice Department to petition Chief Justice Vinson to call an unprecedented special meeting of the Court to review the stay." Vinson granted the petition for a Court hearing, an action that to some seemed to be well beyond his authority, given the Court's tradition of convening a special session only after a vote of the whole body. And knowing that Douglas was gone, the Chief and his colleagues laid plans to meet the next morning and reverse his action, in order to clear the decks for the Rosenbergs to be put to death almost immediately.

By dusk, Douglas had reached a motel in Uniontown, Pennsylvania, southeast of Pittsburgh. Just as he was unloading his bags, the symphony he was listening to on the radio was interrupted by a news flash stating that the Chief Justice had called a special session of the Supreme Court the next morning to reconsider his stay of execution for the Rosenbergs. "The plan was to hold Court without me!!" Douglas later complained to Yale colleague Fred Rodell.

The man from Yakima knew just what to do. He sped into town to find a phone. After calling the Court to confirm the report that the session was to be held at noon on the eighteenth, Douglas told his other secretary, Nan Burgess, to inform the Chief that he would be in attendance. The effort was futile, he knew, but he was not going to give up without a fight. That accomplished, he returned to the motel, retrieved his bags, and drove to the William Penn Hotel in Pittsburgh, where he would stay in order to catch an early flight the next morning.

As soon as Fred Vinson saw Bill Douglas stride into the conference room, he knew that the fight was on. The Court sat briefly in a preliminary conference before their scheduled noon oral argument to determine whether a new hearing should even take place. Hugo Black argued vehemently that the Chief Justice had no power to convene the

Court, saying that it should only be done by a poll of all the Justices. When Douglas said that he would be willing to overlook the matter to get on with the hearing, Black withdrew his objection, and the lawyers' arguments were allowed to proceed.

For several hours the lawyers debated the dual questions of whether Douglas's stay should be vacated and whether the conflict between the penalty provisions of the Espionage Act and the Atomic Energy Act constituted a reviewable question for the Court. The argument took place, Douglas later recalled, "before an audience more tense than any I have ever seen." The government took the position that while Douglas had full power to issue his stay, the Rosenbergs' illegal conduct had occurred before the passage of the 1946 Atomic Energy Act, and thus Judge Kaufman had the legal right to sentence them to death. In response, the Rosenbergs' attorneys bickered with one another in open court about their appellate strategy. New Yorker John Finerty, who had made his reputation in the cases of Sacco and Vanzetti and Tom Mooney, rose and pronounced the judgment against the Rosenbergs to be a "fraud" that had been foisted on the Court by a "crooked" prosecution. After being rebuked by the Court, Finerty added, "If you lift the stay [of the execution], then . . . God save the U.S. and this honorable court."

When the Court moved into conference that afternoon, the atmosphere was charged. Arguments were exchanged on whether the Court should have even been called back into session and whether it had the power to vacate Douglas's stay, as well as on various aspects of the case itself. Several votes were taken, with Justices switching sides each time. Originally, the question was whether to uphold the stay, an action that required a majority vote of the Court. Only Black, Burton, and Douglas voted to uphold it, while Frankfurter abstained and the other five Justices voted no. As a compromise, the dissenters, joined by Frankfurter, proposed a limited extension of the stay to allow for the filing of briefs and additional oral arguments. They lost five to four. Finally came a motion to vacate the stay entirely and allow the execution to proceed. It won by a vote of six to three, with Burton switching to vote with the majority. "Probably a fifth vote could have been summoned [to delay the execution]," Douglas later recalled, but "Vinson was in a towering rage at the suggestion and finally no one pressed the point." Though Frankfurter was still furious with Douglas for making "a grandstand play," he joined Black and Douglas in dissent. The Court was convened again at noon on June 19 when Chief Justice Vinson solemnly announced that the stay was vacated. "We think further proceedings . . . are unwarranted," read Vinson. "A conspiracy was charged and proved. . . . The

Atomic Energy Act did not repeal or limit the provisions of the Espionage Act. Accordingly, we vacate the stay entered by Mr. Justice Douglas." One by one the members of the Court read their individual opinions until the issue reached Douglas, who argued, "Where two penal statutes may apply . . . the court has no choice but to impose the less harsh sentence. . . . I know deep in my heart that I am right." But six of his colleagues did not agree, so the Rosenbergs were electrocuted just after 8:00 P.M. on Friday evening, June 19, around the start of the Jewish Sabbath. Guilty or not, the Rosenbergs lost their bid for delay in part because on a frayed Supreme Court Felix Frankfurter and Robert Jackson were motivated to prevent William O. Douglas from taking the moral high ground.

Six days after the Rosenbergs were executed, an anguished Bill Douglas tried to exorcise these images from his mind. Writing to Fred Rodell, he complained about the haste of the Court's conference to vacate the stay, asking, "Did the Rosenbergs have to die that fast?"

In the politically charged environment surrounding the execution, talk of impeachment swirled around Douglas for the second time in two years. This time, two formal charges were filed in the House of Representatives by W. M. "Don" Wheeler, a Democrat from Georgia. A special five-man subcommittee was selected to investigate the resolutions alleging certain unspecified "high crimes and misdemeanors." By the time the subcommittee was called to order on June 30, Wheeler charged that Douglas was guilty because one of the Justice's speeches had repeated nearly "verbatim" Communist propaganda. Other congressmen argued that Douglas's judicial decisions were motivated by political views. To which an emboldened Wheeler added that the speed with which Douglas had issued his stay indicated that there must have been some sort of advance arrangement with the Rosenbergs' attorneys, which would tend to bring the Supreme Court into disrepute with the American public. The noticeable lack of proof offered to support this allegation moved the other members of the committee to observe that there was no evidence of an impeachable "high crime and misdemeanor." While Wheeler eventually had to admit that his charges were insubstantial, he added that "the country had overextended itself in showing tolerance for 'people who play footsy' with those who would destroy this government." That said, the subcommittee and the judiciary committee let the issue die.

When the Court, in an act of seeming futility, issued its opinion in the *Rosenberg* case nearly a month after the two had been put to death, a still anguished Justice Douglas issued an uncharacteristically personal dissent: "When the motion for a stay was before me, I was deeply troubled by the legal question tendered. After twelve hours of research and study I concluded, as my opinion indicated, that the question was a substantial one, never presented to this Court and never decided by any court. So I issued the stay order. Now I have had the benefit of an additional argument and additional study and reflection. Now I know that I am right on the law." After comparing the timing of the actions for which the Rosenbergs had been charged and the timing of the passage of the Atomic Energy Act to conclude that "the less harsh sentence" should be imposed, Douglas answered the complaint that this appeal was made too late in the process: "No man or woman should go to death under an unlawful sentence merely because his lawyer failed to raise the point. It is that function among others that the Great Writ [of habeas corpus] serves."

The Rosenbergs were dead, but for Bill Douglas the issue lived on. Frequently in talks with close friends he would, without any warning, deliver a virulent diatribe against the bloodthirsty and hasty actions of his judicial colleagues. "The country was out for blood," Douglas later lectured an interviewer. "The Court was blind to any reason. Vinson was filled with passion to such an extent that he could hardly utter a calm word. This was the closest I have ever seen this in my own personal experience. . . . This is the only time I had ever seen the spirit of a mob, the spirit of the streets, dominate a court." For Douglas, this was a "strange orgasm of hate."

Just over two months later, on September 8, Fred Vinson was dead of a heart attack, leading the sometimes cruel Felix Frankfurter, who refused even to attend the Chief's funeral with the rest of the Court, to tell a law clerk, "This is the first solid piece of evidence I've ever had that there really is a God."

As a result of a campaign deal with President Dwight Eisenhower to get the next available Supreme Court seat in return for his delegates' support in the 1952 nominating convention, former California governor Earl Warren was named Chief Justice on September 30. Now it became his task to tame these scorpions in the bottle.

And he would do so with William O. Douglas having demonstrated that he had become a liberal voice fully prepared to act alone.

THE VOICE OF ONE

I suspect that [Douglas] must have come into this world with a rush and that his first cry must have been a protest against something he saw at a glance was wrong or unjust.

—*Hugo Black*

When Earl Warren took over the Chief Justiceship on October 2, 1953, the philosophical balance of the Court was again in a state of flux. Despite the fact that Warren's legal philosophy was more moderate than Vinson's, and that his friendly, charismatic demeanor brought with it a chance of uniting the highly volatile Justices, the Court still tilted toward the conservative side. This became even truer over the next few years after four more appointments by Dwight Eisenhower: John Marshall Harlan, William Brennan, Charles Whittaker, and Potter Stewart. With only Warren and Brennan leaning toward the liberal side among the new Justices, Douglas still found himself uniting all the more frequently in dissent with Hugo Black.

Douglas made clear that he was a sworn enemy of those bent on restricting what they deemed to be undemocratic beliefs. This became clearer in a case involving a doctor from New York named Edward Barsky, who was challenging the power of the State of New York to strip him of his medical license. Barsky had refused to provide a congressional committee with certain papers from the Joint Anti-Fascist Refugee Committee, a suspected subversive organization that he chaired. After Barsky served his time in jail for contempt of Congress, the Board of Regents of the State of New York sought to suspend his license to practice medicine under a state statute authorizing such action against a physician who "has been convicted in a court of competent jurisdiction, either within or without this state, of a crime." After considerable deliberation, the Board of Regents ruled that his license should be lifted for six months.

Speaking for six members of the Court, Harold Burton had no constitutional problem with this action. For the majority, the state had the power to suspend such licenses, even though the conviction was outside of New York and did not involve moral turpitude. For them, this was merely a matter of state supervision of the medical community: "It is equally clear that a state's legitimate concern for maintaining high standards of professional conduct extends beyond initial licensing." Barsky had argued that the state had suspended his license solely because it believed him to be a member of a group on the attorney general's list of subversive organizations. Since that list had been ruled by the Supreme Court in the *Joint Anti-Fascist Refugee Committee v. McGrath* case three years earlier to be open to legal challenges and potentially unlawful, he now claimed that New York had acted unconstitutionally. However, the majority found no evidence to support this charge.

Speaking in dissent, Hugo Black turned this logic on its head and showed that there was no evidence to prove that the State of New York *did not* use this list in making its determination. For him, this action also represented an unconstitutional bill of attainder, punishing people for mere association with others. Thus, he argued that the state violated the federal Constitution at least once and possibly twice.

Douglas was not nearly so technical in writing his own two-page dissent. "The right to work, I had assumed, was the most precious liberty that man possesses," he began. "Man has indeed as much right to work as he has to live, to be free, to own property. . . . To work means to eat. It also means to live." Douglas saw the danger in allowing the government to strip Barsky of his "right to work" as a doctor "not because he was a Communist, not because he was a 'subversive', but because he had certain unpopular ideas." Thus, Douglas argued: "So far as I know, nothing in a man's political beliefs disables him from setting broken bones or removing ruptured appendixes, safely and efficiently. . . . When a doctor cannot save lives in America because he is opposed to Franco in Spain, it is time to call a halt and look critically at the neurosis that has possessed us." Douglas's passionate defense of the "fundamental rights" of this newly articulated right to work and the more traditional right to hold and express unpopular ideas truly set him apart from the majority on the Court.

Douglas's admirers could see what he was doing here. "Bill was a genius and a visionary," explained Hugo Black law clerk Charles Reich. "He had the ability to take you up to the top of the mountain and show you the entire vista of future issues. But then you would come down from the mountain and lose sight of what you had seen. He never did." And here for Reich was an example of that visionary ability: "Douglas wrote the first opinion ever on the Court about the right to work. You talk about vision. Now there is a visionary opinion, in the sense of seeing what's coming. Seeing how people are going to be threatened through their work and regulated through their work." In the end, it was Douglas's broad vision of rights and the ability to enunciate them in such clear language that captured the imagination of the public and pointed the way for the future.

.   .   .

Douglas's courageous willingness to battle against the rest of the government was not limited to his work on the Court. On its editorial page on January 3, 1954, *The Washington Post* endorsed a plan to build the C & O Parkway from Cumberland, Maryland, to the nation's capital along an old 185-mile, 230-foot-wide towpath beside the historic Chesapeake and Ohio Canal. The goal was to provide a sea-level road to Baltimore and Washington for Maryland motorists who were accustomed to risking their lives traveling by car over the treacherous five mountains traversed by U.S. Route 40. The only dissenters were those who walked and rode by horseback along this route, including, as it turned out, one nature-loving member of the Supreme Court: William O. Douglas.

Douglas sent a letter to the editor protesting that this highway would destroy the canal that his predecessor Justice Louis D. Brandeis used to travel by canoe to Cumberland. Even now, he said, "it is a refuge, a place of retreat, a long stretch of quiet and peace at the Capitol's [sic] back door—a wilderness area where man can be alone with his thoughts, a sanctuary where he can commune with God and with nature, a place not yet marred by the roar of wheels and the sound of horns." And, he added, "It is a place for boys and girls, men and women. One can hike 15 or 20 miles on a Sunday afternoon, or sleep on high dry ground in the quiet of a forest, or just go and sit with no sound except water lapping at one's feet. It is a sanctuary for everyone who loves woods—a sanctuary that would be utterly destroyed by a fine two-lane highway." Realizing that these words, no matter how eloquent, would unlikely change the direction of "progress," Douglas then laid down an elegant gauntlet: "I wish the man who wrote your editorial of January 3, 1954, approving the parkway would take time off and come with me. We would go with packs on our backs and walk the 185 miles to Cumberland. I feel that if your editor did, he would return a new man and use the power of your great editorial page to help keep this sanctuary untouched." If he did, the environmentalist jurist insisted, the benefits would be many:

One who walked the canal its full length could plead that cause with the eloquence of a John Muir. He would get to know muskrats, badgers and fox; he would hear the roar of wind in thickets; he would see strange islands and promontories through the fantasy of fog; he would discover the glory there is in the first flower of spring, the glory there is even in a blade of grass; the whistling wings of ducks would make silence have new values for him. Certain it is that he could never acquire that understanding going 60, or even 25, miles an hour.

The plea clearly touched a nerve, as bags of supportive mail poured into the paper and the Supreme Court's offices.

The challenge was just too much to resist for Robert Estabrook, the chief of *The Washington Post*'s editorial page, and Merlo Pusey, the writer of the editorial. "We are pleased to accept Justice Douglas' invitation to walk the towpath of the old canal—the entire 185 miles of it between Washington and Cumberland, if that meets with his pleasure," they responded in a follow-up piece. "He has only to name the time and the starting point of the journey and to prescribe the equipment to be taken along. But it is only fair to warn the Justice that we are already familiar with some parts of the beautiful country that will be traversed. We are sufficiently enthusiastic about it to wear some blisters on our feet, but we do not believe that this back-yard wilderness so near to Washington should be kept closed to those who cannot hike 15 or 20 miles a day." And so the hike was on, and the date was set for March 20.

But if the editors of *The Washington Post* thought that they could outduel Bill Douglas—especially at his favorite avocation of hiking—they were wrong. As physically fit as the two editors were, their fifty-five-year-old travel companion had for years been hardened by the challenge of double-time marches up and down the Wallowa and Cascade mountains. The plan, according to the paper, was for about twenty-five men "to cover the trip in eight days, averaging about 21 miles a day. The first day, though, the goal is about 26 or 29 miles. The hikers will carry packs weighing about 30 pounds, which will hold sleeping bags, tarpaulins, and concentrated foods." Aubrey Graves, the country-life editor, promised that the dried-food diet would be relieved from time to time by what he called "bouillabaisse busts" or mulligan-stew feasts. Graves's small burro, José, would be used to carry supplies, and "some of the party will sleep in sleeping bags under the stars, but the less hardy will repair to nearby farms and towns for the nights."

While the hike was originally set to begin in Washington and go west, Douglas suggested that they reverse the direction, thus affording them maximum publicity opportunities at the finish line. Then the schedule was reset to end by press time the following Saturday, thus guaranteeing a big write-up in the Sunday paper. Once all of the arrangements were set, Douglas, billed by the paper as "the Challenger," arrived at Union Station, carrying only his camera and a small knapsack, to board the special train car that would take them to Cumberland. The other forty hikers, on the other hand, showed up a bit differently prepared for the trek, with a six-ton truck loaded with all their gear and even a motorized commissary carrying their meals.

Douglas surveyed the group of men before him and pronounced the party to be "a little bigger than the Lewis and Clark expedition, and considerably better fed." That said, before they all retired for the evening, the men all joined in one verse of an old canal builders' song ("Oh the old Potomac is rising / And the whesky's running short / We hardly think we'll get a drink / Until we get to Williamsport").

They began their hike in a driving rainstorm, and Douglas immediately set the pace. Marching in the lead at a military double-time pace, somewhere between three and five miles an hour, Douglas moved so fast that, in the words of one participant, rather than looking at the scenery "our eyes were focused for the most part on the fleet-footed jurist who threatened to walk right out of sight away from us. None of us wanted to be left on our own 150 miles or so away from home." Each time they reached a town, the whole community was waiting to join the party for several miles before turning the group over to people from the next town. Every few miles, a new stanza would be added to the canal song, until it grew to an astonishing thirty-one stanzas. "Last night we took to sleeping out / Beneath the open skies / The ground was hard, the dew was wet / But stars were in our eyes!" In reality, rather than "sleeping under the stars" along the way, members of the group stayed in relative luxury at such places as the Cardinal Club in Oldtown, the Woodmont Club (where they feasted on a champagne supper), and the conservation farmhouse for the Bethesda–Chevy Chase chapter of the Izaak Walton League of America, where Boy Scouts prepared buffalo, salmon, and beef steaks for them.

Early in the hike, Merlo Pusey began to see the wisdom of Douglas's viewpoint, writing: "It is good to renew one's contacts with nature. At this point we are torn between a feeling of appreciation to Justice Douglas for luring us into this venture and irritation over the increasingly pathetic condition of our feet. But blisters heal and memories linger. The one conclusion of which we seem capable at this time is that experience on the trail is an excellent leavening influence to which even editors occasionally should be subjected." After 140 grueling miles, Robert Estabrook dropped out and began riding atop an overtaxed horse instead. Then, ten miles later, Pusey had to do the same, choosing to hitch a ride on the truck. Mile after mile, though, a grim-faced, cowboy-hatted Bill Douglas could be seen "marching resolutely" ahead of the party, breaking not only his challengers but in time even the poor horse bearing the heavyset editor.

They averaged twenty-three miles a day, hiking through all kinds of weather, including a freak snowstorm. But nothing stopped Douglas — not fatigue, intestinal problems, or even the bad case of poison ivy he contracted along the way. The grueling nature of the effort was reflected in their latest song stanza: "The knees are slowly playing out / The arches start to drop / If we had John Brown's body here / We'd gladly make a swap." By this time the group had been separated into the duffers, who rode on the truck or the canal boat that was shadowing them; the "dragons," who walked most of the way; "snapdragons," who dropped out from time to time to snap pictures of the trip; and "the simon-pures," who marched every inch of the trip without stopping.

By the end of the eight days, there were still thirty-seven people marching, though not all of them from the original group, and of them only nine, led by Douglas, were simon-pures. One participant recognized this feat with a new verse to the canal song: "The duffers climbed aboard the truck / With many a groan and sigh / But something faster passed them up / The Judge was whizzin' by." Not everyone was as impressed by the liberal jurist's efforts, however, as a sign was tacked on a tree along the way: "Jackasses have traveled this path before."

But for Douglas, who grudgingly admitted that the last three nights had left him "tired," the finish was worth it. They arrived in Washington at Lock Number Five right on schedule, greeted by Secretary of the Interior Douglas McKay. "Justice Douglas I presume," he said, smiling at the dusty jurist and his party. Then they all boarded the *Canal Clipper,* a popular rivercraft, and were pulled by two horses along the final five miles of the trip into Georgetown, accompanied by area residents in canoes carrying signs reading "May Justice Prevail" and "Scratch the Parkway at the Post." Thousands lined the shoreline to cheer as the flotilla went by, and when they arrived in Georgetown a cheering crowd of fifty thousand people waited for them. While the exhausted members of the group remained seated on their boat, wrapped in heavy blankets, Douglas stood in the stern, carrying a fist-

ful of forsythia that had been tossed to him and waving his broad-
brimmed western hat in response to the "roaring welcome." To honor
their feat, Douglas and the eight other simon-pures each received a
Hawaiian lei and heard the final new verse to the canal song: "Glory to
the Immortal Nine / The waiting thousands roared / The Conquering
heroes hit Lock 5 / And hurled themselves on board / And hurled
themselves on board."

The trip achieved Douglas's purpose. On March 31, *The Washington
Post* printed a retraction of their editorial call for the highway, saying:
"We also believe that many semi-wilderness stretches along the old
canal ought not to be disturbed. . . . We urge our readers to investigate
for themselves the wonderful potential of this scenic attraction—with
its respite from daily concerns—so close to the Nation's Capital."
Eventually, the government came to agree with the paper, and the
canal was preserved.

The following year, Douglas called for a reunion hike. The participants were to meet at the Outdoor Club near Cumberland. When the
group arrived though, word came that Douglas was being held up by
Court business and would join them later. So the group hiked to the
designated mountain spot to camp, thinking that the Justice would
get a ride and meet them there, only to discover that the rains had
washed out the road. Instead he arrived, according to *Washington Post*
writer Aubrey Graves, "in typical Douglas fashion":

> Shortly after 9 P.M. those at camp saw a flashlight twinkling
> through the woods. It was Douglas, who, eager to hit the trail, had
> quit the car [driven by his wife] at Paw Paw, W. Va., and in the dark-
> ness started walking the several miles to camp. The gorge below
> Paw Paw tunnel, where the canalway was blasted through deep
> rock, had been a difficult stretch for the early arriving hikers (like
> Bob Estabrook) who came through it in daylight. Douglas plowed
> for some distance through the two-foot-deep water of the canal—
> aided by his flashlight and the moon! He dried out before the blaz-
> ing campfire. A rugged man, that Justice, at 56!

Thereafter, each year in the late spring Douglas would hold a "canal
hike reunion" at which he would set a more leisurely pace, entertain
the group of initial participants, former law clerks, and nature lovers
with stories of the first trip. And, after fifteen miles or so, everyone
would head for a local restaurant.

Having saved the canal, it continued to be Douglas's personal sanctuary from the travails of Washington. On Sundays, Charles Reich

would pick up his phone at 8:30 A.M. or so and hear a western-twanged voice say, without even so much as a hello, "Hey Charlie, wanna go for a walk?"

"There was no mistaking that voice," recalled Reich with a smile. "It sounded like something extraordinary was going to happen." With that, Reich would go meet Douglas, and without a word the two men would start walking between sixteen and twenty-four miles at a pace of three or four miles an hour. The only respite came when they stopped to eat their lunch, which always consisted of a single crushed peanut butter–and–jelly sandwich that each of them carried in his back pocket. A handful of minutes later, it was off on the trail again.

The reason that Douglas spent Sundays walking along the canal was no mystery to his friends. "He had to have something to do," said Charles Reich. "When he was sitting, it would drive him crazy. But walking, he was occupied. . . . And when he was good and tired, that was good, too. He was nicer. . . . He couldn't sit still. Couldn't stand the office. Couldn't relax at home. So going out was an activity for him. . . . Most of the time, it was just doing stuff for the sake of doing it. He just couldn't get enough activity." These walks showed a much different side of Douglas, Reich continued: "When he walked and talked, he mostly looked straight ahead, but every now and then he would say something that he thought was funny, and then he would turn, and you would see that grin, those icy-blue eyes, that sort of burnt, silent laughter. It was a laugh you couldn't hear, but still and all it was a real laugh. He might have told a story about one of his favorite people's foibles, and some of their exploits when they were in law school. And he would turn with that laugh, and I could see there was another part of him."

The discussion on these trips was more a monologue than a conversation. "Almost all that time Justice Douglas was talking," said Reich, "and I was listening. All I had to really show [was] that I was there, was that I was listening, and occasionally I spoke when asked a specific question. The topics on those walks ranged all over, in many, many interests, from the world to the problems of the environment, to the Court, to reminiscences of Yale, to talk about people that he knew, and sometimes whom we both knew. This was an extraordinary experience. It seemed to me that I was the luckiest person in the world— to have been with him and to listen."

These weekly walks did not go unnoticed, and at times others would try to join the pair. But Douglas quickly learned how to deal with them. One time a pair from New York announced that they would be joining the hike, so Douglas picked a spot way out in Maryland to meet them. When they arrived right at the appointed hour, everyone shook hands, and off they went, with Douglas setting a particularly horrific pace. Never once did he interrupt his monologue to notice that the newcomers had quickly disappeared behind them. After several hours, Douglas paused to look around and, seeing only Reich alongside, said, "I wonder what happened to them?"

"I don't know," responded Reich.

"Well," shrugged the Justice, "everyone goes their own pace." And off they went again.

Over the years, Reich noticed, the hikes stopped for only one thing: "Douglas certainly was terribly vain . . . almost in a silly way. . . . The one thing that could stop a hike cold would be the appearance of anybody with a camera. He just loved to have his picture taken. Nothing else would stop him, but a camera would stop him, anytime. I always thought that there is a person who wanted the reassurance that he is someone who is looked up to and who people care about."

Spurred by his love of nature, over the years Douglas would spearhead a number of environmental protests to save natural locations under siege. The natural shoreline at Olympic Beaches in Washington, the Buffalo River in Arkansas, Lake Erie, Lake Tahoe, the Guadalupe Mountains, the Allagash River in Maine, Sunfish Pond in New Jersey, and dozens of other spots all became points of Douglas's concern. But it was the C & O Canal that most identified him as a leader of environmental causes.

.   .   .

Douglas's nonjudicial interests went well beyond the environment. Many thought that Douglas's repeated defenses of likely communists might indicate he was one of them. But nothing could be further from the truth. For the independent-minded libertarian Douglas, there was so much for him to hate in the Soviets: their program of thought control, their militaristic police state, their overarching governmental control, and their repression of religion. But, as in the case of Red China, he knew that only through travel could he learn enough about the people of a country to deal effectively with them in the future. That was why in 1955 he became desperately interested in taking one of his publishing journeys to Russia.

Given the considerable expense, Douglas's literary agent, Helen M. Strauss, arranged for *Look* magazine to pay for the travel, arrange the trip, and supply a top journalistic photographer, in return for several articles written by the Justice. The only stipulation was that all other renditions of the story and all other photographs were embargoed until after the publication of the first piece in *Look*.

With the money in hand, Douglas and Mercedes began to invite some of their friends to join them on the trip. As they did so, Joseph P. Kennedy called Douglas to say that he was "very anxious" that his twenty-nine-year-old son, Robert, then the chief counsel to Senator John McClellan's anticommunist Senate Select Committee on Improper Activities, accompany them. "I think Bobby ought to see how the other half lives," Kennedy told the Justice.

"Joe was convinced that the world was going to go socialist after he died," recalled Eliot Janeway, "and so he had Douglas take Bobby to Russia."

Douglas could see the real reason that Joe Kennedy wanted his son to be exposed to this country: "He had big plans for Bobby and probably thought that the Russian trip would be important in his education."

After the group assembled in Teheran and took a boat up the Caspian Sea to the Azerbaijani port of Baku, the fact-finding visit in August and early September 1955 went well with the exception of Kennedy's behavior. "Kennedy was rude and unduly familiar with the Soviet people that he met," recorded the KGB in its investigative files. As he "mocked all Soviets," Kennedy repeatedly expressed virulently anti-Soviet views, telling his Russian interpreter that there was "no freedom of speech, that the system did not permit any criticism of the Soviet government, and that the Soviet Jews were persecuted" in the country. At the same time, Kennedy ostentatiously carried a Bible wherever he went, all the while taking photographs of the worst things he could find, such as poorly dressed children, crumbling factories, lines at the market, and drunken military officers.

Douglas noticed this ungracious behavior as well, but it seemed to him to be spurred by Kennedy's fear of the country and its repressive government. "Douglas told me that every time they passed a church, Bobby would dive into it and . . . whimper and quiver on the floor," recalled Eliot Janeway.

Kennedy also tried to provoke his hosts with attempts to discover "secret information," with the KGB recording that he told the chief of the Kazakh militia that he "was interested in the techniques of tapping telephone conversations, secret censorship of mail, Soviet intelligence activities abroad, [and] the system of repression, including the means of punishing captured foreign spies." Then he began asking others in the region how many people were being held in Soviet jails and how many others had been forced into Soviet labor camps. The Justice tried to convince him to amend his ways for the remainder of the trip: "I told Bobby—his tendency was to get into arguments with the Communists trying to convince them that they were wrong—and I said 'Bobby, that's whistling in the wind. You never can argue with these fellows, so why don't we just forget about it, and spend an evening doing something else rather than wasting it trying to convert some guy who will never be converted.'"

The "something else" that they did on occasion did not go unnoticed by the KGB either. Both men offered evidence of their real weakness for women during the trip. Soviet intelligence reported to Party Secretary Nikita Khrushchev that Kennedy, then married, had asked his Intourist guide without success to send a "woman of loose morals" to his hotel room. Douglas was no different, though his efforts to find female companionship were made more difficult by the fact that his wife was accompanying him. Still, he boasted in a letter to Clark Clifford that he was able to find ladies in Russia who "went out of their way" in "satisfying his most precious drives." The behavior of both men was ill-advised, given the dictatorial government's predilection for spying on visitors in the hopes of blackmailing them later on. "Douglas was reckless," recalled Eliot Janeway. "He'd say anything to anybody."

By the time the trip ended, both men had learned much about the Soviet people and system of government. As Douglas recalled: "I think Bobby and I both came out of Russia with the feeling that Communism, while it was in control of Russia, was not embraced by more than probably seven percent of the people, and ninety percent of the people couldn't care less. Bobby's impression was that the cadres were in control, but that the Russian people were primarily nationalists and not ideological strays."

But Douglas learned more about the other side of Bobby Kennedy after this trip. When he returned to the United States, the Justice ensconced himself in one of the cottages in the Kennedy compound in Hyannis, Massachusetts, to rest up, work on the backlog of appeals petitions to review for the opening of Court, and write his article on the trip. When the piece was completed, Helen Strauss submitted it to the magazine and arranged for Doubleday to publish an expanded version in book form. But then she received an annoyed phone call from Dan Mich, the *Look* editor on the project, asking, "Have you seen the new issue of *U.S. News and World Report*?" After Strauss responded that she had not, Mich said, "Robert Kennedy has written up the full Russian trip. It's on the stands now. You'll also discover that he had his own photographs taken and that he has sold those to a photographic agency, which is already servicing them to other publications."

When Strauss phoned Douglas with the news about this "conscious and willful betrayal" of their original agreement, the Justice could only say, "There is nothing to be done. That's Bobby Kennedy." Eventually, though, both Douglas's *Look* article and his book, *Russian Journey,* were published. While they might not have had the impact that the publishers hoped they might, for Douglas they kept him on the publishers' agenda.

.   .   .

On the Court, Douglas continued to display a willingness to protect individuals' civil rights and liberties as they continued to come under attack. Such was the case in the appeal of William Ludwig Ullmann, who challenged the constitutionality of the Immunity Act of 1954. This law allowed the granting of a limited form of immunity to people who were called to testify before grand juries or courts about crimes that allegedly endangered national security. Recipients of such immunity could not be tried for any "transaction" about which they had testified. Ullmann had been called to testify before a grand jury regarding his and others' association with the American Communist Party in connection with an espionage case, but even after being granted transactional immunity he refused to testify. His argument was that while he could not be jailed for his testimony, the immunity provisions of the law did not protect him against prosecution under state statutes, the loss of a job, reduction of status in a labor union, the inability to get a passport, or his reduced acceptance by the general public. Ullmann was charged with contempt and convicted. Seven members of the Court, speaking through Justice Felix Frankfurter, upheld the constitutionality of the Immunity Act, arguing that the grant of federal immunity was sufficient to offset the forced loss of protection by the Fifth Amendment right against self-incrimination. Relying on a precedent dating back to the late nineteenth century, *Brown v. Walker,* the guarantees of the Fifth Amendment were held to be satisfied when, as in the case of this grant of immunity, "criminality has already been taken away."

Once more, though, Bill Douglas, joined in dissent by Hugo Black, saw a variety of other negative consequences that resulted from witnesses being forced by the law to reveal information about their associations. Consequences such as being rendered ineligible for employment in the federal government and in defense facilities constituted "real and dread uncertainties that the Immunity Act does not remove. . . . [O]ne protective function of the Fifth Amendment is at once removed when the guarantee against self-incrimination is qualified in the manner it is today." After offering a long, detailed history of the protection against compulsory self-incrimination, Douglas argued that under this law "the privilege of silence is exchanged for a partial, undefined, vague immunity. It means that Congress has granted far less than it has taken away." Having argued that "the law could not be used to pry open one's lips and make him a witness against himself," Douglas concluded that "the Fifth Amendment stands between the citizen and his government. When public opinion casts a person into the outer darkness, as happens today when a person is exposed as a Communist, the government brings infamy on the head of the witness when it compels disclosure. That is precisely what the Fifth Amendment prohibits."

Confronted by the majority's reliance on an opposing precedent, Douglas offered his view on *stare decisis,* the judicial tradition that legal precedents are to be observed: "Finally it is said that we should not disturb *Brown v. Walker* because it is an old and established decision. . . . *Brown v. Walker,* decided by a bare majority of the Court and now 60 years old, has no greater claim to sanctity than the other venerable decisions which history showed had outlived their usefulness or were conceived in error." This confirmed Douglas's earlier argument before the Association of the Bar of the City of New York that "the decisions of yesterday or of the last century are only the starting points. . . . It is better that we make our own history than be governed by the dead." In time, Douglas would shorten this view to write, "I would rather create a precedent than find one." Or, as he told friends defiantly in conversation, "I don't follow precedents, I make 'em."

By end of the Court's 1956–1957 term, Douglas charted in two dissents the far reaches of constitutional protection under the First Amendment. In one case, a man named Samuel Roth was convicted in federal court for sending obscene materials through the mails, while in another a man named David S. Alberts was convicted by the State of California for keeping such material for sale. Faced with the issue of defining obscenity, the Court decided to review the so-called *Hicklin* rule, an English law precedent dating to 1868, which declared that a work was obscene if a small portion of the material had the effect of generating lascivious thoughts in the most impressionable and suggestible members of the community. Justice William Brennan proposed a more modern test, asking "whether to the average person, applying contemporary community standards, the dominant theme of the material taken as a whole deals with sex in a manner appealing to prurient interest." Later, the Court would add that the work also had to be "utterly without redeeming social importance."

Douglas, writing in dissent in *Roth v. United States* with Hugo Black, used an absolutist adherence to the First Amendment to go beyond Brennan's modernized test to state that published material should never be banned. "The test of obscenity the Court endorses today gives the censor free range over a vast domain," wrote Douglas. "To allow the State to step in and punish mere speech or publication that the judge or the jury thinks has an *undesirable* impact on the thoughts but that is not shown to be a part of unlawful action is drastically to curtail the First Amendment." For Douglas, the ruling offered yet one more opportunity for the government to control thoughts:

> Any test that turns on what is offensive to the community's standards is too loose, too capricious, too destructive of expression to be squared with the First Amendment. Under that test, juries can censor, suppress and punish what they don't like, provided the matter relates to "sexual impurity" or has a tendency "to excite lustful thoughts." This is community censorship in one of its worst forms. It creates a regime wherein [in] the battle between the literati and the Philistines, the Philistines are certain to win.

Douglas drove home his point in another dissent to another obscenity case that was also issued that same day. In this case, a challenge was brought by Kingsley Books to a New York obscenity statute under which the chief executive of a municipality could seek an injunction to prevent the sale of allegedly obscene material. Despite the obvious censorship evident in this law, five members of the Court, speaking through Felix Frankfurter, found this to be a valid regulation. Douglas, again dissenting in the company of Black, expressed his horror at a procedure that "gives the State the paralyzing power of a censor," arguing that "free speech is not to be regulated like diseased cattle and impure butter. The audience (in this case the judge or the jury) that hissed yesterday may applaud today, even for the same performance. The regime approved by the Court goes far toward making the censor supreme." Thereafter, Douglas maintained his absolutist stance with respect to allegedly obscene material to the point that, unlike the rest of the Court with the exception of Black, he would refuse in obscenity cases even to read the book or see the movie in question and simply hold for the defendant.

The man who had become an absolutist in the First Amendment area, however, made clear in a prominent contemporary case in June

1957 that he was not yet willing to do the same for criminal defendants. Convicted California murderer Caryl Chessman's nine-year battle to avoid execution reached the Supreme Court with him arguing
that his Fourteenth Amendment due-process rights had been violated
when his trial transcript was prepared by a substitute court reporter
because, with the lengthy appeal, the original official had died before
the task was complete. The Supreme Court held for Chessman, ruling that the manner in which the trial transcript was prepared—
involving the use of shorthand notes from the trial and input from the
prosecutor and police officers who had been witnesses at the trial in a
proceeding at which Chessman and his attorney were not present—
did violate his rights.

But Douglas, in language reminiscent of the stance he first offered
in the *Zap* case, argued "that in substance the requirements of due
process have been fully satisfied, [and] that to require more is to exalt
a technicality." With that, Douglas went into a detailed account of
how Chessman had in fact exercised his right to review the transcript
"with a fine-tooth comb" and noted that many of his suggestions were
in fact used in the final account. As a result, Douglas argued that "it is
impossible to conclude that there is any important, significant prejudicial error in the record on which the appeal in this case was taken."
Clearly not yet an advocate for safeguarding the rights of the accused,
Douglas ruled: "The conclusion is irresistible that Chessman is playing
a game with the courts, stalling for time while the facts of the case
grow cold."

.   .   .

Late in the 1950s, Douglas continued to protect the civil liberties and
rights of those charged with membership in the Communist Party and
other allegedly "subversive" organizations. This was apparent when the
Court heard *Kent v. Dulles,* involving Rockwell Kent and Walter Briehl,
two alleged Communists who were refused passports by the State Department to attend the World Council of Peace in Helsinki, because
of their unwillingness to file a required affidavit stating whether or
not they were members of the Communist Party. When five members of the Court agreed that the relevant statutes—the Immigration
and Nationality Act of 1952 and an Act of Congress in 1926—did not
empower the secretary of state to withhold a passport for this reason, Douglas, the man who loved foreign travel, was chosen to write
the majority opinion. "A passport not only is of great value—indeed
necessary—abroad," wrote Douglas, "it is also an aid in establishing
citizenship for purposes of re-entry into the United States." Then, after

a lengthy examination of the history of passports, Douglas explored what for him had become the major issue here: "The right to travel is a part of the 'liberty' of which the citizen cannot be deprived without due process of law under the Fifth Amendment. . . . Freedom of movement across frontiers in either direction, and inside frontiers as well, was a part of our heritage. Travel abroad, like travel within the country, may be necessary for a livelihood. It may be as close to the heart of the individual as the choice of what he eats, or wears, or reads. Freedom of movement is basic in our scheme of values." For Douglas, this basic liberty was as fundamental as the "right to work," which he had extolled four years earlier in the *Barsky v. Board of Regents* case. It made no difference to him either that no such language can be found in the Constitution or that it was being restricted here for alleged subversives. For William O. Douglas, the civil rights and liberties of accused subversives were paramount, too.

Later that term, Douglas's efforts to protect accused Communists went a step further in dissents to two other cases. The first dispute involved a public-school teacher named Herman A. Beilan, who was fired from the Philadelphia school district for "incompetency." In fact, the action was taken because of his refusal to answer a question from his superintendent regarding his membership in organizations affiliated with the Communist Party. Justice Harold Burton, speaking for five members of the Court, upheld the firing on the grounds that the request for information did not violate his right of "due process." The majority found "no requirement in the Federal Constitution that a teacher's classroom conduct be the sole basis for determining his fitness."

In a companion case, the same issues were raised by a New York City subway conductor named Max Lerner, who was fired under the New York Security Risk Law for refusing to answer questions from his employer regarding his membership in the Communist Party. Here, five members of the Court, speaking through conservative John Marshall Harlan, ruled that this action did not violate Lerner's constitutional rights because the firing was based on a "doubt created as to his 'reliability' by his refusal to answer relevant questions put by his employer, a doubt which the court held justifiable."

Douglas argued that the firings of these two men violated a series of constitutional rights he now found in the First Amendment, including "the right to believe what one chooses, the right to differ from his neighbor, the right to pick and choose the political philosophy that he likes best, the right to associate with whomever he chooses, the right to join the groups he prefers, [and] the privilege of selecting his own

path to salvation." Lacking any evidence of active, treasonous actions
by either man, Douglas clearly saw the problems of punishing people
for their political beliefs:

> The fitness of a subway conductor for his job depends on his
> health, his promptness, his record for reliability, not on his politics
> or philosophy of life. The fitness of a teacher for her job turns on
> her devotion to that priesthood, her education, and her perfor-
> mance in the library, in the laboratory, and classroom, not on her
> political beliefs. . . . It's time we called a halt to government's pe-
> nalizing people for their beliefs. . . . When we make the belief of the
> citizen the basis of government action, we move toward the con-
> cept of *total security*. Yet *total security* is possible only in a totali-
> tarian regime—the kind of system we profess to combat.

In a nutshell, Douglas offered his summary of a decade of thinking and
writing on this topic.

No better example of Douglas's breadth of vision existed than his
use two years later of a little-employed judicial technique of dissenting
to the Court's unwillingness to grant *certiorari* to review a seemingly
very minor case. A group of Long Island, New York, residents, led by
Robert Cushman Murphy, sued to enjoin government officials from
carrying out a planned program of aerial spraying of DDT and kero-
sene to kill the ravaging hoards of gypsy moths in that area. They argued that the danger to their health from this toxic spray violated
their constitutional rights under the Fifth and Fourteenth Amendments. For the Court, the case could not be heard because the spraying
program had already taken place, so they denied the writ of *certiorari,*
thus refusing to hear the case. Douglas, however, believed otherwise
and argued in a dissent that the Court should have taken the case because of its future general applicability: "The public interest in this
controversy is not confined to a community in New York. Respondents' spraying program is aimed at millions of acres of land throughout the Eastern United States." For him, this was "a serious threat to
human health," and "the need for adequate findings on the effect of
DDT is of vital concern not only to wildlife conservationists and owners of domestic animals but to all who drink milk or eat food from
sprayed gardens."

While Douglas "express[ed] no views on the merits of this particular controversy," he left little doubt where he would stand if and when
such an issue was taken up by his colleagues:

We are told by the scientists that DDT is an insoluble that cows get from barns and fields that have been sprayed with it. . . . The effect of DDT on birds and on their reproductive powers and on other wildlife, the effect of DDT as a factor in certain types of disease in man such as poliomyelitis, hepatitis, leukemia and other blood disorders, the mounting sterility among our bald eagles have led to increasing concern in many quarters about the wisdom of the use of this and other insecticides. The alarms that many experts and responsible officials have raised about the perils of DDT underline the public importance of this case.

Typical of Douglas's wide-ranging study on any topic of interest to him, the short dissent was filled with footnotes ranging from agricultural volumes on the effect of DDT in milk to a review of both the federal regulations and popular literature on the topic as well as comments by a congressman in the *Congressional Record* on the dangers of the insecticide. Douglas also included a substantial quotation from author Rachel Carson in *The Washington Post* arguing that "the death of the robins is not mere speculation . . . [but proves] the perils of DDT. . . ." It would be another two years before Carson was to publish her landmark book on the dangers of DDT, *Silent Spring,* and more than a decade before the Supreme Court would begin to consider ruling in the environmental field, but, like an explorer who plants the flag of his nation in a newfound land, William O. Douglas had already staked out his place as a future leader in environmental law.

By early 1960, as a sixty-one-year-old man in the best of health, it seemed to Douglas that he was just hitting his stride for his accomplishments on the Court. The only question remaining for Court observers was what Douglas might do if he could consistently count on four other liberal votes to back him.

But Douglas was not interested in whether that day would ever arrive. He had established his ideological platform, and he planned finally to use it.

CRYING IN THE WILDERNESS

I've never wanted to run for anything. . . . I didn't
have any desire for the [presidential] office. I would
have taken it I suppose if I had been drafted.

—William O. Douglas, 1971

In the summer of 1960, facing his sixty-second birthday, Bill Douglas had finally hatched a plan for his future. On June 27 he wrote his good friend Fred Rodell that he was looking for a "graceful" way to leave the Supreme Court because there was "no point in wasting the rest of my life here." Frustrated by having to serve on a continuingly conservative Court, Douglas was forced to develop his liberal views on civil rights and liberties in dissent, which he had done twenty-three times in the previous term alone. What Douglas carefully left out of his cryptic message to Rodell was just where he now expected to be heading.

Douglas's departure plans had actually begun more than three months earlier, when he spotted Lyndon Baines Johnson, now the Democratic majority leader of the Senate, on a cross-country flight to attend the funeral of their mutual friend, Senator Richard Neuberger of Oregon. With the New Hampshire primary just concluded, Douglas, like the rest of the nation, was intrigued by the Democratic nomination battle shaping up between Senators John F. Kennedy of Massachusetts and Hubert H. Humphrey of Minnesota. With no clear favorite yet established, several quality candidates such as Johnson were sitting on the sideline in case the race became deadlocked. After finding a quiet pair of seats on the plane, Douglas told Johnson that he was willing to resign from the Court to help promote him for the presidency.

It was the second time in eight years that William O. Douglas had offered to leave the Court to campaign for the election of a president. This offer so moved Lyndon Johnson that, unlike Harry Truman, he looked for an opportunity to return the favor. The chance came a month later when Douglas received a letter from Sam Smith, a political operative from San Francisco who, in his "unbounded admiration" for the potential presidential run by Lyndon Johnson, asked: "Has [LBJ] ever thought of making you his running mate? I know if that happened there would be a lot of folks out here really go to town [sic]. . . . The combination of Lyndon and yourself would present a veritable tower of strength. I will deem it a great privilege to put all my efforts into the coming campaign." Douglas immediately sent Johnson a copy of this letter, saying that it was "from a Republican friend who has unbounded faith in you." To which Johnson responded in a *"personal and confidential"* letter: "Mr. Smith seems to be a man of rare discernment since he expresses admiration for both of us. I agree with him that your name would add a 'veritable tower of strength' to any group with which it might be connected." When he saw this response, Douglas sincerely believed that he was now Johnson's personal choice as a running mate.

After a lifetime of trying to get to the White House, Bill Douglas now convinced himself that he was finally on the way to reaching his goal. So, the man who twelve years earlier refused Truman's entreaties to join his ticket as vice president began to pour all of his energy into getting Johnson the nomination that he now believed would become his own means to the White House. Members of Douglas's staff noticed that rather than spending his days at the Court polishing up his judicial opinions, he was constantly on the phone, calling everyone he knew in a position of political power. And his nights were no different. "He went to *every* embassy party that year," recalled one of his assistants. "You don't do that in his position unless you have something else in mind. The thing was, though, that he was terrible at those parties. He would just go and stand in a corner and not speak to anyone." This time there were no doubts heard about whether Douglas would resign from the Court to run for office.

But as a result of his dramatic primary win in West Virginia in mid-May, indicating that a Catholic candidate could indeed win the presidency, it was John Kennedy who received the party's nomination at the Democratic convention in Los Angeles in July. When Johnson was added to the ticket as vice president, the disappointment was just too much for Douglas to bear.

·   ·   ·

In late August, everyone at the Double K dude ranch in Goose Prairie, Washington, knew that time was growing short for pack trips into the mountains before the snows fell. When Bill Douglas said that he wanted to go, Kay Kershaw and Isabelle Lynn agreed to lead a few of their favorite people into the hills. Yakima orchard owner Cragg Gilbert; his wife, Virginia, and father, Elon Gilbert; Pat Keller from Seattle; Douglas's wife, Mercedes, and sister, Martha Douglas Bost, all signed on for the caravan.

They were headed to the high country, to the Big Basin, on a three-night trip that would include the usual long trek to Cougar Lake in between. Off they rode toward Blankenship Meadow, twenty miles into the Nelson Ridge region, where they could find the perfect setting to stop on the first night out. The gentle, rolling meadow was just far enough away from everything that they could put all traces of out-side civilization behind. The day and the scenery could not have been more ideal as they rode. While the countless varieties of flowers were gone—no purple from the lichens or reds from the Indian paintbrush and no fluffy white from the bear grass—there was still plenty of natural grass, and the leaves had started to turn. Rising above them that cloudless day was the looming presence of the 6,400-foot volcanic remnant known as Tumac Mountain. And to their right, a mile or so down the narrow path, was the crystal-clear deep-aquamarine Little Sister Lake.

Everyone looked forward to dinner and the conversation that fol-lowed around the campfire, where Douglas would often sit cross-legged on the wooden supply boxes or on a log by the fire and tell his stories. Looking past the roaring embers, with sparks filling the air around him, he would mesmerize the travelers with his tales of how he had "cleaned up the Street," how he had told Felix to "go to hell," or how close he had come to being vice president and then president in-stead of that haberdasher from Missouri.

But as the pack train moved along on this August day, it soon be-came clear to everyone that something was dreadfully wrong with their famous friend. As they rode, Douglas remained sullen-faced on his mount. The hours passed with his expression hardening and his face getting darker and darker. He was angry, they could soon see—very angry—and no one quite knew why. "I'm gonna get good and drunk tonight," he hissed at Cragg Gilbert. Normally, that would not be an unusual statement, except this time Gilbert could see that Doug-las would be drinking out of anger rather than to amuse himself.

As soon as the procession reached Blankenship Meadow, nearly everyone sprang into action—pitching their tents, getting their water, scouring the woods for kindling, arranging the food and cooking utensils for dinner, and building a campfire. But Bill Douglas did none of that. Instead, reaching into one of his saddlebags, he took out a liquor bottle and just sat down, drinking as fast as his body would allow. With each swig, a deepening anger set in. When the bottle was finished, he simply tossed it aside, returned to the saddlebag, and picked out another one.

As the evening wore on, the others in the party kept glancing over at their friend but said nothing to him for fear of his response. When dinner was cooked, Douglas ate none of it. He just kept drinking. For a long while, Douglas showed no effects from his bender. Finally, though, with the fire roaring and the time for his storytelling session at hand, he began pacing around the fire, pausing from time to time to kick sand into it, as though he wanted to put it out. On and on and on he drank—silently, straight from the bottle, no glass, no mixer, no chasers, no stopping. After a while, the group tried to ignore him and began quietly talking among themselves. But Douglas seemed not to notice.

In time, the man who prided himself on drinking everyone else under the table without getting drunk himself became more drunk than anyone present could ever remember seeing him. Douglas started mumbling, but it wasn't to anyone around him, it was only to himself and in a language only he seemed to understand. Finally, the ravings began to take a pattern. The same phrases were repeated over and over again.

"They bought it!"

"They bought the goddamned nomination!"

"How could this happen?"

"This always happens to me!"

"They bought it!"

"They outright bought it!"

To the others, it seemed as if the drunken Justice was crumbling before their eyes.

Douglas's mumbling eventually ceased, and he began yelling to no one in particular. Streams of obscenities and fragments of sentences all spewed forth, interrupted by swigs from his bottle. His friends looked on in confusion as Douglas became like an old Victrola, stuck in one place on an album. Over and over he repeated his litany of phrases— *"They bought it! This always happens! They outright bought it!"*—but never once explained to anyone what he was talking about. There was no story that day. There was no coherence. Rather, there was a major-league tantrum.

Douglas's ranting continued, until two or three in the morning, when he finally collapsed in a stupor and everyone was able to get some sleep. Usually when Bill Douglas got into one of his black moods he snapped out of it after a good drunk and a better night's sleep. But not this time. As soon as he got up the next morning, he was back at it again. For three days he drank, and for three days he ranted.

When the party got back to the Double K, Douglas had regained enough of his senses to write his traditional salutation in the ranch's guest book. But this time, after describing the trip in the same glowing terms he always did, Douglas added what for him was as close to an apology as he could manage: "Happy Hour was usually a success."

Only later did it slowly dawn on any of them what Douglas had been yelling about. After all, it had been a full six weeks since John F. Kennedy had been nominated by the Democratic party for the presidency. What bothered Douglas, they realized, was not what had already happened, but what he now believed was going to happen in the general election. Joe Kennedy would spend freely for his son's election, and ensure his tenure in the White House. Cragg Gilbert explained: "When Bill found that the Kennedys were going to buy that election, well, he was just incensed. . . . It was quite a show."

This small group had been privileged those August days to peer into the inner soul of Bill Douglas. For the first time in years, they had seen both the little boy named Orville Douglas and the legendary man who had tried to erase his memory—*Justice* William O. Douglas. By that time, though, neither recognized the other.

Once, Justice Douglas had been the youngest person to be mentioned for the White House, the office that Orville's mother had claimed would be his destiny. Now, after flirting with the office for two decades and thinking that he had a solid deal with LBJ, when Kennedy got the nomination instead Douglas knew his chances were gone forever. Eight years of Kennedy rule would simply make Douglas too old for any future presidential run. At age sixty-one, William O. Douglas finally knew what he would be doing for the rest of his life. Douglas realized that he would never reach the summit he sought, the heights he had planned for his career. Rather, he had now been buried alive, trapped forever on the Supreme Court of the United States. And making matters even worse, once again, it was that old family bugaboo — a lack of wealth — that had quashed his chances for escape. The same man who had offered to back him in 1944, and then refused to do so four years later, now through his money and influence would elevate his own son to the Oval Office, where Douglas believed he himself rightfully belonged.

People around Douglas could see that the pain of not getting to the White House never left him. Douglas's longtime secretary Fay Aull Deusterman said: "I think he would have been much happier if he had become president." Mercedes Douglas saw during his trips abroad that "he found an adulation that he didn't get in the United States . . . [because] he chose not to run for president." Even the law clerks at the Supreme Court could see the long-term effect of this disappointment on the Justice. "I always got the impression that he was a very unhappy man," adds former law clerk Peter Kay Westen, who served from 1968 to 1969, "but I never knew what it was that was missing. I suspect that he wanted to be something other than what he was."

Walter Dellinger, later solicitor general of the United States, recalled an occasion during his service as a law clerk to Justice Hugo Black in the 1968–1969 term that told him much about the Justice from Yakima. The clerks had irregular lunches to which members of the High Court were invited to speak on an informal basis. All of the other Justices seemed to like the chance to let their hair down and engage in some lively debate, but, thinking that they were all conservatives, William O. Douglas would have none of it.

Then one day Douglas unexpectedly changed his mind and decided to accept Dellinger's invitation for a lunch date. His first answers to their questions were distracted and monosyllabic, but after a little while it seemed as if he was warming up to the group, which was more liberal than he had realized. Sensing this, Dellinger decided to risk ending the session with a question that had long been on his mind. *Mr. Justice,* he began, *if you had it to do over again would you go onto the Supreme Court?*

"Absolutely not!" Douglas barked without hesitation. This sent the clerks into a tizzy. Why? they asked. "Because the Court as an institution is too peripheral, too much in the backwater on the Court. You're just too far out of the action here," explained the Justice. But what about the cases that had revolutionized society from the Court? they pressed. "They're irrelevant," he answered impatiently. "All of the action is elsewhere. All of the ability to affect action is elsewhere." With that, the lunch was ended. But the clerks who witnessed it were taken aback by the response and the look of determined sadness on the Justice's face as he seemed to renounce his entire judicial career before their eyes. Dellinger concluded from what he heard that what Douglas really wanted to be was president of the United States. With this prize gone forever, though, the question now was what the future held for him.

FELIX'S FINALE

They were almost snarling at one another. . . . Felix regarded him as a turncoat, much as Bill regarded Felix as a turncoat. Consequently, their relations were very strained, to put it mildly.

— *William Brennan*

After the incident in the mountains, Douglas returned to the job he now hated. But he convinced himself that it would not be for long. "I'm going to be named secretary of state by Kennedy," he announced to friends and members of his staff. It would be the crowning achievement for the man who had traveled so extensively worldwide, had dueled with Harry Truman over Red China, and had expressed so many ideas on foreign policy. "There was a feeling in the office [that this would happen]," recalled Fay Aull Deusterman, but they could not figure out how. Would Douglas have been willing to go through what might well be a bruising confirmation hearing even in a Democratic Senate? Would he, at this stage of his career, really be willing to give up his Court seat? And then there was the question of whether he would get the appointment in the first place. "Bobby Kennedy liked him and may well have wanted him as secretary of state," recalled his writing assistant Dagmar Hamilton, "but Douglas was a wishful thinker for the job. He just wasn't a JFK man." To which former law clerk Lucas A. "Scot" Powe added, "He was a mushhead on foreign policy. He had . . . helped to make the senator's reputation in foreign policy, but he was not the man for the job now."

In the end, longtime State Department official Dean Rusk was named the secretary.

·　　·　　·

It was a case of "the more things change, the more they stay the same" for William O. Douglas when Court opened in the fall of 1960. Felix

Frankfurter could still count on four additional conservative votes in Charles Whittaker, Potter Stewart, John Marshall Harlan, and Tom Clark. And by this time the former Harvard professor was trying very hard to expand his influence over the direction of the Court's decisions. As he liked to do at the beginning of each term, Frankfurter had sent all the members of the Court his unsolicited suggestions for how they might improve their work. That year, he recommended shortening the length of time between oral arguments and the release of decisions. He also thought that the Court should immediately release the unsigned, unanimous opinions for the whole Court, known as *per curiam* opinions, rather than allowing any member of the Court to delay the release while giving the matter additional thought. When the latest encyclical reached Douglas's desk, he decided that he had had enough of being lectured on how to do his job, let alone by the man who had once delayed one of the decisions for an appeal by the Rosenbergs for so long. "I vote against a meeting to discuss the proposals," he wrote Frankfurter. "The virtue of our present procedures is that they are very flexible. . . . If we unanimously adopted rules on such matters we would be plagued by them, bogged down, and interminably delayed. . . . If anyone wants delay on a particular case he always gets it. We need not put ourselves in the needless harness that is proposed."

When Frankfurter continued to press his ideas, Douglas decided to widen the scope of the conflict. In a memo to the full Court, Douglas complained: "We are not first-year students who need to be put under strict restraints. . . . The blowing of whistles, the counting to three or ten, the suspension of all activity for a stated time may be desirable and necessary on playgrounds or in sports. But we are not children; we deal not with trivia; we are not engaged in contests. Our tasks involve deliberation, reflection, meditation. When opinions have jelled, the case is handed down. When jelling is not finished, the case is held." Douglas concluded by declaring: "I defend the right of any Justice to file anything he wants. I resist the effort to foist one system on all of us."

After the Court rejected Frankfurter's proposals, Douglas decided to complain about the nature of the two men's associations in a memo to their colleagues:

The continuous violent outbursts against me in Conference by my Brother Frankfurter give me great concern. They do not bother me. For I have been on the hustings too long. But he's an ill man; and these violent outbursts create a fear in my heart that one of them may be his end. I do not consciously do anything to annoy him. But twenty-odd years have shown that I am a disturbing symbol in his life. His outbursts against me are increasing in intensity. In the interest of his health and long life I have reluctantly concluded to participate in no more conferences while he is on the Court. For the cert lists I will leave my vote. On argued cases I will leave a short summary of my views.

After talking to the Chief Justice about this, however, Douglas did not send the letter, knowing full well that the Court cannot function with one of its members operating in self-imposed exile. But privately he began telling interviewers, "We had become more and more suspicious of the good faith of the man [Frankfurter], his intellectual honesty. We disagreed basically with him on so many different things."

With his relationship permanently frayed with the man who now led a majority of votes on the Court, Douglas continued to develop his theories for protecting rights in dissents with Hugo Black. In the 1960 term alone he dissented twenty-nine times, more than in any term since 1952, with another eighteen dissents coming the following term.

Several more Communist Party cases, this time stemming from the investigatory work of the House Un-American Activities Committee (HUAC), came to the Court, allowing Douglas to try to further educate his colleagues and the general public. Arthur M. McPhaul was compelled by a HUAC subcommittee investigating possible Communist activities in vital defense areas to produce "all records, correspondence, and memoranda" relating to the allegedly subversive Civil Rights Congress. When he refused to do so, claiming his Fifth Amendment right against compulsory self-incrimination, McPhaul was indicted and convicted for willful failure to comply with the subpoena. The five conservatives on the Court, speaking through Justice Whittaker, ruled on November 14, 1960, that the government had established a prima facie case proving the failure to comply with the subpoena (McPhaul having offered no reason why he could not produce the documents nor denying that he had them) and saw no constitutional basis in either the Fourth or the Fifth Amendment for overturning the conviction.

Douglas and the other three liberals on the Court—Black, Brennan, and Warren—argued in dissent that "today's decision marks . . . a departure from the accepted procedure designed to protect accused people from public passion and overbearing officials." While the law did indeed prohibit a witness from "willfully mak[ing] default" of documents, Douglas pointed out that there was absolutely no proof by the committee that McPhaul was either an officer or member of the Civil Rights Congress or that he was in possession of the documents being requested. Since the judge instructed the jury that they did not need to ask whether the documents were in the defendant's actual possession, Douglas realized that this charge "permits conviction without any evidence of any 'willful' default." Once more, Douglas mounted his soapbox in the hopes of showing the government the error of its ways:

> Today we take a step backward. We allow a man to go to prison for doing no more, so far as this record reveals, than challenging the right of a Committee to ask him to produce documents. The Congress had the right to get these documents from someone. But, when it comes to criminal prosecutions, the Government must turn square corners. If Congress desires to have the judiciary adjudge a man guilty for failure to produce documents, the prosecution should be required to prove that the man whom we send to prison had the power to produce them.

For Douglas and Black, the issue would be no different if the investigation of allegedly subversive organizations was undertaken by state governments. In another dissent to a case dealing with the attorney general of New Hampshire's power to compel the director of a pacifist summer camp, World Fellowship, to produce the list of names of campers there, Douglas argued that members of all groups, even ones that are allegedly subversive, deserved freedom of association under the First Amendment. For him, such investigations of membership lists threatened "substantial government encroachment" upon important federal rights.

> Can there be any doubt that harassment of members of World Fellowship, Inc., in the climate prevailing among New Hampshire's law-enforcement officials will likewise be severe? Can there be any doubt that its members will be as closely pursued as might be members of [the] N.A.A.C.P. in some communities? If either [the] N.A.A.C.P. or World Fellowship were engaged in criminal activity, we would have a different problem. But neither is shown to be. World Fellowship, so far as this record shows, is as law-abiding as [the] N.A.A.C.P. The members of one are entitled to the same freedom of speech, of press, or assembly, and of association as the members of the other. . . . What is an unconstitutional invasion of freedom of association in Alabama or in Arkansas should be un-

constitutional in New Hampshire. All groups—white or colored—
engaged in lawful conduct are entitled to the same protection
against harassment as the N.A.A.C.P. enjoys.

The Court's review of Communist Party investigation cases by the
HUAC was interrupted by a series of religion cases testing laws requiring businesses to be closed on Sundays, so-called blue laws, in several
states. Was this practice a violation of the First Amendment's admonition that "Congress shall make no law respecting an establishment of
religion"? The majority, speaking through Chief Justice Warren, upheld the Maryland closing law as it applied to a large discount department store where a woman named Margaret McGowan worked, ruling
that the decision to close businesses on Sunday was not based in religious practice and thus did not establish religion in a way that offended the First Amendment: "The State seeks to set one day apart
from all others as a day of rest, repose, recreation and tranquility—a
day which all members of the family and community have the opportunity to spend and enjoy together. . . . Sunday is a day apart from all
others. The cause is irrelevant; the fact exists."

If Douglas were still writing as he had in 1952 in the *Zorach* case,
upholding the public school's "released time" program for religious
education, he also would have upheld this statute. Now, though, he
could see the flaw in the Court's reasoning—that this ruling would
cause a severe hardship for those who did not practice traditional
Christianity and would thus have to close their businesses for an additional day beyond their own Sabbath. As he framed the issue in a dissent, "The question is not whether one day out of seven can be
imposed by a State as a day of rest. The question is not whether Sunday can by force of custom and habit be retained as a day of rest. The
question is whether a State can impose criminal sanctions on those
who, unlike the Christian majority that makes up our society, worship
on a different day or do not share the religious scruples of the majority." Douglas now argued for the freedom of the irreligious and of
religious minorities:

> The First Amendment commands government to have no interest
> in theology or ritual; it admonishes government to be interested in
> allowing religious freedom to flourish—whether the result is to
> produce Catholics, Jews or Protestants, or to turn the people
> toward the path of Buddha, or to end in a predominantly Moslem
> nation, or to produce in the long run atheists or agnostics. On mat-

ters of this kind government must be neutral. This freedom plainly includes freedom *from* religion with the right to believe, speak, write, publish and advocate antireligious programs.

For the home missionary's son to now adopt a "protect the irreligious" stance illustrated a considerable change in his views. Douglas's study of the beliefs and practices of non-Christian religions around the world, based mostly on his travels and reading, left him more open to various belief structures. But more than that, by the spring of 1961 he had been freed from the bonds of political ambition, which likely affected his opinion in the *Zorach* case.

This was made clear the following term. When the Court overturned the use of a twenty-two-word nondenominational prayer by teachers to begin public-school classes in New York, calling it a violation of the "neutrality" of government toward religion implied in the establishment-of-religion clause, Douglas took his position a step further. Rather than arguing that this short, nearly secular prayer coerced anyone or represented an establishment of religion, Douglas suggested that the narrow question in this case was "whether New York oversteps the bounds when it finances a religious exercise." Here, Douglas abandoned his own 1947 view in upholding the use of public funds to bus students to parochial schools and cited instead Wiley Rutledge's dissent, which warned against the dangers of funding of any kind for religious school activities. The disallowance of even a minute of school time for the invocation of this harmless prayer, Douglas argued, "leaves the Government in a position not of hostility to religion but of neutrality."

When the Court considered the power of Congress under the Constitution to investigate Communists and other suspected subversives, Douglas renewed his defense of Bill of Rights protection for everyone. In the first case, the Supreme Court reviewed whether the government had the power under the Subversive Activities Control Act, created to investigate Communists in America, to force the party to register as a Communist-action organization. To no one's surprise, the usual five votes were found to uphold the law, with the opinion this time being written by Felix Frankfurter. For them, although the party had not yet attempted to overthrow the government, the organization could be regulated because it held those objectives. Frankfurter was unwilling to consider the prospect that the entire purpose of Congress's registration requirement was to "outlaw" the party by making it available for future penalties: "It is wholly speculative now to foreshadow whether, or under what conditions, a member of the party may in the future apply for a passport, or seek government or defense-facility or labor-union employment, or, being an alien, become a party to a naturalization or a denaturalization proceeding. None of these things may happen."

But of course, past history had shown that all of these things would happen, and Douglas was not willing to duck these issues in his dissent. After conceding the government its power to register the Communist Party if it could be proved that this group was working to overthrow the American government, Douglas argued that this was regulable "conduct" rather than protected "free speech." But those who feared that Douglas might be joining the conservatives soon saw the trap he had laid: "My conclusion is that while the Communist Party can be compelled to register, no one acting for it can be compelled to sign a statement that he is an officer or director nor to disclose the names of its officers, directors, or members—unless the required immunity is granted." His reasons for opposing a registration law directed at individuals while still allowing the government to require the party to register as an abstract organization were made clear: "Congress (past or present) is attempting to have its cake and eat it too. In my view Congress can require full disclosure of all the paraphernalia through which a foreign dominated and controlled organization spreads propaganda, engages in agitation, or promotes politics in this country. But the Fifth Amendment bars Congress from requiring full disclosure by one Act and by another Act making the facts admitted or disclosed *under compulsion* the ingredients of a crime." For him, "our Constitution protects all minorities, no matter how despised they are."

The Court indicated that same day that it might be willing to consider moving more in Douglas's direction when it ruled in the appeal of Junius Irving Scales. Scales had been convicted under the membership clause of the Smith Act. While the conservative five-person majority upheld the conviction, they added that the government must prove that an individual is an "active member" of the Communist Party or that a person actually "participat[ed] in [the] general affairs of the Communist Party," with the specific intent of bringing about the violent overthrow of the government, as opposed to merely being aware of the organization's activities.

But even in offering more protection to the accused here, Douglas and Black decided that the majority had not gone far enough. Writing in dissent, Douglas argued that this ruling made "serious Mark Twain's lighthearted comment that 'It is by the goodness of God that in our country we have those three unspeakably precious things: freedom of speech, freedom of conscience, and the prudence never to practice either of them." For him, Scales's conviction was based on a charge that fell "well short of a charge of conspiracy." Scales had not been shown, he argued, to be an "active" member of the Communist Party; rather, the indictment was based on "merely belief—belief in the proletarian revolution, belief in Communist creed." Douglas concluded: "When belief in an idea is punished as it is today, we sacrifice those ideals and substitute an alien, totalitarian philosophy in their stead." All that separated Douglas from being able to write his views into law on this question was the lack of the necessary fifth vote.

Two weeks later, when the Court announced its final set of decisions for the 1960–1961 term, Douglas made it clear in the case of *Poe v. Ullman* that he was ready to stake out wholly new legal territory on the right of personal privacy. The Court ruled that three cases challenging the constitutionality of Connecticut's law against the use or sale of— or counseling about the use of—contraceptives by or to married couples were beyond the Court's jurisdiction. Felix Frankfurter argued that since there had been only one prosecution under this anticontraceptive law in the previous seventy-five years, and contraceptives were then being openly sold in Connecticut, there was no "justiciable controversy" with people who had a stake in the case because they had been arrested. Thus, the Court had no place ruling in this case.

After spending a decade thinking about privacy under the Constitution, dating from the three dissents in his "privacy spring" of 1952, Douglas was not prepared to duck this issue. In what was for him an extraordinarily long, forty-five-page dissent, Douglas argued that the Court had the power to hear this case. Regarding Frankfurter's argument that it was not a sufficient "stake" for a doctor or a married couple to sue, he argued: "What are these people—doctor and patients—to do? Flout the law and go to prison? Violate the law surreptitiously and hope they will not get caught? By today's decision we leave them no other alternatives. . . . It is not the choice worthy of a civilized society. A sick wife, a concerned husband, a conscientious doctor seek a dignified, discrete [*sic*], orderly answer to the critical problem confronting them. We should not turn them away and make them flout the law and get arrested to have their constitutional rights determined."

While this would have ended the matter for most Justices, Douglas then went on to leave no doubt that he was prepared to declare the Connecticut law an unconstitutional violation of the right to privacy. The reason, he argued, was that "this Connecticut law as applied to this married couple deprives them of 'liberty' without due process of law, as that concept is used in the Fourteenth Amendment. . . . 'Liberty' is a conception that sometimes gains content from the emanations of other specific guarantees . . . or from experience with the requirements of a free society." Having reasserted the existence of a right of privacy, Douglas then applied it: "The regulation . . . in this case touches the relationship between man and wife. It reaches into the intimacies of the marriage relationship. . . . When the State makes 'use' a crime and applies the criminal sanction to man and wife, the State has entered the innermost sanctum of the home." For Douglas, this law clearly was "an invasion of the privacy that is implicit in a free society." Even though the majority of the Court chose not to rule in this case, close readers of the case could see that a change in both the law and the larger issue of the "right of privacy" might be one vote away from coming into existence.

.   .   .

And the one additional vote was not long in coming. With only three liberal allies—Black, Brennan, and Warren—it had been a very difficult period on the Court for Douglas since the election of John F. Kennedy to the White House. But the forces of nature have a way of changing things on this tenure-based institution. The pressure of work on the Court took such a toll on Charles Whittaker that he was hospitalized for depression and then resigned on April 1, 1962. The first vacancy had been promised by the Kennedy administration to former Connecticut governor and now Cabinet member Abe Ribicoff, but after deciding that life on the Court was not for him he made plans to run for the Senate. In time, Deputy U.S. Attorney Byron White from Colorado was appointed. To the liberal Kennedy's surprise, though, this appointment largely had the effect of trading one conservative vote for another and did not change the final results on the Court.

The following month, though, Felix Frankfurter had a devastating stroke; after weeks of saying that his recovery was progressing nicely, the doctors finally admitted to Chief Justice Earl Warren that it looked hopeless. Perhaps fearing his own mortality, the thought of anyone, even his longtime adversary, having to leave his seat due to health problems now broke Douglas's heart. In penning a note to Frankfurter about how much he would be missed, Douglas added teasingly, "The conferences are *not* shorter by reason of your absence!!" With that, Douglas wished him well and promised to drop by.

When Frankfurter finally retired on August 28, 1962, senators from both sides of the aisle clamored for the appointment of liberal Secretary of Labor Arthur Goldberg to replace him, and the White House agreed. The effect of Goldberg's appointment was transformative. The trade of this extreme liberal activist for the conservative, self-restraint-oriented anchor meant that, for the first time in nearly two decades, there were now five solid liberal votes on the Court. The only question for Douglas would be the nature of his role on what would become the "revolutionary" Warren Court.

WILD BILL

Lead me not into temptation; for I shall surely find
it myself.

—*Anonymous*

After coming to realize that he would never reach the White House,
few men were as well prepared to enjoy life as William O. Douglas.
"Douglas knew how to play the angles," recalled his Court messenger
for nineteen years, Harry Datcher. "He could get on a plane with no
money in his pocket, travel to some exotic location without a ticket,
be fed and housed, and come back with a new girlfriend. . . . He had a
way with women. He could really pick 'em. And I'm not talking about
ugly women either. They were gorgeous women."

Douglas's main problem in satisfying this impulse was not the
Washington press corps, which tended to overlook such philandering
by public officials, but his wife, Mercedes, who suspected his activities
and did not like it one bit. "I was extremely happy with him, until the
neurosis [over women] began to erode on me," she explained. Harry
Datcher saw firsthand the troubles that the Douglases were having: "I
always knew when he was having women troubles, because he'd want
me to take him to the University Club, where he was staying. And in
the early 1960s Douglas was staying at the University Club more and
more."

For Douglas, the quest for new women was constant. The man who
would not even speak to most of the people in the Court building
would see a pretty new secretary and send Datcher to find out her
name. If he liked a woman, Douglas would have his messenger drive
her to the University Club, explain to the attendant at the desk that
she was doing some work for the Justice, and bring her upstairs for a
rendezvous. "If you got to be one of Douglas's lovers, you didn't want

for nuthin'. That's where his money went," recalled Harry Datcher. And others in the Court building all knew it. "If Douglas saw a woman within thirty feet of the Court building, he'd hit on her instantly," recalled former Supreme Court law clerk Walter Dellinger. "And we're not talking about just a case of infidelity here. He had a major problem with women."

It was obvious even to casual observers during the early 1960s that the Douglases' marriage was on the verge of coming apart. "They would stand near Bumping Lake, fighting like cats and dogs," recalled Ira Ford's son, Bob, of Goose Prairie. "They were screeching at each other." "You could tell that things were disintegrating between Merci and him," said Cragg Gilbert, "mainly because of his drinking habits and just completely, you know, going off on his own after other women.... I'm sure Mercedes would ... have been a tremendous asset to him. And I can't understand it." At one point during an argument with his wife in his Court office, Douglas picked up a phone and threw it against the door, later telling his secretary that it had broken falling off his desk. Harry Datcher saw the same problems: "Mercedes had a real sharp tongue, and she wouldn't hesitate to go up and argue with Douglas. She would belittle him, saying something like, 'William, what's all that mess on your tie there?' When I saw the way she talked back to him, and the way she treated him," Datcher concluded, "I knew she wasn't going to last long." In time, the accumulation of all these disputes destroyed the Douglases' marriage.

With no political check restraining him from getting another divorce, Douglas quietly began searching for his next mate. And, just as had happened with Mercedes, the answer came to him in the mail. In the middle of the summer of 1961, a letter arrived from Joan Martin, a senior at tiny Allegheny College in Meadville, Pennsylvania, explaining that she wanted to do a political-science honors thesis on the Justice's political philosophy. Each year, Douglas received dozens of such requests, but this letter was so sweet that he agreed to speak at Allegheny in the fall of 1961.

The attractive, slender, brown-haired Joan was sent to pick him up at the Youngstown, Ohio, airport. And when the two went to a cocktail party, observant faculty members noticed that the sixty-three-year-old Justice was becoming infatuated with the beautiful young coed right before their eyes. Later that night, Joan heard the sound of pebbles pattering against her window in Walker Hall, an all-female dorm on campus. When she opened the window, the pleasant elderly gentleman below said with a crooked smile, "Wanna go for a walk?" Word of the budding relationship spread quickly in rural western Pennsylvania.

Over a hundred miles away, rumors were heard at Penn State University that Douglas had later gone into the women's dorm and that frantic school officials, scared of scandal, were unable to get him out "for days." The story was overblown, explained one school official who was present at the time, saying that it was more like "hours" than "days." But in those days of parietals, even minutes after-hours in a dorm for the other sex meant trouble. Douglas was deeply smitten and told Joan Martin, who drove him back to the airport, that one day they would be husband and wife. All he had to do now was explain this decision to his current wife.

By the time Douglas returned to the Court building, his staff could see immediately that he was once again like a teenager in love. Research assistant Dagmar Hamilton recalled, "[Joan] had drawn a poster announcing the Allegheny speech and drawn in crayons some of the books he had published over the years. So Douglas put the poster up on the wall in his second-floor file room, room 210, and kept it there knowing that Mercedes would never see it." In time, Douglas's risk-taking and self-destructive side began to come out as he placed an unframed picture of the college senior on his mantel in his Supreme Court office. It was only a matter of days before his wife took notice, saying to Douglas's secretary, Fay Aull Deusterman: "I don't think I have anything to worry about, do you?" Deusterman decided not to tell what she suspected.

Joan Martin quickly became the total focus of Douglas's amorous attention. "He wasn't the sweetest person you'd ever want to meet," explained Harry Datcher, "unless you were his current girlfriend." Could they meet at his next speech in Buffalo? he wrote. Could they get together when she came to Washington on an art trip? Would she like a recommendation from him to law school? Would she like copies of his books? When she agreed, one after the other came in the mail. Would she accept a little Christmas present that he had gotten especially for her? Would she accept his phone calls from Washington or whatever port of call he happened to be in at the moment? When her parents came to the city, would they like it if his entire staff was put at their disposal?

For Douglas, this new relationship was the diametric opposite of his current one. Mercedes was more of an equal who could struggle with him on the same plane, while the much younger Joan Martin plainly adored him and put him on a pedestal. When Joan began talking about getting a job in Washington, Douglas saw a chance to use the same ploy that he had used with Mercedes a decade before. Would she like a summer job checking his new manuscript on Abraham Lincoln? he asked. Not realizing that such a position was just part of Douglas's courtship process, she quickly accepted, while also applying for a position at the U.S. Agency for International Development.

.   .   .

The challenge for Douglas in this period was finding the money to pay her. By this time, the confiscatory divorce agreement negotiated eight years earlier by Tommy Corcoran had turned Douglas's life into a financial nightmare. His problems only began with the nearly $11,000 paid annually in alimony and the $145 a month required for the mortgage payment on Mildred's house on Third Street, all paid out of his Court income of $35,000. Because of the vengeful financial-support escalator provision that was activated in 1961, to Douglas's horror nearly one third of every after-tax dollar he was earning under $70,000 and half of every dollar over $70,000 was also going to his ex-wife. This meant that each year from 1961 through 1965 he had to pay Mildred an average of an extra $14,680, none of it tax-deductible.

In any event, his writing career was prospering. In 1961 alone, Douglas made more than twenty thousand dollars in magazine-article commissions. And he used the rough materials for these pieces to deliver speeches around the country for one thousand dollars each, garnering him another ten to twenty thousand dollars a year. Douglas was continuing to dash his books off at the astonishing rate of nearly one a year. After completing a three-book contract with Doubleday, he made a twenty-five-thousand-dollar deal with the same company for five additional books, which proved to be largely forgettable travel and legal-rights tomes. For each new book he received another five thousand dollars, plus any eventual royalties. While all of this extrajudicial work greatly reduced Douglas's time for his Court duties, his speed in producing opinions still enabled him to equal or exceed the output of his colleagues. "I'm just an ordinary person," Hugo Black would tell his former law clerks, "but Bill is a genius. He can get more done in an hour than I can get done in a week."

The problem was that with all of his Court work, travel, and personal appearances, he had little time to produce his book manuscripts. The answer, Douglas decided, was to use the same technique he had adopted at Yale to write his articles and at the SEC to write his reports: take the trips and then find a skilled assistant who could help him write an acceptable manuscript. In the spring of 1962, Douglas hired Dagmar Hamilton, the wife of one of Tom Clark's former law clerks, Robert Hamilton, to work as his research assistant on a book titled *Anatomy of Liberty,* a compilation of lectures he had given at the University of Baghdad. Hamilton's job was to turn the lectures into chapters, check the footnotes, and make sure that the entire manuscript was accurate.

Over the next dozen years, even after she moved with her family to Austin, Texas, Hamilton would work on five more books, even being trusted in time to write portions of chapters when the linkages among existing material were weak. With Hamilton, typing assistance from his office, and an occasional assist from his law clerks, Douglas was able to publish his books without interruption.

But still, he found, the extra money was not enough. When his lecture income dropped dramatically by ten thousand dollars a year between 1959 and 1961, Douglas had to find a new source of revenue. The solution was contained in a handwritten fan letter he had received in 1960 from a Las Vegas businessman named Albert Parvin, who had read the Justice's *America Challenged,* a seventy-four-page compilation of the Walter E. Edge Lectures he had delivered at Princeton, dealing with the dangers presented to America by the growing Communist movement in Latin America. Moved by this book, Parvin wrote the Justice: "It is my desire to endow a trust or foundation for the sole purpose of promulgating and promoting better relations among nations through education." Within two weeks, the two men met at Robert Maynard Hutchins's Center for the Study of Democratic Institutions in Santa Barbara, and Douglas agreed to serve as the president for the new foundation, for which he would receive an annual honorarium of $10,000 (to be increased to $12,000 two years later).

The original plan was to fund through grants of $250,000 to $300,000 two programs to improve America's image abroad: an annual $50,000 cash prize "to the person who has contributed most to the improvement of international relations" and ten fellowships for people from foreign countries to study for a year at Princeton (and later UCLA), followed by a month of travel in the United States. The hope was to educate more people about the operation and benefits of American democracy and in time develop additional programs such as a televised literacy-training program in the Dominican Republic and educational programs throughout Latin America.

Laudable as the goals of this new foundation were, a more cautious man serving on the Supreme Court would have worried about the source of its funding. Parvin had built his forty-two-million-dollar business since 1929 by supplying furnishings around the country, eventually garnering nearly all of the contracts for hotels on the Strip in Las Vegas. In 1954, Parvin had headed a group that bought the financially troubled Hotel Flamingo and gambling casino and five years

The Reverend William Douglas; his wife, Julia; their daughter, Martha; and Orville, called "Treasure"; in Maine, Minnesota. Orville was struck by a life-threatening illness at the age of twenty-two months. His mother treated him as an invalid long after his recovery.

The "poor widow lady" dressed her children—Martha, Arthur, and Orville—in their Sunday best for this formal portrait, circa 1908, Yakima, Washington.

To escape the "pain and poverty" of 111 North Fifth Avenue, Yakima, young Orville would pick up his horseshoe pack and head for the Cascade Mountains, where he developed his love of the outdoors.

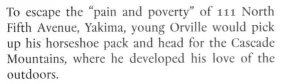

Orville disliked his mother's description of him as "not as strong as other boys," a vestige of her overprotectiveness following his illness as an infant. Though he thought of himself as "puny" and a "weakling," by 1915 he was tall and athletic enough to be the center for the North Yakima High School basketball team.

Orville puts up his dukes while clowning for the camera with his Beta Theta Pi fraternity brothers at Whitman College.

Orville (right) plays Daniel Webster in *The Story of Marcus Whitman*. The "big man on campus," Robert Porterfield (left), plays the lead role of Marcus Whitman, going to Washington to lobby for government help for Oregon.

Orville picnicking with Frances Penrose, a daughter of the beloved Whitman College president Stephen B. L. Penrose. "We lay claim to Orville only for the Whitman era," Frances Penrose would later say. "When he was gone, he was gone. He was no longer Orville Douglas. . . . Oh, we crossed paths over the years, but by then he was slowly becoming someone else. Someone none of us recognized."

Even though his SATC uniform didn't arrive until after World War I ended, Orville asked Frances Penrose to take his picture in it anyway. He hoped the photo would make it into the Whitman College newspaper.

A late addition to the Columbia Law Review, Orville Douglas appears in the back row, second from the right, with Herman Benjamin to his left. Douglas's sometime roommate Carrol Shanks is also in the back row, second from the left. Alfred McCormack, editor-in-chief, and the "star" of the Class of 1925, is at the center of the front row. None of his classmates understood why Douglas's classroom performance increased so markedly after his first year.

Douglas (back row, far right) was recruited to teach at Yale Law School by its dean, the so-called "Boy Wonder," Robert Maynard Hutchins (front row, third from the right). Shortly after this picture of the faculty was taken, Hutchins left Yale to become president of the University of Chicago, causing Douglas to consider moving there as well.

Working with his former student and assistant Abe Fortas on the Protective Committee study and later on the Securities and Exchange Commission, Douglas instructed Fortas to "piss on 'em" when dealing with corrupt corporations.

A new marshal in town: Douglas as chairman of the Securities and Exchange Commission, 1937, prepares to do battle with the New York Stock Exchange, its old guard, and especially Richard Whitney.

Douglas often used this setting, in front of the fireplace of his Silver Spring, Maryland, home, to refine his tall tales about his life and adventures. Here, Mildred, Bill Jr., and Millie help to bring to life one of those tales: that he was a doting husband and father.

About Douglas's Father of the Year Award, his daughter, Millie, said, "My brother and I had a good laugh about that."

The Senate Judiciary Committee considers the nomination of William O. Douglas to the Supreme Court for no more than a few minutes before going into executive session. Contrary to popular belief, Douglas was in fact present, and here he is shown seated between Mildred and Attorney General Frank Murphy.

"A young man in an old man's job," Douglas (standing, extreme right) seems somewhat out of place among the five remaining members of the "nine old men" and the three other Franklin Roosevelt appointees to the Supreme Court. At forty, he was twelve years younger than the next youngest justices, and barely half the age of Chief Justice Charles Evans Hughes. Standing, left to right: Felix Frankfurter, Hugo Black, Stanley Reed, Douglas. Seated, left to right: Harlan Fiske Stone, James McReynolds, Chief Justice Hughes, Pierce Butler, Owen Roberts.

The original of the letter, lost for years, from President Franklin D. Roosevelt to Robert Hannegan, chairman of the Democratic National Party, that determined FDR's vice-presidential running mate in 1944. Douglas always believed that he and not Harry Truman had been FDR's first choice, and that Hannegan had switched the order of the names when a typed version of this letter was created.

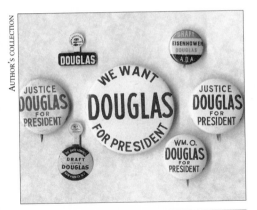

Campaign buttons and a fan from Douglas's short-lived campaign to unseat Harry S Truman for the Democratic presidential nomination in 1948.

Douglas liked to portray himself as a westerner with strong skills as a horseman, but his friend Kay Kershaw of the Double K dude ranch in Goose Prairie, Washington, said of him, "He was a terrible rider. . . . The only reason he survived was he did what we told him to do. 'Bring 'em back alive,' that was my motto. But it wasn't always easy keeping him alive."

After Douglas's riding accident in October 1949, rescuers carry him down the mountain, trying not to injure him further. Douglas broke twenty-three ribs when his borrowed horse, Kendall, reared on a narrow trail and threw him. The horse then rolled over him as they both careened down the mountainside. Except for a few scratches, Kendall was uninjured.

"Nine scorpions trapped in a bottle": The contentious Vinson Court, recently reshaped by the deaths of Frank Murphy and Wiley Rutledge, and the addition of Tom Clark and Sherman Minton, stopped fighting long enough to pose for the annual portrait. Although position is determined by seniority, it seems appropriate that Douglas and Felix Frankfurter are now seated as far apart from each other as possible. Standing, left to right: Clark, Robert Jackson, Harold Burton, Minton. Seated: Frankfurter, Hugo Black, Chief Justice Fred Vinson, Stanley Reed, Douglas.

In 1954, Douglas led the way on a 185-mile hike from Cumberland, Maryland, to Washington, D.C., protesting plans to turn the Chesapeake and Ohio Canal into a highway.

Douglas (right, fourth from the front) brought along Robert F. Kennedy (left, front) when he went on a tour of the Soviet Union in 1955. The trip was paid for in part by *Look* magazine, in return for first rights to publish pictures and accounts of the trip. While Douglas was writing his version for *Look*, Kennedy scooped his host by publishing his own pictures elsewhere.

Douglas with his second wife, Mercedes, in front of the "Marble Palace" in 1962. By this time, the Douglases' marriage was showing signs of breaking down, and Douglas's Court staff dreaded Mrs. Douglas's visits to his office.

Douglas met his third wife when he gave a speech at Allegheny College, where she was a student writing her honors thesis about him. The marriage of the sixty-five-year-old Justice to the twenty-three-year-old Joan Martin was troubled from the start.

When his marriage to Joan ended, Douglas courted Elena Leonardo, a Granger, Washington, artist. Uncertain about becoming the fourth Mrs. Douglas, Elena (shown here in a Hong Kong restaurant) left for a round-the-world tour to think things over. Although they never married, their relationship continued for the rest of Douglas's life.

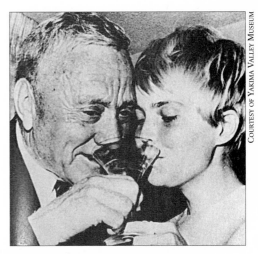

Feeling rejected, Douglas proposed to Cathy Heffernan, a twenty-two-year-old college student/cocktail waitress from Portland, Oregon. Here, Douglas and Cathy drink a toast after their wedding in Encino, California, July 15, 1966.

Sparks fly as "the Storyteller" spins another of his autobiographical tales by the campfire, high in the Cascade Mountains.

Though the legendary Warren Court, pictured here in 1967, finally instituted some of the constitutional changes Douglas had long advocated, he still spoke frequently in dissent. Standing, left to right: Abe Fortas, Potter Stewart, Byron White, Thurgood Marshall. Seated, left to right: John Harlan, Hugo Black, Chief Justice Earl Warren, Douglas, William Brennan.

By 1972, Douglas is the last remaining Court member from the New Deal. In the conservative Nixon/Burger Court, Douglas often found himself dissenting alone. Standing, left to right: Lewis Powell, Thurgood Marshall, Harry Blackmun, William Rehnquist. Seated, left to right: Potter Stewart, Douglas, Chief Justice Warren Burger, William Brennan, Byron White.

September 1975: In an attempt to prove his fitness to continue serving as a Supreme Court Justice, Douglas conducts an impromptu press conference before entering the Yakima County Courthouse to hear an oral argument.

Those closest to Douglas came together one last time to honor the ailing Justice. In a December 6, 1979, ceremony in the Supreme Court building, Columbia University School of Law bestowed upon him an honorary degree of doctor of laws. Standing, center, is Douglas's longtime Court messenger, Harry Datcher. A little more than a month later, the Justice was dead.

His grave marker at Arlington National Cemetery perpetuates Douglas's final legend—that he'd served as a private in the U.S. Army during World War I.

"Bill was a genius and a visionary. He had the ability to take you to the top of the mountain and show you the entire vista of future issues, but then you would come down from the mountain and lose sight of what you had seen. He never did."

—Charles Reich, law clerk to Justice Hugo Black

later sold it for a substantial profit. In the early 1960s, he had bought the Dohrmann Company, a 112-year-old restaurant-supply business, and merged it with his own company to service, among other clients, several Las Vegas hotels. Unknown to the press and the general public, the new foundation was funded by the millions that Parvin was receiving from the proceeds of his sale of the Flamingo, plus stock that he held in the Parvin-Dohrmann Corporation. Eventually, there were suspicions of ties to organized crime.

But such niceties did not bother Douglas. The goals of the new foundation were ones he supported, the obligations involved little more than attaching his name to the enterprise and attending a few meetings each year, and his output was merely spinning off a few ideas for projects. His only concern was his paycheck.

When not even this newfound money proved to be enough, Douglas began donating his sizable personal and office files to the Library of Congress in order to take substantial tax deductions. In 1963, he took a deduction of $17,500 for the first set of private papers; the following year, $30,000. In 1965, more Court material went to the Library of Congress for a deduction of $12,500, a set of biographical interview tapes done by Professor Walter Murphy of Princeton was donated to that university for a $10,000 credit, and Whitman College received a set of pictures and books valued at more than $2,800. Donations in 1966 netted Douglas another deduction of $25,000, with others to follow.

Out of this infusion of funds, Bill Douglas paid Joan Martin to come to Washington, D.C., in the summer of 1962 to help as a second research assistant on his next book, *Mr. Lincoln and the Negroes.* It quickly became clear to others in Douglas's office that Joan occupied a far different position. "I did all of the work on the Lincoln book, and that was OK because I was comfortable doing that," recalled Dagmar Hamilton. "Joan did her work with the Justice." Fay Aull Deusterman confirmed, "[Joan] never worked on his books."

Douglas made little secret of his intentions. Planning a trip to Cape May, New Jersey, in June 1962 to speak to a conference of Quakers, Douglas told his secretaries to get two plane tickets, though Mercedes was not attending. As this revelation became a source of discussion among Douglas's intimates and staff, they all reached their own conclusions as to why he was so interested in a much younger woman. "He was looking for the fountain of youth," argued his law clerk at the time, Jared Carter. "Ponce de León, I think, is what we're looking at." Deusterman saw it a bit differently: "I think the Court was grating on his nerves, because he was there so long. He had to keep changing in his life, so remarrying gives you some change. . . . I felt that he had to have a spark in his life, something to keep him going." Cragg Gilbert agreed with this assessment: "He wanted somebody who had lots of life, to keep up with him, both mentally as well as physically . . . so that meant the young ones. He found them very exciting, and they kept his interest up."

Though in Washington girlfriends are usually kept behind closed doors, Douglas soon began to flaunt his new relationship with "Miss Martin." "Other Justices at the time had mistresses," explained Harry Datcher, "but they would employ them as secretaries or keep them away from the Court building. Douglas, though, did what he did in the open. He didn't give a damn what people thought of him." Just how he did this, though, became the subject of much gossip in the private world of the Supreme Court building.

Court personnel watched in puzzlement in late 1962 and early 1963 as Douglas, who ordinarily never left his desk even to eat lunch with the other members of the Court, began a practice in the middle of the day of putting on his Stetson, picking up a briefcase that otherwise he never carried, and striding out of the building by the front doors. After this had happened on a number of successive days, some members of the staff began to observe the Justice's path. To their amazement, time and time again Douglas would parade out the front of the building, smiling at excited tourists who would recognize the great man in real life, march down the long rows of marble steps to the patio below, walk briskly around to the back of the building, cross Second Street, and then always disappear into a white apartment building. After a couple of hours, he would return to work the same way.

It took them a while to figure out why. That answer first became apparent to Harry Datcher when he tried to solve another mystery. Every day, Douglas liked to have a special brew of oriental tea and some cookies at midmorning. So Datcher was required to fill the Justice's lower desk drawers with boxes of an herbal tea, which he bought with his own money from an oriental grocery store downtown, and some fancy cookies from the Court's cafeteria. Knowing that the impatient Douglas would not wait for his snack while the secretaries found some china and flatware, Datcher would order coffee for himself from the Supreme Court cafeteria, pour it out, clean the china and silverware, and store all of the items in the same lower drawer of the Justice's desk. In time, the drawer was filled with all manner of china, silverware, tea boxes, and finger foods.

Then, one day, to Datcher's horror he noticed that the stash had been disappearing at an alarming rate. Douglas was either on a binge or someone was stealing the stuff, he concluded. Fearing that he would be blamed for it, the startled messenger refilled the drawer as fast as possible, only to see the supply diminish again at an even quicker rate. In time, the poor messenger was having a problem staying one delivery ahead of the thief.

Finally, Datcher whispered about the problem he was having to a couple of building guards, and together they figured it out. Douglas himself, they decided, had to be carrying the items in his briefcase to whomever was in the apartment on Second Street. And, they concluded in unison, the person he was meeting there must be Joan Martin.

Only years later did Datcher learn from Joan Martin that they had guessed correctly. "[Datcher's] either the dumbest man I know or the smartest, because he hasn't said a word about the missing china and food," she quoted the Justice as saying to her at the time.

Members of the Court staff now privately began calling Douglas "Wild Bill," because of both his lifestyle and the hat he wore. When these whispers reached Gloria McHugh, the secretary for Earl Warren, she called up Datcher and ordered him to present himself immediately in the Chief's office. "Datch, the chief heard that you and your buddies in the Court call Justice Douglas 'Wild Bill.' Did you do that?" asked the head secretary sternly.

"Yes," answered Datcher, bracing for what he expected to be an official reprimand.

"That's funny," she said, laughing. "That's what we call him up here as well."

But members of the Court and the staff were not the only ones who used this nickname, though each intended a different meaning. To environmentalists, "Wild Bill" Douglas was the highest legal advocate for the wilderness regions in the government. To the press, "Wild Bill" Douglas was the Justice who liked to wear a Stetson and a western-style coat with no tie, walking around Capitol Hill and conducting life in his own fashion. To the general public, "Wild Bill" Douglas was the only Justice from the far west and the last one from the old American frontier, whose background now led him to reach out on the Court to vote for the downtrodden, the poor, and the oppressed.

But of all these characters, it was the "Wild Bill" Douglas who inhabited and terrorized the Court building who was always one revelation away from bringing the institution into disrepute.

.   .   .

It was not long before Mercedes Douglas began to sense that there was another woman in her husband's life, with her list of suspects including members of the office staff. "She thought Dag [Hamilton] was the other woman," explained Robert Hamilton, "so she went right over to meet her because she is very much a take-charge sort of lady. But after she met my wife she could see that we had two small kids in the house, and she knew it was not her. So they became good friends, and she would drop in from time to time." Eventually, though, Mercedes began to suspect that her husband was interested in his other research assistant, the young graduate from Allegheny College.

When Mercedes began checking on her husband's behavior, the Court building's staff established its version of an emergency drill. The drill's alarm was sounded whenever anyone in the building heard the jingling of a dog collar and the yapping of a small dog. Since few would dare bring a pet of any kind in to disturb the splendid isolation of the Supreme Court, this could mean only one thing: Mercedes Douglas and her miniature collie, Sandy, were in the building on their way to "see" her husband at work.

No one was very fond of Wild Bill, but for the Court staff the harmony of the rest of their day, and perhaps even their jobs, would depend on what they did next. They got on the phone to find out two things: Where was Justice Douglas? And where was Joan Martin? If the answer proved to be "the same place," then the next question was: Where could they hide the young assistant? Jared Carter, Douglas's law clerk for 1962–1963, explained, "It was the silliest thing you could ever imagine. . . . I can remember once she was [hiding] in the closet. I remember Mercedes coming around some weekends or other times looking for him—and pissed off, you know."

Sometimes, as Mercedes moved through the building, the damage-control exercise got quite comical. One day, Douglas had Harry Datcher escort Martin to the Court for lunch. As they were walking toward the Justice's office, Datcher heard the dreaded jingling dog collar just around the corner. Grabbing Martin's arm, Datcher said hurriedly, "We can't go that way." Pushing her into the nearby elevator, he brought her up to Douglas's second-floor file room. By the time Datcher got back down to Douglas's office to tell him where his lunch date was, he found Mercedes standing in front of the Justice's desk, insisting that he take her to lunch. The Justice resisted. When Datcher interrupted to volunteer to retrieve something that Douglas needed from his old files, Mercedes offered to join him for the trip. Instead, Datcher quickly excused himself, raced up to the file room, grabbed Martin, and led her down to the labor foreman's office. If Mercedes Douglas found her there, he decided, then the Justice deserved to be caught. Racing back to the office, he found the Douglases still engaged in a heated conversation. "Judge, you are expected to eat with the other Judges for lunch," the messenger said, intending to be helpful.

"Fine," said Mercedes, "I'll go along with you."

"No, we can't do that," said Douglas, "they are having a birthday party for me." This confused Mercedes even more, who began wondering why all of the other Justices couldn't just bring the cake and party to them.

"Well, you would have to move all of those judges," said Datcher, "and they wouldn't want to move." At which point, Datcher excused himself, saying to the Justice that he would be in the labor foreman's office doing some work, knowing that Douglas would understand the hint. A few minutes later, a call came for Datcher at the foreman's office, with the Justice saying that the way was clear to send Joan Martin up.

The low point in the battle between the Douglases came one Saturday when Mercedes showed up unexpectedly at Douglas's office, knowing that he was not in. The law clerk and secretaries who were working their usual weekend hours watched in amazement as the fashionably dressed woman marched wordlessly through the suite of offices, threw open the door to Douglas's inner office, stormed into the room, and slammed the door behind her. For the next several minutes, all anyone could hear was the noise of moving furniture and shuffling papers. Then, just as suddenly, the sound ceased, and the door flew open once again. With that, the staff looked up to see Mercedes Douglas standing in the entryway, a mixture of triumph and anger on her face. She held in her hand the unmistakable evidence of a recent sexual encounter in her husband's private office; she had obviously fished it out of the trash can lying behind her.

"Shots!" she screamed at the startled staff members. "That lying son of a bitch. I know what kind of shots he needs." That said, she stormed out, carrying the incriminating evidence with her and leaving the astonished office staff to puzzle out what kind of story the Justice had been telling her.

By the beginning of October 1962, the message was now clear. Mercedes Douglas visited Dag Hamilton and offered to drive her to the swearing-in of Justice Arthur Goldberg. "I suppose you know that Bill is in love with Miss Martin," she said softly, "so I guess I'll have to get on with the rest of my life." As her friend gulped, not knowing what to say, the present Mrs. Douglas added, "I'm not going to make it easy for him." Still a compellingly attractive woman in her late forties, Mercedes Douglas appeared to Dag Hamilton to be bitterly hurt by being thrown over by the nearly sixty-four-year-old Justice for a woman in her early twenties. "It took a long time for Mercedes to accept the idea of a divorce," recalled Hamilton.

Upon seeing that his second wife was not willing to end the marriage as quietly as his first, Douglas decided to force her hand. In mid-October, a dozen friends were invited to a buffet dinner at his house on Hutchins Place to jointly celebrate his birthday and Justice William Brennan's wedding anniversary. Joan Martin came, accompanied by the sixty-nine-year-old drafter of the New Deal legislation, Benjamin V. Cohen. "You know what he's done," an angry Mercedes said to those around her. "He's invited the oldest and most unattractive eligible bachelor you can think of so that he will appear to be younger and more virile to her."

Throughout the entire evening, Douglas, who normally demanded to be served by whatever woman was at his side at the moment, instead made an obvious fuss over Joan Martin, ostentatiously refilling her buffet plate and getting her drinks. The tension in the living room continued to rise throughout the evening. With dessert about to be served, Douglas strode to the piano and feebly tried to play a tune. Then, rising from the bench, he announced, "And now, let's hear Miss Martin play the piano." Everyone could see from the reaction on Mercedes's face that a storm was about to blow in.

"Bill," she responded, "I don't think that would be a very good idea. Do you?"

To which Douglas announced, as though he was saying it for the first time, "And now, Miss Martin will play the piano."

"But, Bill," Mercedes responded, unflustered, "people don't really want Miss Martin to play the piano now."

Douglas stared at his wife coldly, walked across the room, gathered up Joan Martin's hand, and directed her to the piano. "Miss Martin is going to play for us *now*," the Justice announced. With that, the Douglases' closest friends knew that the marriage was truly over.

By early 1963, Mercedes had also accepted the inevitable and was trying to work the matter out in letters to Douglas's daughter, Millie: "I feel sorry for him—but I am impotent to help him. He is a great man but an unhappy one. I hope he'll find peace—but we must all pray it will be with someone mature enough to help him."

Friends could accept that Douglas behaved as if he was above the normal rules in living his personal life. As Charles Reich recalled: "Douglas could get away with being a great man, because in the view of history he will be seen as a great man. And you just have to say to yourself, 'You know, enough people are pains in the neck who don't do anything worthwhile in their lives.' And you find somebody who is a good person, you can put up with a lot." But Mercedes Douglas had reached her limit. A month later, she again wrote Millie: "Don't worry—I won't hand him the divorce on a silver platter. . . . He asked for this—so if he's broke after supporting your mom and me—it's his choice."

Douglas tried to avoid that financial fate again, but he had apparently learned nothing from his earlier experience. One day, Mercedes Douglas found in the mail a bill from Saks Fifth Avenue for some clothes that Douglas had bought for Joan Martin but had mistakenly charged to her account. Worse, in that same day's mail Mercedes received a stack of pictures from the Justice's recent trip to Latin America, which should have been sent to the Court but were mistakenly included with a batch of her own pictures. Contained therein were two pictures of Joan Martin, who had been learning from the Justice how to use his Leica camera. With all of the evidence necessary for a divorce victory on the basis of adultery having just been handed to his wife by the mailman, Douglas lamented in a letter to Clark Clifford, "The fates dealt me two losing hands."

With the time at hand to choose up sides in the latest legal round of *Douglas v. Douglas*, Washington attorney Joe Rauh opened his house door one day to find Abe Fortas and Clark Clifford standing there just laughing. "You have been chosen," they told the puzzled Rauh.

"For what?" he replied.

"Bill wants to get another divorce," they said, still laughing. "And we have decided that you should be Merci's lawyer."

"What, no one else wants to take on a Supreme Court Justice?" responded Rauh, as he agreed to accept the draft. In under two weeks, the lawyers hammered out a separation agreement that would provide Mercedes with nearly one thousand dollars a month in living expenses while the divorce was arranged.

Between his alimony from the first marriage, this new separation agreement, and his tangled finances, Douglas had very little money left. His only assets were the home on Hutchins Place and a cabin in Glenwood, Oregon. Since Glenwood had been a gift to Mercedes from Douglas, this property would now be hers. With the Hutchins Place property now worth $60,000 but encumbered by an $18,000 mortgage, Douglas proposed that he take out a second mortgage on it to give her the $20,000 that would effectively divide their community property. So it was arranged that Douglas would pay a lump sum of $10,000 in cash and provide a promissory note for another $10,000 to be paid over a four-year period.

But Mercedes was true to her word to Millie Douglas Read; Bill

Douglas would come to understand that she was not to be trifled with. In addition to insisting that he pay Rauh's fees of nearly $1,500 and $550 a month in alimony until she remarried, she inflicted another escalator clause on him. Accordingly, over and above the indexed payments that he was providing his first wife, Douglas would have to pay Mercedes 15 percent of every dollar over and above his gross Supreme Court income of $35,000, unless she remarried. In forcing this demand on the Justice, who was ready to sign anything by this point in order to be free to marry Joan Martin, Mercedes had made her point. It was hard to see how after taxes and the two sets of divorce payments the Justice would have anything at all.

Then there were lists of property items to be split. An Abercrombie and Fitch ax, two inseparable riding horses, and assorted camping gear were earmarked for him, while some valuable oriental rugs and furniture went to her. On and on the list swapping went. After it was all done, the entire agreement hinged on a beautiful sculpture of a black horse that Douglas had gotten from the wife of onetime Chief Forester Gifford Pinchot. "I remember the horse," recalled Joe Rauh. "I can't remember whether it was Ming Dynasty or some other goddamn horse. It was a shiny black horse about three or four feet long. I remember carrying it over to Ganson [Purcell, whose law firm was representing Douglas] from my office, which was about a block away." Douglas got his horse sculpture, and the divorce was finalized on July 31, 1963, with the vacationing Wild Bill insisting that his ex-wife be out of the Hutchins Place house by the opening of Court.

Hardly willing to let another failed marriage upset him, Douglas borrowed enough money from Clark Clifford to buy a new Jeep to celebrate his freedom. Five days later, on the verge of bankruptcy, the nearly sixty-five-year-old Justice Douglas did what he always did as soon as possible after a divorce: He got married again, this time to twenty-three-year-old Joan Martin. A day after that, Mercedes Douglas remarried as well, this time to Robert Eicholz, a multimillionaire Washington attorney. "It was almost as if each of them were racing the other to see who could get to the altar first," said Dagmar Hamilton, laughing. Ironically, the Eicholz marriage saved Douglas's financial health as it freed him of both the alimony and the escalator payments to her.

.   .   .

Life for the third Mrs. Douglas was even worse than for the first two. "I remember taking a trip to talk to Joanie's parents about [the engagement] and saying, 'This is the dumbest idea I ever heard of in my life,' " recalled Jared Carter. " 'You are going to have a crippled old man on your hands.' And they were beginning to rag each other. You know, call each other liars and hassle and fight, even . . . before they got married." But still the marriage went forward. "You could see that she was not ready for what she would be facing," recalled Fay Aull Deusterman.

The day after the wedding, the couple boarded a plane for Seattle en route to their honeymoon in Goose Prairie. But when they arrived, Douglas began totally ignoring his wife and talking instead with his friends at the Double K ranch. "She was completely out of her arena," recalled Cragg Gilbert of Yakima. "I can remember one time . . . she just sat down and cried all night because he never paid any attention to her." When they heard about these problems, Douglas's office staff thought they knew the issue now that the couple was married. "I think that she was too much in awe of him," explained Deusterman, "and I don't think he liked that. . . . She would try to be a good wife for him at home and have a cocktail ready for him—you know, typical pipe-and-slippers type of thing—and he just rebuffed her. She wasn't enough of a challenge for him, I don't believe."

The truth was that Douglas was now far less interested in his new wife than in replacing the summer home he had lost to Mercedes. However, that was going to require more creative financing. As Harry Datcher put it, in a phrase echoed by others in his office: "He was divorce-broke. In the office we always used to say that the Judge lost one house every time he lost a wife. So he had to keep earning money to get more houses."

When Douglas heard that nine gorgeous forested acres had come on the market in his beloved Goose Prairie, just down the road from the Double K, he turned, as he had done so many times before, to two old friends for help. First, Clark Clifford was able to arrange another bank loan for him in Washington, D.C., to top off some money that Douglas had been able to borrow from the Yakima Federal Savings and Loan. To the disgust of environmentalists in the region, Douglas then clear-cut several acres of the richly treed land to build his house. Then, with no collateral at all, Douglas borrowed another thirteen thousand dollars from family friend Florence Smith, who had helped him recover financially from his last divorce, promising that it would be only short term. It would be eight years and countless numbers of excuses before Douglas was able to repay her.

But that mattered little to Douglas because he could now build his cabin. After hiring a Yakima architect to design a chalet-front, T-shaped ranch house with a deck overlooking Nelson Ridge, Douglas's old mountain friend Ira Ford was put in charge of the construction process. The architect's initial plans for the cottage included a beautiful stone fireplace, a galley kitchen, and a long living room with huge picture windows looking out on Old Baldy and the other mountains. By the time it was finished, though, Douglas's shortage of funds had made it necessary to cut eight feet off the length of the house, making the kitchen very tiny and much too dark. In the end, perhaps because of all the cost cutting, the wooden floor in the living room sloped downward, with parts of the house ending up so warped that some doors could not be shut properly. But when Ford told the Justice the bad news, rather than getting the explosive reaction he expected, he was simply thanked for his effort. When the retreat was finished, Douglas named it Prairie House, and from the moment it was completed he knew that this would become his sanctuary.

Now that the house was ready, though, there was no money left to furnish it. So, once more passing over the ethical niceties of his position, Douglas struck a deal with Albert Parvin. From the same Las Vegas furniture company that was outfitting casinos, Douglas got some used furniture for free. To Joan was left the duty of setting up the household.

It was not long before people began to see evidence that Douglas's latest marriage was in trouble. One Goose Prairie resident was talking to the current Mrs. Douglas at her door when the Justice came out, grabbed his wife, and pushed her back into the house to prevent her from engaging in further conversation. "He used 'em and abused 'em," said longtime Goose Prairie neighbor Bob Ford with a shake of his head. "Once he married 'em, he got sick of 'em and treated 'em badly." Douglas's law clerks saw evidence of the same behavior. "[Joan] called me a time or two, crying and saying that wife-beating was going on," recalled Jared Carter. "I remember I went out to teach at Stanford after clerking, and Douglas came out there to give some speech to somebody. I didn't go. But Joanie called me up, and she said, 'I'm locked in a motel room, and he won't let me out. He beats me up all the time.' And I said, 'Well, why don't you divorce the guy? What are you doing hanging around? Don't whine on my shoulder.'"

These reports soon found their way into the newspapers. "After one tiff, [Joan Douglas] called a cab and began pouring out her heart to the driver," reported investigative columnist Jack Anderson. "She described her celebrated, cerebral husband alternately as 'temperamental,' 'unbearable' and a 'genius.' 'Sometimes he shouts and sometimes he has even whacked me. He never considers a person my age needs affection. . . . I know he'll have several other wives after me, but no one will ever be able to live with him.' " Later, Mrs. Douglas claimed there was a misunderstanding, saying that it was her father and not her husband who had hit her.

In the summer of 1965, after Joan Douglas finished furnishing the retreat, the Justice took a piece of stationery from Portland's Benson Hotel, where he was staying while getting some dental work done in the city, and scribbled out a letter to his wife. Two days later, Ira Ford, now serving as the groundskeeper on the property, looked up to see Joan Douglas running down the driveway, tears streaming down her young face and hysterically waving a letter from her husband. She was so upset, she told Ford, that she could not read beyond the first line, which simply informed her that, after less than twenty-four months of marriage, their relationship was over. When Ford looked at the rest of the note, he was astonished to see that Douglas had demanded that she be out of the cottage and out of his life by the time he returned from Portland. "When Bill made up his mind, it was made up," Ford recalled. But since the Justice had driven away in the only car they owned and allowed her to have no money, his wife was now penniless and trapped deep in the Cascades. It was left to Ira Ford to drive her to the Whistlin' Jack's phone booth, in order to allow her to call her parents in Buffalo, asking them to wire some money to Yakima to help her move back home.

Only later would his friends come to understand that while Joan had been making a home for him, Douglas had been searching for another woman to fill it as his next wife.

BEYOND THE BILL OF RIGHTS

> Once speech, belief, and conscience are placed beyond the reach of government, a nation acquires a spiritual strength that will make it a shining light to all who have never known the blessings of liberty, even to those behind the Iron and Bamboo Curtains.
>
> *— William O. Douglas*

Despite the wildness of his personal life, Douglas did not neglect his work as a jurist in interpreting the Bill of Rights. After a decade of thought and speaking largely through his dissents, Douglas had developed a philosophy that governed his votes. Offered the chance to deliver the fourth James Madison Lecture at the New York University School of Law on January 20, 1963, Douglas titled his speech "The Bill of Rights Is Not Enough." He chose this title deliberately to present the opposing view to a speech given at this same forum by Hugo Black, arguing that the Bill of Rights was sufficient to protect citizens. "People long submerged, who finally win their independence, seem at times to lose their moorings," began Douglas. "Even after independence, equality seems a fragile thing without institutions to espouse and defend it." Then, referring to the Communist Party and the "subversive organization" cases from the last dozen years, Douglas continued, "Constitutions may be undone by erosion through judicial constructions. They are undone by timid popular protests when encroachments are first made on the liberty of a people. They are also undone by sudden convulsions in public affairs." For him, without a vigorous enforcement of the Bill of Rights the dangers to this country were very real. "When ideas become too dangerous to discuss, when advocacy of an unpopular cause becomes a crime, timidity (with its companions, hate and fear) sets the mood of a people."

Douglas made very clear that his mission now on the Court would be to fight against "the default of the judiciary, as respects the Bill of Rights": "It is becoming more and more apparent, as our affairs become more and more complicated, that absent a judicial remedy for a wrong, there will be none within the reach of the average person." This meant devotion to "a renaissance in liberty at home [because m]ore regimentation, more dilution of the Bill of Rights means a lessening of our political ingenuity." And he was ready for the challenge of preventing that "dilution."

William O. Douglas was announcing to the world that with the new liberal majority he felt free to be an aggressive, liberal activist, determined to do anything necessary—including speaking only for himself even on a left-wing Court—to protect the people's freedoms. But he was doing more in this speech: Douglas was also explaining *how* he would fulfill his mission. He was now determined to educate future generations: "The task of any constitutional convention called today would be to increase, rather than merely restore, the original restraints placed on government. Some think that even the original Bill of Rights—particularly the Fifth Amendment—would not be adopted today. I think it would be, if the people gave a second, sober reflection to the problem. But if the Bill of Rights is to be restored in full vigor by the amending process and if additional restraints on government are to be fashioned, an intensive educational program is necessary." While others, like William Brennan, filled the technical requirements of judging, carefully crafting their decision rules based on legal precedent, Douglas was determined to present his legal vision in a manner that all could understand.

The clearest signal of Douglas's change came in 1963 in the case of *Douglas v. California.* Another man named William Douglas and his partner, Bennie Will Mayes, were jointly tried and convicted for thirteen felonies in California with only a single public defender representing both of them. Having dismissed that attorney, they requested new counsel for their appeal. However, the request was denied under a state rule of criminal procedure empowering appellate courts to appoint counsel only if it was determined that such an appointment would be helpful to the defendant or to the court.

It would have been a relatively simple matter for Douglas, who was tapped to write the opinion overturning the rule, to argue that the complicated nature of the appeals process requires that a defendant have the right to counsel under the Sixth Amendment. But he extended the question by taking notice of the defendants' impoverished status and examining the impact of the equal-protection clause of the Fourteenth Amendment on their constitutional rights: "Here the issue is whether or not an indigent shall be denied the assistance of counsel on appeal. In either case the evil is the same: discrimination against the indigent. For there can be no equal justice where the kind of an appeal a man enjoys 'depends on the amount of money he has.' " Thus providing himself with a more or less free hand to explore the unconstitutionality of discriminating between the rich and the poor in the criminal-justice process, Douglas argued: "Where the merits of *the one and only appeal* an indigent has as of right are decided without benefit of counsel, we think an unconstitutional line has been drawn between rich and poor. When an indigent is forced to run this gauntlet of a preliminary showing of merit, the right to appeal does not comport with fair procedure." This was especially true, Douglas added, when such a right to counsel during appeal is available in federal courts. A year later, Douglas's old friend Charles Reich labeled this philosophy "the new property"—the idea that the Fourteenth Amendment's equal-protection clause guarantees certain rights that cannot be denied on the basis of wealth.

When the Warren Court liberals turned to the freedom-of-association area, they did not side as easily with Douglas's views. Theodore R. Gibson, the president of the Miami branch of the NAACP was compelled to testify and present membership lists before a committee of the Florida state legislature investigating the possible infiltration of communists into race-relations organizations. When Gibson refused to produce these lists on the basis of his freedom-of-association rights under the First and Fourteenth Amendments, he was found in contempt and jailed. With Arthur Goldberg now providing the fifth vote to protect these rights, the Court overturned the conviction. The committee, said the Court, had not shown a substantial connection between the issue of communism and the Miami branch of the NAACP, thus the earlier cases permitting such investigations were no longer controlling. "To permit legislative inquiry to proceed on less than an adequate foundation," Goldberg wrote for the majority, "would be to sanction unjustified and unwarranted intrusions into the very heart of the constitutional privilege to be secure in associations in legitimate organizations engaged in the exercise of First and Fourteenth Amendment rights; to impose a lesser standard than we here do would be inconsistent with the maintenance of those essential conditions basic to the preservation of our democracy."

With the implication remaining here that if the NAACP were shown to be communist-influenced, or "subversive" in any way, such a request for membership lists would be permitted, Douglas diverged from the Court. "Joining a lawful organization, like attending a church, is an associational activity that comes within the purview of the First Amendment," he argued in a concurring opinion, adding, "A

Free Society is made up of almost innumerable institutions through which views and opinions are expressed, opinion is mobilized, and social, economic, religious, educational, and political programs are formulated." Within this exalted vision of American pluralism in action, Douglas said, "In my view, government is not only powerless to legislate with respect to membership in a lawful organization; it is also precluded from probing the intimacies of spiritual and intellectual relationships in the myriad of such societies and groups that exist in this country, regardless of the legislative purpose sought to be served. . . . If that is not true, I see no barrier to investigation of newspapers, churches, political parties, clubs, societies, unions, and any other association for their political, economic, social, philosophical, or religious views." For Douglas, only in limiting such investigations can the Court under the First Amendment protect the absolute right to associate with whomever one chooses.

That said, Douglas then suggested that such inquiries also violated another right: that of privacy. "One man's privacy may not be invaded because of another's perversity. If the files of the NAACP can be ransacked because some Communists may have joined it, then all walls of privacy are broken down. By that reasoning the records of the confessional can be ransacked because a 'subversive' or a criminal was implicated," he wrote. While this kind of absolutist language, if offered in the 1940s in agreement with Frank Murphy and Wiley Rutledge, would not have changed the law then, it was helping to change the law now.

Douglas's desire to protect one's freedom of belief led him in another instance to change his view on the issue of the free exercise of religion. This case involved a Seventh Day Adventist in South Carolina named Adell H. Sherbert, whose religious beliefs prevented her from working on Saturdays, when she observed the Sabbath. Since some employers would not hire her as a result, the unemployment commission ruled that she was ineligible for compensation because she had not made herself "available for work." Speaking for the five-person majority, William Brennan ruled that this practice was a burden on Sherbert's free exercise of religion because there was no strong state interest being upheld here and the law forced "her to choose between following the precepts of her religion and forfeiting benefits, on the one hand, and abandoning one of the precepts of her religion in order to accept work, on the other hand."

In his concurring opinion, Douglas, the man who once compared the religious practice of polygamy by the Mormons to illegal prostitution, now saw no reason whatsoever that the state could penalize a person's free exercise of religion, even for a statute that applied to everyone and did not demonstrably discriminate on a religious basis. "Many people hold beliefs alien to the majority of our society— beliefs that are protected by the First Amendment but which could easily be trod upon under the guise of 'police' or 'health' regulations reflecting the majority's views," he explained. Forcing such people to observe "valid secular" regulations that apply to everyone, added Douglas, can also lead to the restriction of constitutional rights: "The harm is the interference with the individual's scruples or conscience— an important area of privacy which the First Amendment fences off from government. The interference here is as plain as it is in Soviet Russia, where a churchgoer is given a second-class citizenship, result- ing in harm though perhaps not in measurable damages." From then on, any claim of free exercise of religion would find an absolutist pro- tector in William O. Douglas.

After the assassination of John F. Kennedy on November 22, 1963, Lyndon Baines Johnson was successful in moving the nation's laws toward allowing greater equality for the races. When the Court next turned to the area of civil rights, Douglas, who had not been a major factor in many of the earlier race cases, now spoke for himself. In the first of these cases, Robert Mack Bell was one of a group of fifteen to twenty African American students who demonstrated against discrimi- nation at Hooper's Restaurant by sitting in at one of their Baltimore establishments, refusing to leave when they were informed that they would not be served because of their race. For this action, they were convicted of criminal trespass. Since the State of Maryland and the City of Baltimore had both, after the arrests were made, enacted pub- lic-accommodations laws, making it illegal to refuse to serve a person based on race, the Court vacated the convictions on the basis that they were no longer crimes in that area. By thus sending the cases back to the lower courts for disposition under the new statutes, in effect, the Justices were ducking the constitutionality of these laws for the mo- ment.

As in the *Poe v. Ullman* case, where the majority also refused to de- cide the case, Douglas wanted to rule on this entire issue now. In a concurring opinion, he argued that "no question preoccupies the country more than this one; it is plainly justiciable; it presses for a de- cision one way or another; we should resolve it. . . . When we default, as we do today, the prestige of law in the life of the Nation is weak- ened." For Douglas, the issue in this case was very simple: "We deal here with public accommodations—with the right of people to eat and travel as they like and to use facilities whose only claim to existence is serving the public. . . . When one citizen because of his race, creed, or color is denied the privilege of being treated as any other citizen in places of public accommodation, we have classes of citizenship, one being more degrading than the other. That is at war with the one class of citizenship created by the Thirteenth, Fourteenth, and Fifteenth Amendments." Douglas was serving notice that he was ready to protect *all* minorities, and in doing so he had no tolerance for the argument that the federal government had no power to prevent private corporations, aided by state action (in this case the State of Maryland enforcing its segregation policies), from discriminating. "There is no specific provision in the Constitution which protects rights of privacy and enables restaurant owners to refuse service to Negroes," he wrote, adding, "Apartheid . . . is barred by the common law as respects innkeepers and common carriers." Taking a unique tack on the issue, Douglas argued that he could protect such rights by extending the constitutionally safeguarded right to travel: "The right of any person to travel *interstate* irrespective of race, creed, or color is protected by the Constitution. . . . Certainly his right to travel *intrastate* is as basic. Certainly his right to eat at public restaurants is as important in the modern setting as the right of mobility. In these times that right is, indeed, practically indispensable to travel either interstate or intrastate."

Douglas had a chance to say more about the right to travel when the Court returned to the issue of governmental regulations of subversive organizations. Herbert Aptheker, the chairman of the American Communist Party and the editor of its "theoretical organ," *Political Affairs,* sued the secretary of state in federal court when he was denied a passport under section 6 of the Subversive Activities Control Act. Five members of the Court, speaking through Arthur Goldberg, ruled that the section was unconstitutional because it "too broadly and indiscriminately restricts the right to travel and thereby abridges the liberty guaranteed by the Fifth Amendment." As Goldberg made clear, there was no link between the penalty and some proof of actual subversive activity by the person: "The prohibition against travel is supported only by a tenuous relationship between the bare fact of organizational membership and the activity Congress sought to proscribe. The broad and enveloping prohibition indiscriminately excludes plainly relevant considerations such as the individual's knowledge, activity, commitment, and purposes in and places for travel." Presumably, though, if such a link could be demonstrated, then travel could be restricted.

Believing that the Court had not gone far enough, Douglas argued in a concurring opinion that the right of "freedom of movement" deserved absolute protection:

Freedom of movement, at home and abroad, is important for job and business opportunities—for cultural, political and social activities— for all the commingling which gregarious man enjoys. . . . This freedom of movement is the very essence of our free society, setting us apart. Like the right of assembly and the right of association, it often makes all other rights meaningful—knowing, studying, arguing, exploring, conversing, observing and even thinking. Once the right to travel is curtailed, all other rights suffer, just as when curfew or home detention is placed on a person.

.   .   .

Douglas's most famous opinion, certainly his most controversial one, was produced when another challenge to Connecticut's "anti-contraceptive law" was brought to the Court by Estelle Griswold, the director of that state's Planned Parenthood League, and one of the litigants from the earlier *Poe v. Ullman* case, Dr. Lee Buxton, the medical director of the league's New Haven center. They were convicted of violating the law for dispensing advice to married couples on the use of birth-control devices and prescribing them. Since the defendants had been penalized under the criminal law, this case, unlike *Poe v. Ullman,* was deemed to be a proper one for the Court to decide.

Having already argued his position on this issue in his extended dissent in *Poe v. Ullman,* Douglas was the most likely choice to author the Court's opinion when nearly all of the Justices voted to overturn the law. Still, when the Chief Justice tapped Douglas to write the landmark opinion, his office staff suspected that the whimsical Warren did so partly because of Douglas's checkered marital history and extramarital dalliances.

Douglas's first draft was scrawled in blue ink on his yellow pad in about the time that it would have taken him in the old days to commute to work into New York City. And it showed. Ten days after the judicial conference on the case, he had produced a five-page, double-spaced opinion that offered the narrowest possible grounds on which to strike down the law.

After relating the facts of the case and explaining why this case was "ripe" for review, Douglas conceded, in the face of Hugo Black's and Potter Stewart's literal reading of the Bill of Rights, that the word *privacy* did not appear there. He also had to admit that the same was true of "marital association": "The association of husband and wife is not mentioned in the Constitution nor in the Bill of Rights. Neither is any other kind of association." But for Douglas there were other ways to safeguard the rights involved here; he argued that on the "periphery" of the right of association protected by the First Amendment were other rights: "The right to educate a child in a school of the parents' choice—whether public or parochial—is also not mentioned. Nor is the right to study any particular subject or any foreign language. Yet the First Amendment has been construed to include certain of those peripheral rights." This sort of extended logic was nothing more than Douglas had been offering with the free-speech decisions in the 1950s and the early 1960s freedom-of-association cases.

After citing a great many of those precedents, Douglas got to the heart of this case: "Marriage does not fit precisely any of the categories of First Amendment rights. But it is a form of association as vital in the life of a man or woman as any other, and perhaps more so. We would, indeed, have difficulty protecting the intimacies of one's relations to NAACP and not the intimacies of one's marriage relation." Douglas closed by arguing the marital relationship's centrality: "We deal with a right of association older than the Bill of Rights—older than our political parties, older than our school system. It is a coming together for better or for worse, hopefully enduring, and intimate to the degree of being sacred. This association promotes a way of life, not causes; a harmony in living, not political faiths; a bilateral loyalty, not commercial or social projects. Yet it flourishes on the interchange of ideas." Opposed to this "sacred" right, Douglas raised in his conclusion the specter of the government in George Orwell's *1984*: "The prospects of police with warrants searching the sacred precincts of marital bedrooms for telltale signs of the use of contraceptives is repulsive to the idea of privacy and of association that make up a goodly part of the penumbra of the Constitution and Bill of Rights." Few could miss the irony of the "sacred" and "hopefully enduring" language linked to marriage from a man with his marital history.

Before he circulated the opinion to the rest of the Court, Douglas sent a copy to William Brennan, the Justice who seemed most in harmony with his views. Seeing that in the entire opinion Douglas had mentioned the idea of privacy only once, and then only casually in the final sentence, Brennan searched for a way to shore up the constitutional justification for this largely unexplored right of personal autonomy. After nearly a decade together on the Court, Brennan had learned that dealing with his senior colleague was a tricky matter: "He had an uncanny ability to see the issues in a case and know how each of his colleagues would react to them." Brennan would watch in amazement as Douglas would write his dissent in a case even before the majority had been written, and then, if the Court was running late into the summer, he would simply pack up and leave. When Brennan would reach him many weeks later to say that the majority opinion in the case was finished and about to be released, Douglas would tell him to go to a drawer in his desk where his dissent could be found. "It always amazed me how closely his arguments would track with those of the final opinion," recalled Brennan.

But Brennan had also learned that because of his colleague's frequent lack of interest in the job, his speed and imprecision in writing could be a detriment. Years later, the usually circumspect Brennan told an interviewer: "[Douglas's] last ten years on the Court were marked by the slovenliness of his writing and the mistakes that he constantly made."

Faced now with an example of Douglas's inattention to detail, which they knew would have the effect of weakening this case as a precedent for future courts, Brennan and one of his law clerks, S. Paul Posner, decided to try to change the direction and focus of this opinion. They were going to try to get more of the right to privacy added to Douglas's language. "While I agree with a great deal" of the opinion, Posner's draft for Brennan's letter to Douglas began, "I should like to suggest a substantial change in emphasis." Brennan's clerk argued that "to bring the husband-wife relationship within the right of association we have constructed in the First Amendment context . . . may come back to haunt us." For him, the absence of any mention in the Bill of Rights of the association of a husband and a wife had become "the obstacle we must hurdle." Perhaps, Posner argued, Douglas could use the notion of rights on "the periphery" of the Bill of Rights to build a case for a larger, protected privacy right. The letter argued, "Why not say that what has been done for the First Amendment can also be done for some of the other fundamental guarantees of the Bill of Rights? In other words, where fundamentals are concerned, the Bill of Rights guarantees are but expressions or examples of those rights, and do not preclude applications or extensions of those rights to situations unanticipated by the Framers. . . . The guarantees of the Bill of Rights do not necessarily resist expansion to fill in the edges where the same fundamental interests are at stake." Thus, several amendments could be cited as a justification for a right to privacy, which could safeguard Douglas's notion of the "right to be let alone." Brennan liked these suggestions so much that he forwarded the letter to his colleague on April 24, saying that there was "a better chance it will command a court."

Douglas knew exactly how to alter his opinion. From the conclusion of his initial draft he decided to expand on the astronomers' notion of a penumbra, a shadow created by the passage of the moon in front of the sun during an eclipse, to explain how this privacy right could be found in the Bill of Rights. In a mere three days, he had written a new draft arguing that the "specific guarantees in the Bill of Rights have penumbras, formed by emanations from those guarantees that help give them life and substance." Now he would find the right of privacy not in one amendment—the First—but in the shadows created by a total of six of them: the right of association in the First Amendment, the protection against having to "quarter troops" in the Third Amendment, the right against "unreasonable searches and seizures" in the Fourth Amendment, the right against "compulsory self-incrimination" in the Fifth Amendment, the Ninth Amendment's promise that "the enumeration . . . of certain rights, shall not be construed to deny or disparage others retained by the people," and the Fourteenth Amendment's protection against the denial of "due process of law." In this way, Douglas argued, "various guarantees create zones of privacy."

Few on the Court could deny that Douglas was dealing, as he said in his closing sentence, with "a right of privacy older than the Bill of Rights," but they did not see it in the same parts of the Constitution that he did. Arthur Goldberg relied on the Ninth Amendment, arguing in a concurrence that the Framers always meant to imply therein the protection of what for them was the most basic right of privacy. John Harlan and Byron White argued in their concurrences that they could accomplish the same result by interpreting the "liberty" wording of the due-process clause in the Fourteenth Amendment in a way that would allow them to overturn the law.

But it was the dissenters who raised the central attack on Douglas's vision. "The law is every bit as offensive to me as it is to my Brethren of the majority," argued Hugo Black in dissent, but he could not conclude "that the evil qualities they see in the law make it unconstitutional." By this time, Black was drifting away from his liberal traveling partner Douglas and using literal constitutional interpretation to offer more and more conservative opinions: "I like my privacy as well as the next one, but I am nevertheless compelled to admit that government has a right to invade it unless prohibited by some specific constitutional guarantee." After a complete review of the meanings of the various provisions of the Constitution in which Douglas professed to find an implied right of privacy, Black concluded: "Connecticut's law as applied here is not forbidden by any provision of the Federal Constitution as that Constitution was written."

Justice Potter Stewart could not find any right of privacy in his copy of the Constitution either. He wanted Douglas to point specifi-

cally to the location of the right of privacy: "In the course of its opinion the Court refers to no less than six Amendments to the Constitution: the First, the Third, the Fourth, the Fifth, the Ninth, and the
Fourteenth. But the Court does not say which of these Amendments, if
any, it thinks is infringed by this Connecticut law. . . . I can find nothing in any of them to invalidate this Connecticut law, even assuming
that all those Amendments are fully applicable against the States." So
for him, like Hugo Black, any repeal of this law should be done not by
the Court but by the "elected representatives" of the state's legislature,
expressing "the standards of the people of Connecticut."

As a result of Brennan's successful lobbying, Douglas was now
credited by his supporters with being even more activist, "inventing"
the right of privacy and "finding" it in the Constitution. His legacy
would be more than the open sale of birth-control devices; it would
also be that the right of privacy for married couples could serve as a
foundation for discussing whether other privacy rights such as the
right to abortion and the right to die could be found in the Constitution as well. It was this opinion that simultaneously made Douglas
both the icon of the liberals and the devil incarnate to generations of
conservatives.

·   ·   ·

When the Court returned to the issue of state control of allegedly subversive organizations, the great dissenter on this issue, William O.
Douglas, was given the honor of putting the issue to rest forever. The
opportunity came in two cases. Hugh DeGregory refused to answer
questions that were put to him by the New Hampshire attorney general about his activities in the Communist Party prior to 1957 and was
jailed for contempt for a year. In the second case, Barbara Elfbrandt, a
teacher in Arizona, refused to sign the state's loyalty oath, knowing
that the law also held criminal penalties and the possibility of removal
from one's job if she remained or became a member of the Communist
Party.

Douglas wrote for the Court in overturning both laws on constitutional grounds. In *DeGregory v. Attorney General of New Hampshire*,
Douglas wrote that the majority was bothered by the historical nature
of the fishing expedition for information on subversives: "The information being sought was historical, not current. Lawmaking at the investigatory stage may properly probe historic events for any light that
may be thrown on present conditions and problems. But the First
Amendment prevents use of the power to investigate enforced by the
contempt power to probe at will and without relation to existing

need." And here, he argued, there was "no showing whatsoever of present danger of sedition against the State itself, the only area to which the authority of the State extends. . . . New Hampshire's interest on this record is too remote and conjectural to override the guarantee of the First Amendment that a person can speak or not, as he chooses, free of all governmental compulsion."

In *Elfbrandt v. Russell,* Douglas and the Court failed to see a showing of "active" membership in the Communist Party and "specific intent" to overthrow the government, both of which were now required by the Court for a conviction. Thus, the state's loyalty-oath requirement infringed on her freedom of association under the First Amendment: "Those who join an organization but do not share its unlawful activities surely pose no threat, either as citizens or as public employees. Laws such as this that are not restricted in scope to those who join with the 'specific intent' to further illegal action impose, in effect, a conclusive presumption that the member shares the unlawful aims of the organization. . . . This Act threatens the cherished freedom of association." After more than a decade of fighting these witch-hunt laws, Douglas had the satisfaction of being on the Court long enough to state for the majority that they had no place in modern America.

.   .   .

When Douglas had a chance in March 1966 to write into law some of his developing views about the rights of the poor under the equal-protection clause, stemming from his earlier *Skinner v. Oklahoma* and *Douglas v. California* opinions, he could see that Hugo Black was now likely to disagree with him vigorously in print.

Annie Harper and Evelyn Butts, both residents of Virginia, brought suit in federal court seeking to have the state's poll tax declared unconstitutional. As part of the state's effort to keep poor people, among them African Americans, off the voting rolls, Virginia charged a $1.50 fee for voting, which was cumulative if left unpaid by nonvoters. Persuaded by the arguments of Solicitor General Thurgood Marshall, six members of the Court decided to rule that the equal-protection clause barred a state from making the payment of up to three years of the unpaid tax a precondition to voting. When Douglas was selected to write the majority opinion, he gave this historic case his usual treatment, saying everything in a handful of pages. "Wealth or fee paying has, in our view, no relation to voting qualifications; the right to vote is too precious, too fundamental to be so burdened," he argued. It bothered Douglas little that twenty-nine years earlier the Court had upheld this very notion in a case coming from Georgia. Precedents now for him were things to be swept away if they interfered with his aims, and he did so here with great dispatch: "*Breedlove v. Suttles* sanctioned [the poll tax's] use as a 'prerequisite of voting'. . . . To that extent the *Breedlove* case is overruled."

The state has the power to confer the right to vote, explained Douglas, but "once the franchise is granted to the electorate, lines may not be drawn which are inconsistent with the Equal Protection Clause of the Fourteenth Amendment." Since states could not thus discriminate against a person's right to vote without a constitutionally permissible basis, Douglas ruled that Virginia could not do so on the basis of financial status: "We say the same whether the citizen, otherwise qualified to vote, has $1.50 in his pocket or nothing at all, pays the fee or fails to pay it. The principle that denies the States the right to dilute a citizen's vote on account of his economic status or other such factors by analogy bars a system which excludes those unable to pay a fee to vote or those who fail to pay."

Citing his *Skinner* opinion, Douglas hinted that his eventual goal for protecting the poor lay in more than just their right to vote: "Wealth, like race, creed, or color, is not germane to one's ability to participate intelligently in the electoral process. Lines drawn on the basis of wealth or property, like those of race . . . are traditionally disfavored. . . . To introduce wealth or payment of a fee as a measure of a voter's qualifications is to introduce a capricious or irrelevant factor. The degree of the discrimination is irrelevant. In this context—that is, as a condition of obtaining a ballot—the requirement of fee paying causes an 'invidious' discrimination." In short, consonant with his arguments on the right to work, the right to travel, the right of privacy, and freedom of belief, wealth or the lack thereof had become another constitutionally protected status upon which the state could not discriminate for any reason.

But Hugo Black, his old and dear ally, would not go with him. Signaling that he and Douglas were parting company on the issue of the role of the Court with respect to both the adherence to precedent and the interpretation of the Constitution, Black wrote a stirring dissent:

> In *Breedlove v. Suttles* . . . decided December 6, 1937, a few weeks after I took my seat as a member of this Court, we unanimously upheld the right of the State of Georgia to make payment of its state poll tax a prerequisite to voting in state elections. . . . I would adhere to the holding of [this case]. The Court, however, overrules *Breedlove* in part, but its opinion reveals that it does so not by using its limited power to interpret the original meaning of the Equal

Protection Clause, but by giving that clause a new meaning which it believes represents a better governmental policy. From this action I dissent.

For him, Douglas and the majority were using the equal-protection clause to put forward their own form of public policy, which he refused to do: "Although I join the Court in disliking the policy of the poll tax, this is not in my judgment a justifiable reason for holding this poll tax law unconstitutional. Such a holding on my part would, in my judgment, be an exercise of power which the Constitution does not confer upon me." And therein lay the difference between these two old friends. Both men agreed that change had to occur, but Black wanted to leave that to the elected legislature or to the constitutional-amendment process, while Douglas believed that it was his job as a jurist to effect change from the Court.

Black notwithstanding, the majority of the Court was now liberal. And it remained so after Arthur Goldberg, who resigned from the Court to become the U.S. ambassador to the United Nations, was replaced by Douglas's old friend Abe Fortas on July 28, 1965. Once more, the liberal votes were present for Douglas to lead the Court if he wished. But his reckless personal life, not to mention his desire to go his own way on the Court, prevented him from doing so.

A TALE OF TWO WOMEN

We went over to the Douglases' at 6:00 for dinner [on October 16, 1966]. . . . A nice evening: same house, same food, same people—different wife.

—Elizabeth Black

By the summer of 1965, there had been only two divorces by Supreme Court Justices in the history of the United States, and both of them were William O. Douglas's. And now he was in the process of bettering his own record.

No sooner had his young wife, Joan, been dispatched to her parents' home near Buffalo, bearing the news that her marriage was now over, than Douglas sought to replace her at Prairie House with another beautiful, even younger woman. He had met a gorgeous, blond artist from Granger, Washington, named Elena Leonardo, who had just graduated from the University of Washington. Beautiful enough to be a model, Leonardo was supporting her artistic endeavors by working in a Yakima travel agency, where she had been helping the Justice. Much like the Justice, she was a free spirit, loved to travel, and had a real sense of adventure. And in a short time, Douglas fell head over heels in love once more. He asked her to have a cup of coffee with him in the Chinook Hotel and then asked her to have dinner in the Four Winds restaurant, where it soon became apparent to the young woman that he was falling in love with her.

After a while, they moved in together at Prairie House, where Douglas was almost childlike and innocent as he made her breakfast in the morning and cooked his favorite dinner of steaks barbecued directly on the coals and barbecued beans that took three days to make. Life for him was fun again as he pulled practical jokes, told his stories, and got to know another young woman. The pain of the impending divorce now behind him, it was not unusual for Douglas to return from a two-week pack trip into the mountains, literally coated with dirt, and have the lovely young blonde bathe him in the tub. By the end of the summer they were nearly engaged to be married, with Douglas insisting on showing her a box of jewels from Falkenberg's in Walla Walla for her wedding ring, but none of them caught her fancy. Justice Douglas seemed to be a man madly in love, writing to Leonardo on September 6 that he was "absolutely wild, wild, wild, wild, wild" about her.

Leonardo had every reason to believe that she was the only object of the Supreme Court Justice's affections that summer. But Damon Trout, an old fishing buddy who always had a surprise or two for his old friend Bill Douglas, had unwittingly helped to complicate things when the Justice came to visit Portland.

No one could fully understand the nature of the relationship between these two old friends, one a brilliant Supreme Court Justice and the other an elementary-school dropout who had gone to sea and was in the marine electrical business. The two men generally behaved like a couple of cowboys on a binge after the cattle had been brought in from the range—cruising various bars, drinking, playing practical jokes on each other, and swapping dirty stories. Sometimes on these visits, Trout performed the same function for Douglas in Portland that Elon Gilbert did in Yakima—finding young women who might catch the Justice's fancy. But in August 1965, after Douglas delivered a speech in Portland, Trout had a special treat for him to take his mind off of his third failed marriage. The night before, he had met a gorgeous young blonde who seemed to be just the Justice's type. Twenty-two-year-old Cathleen Heffernan was an attractive junior studying sociology at Marylhurst College, supporting herself by working as a cocktail waitress at the Three Star restaurant. She stood five foot five inches tall, a slender 108 pounds, and had gentle, twinkling blue eyes and blond hair in a fashionable pixie cut. Inwardly, she had a steely toughness and was able to handle anything life sent her way, but outwardly there was a girlish vulnerability that could make one want to reach out and protect her. "I think she can charm a bird out of a tree," said a later colleague. Indeed, she unknowingly began to charm this elusive Justice right out of his new relationship with Elena Leonardo.

As Cathy chatted at the Three Star for a few minutes with the Justice and his friend in her unaffected and outgoing manner, Douglas found her life story to be a compelling one. She was the only daughter of Curtis and Mary Heffernan, two poor Irish Catholics who had struggled to make ends meet on their salaries as a railroad night clerk and a prison secretary. At eighteen, Cathy had biked and hitchhiked

her way around Europe. Now, in her spare time, she was helping people working with mentally retarded children. Douglas found himself
instantly attracted to her. Would she like to go out on a date the next
night and have some dinner? he asked. When her answer was yes,
Douglas told Damon Trout that he had done a good job. She will be
my next wife, he said. "I loved her the first time I saw her," Douglas
said later.

Douglas was so smitten that he began sending private letters to
Cathy, using Trout as an intermediary to hide the courtship from the
nuns at the college and his girlfriend in Goose Prairie, not to mention
his wife in Buffalo. And he was happy to do whatever favors he could
for her. "One day, four giggling little girls came to my side door," recalled Cragg Gilbert. " 'I'm Cathy Heffernan, and I am here to pick up
a car that Bill Douglas is supposed to have left here.' " When Virginia
Gilbert pointed to the old car in the backyard, they all jumped in "like
school girls" and drove away, leaving the Gilberts wondering what
their old friend was up to now.

Douglas was captivated by the dilemma posed by choosing between his two young girlfriends. So, after returning to the Court
for the October term, Douglas carried on two courtships, sending
love letters to both Leonardo and Heffernan. Initially, though, it was
Leonardo who was the main focus of his attention. "Weekends are interminable waiting to see you," he wrote her in mid-October. He
bought one of Leonardo's paintings to place in his office and arranged
a weekend rendezvous with her at the Hilton in Los Angeles and one
at the Benson Hotel in Portland in conjunction with speaking engagements that he had accepted in those cities. Time and again, the mail
brought her new presents and even money for a new coat and new
dresses at Christmastime, none of which he could afford.

Eventually, the relationship with Leonardo began to deteriorate
somewhat. Why wouldn't she visit him for Thanksgiving instead of
serving as the maid of honor at her girlfriend's wedding? he wondered.
He feared that she would leave him for a younger, more attractive man.
Why couldn't she drive to Portland in the middle of a blizzard to see
him at Christmastime? Communication between the two of them
began to break down. Douglas wasn't mentioning the status of his divorce, and Elena was too polite to ask.

Always one to keep his options open, when Douglas returned to
Portland for another speech in late December 1965, this time it was
Cathy Heffernan whom he asked to join him for dinner at the London
Bar and Grill in the Benson Hotel. When the conversation went well,

he asked her to dinner again the next night and asked to meet her parents. "She just got kind of swept up in it," says her former college roommate, Marty Bagby Yopp. "She was enjoying him and he was pursuing her. Being a bit adventurous and impulsive was not unlike her."

Never very good at hiding these affairs, Douglas again seemed to have learned nothing from the sad ends of his first two marriages. As carefully as he had tried to shield Joan from these new relationships, she accidentally discovered one of Elena Leonardo's letters on the table during a visit with Douglas in Washington and read it. For the third time, Douglas had ruined his chances for a favorable divorce decree.

But, again, that did not matter to Douglas. He was in heaven, with not one but two beautiful young women. "Cathy was a real crutch," Cragg Gilbert recalls from their conversations at the time. "He began to idolize a person, and it was Cathy he was idolizing." To Gilbert, it seemed that by chasing very young women Douglas was trying to fight off the inevitable march of time.

When the time came to negotiate yet another divorce agreement, his tax accountants began to wonder where the money was going to come from. The alimony payments to Mildred and the payments on all of the houses were making it impossible for him to meet his financial responsibilities. The temporary separation agreement with Joan, calling for an additional alimony payment of five hundred dollars a month, was effectively going to take the rest of his disposable income.

As time passed, Elena Leonardo decided to take some time to think her relationship with Douglas over, and without telling him she left in early 1966 for her second trip around the world, sending him a postcard from Tasmania. Douglas was hurt and stunned by the apparent rejection. How could he communicate with someone when he didn't even know where she was? "That makes it *very difficult,*" he wrote. By the time she returned home to the Yakima region, Leonardo was no longer certain what she wanted to do. Should she give up her life and dreams as an artist in order to become the next Mrs. William O. Douglas? She needed some time to sort out her feelings and their relationship. Try as they might to talk to each other, neither Douglas nor Leonardo could explain their own fears or understand those of the other. When the Justice finally proposed that they spend the night together, she refused, saying that she was too tired. So he just left, without any further comment.

Now approaching sixty-eight, the thought that he might not be appealing to younger women was intolerable to Douglas. "I think he felt that at his age he didn't have time to be dallying around, and that I was rejecting him, and that I wasn't going to marry him," said Elena Leonardo, years later.

Nonetheless, Douglas wanted to be married again immediately. He just could not afford to do it. His finances were in total disarray. His divorce from Joan became final on June 24, 1966, saddling him with an agreement to pay her more than $4,000 in annual alimony. This was in addition to the $10,920 he owed Mildred in alimony for that year, the $145 a month he owed on his loan for Mildred's Third Street house, and a $488 tax bill for that house, not to mention the money he still owed Mercedes. The only good news from his latest divorce agreement was that he would not lose a house this time. Instead, in trade for being able to retain possession of the Goose Prairie house, he promised to give Joan a life estate in the property after his death and to bequeath it to the Nature Conservancy thereafter (an agreement that was not kept). Things were so bad, though, that just to renew the $6,150 bank loan on the Goose Prairie property, Douglas had to ask Clark Clifford to cosign for it at the National Bank of Washington, where Clifford served as a director.

The financial noose that Tommy Corcoran had slipped around Douglas's neck in the first divorce settlement continued to cut off his options. Thanks to the escalator clause, in 1966 alone he would have to pay Mildred an extra twenty thousand dollars on his nonjudicial income. When combined with the federal and state tax bite on his high income, Douglas was getting less than thirty cents for every dollar that he earned over seventy thousand. Realizing this, Douglas pleaded with Clifford to try to renegotiate this "oppressive" provision that had been "jammed down my throat by a very vindictive lawyer."

When Corcoran turned a deaf ear, Douglas asked a friend from New York, attorney Sid Davis, to convince his old political ally Ernie Cuneo to serve as an intermediary to Tommy the Cork in an attempt to get the escalator clause canceled. But there was nothing that could be done—Corcoran and Mildred Douglas remembered what he had done to their respective dreams, and neither was willing to let him off the hook. Just to bury the knife a bit further, Corcoran sent word that the Justice should not make such a request again until he had had a good year financially. And with the new alimony payments to Joan, that was not likely to happen.

It was in this mental state, in July 1966, less than three weeks after his divorce to Joan, faced with near bankruptcy and what he perceived to be a devastating rejection from a younger woman, that Douglas impulsively drove over to Portland to see Cathy Heffernan. He had a Ninth Circuit Judicial Conference and a dinner to attend in Los Angeles, he told her. Would she like to come along? She agreed, and once they arrived the two of them went shopping for clothes because she had underpacked for the visit. They should go on another date, Douglas suggested once they were in the dress shop, adding that he was due in Washington for Luci Baines Johnson's upcoming wedding. Would she like to attend with him? When she agreed again, Douglas's impish romantic side took over as he turned to the saleswoman and said: "Well Mrs. Epstein, why don't you bring out a wedding dress for her? . . . If you can convince Cathy to marry me, I'll make you Secretary of the Navy."

The next day, Mrs. Epstein tried to do exactly that, while Cathy tried on one outfit after another. "We might get married," Cathy responded, "but I'm scared to death." The shopkeeper counseled the young girl as best she could about the joys and agonies of marriage. But there was no way she could anticipate the unique joys and agonies of being married to a man who was one of the most visible figures in the nation, nearly three times her age, and contemplating marriage for the fourth time. "We hadn't really talked marriage plans specifically. But it was always in the air," Cathy Douglas said later. And for Douglas, fearful that, just as Mercedes had done, Joan would try to embarrass him by remarrying quickly (even though it would have been to his financial advantage), a new marriage was more in the air than ever.

Finally, Cathy was convinced. "Do you know anyone who can marry us?" Douglas asked Mrs. Epstein on the phone. Why not get married at my daughter's home in Encino? she suggested. When he agreed, the wedding was on. The next day, the happy couple was waiting in front of her store's door when she opened it. "Where [is] the Santa Monica courthouse to get a license?" they asked. A delivery boy was dispatched to help them. After a purchase of matching gold wedding bands and a haircut for the bride, they were ready for the 6:00 P.M. ceremony.

At least, the Justice was ready for it. The prospective bride was no longer so sure. "I don't want to marry anybody," she told the people at the hairdressers'. "I don't care who it is. I can't go through with it. I've got to leave." No amount of reassurance from Mrs. Epstein and the hairdressers seemed to work. By the time she got back to the hotel, Cathy was ready to chuck the whole idea. "I don't want to get married," she cried at Douglas. He started to laugh. The more she cried, the more Douglas laughed. All the while, the phone was ringing, as the rumor of a marriage license being issued for the Justice spread like wildfire. When Douglas opened the hotel door only to find two reporters waiting there for them, the suspicions were confirmed.

"It's no secret anymore," he told Cathy, who was then hiding in the bathroom. "What are we going to do?" Fortunately for Douglas, she had decided that they would be married after all.

But the madness had just begun. After the ceremony, the newlyweds tried to dine with friends at the Del Ray Yacht Club only to find themselves besieged once again. All Douglas wanted to do now was get his new wife out of the city to his retreat in Goose Prairie, where he knew they would be safe from the intrusive press. But just how to accomplish this feat was not clear to him.

As usual, though, the Douglas luck held true to form. When he and Cathy arrived at the Los Angeles airport, he saw an old acquaintance from Yakima, attorney John Gavin, waiting with friends for the plane that was going to take him home from the Ninth Circuit Judicial Conference, which he had also attended. Gavin was already a bit perplexed, having just seen what appeared to him to be a lynch mob of reporters and photographers running by, yelling, "Look for an old man and a young girl!" Then, a few moments later, Bill Douglas appeared from around a corner with a waiflike young woman in tow whom Gavin had never seen before. "This is Cathy," he said breathlessly as they met. "Please stand around her and keep them away. I'll lead them off." With that the Justice turned, saw the next pack of reporters coming toward him, and ran down the airport hallway toward a different plane. Gavin and his friends meanwhile took the woman they soon discovered to be the new Mrs. Douglas with them to Yakima. Finally, Douglas himself escaped to Prairie House, where few reporters ventured because none was welcome.

News of Douglas's impromptu wedding caught those closest to him by surprise. Elena Leonardo, who had so recently spurned his invitation to spend the night, got the word while driving to Seattle to see the Bolshoi Ballet. She heard Paul Harvey say on the radio, "Well he's done it again. . . . He's done it again. . . . He's done it again. . . . Justice William O. Douglas has gone off and gotten married again." Leonardo was so shocked by the news that she nearly drove off the road. Never suspecting that Douglas had been seeing anyone else, let alone planning to marry, she wondered who the new wife might be.

And she wasn't the only one who was stunned by the news. Clark Clifford had said good-bye to his old friend in Washington, D.C., at the end of the Court term, deeply concerned by Douglas's apparent state of depression. So it was with a certain amount of amazement that he read the letter from the Pacific Northwest on July 22 declaring that the new marriage was "the most wonderful thing in my whole life." The ever-faithful Clifford promised to "arrange for Cathy to be happy and content here." But he remained puzzled as to his friend's motivation: "Bill always liked a well-turned ankle. . . . To me it seemed as if he was searching for something—something more—all of his life. But he never found it, and I never really knew what it was. I'm not sure even he knew what it was."

Indeed, within days Douglas began going through his usual "buyer's remorse" with respect to new wives. "Bill was always happy just before a marriage and one week afterward," explained Kay Kershaw. Once he was safely back in Goose Prairie, Douglas snuck away from his new wife to Whistlin' Jack's to call Elena Leonardo in Yakima. He had made a great mistake, he told her. But she was having none of it and hung up the phone. Then Douglas started sending little notes to her. Finally, while the honeymooning couple was shopping in Yakima for supplies and stationery for thank-you notes, Douglas slipped down to the travel agency to peer in the window at her. As soon as she came outside to speak to him, though, Douglas realized how upset he had made his ex-girlfriend. "I knew he was feeling really sheepish," recalled Leonardo, "and I was just so upset. I was just shaking. I could hardly speak. And I said to him, 'Well, Bill, congratulations. I hope you will certainly be very happy.' "

But Douglas was never one to give up easily. Soon came more notes, and in time the offers came to Leonardo to join him on trips. Eventually, the two would resume their romantic relationship. "In the back of my mind, I always figured he would divorce her and that he would marry me," Leonardo said.

Meanwhile, life for Cathy as the new Mrs. Douglas was no easier than it had been for any of the other wives. The Justice decided to introduce her to the rest of his world at Luci Baines Johnson's wedding. "That's the very thing I didn't want him to do!" said Abe Fortas when he saw the crush of reporters around the Douglases at the cathedral. "That was a terrible way to begin your married life in Washington," said Dagmar Hamilton. "Douglas must have enjoyed that because he was upstaging Luci's wedding. And he didn't care that he was using Cathy to do it. . . . I think that wasn't accidental at all. . . . I am sure he enjoyed every moment of the publicity that came to him for his fourth marriage. It must have rejuvenated him."

Douglas, always the subject of controversy, now became the butt of jokes around the country. "Sorry Chief," Douglas says in one cartoon, "I can't make it—I have to find a babysitter for Cathy." The Justice was summarily removed from Washington high society's formal social register, known as the Green Book. It was a slight, commented Hugo Black's wife, Elizabeth, that "I'm sure he doesn't even know hit him."

Family members could see that the Justice's relationship with his new young wife was a complicated one. "My father was certainly a father figure to her. . . . And Cathy was, to my father, a perfect child," William O. Douglas, Jr., explained. "My father was at the age when he began to think about his own mortality. And I think he found in Cathy someone who could follow in his footsteps."

Douglas's third divorce and fourth marriage offended many in his hometown of Yakima, leading them to urge that he be removed from the Bench. "By the 1960s Douglas had become something of a joke in town," explained John Gavin. "Yakima didn't like *anyone* to be remarried, especially not the boy who became such a big man." Others in Washington, D.C., agreed. On July 18, 1966, Congressmen George Andrews of Alabama and Thomas Abernethy of Mississippi, along with three other members of the House, began calling for an impeachment investigation by the Judiciary Committee into Douglas's moral character.

"Well, at least I married mine!" was Douglas's response, referring to the common congressional practice of keeping mistresses on the side. This impeachment threat, however, died as quickly as the previous two in the early 1950s over Douglas's comments regarding the recognition of Red China and his actions in the Rosenberg case.

But the controversy for Douglas was not over that year. Investigative reporter Ronald Ostrow of the *Los Angeles Times* uncovered the Las Vegas–based funding for the Albert Parvin Foundation, and on Douglas's sixty-eighth birthday, October 16, 1966, published a front-page story under the headline VEGAS-LINKED FUND PAYS $12,000 TO JUSTICE DOUGLAS. The appearance of Douglas drawing almost an additional one third of his now thirty-nine-thousand-dollar official salary as the only paid official of the foundation raised substantial questions. Douglas and Parvin quickly argued that the money had not started until 1962, after Parvin had sold the Flamingo, and insisted that it was used "largely as an expense account."

While there was no evidence that the association with the foundation had in any way compromised Douglas's work on the Court, it was not difficult for Ostrow to show how it might violate the judicial canon of ethics, which held that "a judge's official conduct should be free from impropriety and the appearance of impropriety." At that time, for instance, the Supreme Court was considering a tax-evasion conviction by Fred Black, Jr., a business associate of former Lyndon Johnson aide Bobby Baker and of Edward Levinson, both of whom were officers in the Fremont Hotel and gambling casino, in which Parvin also had an interest. Indeed, Levinson himself was suing the FBI for damages in an invasion-of-privacy suit that also had the possibility of reaching the High Court.

Harry S. Ashmore, the secretary of the Albert Parvin Foundation, issued a press release describing its work and explaining that its financial support was being held "in a trust fund administered by the Bank of America . . . and was received as an irrevocable gift from Albert Parvin." Douglas's work, he added, came only "at the insistence of the Board." Douglas sent the release to Chief Justice Earl Warren, hoping that this would put an end to the matter.

But others were not willing to let it go. One foundation board member, Judge William Campbell, objected to this characterization of the organization's payments to Douglas, adding that "the recent regrettable newspaper publicity was my first knowledge of the fact that Justice Douglas was being so compensated." The *Los Angeles Times* editorialized that "acceptance of outside income by a member of the highest court in the land . . . raises grave ethical questions. . . . Justice Douglas said that acceptance of the money poses no problem of ethics. The Times disagrees." Senator John J. Williams of Delaware wrote the Chief Justice that "there is a grave question as to the propriety of [Douglas] accepting such payments, and I would appreciate your reviewing these charges and advising me whether or not the Supreme Court condones such practices and if not, what steps will be taken to protect the integrity of the Court."

With the public-relations heat still rising, Douglas sought to put the matter behind him by writing the Chief Justice a four-page explanatory letter, assuring him that "there has been no conflict whatsoever between the Foundation and my work on the Court." Using this as a basis for his response, Warren then wrote Senator Williams that this issue was now "a matter personal to Mr. Justice Douglas." But while Douglas had also assured the Chief that he was "not sure how much longer I can direct its affairs," when the furor died down the following month he quietly maintained his lucrative association with the foundation.

Having survived the turbulent summer, with Court back in session Douglas was almost relieved to return to the job of being a judge.

KEEPER OF THE CONSCIENCE

The Court is really the keeper of the conscience.
And the conscience is the Constitution.

—*William O. Douglas*

In the fall of 1966, even on a Court where he could command a majority if he wished, Douglas was far happier to speak in dissent. As part of a body in which members dissent in only about one in five cases, Douglas dissented nearly twice that much. Speaking alone, Douglas did not need to worry about shaping his legal positions to suit others for their vote. And speaking alone, he could work quickly and move on to other pursuits that were more interesting to him. At times it seemed to those working in his office that Douglas took positions to ensure that no one would agree with him. And the results showed. Of his 486 dissents over the course of his career, more than half the time Douglas wrote only for himself. More than just the Great Dissenter, Douglas became "the Lone Ranger" on the Supreme Court.

But the question was how long he would fill that role. By now, a series of medical problems were plaguing Douglas. He had been suffering for several years from a combination of hypertension and polycythemia, a thickening of the blood due to excess production of red-blood cells by the bone marrow. While medication kept the disease under control, patients with such an affliction were expected to live only a decade or so. And for a time Douglas's fate appeared to be no different. After his heart developed a symptomatic atrial fibrillation in 1966, he suffered a minor heart failure. Making matters worse, he developed hyperuricemia, an excess amount of uric acid in his blood, which complicated his treatment for the other diseases since it could lead to kidney stones or the gout.

Soon, he began suffering from continual and intense lower gastrointestinal distress, reminiscent of that during his days at the Cravath law firm, for which the doctors could find no medical source. In time, these problems became so severe that Douglas would begin to feel light-headed to the point of fearing that was going to faint. During these attacks, the doctors discovered, his heart was beating so rapidly that it was causing him to slip toward unconsciousness. When none of a series of prescribed medicines effectively controlled his heart's rhythm, Douglas was put on a very high dose of digitalis.

But Douglas was determined to continue with his work on the Court. The opening case of the 1966 term, involving civil-rights protests, showed just how far Black and Douglas had drifted apart. Harriet Louise Adderley and a group of student civil-rights protestors were convicted of criminal trespass when they demonstrated on the grounds of a county jail in which some of their fellow protestors were being held.

Using a close textual analysis of the Constitution and evincing a developing fear of the unruliness of protestors throughout the South, Hugo Black wrote for a five-person majority in upholding the conviction. He was unpersuaded that an earlier precedent allowing protests at the South Carolina state capitol could be used here to uphold the protests because of the difference in the purpose of the areas: "Traditionally, state capitol grounds are open to the public. Jails, built for security purposes, are not. . . . Here the demonstrators entered the jail grounds through a driveway used only for jail purposes and without warning to or permission from the sheriff." For him, the protestors had trespassed rather than expressed their political views as protected by the First Amendment's free-speech provision.

While on the basis of the law there was little to undercut Black's analysis, Douglas, speaking for Brennan, Warren, and Fortas in dissent, cut to the heart of the constitutional issues here: "The Court errs in treating the case as if it were an ordinary trespass case or an ordinary picketing case. . . . The jailhouse, like an executive mansion, a legislative chamber, a courthouse, or the statehouse itself . . . is one of the seats of government, . . . and when it houses political prisoners or those who many think are unjustly held, it is an obvious center for protest." For him, this was just another "right to petition for the redress of grievances" that was deserving of total protection, so long as the protestors were "peaceable":

> Conventional methods of petitioning may be, and often have been, shut off to large groups of our citizens. Legislators may turn deaf ears; formal complaints may be routed endlessly through a bu-

reaucratic maze; courts may let the wheels of justice grind very slowly. Those who do not control television and radio, those who cannot afford to advertise in newspapers or circulate elaborate pamphlets may have only a more limited type of access to public officials. Their methods should not be condemned as tactics of obstruction and harassment as long as the assembly and petition are peaceable, as these were.

Then Douglas asked the central question here: Did the authorities arrest the protestors because of the nature of their speech? If so, as he believed, "by allowing these orderly and civilized protests against injustice to be suppressed, we only increase the forces of frustration which the conditions of second-class citizenship are generating amongst us." Douglas, the jurist who had been protesting against the Establishment for years, was now willing to allow criticism of the government almost anywhere and at any time.

Another civil-rights case in the 1966–1967 term offered Douglas a chance to articulate his views further in dissent. Robert Pierson and others had been arrested by police in Jackson, Mississippi, and charged with breach of the peace for attempting to use segregated facilities at an interstate-bus terminal. After being convicted and given the maximum fine by a municipal justice, Pierson sought to sue the judge and police under section 1983 of the Civil Rights Act of 1871, which made "every person" acting under color of law to deprive others of their civil rights liable for their actions. Eight members of the Court signed Chief Justice Warren's opinion exempting judges from liability under this act. But to William O. Douglas, judges were no different from other governmental actors or from other people, for that matter: "To most, 'every person' would mean *every person,* not every person *except* judges. . . . The congressional purpose seems to me to be clear." To prove his point, Douglas offered a series of examples of potential judicial deprivation of civil rights: "What about the judge who conspires with the local law enforcement officers to 'railroad' a dissenter? What about the judge who knowingly turns a trial into a 'kangaroo' court? Or one who intentionally flouts the Constitution in order to obtain a conviction? Congress, I think, concluded that the evils of allowing intentional, knowing deprivations of civil rights to go unredressed far outweighed the speculative inhibiting effects which might attend an inquiry into a judicial deprivation of civil rights." Once more, Douglas offered encouragement to those who labored on behalf of the oppressed.

.   .   .

The 1967–1968 term presented the Court, which had become even more liberal that summer after the replacement of the retiring conservative Tom Clark with the liberal-activist Solicitor General Thurgood Marshall, the nation's first African American Justice, with the kind of case that Douglas now loved to decide. Under a Louisiana wrongful-death statute, five illegitimate children sued a doctor and an insurance company for the death of their mother even though the law authorized legal action only on behalf of legitimate children. The question was whether this law represented a violation of the equal-protection clause in discriminating against illegitimate children. As Douglas pondered this case, there can be little doubt that he thought about the three little Douglas children who, though legitimate in birth, would have been lost if Julia Fisk Douglas had been taken from them. Why should other children in such circumstances be barred from legal action if the same happened to them just because of the nature of their birth, a condition over which they had absolutely no control? When five other members of the Court agreed with him, Douglas was given the chance to write these views into law.

Douglas began his short, three-page opinion upholding the children's rights from the premise "that illegitimate children are not 'nonpersons.' They are humans, live, and have their being. They are clearly 'persons' within the meaning of the Equal Protection Clause of the Fourteenth Amendment." To determine whether these children had been denied equal protection, the test was whether the law had a "rational basis"—that is, did the classification granting benefits to some and denying them to others constitute an "invidious discrimination against a particular class"? Douglas wondered why corporations could sue as "persons" under the Fourteenth Amendment, even if "its incorporators were all bastards." For Douglas, the thought that guilty parties and insurance companies could walk free just because the litigants were illegitimate children was unacceptable. "Why should the illegitimate child be denied rights merely because of his birth out of wedlock?" he asked. The Louisiana law was struck down as being "invidious discrimination" because "no action, conduct, or demeanor of theirs is possibly relevant to the harm that was done the mother."

Douglas had a chance to explore his developing freedom-of-religion views when the Court returned to the subject of state aid to parochial-school education. A case came from New York testing whether public textbooks could be loaned to parochial schools free of charge so long as they were the same books being used by public schools. Did this financial assistance in the form of books constitute a violation of the First Amendment as an establishment of religion? Six members of the Court, speaking through Justice Byron White, ruled that this was an acceptable form of aid because the books were loaned, only dealt with secular subjects, aided the students and not the schools, and no money changed hands. For the Court, the goal sought by the state was paramount:

> Underlying these cases, and underlying also the legislative judgments that have preceded the court decisions, has been a recognition that private education has played and is playing a significant and valuable role in raising national levels of knowledge, competence, and experience. . . . Considering this attitude, the continued willingness to rely on private school systems, including parochial systems, strongly suggests that a wide segment of informed opinion, legislative and otherwise, has found that those schools do an acceptable job of providing secular education to their students.

While Douglas had been with the majority in *Everson v. Board of Education of Ewing Tp.* in 1947 in allowing the state provision of bus money to students attending religious schools and had allowed a released-time program for religious education from public schools in *Zorach v. Clauson* in 1952, he made clear in this case that his views on what constituted the state's separation from religion had changed. The provision of schoolbooks to parochial schools was for him much different than providing buses: "Whatever may be said of Everson, there is nothing ideological about a bus. There is nothing ideological about a school lunch, or a public nurse, or a scholarship. . . . [However] the textbook goes to the very heart of education in a parochial school. It is the chief, although not solitary, instrumentality for propagating a particular religious creed or faith. How can we possibly approve such state aid to a religion?"

Douglas was troubled that this loan system, under which the schools themselves chose the books and submitted their lists to the school board for approval, might instigate a political civil war: "Can there be the slightest doubt that the head of the parochial school will select the book or books that best promote its sectarian creed? If the board of education supinely submits by approving or supplying the sectarian or sectarian-oriented textbooks, the struggle to keep church and state separate has been lost. If the board resists, then the battle line between church and state will have been drawn and the contest will be on to keep the school board independent or put it under church domination and control." Whoever won this battle, Douglas argued, James Madison's view of the separation of church and state under the religious clause of the First Amendment would be irreparably breached.

.   .   .

With so many opinions in production, life in the Douglas chambers was by no means easy. Every staff member was sure to be at the office before Douglas appeared. "Work is energizing!" he would yell at his exhausted office staff as he arrived and marched double-speed by their desks. The trick, Douglas's messenger and chauffeur Harry Datcher recalled, was to try to stay out of the Justice's way until one could assess his mood. "Mornings were the worst," said Datcher. "We never knew whether he had a lot on his mind or whether he was hung over from the night before, and nobody wanted to be the one to find out. Every worker in the building feared him."

Office training was never a strong suit of Douglas's. "Get me the record," he had barked at secretary Fay Aull on her first day on the job, referring to the legal documents that contained the account of the facts of a particular case. But, never having worked for a judge, the phrase meant nothing to her. So, upon noticing an LP for the musical *Oklahoma* lying on a cabinet, she brought that to the Justice. His piercing, silent glare for a full five minutes told her that she had better get some training from the secretaries in the other Justices' offices.

Douglas's secretaries would watch in terror at the end of the day as he flipped through letters to sign them. Whenever he found the smallest typographical error, rather than give them a chance to make a correction, he would scrawl a giant X on the letter and force them to retype it completely.

After a day of hard work with Douglas, everyone would wait until he departed before leaving themselves—sometimes it was at 6:00 and sometimes as late as 8:00 P.M. When Douglas found out about this practice, he began leaving and then returning ten minutes later to see if the work was still under way. If he saw no one, Douglas asked his secretary the next day, "Where was everyone last night? I came back, and no one was in the office."

On days when they did not all scramble for the door after he had departed, the bottle of vodka in the bottom of Fay Aull's desk might be brought out to celebrate the survival of another day in the Justice's service. One time, the Justice walked in a few minutes later to find a party well under way, said nothing, and went into his office. The next morning, he buzzed for his secretaries and told them, "Somebody is stealing my booze." Knowing that no one would dare touch the ample supply of liquor that he kept in his office, this was merely intended to put them on notice that what he saw should not happen again. All it did, though, was convince them all to wait an extra five minutes before beginning the end-of-day festivities.

The worst nights, though, were the ones when Douglas would leave the lights on in his office to make the staff think that he was still working and quietly sneak out. Since no one dared to peek in Douglas's office, that meant they all stayed well into the night before they realized he had fooled them.

"He wasn't the sweetest person you'd ever want to meet," said Harry Datcher in thinking of his nineteen years in the Justice's service. "He didn't give a damn what people thought of him. No, William O. Douglas was only happy when he had everyone—his wives, his clerks, the workers in the building—in his total control."

No one had it tougher, however, than the Justice's law clerks. Whether he had one, two, or three of them in a given year, to the judge it made no difference. He called them and thought of them by the same name: "the law clerk." And generally he was not very fond of them while they were in his service. "Law clerks are the lowest form of human life," Douglas once told his colleague Harry Blackmun. And he treated them that way. "It is common knowledge that clerking for [Douglas] could be like 52 weeks of boot camp," explained former Douglas clerk Richard Jacobson: "It is difficult to convey, unless you went through it, the absolute terror that a Douglas clerk felt at the thought of making a mistake." To which Fay Aull Deusterman added: "Ten thousand dollars a year did not seem enough for what those boys had to put up with. We all thought they, and we for that matter, should get combat pay in addition."

For all of these people, some of the brightest young legal minds in the United States, selection as William O. Douglas's law clerk represented the highest honor of their developing careers, yet for many of them it also became their worst nightmare. When the clerks arrived at their job during the summer, they would discover that their Justice was in Goose Prairie, enjoying the mountains. Their training, undertaken by the previous year's clerk, was typically brief. Keep up with the work. Give up on lunches. Keep the memos short and on point. And try not to be married, but if you are, don't plan on seeing your wife for the year. Then the pile of petitions for *certiorari* and appeal were handed over. The new clerk was expected to write a memo on each petition, summarizing its contents. And each memo had to be written just the way the Justice liked them.

But since they had not even met him by this point, that was not always easy. Just thirty-two days after Scot Powe began work for the Justice, reviewing petitions and sending them off to Goose Prairie, a harsh letter came back. Writing about his unhappiness over the quality of the memos, Douglas said that this was not the sort of job where "we take it off the top of the head" and asked his assistant whether he believed that he was capable of performing his duties adequately. Now being already threatened with dismissal, Powe told his wife that it was going to be "a very, very hard year on her" and went on to give a distinguished year of service.

Once he was back at work in the Court building, Douglas made it his business to establish in his very first face-to-face meeting with the new assistant just who was boss, in a process that his secretaries called "the Terror."

"What kind of clerks have I got this year, Datch?" the Justice would always ask his messenger.

"Oh, you've got a good batch this year," he would say, knowing that his answer meant little to the man whose mind was already made up on the question.

"I hope so. I hope they are better than last year's."

Douglas would then arrive and slip quietly into his inner office without the clerk noticing. Then the Justice would sit in his office and see how long he could wait before summoning his new victims.

Finally, everyone in the office heard it: *Braaaaaccckkk! Brrrrraaaaaccccckkkkkk!* It was the teeth-chattering sound of the buzzer on the clerks' desk, by which Douglas would summon them into his inner chambers. It was the buzzing sound of a bad dentist's drill that would haunt them for years thereafter. One buzz meant he wanted a secretary (and it had better be the right one). Three buzzes meant that he wanted Datcher (who chose either to answer or not depending on the state of his relations with the Judge at the moment). But two buzzes — *two buzzes* — meant that the Judge wanted a clerk. "I once woke up in the middle of the night, just bolt upright, because I heard that buzzer in my dream," recalled Powe.

Speed in answering the buzzer became the most important skill for a Douglas clerk. If a clerk liked to work in shirtsleeves, he would have to develop the dressing skills of a fireman as the suit coat came off the rack and onto the body while the poor fellow was running for the door. "After that first buzz," said Harry Datcher, "it was like a load off their back. Until then, they waited and looked like they . . . were waiting to be electrocuted."

And that was just how Douglas wanted them to feel.

Douglas did not let up after that initial experience. On occasion, just to keep them off balance, he would stop speaking to one of the clerks for no apparent reason. In 1970 and 1971, Scot Powe of the University of Washington and a UCLA grad named Dennis Brown were chosen as clerks. But for some unknown reason Douglas had decided that he wasn't going to deal with Brown. "The buzzer would come, and the door [to his office] would swing [as you entered] and then close automatically," recalled Powe. "Dennis would get up once [a day]. . . . Douglas would look up at some point while Dennis was walking in and say, 'Where's Powe?' Dennis would then wheel on one foot because the goal was to be able to make it back through the door without having to retouch it. . . . As the door would close, Dennis would say to me, 'Shithead wants you.' And so it went for the rest of the year." This treatment was not a negative reflection on Brown. Year after year, Douglas would, for whatever reason, decide to give this total freeze-out treatment to somebody, whether it was one of his clerks, a secretary, a Court page, a librarian, or a Court marshal.

The law clerks' jobs by now were many. Beyond summarizing appeals petitions for the Justice, their duties included searching out answers to the Justice's steady stream of questions on three-by-five-inch Supreme Court notepaper. When Douglas went to the Bench for an oral argument, a procession of messengers would appear in the office bearing notes for the clerks to follow up on. One problem in deciphering the notes was in trying to figure out what Douglas was working on while the attorneys were speaking before him and just why he wanted this information. Since he was rarely giving full attention to the ongoing argument, in his multitask manner he might be writing on another case, working on a speech or new book, or just playing with a new idea. A typical note came to law clerk Charles Miller during one oral-argument session: "Find out the name of the chief of that Indian Tribe in Nebraska. What's the score of the World Series game? What was the year of the Japanese invasion of Manchuria?" One day Miller got an even more enigmatic request: "What was the case we decided a couple of decades ago when the dissent said something about the overbearing arm of government bureaucrats?" In the days before computer-assisted legal research, such a request was virtually impossible to fill, as the clerks did not even have a list of cases in which Douglas had participated as a starting point.

Frequently, clerks were asked to search out material for extended footnotes. Law clerk Thomas Klitgaard remembers being asked in the 1961 term, "If you have time (and not otherwise) would you send me . . . a paragraph for each case in recent years on the procedural requirements for dealing with obscene literature. You might start with Manual Enterprises and work back. I remember Kingsley from New York and the one from Missouri involving a search warrant so broad that the Sheriff could seize anything that was offensive to him (and by Presbyterian standards that could include everything except algebra)." While Douglas prided himself on doing all of his own work, writing all of his own opinions in the early years, in later years clerks were allowed to contribute more to drafting his judgments.

Because of their crushing workload, Douglas's clerks never had time to eat lunch with the other clerks and exchange views about the Court and its work. And should any of the members of his office want to see the historic oral arguments that were occurring, they would have to stand behind "the Douglas Pillar," so named because the Justice could not see members of the audience in this section of the courtroom from his vantage point on the Bench. "Douglas clerks had to do this because their presence in Court during argument always seemed to pose a challenge to him. It meant that the clerk had run out of work and, since that was intolerable, a note with a research project would shortly arrive by one of the messengers," recalled former clerk Charles Ares.

While the clerks worked around the clock seven days a week, Douglas could not live with the thought that they might not always be busy. So, in the beginning of the Court term, he would assign them "the Term Project." This was a book-length research project, such as "the history of Fourteenth Amendment in race relations," on which the clerk had to work and report at the end of the year. To the best of anyone's knowledge, no one ever had the time to finish one of these projects.

In performing one's duties, one was never permitted to go beyond the limits of the role of an assistant. Shortly after William Reppy began his year of service with the Justice, he learned the lesson well. Having amassed a sterling record at Stanford and having spent a very pleasant year clerking for Justice Raymond Peters of the California Supreme Court, he did not fully comprehend what Tom Klitgaard, who was then empowered by Douglas to hire the law clerks, meant when he warned that "there would be nastiness" during the year. At one point, Reppy was working on a loyalty-oath case, *Whitehill v. Elkins*. The Justice had drafted an opinion just one day after receiving the assignment, ruling the oath unconstitutional, and told his clerk to "check it." To Douglas, this meant confirming the accuracy of the account of the facts of the case, checking all of the case citations, and supplementing footnote sources where the support might be weak. But Reppy, based on his earlier clerking experience, decided to go one step further and redrafted a couple of paragraphs that he found to be a bit garbled, even adding a few sentences resolving a point that had been ignored in the draft. All of these ideas were typed up and carefully attached to the draft for the Justice's consideration.

Brrraaaccckkk! Brrraaaccckkk!! went the buzzer, as soon as the Justice saw the result. When he entered the inner sanctum, Reppy got the same speech that nearly all of the clerks recall hearing at least once. Have you been appointed by the president and confirmed by the Senate? Douglas asked. No sir, came the automatic response. Since that is the case, you are not a Supreme Court Justice, Douglas explained sharply; you should not be writing opinions. Having thus divested himself of this judgment on his assistant's "impertinence," Douglas concluded, "I'll just throw this in the trash then." Then, like so many other clerks before him, Reppy was told to get out and never to return. He had been on the job one week.

"Don't worry," said Douglas secretary Nan Burgess upon hearing about the encounter. "We get fired all the time. Just go home now and come back tomorrow." When he returned the next day, responding to the first double *Brraaaaccckkk,* Reppy got another opinion to work on with a cheerful "Keep giving me your ideas." To the clerk's amusement, he noticed that when the next draft of the opinion was circulated, the offending paragraphs had somehow gotten out of the wastebasket and into footnote two of the final text. "You know," explained Fay Aull Deusterman, "that's the way he treated them. He kept them on their toes by doing things like that."

Law clerks all learned in different ways that none of Douglas's rules was ever to be ignored. *Brraaaccckkkk! Brraaaccckkk!!* rang the buzzer one day in 1965, summoning Jerome B. Falk, Jr. "Did you write in this volume?" asked a furious Douglas, his voice quivering with anger as he held up a *United States Reports* volume containing Supreme Court opinions.

"No sir," responded the concerned young clerk.

"I'm relieved to hear that," said the still angry Justice. "Books are treasures. They are temples of the intellect. They must be cherished and protected. I couldn't imagine that you were the sort of person who would write in a book." Having divested himself of this wisdom, Douglas turned, as was his practice, and pitched the book toward the extended window seat behind him, where Harry Datcher would find them for refiling at the end of the day. But after his fiery speech, he was so pumped with adrenaline that he overshot the window seat and fired the book right out the open office window to its demise on the concrete patio below. Falk simply acted as if the incident had never happened as he spun to return to his desk, and book preservation was never spoken of in the office again.

For some clerks, though, learning Douglas's rules of conduct took a bit longer. The only thing more sacred in the office than the books and the booze was the Justice's private shower. While everyone in the office understood that this was *his* shower, the temptation for his clerks to use it when he was not around was just too much to resist. One summer, Douglas's clerk Richard Jacobson and his colleagues began playing basketball on the "highest court in the land," a low-ceilinged basketball court directly above the marble courtroom. When the games were done, all but Douglas's clerks had permission to use their Justice's shower to clean up. Since Douglas was in Goose Prairie and his office was empty, his new clerks—Jacobson, Bill Alsup, and Ken Reed—reasoned that there would be no harm in using his shower if they kept it clean.

After Douglas returned to Washington, they also saw no point in bothering him with whether they had made the right decision. The clerks simply waited to start their games until after he had left the office. The downfall came when Douglas left the office one Friday in November with plans to go to Emory University the next day to deliver a speech. Since the boss was gone, Jacobson decided to rinse out his gym clothes and leave them drying in the shower until the next morning.

At 7:00 A.M., though, his phone woke him out of a sound sleep. It was Jerry Murphy, a part-time driver for the Court, who was calling to say that Douglas had stopped by his office on his way to the airport, discovered the mess, and instructed him to request an FBI investigation into the nature of the assailant who had broken into his office expressly for the purpose of sullying his shower. "My law clerk's not housebroken," Douglas later complained to Harry Datcher. Only a carefully crafted and plaintive note of admission and apology from Jacobson seemed to mollify him.

But while Jacobson had promised "never to let it happen again," after another Saturday-night game, he decided, before cleaning up the latest mess in the shower, to spend a few moments sitting at his desk clad only in a towel, trying on the phone to convince his girlfriend (later his wife) to go out with him that night. As luck would have it, Douglas walked in, in a suit and tie, pretended not to notice the new casual working attire of his clerk, and marched into his office. All Jacobson could do was dress and sweat out the thirty minutes that crawled by while praying that Douglas would have no reason to visit his bathroom. To his relief, when Douglas reemerged, rather than the expected barrage of obscenities and a quick firing, all he offered was a pleasant "good night," and he was gone. Jacobson rushed into the bathroom, hoping that perhaps his transgression had gone unnoticed, only to find that the shower was more spotless now than when he had first used it. Douglas, the clerk realized to his horror, had actually gotten down on his hands and knees and restored *his* bathroom to the way it should look.

After soliciting advice from all quarters, Jacobson devoted the next thirty-six hours to crafting the perfect 150-word argument as to why he should be given yet a third chance at a career in law. That Monday, Jacobson placed the note on Douglas's desk and waited for the *Brraaacccckkk, Brraaacccckkkk* that would signal the end of his tenure as a law clerk.

Hour after hour went by, and nothing happened. Instead, Douglas left at ten o'clock for oral argument without saying a word. A half hour later, a page brought a note in from the Bench. It was Jacobson's apology, carefully annotated in the margins with Douglas's responses to each of his arguments. At the bottom he wrote: "I came down to take a shower as our water heater had broken down at home. What do I find? Dirt and water everywhere. Where the hell do you expect me to go? Rent a hotel room?" Jacobson was not fired, but never again did he use Douglas's office shower. Only later would he learn from Cathy Douglas that their water heater was just fine and had always been so.

Just why Douglas treated these talented young people so harshly was unclear to those around him. Some thought that he was toughening them up by adverse circumstances, just as had happened to him, so that they could succeed in life. "He was an enigma," explained Deusterman. "He was the type of person that felt that you should be working fifty hours a day, you know. I mean he just pushed, pushed, pushed." Others believed that this legal genius was less patient with others in his field who could not meet his standards. "He had a hard time respecting people that were in his own profession that weren't up to his beat," said Yakima buddy Cragg Gilbert, "but you get him off with someone else like a good old sheepherder or a cowherder or a hiker or climber, any person that he couldn't quite be as good as . . . and he had a tremendous respect for these kinds of people." Still others argue that the workaholic Justice just wanted someone who was as efficient at "getting the work done" as he was. Or perhaps this was simply a chance for Douglas to vent his daily frustrations by lording over his office staff in a tyrannical fashion.

Whatever Douglas's motivation, after watching generations of young assistants come and go, messenger Harry Datcher said: "When you left the judge's office as a clerk, you were prepared for anything."

.   .   .

As the years went on, Douglas grew increasingly disenchanted even with his liberal colleagues. After years of complaining that his Brethren had not gone far enough in their opinions, during this period Douglas resorted to a favorite old technique to illustrate that they were not going fast enough in finding issues to decide. Six times in the 1966–1967 term he tried to persuade his colleagues to change the Court's policy agenda by dissenting to denials of writs of *certiorari,* through which the Court refused to hear an appeal.

The cases dealt with a wide range of topics: civil-rights protests, the right to privacy during police searches and seizures, the use of electronic surveillance, property evictions of the poor, and the safeguards of right to counsel and the right to remain silent during IRS proceedings. A typical effort came in *Williams v. Shaffer,* an appeal of Georgia's accelerated eviction process that was not heard because the tenant had already been evicted. Douglas argued that this case was important enough to be heard because it raised "the larger problem regarding the inability of indigent and deprived persons to voice their complaints through the existing institutional framework, and vividly demonstrates the disparity between the access of the affluent to the judicial machinery and that of the poor in violation of the Equal Protection Clause." For him, the issue should be heard because of the constitutional damage caused by the procedure: "The effect is that the indigent tenant is deprived of his shelter, and the life of his family is disrupted— all without a hearing—solely because of his poverty." For Douglas, the man who liked to portray himself as having grown up desperately poor, this was a devastating consequence.

One other failed *certiorari* petition dealt with another major issue Douglas's colleagues were unwilling to handle: the widening war in Vietnam. David Henry Mitchell III was convicted and jailed for refusing to report for military induction after being drafted, arguing that the Vietnam conflict was in violation of a number of treaties that the United States had signed. One of these, the Treaty of London of August 8, 1945, declared that "waging a war of aggression" is a "crime against peace" imposing "individual responsibility" as to whether to participate. With Mitchell arguing that he did not want to be responsible for this war of aggression, the Court was being asked to declare the war illegal. This the Justices did not want to do, ruling that this was a "political question" for elected officials to decide, and therefore beyond their power. Douglas—who never wanted to be bound by such technical rules—issued a dissent. "There is a considerable body of opinion that our actions in Vietnam constitute the waging of an aggressive 'war,'" argued Douglas. There were, he said, "extremely sensitive and delicate questions . . . [which] should, I think, be answered." He concluded that "we have here a recurring question in present-day Selective Service cases." But his colleagues on the Court did not agree. Once more, just as with his environmentalism, Douglas was years ahead of others in questioning whether this was a matter for judicial resolution.

Time after time, litigants tried to bring the issue of the legality of the growing war in Vietnam before the Court, but they found only one Justice willing to listen. In the years to come, well over a dozen times Douglas single-handedly tried to either stop the war or keep people from being forced to serve against their will.

Douglas's use of dissents to denials of *certiorari* to influence the direction of future policy continued during the Warren Court years at a rate of about seven per term. Beyond that, in the remainder of his tenure on the Court Douglas dissented to denials of *certiorari* 104 times, an average of more than twenty per term.

As time wore on, the war claimed many casualties. The most prominent political casualty was the president himself. In March 1968, in response to growing protests and a credible challenge by Senator Eugene McCarthy for the Democratic party's nomination, LBJ announced that he would not be a candidate for reelection. This tumultuous year included the horrors of a war going badly, race riots in major cities, and the assassinations of both Martin Luther King, Jr., and Robert F. Kennedy. In the midst of this political upheaval, Chief Justice Earl Warren announced his retirement, pending the appointment and Senate confirmation of his successor.

Three times that year, the Court did choose to rule on the operations of the Selective Service system, thus giving Douglas a chance to place his views on this issue next to those of the Brethren. In the first of these cases, announced in May 1968, David Paul O'Brien was convicted in a Massachusetts federal court for burning his draft card as a protest against the war. Such an action violated the 1965 amendment to the Universal Military Training and Service Act of 1948. The question for the Court became whether burning a draft card was "symbolic speech" deserving of constitutional protection under the First Amendment or whether it was "conduct" that was punishable by law. In this case, the Court upheld the conviction by accepting the government's argument that the purpose of the law was to bureaucratically organize the draft for prosecuting a war, a function that was well within federal powers. Here the Court found that the regulation furthered "an important or substantial governmental interest" that was "unrelated to the suppression of free expression" and whose "restriction on alleged First Amendment freedoms is no greater than is essential to the furtherance of that interest." Thus, O'Brien was subject to punishment under federal law.

William O. Douglas emphatically disagreed. In dissent, he took the debate much further by challenging the foundational premise of this argument: whether Congress had at this time the "broad and sweeping" power to conscript men to fight. "The underlying and basic problem in this case, however, is whether conscription is permissible in the absence of a declaration of war," he argued, adding that "this Court has never ruled on the question. It is time that we made a ruling." But with legions of American soldiers now engaged in this conflict, his colleagues did not agree.

Douglas linked this case with two other dissents issued that day for denials of appeals on the operations of the Selective Service system. Albert H. Holmes and Marvin Vondon Hart, Jr., were both Jehovah's Witness ministers seeking draft exemptions as conscientious objectors because of their religious opposition to war of any kind. Holmes's argument, after being convicted for "willful failure to report" for duty, was that "in the absence of a declaration of war . . . a draft is not authorized and is equivalent to involuntary servitude." The *Hart v. United States* case was more focused, in that the petitioner had been denied a ministerial exemption, thus raising freedom-of-religion issues as well when he was commanded to perform alternate service in a hospital and refused.

Focusing on the lack of a formal declaration of war by Congress, Douglas's dissents offered an extended examination of the relevant precedents and statutes to conclude that "there may not be" such power to create a peacetime draft. In the *Holmes v. United States* dissent he stated that "while some decisions suggest that war powers may be exercised in an 'emergency' prior to declaration of war . . . there are other decisions directly linking the power of conscription to Congress' power under Art[icle]. I, 8, cl[ause]. 11 to 'declare war.'" In the end, while Douglas claimed to be "express[ing] no opinion on the merits," his view was plain: "There is a weighty view that what has transpired respecting Vietnam is unconstitutional, absent a declaration of war; . . . that the making of appropriations was not an adequate substitute; and that 'executive war-making is illegal.' " In calling for an examination of the entire conscription system, Douglas concluded: "I think we owe to those who are being marched off to jail for maintaining that a declaration of war is essential for conscription an answer to this important undecided constitutional question." While his colleagues were unpersuaded, Douglas's one-man battle against the Vietnam War was not over.

Douglas's distrust of the Johnson administration was such now that he came to believe that someone, presumably sent by Johnson, had broken into his office and stolen from his desk drawer a critical autobiographical chapter that he was writing on his relationship with the various presidents, including LBJ. Just how the White House knew of this work was no mystery to the increasingly paranoid Douglas: "No one outside the office staff presumably knew that there was such a chapter. In those days when wires were continuously tapped and public institutions such as the Court were under electronic surveillance, word of the existence of a chapter such as this one could spread quickly."

When more and more anti-Vietnam cases flooded the Court's docket, Douglas decided to voice his views more forcefully. He began granting appellants interim stays against deployment to the war zone and referring the cases to the full Court. As soon as these appeals were summarily denied, Douglas then objected vigorously in dissent.

When the Court chose to review the appeal of James J. Oestereich, who challenged the right of the Selective Service in Cheyenne, Wyoming, to revoke his divinity-student exemption after he sent his draft card back to the government as a protest against the war, Douglas was given the chance to produce the majority opinion. Writing for five members of the Court, Douglas ruled that under the First Amendment free-speech clause the draft board could not punish registrants for their political views in this manner unless it was demonstrably related to the merits of granting or continuing that type of exemption. To allow this practice would, in his words, "make the Boards freewheeling agencies meting out their brand of justice in a vindictive manner."

But there was a limit to what Douglas could do from the Bench. In December 1968, when 386 National Guardsmen who were about to be shipped to Vietnam from the State of Washington appealed to him personally as the supervisory Justice for the Ninth Circuit for stays of the departure, he could not help them. Douglas had no doubt of the merits of this claim: "There should not be the slightest doubt but that whenever the Chief Executive of the country takes any citizen by the neck and either puts him in prison or subjects him to some ordeal or sends him overseas to fight in a war, the question is a justiciable one." But the nature of his role did not permit him to make this call now: "I feel precluded from granting a stay on this ground, because, while the Court has not decided the issue, it has refused to pass on it." And for him there had not been "a change in the personnel in the Court indicat[ing] that a different view of the basic constitutional questions might be taken."

Not even when a suit to avoid being sent to war was filed against Clark Clifford, now the secretary of defense, would Douglas duck the case. After the Court denied the petition of Thomas W. McArthur in December 1968, rather than recusing himself Douglas filed another dissent. Here, Douglas increased the level of his rhetoric against the undeclared war: "The spectre of executive war-making is an ominous threat to our republican institutions. What can be done in Vietnam can be done in many areas of this troubled world without debate or responsible public decision." Reminiscent of his language in the Communist-investigation cases of the 1950s, Douglas was comparing the by now deposed Johnson administration to the dictatorships it was trying to overthrow. While Douglas had not been able to keep a single man from going to Vietnam, he won fans across the country for his courageous solo dissents against the war.

SADDLE YOUR HORSES

Just because you're paranoid doesn't mean they aren't out to get you.

—Anonymous

As he contemplated his upcoming seventieth birthday, Douglas became convinced in the early summer of 1968 that the end was drawing near. In the middle of the night he would wake up with his heart racing at two to three times its normal speed. This condition would continue for several hours, with his heart even occasionally skipping a beat as it slowed to its normal pace. Fearing that he would die in his sleep, Douglas developed a severe case of insomnia. Then, while sitting on the Bench listening to oral argument on June 3, he slumped over completely unconscious and had to be carried back to his chambers, where he was revived, only to collapse again.

Once they got him to Walter Reed Army Hospital, the doctors discovered that Douglas had a lower than average heartbeat of sixty-two beats per minute, which slowed in his first two hours of sleep to a dangerously low thirty-eight to forty beats. When this happened, his system would involuntarily "sound a panic button," causing his heart to slip into ventricular fibrillation—a wild, uncontrollable heartbeat that, unlike his earlier bout of atrial fibrillation, can lead to a fatal heart attack. The doctors diagnosed him as suffering from a heart arrhythmia called the Lown-Ganong-Levine syndrome.

Since this latest attack indicated that his drug regimen was not sufficient, the doctors decided to resort to the new pacemaker technology to correct the problem. That same day, they installed in his abdomen a cigarette-pack-sized, battery-driven device that would regulate his heartbeat if it dropped below sixty beats per minute.

Not even surgery could keep the man who loved to play practical jokes from doing so. One night in the hospital, Douglas had to be un-hooked from the electronic heart-monitoring machinery so he could go to the bathroom, but the nurse forgot to reattach the device when he returned to bed. So, after waiting forty-five minutes, Douglas snuck out behind the nurses at the monitoring station and asked quietly, "How's the old judge?" Whereupon, he watched with merriment as the nurses went into a panic seeing the flat line on his monitor, thinking that the Supreme Court Justice in their care had died without them even realizing it.

Still, the operation had a dramatic impact on his outlook. "I do think Dad became more of a hypochondriac after he had the pace-maker," recalled his daughter, Millie Douglas Read. "I think he had a fear of death." His office staff also noticed the difference in his atti-tude. "He had a black loose-leaf book, about the thickness of the city phone book, of doctors and specialists on every possible part of his body," said Harry Datcher. "Every time he had any kind of a pain, and he was having pains all the time, he would come in and say we had to take a ride." Datcher would ask the Justice what was bothering him, flip to the appropriate page in the book for that part of the body, and drive him to that specialist immediately.

Douglas had justifiable reasons for some of his medical concerns when his recovery from surgery developed complications. Despite the heartbeat-regulating device, his more benign atrial fibrillation contin-ued to such an extent that the doctors prescribed another series of drugs, including three times his previous dosage of digitalis, even though Douglas felt that he had already been taking a toxic amount. The use of a catheter while hospitalized aggravated his prostate gland to the point that it had to be removed. In time, Douglas became so ir-ritated by his slow recovery that he checked himself out of the hospi-tal and returned to Goose Prairie.

By the middle of July, with the doctors still debating the proper dosage of digitalis, Douglas became convinced that he was being poi-soned by the drug. He was unable to do more than sit up in bed and was so nauseated that he was unable to eat. When he could finally get out of bed, the man who once tramped over mountains now found that he was too weak to walk more than a few hundred feet. Because of acute diarrhea, he was now unable even to take the two-hour car ride down from the mountain to get treatment, so an Air Force heli-copter pilot who needed more flight time was persuaded to bring the doctors to him. The Army Corps of Engineers also rigged a makeshift field-phone line to Douglas's mountain retreat—the first and only time that it would have such service.

Douglas began pleading with his doctors to adjust his digitalis therapy. But this did not get Douglas much satisfaction, as the doctors reminded him that it was his insistence on leaving their hospital that had made the regulation of his drug therapy so difficult.

In time, the doctors were able to stabilize his health, but Douglas's world continued to fall apart. He watched in sadness as his longtime protégé, Abe Fortas, came under political attack in the summer and fall of 1968 as he was denied confirmation to replace Earl Warren as Chief Justice, leading Warren to announce that he would remain for one more term. This attack deeply affected the normally fiercely independent and implacable Douglas, who thought that he would be next on the conservatives' hit list. Richard Nixon was running for president of the United States on a platform that included a "Law 'n' Order" component that promised the selection of strict constructionists for the Supreme Court who would overturn the decisions of the liberal Warren Court, which made Douglas even more leery of being attacked.

Douglas could not control his health or the choice of his colleagues, so he sought to control those who worked for him. Peter Kay Westen, a prize law-school graduate of the University of California at Berkeley, had survived the rigorous screening process to become Douglas's law clerk for the 1968–1969 term. Trained by the previous clerk, William Reppy, Westen had been on the job for only a few weeks during the summer, sorting and summarizing *certiorari* petitions that were to be sent to Douglas in Goose Prairie for him to decide on. One day, Westen got a message from the secretary at the close of business that he should wait to receive a call from Justice Douglas. Since this would be his first official meeting with his new boss, he was quite understandably nervous. Everyone left the building, and Westen waited for the call. Hour after hour passed, and the phone remained silent. When no call had come by 9:00 P.M., Westen didn't know whether he should leave or not.

Finally at 9:30, the phone rang, and Westen picked it up in the middle of the first ring. "This is Peter Kay Westen in Justice Douglas's chambers," he answered.

"Where's my goddamned pouch!" barked the voice at the other end of the line. Westen was too stunned to do anything but mumble something while he tried to figure out who was on the phone. "Where's my goddamned pouch!" the voice yelled again.

Finally, Westen realized that it was Douglas calling from Goose Prairie, and he was referring to the pouch filled with the *certiorari* petitions for review the following week. "Mr. Justice Douglas," the young man said quietly, "this is Peter Kay Westen, your new—"

"I don't give a damn who you are, where's my goddamned pouch!"

Westen explained the reasons for the holdup, careful to point out that it was not his fault. "Well, don't let it happen again," yelled the voice. And the phone went dead.

Even those outside of the Court were now being subjected to Douglas's desire for control. One day, after he had returned to Washington, he had Harry Datcher drive him to a local automotive dealer, where he bought a new car from a man who agreed to take what Douglas described as his 1963 automobile in trade. But when the Justice showed up to take delivery, the salesman explained that the price would be a bit higher because he could see that Douglas's car was in fact a 1962 model and worth much less in trade. "A contract is a contract, and that is the law. There is nothing you can do about it," shouted Douglas. Coming from a Supreme Court Justice who interpreted the law, it sounded pretty convincing to the salesman, but still he had a living to make.

"I've got five children," he pleaded, "and we make little enough as it is."

"Well, who's at fault for that?" retorted the man who had almost as many wives as the salesman had children.

"I just don't think it is right," said the salesman, "and I can't back down just because you are in the Supreme Court and an important person and I'm not."

"Fine," said Douglas, "we'll take this to court. It'll be *you* a car salesman and *me* a Supreme Court Justice. Who do you think they'll believe?"

"If you want a lawsuit, that's what I'll have to do. Who is your lawyer?" said the salesman.

"Clark Clifford."

"Oh shit. Forget it," said the defeated man as he agreed to make the deal. (When Clifford heard about this incident, the classy lawyer quietly sought out the salesman, explained that the Justice was under a lot of pressure, and reached into his own pocket to pay the difference in the car's cost.)

"What is interesting about this incident," recalled former Hugo Black law clerk Walter Dellinger, "is the way Douglas himself was telling the story around the Court building. The message was very clear to all of us that he felt he could do anything he pleased. 'I can put this over on anyone. I have unlimited power.' "

But when he turned to what he could decide on the Court, Douglas now reluctantly had to admit that there were limits to what he could do from the Bench. Black Panther Eldridge Cleaver appealed to

Douglas when the California Adult Authority revoked his parole without a hearing because he had been in a house where a weapon was present. Since both the California Supreme Court and the U.S. Supreme Court had denied his appeal, Cleaver's lawyers turned to Douglas for relief as the supervisory justice of the Ninth Circuit. Douglas asked Peter Kay Westen for a memo on the issue. The young assistant first studied all of Douglas's earlier due-process opinions. Since there was no Supreme Court precedent to support granting the appeal, Westen bolstered his argument by pointing out that Cleaver's celebrity status, connections, and access to money would induce him not to flee.

Braaackkk!! Braaackkk!! clacked the buzzer on Westen's desk, commanding him to enter the Justice's chambers. "Where did you go to law school, in the gutter?" yelled the Justice. "Even if I voted this way, I would be the only one on the Court who would vote this way. As long as Earl Warren is Chief Justice this Court will never do anything with the California Adult Authority, which deals with paroles. Earl Warren has been an attorney general under the California system, and he regards it as a great liberal advance. The last thing I need is to go out on a limb once more. I'm going to be overturned by the Court anyway. I don't have time to grant this, give it to Thurgood [Marshall]."

So Cleaver's appeal was denied. But the young law clerk realized what was really going on. He could tick off from memory all of the times from the *Rosenberg* case on down when the courageous Douglas had been willing to act on his own. By writing the memo this way, showing precisely where Douglas *wanted* to go and how he had voted in the past, Westen had made it hard to say no to the appeal. But to avoid opening himself up to attack by the new Nixon administration, he was passing the buck to Marshall.

With all of the pressures now working on him, Douglas began treating his staff worse than ever. After rebuking Westen, he said, "By the way, I've got to leave for a speech, and on Monday there will be a woman from the Labor Department in here. She will be my new law clerk, and I'd like you to prepare for her to take over." Though informed by the secretaries that every law clerk had been fired and re-hired at least once in their term, Westen reminded them that it was Friday, and on Sunday he was being married, with a reception in the Supreme Court building, to which Douglas had been invited. Hold the reception anyway, said Fay Aull Deusterman, and see if the Justice shows up. Douglas is eccentric and loves to bully his clerks, but, she added, I have never seen anything quite like this.

So Westen held the reception, expecting to have Douglas come and announce that the young law clerk had been fired. When Douglas appeared at the door with Cathy, Westen held his breath. But the Justice simply came up, all smiles, wished the couple much happiness, and the incident was never spoken of again.

The secretaries were not immune from such treatment. Nan Burgess made the mistake one day of asking Douglas if he wanted to see a female visitor; after he said no, she showed the woman in anyway. The woman happened to be a nun, and Douglas was now stuck with her for several minutes. The Justice was normally so shy with new people that he could not look them straight in the eye, but for some reason that no one understood he was especially nervous around nuns. After the woman left, a furious Douglas buzzed for Burgess, who had served him for nearly twenty years, screamed at her for making the appointment, and then refused to speak to her again. "Tell Burgess to do this," he would say to his other secretary. Or sometimes he would tell Fay Aull Deusterman simply, "Tell the other one what she has to do." The two-month silence nearly drove the sensitive Burgess crazy. "Douglas wasn't a great man," said one staff member who observed this period. "He may have been a great public servant, but he wasn't a great man."

.   .   .

Life for Douglas was no better at home. By the first part of 1969 his fourth marriage was on the edge of collapse. Douglas wrote Clark Clifford with great sadness that his wife was leaving him "for good" on January 10. "Should I retire right soon?" the Justice asked his friend. By now it was apparent that the difference in ages between him and his wife had its effect. "Cathy . . . had all the qualifications that Bill wanted, you know," said Cragg Gilbert. "He wanted somebody that had lots of life to keep up with him both mentally as well as physically at that moment. And Cathy could run circles around Bill physically. And at that point Bill began to disintegrate a little bit physically." For the moment, though, Clifford heard nothing further and put it out of his mind.

Then Douglas was reminded of his own mortality when his first wife, Mildred, succumbed to cancer on February 20, 1969. However, he did not learn about it until days later because by this time his two children were so angry with him, because of his cold treatment of them and their mother, that they had not bothered to tell him about either her illness or her death. "Neither my brother nor I felt the slightest inclination to tell him that Mother had died," explained Millie Douglas Read. "She had been ill for quite a long time. And I guess somebody else rang him and told him what had happened, and he was quite upset that we hadn't notified him." But now that Douglas was released from the oppressive financial terms of his first divorce agreement, the extra thirty thousand dollars or so per year meant that he had a chance to become financially secure.

Spurred by his sense of mortality, Douglas asked his literary assistant Dagmar Hamilton to visit him in the spring of 1969. When she arrived, he asked her to take a walk with him around the block, explaining that he wanted to avoid being overheard by the electronic bugging devices that he still believed were placed in his office by the Nixon administration. Once out on the street, Douglas explained that he had just completed a draft of his autobiography and wanted to publish it while he was still alive. The memoirs project, which had preoccupied his last several years, consisted now of a large, disorganized, stack of manuscript papers, loosely grouped into three large chunks, not even divided into chapters. Decisions had to be made about how much should be published while he was still on the Court, or, for that matter, how much should be published at all. Would she be willing to help? he asked. When Hamilton expressed an interest, Douglas explained that he was going to put it in a warehouse with her name on it and wanted to draw up some papers making her the literary executor of the material. *Why a warehouse?* Hamilton asked. *That doesn't seem too safe.* They have already broken into my office, explained the Justice, and gotten into my desk drawer, and stolen my chapter on the presidency.

Though she was quite shaken by the conversation, Hamilton agreed to help him with the work. Pulling out a fully executed document allowing her to take possession of the work, Douglas quickly finalized the arrangement. Douglas gave her copies of the entire manuscript, and she began the overwhelming task of cutting and pasting the pile of pages into what in time they envisioned to be three books: the pre-Court years, many of the early pages of which were just a rewritten version of his first memoir, *Of Men and Mountains;* the Supreme Court years; and a foreign-policy book on "adventures in friendship."

The autobiographical work stalled when Hamilton realized that for some inexplicable reason Douglas had written absolutely nothing about his years on the SEC, surely one of his most important contributions to American politics and business. That would be left for her to research in the files stored in the sea of cabinets in room 210 of the Court building.

·   ·   ·

Seventeen Justices had come and the same number had left since the young man of forty had ascended to the Supreme Court, but it was the departure that came that spring that hurt the most. After being dragged through the mud in 1968, Abe Fortas now found himself fighting for his professional life. In May 1969, Fortas was again under attack by the Nixon Justice Department and the press because of financial entanglements with a foundation funded by financier Louis Wolfson, who was later indicted for violating the Securities and Exchange Act. Douglas suspected that Nixon was trying to force liberals off the Court in order to appoint conservatives in their place. Given his own similar relationship with the Parvin Foundation, there was no question in his mind who was next on the agenda. So, he and his son, who were by then on better terms, went to see Fortas as the latter debated whether to resign from the Court. At one point in the two nights of discussion, Bill Douglas, Jr., pleaded: "Blood will taste good to this gang. And having tasted it, they will want more." Nevertheless, Fortas decided to resign. Douglas wrote his sister that he and Bill Brennan would likely be under attack soon. "Impeachment proceedings are likely," he wrote his good friend Fred Rodell. He just didn't know when and how. What he did know by June 1969 was that rather than Earl Warren, a conservative Court of Appeals judge from Minnesota, Warren Earl Burger, was Chief Justice. And Abe Fortas's replacement was yet to be chosen.

And soon there were further signs that things were still not right in the Douglas household. On July 15, Douglas's wedding anniversary with Cathy, he wrote to Clark Clifford that his wife had "announced" that she was leaving him the following month and would be attending law school at American University in Washington. The Justice professed not to understand why she was taking this course. However, Douglas added, "Now I figure I *must* retire." To Clifford, it was now clear that his friend felt he had lost control of his own life. The man who three times had dropped spouses now lived in fear that the same would be done to him by his twenty-six-year-old wife.

If Douglas did not know why his marriage was on the rocks, it was because he had a selective memory. It was well-known among Court personnel that he loved to speak to the beautiful young wives of his law clerks and enjoyed eyeing them in their fashionable miniskirts. Once, a clerk for another Justice watched in amazement as Douglas returned from the airport after putting his wife on a plane, only to proposition the wife of another clerk. To the Court staff, it seemed that he had begun to act like a stunted adolescent out of fear of his advancing age.

The simple truth was that his behavior was now totally out of control. One day, Douglas had boarded a plane on the way to a speech when an attractive blond stewardess approached him. Upon seeing the white-haired old passenger in the rumpled suit and mismatched tie, she thought that he had used his life savings to take his first plane trip. "Where are you going?" she asked sweetly.

Douglas smiled at the woman and responded with a crooked grin, "Don't you know who I am?"

"No," she answered.

"I'm Justice William O. Douglas," he said as he handed her his card. "Why don't you come and see me in my office in the Supreme Court of the United States?"

Sure enough, on her next flight to Washington, the young stewardess called Douglas for an appointment. Harry Datcher was immediately dispatched to pick her up and bring her to the Justice's office.

Just a short time after she had entered Douglas's chambers, though, members of the staff began hearing strange sounds from inside—shouts, banging furniture, and running feet. A short time later, the office door flew open and out rushed the young woman, her face all flushed and her clothing badly disheveled, shouting at the startled office staff how outraged and disgusted she was. Douglas, she said, had chased her around his desk, grabbing at her clothes and demanding that they go to a motel immediately for a sexual liaison.

Douglas seemed to be oversexed, and others inside the Washington Beltway became aware of it. One story making the rounds came as a result of a dinner that the Justice had been invited to by television journalist Martin Agronsky, in order to discuss the possibility of doing an hourlong interview on national television. When Douglas arrived at the fancy French restaurant, he passed up the chance to sit next to the journalist and instead insisted on sitting next to Agronsky's pretty, young female assistant. While Agronsky blithely began describing over an elaborate dinner what he had in mind for the show, he seemed not to notice as his assistant began to look more and more uncomfortable. Finally, the young woman excused herself, went across the room, and began motioning to her boss to join her. When Agronsky did, she forcefully explained to him that she was leaving because the Justice had been repeatedly attempting to fondle her underneath the table. With that, the negotiations for the interview were concluded.

Subsequently, when Agronsky did an hourlong interview with Justice Black, it drove Douglas nearly crazy with jealousy. "Hugo can't keep up with the work because he's spending so much time with his Hollywood makeup on!" Douglas complained to his staff. They knew it was linked to the opportunity he had lost.

Despite the marital problems, the Douglases remained together.

Ten days after his startling letter to Clark Clifford, Douglas wrote again to say that Cathy had "changed her mind" and decided that she was not leaving him after all. This decision did not surprise those closest to the Justice. "[Cathy] was determined that she would hold on to the end and become the widow of William O. Douglas," said Harry Datcher. "And as for the judge, if he had lost another wife, all he would have had left was his seat on the Bench."

Convinced that the only way to survive her marriage with the Justice was to go out and lead her own life, Cathy did enroll in law school at American University. It was a decision that changed the nature of their relationship. "[Cathy just kept] hanging in there to continue to go through her life without depending on him. And paradoxically, the more she was determined to graduate from American University, the more attractive she became to him," explained Dagmar Hamilton. "[And the more] she stood up to him, the more he respected her. In that sense, she also was becoming what . . . he made her, in a Pygmalion kind of situation."

Still, determined to show his own kind of independence, as soon as Cathy left Goose Prairie to begin her studies early in the fall of 1969, Douglas invited his old girlfriend Elena Leonardo to come live with him. "Cathy says she doesn't want me, but she won't give me my freedom," he told her at the time.

.   .   .

As Douglas's life continued to spin out of control, President Richard Nixon looked to take advantage. "From the beginning Nixon was interested in getting rid of William O. Douglas; Douglas was the liberal ideologue who personified everything that was wrong with the Warren Court," said Nixon assistant John Ehrlichman. A presidential request to J. Edgar Hoover of the FBI resulted in the collection of more damaging information on Douglas. While the file consisted mainly of unsupported hearsay and negative news clippings, Attorney General John Mitchell instructed his assistant in charge of the Criminal Division, Will Wilson, to expand the file by gathering additional material on Douglas and the Parvin Foundation.

The Nixon administration's attack on Douglas was formulated in mid-August 1969, when the nomination of U.S. Court of Appeals Judge Clement Haynsworth to fill the Supreme Court seat vacated by Abe Fortas ran into trouble. Haynsworth faced questions from the Democrat-controlled Senate about his stock interests in two companies linked to cases in which he had ruled. Nixon was told in early October that some members of his own party were deserting the candidate, and with a final vote still weeks away a majority was not secure in the Senate.

With that news, Nixon began thinking seriously about preemptive revenge. Perhaps the icon of these attacking liberals, William Orville Douglas, could be forced from the Bench just like his protégé Fortas, thus speeding up the process of changing the direction of the entire Court. The president called John Ehrlichman into the Oval Office and said, "Very well, talk to Jerry Ford now." He wanted the congressional minority leader to "move to impeach" William O. Douglas, without making clear the grounds for such an attack. The president added that Ford should take this action "the next day after [the] vote" on Haynsworth, thus leaving no doubt as to the reason for the effort.

A few hours later, Ehrlichman reached Ford, but he found the congressman "to be vague and unfocused much of the time" and got no real assurance that the campaign would be launched. Seeking to light a fire under Ford, the president's assistant began making statements about Douglas's imminent impeachment at various off-the-record gatherings of reporters.

Such prime political gossip began appearing almost immediately in the press. A story in the Washington *Star* exhumed Albert Parvin's Las Vegas connections, implying that Douglas was connected to casino interests. Douglas considered legal action. Friends in the press soon began calling Douglas to warn him that Gerald Ford was planning to draft a bill of impeachment against him. While publicly the Justice could do little more than issue "no comment" responses to such tales, privately he sent word to his lawyer, Clark Clifford, that it was time for them to talk "over a pint of vodka."

Later that month, Douglas learned from another journalist that White House aide Clark Mollenhoff had planted a story that in 1963 Douglas had been in Santo Domingo, Dominican Republic, trying to negotiate with President Juan Bosch to secure a casino for the Mafia. In truth, Douglas had been in the Dominican Republic to set up the televising of an adult-literacy program funded by the Parvin Foundation. With the White House pressing to have the story published even in the face of contradictory evidence, Douglas asked Clifford, "Isn't it time I sued someone?"

Once the groundwork of these critical news articles had been laid, Ford began calling for Douglas's impeachment. The first casualty, though, was not Douglas but Haynsworth, whose nomination went down to defeat in the Senate on November 21. Two months later, when G. Harrold Carswell, another conservative nominee from the

Court of Appeals, immediately ran into confirmation trouble, the rumors about Douglas were renewed.

By early 1970, Douglas had endured enough. Depressed by the unrelenting personal attacks, he began indicating to friends that he was
planning to retire after the current term ended. This was no idle chat-
ter, as he began to hint at the same thing to his colleagues on the
Bench. Shortly thereafter, the Justice called his two secretaries, Fay
Aull Deusterman and Nan Burgess, into the office and said, "I'm thinking of resigning at the end of the term. I'm allowed to keep one secretary, and I'm going to go out to Goose Prairie. I'm going to live out
there. Are either one of you interested in being my secretary and coming out west to live?" The two of them looked at each other, both realizing that he was still not speaking to Burgess, and quickly passed on
the "opportunity."

But by April of that year, it became clear that something had
changed dramatically. After months of silence from Douglas, Nan
Burgess showed up to work one day and got a cheerful "Hi, Nan," from
him. "What happened?" she asked the others in the office. "Why is he
all of a sudden talking to me now?" When Fay Aull Deusterman mentioned that a rumor was floating around that Ford was finally ready to
bring impeachment charges, Burgess said softly, "He knows I am the
one person who could blow the whistle on him." Douglas, it seemed,
had decided to fight. To his friend Charlie Horowitz he wrote that "on
February 6 . . . I was planning to retire this Summer. But now, I understand, there will be impeachment proceedings started against me. So I
do not plan to retire."

Ironically enough, Nixon's effort to have Douglas removed convinced him otherwise. "No way, I'm not resigning," he told his staff
now. "That would look too much like a confession of guilt, and I'm not
guilty of anything. I'm just staying on the Bench."

To those who knew him well, Douglas's reaction was no surprise.
"Fortas thought he could control things with the turn of a legal
phrase, but he was not used to attacks, not used to being out in the
open, and got out of there in a hurry when they came," explained Peter
Kay Westen. "But Douglas was different. When the going got tough, he
was willing to fight."

Attorney General John Mitchell got the word when he phoned
Douglas in mid-April 1970 to tell him formally of the charges. Mitchell
likely expected that Douglas would simply fold his cards, retire to save
his full pension, and take up residence in Goose Prairie. But like
Richard Whitney and his Wall Street buddies three decades before,

Mitchell had a lot to learn about playing political poker with the man from Yakima. "Well, Mr. Attorney General," Douglas responded, "saddle your horses."

So saddle their horses the Nixon administration did. But now they were galloping after a man who not only knew how to ride but had already survived having a horse roll over on him on the side of a mountain.

After his call to Douglas, Mitchell directed Will Wilson to hand his entire "attack" file on the Justice over to Gerald Ford. By this time, Wilson thought that they had solid grounds for an impeachment investigation, having by now collected from the FBI a file that was several inches thick. Contained therein was all manner of unconfirmed evidence about Douglas, involving allegations of attendance at conspiratorial liberal meetings, marathon drinking sessions, and some unusual goings-on in the Pacific Northwest. But it was the financial connection with the Parvin Foundation that seemed to hold the most promise for investigation. "He was the supervising Supreme Court judge for Las Vegas [in the Ninth Circuit]," explained Will Wilson years later,

> and we felt that he was handling the writs for gambling interests in Las Vegas in a way which helped those interests. We thought that was an impeachable offense because the writs are the key instrument used to supervise the lower courts and to make decisions about the ongoing nature of trials for defendants. . . . It would be a thousand-to-one chance even to get to a member of the Supreme Court to have them consider your writ. But with William O. Douglas, they were consistently getting to him to get the writs issued or at least to get the writs considered. They knew they had access to a voice.

While the department conceded that Douglas probably would have voted for the defendants in any event, Wilson believed that doing so while still on the payroll of Albert Parvin gave an "appearance of impropriety" that "had the elements of an impeachable offense." "I recall how incensed I was that Douglas was doing this," said Wilson. "It was almost like Parvin had [a] judicial player on his team."

More than this, when the Justice Department discovered that Douglas was in a position to help dole out money from the Parvin Foundation to Robert Maynard Hutchins's Center for the Study of Democratic Institutions, where he was also an officer, another "appearance of impropriety" was suspected. In addition, Wilson argued, "there was a connection that we could investigate between Albert

Parvin and the Bally Corporation, which was involved in the making of slot machines. . . . [And] with a more direct investigation, we might be able to show a direct connection between the man who is supporting Douglas and the mob's slot machines."

Finally, the Justice Department had uncovered allegations that Douglas had been in the Dominican Republic during the February 1963 inauguration of President Juan Bosch. If he had played an active role in foreign-policy making, offering the private blessings of a prominent member of the U.S. government, he would be in violation of the Logan Act. Recalled Wilson, "The appearance was very bad, and the impropriety was quite clearly demonstrable. . . . I thought at the time we had enough material that, if properly developed, Douglas might be convinced to resign, or in the absence of that he might be impeached."

But the problem for the Justice Department was that they only had a series of charges without sufficient evidence even for a successful indictment. And they knew it. "It was very raw material," explained Wilson, "and it needed a lot of fleshing out and a lot more investigation. At the Justice Department, we thought that Ford was going to make an investigation—have hearings and so forth."

That, however, was not Ford's plan. As soon as he got all of this material, his staff fashioned it into an extended speech calling for the impeachment of Justice William O. Douglas. And, on April 15, the congressman went to the floor of the House to deliver it. Ford began by arguing that "an impeachable offense is whatever a majority of the House of Representatives considers it to be at a given moment in history." Then he launched into a recitation of the charges that might convince a majority of his colleagues to remove Douglas from his position. The Justice had written an article on folksinging for the somewhat pornographic magazine *Avant Garde* and accepted payment from its editor, Ralph Ginzburg, whose libel case was then pending before the Supreme Court, which had once ruled on pornography charges against him. Wasn't that a conflict of interest? Ford asked.

Douglas had just published a short book called *Points of Rebellion,* which was nothing more than a call to arms for the young people of America to revolt against the repressive Establishment, which he likened to Great Britain's King George III. The Justice wrote, "Where grievances pile high and most of the elected spokesmen represent the Establishment, violence may be the only effective response." Did this not prove that Douglas was "one in spirit" with "the militant hippie-yippie movement" while also exhibiting the "first signs of senility"? Ford suggested. When a portion of this book was serialized in an erotic publication called *Evergreen,* which interspersed articles with explicit pictures of sexual acts, and when Douglas wrote other articles for *Play-boy,* Ford had yet another charge.

Then Ford reasserted the now-familiar charges that Douglas's connection with Albert Parvin had compromised his ability to decide cases on the Supreme Court. New evidence, he said, came from a hotel-registration card for the Flamingo Hotel in Las Vegas dated October 22, 1962, which stated that Bobby Baker, an aide to then Senate Majority Leader Lyndon B. Johnson "is with Douglas," implying that they were meeting at the time. If so, Ford argued, Baker's and the Parvin Foundation's subsequent work in the Dominican Republic, linked with Douglas's appearance there, might well prove that the Justice had been illegally helping to draft the country's new constitution in a way that would improve the business opportunities for Las Vegas gambling interests.

On top of this, Ford added, Douglas had continued his association with the "leftist" Center for the Study of Democratic Institutions, which itself was the recipient of money from the Parvin Foundation and helped to convene "militant student leaders." Did Douglas's statements in his latest book constitute the triggering mechanism for future disruptions in this country? asked Ford.

All in all, Ford argued, rather than representing "decent Americans" on the Supreme Court, Douglas protected the gambling, pornographic, and New Left interests. For this, he concluded, Douglas should be impeached for "judicial misbehaviour." When he was finished, all but about ten of the members then on the floor, mostly Republicans, stood and applauded vigorously.

But while they clapped, the Republicans did not realize that they were already in the process of losing the first and most important skirmish in the war. Just as Ford was concluding his speech, a liberal Democrat from Indiana named Andrew Jacobs, Jr., marched to the well of the House and filed his own impeachment resolution against Douglas. In doing so, Jacobs ensured that the matter would be sent by Speaker John McCormack, a Democrat, to the Judiciary Committee, which was controlled by the eccentrically liberal New York Democrat Emanuel Celler. The distress on the faces of Republicans told observers that this had undercut their plan to seek the creation of a select impeachment-investigation committee on which they could play a greater role.

Powerful as the Ford speech was, it infuriated and frustrated the Nixon Justice Department. "Ford blew it," fumed Will Wilson. "You can't believe how raw those files were. We gave [Ford] all of that information, and he just used it to give that dang fool speech. He basically tipped off the opposition to everything that he had in his pocket and had nothing to back it up. He came back to us expecting help, to do more investigating and give him more information, but we didn't have any. So he was kind of sore at me—that we hadn't helped him out. But it wasn't our job to do that."

But the speech was enough to get the wheels of Congress started. The following day, Republican Louis Wyman of New Hampshire filed a bill of impeachment against Douglas cosponsored by twenty-four other members, calling for the creation of a select investigation committee, which John McCormack promptly ignored. When 110 members of Congress subsequently signed a resolution calling for an investigation into the impeachment charges, however, it was clear that the matter was not going to disappear.

This had a powerful impact on Douglas, despite the cavalier manner in which he had responded to John Mitchell. "He was scared stiff," recalled Robert Hamilton. "It was a very serious threat. He realized that in the Parvin relationship, he had done something which he later came to believe that he shouldn't have done." Worse, once set into motion, Douglas well knew, impeachment investigations did not revolve around what was legal or not or even what was "right" or "wrong" but rather what was good or bad politics. Having seen the Fortas, Haynsworth, and Carswell debacles, this seventy-one-year-old man who was married to his fourth wife and seemingly tied to Las Vegas interests knew that he was vulnerable to a congressional inquiry.

By this time, even Douglas's colleagues were concerned about his fate. When some conservative southerners approached Justice Hugo Black, seeking help to get rid of Douglas, he replied: "I have known Bill Douglas for thirty years. He's never knowingly done any improper, unethical or corrupt thing. Tell his detractors that in spite of my age, I think I have one trial left in me. Tell them that if they move against Bill Douglas, I'll resign from the Court and represent him. It will be the biggest, most important case I ever tried." Thus ended the southern attack on Douglas.

While for its target there is no good time for an impeachment investigation, for Douglas this one came at an especially bad time. Such an attack requires a response prepared by a battery of legal advocates, all billing at the top of the rate scale. With his total savings now just under forty thousand dollars, he knew that he could be wiped out financially in no time at all.

Luckily for him, though, Douglas still had a lot of friends—most of whom labored at the top of the legal field. Clark Clifford had appointed himself the headhunter for his legal defense team. After a brief search, Douglas decided to ask his old Columbia Law School classmate Simon Rifkind to undertake the task. "When Douglas came in and asked me to represent him, much to my surprise because I thought he would select somebody with more political status in Washington, instead of so many years in private practice, . . . I was delighted to do it," recalled Rifkind. The choice for Douglas could not have been a better one. Rifkind was both meticulous in his preparation and well versed in the kind of behind-the-scenes bargaining that would be essential in this case. Best of all for Douglas, Rifkind offered not to charge a fee. Whatever other expenses arose in the production of the case would be covered by a fund that had been privately collected from Douglas's most prominent friends.

In addition, Douglas had two powerful tools. First, there was his attitude about working with his attorney. "He was the perfect client," said Rifkind. "Less intrusive than the ordinary corporate clients that I deal with, [Douglas] sat back and attended to his business and just said, 'You fellows do what you have to do.'" And such cooperation was necessary because this was more like a libel trial. Knowing that truth was always the best defense in such cases, Rifkind needed as much information about Douglas's activities as he could find.

Thus, Douglas's second tool in this crisis was his files, which filled room 210 of the Court building. Fay Aull Deusterman recalled that, whenever he went on trips, Douglas continually sent back information to the office on "the back of envelopes, just any old thing, a paper napkin, or something out of a restaurant." All of this was carefully copied and filed in a deliberately redundant three-way system, with material arranged by name, by subject, and chronologically.

For Douglas's attorney, these files were the key to the case. "He was a real pack rat," explained Rifkind. "[Douglas] was the most meticulous hoarder of material. Whenever I asked for something, there it came. I remember that . . . in one incident, we faced an accusation that he had a relationship with a woman in a hotel in Las Vegas, the same time that some gangsters were there. It turned out to be a year or two years later, but it was the same date on the calendar. Not only did Douglas have all this material, but he gave me free access to anything."

Douglas's and Rifkind's plan for his defense was very simple: They would answer any accusation, no matter how trivial, in meticulous detail. When requests came from the House investigators involving Douglas's possible presence in Los Angeles five times over a two-year period, the yearly calendars were used to show conclusively that Douglas was nowhere near that city. When Douglas was accused of various conflicts of interest on the Court, he sent his attorney letter after letter outlining his actions off the Bench and demonstrating how he had recused himself from cases when necessary. When questions were raised about Douglas's involvement in environmental causes, he sent a list of more than eighteen protests at which he had been present, none of which had come before the Court. A question about his speeches off the Court led Douglas to forward a complete list of all his extrajudicial appearances for 1969. In the end, the production of this sort of information was critical. As Douglas explained years later to a clerk, "The House said usually the more we investigate the dirtier the case gets. But this one is unusual, because it just gets cleaner."

But while they labored mightily to mount this defense, in a remarkable irony, Douglas was in the process of being saved by Richard Nixon's concern over giving the right to vote to the same young people that the Justice stood accused of mobilizing. Fearing that eighteen-to twenty-one-year-old voters would "set the [Republican] cause back" by tending to vote Democratic because of their opposition to the war, Nixon instructed John Ehrlichman tersely: "18 year old vote—*must* be defeated." The president predicted that since the House Judiciary Committee would deal with this issue, Emanuel Celler would "kill it in the House" because of his opposition to extending the vote to young people, whom he saw as being too idealistic. But when the Senate attached this provision to the Voting Rights Act of 1970, thus tapping into Celler's concern for civil rights, the president could no longer be certain of the defeat.

Before Nixon could focus on this vote, his agenda was quickly rearranged by outside events. On Monday, April 13, the Apollo 13 space vehicle became crippled on its way to the moon. Such crises captured the president's fancy because of their public-relations possibilities, so he cleared his desk and began to weave various publicity contingency plans. Several days later, when the astronauts returned safely to Earth, a "very cranked up" Nixon, in the words of his assistant H. R. Haldeman, ordered cigars for everyone, called the astronauts' wives, and made plans for a celebration with various congressional leaders. "Isn't this a great day," he said excitedly in a phone call to Gerald Ford, urging him "to give his best to Justice Douglas." The congressman interpreted this statement as continued support for the impeachment effort.

When the president's attention came back to earth, he began to confront once again the realities of dealing with a Congress dominated by the opposing party. After being informed by congressional liaison Bryce Harlow that Speaker McCormack would stop the Douglas impeachment, for Nixon the task now became how to salvage something from the effort. Four days later, Nixon sent word to Attorney General John Mitchell that he was to "go see Ford" and tell him that the administration had decided that it was "not in [its] best interest" to continue the impeachment effort. By acting in this manner, H. R. Haldeman recorded in his diary, the president wanted to appear to "be the good guy." So, less than two weeks after Ford's speech to Congress, Nixon was already preparing to kill the effort.

Nixon now instructed John Ehrlichman to speak with Ford and tell him to offer Celler a trade by which the eighteen-year-old-vote bill would be killed in return for ending the attack on Douglas. The only reason that they were not formally announcing their retreat was that Nixon decided that "it was not a bad idea to keep Douglas worried for a while."

But while the White House was finished with the matter, no one had yet turned off Emanuel Celler. Still believing that he had a constitutional duty to perform, Celler sent a written request for "all relevant reports, documents, or other data [on Douglas] that may be in the possession of the various departments and agencies of the Executive Branch." More than anything, Celler wanted the Treasury Department to release Douglas's income-tax information, which could be done only by executive order. Hoping that the Democrats would do in one of their own without his help, a week later Nixon instructed the executive agencies to be "very forthcoming" to the request. When Douglas's tax returns were finally revealed three days later, they uncovered little that was not already known.

·   ·   ·

By the summer of 1970, the ongoing investigation had a powerful impact on Douglas's state of mind. By this time, Douglas was convinced that the Nixon administration was intercepting and reading his mail. One of his notes to Simon Rifkind took six days to get from Washington to New York, making a meeting between them impossible. Another letter arrived in Rifkind's office a full month after it was sent. As a result, Douglas began sending all important documents to his attorney by personal messenger. Douglas even suggested that Rifkind have the Judiciary Committee chairman request from the FBI all of the wiretap and electronic-surveillance tapes on him, which he had a "moral certainty" actually existed.

Douglas had developed a routine for dealing with this perceived surveillance. He would ask Harry Datcher to drive him around the city in his own pickup truck, rather than using the more visible Court limousine with the license plate 31. The Justice explained that he just didn't want anyone following him. Then Douglas would ask Datcher to drive him to the edge of Rock Creek Park. Before walking into the park, Douglas would tell Datcher to return to the Court building. Only later, did Datcher figure out that Abe Fortas lived on the other side of the park, and Douglas was consulting him on the investigation.

In time, Douglas's own self-censorship spread to other areas. As a result, he wrote to his friend Fred Rodell, it was "turning out to be a long and tedious summer." As much as he wanted to write, the Justice had been urged by his attorneys and advisers to restrain himself. When his former law clerk and now attorney C. David Ginsburg saw the galleys for his next book, to be titled *International Dissent,* he advised Douglas to withhold publication of the book until after the investigation had been completed so as not to "fuel the flames."

The effect of the impeachment threat on Douglas's state of mind became obvious even to those on the storied pack trip in which the three business-suited lawyers tracked the Justice down on the Cascade Mountain trails. After Douglas had written his denial to their appeal and the group had broken camp, it became clear to the others that something was bothering him. "[He was] unusually quiet and moody, and if you spoke to him he would only speak back in one-syllable words," recalled Dagmar Hamilton. "Are you concerned that you denied the appeal in part because you were facing the impeachment?" she asked the Justice at lunch. "Yes," he answered, "that's exactly why I ruled that way." Douglas then explained that this protest case would surely be considered by the Court in October, and he did not think it was right of him to answer the question prematurely by granting the temporary restraining order. "The threat of impeachment caused him to be even more determined to hold up to the ideas which he believed in," explained Hamilton, "[but] the fact that he would spend the morning brooding about it . . . shows that he was not as sure that . . . he had done the right thing." Just as he had in the Eldridge Cleaver episode, "Wild Bill" Douglas was holstering his legal guns for the moment.

But since total self-censorship was not possible for Douglas, he had devoted the summer to working on two plays, each of which, in its own way, revealed his tortured state of mind. The first play, entitled "The Devil and the Lord: Not Guilty," was a revision of a work he had first written in 1969. Created originally for Bill Jr., who was then an actor, to produce and perform in, this was a musical about a debate between William Penn and a man named Bundy over the nature of freedom and legal rights in Great Britain in 1680. Douglas had become fascinated by Penn, a Quaker, being prosecuted in London in 1670 for causing a riot when he had preached a sermon in Grace Church after his own church had been closed under the Conventicle Act.

In its latest revision, the play took on a very different tone as Douglas began to see himself in Penn's role. So, in this play he changed the names of the main characters to William Frazier, a variation of his old pen name, and Rodney Milhous, clearly based on Richard Milhous Nixon. Frazier is a rabble-rousing, nonconformist revolutionary, who is arrested because of the hostile audience reaction to his speech on the nature of legal rights. In pleading for his rights under the Magna Carta, he is opposed by Milhous, who works for the government, hunting down subversives. In a revealing window into the author's mind, Milhous supplies the incriminating evidence in this case by lying under Frazier's bed in order to overhear a conversation he has with his wife.

Frazier's situation seems even more hopeless when his jury is jailed along with him. In a final confrontation between the two characters it becomes clear that only Frazier is interested in equality, privacy, and the diversity of ideas, while Milhous sees all of these as threats to stability that must be crushed by the state. Frazier is freed, and Milhous is left in prison. But once Milhous is released, he decides he should move to America and perform the same "service" that he has done in Great Britain. Frazier pleads in the final scene for Milhous never to seek public office because of the damage he would do to the new nation, suggesting that he would eventually be forced from office. The play clearly shows the author's developing paranoia, not to mention his deep concern over Richard Nixon.

The other play, written that terrible summer of 1970 and entitled "The Couch," was even more revealing of the Justice's state of mind. Here, the action revolves around the problems faced by Sigmund Brock, a psychiatrist and the first occupant of a new cabinet seat designated for the secretary of mental health, who faces a difficult confirmation hearing in the Senate and then, after taking his seat, is threatened with impeachment. The lead character is clearly based on George Draper, Douglas's onetime psychiatrist. In attacking a great many cultural values—religion, criminal punishment, democracy, and the suppression of pornographic material among them—Dr. Brock argues that the root of all problems in the world is motherhood. For him, if mothers were eliminated from the biological equation, all would be right with the world. Such a hyperbolic attack—from a man who would later write that he owed everything to his mother—made it clear that at this time Douglas had, at best, ambivalent feelings about Julia Douglas and her impact on his life.

In the end, Brock comes to the realization that he likes to provoke and irritate the public by his outrageous statements. The message of the play is that the American public is uncomfortable with iconoclastic personalities who are willing to publicly challenge popular beliefs and values. But the submessage is that anyone like this in public office is "trapped" and subject to attacks not only from the press but also from other players in Washington. No depiction could have better described William O. Douglas, who now seemed to be using this theatrical exercise as a way of preparing himself mentally for the prospect of his own Senate impeachment trial.

But the trial did not seem to be imminent. By early October, the battle was now going Douglas's way. The Justice learned from Clark Clifford that a majority of the impeachment subcommittee of the Judiciary Committee had prepared a report arguing that there was "no basis for going ahead on impeachment." Knowing that this might not satisfy the Republicans on the full committee, Douglas's defenders all agreed that his strategy now was to do nothing. "A move might boomerang," argued Clifford. Douglas's marching orders were twofold: regarding the publication of any new books, *"HOLD THEM UP"*; as to giving lectures, he was told to "use [his] discretion" and "do them, but be careful."

The advice proved to be sound. Ten weeks later, on December 15, the nightmare finally ended for Douglas when the subcommittee issued its final report, announcing that by a three-to-one vote it had found no grounds to support any impeachment charges. To be sure, the 924 pages were filled with what many Republican members of the House believed to be proof of Douglas's improper extrajudicial conduct: The Albert Parvin Foundation had underwritten the publication in 1960 of his paperback *America Challenged,* to the tune of $11,250; an annuity had been purchased for the Justice by the Parvin Foundation using $2,400 of the $12,000 paid him in salary; from 1960 to 1969 Douglas had made more money from his extrajudicial income than from his judicial salary (including $96,680 from the Parvin Foundation and $377,260 in writing and lecture fees, as opposed to the $389,749 in salary); and Douglas's connection to the Parvin Foundation had been the subject of an investigation by the Justice Department's organized-crime section (though nothing was found after 30,617 man-hours of work). The committee had also found a number of other highly questionable personal connections between Douglas and Albert Parvin.

When asked by former law clerk Vern Countryman how he had survived the impeachment effort, Douglas responded with an enigmatic smile, "Manny Celler is a very good friend of mine." Indeed, by bottling up the issue in the subcommittee, never even bringing it before the full membership, Celler had preserved both Douglas's reputation and the Court's.

With the attack over, the following day Douglas stepped before the press in the East Conference Room of the Court building to announce, "The Select Committee has now performed its constitutional duties and I will try to continue to perform mine."

THE MAN IN THE SLOUCH HAT

He was "the only known Communist in Yakima County."

—*Robert Mull, quoting locals*

Cragg Gilbert could not quite believe what he saw on a bright sunny day in Yakima as he was driving on the flat old road, coming back to town from the airport. From behind, he could see an old man dressed in a beat-up, dust-filled flannel shirt, a torn work jacket, and the dirtiest old farm blue jeans you could imagine. Stuffed on his head was a crushed sheepherder's cap, and thrown over his shoulder was a beat-up old green duffel bag, so heavy that he had to hunch over as he walked. Rather than walking along the side of the road, the old man meandered across the flat, small grass yards of the houses, weaving toward one house and then away from the next one. People sitting on their porches watched as the old man passed over their property directly in front of them, but they paid him no heed. To them, he was just another deadbeat figuring out where to get his next free meal. But Gilbert thought he saw something rather familiar in this hunched figure. It was something about the way he walked—and the way he didn't really seem to care where he traveled.

As he pulled his truck alongside the man, Gilbert tooted his horn. "Hey, Bill," he shouted through the open window, "what the hell are you doing here?"

"Oh just walking my way back from the airport to the Chinook Hotel," came the response. He had already walked nearly all of the several miles from the airport to the local hotel where he planned to stay for the night while his cottage in Goose Prairie was being prepared for his arrival.

Gilbert shouted, "Well, throw your stuff in the back and jump in

the pickup." With that, William O. Douglas grinned, happy that someone in his old hometown had finally recognized him, and slipped into
Gilbert's truck.

It was always nice for Bill Douglas to see old friends. Despite his
being one of the most powerful political figures in America and having served well over thirty years on the U.S. Supreme Court, most of
the residents of his hometown didn't give a damn about him. To them,
he was just "the man in the slouch hat." "He used to come into Yakima
and walk up and down Yakima Avenue looking in the stores, and visiting friends, and he dressed like . . . he was wrestling steers or something," said Yakima journalist Maurice Helland. When he saw an old
friend, the reaction was often not what he expected. "Some of his former schoolmates, who knew him when he went by Orville or was
called, 'Peanuts,' say they wouldn't say hello if they ran into him on the
street," wrote the *Yakima Herald-Republic*. "But Justice Douglas keeps
coming home." And while he did not like to show it, this attitude
among the hometown folk hurt the Supreme Court Justice very deeply.
"Douglas had a love for Yakima," local attorney and historian George
Martin explained. "But he told me that he was hurt, very much hurt, by
the fact that he was no longer accepted in Yakima."

In his later years, Douglas reciprocated those harsh feelings. "I call
it the love-hate relationship which Bill Douglas and Yakima had for
each other," explained Robert Lucas, a Douglas intimate and a former
editor of the *Yakima Herald-Republic*. "Bill's love for Yakima was its association with the West and the country he explored around it—
of his experiences in the Cascades as a kid, and his valued friend-
ships. But he also seemed to have been embittered by the fact that he
thought Yakima was a feudal community in that it was very class-
conscious. . . . I think that left its mark on him."

But Yakima was not the only thing that had left its mark on him. By
this time it was clear to Douglas's friends that he had been deeply affected by the impeachment threat. "You would listen to Justice Douglas in the later years," recalled Robert Hamilton, "and you would think
that he was a raving paranoid. Then sometime later you would find
out that about ninety percent of what he had said was absolutely true."
Court messenger Harry Datcher observed: "Douglas was one of the
most paranoid people I have ever seen. He was afraid of almost everything and looked out for things everywhere."

By this time he was especially suspicious of the FBI. Upon noticing
men in dark suits loitering around his summer house, Douglas began
to investigate their mission. "I wrote you last fall or winter that federal
agents were in Yakima and Goose Prairie looking me over at Goose

Prairie. I thought they were merely counting fence posts," Douglas wrote his friends at the Double K ranch in the spring of 1970. "But I learned in New York City yesterday that they were planting marijuana with the prospect of a nice big TV-covered raid in July or August. I forgot to tell you that this gang in power is not in search of truth. They are 'search and destroy' people. . . . It would be ironic if they planted it in Ira [Ford]'s yard, not mine!" But no such marijuana raid was ever staged.

.   .   .

Back on the Court, much had changed since Abe Fortas and Chief Justice Earl Warren had left. Reminiscent of the change in the Court's voting direction due to the sudden loss of Murphy and Rutledge in 1949, this loss of Douglas's two liberal allies once again meant a huge change in the philosophical direction of the Court, toward the conservative view. Chief Justice Warren Burger was proving to be just as reliably conservative a vote as Richard Nixon had hoped for in appointing him. And, after the confirmation failures of Haynsworth and Carswell for Fortas's vacant seat, Richard Nixon's appointment in April 1970 of Court of Appeals Judge Harry Blackmun, a friend of Burger's from Minnesota, added a vote that was initially so similar to the new Chief's that Blackmun was nicknamed "Hip-Pocket Harry" or the "Minnesota Twin."

Despite the conservative Court, Douglas was determined to have his say. He was once more issuing his clarion calls in dissent after dissent so that future generations and future majorities could see the error of the current Court's ways. Among the many issues of importance to him, he still wanted to force the Brethren to rule on the constitutionality of the Vietnam War, protect the poor, end racial discrimination, solidify the protection of privacy, and raise the public's consciousness of the environment.

In the middle of the 1970–1971 term, the Court turned to the constitutional protections connected to the welfare system. Barbara James, a recipient of Aid to Families with Dependent Children in New York, objected to the state's practice of sending a caseworker to check on her lifestyle by visiting her home. James offered to supply any information that was needed, but when she refused to allow the visit, her AFDC was terminated. For the majority, Justice Blackmun wrote that while this was not a "search," even if it were it would be considered "reasonable" because the sole purpose was to serve a valid administrative purpose.

For Douglas in dissent, the starting point was the constitutional nature of the government's subsidy: "We are living in a society where one of the most important forms of property is government largesse which some call the 'new property.' " After mentioning the benefits offered to businesses by government-issued defense contracts, highway deals, transportation subsidies, and media licenses, Douglas noted: "Our concern here is not with those subsidies but with grants that directly or indirectly implicate the *home life* of the recipients." So for Douglas, "the central question is whether the government by force of its largesse has the power to 'buy up' rights guaranteed by the Constitution." And, of course, when the right was that of privacy, for Douglas it did not. For Douglas, the right to privacy protected one's home, no matter what the nature of the government program: "If ... [Barbara James] ran a small factory geared into the Pentagon's procurement program, she certainly would have a right to deny inspectors access to her *home* unless they came with a warrant. . . . It is a strange jurisprudence indeed which safeguards the businessman at his place of work from warrantless searches but will not do the same for a mother in her *home.*"

Two months later, Douglas found himself writing once more on the welfare system, this time Connecticut's. Gladys Boddie, a female welfare recipient, was prevented from getting a divorce because she could not afford the fees and costs required for the process service necessary to gain access to the courts. Here the Court, speaking through John Harlan, voted for the poor: "Given the basic position of the marriage relationship in this society's hierarchy of values and the concomitant monopolization of the means for legally dissolving this relationship, due process does prohibit the State from denying, solely because of inability to pay, access to its courts to individuals who seek judicial dissolution of their marriages." But since the Court used only the due-process clause of the Fourteenth Amendment to offer protection, Douglas was still not satisfied. "Here Connecticut has provided requirements for married couples to obtain divorces and because of filing fees and service of process one of the requirements is having the necessary money. The more affluent can obtain a divorce; the indigent cannot," he wrote in a concurring opinion. Mixing his concern for the poor with the question of access to the courts that he had first raised in 1963 in *Douglas v. California,* Douglas thus saw discrimination here that was barred by the equal-protection clause as well.

In a somewhat bizarre reversal of jurisprudential roles, the activist Douglas objected to the conservative, self-restraint-oriented Harlan's willingness to stretch the due-process clause to protect new rights:

The Court today puts "flesh" upon the Due Process Clause by concluding that marriage and its dissolution are so important that an unhappy couple who are indigent should have access to the divorce courts free of charge. Fishing may be equally important to some communities. May an indigent be excused if he does not obtain a license that requires the payment of money that he does not have? How about a requirement of an onerous bond to prevent summary eviction from rented property? The affluent can put up the bond, though the indigent may not be able to do so. . . . Is housing less important to the mucilage holding society together than marriage? The examples could be multiplied. I do not see the length of the road we must follow if we accept my Brother Harlan's invitation.

For Douglas, the more "definite guidelines" against discrimination in the equal-protection clause were a better choice here: "The power of the States over marriage and divorce is, of course, complete except as limited by specific constitutional provisions. But could a State deny divorces to domiciliaries who were Negroes and grant them to whites? Deny them to resident aliens and grant them to citizens? Deny them to Catholics and grant them to Protestants? Deny them to those convicted of larceny and grant them to those convicted of embezzlement? Here the invidious discrimination is based on one of the guidelines: *poverty*." Extending the full reach of the equal-protection clause had become one of the goals that Douglas was trying to achieve in what he knew were his final years on the Court.

. . .

By the spring of 1971, Douglas's heart problems began to plague him once again. When his pacemaker began to fail, Douglas traveled to Boston on May 3 to have it replaced. Within two days, however, that new device also showed signs of failing, and Douglas was back in the hospital to get another device. Once he was assured that this one was working, the Justice returned to Washington on May 8. Late that week, though, one of the secretaries entered the Justice's office to find him slumped over, unconscious, on the papers on his desk.

After he was revived and tested, Douglas was told that yet another new pacemaker would have to be inserted in his chest. Once more, he began to fear that he was about to die. Faced with the question of how to spend what he thought would be his last weekend on earth, rather than spend that Saturday with his wife, Douglas went to the office, where a pile of letters and unfinished judicial opinions awaited him. If he was going to die, he decided, it would be with a clean desk. "It was clear to me that he knew that things were really, really wrong [with the pacemaker]," recounted that year's law clerk, Scot Powe. Rather than work, though, Douglas went into the outer office, sat next to his clerk, and began to talk. For one of the very few times in his judicial career, he became for his law clerk "the Storyteller," who was usually evident only in the Cascade Mountains. He talked about everything—his life, the New Deal, FDR, the early years on the Court, Felix Frankfurter, and whatever else crossed his mind. "We talked more than we did at any other period of time during the term," said Powe. "And it was quite apparent to me that he thought he was dying. And he was searching for some closeness at that time."

At the end of the following week, when the second pacemaker began to fail, too, Douglas underwent his third chest operation in eleven days. When the procedure was completed, Douglas wrote his son that had he not gone to the hospital he "would have probably been shaking hands with the Old Man." Once the doctors assured Douglas that his heart problems were finally under control, Douglas and his law clerk went back to the usual master-slave relationship.

.   .   .

On the Bench, it became evident how far apart Douglas and the increasingly conservative Hugo Black had become on the question of race. Hazel Palmer and others had taken the city of Jackson, Mississippi, to federal court because of the city's policy toward the use of the public pool facilities. After the city's segregation of public swimming pools was declared unconstitutional, Jackson had closed all of its pools, allowing them to be operated on a private basis by and for Caucasians only. For African Americans, this now meant that no pool facilities were available. Writing for the majority, Hugo Black found no constitutional violation here, supporting the city's arguments that the pools were closed due to safety and budgetary considerations. Once more, this was a question of the limits that Black saw to his role as a judge: "Probably few persons, prior to this case, would have imagined that cities could be forced by five lifetime judges to construct or refurbish swimming pools which they choose not to operate for any reason, sound or unsound."

Seeing this action as the kind of unconstitutional segregation that the *Brown v. Board of Education* school-desegregation case had promised to eliminate, William O. Douglas dissented vigorously. Yet while this program was, for him, a violation of the Thirteenth, Fourteenth, and Fifteenth Amendments, he worried about the limits here on the federal government's ability to force states to desegregate: "Is there anything in the Constitution that says that a State must have a public school system? Could a federal court enjoin the dismantling of a public school system? Could a federal court order a city to levy the taxes necessary to construct a public school system? Such supervision over municipal affairs by federal courts would be a vast undertaking, conceivably encompassing schools, parks, playgrounds, civic auditoriums, tennis courts, athletic fields, as well as swimming pools." So, Douglas expanded his search for additional weapons in the Constitution for use by activist federal judges to regulate these areas. The answer, he began to think, lay in the Ninth Amendment, which states that "the enumeration in the Constitution, of certain rights, shall not be construed to deny or disparage others retained by the people." For him, this meant that federal judges might be able to protect rights that "have at times been deemed so elementary to our way of life that they have been labeled as basic rights." Using this power, the man who wrote so eloquently about hiking in the Cascades now found a right of recreation in his version of the Constitution: "There is, of course, not a word in the Constitution, unlike many modern constitutions, concerning the right of the people to education or to work or to recreation by swimming or otherwise. Those rights, like the right to pure air and pure water, may well be rights 'retained by the people' under the Ninth Amendment." Thus, Douglas believed that federal judges were obligated to safeguard them.

Douglas then supplemented this position with his long-held arguments about the need to avoid discrimination against the poor: "Though a State may discontinue any of its municipal services—such as schools, parks, pools, athletic fields, and the like—it may not do so for the purpose of perpetuating or installing apartheid or because it finds life in a multi-racial community difficult or unpleasant. If that is its reason, then abolition of a designated public service becomes a device for perpetuating a segregated way of life. That a State may not do." It now seemed in this case and others as if Douglas was trying, like Einstein in his final years, to work out some kind of unified theory. He sought to expand the Ninth Amendment and tie it to the equal-protection clause to accomplish many of his aims.

When the Court turned in the *Lemon v. Kurtzman* case to the question of the constitutionality of state aid to parochial schools, Douglas refined his interpretation of the separation of church and state in the establishment clause of the First Amendment. In a trio of cases, the Court explored whether Pennsylvania and Rhode Island could provide aid to religious schools for such items as partial salaries for teachers, textbooks, and instructional materials for secular subjects. Here the Court introduced the *Lemon* test for judging permissible state aid to education, which would govern the area for decades to come: "First, the statute must have a secular legislative purpose; second, its principal or primary effect must be one that neither advances nor inhibits religion . . . finally, the statute must not foster 'an excessive entanglement with religion.'" In these cases, the need to monitor the teachers in their classrooms to make certain that only secular subjects were being taught triggered the "excessive entanglement" of government with religion, thereby making those parts of the statutes impermissible.

Douglas, in concurrence, had no tolerance for such fancy tests when it came to defining the acceptable level of the separation of church and state and in this manner safeguard the diversity of religious practices and freedom of belief. With teachers able to teach any way they like, Douglas could see that religion could be injected into any class, regardless of the state's intention: "Sectarian education, in which, of course, a State may not indulge, can take place in a course on Shakespeare or in one on mathematics. No matter what the curriculum offers, the question is, what is *taught*? We deal not with evil teachers but with zealous ones who may use any opportunity to indoctrinate a class." For Douglas, any effort by the state to monitor and perhaps limit the academic freedom of these teachers under the guise of preserving the First Amendment's admonition against the establishment of religion would "breed division and dissension between church and state." In writing this way, a more experienced Justice Douglas was now echoing the argument first made by his long-missed colleague Wiley Rutledge in the 1947 *Everson* case, which he did not embrace at that time, for a "high wall of separation" between church and state.

The 1970–1971 term ended with a bang when two expedited appeals came to the Court seeking to explore whether the U.S. government could restrain *The New York Times* and *The Washington Post* from publishing the contents of the classified study entitled "History of U.S. Decision-Making Process on Viet Nam Policy," more popularly known as the Pentagon Papers. By the time the cases came to the Court in its final conference, on June 25, Douglas had already left for Goose Prairie and had to phone in from Whistlin' Jack's his desire to hear the appeal. When the cases were accepted for review, it meant that for one of the rare times in his judicial career he had to interrupt his summer solitude to return to the nation's capital.

Taking very seriously the military's claim that the secrecy of this history was in the "national interest," the Chief Justice had the record for the case placed in the conference room, under security guard, and members of the Court were instructed to read it there. Just to tweak Burger, though, and to illustrate to his colleagues that he saw nothing dangerous to anyone here, Douglas would take the materials back to his chambers and allow his law clerks to peruse them.

The Court voted six to three to uphold the interests of the press, arguing in a brief *per curiam* opinion that the government's right to censor material prior to publication was very marginal. In this case the government had failed to meet its "heavy burden of showing justification" for this restraint. Of the various tests offered in separate opinions by those in the majority to measure this burden, the most memorable phrase was offered by Justice Potter Stewart in concurrence: The government must first prove that "disclosure of any of [the articles] will surely result in direct, immediate, and irreparable damage to our Nation or its people." For William Brennan, this meant that "only governmental allegation and proof that publication must inevitably, directly and immediately cause the occurrence of an event kindred to imperiling the safety of a transport already at sea can support even the issuance of an interim restraining order."

But the old absolutists, William O. Douglas and Hugo Black, would not even allow that much government censorship power. For Douglas, in an opinion that he dashed down in a day and a half before flying back to Washington, there was "no room for governmental restraint of the press." After so many years of arguing the issue of the legality of the Vietnam War in obscure dissents to *certiorari* writs, Douglas finally got to make his argument in a case holding. In conceding that "any power that the Government possesses [to restrain publication during wartime emergencies] must come from its 'inherent power,' " Douglas argued that because of the nature of this war there could be no such power: "The war power stems from a declaration of war. The Constitution by Art. I, Section 8, gives Congress, not the President, power '[t]o declare War.' Nowhere are presidential wars authorized. We need not decide therefore what leveling effect the war power of Congress might have." For him, the government was trying to suppress critical speech and not dangerous information, a goal that was anathema to the Bill of Rights: "The dominant purpose of the First Amendment was to prohibit the widespread practice of governmental suppression of embarrassing information. It is common knowledge that the First Amendment was adopted against the widespread use of the common law of seditious libel to punish the dissemination of material that is embarrassing to the powers-that-be." For Douglas, this material was "highly relevant to the debate in progress" over the government's posture in Vietnam, as he argued with his now familiar anti-Establishment flair: "Secrecy in government is fundamentally anti-democratic, perpetuating bureaucratic errors. Open debate and discussion of public issues are vital to our national health. On public questions there should be 'uninhibited, robust, and wide-open' debate."

But this was not absolutist enough for Hugo Black. With superb eloquence, Black explained what the "Congress shall make no law" language really meant in the First Amendment: "The Government's power to censor the press was abolished so that the press would remain forever free to censure the Government. The press was protected so that it could bare the secrets of government and inform the people. Only a free and unrestrained press can effectively expose deception in government. And paramount among the responsibilities of a free press is the duty to prevent any part of the government from deceiving the people and sending them off to distant lands to die of foreign fevers and foreign shot and shell." So Black pleaded for the protection of the free press against government power: "To find that the President has 'inherent power' to halt the publication of news by resort to the courts would wipe out the First Amendment and destroy the fundamental liberty and security of the very people the Government hopes to make 'secure.'"

This would prove to be Black's valedictory opinion on the Court. On September 17, 1971, with his health failing rapidly, Black resigned. Less than a week later, with his eyesight gone and his health collapsing, the learned and scholarly John Harlan did the same. Just eight days after his resignation, Black would be dead, and by the end of the year, the same would be true of Harlan. When they were replaced by conservatives Lewis Powell and William Rehnquist, William O. Douglas knew that his own time on the Court was rapidly dwindling.

THE LAST NEW DEALER

Douglas had the best idea of any person that I knew
in my whole life . . . of the direction of the country. . . . That look in his eye was always a faraway
look. . . . He seemed to be looking into the distance.

—*Charles Reich*

With Hugo Black's retirement and death, William O. Douglas was
now the last New Dealer on the Court. He had outlasted them all—
Frankfurter, Black, Murphy, Rutledge, Jackson, Byrnes, and Reed—
and now this relic of the past was determined to create a judicial
legacy by crafting his constitutional vision for the young decade.

The first opportunity to do so came in an appeal concerning the vagrancy law in Jacksonville, Florida, and resulted in Douglas writing
what proved to be one of his all-time favorite opinions. Eight people,
headed by Margaret Papachristou, were arrested under a city ordinance that levied criminal penalties against so-called rogues, vaga-
bonds, beggars, common gamblers, jugglers, drunkards, nightwalkers,
thieves, pilferers, pickpockets, habitual loafers, vagrants who were
"prowling by auto," and disorderly persons.

A unanimous Court ruled that the Jacksonville ordinance was unconstitutional because of its vagueness under the due-process clause,
affording the police too much discretion in deciding whom to arrest.
When he was assigned to write the majority opinion, Douglas, the
longtime nonconformist who loved to tramp around Yakima dressed
like a vagabond, decided to use the occasion to protect the rights of
others to do the same wherever they lived.

Douglas wrote here that walking around in old clothes was "his-
torically part of the amenities of life as we have known them." On the
other hand, the vagrancy law was so vague that it criminalized persons
merely for "wandering or strolling," an activity that had once been extolled by authors such as Walt Whitman and Henry David Thoreau

and was undertaken even by "many members of golf clubs and city clubs." For Douglas, "arresting a person on suspicion, like arresting a person for investigation, is foreign to our system, even when the arrest is for past criminality. Future criminality, however, is the common justification for the presence of vagrancy statutes." In concluding, Douglas made very clear that such vague laws would never pass muster for him: "A presumption that people who might walk or loaf or loiter or stroll or frequent houses where liquor is sold, or who are supported by their wives or who look suspicious to the police are to become future criminals is too precarious for a rule of law. . . . The rule of law, evenly applied to minorities as well as majorities, to the poor as well as the rich, is the great mucilage that holds society together."

With his time on the Court now limited, Douglas looked for opportunities in the cases that followed to handle issues beyond what the Court majority considered. This was true in a dispute brought from Louisiana by Claude Alexander, an African American who had unsuccessfully tried to have a rape charge against him dismissed on the grounds that the grand jury that had indicted him had excluded both people of his own race and women. Writing for a unanimous Court, Byron White found this to be an invidious racial discrimination, arguing that the state had not proved that "racially neutral" selection criteria had been used. In a concurring opinion, Douglas argued that his colleagues should have taken the additional step here of ruling on women's rights for representation in jury trials as well. Had they done so, Douglas made very clear which way he would have ruled: "I believe that the time has come to reject the [1880] dictum in *Strauder* v. *West Virginia* . . . that a State 'may confine' jury service 'to males.'" Douglas believed that the lists for grand-jury service, like those for trial jury, should "reasonably reflec[t] a cross-section of the population" of the community. "If the shoe were on the other foot," he wrote, "who would claim that a jury was truly representative of the community if all men were intentionally and systematically excluded from the panel?" Thus for Douglas, "The absolute exemption provided by Louisiana, and no other State, betrays a view of a woman's role which cannot withstand scrutiny under modern standards."

Douglas also searched for every opportunity he could to advance his legal-agenda in cases where he was not able to write a full opinion. After dissenting to the *certiorari* denial in 1960 on the question of DDT spraying on Long Island, Douglas had been waiting for another chance from the Court to help preserve the environment. Finally, in 1972, he seized the opportunity to consider the level of constitutional protection afforded the environment in a case called *Sierra Club v. Morton,* involving a proposed vacation-resort development by the Walt Disney Corporation.

Disney had secured the U.S. Forest Service's approval to put a thirty-five-million-dollar skiing and swimming resort in the Mineral King Valley of California's Sierra Nevadas—sort of an alpine Disneyland—next to Sequoia National Park. The Sierra Club, a conservationist group, brought suit to stop the development, alleging its "special interest in the conservation and sound maintenance of the national parks, game refuges and forests of the country, regularly serving as a responsible representative of persons similarly interested."

By now Douglas felt these losses of natural resources greatly, as was evident to all around him. Fay Aull Deusterman recalled the day that Douglas dragged himself into the office, peered sadly at her, and cried out, "Lake Erie is dying!"

Not realizing the full level of his distress, she looked up from her pile of typing and said flippantly, "Oh really? I didn't even know that it was ill." Only when he ceased speaking to her for a while did she realize that her boss really meant it.

A law professor named Red Schwartz recalled the time that Douglas came to lecture at the State University of New York at Buffalo Law School and could not even eat dinner because he was so upset. "When I ventured to ask what was wrong, he said that he was virtually in a state of despair," said Schwartz. "He was deeply distressed at the polluted condition of the environment, blaming it all on the work of giant corporations."

"I'm ready to bend the law in favor of the environment and against the corporations," Douglas revealed to Schwartz, giving no specific example as to why he was reaching this conclusion.

The great naturalist on the Court now found a way to "bend the law" to fight for the Mineral King area. The conservative Burger Court ruled that the Sierra Club lacked standing to sue—that is, to take their case before the Court—because they could not prove that they had a sufficient stake in the controversy, meaning that they were not likely to be personally affected by the outcome in this case. Douglas, on the other hand, given his love of nature, cared not a whit about this legal technicality. Instead, he argued that the Court should still decide the case: "The critical question of 'standing' would be simplified and also put neatly in focus if we fashioned a federal rule that allowed environmental issues to be litigated before federal agencies or federal courts in the name of the inanimate object about to be despoiled, defaced, or invaded by roads and bulldozers and where injury is the subject of public outrage." Noting that many other "inanimate objects" now had legal standing, such as ships and corporations, Douglas now argued that "valleys, alpine meadows, rivers, lakes, estuaries, beaches, ridges, groves of trees, swampland, or even air" should have legal rights too. So, "those people who have a meaningful relation" to those natural bodies, whether they be "fisherman, a canoeist, a zoologist, or a logger— must be able to speak for the values which [they represent and] . . . are threatened." Only by having environmental issues brought to the Court by the inanimate object itself, Douglas concluded, will there "be assurances that all forms of life which it represents will stand before the court—the pileated woodpecker as well as the coyote and bear, the lemmings as well as the trout in the streams. Those inarticulate members of the ecological group cannot speak. But those people who have so frequented the place as to know its values and wonders will be able to speak for the entire ecological community." For Douglas, trees and other natural life-forms should have the right to sue in federal courts.

This was the Reverend William Douglas's son preaching with all of his power from his pulpit on the Court. And this was Justice William O. Douglas, the man who had longed to be president, ready as an activist jurist to "bend the law" to protect nature. Little wonder then that Douglas would later be hailed by the Sierra Club as "the highest-placed advocate of wilderness in the United States."

What at first seemed like a hopeless cause in fact helped the environmental advocates. The Sierra Club Legal Defense Fund, which had been created initially for this fight, soon became the first public-interest law firm devoted exclusively to instituting environmental litigation. After five years of additional litigation, using a loophole suggested by Justice Stewart to create an acceptable standing to sue in the case, the Mineral King Valley was saved from the bulldozer's scars and made part of Sequoia National Park in 1978.

. . .

In March 1972 Douglas found himself in dissent against the army in a case involving the use of the military by the Nixon administration to spy on civilian antiwar protests. The effect of the conservative Nixon appointments to the Court became evident as five of its members, led by Chief Justice Warren Burger, found a way to duck hearing this case on the grounds that the appellants had not established a specific harm to their interests. Having warned against an intrusive, omnipresent government since the 1950s, Douglas did not miss this new chance to lambaste his colleagues in a dissent offering an Orwellian societal vision. Congress, he pointed out, had no authority to create a system of military surveillance over domestic groups and citizens, and the Framers never would have offered this power: "Our tradition reflects a desire for civilian supremacy and subordination of military power. The tradition goes back to the Declaration of Independence in which it was recited that the King 'has affected to render the Military independent of and superior to the Civil Power.' " Thus, for Douglas, "The act of turning the military loose on civilians even if sanctioned by an Act of Congress . . . [s]tanding as it does only on brute power and Pentagon policy, . . . must be repudiated as a usurpation dangerous to the civil liberties on which free men are dependent." That said, Douglas concluded by offering his most eloquent call for constitutional vigilance: "This case involves a cancer in our body politic. It is a measure of the disease which afflicts us. Army surveillance, like Army regimentation, is at war with the principles of the First Amendment. Those who already walk submissively will say there is no cause for alarm. But submissiveness is not our heritage. The First Amendment was designed to allow rebellion to remain as our heritage. The Constitution was designed to keep government off the backs of the people." "Keep government off the backs of the people"—there could be no better description of what Justice William O. Douglas was trying to accomplish now from the Bench. Dissent as he might, though, against the powerful tide of the Burger Court, Douglas had by this time become like King Canute, sitting on the seashore unsuccessfully commanding the tide to cease coming in.

.   .   .

By this time, Douglas's advancing age was having an impact on the personal relations in his Court office. In the summer of 1972, Fay Aull Deusterman decided that she had been abused by a letter from the Justice, who was vacationing in Goose Prairie, for the last time. Fearing that Douglas would fire her on the spot if she tried to resign from her job, thus preventing her from getting her full pension, Deusterman consulted with Justice Brennan. "Well, I don't think Bill would do that, but let me check with the chief," Brennan told her. When she was assured that she would be given a job in the typing pool if she was fired, Deusterman wrote Douglas a note saying that she had decided to retire at the end of October, citing the fact that she would have thirty years in the government. But Douglas turned out to be far from heartbroken. "Datch," he asked his messenger by phone from Goose Prairie, "who was that pretty young girl in the clerk's office?" Upon being told that her name was Sandy Phillips, the Justice hired her for his office.

Soon it was not just the office staff that was facing Douglas's wrath; his conservative colleagues felt it as well. He celebrated his seventy-fourth birthday, on October 16, 1972, by objecting to twenty-six denials of writs of *certiorari,* offering full dissents in ten of them. Douglas was objecting to the Court's unwillingness to hear all manner of cases: antimonopoly laws, airport zoning statutes, state support for parochial-school education, employment liability, destruction of war materials, the constitutionality of chain gangs, and the rights of the poor in filing for criminal-trial transcripts. By this time, Douglas was so anxious to show his displeasure with his colleagues that when four members of the Court voted to accept a case, he objected to that as well. But with four Nixon appointees now dominating the Burger Court, it was all to no avail.

Douglas had an opportunity to offer his views on the right of privacy of single women to get abortions this term when the Court explored the reaches of its landmark *Roe v. Wade* pro-abortion-rights decision in a companion ruling issued on the same day, *Doe v. Bolton,* from Georgia. In *Roe,* the Court had overturned Texas's ban on abortions by creating a trimester system regulating the ability to secure abortions based on the differing interests of the three parties involved in the dispute: the mother, the unborn fetus, and the state. While the mother had an unlimited right to get an abortion in the first three months of a pregnancy, and the state had the right to prevent an abortion in the last three months to protect the fetus, in the middle trimester a state could only regulate the decision to get an abortion based on the need to protect the health and life of the mother. *Doe* turned on whether Georgia's requirement that abortions could be obtained only in hospitals, and with the permission of abortion committees and various physicians, represented an unconstitutional limitation on this new right to get an abortion. Speaking through Justice Harry Blackmun, the Court also overturned this law.

While promising to add only "a few words" to the Court's judgment with his concurrence, Douglas's twelve-page opinion was longer than a great many of his landmark decisions. For him, the Georgia statute was "overbroad" in failing to "closely correlat[e the law] to the aim of preserving prenatal life," such as by permitting abortions for females under the age of consent but proscribing them in cases where "severe mental disorders" will be the result. Thus the law was "at war with the clear message of these [precedential] cases—that a woman is free to make the basic decision whether to bear an unwanted child." Once more he indicated an affection for considering the protections that might be afforded here by the Ninth Amendment as they were applied to the states through the due-process provision of the Four-

teenth Amendment: "The Ninth Amendment obviously does not create federally enforceable rights. . . . But a catalogue of these rights
includes customary, traditional and time-honored rights, amenities,
privileges, and immunities that come within the sweep of 'the Blessings of Liberty' mentioned in the preamble to the Constitution. Many
of them, in my view, come within the meaning of the term 'liberty' as
used in the Fourteenth Amendment."

Using the instruction of the Ninth Amendment to safeguard
"rights . . . retained by the people," Douglas argued that the first of
these rights was "the autonomous control over the development and
expression of one's intellect, interests, tastes, and personality." Second
on this list of rights for Douglas was the "freedom of choice in the
basic decisions of one's life respecting marriage, divorce, procreation,
contraception, and the education and upbringing of children." Finally,
as he had argued in his *Papachristou v. Jacksonville* decision, Douglas
also sought to protect "the freedom to care for one's health and person, freedom from bodily restraint or complusion, freedom to walk,
stroll, or loaf." Citing precedent after precedent, Douglas explained
that these rights were so " 'fundamental' that they could only be overcome by a narrowly and precisely drawn statute that supported a
'compelling state interest.' " Though no one else would sign his opinion, William O. Douglas had written here much like a Framer, creating
his own threefold supplement to the Bill of Rights.

.   .   .

Douglas's now annual assault against the Court's denial of Vietnam-
related appeals resumed on January 22, 1973, just five days before the
announcement of the signing of a cease-fire agreement, when the
Court denied a writ of *certiorari* for antiwar protestors Reverends
Philip and Daniel Berrigan. The two ministers, who had been convicted of charges relating to one of their protests, were being prevented by their parole board from traveling to the war region on a
peace mission because the State Department had determined that
their possible contact with a Communist regime was "not in the national interest." When the Court refused to hear their appeal, Douglas, picking up on the thread of his ruling in the 1958 *Kent v. Dulles*
passport-denial case, argued that "the right to travel is a peripheral
right of every citizen under the First Amendment." Douglas now saw
no "national interest" that outweighed this constitutional right: "To
the contrary, the national interest embodied in the First Amendment
right to freedom of speech and information would be furthered by such
a visit. . . . Keeping alive intellectual intercourse between seemingly

opposing groups has always been important and is even more important in view of the bridges of communication long destroyed between
this country and North Vietnam which are now being restored." For
him, preserving the right to travel for others had now become a sacred
mission: "The ability to understand this pluralistic world filled with
clashing ideologies is a prerequisite of any hope for world peace. . . .
One of the best ways to insure this knowledge and understanding is to
allow the people of the world to mingle freely with one another."

With his hiring of one new young secretary, everyone in the building knew what was coming next. Fay Aull Deusterman had been the
workhorse, doing all of the typing of the opinions and most of the letters, while Nan Burgess had worked the phones and served as the re-
ceptionist. When the attractive Sandra Phillips arrived, Burgess decided
to make clear who was boss. Phillips got all the close-to-the-deadline
typing work, and it was often not dumped on her desk until just as she
was about to leave at 6:00 P.M. It was not long before the pile of unfinished work began to grow.

After a few weeks, Burgess went to apologize to Douglas for the
slowness of the production of the office work and suggested that the
new secretary was not working out. As soon as Burgess left the office,
the buzzer clattered, summoning Phillips into the Judge's chambers.
"Leave the door open," Douglas said, loud enough for everyone in the
outer office to hear. "I just want to tell you how good a job you are
doing."

Whereupon Burgess marched back into his office. "Judge, I've had
all I can take," she told Douglas, expecting him to offer to fire the new
appointee and let her choose a more "acceptable" coworker.

Without saying a word to her, Douglas picked up the phone to dial
his wife: "Cathy, who's that friend you have who needs work?" With
that, Cathy Douglas's roommate from her freshman year in college,
Marty Bagby, was hired to replace the "retiring" Nan Burgess by the
first week in July 1973. "In this way," chuckled Court messenger Harry
Datcher, "the judge changed from the old-timers to two young girls
who could cross their legs and take dictation."

Bagby's indoctrination was a unique one. After just one month on
the job, a long-distance phone call came to the office, and just above
the loud static Bagby could hear the unmistakable high-pitched,
craggy voice of her boss from the Pacific Northwest. *Listen up,* Douglas
said abruptly, *this call will have to be quick.* Then he explained that he
was locked in a desperate struggle against the Nixon administration
over an expansion of the Vietnam War.

The incident had started several days before. Doug Williams, the owner of Whistlin' Jack's Motel, had taken a rare early-morning phone call on Sunday, July 29. Someone whose name Williams did not quite get said that he was from the ACLU and wanted to convey a "top secret" message to Justice William O. Douglas. The Nixon administration was bombing the neutral country of Cambodia, the man began, and Representative Elizabeth Holtzman as well as four Air Force officers had sued in federal court to halt the offensive. While Judge Orrin G. Judd in the district court of New York had ordered that the bombing be halted at 4:00 P.M. on July 27, that judgment was overturned by the Circuit Court of Appeals. That much was known, but now, with the Supreme Court out of session, the only option for the war's opponents to stop the bombing was to find as quickly as possible an individual Justice who would issue a stay in their favor until the full Court met in the fall. While Congress had already voted to cut off funds for the bombing as of August 15, thus rendering the entire issue moot in seventeen days, the symbolism of having the Court stop the war for any period of time, no matter how small, could not be overlooked. Congresswoman Holtzman had asked Justice Thurgood Marshall to issue an order immediately ending the bombing in Cambodia, but he was expected to refuse, and now they wanted Douglas to stand ready to rule on the matter. Can you help get him the message? the man pleaded.

Doug Williams carefully took down all this information on several sheets of hotel stationery and then raced to the top of the mountain to find Douglas. As angry as Douglas was to be disturbed at his cottage on a Sunday morning, after snatching the note out of the breathless man's hands he stared at it in disbelief. "You took this down over the phone?" Douglas barked at the startled visitor.

"Yes," said Williams.

"You still have a four-way party line down there. Those dumb bastards!" he responded. Convinced that Nixon now had advance notice of what he would do, Douglas was determined not to make the same mistake that he had made in the *Rosenberg* case twenty years before, when he had informed his colleagues—Frankfurter, Jackson, and Vinson—in advance as to how he would rule. Ignoring the custom that a second Justice asked to issue a stay in a case either defers to the decision of the first Justice or else waits for the full Court to convene to consider the issue, Douglas immediately returned to Whistlin' Jack's prepared to lay the groundwork for making a decision. Calling from the pay phone next to the street, so that he would not be overheard by any electronic surveillance that he suspected existed inside the hotel, he informed the ACLU that he would rule on the issue after conducting an open hearing in the Yakima County Courthouse. With that, they waited for Marshall's ruling.

On August 1, Marshall refused to rule on the case because the Court had repeatedly refused to rule on the constitutionality of the Vietnam War. Now it was William O. Douglas's turn.

The hour-long hearing was held on Friday, August 3. As much as many disliked him, Yakima residents could not resist witnessing a single Supreme Court Justice in their federal courthouse deciding whether the government should stop sending waves of bombers half a world away. A packed courtroom audience watched as U.S. Attorney Dean Smith of Spokane submitted an affidavit from Secretary of State William Rogers alleging that any halt in the bombing would do "irreparable damage" to United States foreign-policy interests and to the military forces, which would be exposed to enemy fire. "Irreparable injury?" responded Douglas sharply. "Who to, the peasants of Cambodia who get bombed? I don't know what you mean." Arguing for the bombing to be halted, prominent ACLU lawyer Burt Neuborne said, "Twelve more days is a lot of people placed in jeopardy from the bombing, $5 million a day more in American money spent."

Douglas told the attorneys that he would have to take some time to consider the case and would be releasing his decision through the Supreme Court in Washington. As he left the courtroom, Douglas vowed to the local press that even though there were now only eleven days left in the bombing, "I will not let it become moot."

But as he walked out of the courthouse, Douglas knew exactly how he would rule. He walked around the block to make sure no one was following him and found a vacant phone booth. With the three-hour time difference, Marty Bagby was on her way out the door to attend a 7:30 dinner party when the phone rang. "Get your pen, and get everyone in the office on the phone lines," barked the Justice. "Your weekend will have to wait. I'll be calling back from another location, and I want you to start taking down this ruling." Then the phone went dead.

For the next forty-five minutes the two secretaries and the two new law clerks, Richard Benka and Michael Clutter, stood by their phones. After they finally rang, Douglas said that he was calling from a truck stop and, without any further explanation, began dictating the first paragraphs of his decision to halt the bombing in Cambodia. The problem for his staff was that they could not understand him over the sound of traffic and telephone static. "All four of us were on the phone in the office," recalled Bagby. "I tried to take it down verbatim, Sandy [Phillips] tried to take it down stenographically, and the two law clerks who were there listened for the case names." Finally they just gave up and rotated trying to take down every fourth sentence or so.

Just when they were beginning to get into a workable system, the four of them heard "Call you later." The phone was dead once again. Douglas moved to a new location and another safe phone farther up Route 410 on his way to Goose Prairie. Several minutes later, the phone rang again, and the voice they knew all too well simply began dictating the next part of his judgment. Then he was gone again. Several minutes later, the phone rang again. "Alert the printer!" the voice on the line shouted without even saying hello, explaining that he was calling from the phone booth outside of Whistlin' Jack's. It was Douglas's version of "stop the presses," they all decided. Then without any further formalities, he began dictating the final paragraphs of his opinion. The only indication that he was done came when, without any warning, the phone went dead once more, and he did not call again soon.

Several hours later, dinner parties long since a distant memory, the Douglas office staff was still laboring on the opinion when the phone rang for the fifth time. "Read it back to me," commanded the distant voice. While Benka did his best to make sense of their scribbling and hours of mutual deciphering, the rest of them wondered just where Douglas was calling from now, since they all knew that there was no phone between Whistlin' Jack's and Goose Prairie.

As he listened to the reading, Douglas edited the opinion from 2,300 miles away. When he was finally satisfied, he told the staff to have the Court release it immediately. The fact that there was no one left in the building except his office staff, the printers, a couple of guards, and the night janitors was of no consequence to the man who was trying to stop the Vietnam War all by himself.

The opinion, *Holtzman v. Schlesinger,* offered in Douglas's familiar plain-speaking manner, used the logic of death-penalty cases to make clear that the Nixon administration was not going to drop one more bomb in the area if he could help it:

> The classic capital case is whether Mr. Lew, Mr. Low, or Mr. Lucas should die. The present case involved whether Mr. X (an unknown person or persons) should die. No one knows who they are. They may be Cambodian farmers whose only "sin" is a desire for socialized medicine to alleviate the suffering of their families and neighbors. Or Mr. X may be the American pilot or navigator who drops a ton of bombs on a Cambodian village. The upshot is that we

know that someone is about to die. Since that is true I see no reason to balance the equities and consider the harm to our foreign
policy if one or a thousand more bombs do not drop.

Douglas then turned to the argument against the war, which he had
been making so often: "It has become popular to think the President
has that power to declare war. But there is not a word in the Constitution that grants that power to him. It runs only to Congress." But for
him, this extension of the conflict was much different:

> I do not sit today to determine whether the bombing of Cambodia
> is constitutional. Some say it is merely an extension of the "war" in
> Vietnam, a "war" which the Second Circuit has held . . . to raise a
> "political" question, not a justiciable one. I have had serious doubts
> about the correctness of that decision, but our Court has never
> passed on the question authoritatively. I have expressed my doubts
> on the merits in various opinions dissenting from denial of certio-
> rari. But even if the "war" in Vietnam were assumed to be a consti-
> tutional one, the Cambodia bombing is quite a different affair.

For Douglas, it was now just a matter of using his power on the
Court: "The merits of the present controversy are therefore, to say the
least, substantial, since denial of the application before me would
catapult our airmen as well as Cambodian peasants into the death
zone. I do what I think any judge would do in a capital case."

The order was issued late on Friday, August 3. But if Douglas was
hoping for a dramatic full Supreme Court hearing on the war, just as
had occurred during the *Rosenberg* dispute in 1953, he was to be disappointed. When the government attorneys appealed to Thurgood
Marshall, he immediately polled the rest of the Court by phone; a mere
six hours after Douglas's ruling had been released, the Court announced that all eight of his colleagues had overturned it. Nevertheless, though the bombing continued without interruption even during
the few hours when Douglas's injunction was technically in effect, the
point had been made. After all those years of begging his colleagues to
do something about the carnage, Douglas had become the one person
to single-handedly stop the war, if only symbolically, for a handful of
hours.

Douglas did not appear to be upset by the reversal. "I expected to
be overturned," Douglas told Bagby cheerfully, "but I didn't think it
would happen so fast. I really wanted a full hearing, but at least I got
my say." As expected, he issued a dissent against Marshall's action,

protesting that "seriatim telephone calls cannot, with all respect, be a lawful substitute" for the practice of summoning the Court to a special term: "I do not speak of social propriety. It is a matter of law and order involving high principles. . . . A Gallup Poll type of inquiry of widely scattered Justices is, I think, a subversion of the regime under which I thought we lived." Mostly he objected to the fact that only a few of his colleagues had even seen his opinion when they reversed it. To the outside world, that was the end of the issue, but Court insiders witnessed the appearance of the other, more private and paranoid, Douglas.

The more he thought about what Marshall and the other Justices had done, the more Douglas began to wonder how they could have acted so quickly. After fussing and fuming for a while, Douglas decided that the only answer was that the phone at Whistlin' Jack's had been tapped by the FBI, meaning that his initial call to the ACLU had been intercepted and passed on to Marshall. Douglas believed that he had used that advance warning to prepare the Court's quick reversal in advance of his ruling. Now furious, he phoned for help from his longtime aide-de-camp Abe Fortas, then practicing law in Washington. *They tapped my phone at Whistlin' Jack's,* he told Fortas, *look into it for me.* Douglas said that he wanted to sue the phone company in Seattle for its "cooperation" with the government in allowing the tap.

Fortas, who remained convinced that he himself had been forced off the Court by just such nefarious governmental means, went into full legal confrontational mode. He called up Pacific Northwest Bell in Seattle and in what was described by the recipient as a "rude" and "high-handed" manner accused a manager who oversaw the Yakima region of leaking the contents of Douglas's judicial opinion to someone in Washington, D.C. The startled man said that he would investigate the charge immediately and report back.

When the matter came to the attention of John Rupp, the general counsel for Pacific Northwest Bell, he decided to deal with the legendary Washington lawyer personally. Someone has intercepted information from one of Douglas's phone calls, said Fortas, and we will be suing your company as a result. He doesn't have a phone, replied Rupp, adding that in fact the Naches Telephone Company, rather than his firm, serviced that area. That doesn't matter, Fortas responded, we will be suing you, your phone company, the FBI, the CIA, and everyone else. "But what is your evidence of a wiretap?" Rupp responded with a chuckle. "Nobody in Yakima listens to Douglas anyway." Fortas said that he knew the tap existed because material on Douglas had come before him with the name "Whistlin' Jack's" on it—obviously a government code name for the jurist. "That's a real place," Rupp said, trying to suppress a laugh. "It's a motel up in Cliffdell and the public phone there has no door, no glass in the window, and is right by the road. Anyone could have overheard him if they were standing in line waiting to use it." Then he added that the wires to this phone booth went right past one of the motel's windows, making it easy for any resident there to tap the line if they really wanted to. But, Rupp assured Fortas, they had already checked at Whistlin' Jack's, and no one saw any wiretapping or eavesdropping taking place. Finally, Rupp added, if the information was all that confidential, then why was Douglas putting it over the line of a public pay phone?

Unfazed by these arguments, Fortas pressed on. A long-distance phone call from Whistlin' Jack's had to be manually switched by an operator in Yakima to Pacific Northwest Bell's long-distance service, he argued. "That operator could listen to the call," said Fortas. Rupp explained that not only would this violate company policy, but operators were just too busy to listen in to any calls. Finally, Fortas revealed his "smoking gun" piece of evidence, "Yes I know . . . but Bill Douglas says there was something fishy about that call. He told me that the person he talked to was not an operator. It was a man!"

Rupp quickly pointed out to Fortas that there were indeed three male operators in Yakima, one of whom was blind. "You know, I think you're looking at the wrong end of the line," said Rupp. "Bill Douglas was brought up in the Yakima country, and the people there take him for granted. They don't pay much attention to him. And when he does come into town from his ranch he looks like any other farmer. I think he likes it that way. And I don't think those Yakima folks are much interested in what he might do about Vietnam. Don't you think that, if there was a leak, it was in Washington D.C.? I gather that leaks are a way of life there." Seeing the wisdom of the argument, Fortas decided to drop his "investigation" and Douglas's "suit."

But Douglas had the last word. Someone sent him an editorial cartoon showing an American military bomber marked the "Defense Department" leading waves of other planes in bombing not Cambodia but a cabin and a billboard reading, "WELCOME TO GOOSE PRAIRIE, WASH. HOME OF JUSTICE DOUGLAS," with the pilots cavalierly saying "OOPS!!!" He framed the cartoon and hung it in a place of honor on the wall of his office, right across from his desk.

·   ·   ·

The 1973–1974 term offered Douglas the opportunity to deal with the growing number of programs offering preference based on race to law-school applicants. Marco DeFunis, Jr., a Caucasian, was suing the

University of Washington Law School for denying him admission while admitting under its "affirmative action" program minority applicants with lesser qualifications. DeFunis argued that this denial was discriminatory and thus violated the equal-protection clause of the Fourteenth Amendment. After winning his case in trial court, DeFunis was admitted to the law school. Thanks to a stay issued by Douglas, sitting as the supervisory Justice of the U.S. Court of Appeals Ninth Circuit, DeFunis was allowed to remain in school during the appeals process and was about to graduate with his class by the time the case reached the Court.

After being alerted by his law clerk Ira Ellman that he should vote to take this case because "there really was some kind of quota here," Douglas could see that he would be the swing vote on whether to grant *certiorari*. Douglas was uncharacteristically uncertain as to how he would decide. So he told Ellman to draft an opinion. "I don't know about these tests," said Douglas, referring to the Law School Admissions Test (LSAT), which is used to test the aptitude of prospective law-school applicants. Three days later, after the Court decided not to hear the case because DeFunis was about to graduate, Douglas decided to write a dissent to the denial. The reason, he explained to his clerk, was simple: "I might not be around next time this issue comes up."

After considerable back and forth with his clerk in writing the opinion, Douglas's arguments against affirmative-action programs were instructive. First, he vigorously attacked the LSAT, even without evidence to prove his point, as being so racially biased that on occasion there must be reverse bias by a law school to correct it. The only requirement for him was that "the consideration of each application [be done] *in a racially neutral way*. Since [the] LSAT reflects questions touching on cultural backgrounds, the Admissions Committee acted properly in my view in setting minority applications apart for separate processing. . . . The melting pot is not designed to homogenize people, making them uniform in consistency. The melting pot as I understand it is a figure of speech that depicts the wide diversities tolerated by the First Amendment under one flag." To bolster his argument for the need to consider diversity in admissions, Douglas offered examples from his life experience:

I do know, coming as I do from Indian country in Washington, that many of the young Indians know little about Adam Smith or Karl Marx but are deeply imbued with the spirit and philosophy of Robert B. Jim of the Yakimas, Chief Seattle of the Muckleshoots,

and Chief Joseph of the Nez Perce which offer competitive attitudes towards life, fellow man, and nature. . . . At least as respects
Indians, blacks, and Chicanos—as well as those from Asian cultures—
I think a separate classification of these applicants is warranted,
lest race be a subtle force in eliminating minority members because
of cultural differences.

Douglas made very clear, however, that he had no tolerance for a
quota system, by which a certain number of the seats for the incoming
class were reserved for certain minorities: "The reservation of a proportion of the law school class for members of selected minority
groups is fraught with similar dangers, for one must immediately determine which groups are to receive favored treatment and which are
to be excluded, the proportions of the class that are to be allocated to
each, and even the criteria by which to determine whether an individual is a member of a favored group." Only a policy of admissions
based on racial neutrality was the answer: "The purpose of the University of Washington cannot be to produce black lawyers for blacks, Polish lawyers for Poles, Jewish lawyers for Jews, Irish lawyers for Irish. It
should be to produce good lawyers for Americans and not to place
First Amendment barriers against anyone. . . . A segregated admissions
process creates suggestions of stigma and caste no less than a segregated classroom, and in the end it may produce that result despite its
contrary intentions." For Douglas, who had once been denied access
to the undergraduate portion of this very school because of his
family's finances, the programs of affirmative action, which diminished the use of merit as an admissions criterion, were not permissible:
"All races can compete fairly at all professional levels. So far as race is
concerned, any state-sponsored preference to one race over another in
that competition is in my view 'invidious' and violative of the Equal
Protection Clause." He was prepared to send this case back to the
lower court to determine both the impact of the LSAT and this application process on various groups.

In offering these views, Douglas had done more than preview much
of the Court's debate in the landmark affirmative-action case, *Regents of
the University of California v. Bakke,* which was to be announced four
years later. In fact, his argument that admissions programs should be
racially neutral and based more on merit foreshadowed debates that
would rage in the United States decades later.

The following day, April 24, 1974, the Court announced its ruling
in a Florida case brought by Mel Kahn, challenging the state's annual
five-hundred-dollar property-tax exemption for widows but not for

widowers. This was normally the kind of discriminatory law that Douglas would bludgeon to death using the Fourteenth Amendment equal-protection clause. But in this case Douglas wrote with conservative William Rehnquist and Warren Burger to uphold the law, while the other liberals, William Brennan and Thurgood Marshall, were making his usual arguments against him in dissent. Douglas's four-page majority opinion, one of a number nicknamed "plane-trip specials" by his staff because they were actually drafted very quickly during his Friday plane trips to one of his many weekend lecture sites, was hardly typical of his liberal views. The man who for years had pleaded for the imaginative use of the equal-protection clause to force the states to protect poor people now sounded instead like a Burger Court regular in finding this to be a constitutionally justifiable policy: "There can be no dispute that the financial difficulties confronting the lone woman in Florida or in any other State exceed those facing the man. . . . While the widower can usually continue in the occupation which preceded his spouse's death, in many cases the widow will find herself suddenly forced into a job market with which she is unfamiliar, and in which, because of her former economic dependency, she will have fewer skills to offer." For him, this law protecting women should be upheld: "We deal here with a state tax law reasonably designed to further the state policy of cushioning the financial impact of spousal loss upon the sex for which that loss imposes a disproportionately heavy burden." It was left to Brennan and Marshall to point out in dissent that not all widows are poor. That being the case, they asked, why not closely tailor your law to protect only the poor widows but not the rich ones who do not need such clearly discriminatory help?

When his clerks asked why he was ruling this way, Douglas looked at them squarely and said simply, "I've known a lot of starving widows." Law clerk Richard Benka conjectured, "Perhaps he was thinking of his own mother, for he had at the time been working on his autobiography. . . . The Justice was voting to uphold the statute—no doubts, no second thoughts, no more discussions." None of the assistants could know that in fact Julia Fisk Douglas, who was far from "starving" when Douglas was young, would have found the property-tax exemption quite useful in relieving her of the burden of taxes on the various plots of land that she owned in Yakima.

·   ·   ·

In the summer of 1974, Douglas's sense of justice was sated when the tables turned for one of his tormentors: Richard Milhous Nixon. By this time, Douglas was making it very clear what he thought of Nixon.

Asked earlier that year by a student at the University of Delaware whether he would retire, Douglas spat out: "Not as long as that no good, goddamned son of a bitch is still in the White House. If they cut off my head, I'd simply tuck it under my arm and march right back to the Bench."

With the Watergate case unfolding, the Court heard the expedited appeal raising the question of whether Nixon, relying on the power of executive privilege to keep discussions with advisers and subordinates secret, could refuse to turn over his tapes of Oval Office conversations to the Watergate special prosecutor, the Senate, and a grand jury. For Douglas, this case was one of just deserts. Now the man whom he was still convinced had been tapping and bugging the Court's conversations over the years faced being destroyed politically by his *own* taped conversations.

Even though the Court was still in session when the case of *United States v. Nixon* was considered, Douglas was not in Washington. With his own work completed for the regular term, he had left early for Goose Prairie. His initial thirty-page explanatory memorandum on the case, drafted from his cottage with the long-distance telephone assistance of his law clerk Don Kelley, was circulated three days before the oral argument.

After explaining that the Court had the power to hear this case, Douglas argued that "no executive privilege of the President . . . justifies withholding these materials from the District Court." For Douglas, "to allow [Nixon] to conceal from a court information which may be critical to the fairness of a trial of named defendants would be a monstrous affront to the rule of law under which we live." With each new draft, Douglas's level of hyperbole against this use of executive privilege increased, until he was writing that "every citizen, high or low, has a right to privacy and confidentiality concerning his conversations except as they be reached by process for use in a civil or criminal trial. This present controversy is a prelude to a serious criminal trial. In that setting it stands on no higher footing than does a subpoena against a member of the Mafia."

For the final time in his career, Douglas interrupted his summer vacation to return to the capital for the oral argument on July 8, to be followed the next day by the Court's conference deciding the case. Even the law clerks could see the salutary effect of this case on Douglas's temperament. As soon as he walked into his chambers and saw his law clerks, the Justice went over to the one he had not yet met—Jay Kelly Wright—and briskly shook his hand while saying "welcome." Wright's coclerk, Alan Austin, said that this was the warmest greeting that any of them had received, but warned he "should not let this go to [his] head."

As soon as the Court's conference ended, Douglas returned to his chambers and began hitting his buzzer repeatedly, indicating that he wanted to see all of his law clerks immediately. As the young men filed into his office, expecting to be rebuked as a group, they noticed that they were being followed by Harry Datcher, who was carrying a beat-up old cardboard box that made clinking noises with each of his steps. Once the group was fully assembled, Douglas marched over to the box, grabbed a bottle of scotch from it, and began pouring shots for everyone. The Justice poured a Dubonnet for himself, saying that by now any other kind of liquor made him sneeze, and then raised his glass in a toast to celebrate the Court's unanimous vote ordering Nixon to turn over the tapes to the special prosecutor. This decision, he explained, would confirm the notion of all members of the "government being bound by the rule of law."

In the end, Douglas withdrew his draft opinion, as did all his colleagues, in order to allow a compromise unanimous opinion to be authored under the Chief Justice's name. Thus, the Court ruled that while the inherent power of executive privilege did in theory exist, it could not override the needs of the federal courts and the Senate, absent any compelling presidential justification, such as national security or military secrets. With no further basis for withholding the tapes, Nixon turned them over, and on August 9 resigned his office, being replaced by his vice president, Douglas's onetime inquisitor during his impeachment fight, Gerald R. Ford.

It was in one other opinion at the end of that term that Douglas raised real questions about his state of mind, if anyone had known his actual early life history. On July 8, Douglas was in dissent again on the Vietnam issue, when a majority of the Court was unwilling to review the appeal of Mark Avrech, a Marine who had been court-martialed for criticizing the willingness of the South Vietnamese allies to fight and arguing that "the United States has no business over here." For Douglas, free speech should always be protected: "Talk is of course incitement; but not all incitement leads to action. What appellee in this case wrote out with the purpose of showing to the Marines in his unit, might, if released, have created only revulsion. . . . Secrecy and suppression of views which the Court today sanctions increases rather than repels the dangers of the world in which we live. I think full dedication to the spirit of the First Amendment is the real solvent of the dangers and tensions of the day."

What made this statement most unusual was his evidence to justify this holding: "Soldiers, lounging around, speak carefully of officers who are within earshot. But in World War I we were free to lambaste General 'Black Jack' Pershing who was distant, remote, and mythical. We also groused about the bankers' war, the munitions makers' war in which we had volunteered. What we said would have offended our military superiors. But since we could write our Congressmen or Senators about it, we saw no reason why we could not talk it out among ourselves." Reading this, one could almost see young Bill Douglas sitting in the enlisted men's mess in the trenches in Europe, complaining to his fellow soldiers. With few knowing the true story of his very limited Students' Army Training Corps service at Whitman College during the war, Douglas was now freely rewriting his legend into case law.

.   .   .

But that was not the only place where he was recrafting his public image.

THE APPROXIMATE
MR. JUSTICE DOUGLAS

The Douglas I knew . . . is as different from the
Douglas the public knows as any two people alive.

—*Simon Rifkind*

By this time, Douglas's perception of his life and career on the Court
had changed so much that the initial Horatio Alger/Crown Prince images he had created in his early memoirs no longer fully explained who
he saw in his mirror. Douglas now had a sense of a life misspent and
opportunities lost. Why had he not been able to afford to go to the
University of Washington, which would have gotten him the Rhodes
scholarship? Why had he not gotten the clerkship with Harlan Fiske
Stone? Why had his law career not worked out on Wall Street? Why
had he missed out on the vice presidency that FDR once wanted for
him or the presidency that should have been his? While others would
look at William O. Douglas's life and be awestruck by his fabulous
achievements, the Justice himself was troubled by the might-have-
beens. Given the way that the public now perceived him, these became
the questions that Douglas was trying to work out in print. Like a master portrait artist reusing canvases, Douglas now tried to cover his old
images with a completely new autobiographical portrait.

While Dagmar Hamilton labored on revising his memoirs, Douglas
could not resist trying out one of his new tales on an audience. The opportunity came when he journeyed to Low Memorial Library at Columbia University on April 7, 1973, for a celebratory gathering of his
old law-school classmates of the now legendary class of '25. From
among dozens of legal titans present, Dean Michael Sovern chose to
confer the Columbia Law School Association's much coveted Medal of
Excellence on both Douglas and Judge Simon Rifkind, now recognized as the "lawyers' lawyer" in New York.

When Douglas rose to speak, in his rehearsed, impromptu-appearing storytelling fashion, he offered his recollections of law school. Harlan Fiske Stone was appointed to the Supreme Court in 1925, he began, and it surprised no one that he immediately looked to his old law school for his first law clerk. Since Alfred McCormack had graduated first in the class of '25, and he, Douglas, had been second, Stone chose McCormack instead of him. That decision, Douglas recalled, had depressed him for days. And so McCormack went to Washington while Douglas went to work in a Wall Street law firm. In telling this tale, Douglas expected that his distinguished and learned audience could easily draw the ironic lesson here: Now he was the Supreme Court Justice picking the law clerks.

But as he finished this tale, rather than nodding in agreement, his classmates began looking at one another quizzically. The real truth, they all knew, was that the Yakima Apple Knocker had been nowhere close to graduating second in his class or, for that matter, to the law clerkship. Herman Benjamin, a Law Review compatriot who is acknowledged as the class's historian, remembered, "Not only can I assure you that Al McCormack was the universal and obvious choice for the clerkship, but . . . if Douglas was competing for anything with McCormack, it was for no better than *fifth* in the class. . . . Douglas's memory on this matter is never very precise. I have concluded that he is always a little general about the facts."

Douglas's classmates also recognized the real origin of his story of missing out on the Supreme Court clerkship to Alfred McCormack. One of the reasons that McCormack's law-clerk selection had been so easy, everyone knew, was because of his service as editor-in-chief of the Law Review. And, they all recalled, since this position had been first offered to Herman Benjamin, who turned it down for the post as associate decisions editor, and given his higher class standing than both of them, it was he rather than Douglas who would later have been the likely nominee. "I've often wondered how my life would have been different if I had accepted the offer," Benjamin mused. So it was then that Douglas's classmates decided to change their old nickname for him to a new one, which now seemed to suit him better: "The Approximate Mr. Justice Douglas."

·   ·   ·

By 1973, the public, like his classmates, believed that after his nearly four decades on the public stage it knew everything that there was to know about William O. Douglas. But in reality people did not know him at all. Now, fearing that time was running out and that his public legacy was not secure, Douglas decided to do what he had been doing so successfully for years: reintroduce himself to the public through his newly revised memoirs. In so doing, he set out to create one final, indelible character: "*Justice* William O. Douglas."

Go East, Young Man was published to much fanfare in 1974. After years of retelling the story of his life, "the Storyteller" finally got his tale just the way he wanted it: the brush with death from polio, James O. Cull cheating the family, the family's desperate poverty, battling poverty at Whitman College, "riding the rods" to law school, abandoning a lucrative living on Wall Street to work in a small firm in Yakima, leaving Columbia with no job in hand after a courageous fight against the school's president, and the fabulous offer from Robert Maynard Hutchins to work at Chicago that he never fully accepted. After *Go East, Young Man* everyone understood completely how this iconoclastic, fiercely independent, courageous protector of the common man and underdog on the Supreme Court had been shaped this way from birth.

Once again, the critics loved his autobiographical effort. Nat Hentoff gushed in *The New York Times Book Review* that the book was "so continually arresting that it reads like the kind of novel one wishes would not end." *Time* added: "This volume . . . often seems extraordinary enough to match many of the stories that surround the forging of America's great men." And now, these tales became the foundation for virtually every subsequent journalistic and academic portrait of Douglas's life and work.

The new memoir turned out to have only one flaw: It was no more accurate than the story he had told to his law-school classmates the year before. Gone was the insecure Orville Douglas, the boy who had lived a relatively normal life but had been overprotected by his mother and misled into thinking he was desperately poor. Gone, too, was the real Bill Douglas, the insecure young attorney who kept quitting his jobs, could not get his career started, and by his own admission had a "macaroni spine." And gone was the actual Professor Douglas, the ambitious legal scholar who used his staff and played Yale and Chicago against each other for his services while he decided his career direction. Now, with this new image, he sought to bury forever the true origins of the man Douglas had grown to be.

In its place was a largely new story of the confident, self-reliant, and uniquely talented young man who would one day become "Justice William O. Douglas." The portraits of various members of Douglas's family were changed to fit the heroic ancestral image that he now preferred. His grandfather, Orville Fisk, the two-time deserter of the Union army, became "barely sixteen when Lincoln was elected in 1860 but answered the call to arms and ended up with Grant at Vicksburg. . . . When [he] returned from the Civil War, he brought with him a bad case of malaria from which he never completely recovered." His father, Reverend William Douglas, the man who had ignored his family in pursuit of his religious calling, became instead a warm, loving family man who would "lift me high in the air, to squeeze my hand and give me masculine praise . . . [with] the laugh, [and] the jingle of coins in the pockets."

The rest of the "characters" in Douglas's life story were similarly reconstructed. His mother now became a poor, oppressed widow who had been cheated of her life savings by James O. Cull when Douglas was a child of six. Put in different hands, the story of Douglas's early life could easily have been the dramatic tale of the feisty and independent widow striving with success to keep her family afloat financially, even at the cost of her own psychological well-being, and producing a feisty and independent son. By erasing the details of his early life, he became the poor young lad who overcame adversity all on his own.

He also added much more compelling detail to his polio story. After having stated in *Of Men and Mountains* that he "did not recognize [the infantile paralysis] for what it was until years later," he now explained for the first time the interesting tale of how he eventually learned of the diagnosis. Here he revealed that it was polio expert Dr. George Draper, "the main seminal influence" in his life, who had played the key role in helping him to deal with the psychological effects of the disease.

According to the Justice's account, once he learned of Douglas's early polio episode, Draper said, "Tell [FDR] of your own polio experience." But, Douglas wrote, "I never did. I felt it would be like talking to the President about his own illness, and I never mentioned that either directly or indirectly. So far as I know, FDR was never aware of the fact that I went through as a boy what he experienced as a man."

With this newly revised account, Douglas had bolstered his own pedigree on the disease by claiming that FDR's own doctor had confirmed the diagnosis. And Douglas did so without fear of contradiction from the man who had once written that the Justice had actually suffered from a "severe and prolonged intestinal colic" as a young boy, because Draper had by this time been dead for fifteen years.

Douglas also now wrote engagingly about his repeated clashes with the "pompous" and "pseudo-intellectual" Whitman College president, Stephen B. L. Penrose, who had "the instincts of a stuffed shirt." As the developing young campus rebel, Douglas wrote, he had helped his classmates saw partly through a short staircase connected to a temporary dock on the campus's small pond, Lakum Duckum. As President Penrose, singing from a boat during an outdoor opera, stepped onto this dock, it collapsed, causing him to fall in the water. But Frances Penrose Owen and her older sister, Mary, the daughters of Penrose, both of whom attended Whitman College during Douglas's years there, were quite offended by what they perceived to be Douglas's inaccurate portrait of his relationship with their father. One of Frances's prize mementos from those years was an enlarged photo, taken at a Beta Theta Pi picnic, showing a very attractive Frances and a rail-thin Orville Douglas sitting near a pile of logs by Mill Stream, eating their sandwiches. The looks in their eyes and the smiles on their faces indicated that they knew each other well and liked each other a great deal.

"You see," said Frances Penrose Owen carefully, "*I* was the girl he saw as much of as anybody at that time." Pointing out that he had brought the president's daughter to the picnic and to the yearly Beta dance, Owen made clear that contrary to Douglas's carefully honed images of revolting against "the Establishment" at Whitman College, he had literally courted it.

Douglas exercised his literary license further about his college years. He wrote about how desperate he became, with war fever sweeping Whitman College, to join the army. After deciding not to join the Marines, in April 1917, because "mother was dependent on me . . . [for] the necessary twenty dollars a month," Douglas wrote of his difficulties in trying to join the military because his green-red color blindness made it difficult to pass the eye examination. Only the armistice, he wrote, prevented him from reporting to artillery school, orders that had been "held up for days."

But color blindness did not exclude *anyone* from either the army or the Students' Army Training Corps (SATC) during World War I. In fact, had he really wanted to enter the war the medical examination would have presented no problem for him. Douglas's classmate Hallam Mendenhall, the brother of Jack Mendenhall, who joined the SATC regiment along with him, remembered: "They had to get people, and fast. So there wasn't any physical exam at all. If you could walk into the registration center, you passed the medical exam. We didn't take any color-blindness test or any other type of medical test for that matter." The truth was that Orville Douglas's sole obstacle to joining the armed forces before August 31, 1918, was that any applicant under the age of twenty-one needed parental permission to join. He knew that his mother never would have sent her "Treasure" to war.

But if Douglas wanted to portray himself as being so patriotic and desperate to join up, what happened after the law was changed and those over eighteen years old were made eligible said a great deal about his actual desire to serve in the military. The fact, of course, was that rather than enlisting, Douglas's service was limited to two months and ten days, from October 1 to December 10, 1918, as a "Pvt. S.A.T.C." who marched on Whitman's campus and got the flu. By the time the war ended, as the discharge papers filed for Douglas by Captain Chris Jensen, U.S. Army Infantry at Whitman College, made clear, there was no record of his induction into the army. But it made no difference to Douglas that he had not been an army private fighting in the trenches in France in 1918 as he posed, after the war was over, for his senior class picture in his newly arrived uniform. Hallam Mendenhall recalls: "We all knew we were not in the military. We marched around campus like we were in the infantry. And we took classes in military subjects to get ready to be a soldier, and we learned discipline and such. But we all knew we were not in the military."

The real reason for Douglas's decision to join the college's SATC was plainly apparent to his college chums at the time. Hallam Mendenhall recalled: "We all *had* to be there [in the SATC]. If we hadn't— we'd have been drafted." Indeed, when the draft age was reduced from twenty-one to eighteen, on August 31, 1918, nineteen-year-old William O. Douglas, unmarried and absolutely healthy by military standards (in spite of his color blindness), immediately became prime draft material. As one of only four men in his Whitman class who remained behind "to serve" in the SATC unit rather than a military unit in Europe, Douglas was also one of only a handful of males in his class who would be able to graduate on time.

·   ·   ·

His Columbia Law School classmates were just as surprised by the rest of Douglas's new tale in his memoirs of how he had gone to school as they had been the year before by the "lost clerkship" story. It was Douglas's description of the timing of his marriage that troubled classmate Simon Rifkind the most. "Through my tutoring service," Douglas wrote, "I struck it rich at Columbia. I not only paid all my expenses, I also banked a couple of thousand dollars, enough so that in 1924 I was, for the first time in my life, fairly well set up financially. That summer I returned West and married Mildred Riddle, graduate of the University of Oregon, resident of LaGrande, Oregon, and Latin teacher in the Yakima High School, where I had met her. . . . While we were living in New York, Mildred taught in suburban schools around the metropolitan area, though never in the city itself." However, the Douglases' marriage certificate in the La Grande, Oregon, county records shows that the marriage occurred on August 16, 1923, a full year earlier than the Justice now claimed. Rifkind knew that his classmate was deliberately changing the date of his marriage to hide the fact that Mildred had put him through his last two years of law school. But this was no mere typographical error; rather, it was the way Douglas had been telling the story for thirty years.

This time, though, rewriting history proved to be not so easy. By writing a year of his marriage out of existence, Douglas had robbed the longtime residents of the town of Bernardsville, New Jersey, where Mildred had lived while supporting his law-school studies, of a tiny contribution to American history. So they decided to get even. In a feature article for the Bernardsville News in late 1975, Mary Louise Shaw observed: "Douglas's memory seems a bit hazy on the year of their marriage. In 'Go East Young Man' he puts their wedding date as summer, 1924. And yet the Bernardsville News of October 18, 1923, records the hiring of 'Mrs. Mildred Riddle Douglas.'" "Although his wife was universally admired," the reporter explained after canvassing local residents for their recollections of the Douglases, "Douglas did not appear to have made a favorable impression locally." By burying the true tale of how others had aided his rise to prominence, Douglas created a new story of "pulling himself up by the bootstraps."

As soon as the book was published, though, the people in his hometown of Yakima also realized that they could not rely on William O. Douglas's account. In recounting how he had returned to work in 1926 with James O. Cull in Yakima, rather than, as it had actually happened, in 1927, Douglas was able to write out of his fictional life the breakdown that compelled him to leave the Cravath firm, the period of unemployment when he was supported by his wife, his second failed stint with that firm, and the abysmal four-day (not as he wrote the "few months") trip to work with Cull in Yakima before fleeing back to New York to the Columbia Law School job, which he had never relinquished. But there would be no objection from James O. Cull, as his death sixteen years earlier ensured his silence.

Still, too many people knew the truth to fail to notice. Attorney Fred Velikanje, who practiced law in Yakima in the 1920s, was baffled by Douglas's account. Just a few years earlier at an American Bar Association midyear meeting in Chicago, Velikanje had been standing in the lobby of the Palmer Hotel when Douglas, who was in town for the same convention, suddenly approached him. "Fred," said the Justice, "I've been meaning to call you. I have a question for you."

"What's that, Bill?" replied the surprised Velikanje.

"Do you remember who I practiced law with in Yakima in the 1920s?" asked the Justice.

Velikanje was stunned by the question, because he and all of his old legal friends remembered it very well. "Why, it was James O. Cull of course!" he said quickly.

"That's right," said Douglas. "I'm writing my memoirs, and for the life of me I just couldn't remember who I practiced law with then." Without another word, Douglas spun on his heels and was gone, leaving Velikanje shaking his head. This he would do again when he read the new book.

Whatever the errors or exaggerations in his new memoirs, Douglas had finally written an autobiographical portrait that for him was just right.

A POOR OLD MAN

You see me here, you gods, a poor old man, As full
of grief as age; wretched in both!

—*William Shakespeare,* King Lear

Christmas was fast approaching in late 1974, and Douglas's office staff
braced for his annual Ebenezer Scrooge imitation. This was the time of
the year when he frequently reminded them of his impoverished childhood, as he drove them all to work even harder. But now, instead of
snarling, he uncharacteristically offered them some time off. Douglas
explained with a wide smile that even though he was fighting a
bronchial infection, he was going on a New Year's Day vacation. And,
he added, rather than taking work along, he would be reading James
Michener's *The Drifters.*

What seemed most strange was his choice of vacation spot: the
beach at Nassau in the Bahamas. Normally, the light-complected Justice preferred to go to the mountains because of his tendency to get
sun sickness. But, he said, Cathy wanted to go to the beach, so that was
where they were going. Then, putting on his tweed hat, Douglas jaun-
tily waved good-bye to his entire staff, wishing them a good New Year.

Once she and Douglas arrived on the island and settled into their
hotel room, Cathy announced that she was going downstairs to buy
some magazines. Douglas, though, had learned to his distress that a
lawyers' convention was in the same hotel, making it impossible for
him to leave the room without being accosted. So he said that he
would confine himself to the room. When his wife returned from her
trip, she found him lying crumpled on the floor.

Douglas was semiconscious, moaning in severe pain and unable to
move the entire left side of his body. His upper dental plate lay broken
on the floor. A local doctor was called, and the diagnosis was not

good. He had suffered a massive stroke, and, in a crisis in which speed of treatment is of the essence, he was a plane trip away from the best medical facilities.

Ironically, his fate now lay in the hands of the man who had once tried to mount Douglas's head on his political trophy wall. As soon as President Gerald R. Ford, then at his vacation retreat in Vail, Colorado, was notified of the crisis, he immediately ordered a military jet to transport the Justice's personal physician, Dr. Thomas Connolly, to his side and then ferry them home. For Douglas, it was the cruelest of ironies. "My God," he mumbled with great difficulty to his wife, "you know they'll drop us in Havana."

Once he arrived at Walter Reed Army Hospital, three doctors labored over him, concluding that only his fabulous physical condition for his age had kept him from dying immediately. An IQ test was administered with some difficulty, only to reveal a score of 100, which while well below his normal genius level was still acceptable for a severe stroke victim. But with doctors disagreeing on the best form of drug therapy, Douglas was kept in a twilight zone of narcotic reverie.

While Douglas had never been a good patient, the bedside manner of the staff at Walter Reed did little to improve his demeanor. A young nurse came in and, without any introduction, began asking him a series of very basic questions to test his mental alertness. What month was it? What was his name? Could he tell her which month Christmas came in? Was July hotter than the winter? Ever the feisty soul, even in his painful condition, he mumbled back a quiz of his own for the young woman: How do you know if you are sleeping with an elephant? When she could not answer, he told her with supreme satisfaction that you look for the *E* on his pajamas. And then he refused to speak to her again.

A while later, one of the hospital's psychiatrists came in and began reading Douglas's mail, leading him to feel that his privacy was being invaded. After explaining that he was there to determine whether the Justice was mentally competent, the doctor asked whether some legal opinion in the stack of papers around the room might demonstrate his state of mind. The Justice directed him to a complicated portion of an opinion dealing with Wharton's Rules of Evidence, only on the condition that the doctor submit to an examination about its contents after reading it. When the doctor's eyes glazed over after just a few pages of reading, he complained that the material was incomprehensible to him. Douglas responded that in this case perhaps the doctor, and not the patient, was *non compos mentis*.

With the press clamoring for some word on Douglas's condition,

Barrett McGurn, the secretive Supreme Court press officer, released an encouraging report on the morning of Friday, January 3: "Justice Douglas spent a restful night and has shown improvement in his left-side weakness. He continues on anticoagulants and began physical therapy yesterday. He is alert, on a full diet and has an excellent appetite. His vital signs remain stable and he is resting comfortably." But insiders knew the truth; a quick death would have been more kind.

But Douglas was determined not to give in. To hell with intensive care, he decided. Work had to be done. "Where's Bagby? Where's Bagby?" he mumbled over and over again. Not knowing what a "Bagby" was, the hospital staff became concerned that the Justice was regressing mentally, until someone learned that he was actually calling for his secretary Marty Bagby. A call was made and Marty Bagby fought her way through a raging snowstorm to the hospital. When she walked into her boss's hospital room, she found him sitting in a wheelchair in the same checked shirt he had packed for his vacation. "What took you so long?" he barked. From that moment on, she knew, it would be business as usual, or as usual as he could make it.

To stave off any rumors of an impending retirement, Douglas's office staff quickly put out the word that his work output was back to normal, with him continuing to rule on appeal petitions and write his opinions. In fact, during his few moments of lucidity, the work style was very different. "It was like spinning judicial roulette," explained Dagmar Hamilton. "The Justice had a hundred-and-three-degree fever and was basically *non compos mentis*. They would hold out the briefs in front of him and say, 'What do you think of this one, Mr. Justice?' And he would just say yes or no; you just didn't know how he was going to vote."

As bad as things had been for Douglas, though, the worst was yet to come. His kidneys began to degenerate, causing fluid to build up in his lungs, and the doctors feared that a blood clot might break off and kill him. So, on January 12 they put him in a circular aluminum stretcher device containing a weblike structure of leather straps with which a patient can be immobilized while tipping his body upside down. When the attendant tried to place Douglas's head into the contraption's leather, nooselike neck restraint, the Justice resisted, fearing that he would be unable to look around. But soon his breathing got so labored that he became dizzy and passed out, and the deed was done.

Now victimized by both the severe paranoia and the confusion that can be brought on by a stroke, Douglas had become convinced that his medical treatment constituted torture by his enemies from the far right. To him, they were seeking to gather enough information for another impeachment effort, and he wondered if the government was treating him like the Soviet dissenters whom Nikita Khrushchev had once sent to insane asylums for "treatment."

When Marty Bagby returned to the hospital the next day, she found her boss helpless, hanging upside down. "Get your pad and come over here," she heard him gurgle through the leather noose. Douglas explained that he was being "stretched" for political information in some kind of rack-and-screw device left over from the Spanish inquisition. And, he mumbled, he was ready to fight it in the only way he knew how. So, seated with her ear placed next to his mouth, Bagby took down Douglas's words as he literally choked out a Supreme Court opinion. Like so many other Douglas opinions, this one drew upon his classic positions—antigovernment, antibureaucracy, and pro–oppressed common man—only now the person being oppressed by the government bureaucracy was himself. If this was how the Walter Reed Army Hospital would treat him, a man who had served his nation honorably in World War I, he argued, what hope was there for those draftees who opposed the Vietnam War?

By mid-March, Douglas decided that he had endured enough of the army's "torture." When Justice Harry Blackmun came to visit, Douglas asked if he would help to spring him from his confinement. Blackmun would not play along, so for days Douglas planned his escape with his messenger, Harry Datcher. Observing an unguarded door down the hall from his therapy room, Douglas planned his dash to freedom. "The door became an obsession," said one observer. "He saw it as the perfect escape route back to the court." And they might have succeeded, too, had the doctors not discovered the conspiracy. Since this was the first evidence they had seen of Douglas's improvement in condition, though, they decided to grant him a twenty-four-hour pass to return home. But typically, rather than going home, Douglas ordered Datcher to drive him to the office, where he knew a pile of work awaited him. When he adamantly refused to return to the hospital, the doctors agreed to release him, but only if he promised to return three times a week for therapy sessions.

All Bill Douglas wanted now was to return to his normal life and resume his work. But the press was not willing to let him do so. No sooner had he arrived home than he was accosted by a television reporter who had staked out the residence. Upon being asked about his physical condition, Douglas responded as he long had, mumbling a challenge to the man to hike with him on the C & O Canal in late April.

But Douglas's body told him otherwise. When he returned to hear oral argument for the first time, on March 24, his staff continued to try to present the image that the situation was normal. "He was screaming at us again, writing his usual terse notes," they insisted. But the glassy look in his eyes, the sling on his left arm, and the frequent lapses in his conversation told members of the press that it was not true. The following day, even Barrett McGurn distanced himself from the situation by issuing a carefully worded Court press release in Douglas's name: "The justice is using a sling on his left arm which he said he injured in a fall against a wall at the time he became ill."

When the rumors persisted, Douglas decided to break the Court's secrecy tradition by giving a televised interview with reporters. As the members of the press trooped into his office, they found Douglas seated behind his desk, looking as casual as possible. But as soon as he spoke, his slurred speech gave them license to go for the kill.

After a half-dozen basic questions about his general state of health, someone asked, "Have you thought of whether there are any circumstances in which you would consider stepping down from the Court? . . . Have you said, if I'm not able to walk by the end of this term, if I don't have my strength back by the end of this term, I'll step down?"

"No," responded Douglas, "but walking has very little to do with the ability to discharge the duties of the Court."

Then another question was shouted out: "Mr. Justice, I've read in the newspaper that you just walked out of the hospital and didn't tell your doctor. Is that true?"

By this time, though, Douglas's concentration had begun to wane, and he started staring at his desk as though he had heard nothing. When he then began responding to every question with one-word responses, Press Secretary McGurn broke in to say, "The Justice is due on the bench at 10:00. I think there is time for one more question."

With that, one of the newsmen shouted out the question that was on all of their minds: "Mr. Justice Douglas, do you have any feeling about staying on the bench long enough so that someone other than President Ford would name your replacement?"

The mere question seemed to snap Douglas back into gear as he stared back at the questioner angrily for several moments and then stammered as clearly as he could: "That's not a factor in any of my calculations." And with that, the news conference was over.

Reports of this shaky performance so disturbed the Chief Justice that he began to wonder what to do about his senior colleague. And his concern was well justified. Douglas was now reduced to making cameo appearances on the Bench, being present for only eleven hours of oral argument that spring. And doing even that was not easy. Just to hear the arguments, the marshals had to lift him into his specially equipped chair as his colleagues walked to their seats. Never very vocal on the Bench, Douglas now never said a word. When the day's arguments were over, and the Justices exited behind the purple velour curtains, Douglas would remain seated, staring helplessly at the audience from his chair as he awaited help to depart.

Even the simplest aspects of daily life now seemed almost overwhelming for the Justice. His unwillingness to use his new ill-fitted upper dentures to replace the broken dental plate made it difficult for him to speak clearly. By this time, his normally high-pitched voice had also taken on an unnatural shrillness, making him sound like some sort of spirit coming from a distant past. Because of his impaired eyesight, reading was now virtually impossible. The drug therapy, which lessened the incessant pain on his left side, had cut his usual twelve- to fourteen-hour workday down to only three or four hours. And not being able to perform his duties became psychologically crushing to him. "He couldn't use his left arm, or his hand," remembered his son, Bill Jr. "And it is terribly difficult to open up a law book and hold it open and take notes [with one hand]. . . . [The books] would close up on him, [and] they would fall off the desk. And it was frustrating beyond belief to him."

Despite these problems, the work on the closely divided Court was too important for the Justice to give it up. On April 21, he sat on the Bench to hear ninety minutes of the most visible oral arguments of the year, concerning a challenge to the death penalty. To those seated in the audience, the once vibrant Wild Bill now looked more dead than alive. His face was as white as chalk and appeared horribly gaunt. His mouth hung half open from one side, with his eyes glazed and seeming to bulge unnaturally out of his head as he sat slumped to one side of his chair. At one point in the proceedings, rather than focusing on the arguments, Douglas tried instead to write one of his legendary notes on a four-by-four-inch pad, but when he was finished the audience suffered in silence as he tried fruitlessly to separate the page from the rest of the pad with his one good hand. Only when Douglas began beating the pad against the bench did a marshal scurry up behind him to help.

The next day, Douglas was transported to the Rusk Institute of Rehabilitation Medicine in New York for intensive six-hour-a-day therapy. His only lifeline seemed to be the pile of work that he insisted be delivered to him despite his enfeebled condition. Longtime girlfriend Elena Leonardo went to his side to help him with the stacks of legal documents to be considered. "We didn't want the liberals to lose the seat on the Court, so we just had to get through all of the work that the healthy Justices were doing," Leonardo recalled. Realizing that he would need even more help to keep up with his duties, Douglas began demanding that his Court staff join him. Despite their past difficulties, as soon as Chief Justice Warren Burger learned about the request, he gave the staff the use of a new station wagon and a gas card to answer the call to duty. From then on, every weekend, Harry Datcher, Marty Bagby, and Sandra Phillips would pile into the car, drive up to New York, stay for free in a nearby Statler because of Arthur Douglas's past connection to the chain, and keep the Justice company.

The challenge for Douglas's staff became just how to shield his true condition from the other members of the Court. On the Justice's orders, his staff hid the medical reports so that Chief Justice Burger wouldn't see them (though Douglas was convinced that Burger was getting information from the institute's nurses). Nonetheless, the Brethren privately agreed not to accept any future appeal on which they were closely divided, fearing that an impaired Douglas would cast the deciding vote.

Unaware of this action, Douglas instructed his law clerk Alan Austin to draft some thoughts on the death-penalty case, which dealt with a claim of unconstitutional arbitrariness in its use in North Carolina. Then the Justice pulled out a yellow legal pad and tried to produce his own draft, as he had done so many times before.

Douglas's process of writing this opinion said much about his condition. Once, he would have effortlessly scribbled an entire opinion in a single sitting, composing an impassioned and brilliant analysis of the vital issues. Now, all he could manage was to scrawl in nearly indecipherable handwriting on the first page that he would be dissenting. Then, with his pad sliding around and the ideas in his head now too scrambled to be captured and transferred to the page, Douglas produced on the next page a handful of short, sloped sentence fragments, which had little connection to one another. After a page and a quarter of labored effort, Douglas just gave up. When they received this "opinion" for typing, even his secretaries, who were so skilled at deciphering what now passed for his penmanship, were stymied. All they could do was circle the words they could not read and leave spaces in their draft in the hopes of working out their meaning later on.

When Alan Austin saw the effort, he did not know what to do with it. How could Douglas dissent when no vote had yet been taken in the case? Should the wording of his opinion match that of Justice Brennan, with whom Douglas seemed to want to agree? Which quotations from the landmark 1972 *Furman v. Georgia* case on the unconstitutionality of the biased and inequitable imposition of the death penalty did he want to be used here? Until these and other questions could be answered, the draft could not be sent to the printer.

By the middle of May, Douglas's law clerk and secretaries had turned out an impressive four-page draft that sounded like a healthy Justice had written it. But his colleagues were not fooled. The work contained Douglas's views, but its wooden academic style lacked his passionate fire on such a civil-liberties question. So the other members of the Court took the next step in dealing with their infirm colleague by agreeing not to issue any opinions in close cases. For all intents and purposes, they had retired him.

When Douglas demanded to see the other circulating opinions in the death-penalty case, his clerk learned from the grapevine that the Court had scheduled it for reargument the following term. Alan Austin tried to cushion the blow by telling Douglas that the Court was looking for a different kind of case on which to further explore the constitutionality of the use of the death penalty. While a healthy Douglas would have seen through this explanation immediately and fought it, now he simply accepted the action.

But he was still able to have his say on issues of importance to him by dissenting on his own to denial of *certiorari* opinions. Late that June, the Court denied standing to a group of people and organizations in Rochester, New York, that claimed that the zoning regulations of a nearby suburb called Penfield were being fashioned to exclude people of low and moderate income. When the Court refused to hear the appeal because no one in this case had sufficient "injury" to raise it, Douglas dissented that his colleagues were reading "the record with antagonistic eyes." For him, there was another right in this case that the Court had not yet explored: "A clean, safe, and well-heated home is not enough for some people. Some want to live where the neighbors are congenial and have social and political outlooks similar to their own." For Douglas, this was no different from the cases in which the Court had previously ruled in favor of the NAACP's efforts to desegregate communities.

Believing that his colleagues were ducking their constitutional responsibility, Douglas made it very clear that he was ready to rule all the time: "Cases such as this one reflect festering sores in our society; and the American dream teaches that if one reaches high enough and persists there is a forum where justice is dispensed. I would lower the technical barriers and let the courts serve that ancient need." Despite his crippled body, unmoving hand, and periodically clouded mind, Douglas now all but accused his colleagues of shirking their duty by lessening their caseload through such legal technicalities: "In all frankness, no Justice of this Court need work more than four days a week to carry his burden. I have found it a comfortable burden carried even in my months of hospitalization."

With the world waiting to see whether Douglas would return to his full powers, he reaped the rewards of a distinguished career. In June 1975, Douglas and Simon Rifkind were honored by the members of their legendary Columbia class of '25 at their fiftieth reunion. "It took enormous will power [for him] to attend that reunion, wheelchair and all," Rifkind recalled. His classmates presented him with an ornate scroll testifying to their admiration of his work, reading in part: "Constitutionalist, Environmentalist, and World Traveller, William O. Douglas has deeply influenced the life of his times. . . . By his fighting qualities of mind and heart, his rugged independence of thought and his steadfast integrity of purpose, he exemplifies the truest of American traditions and has endowed the profession of the Law with dignity and honor. We, the members of the Class of '25, salute him on this occasion of our Fiftieth Reunion, and extend to him our continued high regard and our undiminished affection." Douglas's incapacitated condition on this occasion raised new questions in the press as to whether he would return to the Bench the following term. But the Justice was unaffected by such speculation. "There's no chance I'll retire. I'll be there in October, positively," he promised *The New York Times*.

It took the simplest act that summer, though, to suggest otherwise to Douglas. He had returned to Goose Prairie, hoping that the cool, crisp mountain air would rejuvenate him. The Double K gals—Kay Kershaw and Isabelle Lynn—were told that if they would get a wrangler to saddle up one of their horses, he would ride again. "He didn't go easily into death," they recalled with admiration. "No, he fought it all the way."

But when the Douglas car drove up to their ranch house, the Justice had such trouble getting out that his son, who had come to visit, rushed to his aid. But the Justice shook his head vigorously and spat out, "I'll be goddamned if they carry me into the Double K." Only through sheer determination did Douglas make it into the house with his walker.

But later that summer, when Douglas was driven right up to the door of Prairie House, try as he might he could not repeat the feat. It was the last time he would ever attempt to walk. The effect of this incident was evident to those around him. "I thought his mind was reasonably active and alert long past the stroke," recalls William Douglas, Jr. "But I think [it] began to debilitate when he realized that he was not going to walk again. . . . He was a fiercely independent man, . . . [and] it was devastating to him." Douglas's closest friends heard about his declining condition and decided to visit the tiny hamlet for one last communal visit. Isabelle Lynn and others hiked up to the Justice's beloved Blankenship Meadow to collect a bouquet containing every flower in the region for him. But when his son raised the question of his future, the Justice made clear that he could not bring himself to quit. "What will I do? Who will I be without the Court?" he asked with a pained expression on his face.

Determined to quash this talk, when a delegation of lawyers approached him in early September asking for a hearing, Douglas seized the opportunity to prove he could still do the work of a Supreme Court Justice. The lawyers were appealing on behalf of C. Arnholt Smith, a San Diego millionaire who was seeking a temporary injunction to prevent California authorities from gaining access to secret grand-jury evidence on a series of banking charges while his case proceeded through the courts. In an earlier time, the lawyers would have been told to return the next day to a spot in the mountains, only to find the word *Denied* on a piece of notebook paper tacked to a tree. But this was a different William O. Douglas. Now he told them that he would personally hear the case in the Yakima County Courthouse. "I am returning to my spot on the Court because I can still do the job," he told the press and, indirectly, his friends.

Others close to him, though, were not so sure, and they begged him not to do it. "He was in and out, and we just didn't want to roll the dice to see which Douglas would show up on the bench," said Elena Leonardo, who was staying with him at Goose Prairie and who helped him attend the hearing. By this time, the Double K gals were writing friends that Douglas was bordering on "the vegetable state."

When Douglas arrived at the courthouse, a horde of reporters and photographers surrounded his car and peppered him with questions as to when he would be returning to Washington. "Within a week or so," he mumbled as his son wheeled him into the courthouse. One of the journalists surreptitiously followed Douglas around, learning that he had already decided to block the State of California from the evidence and was dictating the decision over the courthouse phone to Washington before the argument took place.

But Douglas was there to prove his point by giving the lawyers their day in court. After the Justice's wheelchair was raised to the bench, the argument began. For an hour and forty minutes, the legal pyrotechnics raged as Douglas quizzed both attorneys aggressively, challenging and pinning them on several legal points. After this bravura performance, though, Douglas's friends drew in their breath when he proposed a 12:30 recess, even though it was actually 1:00 P.M. Only when they realized that the only clock the immobile Justice could see from his vantage point was out of order, with its hands permanently stuck at 11:30, did they breathe a sigh of relief. After the break, the hearing continued. When the argument concluded, the time had come for Douglas to render his decision. Every eye in the room was fastened on him. But Douglas did not say a word, did not move a muscle, and instead just stared back at them wordlessly. A full minute went by, then another, and then yet another. The Justice was just taking longer than usual to issue his verdict, everyone concluded. But when five full minutes passed by and Douglas still had not moved, spectators began to shift nervously in their seats. It seemed as though he was no longer mentally in the room. "Friends of mine who saw it told me that it was the saddest thing they had ever seen," said Yakima attorney John Gavin. "He just said nothing—nothing at all."

After a full nine and a half minutes of silence, Douglas finally began to mumble with obvious difficulty. But rather than issuing a formal decision in the case, he began offering some random comments on the arguments before inviting both attorneys to come see him at his home in Goose Prairie. "It is a very beautiful place—a jewel of the American countryside," he said, "with pristine air and abundant wildlife— the climate is salubrious." Sensing a problem, Douglas's son quickly mounted the platform behind the bench and interrupted the "ruling" to wheel the Justice away, trying to shield him with his body from the puzzled looks on the audience's faces. The performance had completely backfired. "Back to work in a week?" asked the *Yakima Herald-Republic* in its account.

Upon seeing the disaster in the courthouse, Douglas's family and friends knew that the time had come to persuade him to retire. Bill Douglas, Jr., Isabelle Lynn, and Kay Kershaw decided that the only person with the necessary stature and impartial distance to tell him that it was time to leave was Charles Reich, the former Hugo Black law clerk who had walked with Douglas so many times on the C & O Canal. "What are we going to do?" Isabelle Lynn asked Reich on the phone. The San Francisco attorney promised to consider the question and shortly thereafter sent back a long letter outlining all of the reasons why Douglas should leave the Court, instructing them to give it to him. But no one in Goose Prairie could bear to do it, believing that in his present mental state he would not accept such advice. So Lynn invited Reich to come for a visit, make his own appraisal of their friend's competence; if in his mind things were as bad as they thought, perhaps he could convince the Justice to retire. *I won't come,* responded Reich, *unless the Justice or Cathy invites me.* Once the invitation was arranged, the discussion was scheduled for September 25.

As soon as Reich arrived and saw the condition of his old friend, he knew what he had to do. "You're in no shape to continue," said Reich, "and besides that, who needs this? You have this great record on the Bench, why jeopardize it?"

Douglas's response was poignantly simple, "Well, my life will be over." Realizing that there was no adequate answer here, Reich suggested that they adjourn their discussion until the following day.

When the two men resumed their talk, Reich opened by suggesting to Douglas that his life already was over. For hours, he explained that the job was stressful enough when he was in perfect health, and now he was in no shape to perform the same tasks. "I didn't feel very convincing," the skilled legal advocate said years later. And Douglas proved the point by indicating that he was not ready to give up the fight. "Maybe there will be some case where there is a Chicano or a black or something, and my vote will make a difference, even if I'm a wreck," he said.

"Well, you can't stay on for that kind of a reason," responded Reich, adding:

> It's perfectly true what you say, but you will hurt yourself publicly and you will hurt your reputation. . . . If you go on the Bench, you will perhaps excite gossip, whether you are competent to be on the Bench. The rumors will start that you may make some slips, or it may seem you are inattentive. You will have everybody's knife out for you. And who needs it, you know? You've done your time, made a great contribution, and you are entitled to get old. Get off now, while you are standing up straight. While you look good. Not in a barrage of criticism.

With that, Douglas simply stopped listening and began staring off into space. But Reich decided to press on, confronting the feeble Justice with the horror of his condition. "Look, you have to be carried from one room to the other. Do you really think you can function as a Justice?" he argued. It wasn't easy to do, but Reich knew that somebody had to say it.

For three days the discussion raged on. Douglas was not taking the news well, having already hit his wife, who had returned to Goose

Prairie, with his one good hand and ordered Bill Jr. from his house when they supported Reich's view. Every time the Justice turned stone silent, someone would carry him out of the room for an hour's rest, and then they would bring him back for more discussion. Finally, Douglas began to admit that maybe he should leave, but just as immediately he would back away. "I'll just go back and see what it feels like," he offered.

Seizing upon this opening, Reich turned to the most powerful argument in his arsenal: "You know, I think Hugo Black would have told you to retire. He would have said it is time to get off for your own good and for the best of everyone."

For just a moment, the years seemed to melt away as Douglas stared back at Reich with the same cold blue eyes that had withered so many others in his heyday, and, contrary to what he had told reporters in late March, he spat out his worst fear in response: "Ford will appoint some bastard." By this time, Douglas's greatest paranoid fear was that that "bastard" would be Richard Nixon. The debate, Reich realized, was over. He rose and shook the old man's hand, wished him the best, and left for the Double K to pack for his flight home.

By the time Reich returned to Prairie House to say good-bye, he found Douglas already sitting in the car, waiting to be driven back to Washington. So anxious was the old man to get away that they left Prairie House without even locking it and with several horses uncared for outside. Only when the Double K gals heard on the radio that Douglas had returned to the Bench did they realize that the retirement-intervention effort had failed.

But Charles Reich was right. Life back in the capital proved to be just as difficult as he had predicted. Unable to do any work because of his degenerating health, the Justice could now only check himself in and out of Walter Reed for therapy. Concluding that Douglas's life would only improve if he chucked the burden of work on the Court in favor of extended rest, his friends Clark Clifford and Abe Fortas began to work on a draft of a resignation letter, just to have it ready when needed.

Despite his condition, Douglas never ceased fighting for his causes. On November 11, he issued yet another short opinion, this time on the subject of the environment. The Atomic Energy Commission (AEC) had issued a permit for the construction of a nuclear-power plant on the south shore of Lake Michigan. But that permit had been set aside by the Court of Appeals as violating the agency's own rules dealing with the necessary minimum distance of such construction from population centers. When the Supreme Court ruled in an unsigned *per curiam* opinion that the lower federal court should not have over-turned the AEC's interpretation of its own rules, Douglas voted with them. However, he was so disturbed that the AEC's successor agency, the Nuclear Regulatory Commission, had issued an ad hoc amend-ment to its regulations that in effect ratified this decision after the fact that he issued a special concurring opinion. "A certain danger lurks in the ability of an agency to perfunctorily mold its regulations to con-form to its instant needs," wrote Douglas. "The power to change the rules after the contest has been concluded would once more put the promotion of nuclear energy ahead of the public's safety."

These were the last words that Douglas ever wrote on the Court. Sitting on the bench on November 12, while trying unsuccessfully to focus on the words of the arguing attorneys, the fight finally left him. While the verbal combat continued, he picked up a sheet of paper and with his one good hand painstakingly began to write:

Dear Mr. President:

It was my hope, when I returned to Washington in September, that I would be able to continue to participate in the work of the Supreme Court.

I have learned, however, after these last two months, that it would be inadvisable for me to attempt to carry on the duties re-quired of a member of the Court. I have been bothered with inces-sant and demanding pain that depletes my energy to the extent that I have been unable to shoulder my full share of the burden.

Therefore, pursuant to the provisions of Title 28, U.S. Code Sec-tion 371 (b), I hereby retire at the close of this day from regular ac-tive service as an Associate Justice of the Supreme Court of the United States.

During the hours of oral argument last week pain made it nec-essary for me to leave the Bench several times. I have had to leave several times this week also. I shall continue to seek relief from this unabated pain but there is no bright prospect in view.

Chief Justice Burger and my other colleagues on the Bench have extended to me every courtesy and generous consideration. I have appreciated their thoughtfulness and I shall miss them sorely, but I know this is the right decision.

When Marty Bagby received the note by messenger, with tears in her eyes she quickly prepared it for the Justice to sign when the argu-ment ended at noon. It was a remarkably eloquent document, she thought, done in one draft without a single word crossed out.

But before the letter could be released, Douglas was determined to observe a Court formality that he had seen so many times before. He asked Harry Datcher to wheel him to the Justices' upstairs dining room, where he had eaten so few meals and where his colleagues were now enjoying their lunch before celebrating Harry Blackmun's birthday. At the end of the festivities, Chief Justice Burger said to the others, "Bill wants me to tell you he's written a letter to the President." Old battles were forgotten now as Douglas signaled his respect for the office of the Chief Justice by asking Burger to read it aloud.

After they heard the news, one by one each member of the Court walked over to shake their senior colleague's hand and wish him well. Then, as Douglas was quietly wheeled to the door, he raised his good arm and, with some difficulty, expressed to his old colleagues what had become his mantra in his waning years: "Keep the Faith!" With Douglas's record-making legacy of 1,164 full opinions, including 486 full dissents (not to mention his thirty-two books and hundreds upon hundreds of public speeches), now complete, for the first time in more than thirty-six years the guardianship of the Constitution was in others' hands.

ALONE

He didn't have his children around him. He didn't have his friends around him. He was alone at the end. And that needn't be.

—*C. David Ginsburg*

In the days following his resignation, Douglas's life was still centered around the Supreme Court. Recalling that his Brethren had written to him upon his retirement that "we shall expect you to share our table as usual, for you remain Senior Justice Emeritus," he believed that he was being offered a continuing role on the body. He went to the Court building office assigned to him as a retired Justice and showed he had lost none of his irascibility. Once ensconced in a special reclining chair that raised his stroke-damaged leg to ease his pain, the first thing Douglas did was press his buzzer, looking for one of his law clerks. But no one burst through the door. So he pressed the buzzer again for a longer spell. Once more, no one came. Finally, Douglas leaned on the buzzer with all his might. This brought only a visit from his secretary. "Where are the clerks?" Douglas barked at Marty Bagby.

"There are no clerks," she responded, explaining that the Chief Justice had reassigned them to active members of the Court.

"How can I do my work without [my] assistants?" the ill man asked. Douglas found out where one of his clerks was and summoned him to his chambers, and they got to work.

One of his first orders of business was to write a letter of protest to the Chief Justice about the reassignment of his assistants. How could he maintain his voluminous correspondence files? he asked. When his letter got no response, Douglas circulated a copy of it to his former colleagues, hoping to get some support. He needed the help, Douglas explained, because in addition to his usual workload he had promised a member of the faculty of Fairleigh-Dickinson University that he would write a two-hundred-year history of the Supreme Court. Just the mere fact that he thought that he could perform this task indicated once again to those around him how unwilling he was to admit his infirmity.

Two days later, on December 19, 1975, Douglas was wheeled into the Court's chamber to witness the swearing in of his replacement, Court of Appeals Judge John Paul Stevens. When President Ford spotted Douglas in his wheelchair in a corner of the room, he walked over and said, "Good to see you, Mr. Justice."

Hardly impressed by the gesture, Douglas muttered, "Yeah. It's really nice seeing you. We've got to get together more often." Then, with a wave of his good arm, Douglas had Harry Datcher wheel him out of the room.

With the completion of the new appointment, Douglas became obsessed with the question of what role he would play on the Court. So when he learned that the Court was considering the *Buckley v. Valeo* case, dealing with the constitutionality of the 1974 campaign-finance law, Douglas sent word to the chief that he was drafting his own memorandum on the case and trying to reschedule an operation at Walter Reed Army Hospital to allow him to attend the Court's conference.

When Burger ignored the message, Douglas had his thirteen-page memorandum on the *Buckley* case printed a month later. The meandering essay was devoted much more to the question of whether he should have the right to serve as a voting member of the body than it was to the issues in the case itself. "Bill is like an old firehouse dog," Chief Justice Burger told one of his clerks after reading the effort, "too old to run along with the trucks, but his ears prick up just the same."

The Chief responded in a three-page memorandum stating that, as a retired Justice, Douglas was not qualified to sit in any pending cases unless he was specifically requested to do so by the full conference. And no such request had been, or would be, made. But even in his crippled state Douglas was still not a man to be denied. He told his staff that he would circulate the memo to the other chambers anyway. When Douglas found out that the Court would announce its ruling on January 30, he told his clerk to release his opinion to the press at the same time. "I won't do it," said the clerk.

"You are a traitor," responded the old man. "I will get it down there myself." Only when everyone in the building was told to ignore Douglas's efforts was the matter dropped.

But Douglas was not deterred. When he learned in late March that the Court was about to hear a reargument of the death-penalty cases, he drafted another memorandum informing his colleagues that he would be filing an additional opinion in this new case. The promise, though, was more than he could fulfill. Douglas took out a small pad of unlined notepaper and after hours of labor produced a short, illegible document. When his secretaries finally decoded it, the less than two-page typewritten essay again seemed more concerned with his exclusion from sitting on the Court than with the peril facing the 450 people then on death row. Only when this document was also ignored by his old colleagues did Douglas finally accept that he was no longer serving on the Supreme Court.

.   .   .

The nation was told that William O. Douglas was enjoying his retirement. "The former justice still goes to the court every day for a few hours," reported *The Washington Post.* "He writes letters, talks to people on the phone, talks with his secretaries and others he sees about current events." The image presented was that of a man making progress in his physical therapy and tying up the loose ends of his life, all the while surrounded by members of his family, his friends, and his staff.

But those closest to Douglas knew that the truth was much sadder than that. Physically, Douglas was now little more than a breathing corpse, dying a very slow, lingering death. When Douglas felt well enough on weekdays, he tried to keep up with his correspondence or to push around some paragraphs in the second volume of his memoirs. Periodically, his staff would carefully arrange heating pads around his leg while he sat in his reclining chair to keep the blood flowing and wrapped the rest of his lower body in blankets to keep him warm. Becky McGuire, the Court nurse, came up three times a day to check his hot packs and put the Justice through a series of painful stretching exercises in the hopes of getting back some of his movement. But by now the atrophy of the muscles was permanent.

All too frequently Douglas's mind would slip out of gear, with cogent periods followed by times when his memory completely failed. People never knew what they would find when they entered the Justice's chamber. Sometimes Douglas would entertain them by telling delightful tales of his past, recalling political conquests or offering a ribald story. But just as frequently he would either sit in stony, sullen silence or break into tears at the thought that his time was coming to an end.

It was in this condition that Douglas was now directing the revision of yet another memoir, taking up his story where *Go East, Young*

Man left off. This account of his years on the Court was to become one
on which scholars and journalists later relied for interpretations of
his life. One of his main preoccupations was his literary portrait of his
nemesis, Chief Justice Burger, who never realized that every time he
stopped by to chat, often bringing a favorite wine or a jar of homemade
preserves, Douglas would remove another negative comment from his
literary portrait. "They never should have published that second volume of his memoirs," said Abe Fortas years later. "People don't realize
that Douglas was a very sick man by then." In making his revisions,
Douglas was totally unaware that his editor at Random House, Charlotte Mayerson, had decided to hold off the release of the volume until
after his death, in the hopes that the publicity would help them make
back the $166,000 in unrecovered advances from the well-reviewed but
poor-selling *Go East, Young Man*.

Since serious writing is not possible if you cannot keep the
thoughts in your head, when he was awake Douglas mostly liked to
reminisce. Every few minutes he would seek an audience by leaning on
the buzzer that had once terrorized generations of law clerks. "You are
going to get calluses on your finger the way you keep punching that
buzzer," his daughter, Millie, wrote him. As he got older and feebler,
though, Douglas's biggest fear was that he would not be able to reach
or operate the device that enabled him to summon help.

All he really wanted to do now was to get out of the chair and be
young again, but he knew it would never happen. Instead, his new law
clerk, Montana Podva, who had training as a physical therapist, and
Podva's wife, Rebecca Judge, a blond Scandinavian beauty who was a
nurse, helped to look after his needs. Tears would fill Podva's eyes as
he saw his young daughter trying to steady herself against Douglas's
wheelchair as she learned to walk, while this mere husk of a man, now
helplessly slumped over in his chair, tried futilely to stroke the hair of
the little blond girl. Douglas told his assistant that the best times for
him now were when he was able to sleep soundly enough to dream of
the days when he was still walking in the mountains and enjoying his
adventures.

The weekends were sheer torture because he could not go to his office. So he would ask Harry Datcher, then on his own time, to drive
him somewhere to see people. In the fall, they would go to an occasional football game at RFK Stadium or at the University of Maryland.
It didn't matter that they had no tickets or that the stadium was sold
out, seats near the fifty-yard line were always found for the legendary
jurist and his friend. Sometimes Datcher would take him to a local

restaurant, knowing that the patrons, upon seeing the last New Dealer, would always rise as one and give him a standing ovation. "He was a folk hero outside," said Datcher years later, "but not at home."

Indeed, as bad as his physical condition was, Douglas's psychological environment was much worse. The man who had always been so hard on those around him now reaped the consequences of his behavior. Neither of the children he had pushed away when he was active was close to him now. His daughter, Millie, had long ago married an Englishman named Norman Read and was teaching school and raising her family in Great Britain. His son, William Jr., was living on the West Coast, pursuing an acting career, and later attempting a career in restaurant management. "The fact is that neither of his children really had much respect for him. This is what hurts," recalled old Yakima buddy Cragg Gilbert. "They just deserted him like he deserted them."

Eventually, even his old friends began to distance themselves from him. "We finally quit calling him," said his childhood chum Al Egley. "I just didn't have the guts to call anymore. It hurt him as much to be that way as it hurt me to hear him. That last time, he broke down and cried, and we didn't want to upset him anymore."

Knowing that he needed round-the-clock care, Douglas's intimates began to raise questions about who was looking after him. Martha Douglas Bost would call her brother's home at all hours of the day and night checking up on his well-being. Whenever she could not immediately find Cathy, she would then call Harry Datcher and scream, "Where's Cathy?" Her fears were not eased when Douglas wrote that his wife had told him that he was no longer welcome in his own house. Whether this had actually happened or was just a product of his stroke-ravaged mind, Bost took it as gospel truth. Writing to her brother, she said that he should not be forced to leave his own house; instead, Cathy should go. Bost was not alone with her concerns. Douglas's friend and New York attorney Sid Davis would also pester Harry Datcher about Cathy's whereabouts. "Where's Cathy?" he would say in a slow, concerned voice. "Where does she go? Where does she stay? Shouldn't she be home with Bill?"

A high point of Douglas's week now would be when Monty Podva and his wife took him out to eat. But it was not always a pleasant occasion. When one lunch ended, Douglas refused to leave the restaurant, yelling that he intended to stay forever unless his wife joined them. Finally, Podva persuaded him to leave by saying that the men's room in the establishment was closed for the day, meaning that Douglas would have to return to the Court building. "He became obsessed with having Cathy around," confirmed Dagmar Hamilton. "If you went to lunch with him and she wasn't there, he wouldn't eat a bite of his food until they placed the telephone at his table and he could call." Hamilton, who had seen how badly Douglas treated his wives over the years, saw the irony in the situation: "It was as though he now feared that she wouldn't need him. I mean the roles were reversed. . . . Now he was totally dependent on her." Concluded Hamilton: "To the man from the strongly Calvinistic Presbyterian upbringing, it must have seemed as though the stroke was God's way of repaying him for all of the terrible things he had done [to his wives] in the past."

Former law clerk C. David Ginsburg now saw in Douglas an intense jealousy: "The sense of weakness and age led him to the feeling that she must be interested in somebody else. Absolutely nothing to that. But it was a terrible period for him, everybody around him. How Cathy managed it, I don't know. I never heard her say anything other than supportive things about him. At that time, and since, I had a real respect for that girl."

Despite the criticism of others around her husband, Cathy Douglas did what she could for him. Harry Datcher, who saw everything in those days, explained: "Cathy loved him, but she just didn't ever expect him to get old and sick. So she wasn't around very much. He got the best of care, though. . . . 'Take care of the judge, give him anything he wants,' she would say." Friends point out that to her credit, rather than putting her husband in a nursing home, she turned the L-shaped dining room into a makeshift bedroom on the first floor. There was just enough room there to put a hospital gurney, a bedside table, and a chair for visitors alongside an array of medical machinery. And she insisted on hiring a series of nurses at great expense to care for him at their home on Hutchins Place. Only when she looked into the prospect of putting a ramp for him up to the front door of their home did Douglas object, fearing that it would signal to the neighbors and the press that he might not recover from his illness.

As for the absences from the house that concerned Martha Bost and others, friends are quick to point out that they are easily explained. They needed her income and benefits from practicing law to supplement his Court retirement income. "Some people thought that Cathy should quit her job and be with the Justice all the time, but the only way he got into the Rusk Institute [sic] and the other good medical care was that the insurance policy from her law firm paid for all of it," recalled Marty Bagby Yopp. "Douglas's retirement pay and the standard federal insurance policy was not going to cover the one-million-dollar bill just for the Rusk Institute stay alone. Then there was the battery of nurses for the home care, the cost of the drugs, and the doctors, and everything else." Concluded Yopp, "Cathy had to work [to pay for it all], and besides it would have driven her crazy not to do so." To which C. David Ginsburg added: "It was so painful, and his demands on Cathy were so enormous. He wanted her with him all of the time, and she couldn't have been. He had also taught her—he insisted—that she become a lawyer. He insisted that she go into private practice. He insisted that she should be able to earn her way, because he couldn't leave very much, if anything. And now he needed her. I mean this was so sad."

With his wife, his children, and his friends all off living their own lives, Douglas's immediate world now consisted of Harry Datcher, Marty Bagby, Sandra Phillips Flax, Montana Podva, and Rebecca Judge. "In his last years," recalled Dag Hamilton, "Monty Podva and Rebecca Judge were the only family that Douglas ever really had." For the man whose empire of friends and associates once circled the globe, it was a small group indeed.

Despite Douglas's personal loneliness, America had not forgotten him. On May 17, 1977, several hundred people gathered at Lock Number One of the C & O Canal Towpath to commemorate the establishment of the area as a national park in his name. Senators Henry M. Jackson, Thomas Eagleton, and Edward Kennedy, Congressmen Richard L. Ottinger and Don Edwards, various members of the Supreme Court, and hundreds of common folk on the terraces of nearby office buildings watched as Cathy Douglas pulled the sheet off the magnificently lifelike bronze bust of Douglas, sculpted by Wendy Ross. When Douglas saw the bust, he mumbled with great difficulty, "By God, that is the face I shave every morning!" The marble column supporting it read: "In Recognition of Justice William O. Douglas for His Contributions Toward the Establishment of the Chesapeake and Ohio Canal National Historical Park."

Even in the midafternoon heat, the wheelchair-bound Douglas was not willing to give in to his physical difficulties. "He sat in [the] shade of a tree, his jaw slack, his face expressionless, not smiling, not laughing, not showing in any way that he was hearing what was being said," reported *Washington Post* journalist Richard Cohen. He wore a hat and a blue suit, with his tie, bound by an overly large knot, hanging loosely around his neck, as he sat listing to the left during the proceedings. "There was something about the way he was dressed to indicate that something was wrong—that maybe he had not dressed himself or maybe, on the other hand, he had," added Cohen. Still, the reporter added, Douglas had "the fierce, proud eye of an eagle."

Even his former colleagues on the Court noticed. "There are seven other Justices back in the shade," said Chief Justice Warren Burger, "because they couldn't take the sun."

"That's more than a quorum," replied Douglas. "I was never able to entice any of them the whole distance [of the canal] anyway, but I promise when I'm well we'll take the hike. As a matter of fact, I think we should rededicate the day to a hike, not for today, but another May 17th." But observers who could plainly see that it would never happen openly wept during the proceedings.

When it came the honored guest's turn to speak, and the microphones were lowered to his level, Douglas tried to address the crowd in his high, halting voice. Speaking without a text, he recalled how he had replaced Benjamin Cardozo on the Court, who had also traveled up the Potomac in his canoe. No one in the crowd cared now that Douglas's predecessor and fellow canoeist was in fact Louis D. Brandeis. Instead, their hearts went out as the stricken jurist struggled to speak. After each sentence, Douglas would pause and seem to fade out for long moments until his wife nudged him and he would begin again. At one point, he became so tongue-tied that Cathy had to whisper into his ear, causing the Justice to add, "What I've been trying to say is that many Presidents and numerous public officials have helped with this canal project. I thank you all for coming. I thank all those who have no portfolio but who have two strong legs and like to hike." With that, he closed with a promise "to get well and to be able to walk again."

When Douglas finished, the crowd, many with tears streaming down their cheeks, rose to their feet and cheered, suspecting that this was his farewell address. And, as he was wheeled out of the proceedings, members of the audience leaned over one another to touch him.

.   .   .

More and more, Douglas's conversations in his final years were devoted to lamenting the choices that he had made during his life. Serving on the Court, he made clear to Monty Podva, was not what he had really wanted to do. Quoting Oliver Wendell Holmes, he explained: "Being a judge is like being an oyster: You've got to wait for the food to come washing up to your mouth with the high tide. And you watch many of the best mussels float by." It was not the power of the Oval Office that Douglas sought, he explained, but rather the total freedom to explore in a timely fashion all of the important issues of the day.

Even at this late date, there were still some personal fences to mend. Douglas had yet to deal with the ex-friend who had financially destroyed him: Tommy Corcoran. Fearing that these two former political allies, who had not spoken since the early 1950s, would go to their graves without ever reconciling, Eliot Janeway, the last man in this political triangle, arranged a luncheon at the Cosmos Club in November 1978, without telling Douglas the name of the third person at their table. On his way to the festivity, Tommy the Cork appeared at Douglas's Supreme Court office door and bowed as he entered the room. Not even this dramatic greeting however could engage Douglas, who refused to acknowledge the visitor with anything beyond a perfunctory handshake. But at the lunch table, when Corcoran pressed a bit further, Douglas's frostiness melted. Forming his words with considerable effort, Douglas said simply, "Tommy, I guess I always knew you were my best friend." This judicial pardon brought tears to the eyes of the hardened political infighter, as he jumped from his seat to clasp the old jurist's one good hand with both of his own.

.   .   .

By late 1979, word reached Douglas that he had been voted the greatest honor that his alma mater, Columbia University, had to offer: an honorary degree of doctor of laws. Informed by school officials that for the first time in 119 years they would be traveling off campus to make the award, just as had been done for Abraham Lincoln on June 26, 1861, the Justice joked, "I suppose the next thing to happen to me is that I'll be shot."

One hundred and fifty people—fellow Justices, family members, friends, and university representatives—gathered on December 6, 1979, in the East Conference Room of the Supreme Court building for the ceremony. "It was quite an occasion," remembered Marty Bagby Yopp, "because it was the last gathering of his friends." After a full academic procession marched into the room led by law-school dean Albert J. Rosenthal, bearing the silver mace, followed by President William J. McGill and various other university dignitaries, Douglas was draped in an academic gown for the last time. Provost and Executive Vice President for Academic Affairs Michael Sovern told the gathering solemnly: "The lessons he has taught on the Court and off, are as old as man's spirit, always in jeopardy and ever dependent on the courage, vision and eloquence of those who know where man must go. . . . For Mr. Justice Douglas it has never been enough simply to discover the law and leave it where he found it—he has insisted that the law be shaped, to bear witness to the moral development of society. The result has been an original and profound vision in the role of law."

With this award, William O. Douglas had finally reached the top of his law-school class. Simon Rifkind could see the impact that this ceremony had on his old friend: "By this time, his strength had ebbed but his spirit shone brightly in his eyes. It was plain that he was glad to receive this honor from his alma mater. To me it seemed that he greatly honored Columbia University by accepting the degree." As the guests gathered around the wheelchair to congratulate the ailing Justice, they knew that the nation would never see his like again.

And they were right. On Christmas Eve 1979, the Justice's respiration became so labored from a new bout of pneumonia that his wife took him to Walter Reed. But before he left his gurney, there was one last message he wanted to convey.

When Cathy Douglas brought him something from another room, he grabbed her hand. "I want you to know something," he mumbled softly, adding: "I want you always to know that no one has ever been better to me since my mother."

They were the last words he ever spoke. While Cathy Douglas took comfort from these words, others saw a very different message here. "It was clear to me that Dad meant this as no compliment," explained Millie Douglas Read, thinking about her father's private hostility toward his mother.

"Cathy just didn't get it," said television documentarian Walter Lowe after his extensive research on the Justice. "His mother didn't treat him well at all. Douglas's last words were obviously an inside joke."

.   .   .

For eight days, Cathy Douglas, Dagmar Hamilton, Marty Bagby, various members of his office staff, and others stood watch over Douglas in Walter Reed Army Hospital as he slipped in and out of a light coma. He was put on life support in the intensive-care unit. Though he was in a semi-private cubicle, the hospital authorities made some allowance for Douglas's station in life by putting him in a small corner of the unit ringed by curtains and reserving a small room off of this area for those maintaining the vigil.

With his kidneys now failing, all of the fluids from his intravenous feeding caused the Justice's gaunt facial features to fill out, until he looked like a middle-aged man. By ignoring all of the hospital equipment hooked up to him, his friends could fool themselves into believing that he was just sleeping lightly before rising to terrorize a clerk or harass Felix Frankfurter. But now, when Douglas's eyes opened, they would stare vacantly at the ceiling.

However, the man who loved life so much was not ready to give it up just yet. "The gauges would all go down, and we thought it was over," recalled Marty Bagby Yopp. "Then in a few moments they all went up again without explanation." The truth was that no one around him really trusted that it was over.

"He still scared us so much, he had pulled through so many times before," said Harry Datcher, "that anytime we wanted to talk about him someone would say, 'He can still hear us, let's go outside.' And so we left the room."

For some friends, Douglas's last moments on earth became a mirror in which they could reflect on their own life. When Monty Podva noticed the sadness on the face of Abe Fortas, he said cheerily: "Hey, he looks better than he did before he got pneumonia."

"Yeah, he does," replied the disgraced former Justice. "He looks just like he used to look."

"Isn't that interesting, that only in death was he able to get at least the physical appearance that he had strived for during the last few years," said Podva, adding reassuringly: "He's a fighter. He's gonna fight it as long as he's got any chance."

"Yeah, I know," responded Fortas. "In fact, last night he and I talked about a fight when I was being chased off the Court. He had told me not to resign." Podva was puzzled for a moment, realizing that since Douglas had been unable to speak for days, this "talk" had been entirely one-sided.

"He told me that story," Podva said. " 'As soon as they get you, Abe,' he told you . . . 'the hounds are gonna be after me.' "

"Yep," said Fortas, "and he was exactly right. When he goes, there will be no one else to keep the faith. . . . Those times will never be again." And both men knew, looking at the direction of the Burger Court on the Bill of Rights, that Fortas was right.

With the Justice now being kept alive only by machines, Cathy Douglas was asked to make the difficult decisions as to how far to extend these life-prolonging measures. Should they use the lung machine to keep him breathing? Yes, she said. What about the heart machine? Yes again, she responded. Ironically, she would not have been able to make these decisions had it not been for her husband having created such rights of personal autonomy through his decisions on the Court. Finally, when jaundice set in and Douglas's kidneys were about to fail completely, Cathy was asked whether the dialysis machine should be set up. At this point, she said there was no purpose in continuing the futile fight. It was time to let him climb his final mountain on his own.

By this time, Cathy Douglas had stayed up forty-eight hours straight, and Abe Fortas and Sid Davis were called in to take a spell at the bedside. As he stood over Douglas's supine body on Saturday morning, January 19, 1980, watching his mentor's labored attempts to continue breathing, Fortas's mind inexplicably began flashing back:

> I saw Douglas about forty-five years ago, in our days at Yale in his New Haven house, playfully presiding at a pretended meeting of the mythical Hunt Club that he and Thurman Arnold invented. . . . And I saw Douglas, who fancied himself a great outdoor chef, throwing a preciously expensive steak directly on a charcoal fire, at a cookout in our back yard. And I saw him slyly letting us know that it was he who had induced our Dean at Yale to board the train to Boston instead of New York where the Dean was scheduled to speak. And I saw him, much later, with Cathi [sic], happily striding along the C & O Canal.

And that was how he would remember Douglas when, at age eighty-one, he passed into eternity shortly after ten o'clock that evening.

.   .   .

Douglas's remains were removed to the First Presbyterian Church of Washington, where he lay in state in the building's great hall for the next day's viewing by the long lines of commoners, for whom he had fought so long. Groups of his law clerks were asked to stand in an around-the-clock vigil next to the coffin, much like a military honor guard. "This often amused me," recalled former secretary Fay Aull Deusterman. "I often wondered after all the hell he had put them through what the law clerks talked about at three in the morning when nobody was there." Perhaps, she decided, they considered opening up the coffin and peering inside just to make sure that Douglas was not being buried along with his buzzer.

William O. Douglas was gone, but one final legend about him had yet to be written.

EPILOGUE

PRIVATE DOUGLAS

Things are seldom what they seem.

—*Sir William Schwenck Gilbert*

The dark-clad figures stood somberly and motionless in the freezing cold, under the overcast skies, watching William O. Douglas's last journey. Just as he had planned for his final public appearance, the military pallbearers slowly carried the simple wooden casket, draped with an American flag, past a cordon of ten sitting and former Supreme Court Justices, and laid him to rest on a shady knoll in Arlington National Cemetery.

Reverend Edward Elson said a few words at the gravesite to comfort the two hundred or so witnesses present. Three volleys of rifle fire rang out from the military firing squad. Master Sergeant Patrick Mastroleo solemnly played "Taps." The crisply folded flag from Douglas's coffin was presented to his widow, Cathy. After more than eight decades of memories, the simple six-minute ceremony ended a remarkable life.

The news media loved it, describing the funeral more in the fashion of a movie review than a news event. "William Orville Douglas was buried . . . after a funeral that he had arranged in his own inimitable, individualistic style. . . . [He] went to his grave as unawed as ever by the high and the mighty," reported the *Los Angeles Times*. *The New York Times* added that "as a Supreme Court Justice for 36 years, William O. Douglas had not lacked opinions and he had decided, too, on how it was to be after his death."

But no one realized the significance of where Douglas had chosen to be buried, or the way that his final resting place would be commemorated. He had considered being buried in the family plot in

Yakima or, even more romantically, being cremated and placed in an urn near his favorite hiking trail on the American Ridge in Goose Prairie. But then he came up with a better solution. "Dear Cathy," Douglas wrote his wife on June 28, 1977, "I've remembered that I would qualify for burial in the Arlington National Cemetery since I was in World War I. I wasn't very high—Private First Class—but I was honorably discharged." The man named for the military "hero" in his family now wanted to be buried as a soldier. Perhaps now he even believed this story himself.

No one would deny that after Douglas's great service to the nation on the Supreme Court he deserved to be buried in Arlington. However, because of the demands placed on the facility after the highly visible burial of John F. Kennedy in the cemetery in 1963, and because of the Vietnam War, a decision was made to tighten the requirements for interment there. For burial as a member of the armed forces in the national shrine of America's military heroes, a military veteran now had to have achieved a Silver Star or higher honor, died on active duty, or served at least twenty years of active duty. Burial for a nonmilitary national figure was possible, but it usually required a presidential exception.

Service as a private in the Students' Army Training Corps for ten weeks at the end of World War I did not qualify one for burial in Arlington as a military figure. But Douglas knew that he had an ace to be played. So, he added in the letter to his wife, "If you want to pursue it Clark Clifford would be the one to talk to because he knows all the ropes." If the king of the Democrats could not get this done during the administration of Democratic president Jimmy Carter, Douglas knew, then he was unworthy of the title.

After receiving the request from Cathy Douglas, who herself had no reason to doubt her husband's story, the administrative office of the cemetery began a routine inquiry into Douglas's eligibility. The performance of these record checks in the Military Personnel Records Department of the National Personnel Records Center in Saint Louis was complicated by a huge fire in 1973 that destroyed a great percentage of the records. Normally, this blanching of the record did not affect famous Americans because their records had already been gathered and stored in a fireproof vault. However, William O. Douglas's record was not in the vault. Assuming that there had been some bureaucratic oversight in failing to preserve these records—rather than that they never existed at all—this civil servant almost certainly did the only thing possible: He went to secondary reference materials. And the evidence to support this request was there. *Who's Who in America* contained an entry written and checked by Douglas himself, which said that he had been a "Pvt. U.S. Army, 1918." A Douglas newspaper obituary also noted: "Mr. Douglas served as a private in the Army during World War I." And finally, Douglas's own *Of Men and Mountains* and *Go East, Young Man* detailed the entire story of his military career. When a check was made through the various Students' Army Training Corps lists, Douglas's record at Whitman College was located. Assuming that his service in the war had followed, the clerk compiled Douglas's military-service folder to sanction his burial in Arlington as a military figure, along with a note that it had been "reconstructed on the death of the individual." Thus, the cemetery's records show that Douglas was buried on the basis of his three months of military service as a private in the U.S. Army during World War I.

Even in death, Douglas's final autobiographical legend was duly written on the face of his dark-gray granite tombstone:

William O. Douglas
Private
United States Army
October 16, 1898
January 19, 1980

On the other side of the stone is carved the real reason that Douglas should be buried in Arlington:

DOUGLAS
Associate Justice
United States Supreme Court
April 17, 1939–November 12, 1975

But Douglas did not have total control over the symbolic meaning of his burial. As high as this tomb is on the ridge, Douglas's burial site is 150 feet below the gravesite of President John F. Kennedy, a man whose family's wealth allowed him to reach the summit that twice eluded William O. Douglas.

Even still, Douglas's final resting place, burial plot number 7004-B-1 in section V of the cemetery, could not have better encapsulated the full meaning of his life. Just a few paces away from his site is that of the other great dissenter on the Supreme Court, Oliver Wendell Holmes. Moreover, this man of nature, who so loved climbing mountains, rests on a gentle knoll in a stand of beautiful trees. And finally, for this man of such vast intellectual vision, his resting place overlooks the entire vista of Washington, D.C.

And so, as they laid him to rest, Douglas put down the burdens of his mother's expectations, his personal insecurities, and his own unfulfilled ambitions. He was finally free.

AUTHOR'S NOTE

Nearly fifteen years ago, I began a journey to discover the real William O. Douglas. The reason for the length of this task, the period of which has seen my seven-year-old daughter grow up to help edit this book and my four-year-old son head off to train in New York City to become an actor, requires some explanation.

After I finished my second judicial biography, on Abe Fortas, I was speaking with Professor Raoul Berger of Harvard University when he said, "I've been giving a lot of thought to your next project. I think you should do Douglas. I got to know him a little bit, and I have to tell you that William O. Douglas was the oddest duck to ever serve on the United States Supreme Court." The fact was that I had already been playing with this idea for a topic. I was also struck by the similarity between Berger's statement and one from journalist James J. Kilpatrick's column on Douglas after his death: "The historian who sets out to write an honest biography of William O. Douglas will have his hands full—search Supreme Court histories as you will, you will not find among the 101 justices a life more colorful than the life of Douglas. Like him, or loathe him, there was a man." Indeed, who could resist researching and writing the life of the man who set records for serving the most years, issuing the most opinions, writing the most dissents, writing the most books, giving the most speeches, having the most wives, suffering the most divorces, and being threatened with the most impeachments of any Justice in the history of the U.S. Supreme Court? What I did not know when I started my research was that Douglas also had the most fertile imagination in writing his memoirs.

It seemed at first that it would be an easy task. Douglas had written three autobiographies, so all I had to do, I thought, was to use that material to guide me through the Justice's recently opened private and professional papers in the Library of Congress and to interview the sources who could confirm his accounts. It seemed I was embarking on the same six-year cycle that I had gone through for my first two biographies. Very quickly, though, I discovered that I now faced the Mount Everest of judicial biographies—only to this point I did not realize that there had been no Sir Edmund Hillary to blaze the way.

The challenge became clearer as I went off to meet one after another of the people who were described and quoted in Douglas's memoirs. Finding the real Douglas, I soon learned, required a nationwide search. Thanks to Kay Kershaw and Isabelle Lynn, I spent two thrilling weeks actually living in the mountain cabin at the Double K ranch in tiny Goose Prairie, Washington, where Douglas hid from his family and the nation while he caroused and wrote his books. I climbed the same mountain paths in the Cascades (complete with mountain-lion tracks) where he had hiked and ridden horses. I drove to Oregon to meet Douglas's daughter and see his family's other cabins in the Wallowa Mountains. I met his surviving Columbia Law School classmates, Simon Rifkind in New York and Herman Benjamin in Florida. I spoke at great length with his research assistant, Dagmar Hamilton, in Austin, Texas, and with his former secretaries Marty Bagby Yopp in Moscow, Idaho, and Fay Aull Deusterman in Orlando, Florida. People such as lawyer and presidential adviser Clark Clifford, artist Elena Leonardo, former law clerk Montana James Podva, Whitman College classmate Frances Penrose Owen, and many others literally dug into their attics and closets to find long-hidden records of Douglas's life. Two things united these people: They all wanted the real story of Douglas's life to be told, and they all said more or less the same thing when I asked them about any particular story from Douglas's memoirs about their roles in his life: "Oh, that part's not true, but I'm sure the rest of the memoir must be." When I could not find a single person who could confirm a single account dealing with them in one of Douglas's books, the warning signs were very clear. And they became clearer still when I realized that, over the years—other than James F. Simon, who had published a fine biography of Douglas before the Justice's papers were available for research—no fewer than a half dozen other people had begun full biographies of Douglas and not one of them had finished the task.

The challenge was clear. Douglas's life was the stuff of novels. Unfortunately for me, he had already written those novels in the form of his memoirs. As a result, it was my task to research and write the accurate account of his life, all in a single volume. And it was no easy task, given the vastness of the unpublished and published material on Douglas. Douglas's own unpublished papers are divided among 1,784 boxes of documents in the Library of Congress, in Washington, D.C., and hundreds of his speeches are on file in the Yakima Valley Museum and Historical Association. Other materials are scattered all over the country. I was able to examine eighty-six collections of manuscripts and personal sets of unpublished papers, interview more than one hundred people (many of whom are no longer living and all of whom I thank for taking the time to speak with me, sometimes for days on end), and analyze nearly one hundred oral histories.

I greatly benefited from the prior work on Douglas by two talented video documentarians, which pointed me in the right direction, toward the "real" William O. Douglas. Walt Lowe, along with Don Heinen at KYVE-TV in Yakima, kindly made available to me thirty-three video-taped interviews that were very helpful to my research. I also benefited from the kindness of documentarian Robert W. Mull, who made available to me two very useful interviews from his own research. My work was also made easier by being granted access to the transcripts of the interviews with Douglas by Professor Walter Murphy of Princeton University, done in the early 1960s. Using all of this material, I was able to produce a manuscript that was 2,700 pages long.

Paring this down to its present size and shaping its tone would not have been possible without the wisdom and incredible patience of the legendary Robert Loomis of Random House, a man whose reputation as one of the most skilled and author-friendly editors is well deserved. I am also grateful to David Rosenthal, who, along with Sam Vaughan and Charlotte Mayerson, originally signed the book. I also want to thank the enormously talented copy editor Timothy Mennel for saving me from countless errors.

My gratitude is extended to agent Robert Gottlieb, then at William Morris, for arranging the original book contract and for encouraging me to stick with the plan of doing a one-volume biography.

Three people were indispensable in guiding my early research. Dagmar Hamilton offered countless insights based not only on her work as Douglas's research assistant but also on her years of studying and teaching the Justice's work. Early in the project, Suzanne Wills, then of the Pennsylvania State University Gerontology Study Group, suggested I familiarize myself with the "life cycle" research of Erik Erikson and Daniel Levinson, which helped me to explain Douglas's life. I am also grateful to Scot Powe for the wisdom of his seminal article on Douglas ("Evolution to Absolutism: Justice Douglas and the First Amendment," *Columbia Law Review* 74 [1974]).

This project was begun when I was teaching at the Pennsylvania State University, University Park. I want to thank the directors of the Institute for the Arts and Humanistic Studies—Stanley Weintraub, George Mauner, and Robert Edwards—its fellows, and its assistants—Shirley Rader and Sue Reighard—for providing such encouragement and support. The remarkable staff at Pattee Library during Nancy Cline's deanship, especially Kevin Harwell and the other reference librarians, provided much-needed answers without complaint. My thanks to then-Provost William C. Richardson and to his successor, Charles Hosler, for their support. Thanks also go to the clerical staff for typing the mountain of transcripts of my interviews. Mostly, though, my thanks from that era of my life go to colleagues such as Bob Harkavy, Jackson Spielvogel, Arthur Goldschmidt, Dan Walden, Phil Klein, John Buck, John Moore, Jim Moeser, Wendell Harris, Bob Maddox, Dan Katkin, and so many others who kept alive the spirit of teaching excellence there during difficult times.

For the latter phases of this project, I want to thank Fred Morgan Kirby and his family for creating and supporting the wonderful professorship in civil rights for the Government and Law Department at Lafayette College, in Easton, Pennsylvania, and to President Arthur Rothkopf and Provost June Schlueter for hiring me to fill it. My thanks also go to my assistant, Carmela Karns, for her untiring and upbeat assistance, to reference librarian Mercedes Sharpless and the other librarians at Skillman Library for searching out answers to countless queries, and to Government and Law Department head John McCartney and secretary Ruth Panovec and my colleagues there and in other departments for providing a harmonious academic community.

At various points, I have had the help of many people. Berneice Holt, Torri Jon Estrada, and William McIntosh were kind enough to search out files in distant locations. I also want to thank a number of research assistants for their diligent efforts: Douglas Kachadorian, Andrew Sieg, Tanya Baronti, and most especially Kenneth Mash and Laura Gordon-Murnane. Thanks go to Frances Hare and Marty Humphrey at the Yakima Valley Museum and Historical Association, Cynthia Garrick at the Yakima Public Library, Larry Dodd at the Whitman College Archives, and Dennis Bilger at the Harry S Truman Presidential Library for many kindnesses. Thanks also go to the research-library staffs at the Manuscripts Division of the Library of

Congress, the Columbia Oral History Collection, and the Franklin D. Roosevelt, Lyndon B. Johnson, Harry S Truman, Gerald R. Ford, and John F. Kennedy presidential libraries. My thanks also for the research grant that allowed me to travel to the Gerald R. Ford Presidential Library. I deeply appreciate the efforts of Lisa Reid Ragan for helping me gain access to Douglas's SEC files. Thanks to Marty and Ruth Orland for providing shelter during my early research trips to Washington, D.C.

My thanks to Mike Siebol and David Lynx of the Yakima Valley Museum and Historical Society in Yakima, Washington, Annie Miller and Franz Jantzen of the Supreme Court Curator's Office, Hayley Miller of Columbia University, and David Burgevin of the Smithsonian Institution for their help in securing copies of, and permission for using, the images that appear in the photo section of the book. Thanks also to Daniel Meyer of the University of Chicago Library for securing permission to quote from the Robert Maynard Hutchins papers. And thanks to Montana James Podva for granting me permission to quote from his personal diary.

Thanks go to Eliot Janeway for patiently explaining Douglas's campaign for the presidency and to attorney Jonathan Cuneo for pointing the way to his father, Ernie's, unpublished papers, which helped to untangle this story. My thanks also to Harry Datcher and Charles Reich for taking so much time to explain Douglas's behind-the-scenes life at the Court.

As always, I salute my four mentors—Henry J. Abraham, Dean Alfange, Jr., Sheldon Goldman, and the late Robert Harris—for giving me such a wonderful start on this career. Thanks also go to Larry Berman, F. Graham Lee, Charles Neal, Bruce Auerbach, and Beth Specker for their support over the years.

I am saddened that Alfred E. Coe, Harold M. Wright, and James Milholland did not live to see this book completed. I am so grateful, though, that my mother, Jean H. Coe, and my mother-in-law, Patricia G. Wright, will finally see that I wasn't kidding when I claimed for so long to be working on this book.

There is no way that I can adequately express my thanks to the members of my family, who have been so unfailingly encouraging and supportive throughout this seemingly endless biographical journey. My daughter, Emily, a writer in her own right, has offered many keen editorial insights at various points in the manuscript, and my son, Geoff, has helped me keep my sense of humor. This effort would simply not have been possible, though, without my wife and soul mate, Carol Lynn Wright, who kept me as sane as humanly possible over the years as she edited countless drafts of each chapter of the manuscript. It was truly the constant love and encouragement from these three people that made it possible for me to climb this personal mountain by completing this book.

Bruce Allen Murphy
Center Valley, Pennsylvania
August 6, 2002

ABBREVIATIONS

AI   Author's interview

Clifford private papers   Clark Clifford's Office Legal Files for William O. Doug-
                                las, Clifford and Warnke law firm, Washington, D.C.

COHC   Columbia Oral History Collection, Butler Library, Co-
                                lumbia University, New York, N.Y.

Corcoran Transcripts   "Summaries of Conversations [of Thomas Corcoran],"
                                President's Secretary's File, Box 336, Harry S Truman
                                Library, Independence, Mo. Copies in the Reading
                                Room, FBI Headquarters, Washington, D.C.

Cuneo Papers, FDRL   Ernest Cuneo Papers, Franklin D. Roosevelt Library,
                                Hyde Park, N.Y.

Douglas Conversations   "Transcriptions of Conversations Between Justice
                                William O. Douglas and Professor Walter F. Murphy,
                                1961–1963," Special Collections, Seeley G. Mudd Li-
                                brary, Princeton University, Princeton, N.J.

Douglas Impeachment   The Special Subcommittee on H. Res. 920 of the Com-
Hearings   mittee on the Judiciary, *Associate Justice William O.
                                Douglas: Final Report*, 91st Cong., 2d sess., 9/17/70,
                                pp. 484–552.

Douglas Military   "Final Statement of William O. Douglass [*sic*], serial
Record   no. 5900189," and *Report of Changes Enlisted Men*. Na-
                                tional Personnel Records Center, Military Personnel
                                Records, Saint Louis, Mo. Supplied by W. G. Seibert,
                                archivist and chief, Appraisal and Disposition Sec-
                                tion.

Douglas Remembrances   "Remembrances of William O. Douglas by His Friends
                                and Associates: In Celebration of the Fiftieth Anni-

versary of His Appointment as Associate Justice of the Supreme Court of the United States of America, 1939–1989." Ed. William Tod Cowan and Catherine Constantinou. Washington, D.C.: Supreme Court Historical Society.

Ehrlichman Presidential Notes
John Ehrlichman, meeting notes, John R. Ehrlichman Papers, Richard M. Nixon Presidential Papers, National Archives Storage Facility, College Park, Md.

FDRL Papers
Franklin D. Roosevelt Presidential Papers, Franklin D. Roosevelt Library, Hyde Park, N.Y.

Fisk Removal of Desertion File
P. J. Lockwood, "Application for Removal of Charge of Desertion," Adjutant General's Office, Washington, D.C., December 1888, Enlistment Branch File EB 10750 A 1888 for Orville Fisk, Location 9W3 R24 C14 SC, Box 3862, National Archives and Records Administration, Washington, D.C.

Frankfurter Rosenberg Addendum
Felix Frankfurter, "Addendum—June 19, 1953," to the Frankfurter Rosenberg Memo.

Frankfurter Rosenberg Memo
Felix Frankfurter, "Rosenberg Memorandum," 6/4/53, Box 65, File 1, Felix Frankfurter Papers, Harvard Law School, Cambridge, Mass. (microfilm).

Frankfurter Scrapbook
Felix Frankfurter, Supreme Court Scrapbook, Felix Frankfurter Papers, Harvard Law School, Cambridge, Mass.

Haldeman Diaries
H. R. Haldeman, *The Haldeman Diaries: Inside the Nixon White House,* multimedia CD-ROM. Sony, 1994.

Ickes Diary
Unpublished Diary of Harold Ickes, Manuscripts Division, Library of Congress, Washington, D.C. (microfilm).

Lowe Videos
Uncut videotaped interviews by documentarian Walter Lowe for *William O. Douglas: A Life on the High Court,* KYVE-TV, Yakima, Wash., 1988.

Podva Diary
Personal Diary of Montana James Podva, Willits, Calif.

RMHP
Robert Maynard Hutchins Papers, University of Chicago Library, University of Chicago, Chicago.

Salome Fisk Pension File   Pension Records, Orville T. Fisk, File Designation: Fisk, Orville T., WO373-092, Adjutant General's Office, National Archives and Records Administration, Washington, D.C.

Whitman Archives   Special Collections, Penrose Memorial Library, Whitman College, Walla Walla, Wash.

WOD   William O. Douglas

WODP   William O. Douglas Papers, Manuscripts Division, Library of Congress, Washington, D.C.

WOD/SEC   William O. Douglas SEC Commissioner Files, Securities and Exchange Commission, Washington, D.C.

WODY   William O. Douglas Materials, Yakima Valley Museum and Historical Association, Yakima, Wash.

Yakima City Directory   *R. L. Polk and Co.'s Yakima City Directory, Yakima, Washington.* Copies in the Yakima Genealogical Society, the Yakima Public Library, and the City Directories Room, Library of Congress, Washington, D.C.

Yakima Valley Genealogical Society   *Yakima Valley Genealogical Society* 11, no. 1 (January 1979).

Yale Archives   Manuscript Division, Sterling Library, Yale University, New Haven.

NOTES

PROLOGUE

xiii **He sure didn't** The description of WOD on the trail relies on a number of interview sources. Everyone has a favorite height for the Justice. Many of his friends recall him as being anywhere from just a shade to an inch over six feet tall (AI, Sheldon Cohen, 5/13/93, Washington, D.C., and Cragg Gilbert, 8/17/90, Yakima, Wash.). However, the *Current Biography* year-book from 1950 (New York: H. W. Wilson, 1950, p. 128) used a compendium of available biographical accounts of Douglas to describe him as "a little under six feet tall." While it is admittedly inexact, a measurement of Douglas's judicial gown, which in 1990 was on display in a mock-up of his Supreme Court office at the Yakima Valley Museum and Historical Association, indicates that the Justice stood just under six feet tall.

    The description of the disheveled Douglas relies on the following author interviews: Kay Kershaw and Isabelle Lynn, 8/6–23/89, Goose Prairie, Wash.; Cragg Gilbert, 8/17/90, Yakima, Wash., Dagmar Hamilton, 2/23–3/2/90, Austin, Tex.

xiii **As he rode** The liquor-bottles description comes from AI, Kay Kershaw, 8/7/89, Goose Prairie, Wash. The pant-leg description comes from AI, Cragg Gilbert, 8/17/90, Yakima, Wash.

xiii **Douglas was dressed** The narrative of this trip is based initially on the multiple accounts by Dagmar Hamilton. Her initial public account came in a speech at the William O. Douglas Commemorative Symposium, 1939–1989, sponsored by the William O. Douglas Institute, at the University of Washington, Seattle, 4/17/89. This account was repeated at the Supreme Court reception for Douglas in May 1989 and titled "Douglas the Man, Douglas the Myth: A Personal View." Further details about this trip were gleaned from the author's conversations with Hamilton from 2/23–3/2/90. Hamilton's recollections were confirmed and supplemented by author interviews with the following people, who were also on that trip: Kay Kershaw and Isabelle Lynn, 8/6–23/89, Goose Prairie, Wash., and Eileen Ryan, 8/10/89, Yakima, Wash. The trip can be precisely dated by the guest book at the Double K ranch, Goose Prairie, Wash., which shows that it ended on 9/2/70.

xv **"I'm not going"** AI, Kay Kershaw, 8/8/89, Goose Prairie, Wash.

CHAPTER 1

3   **"With a good"** Martha Douglas Bost to WOD, n.d. [Friday P.M. (1958)], WODP, Box 238; and see "Arthur and William Douglas," *National Biographic* 1:8 (May 1954): 2, in Yakima Valley Genealogical Society files, Yakima, Wash.

3   **Julia had named** WOD, *Go East, Young Man: The Early Years: The Autobiography of William O. Douglas* (New York: Random House, 1974), pp. 3–4, 12. Here, based on his mother's stories and faulty information from archivists, Douglas wrote that his grandfather "was born in Moreton, Vermont . . . [and was] barely sixteen when Lincoln was elected in 1860 but answered the call to arms and ended up with Grant at Vicksburg." He recalled how his father "lift[ed] me high in the air, . . . squeez[ed] my hand and [gave] me masculine praise." Douglas got this information from Charles T. Morrisey, director of the Vermont Historical Society, 5/10/67 (Box 912, WODP), who wrote that Orville Fisk was born to Eddy and Ursula Fisk of Moretown, Vermont. Indeed, sixteen-year-old Orville Fisk appears in the census records for Moretown, Vt. (Family History Center, State College, Pa.). However, while this man may have served with Grant in the Civil War, he was neither the husband of Salome Richardson nor the grandfather of William O. Douglas. In fact, the U.S. Census Reports from Irasburg, Vermont, for 1850 and 1860 (Family History Center, State College, Pa.) reveal that the Orville Fisk of Irasburg was the son of James and Rebecca Fisk. The Canadian Census Reports for 1871 (Boulton Centre, Quebec) and the U.S. Census Reports for 1880 (Family History Center, State College, Pa.), reveal that it was this Orville who married Salome Richardson. The actual behavior of Reverend William Douglas is made clear below.

3   **A New England** Private Orville Fisk, Civil War enlistment papers, "Company Description Book" (hereafter Orville Fisk Military Records), Sixth Regiment, Vermont Infantry, contained in Pension Records, Orville T. Fisk, File Designation: Fisk, Orville T., WO373-092, National Archives, Washington, D.C. (hereafter Salome Fisk Pension File), Adjutant General's Office, National Archives and Records Administration, Washington, D.C. My sincere thanks to William E. Lind, Military Reference Branch, Textual Reference Division, for locating all of these files and explaining them in a letter, 1/30/92.

4   **In 1861** For information on Salome Richardson Fisk's birthday, see U.S. Census Reports for 1850, 1860, 1880, and 1900 (Family History Center, State College, Pa.). For the marriage on 5/12/1861, a handwritten copy of the certificate can be found in "Copy from the record of Marriages in the town of Glover, Vt. for the year 1861," in the Salome Fisk Pension File. Here, the ages of the two are confirmed as twenty-four for Orville and thirty for Salome. These ages are also calculated from "Certificate of Death Record," Orville T. Fisk, 5/15/1885, and Salome Fisk, 3/1/12, County of Otter Tail, Minnesota, signed on 4/14/92 by Christie J. Buckmeir, deputy county recorder, Fergus Falls, Minn. These ages are contained in their obituaries: *Fergus Falls* (Minn.) *Journal,* 5/21/1885, p. 1 (Orville), and ibid.,

3/5/12, p. 4 (Salome), both on microfilm at the Minnesota State Library, St. Paul. Salome's funeral is described in ibid., 3/14/12, p. 3.

4   **Like so many** Orville Fisk Military Records, contained in Salome Fisk Pension File.

4   **But while his regiment** For Orville Fisk's behavior, see Orville Fisk Military Records, contained in Salome Fisk Pension File. For the record of the Sixth Regiment from Vermont during this period, see Frank G. Butterfield, *Revised Roster of Vermont Volunteers, 1861–1866* (Carlisle, Pa.: Military History Institute Collection), pp. 177–80, and a summary of Orville Fisk's military record on p. 194. See also G. G. Benedict, *Vermont in the Civil War: A History of the Part Taken by the Vermont Soldiers and Sailors in the War for the Union, 1861–65,* vol. 1 (Burlington, Vt.: Free Press Associates, 1886), pp. 208–33. See also *Revised Roster of Vermont Volunteers and Lists of Vermonters Who Served in the Army and Navy of the United States During the War of the Rebellion, 1861–66,* compiled by authority of the General Assembly under the direction of Theodore S. Peck, adjutant-general (Montpelier, Vt.: Watchman Publishing, 1892), pp. 213ff. See also Emil and Ruth Rosenblatt, *Hard Marching Every Day: The Civil War Letters of Private Wilbur Fisk: 1861–1865* (Lawrence: University Press of Kansas, 1992), passim.

4   **Orville convalesced** See Orville Fisk Military Records, contained in Salome Fisk Pension File. Orville actually got off lightly for his desertion charge, as made clear in Ella Lonn, *Desertion During the Civil War* (New York: Century, 1928), pp. 178–82.

4   **Finally, in June** See Orville Fisk Military Records, contained in Salome Fisk Pension File. For information on the reenlistment plan, see General Order no. 191, War Department, Series 1863, War Department Adjutant General's Office, Washington D.C., 6/25/1863, contained in *General Orders Affecting the Volunteer Force Adjutant General's Office, 1863* (Washington, D.C.: Government Printing Office, 1864), pp. 134–37.

5   **Knowing that the** This deal is recorded in deed 3899, entered in the registry of Brome County, Canada, on 6/30/1864, Gouvernement du Quebec, Ministere de la Justice, Archives Nationales du Quebec, Sherbrooke, Quebec. My sincere thanks to Simon Beauregard for his help in locating this document.

5   **While his old** For the birth dates and locations of the Fisk children, see Canadian Census for 1871, Brome County, Bolton Centre, Quebec; and the U.S. Census Material for 1880 and 1900 in Otter Tail County, Maine, Minn. (Family History Center, State College, Pa.). Walter's dates can be confirmed in *Fergus Falls Journal,* 8/2/34, p. 6.

5   **After nearly eight years** On the deal by Orville Fisk to get the land in Maine, Minn., see Homestead Patent, 8/12/1882, Recorder vol. 5, p. 497, by S. W. Clarke, Recorder of the General Land Office, Otter Tail County Recorder's Office, Fergus Falls, Minn. On the trip west, see Martha Douglas Bost to WOD, n.d., Box 238, WODP, and Douglas, *Go East,* p. 3. On the settlement of the Otter Tail County region, see John W. Mason, ed., *The History of Ottertail County, Minnesota* (Indianapolis: B. F. Bowen, 1916), pp. 479–647.

5   **Soon after their** Birth date for Julia can be found in the Julia Fisk Douglas

files, Yakima Valley Genealogical Society, Yakima, Wash., confirmed by the U.S. Census Reports for 1880, 1890, and 1900 (Family History Center, State College, Pa.). The correct birth date for Julia is listed in the Salome Fisk Pension File. We know that the family arrived in Maine about six weeks before her birth from the death certificate of Rebecca Fisk, Orville's mother, who traveled with them. Upon her death, on 7/3/1881, she was listed as having arrived in Minnesota on 5/9/1872 (Certificate of Death Record, Otter Tail County Recorder's Office, Fergus Falls, Minn.). The description of Julia as a young girl comes from Douglas, *Go East,* p. 3.

5   **While Salome raised** For more on Orville's illnesses, see Salome Fisk Pension File. For information on Orville's life in Maine, see his obituary in *Fergus Falls Weekly Journal,* 5/21/1885, p. 1. Salome's life in Maine is described in Douglas, *Go East,* p. 4.

5   **Besides keeping the** On Orville's death, of "Billious fever," the *Fergus Falls Weekly Journal,* 5/21/1885, p. 1, incorrectly listed the date of death as 4/15/1885. His death certificate on file in the Otter Tail County Recorder's Office, Fergus Falls, Minn., correctly has it as 5/15/1885. See also Orville Fisk's probate records for the farm in Maine, Minn., on 5/27/1895, Otter Tail County Recorder's Office, Fergus Falls, Minn.

6   **Despite the** See Salome Fisk Pension File.

6   **Not satisfied with** See Fisk Removal of Desertion File.

Because of the government's filing requirements designed to prevent fraudulent claims, making such an application often became a town affair. At least three citizens were required to submit supporting affidavits stating that they knew the claimant and her deceased husband, that the two of them were indeed married, that the veteran was a man of good character, that his death was caused by war-related injuries, and that they wrote their statements without any expectation of compensation.

The conclusion that the removal of the desertion charge was denied is confirmed by a reading from William E. Lind, Military Reference Branch, Textual Reference Division, National Archives and Records Administration, Washington, D.C.

6   **She argued that** Fisk Removal of Desertion File. "Dear Sir," the adjutant general wrote Attorney Lockwood on 1/9/1889, in response to this request:

> Inasmuch as [Private Fisk] did not return within a reasonable time from his first desertion, and as the testimony submitted cannot be accepted to establish that he was prevented from completing his re-enlistment contract by reason of wound received or disease contracted in the line of duty—or was ever found upon examination to be physically disqualified from performing the onerous duties of a soldier, not accepted as veteran volunteers, it must be assumed that this man was in good health when furloughed. There is no provision of law under which either charge of desertion can be removed, and the application must accordingly be denied.

While the military board missed the fact that Salome had come from Canada, Orville Fisk's obituary in the *Fergus Falls Weekly Journal* on 5/21/1885 mentioned that "after the war [he and his new wife, Salome] moved to Canada where he dwelt until he came to this state in the spring of 1872" (p. 1). Salome's own obituary would later confirm that "for a number of years their home was in Canada" (*Fergus Falls Weekly Journal,* 3/5/12, p. 4).

6   **While for most** *Fergus Falls Weekly Journal,* 7/10/1890, p. 8, and 9/4/1890, p. 8.

6   **But that did** Ibid., 3/7/1889, p. 8.

6   **But on October** Ibid., 10/24/1889, p. 5.

7   **Years later** Martha Douglas Bost to WOD, n.d. [Friday P.M. (1958)], WODP, Box 238; "Arthur and William Douglas," *National Biographic*. For the account of the three Fisk daughters leaving for their teaching jobs, see *Fergus Falls Weekly Journal,* 4/17/1890, p. 8.

7   **Just three days** *Fergus Falls Weekly Journal,* 10/31/1889, p. 6, and Douglas, *Go East*, p. 184.

7   **The loss of her** Douglas, *Go East,* pp. 19, 184.

7   **By the middle** *Fergus Falls Weekly Journal,* 4/17/1890, p. 8.

7   **Julia decided** Ibid., 9/20/1894, p. 8, and 2/27/1896, p. 8.

7   **Standing more than six feet** For William Douglas's age and early life, see the files on him at the Yakima Valley Genealogical Society. The physical description comes from letters by Martha Douglas Bost to WOD, quoting their mother, 5/3/62 and 5/2/73, WODP, Box 238. For his early connection with the First Presbyterian Church in Maine Township, see history prepared for the church's fiftieth anniversary on 9/16/36, available at the church in the Yakima Valley Genealogical Society files (hereafter Maine Church History).

7   **After hearing about** For the story of Douglas's failed career in Shandon, see his application for admission to the Bible Institute, Chicago. Thanks to Lynn Owens of the Alumni Office of the Moody Bible Institute for making this material available.

7   **Taking this as a signal** Ibid. This file lists Douglas as having applied on 5/3/1894, been accepted on the same day, entered two days later, and left on 6/12/1894. See also Gene A. Getz, *MBI: The Story of the Moody Bible Institute* (Chicago: Moody Press, 1969); Bradley J. Longfield, *The Presbyterian Controversy* (New York: Oxford University Press, 1991); James Findlay, "Moody, 'Gapmen,' and the Gospel: The Early Days of the Moody Bible Institute," *Church History* 31 (September 1962); and Lefferts A. Loetscher, *The Broadening Church: A Study of Theological Issues in the Presbyterian Church Since 1869* (Philadelphia: University of Pennsylvania Press, 1954).

8   **Despite his lack** Ibid.

8   **To their surprise** *Fergus Falls Weekly Journal,* 9/6/1894, p. 8; 9/13/1894, p. 8. In the account of her twin sister Jennie's wedding, this appears to be the first time that Julia sees William (see 9/20/1894, p. 8). See also Maine Church History.

8 **When Douglas arrived** *Fergus Falls Weekly Journal,* 9/20/1894, p. 8; 10/25/1894, p. 8; 11/15/1894, p. 5; and 11/29/1894, p. 5.

8 **When he finally began** Application for Marriage License, 4/13/1896, Otter Tail County Recorder's Office, Fergus Falls, Minn.; Julia and William Douglas File, Yakima Valley Genealogical Society; *Wheelock's Weekly,* 4/23/1896.

8 **Since for William** *Fergus Falls Weekly Journal,* 9/17/1896, p. 8. For more on the life of a typical Presbyterian Home Missionary and his wife, see "Experiences of a Home Missionary," *Rocky Mountain Presbyterian* 4, no. 10 (October 1875); Rev. E. F. Pratt, "Self Sacrifice of Home Missionaries—Personal Reminiscence," ibid., 4, no. 2 (February 1875); Mary Kelsey, "A Home Missionary Wife," ibid., 6, no. 4 (April 1877); and "20 Years on the Mission Field in Iowa," ibid., 5, no. 4 (April 1876).

9 **Beyond dealing with** *Wheelock's Weekly,* 4/8/1897, 4/15/1897, 4/22/1897, and 4/29/1897. See also *Fergus Falls Weekly Journal,* 5/27/1897, p. 8.

9 **For Julia** *Wheelock's Weekly,* 6/17/1897, and *Fergus Falls Weekly Journal,* 6/17/1897, p. 8.

9 **Then, a month later** *Wheelock's Weekly,* 7/15/1897 and 8/5/1897. See also *Fergus Falls Weekly Journal,* 8/5/1897, p. 8.

9 **Life for the Douglas family** *Wheelock's Weekly,* 2/17/1898, p. 5.

10 **For Julia** *Fergus Falls Weekly Journal,* 4/21/1898, p. 4. Birth certificate for WOD can be found in the County Recorder's Office, Otter Tail County, Fergus Falls, Minn.

10 **Relays of neighbors** *Wheelock's Weekly,* 10/20/1898, 10/27/1898, 11/3/1898, 11/10/1898, 12/1/1898, and 12/22/1898.

10 **Only when Julia** Ibid., 12/29/1898.

10 **Thereafter, for the Douglases** For a complete account of the traumatic life of the Douglases during this period, see ibid., 1/2/1899, 1/26/1899, 2/9/1899, 3/9/1899, 3/30/1899, 5/18/1899, 7/13/1899, 8/10/1899, 8/17/1899, 8/24/1899, 9/7/1899, 9/14/1899, 9/28/1899, 10/19/1899, 10/26/1899, 12/7/1899, 3/8/00, 3/22/00, 5/3/00, 5/17/00, 5/24/00, 6/7/00, 7/5/00.

10 **By mid-July** Ibid., 7/12/00.

10 **In early August** Ibid., 8/2/00, 8/9/00, 8/23/00. See also *Fergus Falls Weekly Journal,* 8/9/00, 8/16/00. On Reverend Douglas's vacation, see *Wheelock's Weekly,* 8/2/00, 8/9/00, and 8/16/00.

10 **Abandoned once again** *Fergus Falls Weekly Journal,* 8/16/00, and *Wheelock's Weekly,* 8/9/00.

10 **This time, though** *Wheelock's Weekly,* 8/23/00 and 8/30/00.

10 **Soon the papers** *Fergus Falls Weekly Journal,* 8/30/00, and *Wheelock's Weekly,* 8/30/00.

10 **While the precise nature** *Fergus Falls Weekly Journal,* 8/30/00.

10 **In fact** Ibid., 9/6/00 and 9/13/00.

10 **For a time,** Ibid., 9/6/00, and *Wheelock's Weekly,* 9/6/00.

10 **By the time** *Wheelock's Weekly,* 9/13/00, and *Fergus Falls Weekly Journal,* 9/13/00.

11 **The doctor** Martha Douglas Bost to WOD, 2/12/73, WODP, Box 238.

Douglas repeats part of this story in his memoir *Of Men and Mountains* (New York: Harper and Brothers, 1950), pp. 31–32, and in Douglas, *Go East,* pp. 32–33. For the doctor's history, see Mason, *History of Ottertail County,* p. 356. Dr. Leonard is mentioned often in *Wheelock's Weekly* and the *Fergus Falls Journal* during this period and was a close friend of the Douglases.

11   **It seemed to Julia** *Wheelock's Weekly,* 9/13/00 and 10/4/00.

11   **But nothing she did** Ibid., 9/27/00 and 10/4/00.

11   **Martha later told** Martha Douglas Bost to WOD, 2/12/73, WODP, Box 238.

11   **But despite these efforts** *Wheelock's Weekly,* 9/27/00.

11   **By early October** *Fergus Falls Weekly Journal,* 10/4/00.

11   ***Wheelock's Weekly*** *Wheelock's Weekly,* 10/4/00.

11   **Then, without warning** Ibid., 10/11/00. On the waves of typhoid in the region, see *Fergus Falls Weekly Journal,* 10/11/00.

11   **The *Fergus Falls Weekly Journal*** *Fergus Falls Weekly Journal,* 10/11/00.

11   **For the little boy's** Douglas, *Go East,* p. 184. In a very revealing passage for understanding Douglas's later life, he writes of his "liking for baked beans, my favorite dish to this day." When his infant illness ended, "I craved baked beans. Baked beans became a symbol of my return to a haven of security, which of course was my Mother."

11   **Just one week** *Wheelock's Weekly,* 10/18/00.

12   **Having already lost** Douglas, *Of Men and Mountains,* p. 32; see also Martha Douglas Bost to WOD, 10/5/64, 11/2/71, 2/12/73, and 9/10/74, WODP, Box 238.

12   **God had spared** WOD, *The Court Years: 1939–1975: The Autobiography of William O. Douglas* (New York: Random House, 1980), pp. 393–94. See also chapter 19 below.

12   **As a result** Martha Douglas Bost to WOD, 11/2/71, WODP, Box 238. See also ibid., 10/5/64, 2/12/73, and 9/10/74.

12   **After more than** *Wheelock's Weekly,* 4/17/02; *Fergus Falls Weekly Journal,* 4/24/02. For a small sample of Reverend Douglas's many duties and illnesses, see *Wheelock's Weekly,* 1/17/01, 1/24/01, 2/7/01, 2/14/01, 2/21/01, 2/28/01, 3/7/01, 4/18/01, 5/16/01, 6/13/01, 10/17/01, 10/20/01, 11/28/01, 12/26/01, 1/2/02, 1/9/02, 1/16/02, 1/23/02, 2/6/02, 3/6/02, 3/13/02, 4/3/02, and 4/20/02.

12   **Even more oddly** AI, John LaCoco, state clerk of the Presbytery of San Jose, Calif., who searched the records on the church's actions during that period, 11/20/91. No record exists either in the Department of History for the Presbyterian Historical Archives (U.S.A.) in Philadelphia or in the minutes of the 1902 Presbyterian General Assembly contained therein, of any call being made by that church for Reverend William Douglas. My thanks to Reference Librarian Kenneth J. Ross for guiding me in this search.

12   **"He just *arrived*"** AI, Ross McMillan, 12/13/91, Santa Cruz, Calif. (phone).

12   **After visiting friends** The description of Shandon and the Douglases' time there comes from the following phone interviews: Alta McMillan, 12/13/91, Shandon, Calif.; Eben McMillan, 12/13/91, Shandon, Calif.; Ross

McMillan, 12/13/91, Santa Cruz, Calif.; and Betty Lou Cokum, 12/13/91, Shandon, Calif. An excellent portrait of the area can be found in *La Vista* 3, no. 1 (June 1972), published by the San Luis Obispo County Historical Society, San Luis Obispo, Calif. Many thanks to Mark P. Hall-Patton of the Historical Society Museum in San Luis Obispo, who helped to provide this document and to guide my research in this region. See also the 1903 records of the General Assembly of the Presbyterian Church, Department of History for the Presbyterian Historical Archives (U.S.A.), Philadelphia.

13   **Entrusting Martha** AI, Ross McMillan, 12/13/91, Shandon, Calif. (phone); and Eben McMillan, 12/13/91, Shandon, Calif. (phone).

13   **Alex McMillan drove** AI, Eben McMillan, 12/13/91, Shandon, Calif. (phone).

13   **"The community didn't like"** Ibid.

13   **"In the end"** Ibid., and AI, Ross McMillan, 12/13/91, Santa Cruz, Calif. (phone).

13   **So, in April** AI, Eben McMillan, 12/13/91, Shandon, Calif. (phone).

14   **Just as two years** Search of the Central Washington Presbytery Minutes, 1902–1904, and the 1904 records of the General Assembly of the Presbyterian Church.

14   **Though he had no job** Ibid. Also, AI, Herbert Matsen, Yakima, Wash., 4/18/90. *A History of Klickitat, Yakima, and Kittitas* (Yakima: Yakima Valley Genealogical Society, 1904). (Also found as *An Illustrated History of Klickitat, Yakima, and Kittitas Counties* [Chicago: Interstate, 1904].)

14   **"Do you know me?"** Martha Douglas Bost to WOD, dated only "Thursday," WODP, Box 238; William Douglas File, Yakima Valley Genealogical Society; Central Washington Presbytery Minutes, 9/27/04.

14   **Three days later** William Douglas File, Yakima Valley Genealogical Society; Martha Douglas Bost to WOD, dated only "Thursday," dated only "Thurs. P.M.," and 6/17/67, WODP, Box 238.

14   **Days later** Ibid.; Douglas, *Go East*, p. 13.

15   **But there was no peace** Martha Douglas Bost to WOD, dated only "Thursday," WODP, Box 238.

15   **For the rest of her life** Ibid.

CHAPTER 2

17   **"Douglas was a screwball"** AI with Walter Lowe for his documentary on WOD, 4/27/89, Seattle (phone).

17   **"All I remember"** AI, Harry Datcher, 5/5/90, Washington, D.C.

17   **As the members** The material on early Yakima comes from a variety of superb sources available in the Yakima region and the Yakima Public Library: W. D. Lyman, *History of the Yakima Valley, Washington* (Chicago: S. J. Clarke, 1919); Gary L. Jackson, *Remembering Yakima: By Those Who Were There* (Yakima: Golden West, 1975); Click Relander and George M. Martin, *Yakima Washington Jubilee, 1885–1960* (Yakima: Franklin Press, 1960); George M. Martin, Paul Schafer, and William E. Scofield, *Yakima: A Centennial Reflection: 1885–1985* (Yakima: Shields Bag and Printing, 1985);

Maurice Helland, *Tent to Tower, 1885–1985* (Yakima: Yakima Presbyterian Church, 1984); and Jeanne R. Crawford, ed., *As the Valley Was: A Pictorial View* (Yakima: Yakima Federal Savings and Loan Association, 1968). Many thanks to the noted Yakima historian George M. Martin, and Yakima librarian Cynthia Garrick for leading me to these sources.

17 **The reason for this appearance** Douglas, *Go East,* p. 23.

18 **The topography** Calvin B. Coulter, "The Victory of National Irrigation in the Yakima Valley, 1902–1906," *Pacific Northwest Quarterly* 42 (1951): 100.

18 **The secret to the future** Robert C. Nesbit and Charles M. Gates, "Agriculture in Eastern Washington, 1890–1910," *Pacific Northwest Quarterly* 37 (October 1946): 288–89; and Douglas, *Go East,* pp. 17–18, 24.

18 **But in fact finding** *Yakima Signal,* 2/24/1883, available on microfilm from the Washington State Historical Society; and Martin, et al., *Yakima,* pp. 17–18. See also Louis T. Renz, *The Construction of the Northern Pacific Railroad Main Line During the Years 1870 to 1888* (Walla Walla: privately printed, 1973).

18 **In the early 1880s** While all of the Yakima sources have versions of this legendary city move, see specifically Martin, et al., *Yakima,* pp. 26–30; Relander and Martin, *Yakima Washington Jubilee,* pp. 18–29; and Jackson, *Remembering Yakima,* pp. 13ff. These accounts were supplemented by AI, George M. Martin, 6/5/90, Yakima, Wash.

19 **Thus began** Maurice Helland, *They Knew Our Valley* (Yakima: privately printed), p. 78; and ibid.

19 **While the new buildings** Martin et al., *Yakima,* pp. 28–29.

20 **With Yakima City** Ibid., p. 30.

20 **By the time** Jackson, *Remembering Yakima,* p. 18.

20 **She looked** AI, George M. Martin, 6/5/90, Yakima, Wash.

20 **Fortunately for Julia** This pension was from the Corporation for Relief of Poor and Distressed Presbyterian Ministers and from the Poor and Distressed Widows and Children of Presbyterian Ministers, a program that had existed since 1759. See R. Douglas Brackenridge and Lois A. Boyd, *Presbyterians and Pensions: 1917–1988* (Atlanta: John Knox, 1988), pp. 7–19; for the range of these pensions, see the minutes of the 1903–1905 General Assembly for the Presbyterian Church and the Central Washington Presbytery Minutes. Reverend Douglas's personal pension records could not be located in the files of the Presbyterian Historical Society or the Yakima or Cleveland, Washington, Presbyterian churches.

20 **Because Julia's brother-in-law** See *Wheelock's Weekly,* 8/18/04, and the *Fergus Falls Weekly Journal,* 8/18/04, filed in the Otter Tail County Historical Society, Fergus Falls, Minn.

21 **After the burial** The range of Julia's initial financial stake following her husband's death has varied among the stories told by her offspring. In "Arthur and William Douglas," *National Biographic,* the figure is put at $1,800. In Douglas, *Go East,* the figure is put at $2,500 (p. 17). As will be outlined below, Julia Douglas had around $3,000.

21 **Finally, the local** See Julia Fisk Douglas to WOD, dated only "Tuesday, P.M." [1926], WODP, Box 241, "Julia Douglas, Death of," file.

21　　**By supplementing** See Maurice Helland's interview with Douglas child-hood friend Al Egley in *Yakima Valley Genealogical Society,* 31–32.

21　　**The question now** Land Title, George E. Wise and Sadie W. Wise to Julia B. Douglass [*sic*], 12/13/04, Yakima County Book of Deeds, vol. 32, p. 27, Yakima Title Guarantee Company (as well as Yakima Recorder of Deeds office); thanks to Betty McGillen, Yakima county clerk, and Kathy at the Yakima Title Guaranty Company for their help in retrieving these docu-ments. Yakima City Directory, 1905, gives the precise listing of the Doug-las home; confirmed by U.S. Census Materials for Yakima, 1910, Yakima Valley Genealogical Society.

21　　**Since the house** See Yakima City Directories, 1903–1904 to 1911.

21　　**The Douglas home** Taken from the U.S. Census Materials for Yakima, 1910. By 1916, the census materials make clear, the social class of the neighbor-hood had improved. U.S. Census Materials, Yakima, 1920, matched with the Yakima City Directory, 1916.

21　　**"[We] never thought"** See Maurice Helland, interview with Al Egley, *Yakima Valley Genealogical Society,* 31–32.

21　　**John Gavin** AI, John Gavin, 2/10/92, Yakima, Wash. (phone).

22　　**Indeed, until 1909** Yakima City Directory, 1909, makes it possible to sta-tistically compare the taxes paid by Julia Douglas to those paid by other residents.

22　　**But disaster loomed** Ibid., 1910–1911 and 1911–1912.

22　　**In just two years** The statistical analysis of Yakima occupant-tax payments in 1910 indicates that the median payment figure was $497.89 (though this figure could be high because many occupants did not declare any holdings at all). In 1910, 24 percent of the respondents fell between $200 and $300 in taxes, another 24 percent fell between $300 and $500. Only 18.4 percent fell in Julia's tax category of $100 to $200, well within the bottom quarter of Yakima society. The total number of tax entries was 4,274.

22　　**"Cull didn't attempt"** AI, Chalmer Walter, 12/23/91, Yakima, Wash. (phone).

22　　**"Jim did mostly"** AI, Fred Velikanje, 12/23/91, Yakima, Wash. (phone).

22　　**Normally for Cull** AI, George M. Martin, 6/5/90, Yakima, Wash. And George M. Martin, interview of Bruce Mallard (cousin of James O. Cull), reported to the author, 9/17/91 (phone).

22　　**Rather than offering** Information on this transaction comes from Yakima Book of Deeds, vol. 74 (1911), p. 415; vol. 90 (1912), p. 110; Terrace Heights Subdivision no. 1, January 1911; Yakima County Assessor's Office (provided by Linda Huebner of that office); and, for the current day, Yakima County Assessor's Plat, NW 1/4 Section 22 Township 13, North Range, 19 E.W.M. (Formerly Terrace Heights Subdivision #1, Lot 154, now Charline Heights and Charline Heights Replat). See also below and chap-ters 5, 7, and 36. See Douglas, *Go East,* p. 17, for his remarkably different account of this deal (in terms of timing, investment target, and success), in which he claims that Cull, "the devil incarnate," persuaded his mother to invest her money in 1904 (when Douglas was only six) in a failed irri-gation project, which went bankrupt, ruined them financially, and "caused us to start life penniless." The real estate and financial records for Yakima in the Registrar of Deeds Office indicate very clearly that Julia and Cull's first land deal and many others were quite successful and began in 1911, when Orville was thirteen and in high school.

23   **But Julia may not** Yakima City Directories, 1910–1911, 1911–1912; AI, John Gavin, 2/10/92, Yakima, Wash. (phone); and Douglas, *Go East*, p. 26.

23   **For the remainder** Yakima Book of Deeds, vol. 77 (1911), p. 191, and vol. 78 (1911), p. 290. These Yakima Title Company documents are in the possession of the author.

23   **However, investors** This suit was canceled pursuant to an order of the Superior Court of Yakima City, Wash., 1/30/13, recorded in Superior Court Journals, vol. 6, p. 339. Suit found in Yakima Book of Deeds, vol. 74, p. 415; case no. 8031, Superior Court Records, *Julia B. Douglass v. A. A. Nicol, Ruby A. Poole, and Nina L. Poole,* filed 12/14/12.

23   **To Julia's dismay** Julia was paid some seventy-two dollars in back interest on 8/28/15 and got the remainder of the $124 owed her in interest some three months later. See Deed no. 107442, 4/10/17, in Yakima Book of Deeds, vol. 169, page number unreadable. (Thanks to the Yakima Title Guarantee Company for providing this document.) See also "In the Matter of the Estate of James H. Thomas, Deceased," Superior Court of Washington Order no. 23800, 6/15/18, signed by Judge Harcourt M. Taylor, provided to author by Tracy Slagle of the Yakima County Clerk's office (including Exhibit A, a quitclaim deed, Maud Granger et al. to Lucy B. Thomas, 5/26/15, and Exhibit B, the claims against the Thomas estate).

23   **Upon learning** Yakima County Book of Deeds, vol. 187 (1919), p. 871, June 3.

24   **The dramatic impact** See Yakima City Directory, 1914 (also 1911–1913), and statistical analysis of the tax entries for the entire city. Only when Pettit's grocery store began to make money in 1916 did he pull slightly ahead of Julia in the tax listings. However, three years later, he fell behind her again when his business experienced a downturn.

24   **Just two years later** See ibid., 1915 and 1916. While Yakima's average tax base had increased by 1916 to $620.81, Julia's $300 tax base now placed her higher than 60 percent of the other taxpayers in the city. Julia was at the absolute top of the largest category of taxpayers, which comprised 53 percent of the city. Julia's investments had allowed her to move from the bottom quarter of the city's society in 1910 to the top 40 percent of Yakima society in 1916 (total of 2,086 tax entries).

24   **Just a few months** The mortgage obligation was marked "satisfied and cancelled" on 8/14/16 on *Lis Pendens,* case no. 8031, Superior Court Records, *Julia B. Douglass, Guardian v. A. A. Nicol et al.,* 12/14/12, p. 435. Also marked "full and complete satisfaction" on original handwritten form of the Poole company mortgage.

24   **By this time** All of these financial calculations match up as well with a series of undated letters from Julia to WOD in 1926, outlining her finances in this period, WODP, Box 241, "Julia Douglas, Death of" file. See chapter 5, below.

24   **But having endured** AI, George M. Martin, 6/5/90, Yakima, Wash.; and AI,
      Isabelle Lynn, 4/19/89, Goose Prairie, Wash. Julia refers to herself as a
      "widow lady" in an undated letter to her son written in late 1925 or early
      1926. See Julia Douglas to WOD, "Monday, P.M.," n.d., WODP, Box 241,
      "Julia Douglas, Death of," file.

24   **And she could not** Interview, Cathy Douglas Stone, 5/17/88, Lowe Videos.
      Confirmed by Douglas, *Go East,* p. 17, where he writes: "It was the ten or
      fifteen cents that we brought home each evening that often meant the dif-
      ference between dinner and no dinner." Cathy Douglas also wrote how her
      husband recalled Julia saying at breakfast, "Easy on the butter, boys, its [*sic*]
      ten cents a pound!" Cathy Douglas, "William O. Douglas: The Man,"
      Supreme Court Historical Society 1982 Yearbook, Supreme Court Historical So-
      ciety, Washington, D.C., website, found at www.supremecourthistory.org.

24   **Young Orville** Martha Douglas to WOD, "June 20," n.d., WODP, Box 238;
      Interview with Cathy Douglas Stone, 5/17/88, Lowe Videos; Douglas, *Go
      East,* pp. 59–60.

24   **Some of these jobs** AI, Ira Ford, 8/20/89, Yakima, Wash. Whitman class-
      mate Hallam Mendenhall stated that he and his friends heard the same
      story from Douglas in college, AI, Hallam Mendenhall, 2/27/92, Ocean
      City, N.J. (phone). Both men drew the same conclusion from Douglas's re-
      peated tales that he likely lost his virginity in this brothel. Mendenhall
      also says that he and his college friends believed that this incident later
      "colored Douglas's association with the issue of pornography on the
      Court for many years." This story is also significant because by the time
      Douglas retold it in his memoirs, he told a tale of being used by the Es-
      tablishment in Yakima to try to trap the ladies in the brothel into solicit-
      ing an underaged client, thus sickening him toward these town and
      church leaders (see Douglas, *Go East,* pp. 60–62). Showing the impact of
      these and other autobiographical tales on Douglas's later image, this story
      was used by playwright Douglas Scott as the key dramatic device for his
      superb Off-Broadway play on Douglas's life, "Mountain," staged in the
      Lucille Lortel Theater and seen by the author in 1990, starring Len Cariou.

25   **Having already lost** Douglas, *Of Men and Mountains,* p. 32.

25   **In time, Orville** See Maurice Helland, interview with Al Egley, *Yakima Val-
      ley Genealogical Society,* 31–32. As outlined below, though, Douglas's
      friends did not believe this or see him as any different from them. See
      also Douglas's own account of his appearance in *Of Men and Mountains,*
      pp. 32–33, and *Go East,* pp. 33–35.

25   **Throughout his life** AI, Frances Penrose Owen, 9/9/90, Seattle.

25   **To build up** Douglas, *Court Years,* pp. 393–94.

25   **Despite Julia's** See Maurice Helland, interview with Al Egley, *Yakima Val-
      ley Genealogical Society,* 31–32.

26   **Every time Orville** See comments by WOD childhood buddy Paul L.
      Marble in "Douglas, Now Justice, Was 'Peanuts' to Chums," *Seattle Post-
      Intelligencer,* 3/26/39, p. 3.

26   **Embarrassed by his physique** *Yakima Wigwam,* North Yakima, later A. C.
      Davis, High School yearbook, vol. 4, no. 8 (May 1916), Yakima Public

Schools (thanks to Lynne Greene, librarian, for providing the copy) (hereafter *Yakima Wigwam*). On WOD's recovery technique, see Douglas, *Of Men and Mountains,* chap. 3, and Douglas, *Go East,* chap. 3.

26   **Prior to this** Douglas, *Of Men and Mountains,* p. 33.

26   **Julia encouraged** Martha Douglas Bost to WOD, 2/12/73, WODP, Box 238. See also James F. Simon's biography of Douglas, *Independent Journey: The Life of William O. Douglas* (New York: Harper and Row, 1980), chaps. 2–4, for a fine account of Douglas's Yakima childhood.

26   **Blessed with a photographic memory** AI, an anonymous representative in the personnel office, Educational School District (ESD) offices, Yakima School District, 4/24/90. This woman was looking at the Douglas school files at the time, but, according to Yakima school policy at the time, for privacy reasons she could not release the information.

26   **When her children** Jack Alexander, "Washington's Angry Scotsman," *The Saturday Evening Post,* 10/17/47, pp. 9–10, 102–7. On Douglas's Yakima years, see also Milton Viorst, "Bill Douglas Has Never Stopped Fighting the Bullies of Yakima," *The New York Times Magazine,* 6/14/70, pp. 8ff.

27   **In time, this routine** Besides becoming somewhat sick of the church services, Orville experienced a kind of split in his religious personality, as the more forgiving Social Gospel doctrine that he now heard from the Yakima pulpit differed from the "hellfire and brimstone" sermons that were delivered by his father in years past (and would be evident in the old sermons that Julia had her children read repeatedly). So, by his teenage years, Orville began looking to other churches for guidance. See Alexander, "Washington's Angry Scotsman"; Viorst, "Bill Douglas Has Never Stopped"; and Douglas, *Go East,* pp. 13–16.

27   **Orville also joined** *Yakima Wigwam,* 1916, and *Yakima Valley Genealogical Society,* passim.

27   **Hampered by a combination** Maurice Helland, interview with Eddie Thompson in *Yakima Valley Genealogical Society,* p. 26.

27   **One of Douglas's** Comments by Paul L. Marble, in "Douglas, Now Justice," p. 3. See also *Yakima Wigwam,* 1916. It is clear from the yearbook photo of WOD and photos of him at Whitman College (in Douglas, *Go East*) that he wore this checkered suit throughout the end of his high school and into his college years. This cartoon and the name stung WOD deeply. Marble recounts that years later, in presenting himself to Justice Douglas, his outstretched hand was ignored while the Justice turned to his wife to introduce him as the classmate who had drawn "that horrible picture" of him in high school.

28   **Burdened by his** AI, Cragg Gilbert, 8/17/90, Yakima, Wash.; Douglas, *Go East,* chap. 4. Douglas claims in *Go East,* p. 19, that he began these trips at the age of eleven. However, his sister recalls his July 1915 trip as his first, making him nearly seventeen years old (see Martha Douglas Bost to WOD, 2/12/73, WODP, Box 238). Indeed, the only surviving pictures of WOD on such camping trips show a strapping late teenager carrying a horseshoe pack over his shoulder and next to a horse.

28   **Then the fun** Ibid.

28   **For the overprotective** Martha Douglas Bost to WOD, n.d., "Saturday," likely 1974 or 1975, WODP, Box 239.

28   **Despite his mother's** See Douglas, *Of Men and Mountains,* passim.

CHAPTER 3

29   **"We lay claim"** AI, Frances Penrose Owen, 9/9/90, Seattle.

29   **It was money** Douglas, *Go East,* p. 97.

29   **There was just** AI, Jerry Cundiff, Jr., 5/31/90, Walla Walla. Also, see Robert Mull, interview with Chester Maxey, 9/22/81 (provided to the author by Mull). Also see *Walla Walla Union,* 5/7/17, p. 2.

30   **Since these boys** Ibid.

30   **But even this fine job** AI, Jerry Cundiff, Jr., 5/30/90, Walla Walla; also see "William O. Douglas: The Man, His Life, His Views," campaign document by the Research Division of Americans for Democratic Action (ADA) (Washington, D.C., 1948). The author's thanks to Ed Mitchell for providing a copy of this document from his collection, Malibu, Calif.

30   **For Orville** AI, Frances Penrose Owen, 9/9/90, Seattle; see also Douglas, *Go East,* p. 101.

30   **And what an education** Chester Maxey Oral History, 1/16/76, Whitman Archives (with thanks to Larry Dodd for leading me to this material); and AI, Frances Penrose Owen, 9/9/90, Seattle.

30   **A semester of living** Douglas, *Go East,* p. 100.

30   **In those days** AI, Jack Mendenhall, 3/4/92, Portolla Valley, Calif. (phone); and AI, Hallam Mendenhall, 2/27/92, Ocean City, N.J. (phone). The Mendenhall brothers were members of the rival Phi Delta Theta fraternity.

31   **Once he had pledged** This account is taken from the Whitman College Beta Theta Pi chapter's letter and notes, 4/12/17, Beta Theta Pi Historical Records, Oxford, Ohio. With thanks to national fraternity officer H. H. Stevenson for his help in locating and providing these documents.

31   **The ceremony had** Ibid., 6/7/39. By the time Douglas was writing his memoirs, he said of these organizations: "I concluded that fraternities were a form of feudalism and that feudalism on a college campus paid few dividends" (Douglas, *Go East,* p. 100).

31   **Now free from Julia's** WOD daily diary, 2/14/17, "School papers, Whitman College," WODP, Box 1771 (hereafter WOD School Diary). Also quoted in David J. Danelski, "The Origins of William O. Douglas's Jurisprudence," *Whitman: The Quarterly Magazine of Whitman College* 13, no. 3 (summer 1991): 4.

31   **He also went** WOD School Diary, 2/6/17–5/9/17.

31   **"Guess I'm too strong"** Ibid., 2/21/17.

31   **Finally, the effect** Ibid., 2/26/17.

31   **For the first time** Simon, *Independent Journey,* p. 50.

31   **When the family** AI, Frances Penrose Owen, 9/9/90, Seattle.

31   **All of this socializing** WOD School Diary, 2/28/17.

32   **And a week later** Ibid., 3/5/17.

32   **Toward the end** Ibid., 3/24/17.

32   **International events** See Woodrow Wilson Presidential Proclamation,

8/31/18, *Congressional Record;* 66th Cong., 11/14–19/19, vol. 58, pt. 9: 1840–42. On the pressure said by WOD to be felt to join the military, see WOD School Diary, 4/9/17, and Douglas, *Go East,* pp. 87–95. See chapter 37 about WOD's actual views toward military service.

On the "war fever" at Whitman, see WOD School Diary, 4/17/17 and 6/17/17, and among others, the following college-newspaper articles: "Whitman Obtains Unit of R.O.T.C.," 12/14/17; "Whitman Men to Go to Seabeck," 5/17/18; "Whitman Men in Summer Camps," 10/15/18; "Men Inducted into S.A.T.C.," 10/3/18; *Whitman College Pioneer,* Whitman Archives.

32 **Age did not prevent** AI, Jack Mendenhall, 3/4/92, Portolla Valley, Calif. (phone). This sort of service was not atypical. Douglas's later friend Robert Maynard Hutchins served in the war as an ambulance driver for two years even though he was younger than Douglas. Mary Ann Dzuback, *Robert Maynard Hutchins: Portrait of an Educator* (Chicago: University of Chicago Press, 1991), p. 15.

32 **Instead, in the fall** Stephen Penrose, "S.A.T.C—A Comedy," *Outlook,* 2/19; a copy appears in his college history/memoir, *Whitman: An Unfinished Story* (Walla Walla: Whitman Publishing, 1935), pp. 187–92. For more on how the SATC was supposed to operate, see Ralph Barton Perry, "Students' Army Training Corps," *National Service* 6 (1919): 77–84.

32 **In this setting** Blaine Hallock to S. T. Anthon, 2/20/50 (plus attached personal memoir), WODP, Box 1032.

32 **But beyond these runs** Penrose, "S.A.T.C.—A Comedy."

32 **Equipment problems** AI, William Pugh, 2/27/92, Yakima, Wash.; confirmed by entry in Walla Walla phone book, 1939. See also *Whitman College Pioneer,* 10/15/18, Whitman Archives.

33 **Despite the limited nature** Photo from her collection, now in the possession of the author. Thanks to Frances Penrose Owen for providing it.

33 **One classmate** AI, Frances Penrose Owen, 9/9/90, Seattle.

33 **And in the 1919** Yakima City Directory, 1919.

33 **As his college years** See the *Whitman College Pioneer,* 1916–1920; for instance, 3/1/18, 3/11/19, 1/12/17, 5/3/18, 5/10/18, 10/8/18, 2/18/19, 3/11/19, 6/13/19, located in the Whitman Archives. Also see WOD School Diary. Also confirmed by a review of the photo album from her college years with WOD in possession of Frances Penrose Owen, 9/9/90, Seattle, and other photos now in the possession of the author.

34 **Just three weeks** *Whitman College Pioneer,* 10/27/16, Whitman Archives.

34 **The search at Whitman** See Whitman College Catalog, 1917, p. 98, ibid.

34 **But Douglas accomplished** *Yakima Wigwam,* 1916. *Whitman College Pioneer,* 3/1/18 and 4/15/18.

34 **When the school's** *Whitman College Pioneer,* 3/14/19, Whitman Archives.

35 **As the more experienced** Ibid., 2/25/19.

35 **In the hopes** The account of this pivotal debate comes from AI, Frances Penrose Owen, 9/9/90, Seattle. Owen was consulting her personal journal from her college years and her contemporaneous notes. Her account is confirmed by the recollection of their classmate Bill Wilson, who told

James F. Simon: "[Douglas] just knocked their ears down with two or three sentences in rebuttal." See Simon, *Independent Journey*, p. 55.

35   **For an hour and** Ibid.

35   **"Orville gives"** Ibid.

35   **With one dramatic performance** Whitman College Catalog, 1919, p. 102; and *Whitman College Pioneer*, 4/23/20, both in Whitman Archives.

36   **But soon thereafter** See letters, Martha Douglas Bost to WOD, dated only "Saturday" [1975], WODP, Box 239; and "June 20," WODP, Box 238. In the "Saturday" letter, Martha writes: "I'm sorry you felt you had to send mother $20 a month when you were working your way thru [*sic*] college. Mother, Arthur, and I were getting along all right on my teaching salary— plus the extra day Art and I spent in the [fruit] packing house." These events can be cross-checked by Martha's absence from Whitman and presence in Yakima in the Whitman College Catalogs, 1917–1920, and the Yakima City Directories, 1917–1920. These records show that initially WOD was a freshman when Martha was a sophomore, but he was a senior when she was a junior. Also confirmed by Chester Maxey Oral History, 1/16/76, Whitman Archives.

36   **Then one day** Douglas, *Go East*, p. 105.

36   **But fate intervened** Yakima County Book of Deeds, vol. 187, p. 871, 6/3/19. These deals had a positive impact on Julia's financial status, and it was this improved financial position that not only allowed WOD to remain in school but also allowed Martha to return in the 1919–1920 academic year. Once more, this account matches up exactly with the series of undated laters from Julia Fisk Douglas to WOD, late 1925 and 1926, WODP, Box 241, "Julia Douglas, Death of" file. For more, see chapter 5 below.

36   **Julia now felt** See undated letters, Julia Fisk Douglas to WOD, late 1925 and 1926, WODP, Box 241, "Julia Douglas, Death of" file. For more details on this trust certificate and the effect on Douglas's life, see chapter 5, below.

36   **Going into his senior year** AI, Frances Penrose Owen, 9/9/90, Seattle, and *Whitman College Pioneer*, 11/7/19, and 2/27/20, Whitman Archives.

37   **If Orville had quit** *Whitman College Pioneer*, 4/23/20, and Whitman College Catalogs, 1916–1917 and 1919–1920, all in Whitman Archives. Douglas never received the yearly departmental honors in either English or economics.

37   **Orville did not fully** *Whitman College Pioneer*, 10/1/21, Whitman Archives.

37   **Despite her son's dismay** "William O. Douglas" file in the Yakima Valley Genealogical Society office; and "William O. Douglas" issue, *Yakima Valley Genealogical Society*, and Yakima City Directories, 1920–1922, passim; see also Douglas, *Go East*, chap. 9.

37   **Orville hated the job** Maurice Helland, interview with Al Egley, *Yakima Valley Genealogical Society*, 31–32.

38   **In his spare time** See *The Diary of William Fraser, August 1834 to July 1835* (London), and *The Emigrants Guide, or, Sketches of Canada: with some of the Northern and Western States of America* (Glasgow: Porteus Brothers, 1867).

38 **As soon as he saved** Alexander, "Washington's Angry Scotsman," pp. 9–10, 102–7.

38 **Teaching high school** Maurice Helland, interview with Maxine Moore, *Yakima Valley Genealogical Society,* 29–30.

38 **The truth was** See Yakima City Directory, 1921 and 1922, showing that WOD lived with his mother in the family's North Fifth Avenue home.

38 **Everything changed** The reason Mildred moved to Yakima for her senior year is unknown. See *Yakima Wigwam,* 1911 (with thanks to Lynne Greene, librarian, for providing the copy). University of Oregon records also note that she matriculated there after Yakima High School (AI, anonymous school official, 10/20/91, University of Oregon alumni office [phone]). Whether she met Orville or knew of him at that time is not known. With thanks to Jack Evans of La Grande, Oreg., for helping to track down some of this information and providing it to the author by phone, 10/19/91.

38 **Mildred had** The *Mimir,* academic yearbook for La Grande, Oreg., High School, 1917–1920; and interview with a school official in the Educational School District office for Lostine, Oreg., 10/18/91 (phone).

38 **In addition to being** AI, Millie Douglas Read, 8/20/89, Lostine, Oreg., and with John Evans, 10/19/91, La Grande, Oreg. See also Singrid Arne, "Douglas Has Good Head for Law But Wife Must Mind the Finances," Washington *Star,* 4/26/39, Martin Luther King Library, Washington, D.C.; and "Blonde Mrs. Douglas, to Be Youngest Court Wife," *The Washington Post,* 3/21/39, p. A5.

39 **When Mildred and Orville** The Yakima City Directory, 1922, shows that Mildred lived at 204 Hall Avenue, which was roughly seven blocks west of 111 North Fifth Avenue.

39 **As soon as she learned** See U.S. Census Materials for La Grande (Union County), Oregon, 1900. Information in the La Grande area genealogical society typed from her obituary shows that even it was initially fooled, as Mildred's original birth date of 1900 was crossed out, replaced by the correct date of 1892. Many thanks to genealogical researcher Christine Isaacson, who helped find these documents.

While Mildred and Bill's daughter, Millie, did not know her mother's exact age, she became aware over the years that she was older than her father: "No one knew that Mother was actually 8 years *older* than Dad. And she went to considerable pains to keep that fact private." AI, Millie Douglas Read, 8/20/89, Lostine, Oreg.

39 **Mildred became the subject** Based on a review of Mildred's letters to WOD, WODP, Box 241.

39 **In time** Douglas, *Go East,* p. 123; confirmed by George Draper to WOD, 4/19/46, and undated letter titled only "Dear Mr. Douglas," WODP, Box 324.

39 **And then there was the** George M. Martin, interview of Bruce Mallard, 9/17/91, Yakima, Wash. (phone). It makes perfect sense that Douglas would consult Cull, who was still the family lawyer at the time, as confirmed by the Yakima County deed and court records from that period.

Surely, Douglas, fatherless, would have talked to such a close family associate, who actively practiced law, about this career.

However, see also Douglas, *Go East,* pp. 122–25. While Douglas, for reasons that are made clear below, refused to credit Cull publicly with his role, it did not bother the crusty old attorney, who loved to tell relatives such as Bruce Mallard at family picnics: "I want no credit or blame for Douglas's legal career. How could the conservative young man I counseled in Yakima become such a revolutionary Communist on the Supreme Court? I don't want to be known as the man who had foisted such a blight on the nation." Mallard interview cited above.

39 **After several dates** AI, Millie Douglas Read, 8/20/89, Lostine, Oreg.

39 **Now all Orville** Douglas, *Go East,* p. 124.

40 **When Orville told Mildred** Mildred Riddle to WOD, November 1922, WODP, Box 241. Information confirmed by Yakima City Directory, 1923. Eventually, she returned to La Grande to teach Latin.

40 **"Lord, that was luxurious"** Chester Maxey Oral History, 1/16/76, Whitman Archives; Robert Mull, interview with Chester Maxey, 9/22/81, Walla Walla. As will be outlined below, it was not clear just how far Douglas traveled on this sheep train.

40 **When the arrangements** Douglas, *Go East,* p. 127.

40 **The next morning** As will be outlined below in chapter 12, the precise amount of the money is in serious dispute. It could have amounted to as little as seventy-five dollars. Douglas, *Go East,* pp. 127, 133, uses this figure, as does Simon, *Independent Journey,* p. 62. What is known, though, is that it did not last for all of Douglas's trip. (See tales in "Arthur and William Douglas," *National Biographic,* and all of the sources cited and discussed in chapter 12.)

40 **Julia cupped** Douglas, *Court Years,* p. 394.

40 **Plan as young** Editors' answer to letter from Silvanus Kingsley of Portland, Oreg., *Newsweek,* 4/10/39. As will be outlined in chapter 12, Douglas told many versions of this tale, but this appears to be the most correct one. It also confirms the story that he told longtime friends from Whitman College such as Frances Penrose Owen (AI, 9/9/90, Seattle) and from Columbia Law School such as Herman Benjamin (AI, 11/10/91, Palm Beach, Fla.). See chapter 12 for a discussion of the authenticity and reasons for Douglas's tale.

41 **When he arrived** Ibid. See also Marquis W. Childs, "The Next Member of U.S. Supreme Court," *St. Louis Post-Dispatch,* 4/2/39, p. 3. Much later, Douglas would claim in *Go East,* pp. 133–35, to have come into New York City on a freight train.

41 **Just as Douglas was** Bill Wilson told this story to Frances Penrose Owen (AI, 9/9/90, Seattle). See also Douglas, *Go East,* p. 134.

41 **After the explanations** Ibid.

42 **Now "Bill"** "Orville? Oh, he did hate that name. But it was the one his mother insisted on" (AI, Frances Penrose Owen, 9/9/90, Seattle). And see Douglas, *Go East,* p. 428: "As I have written, I always disliked the name Orville, though it followed me like a shadow right through high school.

I got mostly rid of it in college and completely so in law school." Thereafter, the only people who called Douglas "Orville" were members of his family, old college and high school classmates, and, for reasons that are unclear, Robert Maynard Hutchins.

CHAPTER 4

43   **"Bill used to write"** AI, Simon Rifkind, 8/4/89, New York.

43   **Nothing in Bill Douglas's life** AI, Herman Benjamin, 11/10/91, Palm Beach, Fla.

43   **There were no more** Information from student listings in the Columbiana Room, Columbia Law School Historical Archives, Columbia University, New York; for the listing on Shanks, see also the *Columbia University Bulletin of Information: School of Law Announcement* (hereafter *Columbia Law Bulletin*), 1923–1924 and 1925–1926, in author's possession (with thanks to Whitney Bagnall of the Columbia Law School's Alumni Office for making these catalogs available for purchase, 9/18/91). Copies also available in the Columbia Law School Library. By his senior year, Shanks was listed as being from Fayette, Idaho.

43   **By now, Douglas** *Columbia Law Bulletin*, 1922–1923, p. 18. It is not clear from the records in the Columbiana Room how much of the year Douglas remained in the Beta house, but he is listed in the catalog as living in Furnald Hall.

43   **To get through** Carrol M. Shanks, "Classmate Recalls W. O. Douglas' Columbia Exploits in Winning Honors While Working His Way Through," *Columbia Law Alumni Observer*, 4/14/39, p. 9, in the Columbiana Room, Columbia University, New York. Herman Benjamin recalls it a bit differently: "I would never disagree with Carrol, but Bill couldn't have done much tutoring. He didn't have the time." AI, Herman Benjamin, 11/10/91, Palm Beach, Fla.

43   **By Christmastime** Ibid. Compare to Douglas's version in *Go East*, pp. 135–36.

44   **"The thing that really"** AI, Herman Benjamin, 11/10/91, Palm Beach, Fla.

44   **Indeed, in an entering class** Ibid., and *Columbia Law Bulletin*, 1922–1923.

44   **Embarrassed by this** AI, Herman Benjamin, 11/10/91, Palm Beach, Fla.

44   **"The nickname"** Ibid., and *Columbia Law Bulletin*, 1922–1923. In *Go East*, Douglas claims to have saved his "nickels and dimes" and sat in the rafters to hear Enrico Caruso sing at the Metropolitan Opera in the winter of 1922–1923 (pp. 143–44). And had the famous tenor not died the year before Douglas arrived in New York, maybe that would have happened.

45   **Now all this hayseed** Much later, Douglas would claim that "on the whole, the intellectual competition at Columbia was not as keen as I had expected. This is not to say I did not have to compete." See Douglas, *Go East*, p. 148.

45   **Beyond the high caliber** *Columbia Law Bulletin*, 1922–1923.

45   **This combination** See ibid., 1924–1925, p. 19, for the listings of the Kent Scholars. I am indebted to Dean Arthur Kimball of the Columbia Law School (AI, 8/21/91 [phone]) and Herman Benjamin (AI, 8/21/91 [phone]) for explaining the meaning of this honor.

45   **"Douglas was not well-off"** AI, Herman Benjamin, 11/10/91, Palm Beach, Fla.

45   **As disappointed** See the listing of the new members of the Law Review in the *Columbia Law Review,* November 1923 (published monthly at that time by the Columbia Law School). Compare the class of '25 student listings in the *Columbia Law Bulletin,* 1922–1923 and 1923–1924. Also, AI, Herman Benjamin, 11/10/91, Palm Beach, Fla.

46   **A month later** See *Columbia Law Review,* December 1923, and the class of '25 student listings in the *Columbia Law Bulletin,* 1922–1923 and 1923–1924.

46   **Two months later** See *Columbia Law Review,* February 1924, and compare the class of '25 student listings in the *Columbia Law Bulletin,* 1922–1923 and 1923–1924.

46   **In the summer** See Affidavit for Marriage License, William O. Douglas and Mildred M. Riddle, 8/15/23, signed by L. B. Pierce; and Marriage Certificate, William O. Douglas and Mildred M. Riddle, 8/15/23; and Medical Certificate for Marriage License, 8/15/23, signed by J. L. Ingle, located in the Union County Clerk's office, La Grande, Oreg. (with thanks to R. Nellie Bogue, Union County county clerk, for assistance in obtaining these documents). For problems in Douglas's account of the date for his marriage and their implication for his story, see chapter 37 below.

47   **But strangely** AI, Herman Benjamin, 11/10/91, Palm Beach, Fla. Carrol Shanks never mentioned her in "Classmate Recalls Douglas." And Simon Rifkind recalled that he did not learn about Douglas's wife until after their law-school career. AI, Simon Rifkind, 8/4/89, New York.

47   **The way that Douglas** Others did not view the manner in which Douglas treated this relationship as charitably. See Mary Louise Shaw, "Justice Douglas Once Lived Here; First Wife Taught in Local School," *Bernardsville News,* 11/20/75, p. 1. Also see chapter 37 below.

47   **With married students** *Columbia Law Bulletin,* 1922–1923 and 1923–1924.

47   **Try as she might** *The Bernards Crimson* 8, no. 2 (11/7/23), in Bernardsville Historical Society.

47   **The problem with the job** AI, Marion Kennedy, town historian, Bernardsville, N.J., library, 10/24/91. Kennedy also kindly consulted city records and searched out information. See also Shaw, "Justice Douglas Once Lived Here," p. 1.

47   **The only passenger** AI, June Kennedy, township historian, 7/30/2002, Bernards Township, N.J. (phone), and AI, Marion Kennedy, town historian, 7/30/2002, Bernardsville, N.J. (phone).

47   **Never telling the law-school** *Columbia Law Bulletin,* 1924–1925.

48   **In an era** Shaw, "Justice Douglas Once Lived Here," p. 1.

48   **Thanks to his wife's** *Columbia Law Bulletin,* 1924–1925; AI, Herman Benjamin, 11/10/91, Palm Beach, Fla.; Shanks, "Classmate Recalls Douglas." Also see Douglas, *Go East,* chapter 10.

48   **The first professor** The account of Moore's teaching style also draws upon the recollections of those who later studied under him at Yale: Thomas I. Emerson Oral History, COHC; and Frank R. Strong, "Reminiscences of Yale Law School of Fifty Years Ago," *Yale Law Report* 28, no. 3 (spring/summer 1982): 14–18.

49 **Bolstered by Mildred's** See *Columbia Law Review,* May 1924, which listed, likely to his dismay, the newest member of the Review as "W. Orville Douglas."

49 **"Class work was sort of"** AI, Herman Benjamin, 11/10/91, Palm Beach, Fla.

49 **On the opposite page** See *Columbia Law Review,* May 1924.

50 **But as Bill Douglas** Mildred's change of address comes from the alumni files, University of Oregon Student Records Office. See also Shaw, "Justice Douglas Once Lived Here," and Shanks, "Classmate Recalls Douglas," and also AI, Herman Benjamin, 11/10/91, Palm Beach, Fla.

50 **Knowing that a great** This account is drawn from Shanks, "Classmate Recalls Douglas."

50 **Despite all of his labors** See *Columbia Law Bulletin,* 1926–1927, p. 20.

51 **Powell loved two things** While the records of class performance were not made available to the author, and indeed may not even still exist, this is the recollection of the order of standing according to the acknowledged class of '25 historian Herman Benjamin. AI, Herman Benjamin, 11/10/91, Palm Beach, Fla. See also Douglas, *Go East,* pp. 147–48; and Melvin I. Urofsky, " 'Dear Teacher': The Correspondence of William O. Douglas and Thomas Reed Powell," *Law and History Review* 7 (fall 1989): 331–86.

51 **As the spring term** See Simon, *Independent Journey,* p. 79; Douglas, *Go East,* p. 149.

51 **"The outstanding member"** Milton Handler to author, 7/10/91.

51 **"The news reached"** Douglas, *Go East,* pp. 148–49. While this makes a very dramatic tale, the real events were quite different. According to Herman Benjamin (AI, Herman Benjamin, 11/10/91, Palm Beach, Fla., and Benjamin to author, 12/7/91), the actual order of finish for the class was Carrol Shanks in first; Arthur Kramer and Herman Benjamin tied for second; Irvine Shubert fourth; and Alfred McCormack in fifth place. This is also the recollection of Milton Handler (Handler to author, 7/10/91). These recollections can also be confirmed through rough calculations based on the number of times that members of the class of '25 were named Kent Scholars. The fact that WOD was never once so named indicates that, *at best,* he was sixth in the class. For more on this discrepancy and its consequences, see chapter 37 below.

51 **He and Carrol Shanks** See *Columbia Law Bulletin,* 1925–1926.

CHAPTER 5

53 **"Something's crooked"** Julia Douglas to WOD, undated letter headed "Wednesday P.M.," WODP, Box 241, "Julia Douglas, Death of" file.

53 **For Mildred** Mildred Douglas to WOD, 8/12/26, WODP, Box 5 (discusses the concerns that she had had for the past year). The bar results were announced on 9/7/25; see "506 Students Pass Bar Examinations," *The New York Times,* 9/9/26, p. 27.

53 **Reasoning that Bill's** On the Douglases in Pelham, N.Y., see the *Pelican,* the Pelham Memorial High School yearbook, 1926, 1927, 1928 (provided by Pelham Memorial High School); and the Pelham street directories, 1925 and 1928, Town Historian's Office, Pelham (with thanks to Pelham

town historian Susan Swanson for researching this information and making it available). And see the Westchester County telephone directories for 11/9/25, 5/5/26, 11/8/26, 5/5/27, 11/1/27, and 5/11/28, Phone Directory Collection, Library of Congress, Washington, D.C. These records show that the Douglases lived in the Peldale Apartments from the winter of 1925–1926 to the winter of 1926–1927, when they moved to Peldean Court. See also Mary Louise Shaw, "Justice Douglas Once Lived Here," p. 1. On the problems of the move, see Mildred Douglas to WOD, 8/12/26, WODP, Box 5.

54   **But Douglas quickly learned** Leonard Mosley, *Dulles: A Biography of Eleanor, Allen, and John Foster Dulles and Their Family Network* (New York: Dial Press, 1978), pp. 76–77; and Nancy Lisagor, *A Law Unto Itself: The Untold Story of the Law Firm Sullivan and Cromwell* (New York: Paragon House, 1989), pp. 100–101. Also, AI, Herman Benjamin, 8/21/91, Palm Beach, Fla. Douglas's account differs from all of these; see *Go East*, pp. 149–50.

54   **After being passed over** This is according to Roxanne Piquero, Personnel Office, Cravath, Swaine & Moore law firm, who kindly consulted the firm's employment records (AI, 9/17/91, New York). These records confirm the information, though not the title of the firm used in *Go East* (p. 150), about Douglas's employment in Robert T. Swaine, *The Cravath Firm and Its Predecessors, 1819–1948*, vol. 2 (New York: privately printed, 1948), p. xv, n. 177, and p. 120; Mildred Douglas to WOD, 8/12/26, WODP, Box 5. On McCloy's reaction to WOD see Simon, *Independent Journey*, pp. 79–82. Simon reports that, according to McCloy, "when [Douglas] came in, he looked like he had come off a hike. He was not one of the usual Brooks Brothers set. In fact, he looked like a singed cat" (p. 81).

54   **In order to give him** Confirmed by AI, Pearl Sparrow, consulting the records of the personnel office, Columbia University, New York, 10/14/91. The extension school is now called the School of General Studies. Also see Columbia University Extension Contract for William O. Douglas, signed by Frank D. Fackenthal, 10/5/25, and [Dean] Huger W. Jervey to WOD, 12/28/25, WODP, Box 22. See also the *Columbia Law Bulletin*, 1925–1926.

54   **Like all new Cravath** See Simon, *Independent Journey*, pp. 79–91; and Douglas, *Go East*, pp. 150–58.

55   **With each passing day** For more on this illness, documented in Douglas's numerous letters to A. Howard Meneely, see below in chapter 6. See also Simon, *Independent Journey*, pp. 86–87, and Mildred Douglas to WOD, 8/12/26, WODP, Box 5.

55   **When the physical pains** Simon, *Independent Journey*, pp. 86–87, based on his interview with Wilson.

55   **Any changes** Obituary, Sara Stone Riddle, 12/28/25, *The Observer*, La Grande, Oreg. (Thanks to Christine Isaacson for assistance in locating this document.)

55   **Mildred packed** Julia Douglas to WOD, undated letters, "Tuesday P.M.," "Wednesday P.M.," and "Tuesday Morning," WODP, Box 241, "Julia Douglas, Death of" file. These letters were written in either late January or early

February 1926, because Julia mentions that Mildred has been away from WOD for a month, after the death of her sister. The letters can also be dated by Julia's discussion of the botched real-estate deal with the Coopers, discussed below.

55   **With pressure** Ibid. Julia does not appear in the Yakima City Directory in 1925 (published in September that year) and instead appears in the Minneapolis City Street Directory for that year, 1926, and 1927, with Martha at 315 West Fifteenth Street, apartment 44. Martha worked as an "assistant employee superintendent" at "L. S. Donaldson's Co." (1925 Directory, p. 683). Additionally, the Yakima City Directory lists the Coopers at 111 North Fifth Avenue in 1926 and 1927.

56   **The effect of this loss** Yakima City Directory, 1919 and 1921.

56   **Then, in November 1921** The information in this paragraph is taken from Julia Douglas to WOD, undated letters, "Tuesday P.M.," "Wednesday P.M.," and "Tuesday Morning," WODP, Box 241, "Julia Douglas, Death of" file. The precise nature of the trust arrangement between Julia and Cull is reprinted in the letter marked "Wednesday, P.M." The difficulty is that Julia misdates the deal as being in 1928, though this numeral is difficult to decipher and could be 1923, and her account from memory in the "Tuesday P.M." letter differs in some key respects from the actual document reprinted in the "Wednesday P.M." letter. This letter was almost certainly written in January or early February 1926, making all of the dates in her calculations from memory highly suspect and quite likely inaccurate. See also letters marked, "Friday P.M.," "Sunday P.M.," "Thursday P.M.," and "Monday P.M." This arrangement appears not to have been recorded in the Yakima City records, as searches by the author, the staff of the Recorder of Deeds in the early 1990s, and the Yakima Valley Title Company all failed to uncover this document. However, the amount of money that Julia talks about at that time squares with the calculations of the money available to her from her earlier real-estate deals.

The problem with the account that she told her son is that, likely because of a failure of memory due to old age, it is incomplete. She told him, likely in 1926, that she invested $2,100 "about 15 years ago" with Cull and Rankin. However, she left out her earlier real-estate investments. It is possible that she actually had more money than I have outlined, but I have used the most conservative calculation in reconstructing these events. I am reassured in these calculations that the numbers match, as all of these real-estate deals would have given her $3,000 in 1919, and the unrecorded note that she discusses in the "Tuesday P.M." letter recalls that her deal with Cull in 1921 was for $3,010. This is almost certainly the failed "irrigation deal" between Cull and Julia that Douglas discussed in *Go East*, p. 17.

Compounding the $3,010 figure does indeed generate just more than the $3,500 figure ($3,521.25) that she mentions being owed by the Cull firm in 1925. This provides further indication of the veracity of her claims and the earlier determination of her investment nest egg.

56   **On top of all this** See Warranty Deed no. 371192, Julia B. Douglass [*sic*] to

Charley Cooper and his wife, Elizabeth J. Cooper, filed 1/9/26 (referring also to the mortgage on 111 North Fifth Avenue of $1,200, 8/24/23, which still had $885.62 outstanding), vol. 244, Yakima Registry of Deeds Office, provided to the author by the Yakima Valley Title Guarantee Company. See also Julia Douglas to WOD, "Thursday P.M.," "Monday P.M.," and "Tuesday P.M.," WODP, Box 241, "Julia Douglas, Death of" file.

57 **"You can see"** Julia Douglas to WOD, "Thursday P.M.," WODP, Box 241, "Julia Douglas, Death of" file.

57 **"Hope you get"** See ibid., "Tuesday P.M.," and also "Wednesday P.M." and "Tuesday Morning," WODP, Box 241, "Julia Douglas, Death of" file.

57 **But this time** Later in life, Douglas wrote his sister about Cull as the man "who skinned Mother out of her small inheritance." But it was not until the middle 1920s that both of them realized this had been the result of bad, or ill-advised, investments. WOD to Martha Douglas Bost, 9/28/56, WODP, Box 238.

57 **As for the problem** This story has something of a happy ending for Julia. The Coopers, through James O. Cull, transferred the North Fifth Avenue house back to Julia for a fee of ten dollars. (See quitclaim deed no. 418840, "Charley Cooper and Elizabeth J. Cooper" to "Julia B. Douglas, a widow," 4/22/27, vol. 260, Yakima Registry of Deeds office.) Three years later, Julia sold the property to Sadie Bunch; see Deed no. 556278, 12/23/30, vol. 290, Yakima Registry of Deeds, provided to the author by the Yakima Valley Title Guarantee Company.

58 **In a matter of days** AI, Roxanne Piquero, 9/17/91, New York, confirming Swaine, *Cravath Firm,* p. 120. Douglas argues, contrary to these records, that he remained with the firm for almost a year and left despite the efforts by Robert Swaine to keep him (see Douglas, *Go East,* pp. 156–57). It is possible given the timing of the departure that Mildred was not even in New York when Douglas quit his job.

58 **When Mildred returned** See the *Pelican,* the Pelham Memorial High School yearbook, 1926. See also Shaw, "Justice Douglas Once Lived Here," p. 1.

58 **Meanwhile, Douglas tried** On his fees, see the Columbia University Extension School agreement for WOD, 10/5/25, and Dean Huger W. Jervey to WOD, 12/28/25, WODP, Box 22. See also Frank D. Fackenthal, secretary of the university, to WOD, 2/4/26, WODP, Box 22. The records of the Columbia University Personnel Office confirm that WOD did in fact continue to teach part-time at Columbia Law School both in the day division and in the extension school during the spring of 1926. AI, Pearl Sparrow, who was consulting WOD's file, 10/14/91 (phone).

Figures comparing WOD's teaching salary with what he would have received from the Cravath firm vary depending on the length of the spring term. Conservatively assuming a four-month term, Douglas would have received $600 from Cravath. During this time, Douglas received $2,600 from Columbia.

59 **By quitting the Cravath** I am indebted in the analysis for this chapter— and, frankly, in the construction of the framework of this book—to the seminal work of psychologists Erik Erikson and Daniel Levinson on the

"life cycle" of human beings. Erikson writes that in a normal life cycle, a person will have a crisis, which varies in severity, between the ages of twenty-five and thirty-two as he or she breaks away from family teachings and plans and societal expectations to follow his or her own path. In *Young Man Luther: A Study in Psychoanalysis and History* (New York: W. W. Norton, 1958), Erikson uses this analysis to explain Martin Luther's famous and pivotal "fit in the choir." For Douglas, this 1926 "breakdown" was his "fit in the choir." My analysis is informed also by the extending work of Daniel Levinson, *Seasons of a Man's Life* (New York: Ballantine, 1978), which argues that this life crisis will recur numerous times. These crisis periods, sandwiched by periods of stability, create the four seasons of a life. Critics argue that Levinson's pathbreaking line of research applies only to his sample—largely white males. Regardless, this is precisely the description of WOD. I am greatly indebted to psychologist/gerontologist Suzanne Wills of State College, Pennsylvania, for pointing me in this direction for my analysis.

In later describing this period in his life (*Go East,* chaps. 10 and 11), Douglas hid this crisis, thus misleading readers. Instead, Douglas argues that every move made by him in this period was his choice and had positive results. (See chapter 37 below.)

59   **"Lovingest boy"** Mildred Douglas to WOD, "Thursday, Aug. 12" [1926], WODP, Box 5, referring to the long letter she had just received from WOD "telling about the apt. + boy might come etc." See also Mildred Douglas to WOD, "Sat. Pm Aug. 14" [1926], WODP, Box 5.

60   **"If we have"** Ibid.

CHAPTER 6

61   **"People will say"** Douglas, *Go East,* p. 182.

61   **On August 24** "Valentino Passes with No Kin at Side," *The New York Times,* 8/24/26, p. 1.

61   **But the strangest reaction** The first account of the movie star's illness that Douglas would have seen was in *The New York Times,* 8/16/26, p. 1. On Douglas's reaction to this story, see Douglas, *Go East,* p. 184. Compare George Draper, *Disease and the Man* (New York: Macmillan, 1930), pp. 155–57, esp. p. 156. As will be explained below, the eerie similarity of these two accounts is not accidental and very instructive for a full understanding of Douglas's life.

61   **This most recent** This would be followed by courses in damages and bankruptcy and insolvency in the spring term. See *Columbia Law Bulletin,* 1926–1927; also AI, Pearl Sparrow, 10/14/91 (phone); on the Cravath firm reemployment, AI, Roxanne Piquero, 9/17/91, New York, confirming Swaine, *Cravath Firm,* vol. 2, p. xv, n. 177, and p. 120. On the firm's salary for Douglas, see Simon, *Independent Journey,* p. 88, citing interview with John J. McCloy.

62   **Since he had agreed** Douglas, *Go East,* pp. 150–51.

62   **For the first time** See the Pelham, N.Y., street directory for 1928, Town Historian's Office, Pelham (with thanks to Pelham town historian Susan

Swanson for researching this information and making it available). And
see the Westchester County telephone directories for 11/1/27 and 5/11/28,
Phone Directory Collection, Library of Congress, Washington, D.C.

62   **The only troubling issue** WOD to A. Howard Meneely, 2/27/27, WODP,
      Box 10.

62   **But by early 1927** Ibid., 1/4/27, WODP, Box 10.

62   **Despite his earlier misgivings** Ibid. This squares with Douglas's account of
      his dislike of working at Cravath in *Go East,* pp. 150–58.

63   **"The faculty is all for me"** Ibid., 1/4/27, WODP, Box 10.

63   **"There is a big piece"** Ibid.

63   **"Ye Gods"** Ibid.

63   **Douglas confessed** Ibid., for all of these quotations.

64   **After much reflection** Ibid., 2/7/27, WODP, Box 10.

64   **Return home to the west** Ibid., 2/27/27.

64   **"I have been seriously"** Ibid.

64   **Thinking that the time** Ibid. There is no record whether such a meeting
      ever took place.

64   **"At last I have found"** Ibid., 4/20/27, WODP, Box 10.

64   **Because of a sheer** At the time, Draper was an associate professor of clini-
      cal medicine at the College of Physicians and Surgeons, Columbia Univer-
      sity, and an associate attending physician at Presbyterian Hospital. For
      Douglas's account of this relationship, see *Go East,* pp. 177–84. For an-
      other of his versions, see below, chapter 34. See Draper's obituary in *The
      New York Times,* 7/2/59, p. 26.

65   **His 1917 volume** *Acute Poliomyelitis* (Philadelphia: P. Blakiston's Sons,
      1917). See also Kenneth S. Davis, *FDR: The Beckoning of Destiny: 1882–1928:
      A History* (New York: G. P. Putnam's Sons, 1971), pp. 657–61; and Geoffrey
      Ward, *A First-Class Temperament: The Emergence of Franklin Roosevelt* (New
      York: Harper and Row, 1989), pp. 576–99.

65   **Despite these accomplishments** George Draper, *Human Constitution: A Con-
      sideration of Its Relationship to Disease* (Philadelphia: W. B. Saunders, 1924).

65   **While normally** The pivotal stomach attack for Douglas occurred in May
      1927, not, as he indicates in his memoir, following Valentino's death in
      August 1926. We know that Douglas had just begun work with a new
      "A1" doctor. Draper's account of his medical analysis of "Lawyer, Aged
      37," while misdated as to WOD's actual age at the time (either an error on
      Draper's part or an effort to preserve patient confidentiality) has a star-
      tling similarity to that of Douglas in *Go East,* pp. 183–84. Note especially
      here the reference in both accounts to the association of the attacks with
      Valentino's death, the relation to stomach problems of "an old family
      friend"—almost certainly Julia's brother Milo—the medical problems of
      the patient at a very early age, and, most especially, the craving for baked
      beans following every attack. Literally every one of Douglas's friends who
      visited him or knew him in Goose Prairie recalled that baked beans were
      one of his favorite dishes (one of the others being steaks grilled right on
      the charcoal) (AI, Kay Kershaw and Isabelle Lynn, 4/19/89, Goose Prairie,

Wash.; Elena Leonardo, 8/21/89, Sunnyside, Wash.; Dagmar Hamilton, 3/1/90, Austin, Tex.; Millie Douglas Read, 8/20/89, Lostine, Oreg.).

Any remaining ambiguity as to the identity of the patient is removed by analysis of the timing of these sessions as recounted by Draper, a narrative that was written more contemporaneously than Douglas's memoir, likely with reference to his session notes, and without the agenda that Douglas would have had. See Draper's *Disease and the Man,* pp. 155–57, relating that the triggering mechanism to "Lawyer, Aged 37"'s final stomach attack occurred "two weeks before. . . . He remembered the day quite definitely, he said, because the pain began a short time after his neighbour had come in to announce the death of his son from peritonitis" (p. 155). An account of the only child to have died from peritonitis in the Pelham area at that time can be found in "Jackie Landstreet Dies Following Relapse," *The Pelham Sun,* 5/6/27. Susan Swanson, the Pelham town historian, revealed that Jackie Landstreet and his family lived in Pelbrook Hall, which was "the apartment building right next door to Peldean Court," where the Douglases lived (Swanson to author, 9/20/91).

65   **This fascinating case** See Draper, *Disease and the Man,* p. 155, and see also pp. 155–57, on which the account below relies. Draper's other textbook case was "Mrs. M," a fifty-nine-year-old woman whose complaint of incurable insomnia was solved when she was forced to confront the connection of this ailment to the death of her infant son of pneumonia (pp. 157–61).

65   **Draper wrote that** Ibid., pp. 155–56.

65   **Draper searched** All from ibid., p. 156.

66   **Draper reasoned** Ibid., pp. 156–57.

66   **Having worked on** Ibid., p. 157.

66   **This Douglas did** AI, Roxanne Piquero, 9/17/91, New York. Cravath files confirm that Douglas left the firm on 6/30/27. See also Swaine, *Cravath Firm,* p. xv, n. 177, and p. 120. On Douglas's intention to reduce his work, see WOD to A. Howard Meneely, 4/20/27, WODP, Box 10.

66   **"I hate to sever"** WOD to A. Howard Meneely, 4/20/27, WODP, Box 10.

67   **And, rather than** Ibid., 4/20/27, 5/19/27, and 5/29/27, WODP, Box 10.

67   **Since family finances** Whether Douglas had informed Columbia of this intention cannot be known, but given later events it appears highly unlikely. See ibid., 5/19/27, WODP, Box 10.

67   **"I hated like hell"** Ibid., 5/29/27, WODP, Box 10. Date of departure is set in ibid., 5/19/27.

67   **"Of course"** Ibid., 5/29/27.

67   **Had Meneely known** Ibid. That Cull had invited him was confirmed by George Martin, interview of Bruce Mallard, 9/17/91, Yakima, Wash. (phone); that Douglas worked with Cull was confirmed by AI, Fred Velikanje, 12/23/91, Yakima, Wash. (phone).

67   **Of all the places** The number of attorneys comes from the Yakima City Directories, 1926, 1927. As will be outlined below, Douglas was not there long enough to be included on the list.

CHAPTER 7

68   **"Get the hell out"** WOD to A. Howard Meneely, 7/31/27, WODP, Box 10.

68   **"Cull was full"** Ibid. Douglas's account dates his trip to Yakima to work with Cull in 1926, thus linking it with the Valentino episode (Douglas, *Go East*, p. 157). As is now clear, the trip actually occurred in 1927.

It is not clear whether, in going to Yakima, he actually backed out of his Columbia commitment, as he had contemplated in his correspondence with Meneely, or just failed to tell the university that he might be leaving, after a summer of testing the water elsewhere. Columbia has no record of his resignation from this era (AI, Pearl Sparrow, 10/14/91 [phone]). Douglas's letter of 7/31/27 seems to indicate that he never told Columbia he was leaving. Given his risky departures from Cravath with no job in hand, this would seem to have been the more prudent course of action.

68   **The truth was** The documentary record shows that Douglas was in the process of applying for his bar license. See "In the Matter of the Application of William Orville Douglas for Admission to the Bar," WODP, Box 234, including recommendations to the Washington State Bar Association from Carrol Shanks, Bruce Bromley, and William Mallard, 5/19/27; also A. S. Reinhard, clerk of the Washington Supreme Court, to WOD, 4/29/27, WODP, Box 234. Members of the Yakima bar at the time still remember Douglas coming to town in 1927, intending to practice law: AI, Fred Velikanje, 12/23/91, Yakima, Wash. (phone); AI, Chalmer Walter, 12/23/91, Yakima, Wash. (phone); AI, George M. Martin, 6/5/90, Yakima, Wash.

68   **"The old town got me"** WOD to A. Howard Meneely, 7/31/27, WODP, Box 10; see also Douglas, *Go East*, pp. 157–58.

68   **Douglas's paralyzed** The account that follows is the story that Cheney, now dead, told frequently to his law partner John Gavin (AI, John Gavin, 2/10/92, Yakima, Wash. [phone]). Douglas wrote in *Go East*, p. 158, of how life as a Yakima lawyer was not what he had expected:

My first legal assignment in Yakima was drafting a mortgage on a farmer's chicken pens. I worked assiduously on it, spending most of one day, as I recall. The last mortgage I had drawn was on the Chicago, Milwaukee & St. Paul Railway Company when I practiced in Wall Street. My chicken-coop mortgage had a like detail and finesse. I took it into Cull's office, and he first complimented me on it, then admonished: "Our fee for this is fifteen dollars and you have put in at least fifty dollars' worth of work."

As great as the tale was, the Yakima attorneys who had practiced law during that era knew that it couldn't be true. "How could he do legal work?" asked Yakima attorney John Gavin. "He hadn't passed the bar yet."

69   **"They were a backslapping"** WOD to A. Howard Meneely, 7/31/27, WODP, Box 10.

69   **Then there was** Ibid.

69 **"I was opportuned"** Ibid.

70 **For his part** AI, George M. Martin, 6/5/90, Yakima, Wash., and George M. Martin, interview of Bruce Mallard, related to the author on 9/17/91 (phone).

70 **"I could not have stayed"** WOD to A. Howard Meneely, 7/31/27, WODP, Box 10.

70 **"As soon as I crossed"** Ibid.

70 **Still, Douglas** The number of firms that Douglas visited ranges from the high of thirteen that he claimed in his letter to Meneely of 7/31/27 to the low of nine that are documented in the "Admission to Bar of State of Washington, 1927" file, WODP, Box 234.

70 **Several firms** See WOD to A. Howard Meneely, 7/31/27, WODP, Box 10, and "Admission to Bar of State of Washington, 1927" file, WODP, Box 234.

71 **"I have accepted"** Ibid., 7/31/27, WODP, Box 10.

71 **"I am confident"** Ibid.

71 **"We fished all day,"** Simon, *Independent Journey,* p. 93, citing an interview with Wilson.

71 **"The future seems"** WOD to A. Howard Meneely, 8/27/27, WODP, Box 10.

CHAPTER 8

72 **"The old school"** WOD to A. Howard Meneely, 5/26/28, WODP, Box 10.

72 **"The first time"** Ernest Cuneo, "The Near-Presidency of Supreme Court Justice William O. Douglas," Cuneo Papers, FDRL.

72 **"He was all over"** Ibid.

72 **Accustomed to working** See *Columbia Law Bulletin,* 1927–1928. Also, Milton Handler to author, 7/10/91.

72 **Lunch was** Ibid. Milton Handler's observations are confirmed by Douglas's own account in a year of long diary-like letters to A. Howard Meneely. Handler, however, recalled that the events in this chapter were not mentioned to him until the end of the academic year. Likewise, Douglas never mentioned these disputes until the end of the year. See WOD to A. Howard Meneely, 1927, WODP, Box 10.

73 **Columbia's foray** Julius Goebel, Jr., *A History of the School of Law, Columbia University* (New York: Columbia University Press, 1955), pp. 135–305, esp. pp. 275–305.

73 **This new movement** "Report of the Dean of the School of Law for 1928," *Columbia University Bulletin of Information,* 29th series, no. 9, 12/1/28, Columbiana Room, Columbia University Archives, p. 28, and Milton Handler to author, 7/10/91. The spelling of Berle's first name varies in sources between *Adolf* and *Adolph.* My spelling is that in Yale Law School, "Report of Dean of the School of Law for 1929," 2/1/30, p. 9, Sterling Library, Yale University, New Haven.

73 **Like most academic debates** Milton Handler to author, 7/10/91.

73 **The reform forces** Goebel, *History,* p. 299ff.

74 **Under Jervey's direction** "Report of the Dean," 1928, pp. 12–20. See also Goebel, *History,* chap. 12.

74 **In the end** Milton Handler to author, 7/10/91. Handler has a very different

account of this year than Douglas's in *Go East,* chap. 11. Goebel, *History,* and the documentary files and letters from this period support Handler's recollection.

74   **While all of this** Milton Handler to author, 7/10/91.

74   **But Douglas's effort** WOD to A. Howard Meneely, 4/23/28, WODP, Box 10. Douglas refers to the town here only as Baker.

74   **In a fortnight** Milton Handler to author, 7/10/91; Goebel, *History,* pp. 303–4.

75   **On Wednesday, May 2** Nicholas Murray Butler to "Professor" Douglas as "Members of the Faculty of Law," 5/2/28, WODP, Box 1. See also Goebel, *History,* p. 303.

75   **"If the appointment"** WOD to A. Howard Meneely, 5/5/28, WODP, Box 10.

75   **"Your decision to nominate"** WOD to Nicholas Murray Butler, 5/5/28, WODP, Box 1, also quoted in Melvin Urofsky, ed., *The Douglas Letters: Selections from the Private Papers of Justice William O. Douglas* (Bethesda: Adler and Adler, 1987), pp. 4–6, but misdated as 4/5/28. See also WOD to Stephen G. Williams, 5/5/28, WODP, Box 22. In seeking to ensure that everyone knew his position, Douglas forwarded a copy of his letter to the Committee on Education of the Board of Trustees as well.

75   **After reviewing all** Ibid.

75   **For the man** Respected Douglas scholars have differed over the years on the question of whether Douglas resigned from Columbia without having another job in hand. Law professor James Simon, in his *Independent Journey,* sees a cagey Douglas, acting to preserve his own options: "Douglas distorted not only the facts in dispute at the Columbia Law School, but also the circumstances surrounding his resignation." Simon discovered that Douglas had attended a faculty meeting on 6/1/28, four weeks after the announcement of Smith's appointment, and accepted an appointment to the faculty scholarship committee for the following year, indicating that he had no plans to leave at that time. By the time Douglas's resignation from Columbia was announced in the fall, he had already landed elsewhere. "In his autobiography," Simon concluded,

> Douglas's version of the Battle of 1928 revealed more about the author than about his role in the Columbia dispute. Though he certainly did support the Oliphant forces, he was not the outspoken Young Turk that he later claimed. . . . Because he played a major role in so many important struggles for reform in his later life, Douglas seems to have reasoned backward that this was always so. It was not. [p. 99]

Political scientist Philip Cooper sees it differently: "Douglas's story of his resignation has been disputed. . . . Even so, the evidence suggests considerable independence and courage for someone so early in an academic career at a leading institution" (Howard Ball and Philip Cooper, *Of Power and Right: Hugo Black, William O. Douglas, and America's Constitutional Revo-*

lution [New York: Oxford University Press, 1992], pp. 41–42). His reading of letters that were not available to Simon indicate that Douglas had made the psychological commitment to leave Columbia long before the formal transactions occurred.

Historian Melvin Urofsky takes more of a middle ground: "It appears more likely that although he intended to resign, WOD did not do so until assured he would have a place at Yale" (Urofsky, *Douglas Letters,* pp. 6–7).

In arguing that Douglas was actually considering a move back to private practice, this volume argues that while Douglas did not finalize his departure until after he knew the nature of his next position, he acted as if ensuring his departure even without having that job. This measure of courage, principle, and recklessness was born of the fact that he did not really care whether he remained in the teaching profession or returned to the practice of law. Only the unforeseen events outlined below determined his fate.

75 **But Douglas had also** Nicholas Murray Butler to "Professor Douglas" as "Members of Faculty of Law," 5/8/28, WODP, Box 1.

75 **Instead, Douglas** See "Richard J. Walsh Succeeds to Presidency of Pelham Men's Club; Presentation to Lockwood Barr" [*sic*], 5/11/28, *The Pelham Sun,* Pelham, N.Y., Historical Society Archives; also, Susan Swanson to author, 10/14/91 and 11/8/91.

76 **Douglas had been** Ibid. See also "Men's Club Promises Big Time at Annual Dinner Tuesday Night," *The Pelham Sun,* 5/4/28, Pelham, N.Y., Historical Society Archives.

76 **"Most American boys"** Ibid.; supplemented by anonymous interview, Pelham Country Club, 10/18/91 (phone).

76 **To Bill Douglas** For more on Hutchins, see Harry S. Ashmore, *Unseasonable Truths: The Life of Robert Maynard Hutchins* (Boston: Little, Brown, 1989); Mary Ann Dzuback, *Robert M. Hutchins;* and William H. McNeill, *Hutchins' University: A Memoir of the University of Chicago, 1929–1950* (Chicago: University of Chicago Press, 1991).

77 **Mornings are tough** Overall account of this conversation is drawn from Impromptu Speech Notes, 4/30/60, Yale Alumni Association Luncheon, New Haven, WODY. Also see Douglas, *Go East,* p. 163.

77 **Still trying to place** WOD to A. Howard Meneely, 2/2/29, WODP, Box 10. Douglas's account of the contract amount varied widely (see the seven-thousand-dollar figure he claimed on p. 106 in Alexander, "Washington's Angry Scotsman," pp. 9–10, 102–8), but the account in the Meneely letter is more contemporaneous and thus more reliable.

77 **Douglas realized** Three fine accounts of this incident can be found in John Henry Schlegel, "American Legal Realism and Empirical Social Science: From the Yale Experience," *Buffalo Law Review* 28 (1979): 459–586, esp. pp. 491–95; Laura Kalman, *Legal Realism at Yale, 1927–1960* (Chapel Hill: University of North Carolina Press, 1986), esp. chap. 4; and Robert Stevens, *Law School: Legal Education in America from the 1850s to the 1980s* (Chapel Hill: University of North Carolina Press, 1983), esp. chaps. 8 and 9.

77   **Two days after** "Minutes of the Yale Law School Faculty," 5/10/28, Manu-
        scripts Division, Sterling Library, Yale University, New Haven (hereafter
        Yale Law Minutes).

78   **Hutchins's discussions** Yale Law Minutes, 5/18/28; Milton Handler to au-
        thor, 7/10/91; and Schlegel, "American Legal Realism," pp. 491–95.

78   **Hutchins reported** Kalman, *Legal Realism,* pp. 111–12.

78   **"Well the jig is up"** WOD to A. Howard Meneely, 5/12/28, WODP, Box 28.

78   **"Subsequent to the announcement"** Milton Handler to author, 7/10/91.

79   **Meanwhile, Hutchins's** Schlegel, "American Legal Realism," pp. 491–95.

79   **"The Yale proposition"** WOD to A. Howard Meneely, 5/26/28, WODP,
        Box 10. See also Yale Law Minutes, 5/31/28, 5/18/28, and also 5/10/28.

79   **During all of Hutchins's** Yale Law Minutes, 5/31/28; and WOD to James
        Rowland Angell, 6/12/28, cited in Urofsky, *Douglas Letters,* p. 7.

79   **Before that meeting** Milton Handler to author, 7/10/91; Schlegel, "Ameri-
        can Legal Realism," pp. 491–95; Kalman, *Legal Realism,* pp. 111–12 (from
        which the term "neighbor's cook" is drawn); Goebel, *History,* p. 305.

        Underhill Moore backed out because of his concerns about the fund-
        ing situation and remained at Columbia for another eighteen months
        before finally accepting Hutchins's call to Yale. But Hutchins, who was
        perpetually optimistic about the outcome of his machinations, was very
        pleased by this. By successfully luring Carrol Shanks back to academia
        from Wall Street, Hutchins believed that he had hired both parts of the
        foremost legal scholarly team on business law.
        Compare with Douglas, *Go East,* pp. 162–63.

80   **"I have accepted"** WOD to A. Howard Meneely, 6/8/28, WODP, Box 10.

80   **"The reason for this action"** WOD to Nicholas Murray Butler, 6/11/28,
        WODP, Box 1, also quoted in Urofsky, *Douglas Letters,* p. 6.

80   **Bill Douglas was on** Frank B. Fackenthal to WOD, 6/22/28, Records of the
        Columbia University Secretary's Office, with thanks to Diane Pierce for
        providing this document. On Yale's appointment of WOD, see AI, Donna
        Fleming, 1/18/92, Yale University Provost's Office, New Haven (phone).
        Fleming was consulting Douglas's personnel records.

CHAPTER 9

81   **"It never occurred"** Thomas I. Emerson Oral History, COHC.

81   **Nobody could have been happier** Robert Mull, interviews with William O.
        Douglas, Jr. (with thanks to Mull for making this recording available), and
        interview with William O. Douglas, Jr., 2/13/88, Lowe Videos.

81   **The choice turned out** The initial street address of the Douglas home can
        be found in WOD to A. Howard Meneely, 9/3/28, WODP, Box 10. The
        Willow Street address is in Douglas, *Go East,* p. 167.

82   **"The prospects for business expansion"** WOD to A. Howard Meneely,
        12/18/28, WODP, Box 10.

82   **"The thing that strikes"** Ibid.

82   **For the man whose stomach** In his sessions with George Draper, Douglas
        had mentioned that one of his career goals was to become a judge. Draper
        to WOD, n.d. (ca. 1946); also see Draper to WOD, 4/19/46, WODP, Box 324,

and 4/26/50, WODP, Box 1030. In these letters, Draper continually warns Douglas that he is more temperamentally suited to the Court and should remain there rather than move to politics.

83 **Upon deciding** WOD to A. Howard Meneely, 1/1/29 and 1/8/29, WODP, Box 10.

83 **Douglas was unpersuaded** Ibid., 2/2/29, WODP, Box 10.

83 **Meanwhile, Douglas** Ibid.

83 **The dean did not** Catalog, Yale University School of Law, 1930–1931, 26th series, no. 20, Manuscripts Division, Sterling Library, Yale University, New Haven (hereafter Yale Law Catalog).

83 **"Law as a social science"** WOD to A. Howard Meneely, 2/2/29, WODP, Box 10.

83 **Moreover, when Hutchins** Ibid., 4/16/29, WODP, Box 10.

84 **Just then, though** See chap. 6 of Ashmore, *Unseasonable Truths*.

84 **"I meant to get"** WOD to A. Howard Meneely, 4/26/29, WODP, Box 10.

84 **But he also decided** While it is possible that Columbia had called by sheer coincidence, it seems far more likely that Douglas had begun privately shopping his services around once again.

84 **In truth** WOD to Nicholas Murray Butler, 4/5/28, WODP, Box 1.

84 **"The conditions under which"** WOD to A. Howard Meneely, 4/30/29, WODP, Box 10.

84 **"The challenge to my"** Ibid.

84 **"I hardly know"** Ibid. See also WOD to A. Howard Meneely, 4/24/29, WODP, Box 10.

84 **"Yale of course"** Ibid., 4/30/29, WODP, Box 10.

84 **"here is the secret"** Ibid.

85 **"Yale it is"** Ibid., 5/10/29, WODP, Box 10; for salary figures, see Charles Clark to Charles Seymour, 4/1/30, Angell Presidential Papers, Box 120, Law School 1930 folder, Yale Archives. In fact, Douglas received even more than that: $11,000, see Charles Clark to Charles Seymour, 12/11/30, Angell Presidential Records, Box 2-A-14, Yale Archives.

85 **With Carrol Shanks's** WOD to A. Howard Meneely, 5/10/29, WODP, Box 10.

85 **"[Douglas was] considered"** Thomas I. Emerson Oral History, COHC, pp. 123–24.

85 **A former teaching colleague** Simon, *Independent Journey,* p. 105.

85 **"Douglas came to Yale"** Thomas I. Emerson Oral History, COHC.

86 **"In those days"** Oral History for Judge Gerhard Gesell in Katie Louchheim, *The Making of the New Deal: The Insiders Speak* (Cambridge, Mass.: Harvard University Press, 1983), p. 136.

86 **"Who are those"** Fred Rodell, "For Charles E. Clark: A Brief and Belated Fond Farewell," *Columbia Law Review* 65 (1965): 1324–26; see also Kalman, *Legal Realism,* p. 117.

86 **On Monday morning** In a pair of subsequent letters to the president, Clark relayed their profuse apology, explaining that they were a little spoiled, and being so young they were unable to hold the small bit of liquor they had consumed that evening. And besides, hadn't he also heard that even

the faculty at Columbia was drunk at a recent banquet, as well as the partners of a prominent New York law firm at their annual dinner? (This became a favorite story of Douglas's about his time at Yale; see Impromptu
Speech Notes, 4/30/60, Yale Alumni Association Luncheon, New Haven,
WODY.)

86   **"His contribution was somewhat"** Thomas I. Emerson Oral History,
COHC, pp. 123–24.

87   **"He had a way"** Interview with Judge Gerhard Gesell, 5/16/88, Lowe
Videos.

87   **"Evening use"** Strong, "Reminiscences of Yale Law School," p. 17.

87   **For the first time** Schlegel, "American Legal Realism," p. 478.

87   **Douglas's idea** Richard W. Jennings, "Mr. Justice Douglas: His Influence
on Corporate and Securities Regulation," *Yale Law Journal* 73 (1964): 920.

88   **Since these courses** Yale Law Minutes, 5/10/28. See also Kalman, *Legal Realism,* p. 136. While the idea never developed a large or stable student or
faculty constituency, Douglas's interaction with the business school enabled him to draw even more connections among the areas of study.

88   **Outside of the classroom** I am indebted in writing this account to Schlegel,
"American Legal Realism," passim. His seminal account, informed by the
interviews he conducted at the time with people who had worked with
Douglas at Yale Law School but who were no longer living when I began
my research, greatly aided in my interpretation of these events.

88   **In researching the bankruptcy field** See speech by WOD, National Aca-
demy of Bankers (1928), WODY. See Schlegel, "American Legal Realism,"
pp. 522–32; see also John W. Hopkirk, "The Influence of Legal Realism on
William O. Douglas," in *Essays on the American Constitution* (New York:
G. Dietz, 1964), pp. 59ff.

89   **Teams of unpaid** Schlegel, "American Legal Realism," pp. 522–26.

89   **Never one to waste time** WOD and J. H. Weir, "Equity Receiverships in the
United States District Court for Connecticut: 1920–1929," *Connecticut Bar
Journal* 4 (1930): 1ff.

90   **The combination** This was done even though the funds were supposed
to launch new studies rather than back ongoing departmental or school
projects.

90   **Having accomplished** See Douglas, *Go East,* pp. 174–75, where he remembered the study with great fondness: "I would make the 5:15 A.M. train out
of New Haven on Monday mornings, arrive in Newark at eight o'clock and
interview bankrupts all day, and return to New Haven late the same night."

90   **Since he relied** William Clark, WOD, and Dorothy S. Thomas, "The Business Failures Project: A Problem in Methodology," *Yale Law Journal* 39
(May 1930): 1013ff; and WOD and Dorothy S. Thomas, "The Business Failures Project II: An Analysis of Methods of Investigation," *Yale Law Journal*
40 (1931): 1054. See also Schlegel, "American Legal Realism," pp. 527–31.

90   **In the fall of 1930** WOD, "Some Functional Aspects of Bankruptcy," *Yale
Law Journal* 41, no. 3 (January 1932): 329ff. WOD and J. H. Marshall, "A
Factual Study of Bankruptcy Administration and Some Suggestions," *Co-
lumbia Law Review* 32 (1932): 25ff.

90 **Realizing that the search** *Strengthening of Procedure in the Judicial System,* 72d Cong., 1st sess., 1932, S. Doc. 65, pp. 4–45.

91 **Once again,** See, for example, the plans that Douglas previewed in WOD to Robert Maynard Hutchins, 4/15/32 and 2/2/33, RMHP.

91 **It was not all work** AI, Irene Hamilton, 5/16/90, Washington, D.C. See also the description of Yale Law School at that time in Simon, *Independent Journey,* p. 116.

91 **When exercise** Abe Fortas, "In Memoriam," *American University Law Review* 29 (1979): 8–9.

91 **At other times** Ibid., and see Douglas, *Go East,* pp. 168–69, and Simon, *Independent Journey,* p. 117.

92 **For many of these men** AI, Irene Hamilton, 5/16/90, Washington, D.C.

92 **"Bill was a free spirit"** Ibid.

92 **"how she had worked"** Ibid., and see Douglas, *Go East,* p. 174.

92 **Having abandoned** Schlegel, "American Legal Realism," pp. 495–504.

93 **Such calculation** Dean Charles Clark to Claire Wilcox, 5/1/31, cited in Schlegel, "American Legal Realism," p. 503, n. 215.

93 **Despite these problems** Schlegel, "American Legal Realism," p. 504.

94 **However, since nonreformist** Eventually, money would be found by the Yale group to complete a small part of the study, but it would be several years before any part of it was published.

CHAPTER 10

95 **"I never understood"** Simon, *Independent Journey,* pp. 110–11.

95 **When Robert Maynard Hutchins** Hutchins's first choice to raid was Columbia philosopher Mortimer Adler, whose hiring as a full professor at a salary of six thousand dollars caused the three top men in the department to resign in protest in January 1931 and jump to other schools (Ashmore, *Unseasonable Truths,* pp. 85–105).

   For more, see Ashmore, *Unseasonable Truths;* Dzuback, *Robert M. Hutchins;* and McNeill, *Hutchins' University.* The Chicago Board of Trustees had been investigating the "boy wonder" for such a lofty position for more than a year. At first, Hutchins had assumed that he was being considered for the position of dean of the Law School. But Chicago had much bolder plans. While his youth terrified some members of the board, the aggressive and innovative school was willing, in the words of one trustee, to take "a gamble on youth and brilliancy" (Ashmore, *Unseasonable Truths,* p. 59). The only dissenting vote was that of President James Rowland Angell of Yale, who warned the trustees that "if [Hutchins] develops as he now promises, he should in five or ten years be an extraordinarily able and well trained man. I cannot believe that at present he is mature enough wisely to shoulder so grave and critically important a task as that of your presidency" (Ashmore, *Unseasonable Truths,* p. 60). While Angell obviously had his own interests to protect, his sentiments were to prove prescient in the short run.

95 **Work was going** WOD to Robert Maynard Hutchins, 11/14/29, RMHP.

95 **Thicker and thicker** WOD to Robert Maynard Hutchins, 2/18/30, 3/4/30,

3/29/30, 4/12/30, 5/2/30, and also Robert Maynard Hutchins to WOD, 3/10/30, RMHP.

95   **Finally, Douglas began** WOD to Robert Maynard Hutchins, 5/14/30, RMHP.

95   **A week later** WOD to Robert Maynard Hutchins, 5/22/30, RMHP.

96   **Only toward the end** Douglas also claimed to have tried to hire someone on the faculty who could do the bankruptcy project while he directed it from Chicago but said that the effort had been unsuccessful. No such evidence of this effort exists in the Yale Law Minutes. WOD to Robert Maynard Hutchins, 6/10/30, RMHP.

96   **What Douglas failed** There is no record of just how much Hutchins was offering in this initial bid, but Clark described it as "a very determined effort to secure his services, offering him a professorship and a very high salary." Dean Charles Clark to Provost Charles Seymour, 12/11/30, Angell Presidential Records, Box 2-A-14, Yale Archives; also AI, Donna Fleming, Yale University Personnel Office, New Haven, 1/18/92.

96   **But Robert Maynard Hutchins** WOD to Robert Maynard Hutchins, 6/10/30, RMHP.

96   **"You are, of course"** Robert Maynard Hutchins to WOD, 6/12/30, RMHP.

96   **"I have a letter"** Robert Maynard Hutchins to Dean Harry Bigelow, memo, 6/12/30, University of Chicago Presidential Papers, 1925–1945, Box 112.

96   **By the end** Dzuback, *Robert M. Hutchins*, pp. 178–79; and George Wilson Pierson, *Yale: College and University, 1871–1937*, 2 vols. (New Haven: Yale University Press, 1952).

96   **When they met** Charles E. Clark to Provost Charles Seymour, 12/11/30, Angell Presidential Records, Box 2-A-14, Yale Archives.

96   **Two days later** Minutes of the Chicago Board of Trustees, 12/11/30, University of Chicago Library, vols. 20–22, p. 16. Douglas asserted later in *Go East*, p. 164, that he was offered twenty-five thousand dollars. Beardsley Ruml was offered the same amount of money in that meeting to become the dean of social sciences. Perhaps Douglas got his figure from the amount that Hutchins was in fact paid by the university (though with considerable entertainment and living expenses added to it) (Ashmore, *Unseasonable Truths*, p. 64). It seems inconceivable that Hutchins would have offered to pay a faculty member as much. Such a salary was indeed exorbitant even for Chicago, where the salary of its well-paid full professors topped out at eight thousand dollars.

96   **"Think of the jealousy"** AI, Judge Charles Wyzanski, 1/13/77, Richmond, Va.

97   **Nevertheless, recognizing** Minutes of the Chicago Board of Trustees, Jan. 1931, vol. 20–22.

97   **"The most outstanding"** Ibid., p. 16. See also Douglas, *Go East*, p. 164.

97   **The truth was** In addition to the previously mentioned article on equity receiverships, see WOD, "Functional Approach to the Law of Business Associations," *Illinois Law Review* 26 (March 1929): 673–82; WOD, "Vicarious Liability and Administration of Risk II," *Yale Law Journal* 38 (April 1929): 720 ff.; and WOD and Carrol M. Shanks, "Insulation from Liability Through Subsidiary Corporations," *Yale Law Journal* 39 (December 1929): 193ff.

97   **But the Yale** Dean Charles E. Clark to Provost Charles Seymour, 4/1/30; salary lists constructed by Clark, 10/7/33 and 6/11/34, Angell Presidential Papers, Yale Archives, Box 121, "Law School Faculty" folder, referring to the salaries for the preceding three years. Compare this with the salary list in Kalman, *Legal Realism,* p. 270, n. 130, showing WOD's salary as being first thirteen and later fourteen thousand dollars.

97   **"This difference is so large"** Charles E. Clark to Charles Seymour, 12/11/30, Angell Presidential Papers, Box 2-A-14.

98   **"It would be most distressing"** Ibid.

98   **President Angell agreed** WOD to James Rowland Angell, 12/19/30, Angell Presidential Papers, Box 2-A-14.

98   **To Dean Clark** Charles E. Clark to James Rowland Angell, 12/20/30, in ibid.

98   **Indeed, it was** WOD to Robert Maynard Hutchins, 12/31/30, University of Chicago Presidential Papers, Appts and Budgets, 1925–1940, Box 44.

98   NEW PROFESSOR TO AID *Chicago Tribune,* 1/2/31, p. 4.

98   **Hutchins sent** Robert Maynard Hutchins to WOD, 1/3/31, University of Chicago Presidential Papers, Appts and Budgets, 1925–1940, Box 44.

98   **When the announcement** Charles Clark to James Rowland Angell, 1/2/31, Angell Presidential Papers, Box 2-A-14.

98   **Angell decided** Kalman, *Legal Realism,* p. 129.

98   **Seemingly unaffected** WOD to Robert Maynard Hutchins, 3/12/31, 3/17/31, 3/19/31, and 3/23/31, University of Chicago Presidential Papers, 1925–1945, Box 112.

99   **And Douglas crowed** Ibid., 3/23/31.

99   **"Dear Orville"** Robert Maynard Hutchins to WOD, 3/23/31, in ibid.

99   **Given "your desires"** WOD to Robert Maynard Hutchins, 3/26/31, in ibid.

99   **The more he thought** Ibid., 3/30/31.

99   **Hutchins failed to see** Telegrams, WOD to Robert Maynard Hutchins, 4/11/31 and 4/18/31, University of Chicago Presidential Papers, Appts and Budgets, 1925–1940, Box 44.

99   **After meeting** Ibid., 5/9/31.

99   AM REGRETFULLY WILLING Robert Maynard Hutchins to WOD, 5/13/31, in ibid.

100   **Unknown to Hutchins** Charles E. Clark to Charles Seymour, 5/15/31, Provost's Records, Box 3-A, Yale Archives.

100   **Clark well knew** AI, Donna Fleming, 1/18/92, New Haven (phone).

100   **Furthermore, Douglas's** WOD and Carrol M. Shanks, *Cases and Materials on the Law of Corporate Reorganizations* (Saint Paul: West, 1931); WOD with Carrol M. Shanks, *Cases and Materials on the Law of Financing of Business Units* (Chicago: Callaghan, 1931); and WOD with Carrol M. Shanks, *Cases and Materials on the Law of Management of Business Units* (Chicago: Callaghan, 1931).

100   **When the faculty** Charles Clark to Charles Seymour, 5/15/31, Provost's Records, Box 3-A.

100   **"In this Douglas matter"** Charles Seymour to Charles Clark, 6/9/31; Charles Clark to Charles Seymour, 12/11/30, cited in Kalman, *Legal Realism,* p. 270 n. 130.

101   **So, in telegraphing** WOD to Robert Maynard Hutchins, 5/15/31, University of Chicago Presidential Papers, Appts and Budgets, 1925–1940, Box 44.

101   **Stock in Western Union** Robert Maynard Hutchins to Charles Clark, 5/21/31, and Charles Clark to Robert Maynard Hutchins, 5/21/31, in ibid.

101   **Caught in the middle** WOD to Robert Maynard Hutchins, 6/4/31, University of Chicago Presidential Papers, 1925–1945, Box 112.

101   **Still unaware** Minutes of the University of Chicago Board of Trustees Minutes, 6/11/31, vols. 20–22., p. 3.

101   **But Clark was not done** Yale Law Catalog, 1931–1932; and WOD to Robert Maynard Hutchins, 6/23/31, University of Chicago Presidential Papers, 1925–1945, Box 112.

101   **Douglas could see** WOD to Robert Maynard Hutchins, 6/23/31, University of Chicago Presidential Papers, 1925–1945, Box 112.

102   **"You should be flattered"** Robert Maynard Hutchins to WOD, 6/25/31, in ibid.

102   **Try as he might** WOD to Robert Maynard Hutchins, 6/4/31 and 6/23/31, in ibid.

102   **But Hutchins wasn't ready** Ibid., 11/13/31; Harriet Servis to Robert Maynard Hutchins, 11/16/31; and WOD to Robert Maynard Hutchins, 11/20/31, all in University of Chicago Presidential Papers, 1925–1945, Box 112.

102   **Those discussions with Dean Bigelow** WOD to Robert Maynard Hutchins, 12/16/31, University of Chicago Presidential Papers, Appts and Budgets, 1925–1940, Box 44.

102   **A delighted Hutchins** Robert Maynard Hutchins return note, handwritten on ibid.

102   **Believing that he was still** Copy of WOD's telegram to Bigelow contained in telegram to Robert Maynard Hutchins, 12/19/31, in ibid.

102   **Complaining that he was** Telegram, WOD to Robert Maynard Hutchins, 12/19/31, in ibid.

103   **Hutchins called Douglas** Robert Maynard Hutchins, marking on ibid; and WOD to Robert Maynard Hutchins, 12/28/31, University of Chicago Presidential Papers, Appts and Budgets, 1925–1940, Box 44.

103   **Once more, the personal** WOD to Robert Maynard Hutchins, handwritten, 3/1/32, RMHP. Hutchins had already failed to hire Dean Clark away from Yale, thus ending the chance to eliminate his major rival in the battle for William O. Douglas.

103   **While various members** WOD to Robert Maynard Hutchins, 4/15/32, RMHP.

103   **Then, even though** AI, Donna Fleming, 1/18/92, New Haven (phone).

103   **With all of the obstacles** See Charles Clark to Charles Seymour, 6/11/34, Angell Presidential Papers, Box 121, "Law School Faculty" folder; and salary list cited in Kalman, *Legal Realism,* p. 270, n. 130. In a year that would be increased to fifteen thousand dollars. (See "School of Law Leaves of Absences Granted since 1931," Seymour Presidential Papers, Box 94, Yale Archives.)

103   **Hutchins tried to pass** Robert Maynard Hutchins to WOD, 4/4/32, RMHP.

103   **Faced with the hint** Douglas refers to this sudden and sharp drop in his proposed salary in WOD to Robert Maynard Hutchins, 4/15/32, RMHP.

104   **But still Douglas** Ibid., 4/14/32.

104   **So the next day** Ibid., 4/15/32, handwritten. Ironically, Douglas could not know that in a short time the finances of Yale were such that it, too, would consider lowering the salaries of their top men, including him. Charles Clark to Provost Charles Seymour, 10/7/33, Angell Presidential Papers, Box 121, "Law School Faculty" folder.

104   **While he still wanted** WOD to Robert Maynard Hutchins, 4/15/32, handwritten, RMHP.

104   **"A good letter"** Untitled note signed H.H.B. [Dean Bigelow to Hutchins], 4/18/32, RMHP.

104   **"Professor William O. Douglas"** Charles E. Clark, dean's report, 1931–1932, cited in Simon, *Independent Journey,* p. 110.

CHAPTER 11

106   **"No one in Washington"** AI, Irene Hamilton, 5/16/90, Washington, D.C.

106   **Having conquered** Years later, Douglas would insist that Washington just came calling because of his expertise in business and financial matters, taking him away from his fulfilling academic work at Yale (Douglas, *Go East,* p. 258). But the truth was that the calling had gone very much in the opposite direction.

106   **"He was terribly ambitious"** AI, Irene Hamilton, 5/16/90, Washington, D.C.

106   **By the summer of 1933** Kalman, *Legal Realism,* pp. 130–32.

106   **Since who he knew** WOD and G. E. Bates, "Some Effects of the Securities Act Upon Investment Banking," *University of Chicago Law Review* 1 (November 1933): 283–306; WOD and G. E. Bates, "Stock 'Brokers' as Agents and Dealers," *Yale Law Journal* 43 (November 1933): 46–62; WOD and G. E. Bates, "Federal Securities Act of 1933," *Yale Law Journal* 43 (December 1933): 171–217; WOD, "Protective Committee in Railroad Reorganizations," *Harvard Law Review* 47 (February 1934): 565–89; WOD, "Protecting the Investor," *Yale Review* 23 (March 1934): 521–33; and WOD, "Directors Who Do Not Direct," *Harvard Law Review* 47 (June 1934): 1305–34.

107   **For all his careful** See Jordan A. Schwarz's excellent *The New Dealers: Power Politics in the Age of Roosevelt* (New York: Alfred A. Knopf, 1993), p. 166.

107   **As it happened** WOD, "Protective Committee," 565–89. See also Joel Seligman, *The Transformation of Wall Street: A History of the Securities and Exchange Commission and Modern Corporate Finance* (Boston: Houghton Mifflin, 1982), pp. 110–11.

107   **Relying on both** James Landis Oral History, COHC, pp. 232–33; Seligman, *Transformation of Wall Street,* pp. 110–11; and WOD to James Landis, 7/18/34, in Urofsky, *Douglas Letters,* pp. 28–29.

107   **Despite working** Douglas, *Go East,* p. 264. These chapters on the SEC years are more reliable than others because their drafting was overseen closely by his assistant Dagmar Hamilton after his editor, Charlotte Mayerson,

asked that they be added. Hamilton drafted these chapters with careful attention to Douglas's files in room 210. AI, Dagmar Hamilton, 3/1/90, Austin, Tex. Also, interview of Cathy Douglas, 5/17/88, Lowe Videos.

107 **By commuting part-time** Landis gave Douglas permission to do this in his acceptance letter (WOD to Landis, 7/18/34, in Urofsky, *Douglas Letters,* pp. 28–29; also William O. Douglas personnel records, Yale University Provost's office, AI, Donna Fleming, 1/16/92; confirmed by both "School of Law Leaves of Absence Granted since 1931," Seymour Presidential Papers, Box 94, Yale University Manuscripts Division, Sterling Library, Yale University, New Haven, and also "Protective Committee Study Staff" [salary list], WODP, Box 30). For Douglas's own views, see Douglas, *Go East,* pp. 258–60.

107 **The day-to-day administrative** WOD to Landis, 7/18/34, in Urofsky, *Douglas Letters,* pp. 28–29. As a result, while Douglas wrote years later that his government service forced him to get "a semester's leave of absence" from Yale, to be followed by "repeated leaves" thereafter, the truth was that Bill Douglas never took a leave while serving on this committee. (See "School of Law Leaves of Absence Granted since 1931," Seymour Presidential Papers, Box 94. The Douglas entry shows that Douglas requested and was granted leave only after he went on to the SEC full-time.)

107 **To Douglas, this** AI, Irene Hamilton, 5/16/90, Washington, D.C.

108 **"None of us took"** Ibid.

108 **Indeed, when Douglas's** "Brown Admits Frisco Deals on Own Authority," New York *Herald Tribune,* 5/28/35, p. 33; and "Frisco Financing Traced at Hearing," *The New York Times,* ibid., p. 41.

108 **But Douglas's friends** Bruce Allen Murphy, *Fortas: The Rise and Ruin of a Supreme Court Justice* (New York: William Morrow, 1988), pp. 22–24.

108 **With the subsequent** For all of Fortas's ambivalence, not only did this jump to the Protective Committee study make his career, it saved it. Within a matter of months, the top leadership of the AAA was purged, followed a year later by the firing of Frank himself and most of his legal team (no doubt likely to have taken Fortas with him). Shortly thereafter, the entire agency was found unconstitutional by the Supreme Court.

109 **"Piss on 'Em."** Schwarz, *New Dealers,* p. 173.

109 **"Douglas would sit"** AI, Abe Fortas, 8/7/81, Washington, D.C.

109 **The same was true** AI, C. David Ginsburg, 8/28/89, Washington, D.C.

109 **"Bill was a great man"** AI, Abe Fortas, 8/7/81, Washington, D.C.

109 **For all his efforts** George Creel, "The Young Man Went East," *Collier's,* 5/9/36, pp. 9, 95ff. And see John W. Hopkirk, "William O. Douglas: His Work in Policing Bankruptcy Proceedings," *Vanderbilt Law Review* 18 (1965): 667, citing interview with Samuel O. Clark.

109 **After sending out** William T. Raymond, "New SEC Rules in the Making," *Barron's,* 2/18/35, p. 20.

109 **To their surprise** Kalman, *Legal Realism,* pp. 53–61.

109 **After six months** "Celotex Inquiry Starts," *The New York Times,* 2/16/35, p. 23.

109 **At the two-day public** Ibid., p. 29. They created two other companies,

Phoenix, a newly formed investment trust, and Red Crest, a company headed by the president of Celotex, which combined to take over 50 percent of a new company called Central Securities. Through this enterprise, they could finance the reorganization of Celotex by giving Phoenix fifteen thousand shares in the new company, along with an option to purchase an additional one hundred thousand shares at ten dollars a share (then a good price), and exercising the right to name three of the five directors of the new company.

110　**When Douglas confronted** "S.E.C. May Recommend New Laws on Protective Groups," *The Wall Street Journal*, 2/7/35, p. 2.

110　**Upon the completion** Raymond, "New SEC Rules," p. 20.

110　**Thanks to a tip** Later, Douglas described Kintner, whom he called "Kittner," as a man with whom he had "a long, warm friendship" and who "wrote scintillating articles [on the SEC], each one painstakingly accurate." Douglas, *Go East*, p. 259.

110　**More publicity** "S.E.C. Reveals Dual Interests in Receivership," New York *Herald Tribune*, 4/18/35, p. 29; "S.E.C. Delves into Actions to Reorganize," ibid., 4/17/35, p. 35.

110　**Adding to the drama** "Treasury Action on Frisco Is Told," *The New York Times*, 5/29/35, p. 31; "Details of Fight on Frisco Plan Told to S.E.C.," New York *Herald Tribune*, 5/30/35, p. 23. See also "Brown Admits Frisco Deals on Own Authority," ibid., 5/28/35, p. 33.

111　**Why then, Douglas asked** "Hearing Bares $400,000 Paid Frisco Board," New York *Herald Tribune*, 6/1/35, p. 25. See also "Details of Fight on Frisco Plan," ibid., 5/30/35, p. 23.

111　**This led Swaine** William T. Raymond, "SEC Not Affected by NRA Defeat?" *Barron's*, 6/3/35, p. 24.

111　**When Douglas discovered** "Swaine Admits Part in Writing Bankruptcy Act," New York *Herald Tribune*, 6/8/35, p. 21.

111　**Swaine admitted** Ibid., and "Swaine on Stand in Frisco Inquiry," *The New York Times*, 6/8/35, p. 25.

112　**Despite this success** "S.E.C. Faces Fire on Its Legality in Opening Jones Hearing Today," New York *Herald Tribune*, 6/18/35, p. 27. See also Douglas, *Go East*, p. 260.

112　**But from the very** "Bankers' Gain in Paramount Plan Revealed," New York *Herald Tribune*, 6/19/35, p. 25; and "S.E.C. Opens Hearing in Paramount Case," *The New York Times*, 6/19/35, p. 29.

112　**Try as he might** "Bond Group Held No Stock in Paramount," New York *Herald Tribune*, 6/20/35, p. 30.

112　**Only when Douglas** Ibid.

112　**However, the banker** William T. Raymond, "SEC Probes Paramount Reorganization," *Barron's*, 6/24/35, p. 24.

113　**As a result of** The press later printed that "according to best SEC authorities, the report will go a long way toward complete revision of present policies" in the bankruptcy area. Ibid.

113　**"Bill was very"** AI, Herman Benjamin, 11/10/91, and 8/21/91, Palm Beach, Fla. (phone).

113 **His next witness** "Banker Tells of Paramount 'Stabilization,'" New York *Herald Tribune*, 6/21/35, p. 31; "Assails Financing of Old Paramount," *The New York Times*, 6/21/35, p. 34.

113 **By now, the arguments** "Topics in Wall Street," *The New York Times*, 7/12/35, p. 27.

113 **Douglas was jubilant** "Assails Financing of Old Paramount," *The New York Times*, 6/21/35, p. 34.

113 **"Once he broke"** AI, Herman Benjamin, 11/10/91, Palm Beach, Fla.

113 **In his subsequent** For more on Douglas's work on the protective committee, see Milton Freeman Reminiscences in Douglas Remembrances, p. 24. Later published in *Journal of Supreme Court History: 1990 Yearbook of the Supreme Court Historical Society* as *Remembrances of William O. Douglas on the 50th Anniversary of His Appointment to the Supreme Court.* (The unpublished version was generously supplied by Gail Galloway, then the curator for the Supreme Court). See also Oral History of Abe Fortas in Louchheim, *Making of the New Deal*, pp. 220–24.

114 **Though the two** Kalman, *Legal Realism*, relates the engaging story of how Fortas got this information from Siegfried F. Hartman (pp. 56–58).

114 **When Douglas raised** "S.E.C. Studies Krueger and Toll Fee for Davis," New York *Herald Tribune*, 8/14/35, p. 21.

114 **"No," responded Dulles** Ibid.

114 **Suspecting otherwise** The comptroller of the SEC refused to reimburse Douglas for the five-hundred-dollar expense of bringing along Draper, saying, "Why a lawyer at the SEC needs a doctor to help him make an investigation is a mystery. Moreover, there is no provision in the budget or the regulations authorizing it." Douglas, *Go East*, pp. 263.

115 **Other members of** "S.E.C. Scans Cuba Cane Sugar in Study of Reorganization," New York *Herald Tribune*, 8/21/35, p. 23; "Banks Controlled Cuban Sugar Group," *The New York Times*, 8/22/35, p. 27; Abe Fortas to Joel Seligman, 7/29/80, cited in Kalman, *Legal Realism*, p. 56; "Option Pool in Cuba Cane Sugar Shown," New York *Herald Tribune*, 8/23/35, p. 25.

For more on the committee's other work during this period, see: "Cuba Cane Records Subpoenaed by S.E.C.," *The New York Times*, 8/30/35, p. 25; "Hayden Affirms Right to Trade in Cuban Cane," New York *Herald Tribune*, 8/30/35, p. 27; "Banker Defends Sugar Bond Action," *The New York Times*, 8/23/35, p. 25.

115 **Soon thereafter** "S.E.C. to Scan McLellan Store Reorganization," New York *Herald Tribune*, 9/5/35, p. 25; "McLellan Assails Deposits Seizure," *The New York Times*, 9/7/35, p. 32; "McLellan Cash Seized by Banks Prior to Failure," New York *Herald Tribune*, 9/7/35, p. 19; "McLellan's Acts to Keep Stores Alive Praised," ibid., 9/8/35, p. 11; "McLellan Rescued Bankrupt Chain," *The New York Times*, 9/8/35, sec. 3, p. 1; "Hedden Profit Half-Million in McLellan Deal," New York *Herald Tribune*, 9/10/35, p. 27; "Hedden Defends Buying of Claims," *The New York Times*, 9/10/35, p. 32; "Lawyer Assails Banks Interests in Bond Group," New York *Herald Tribune*, 9/11/35, p. 33; "S.E.C. Ends Hearing of McClellan Stores," *The New York Times*, 9/11/35, p. 39; "Cuban Cane Products Hearing Resumed," *The Wall Street*

Journal, 8/30/35, p. 2; "Cuba Cane Records Subpoenaed," *The New York Times,* 8/30/35, p. 25.

115 **Despite these successes** Robert E. Kintner, "Financial Washington," New York *Herald Tribune,* 8/25/35, sec. 2, p. 11.

115 **The timing of this leak** "Florida Issues of Bonds Kept in S.E.C. Study," New York *Herald Tribune,* 9/13/35, p. 27.

115 **Joe Kennedy had just** Francis Maloney to FDR, 12/7/35, FDRL Papers, cited in Simon, *Independent Journey,* p. 152.

115 **Douglas also asked** Corcoran later claimed in his memoirs to be responsible for the appointment. See Thomas Corcoran, "Rendezvous with Destiny," Unpublished Memoirs, Thomas Corcoran Papers, Manuscripts Division, Library of Congress, Washington, D.C., chap. 10, p. 33, and preface, p. 5; see also interview with Corcoran in Simon, *Independent Journey,* in which he states, "Ben [Cohen] and I chose Bill" (p. 153); and Joseph Alsop and Robert Kintner, *Men Around the President* (New York: Doubleday, 1939), pp. 93–94. On the other hand, Ralph F. DeBedts, *The New Deal's SEC: The Formative Years* (New York: Columbia University Press, 1964), p. 156, relies on an interview with Ben Cohen to say that they did *not* support Douglas, but it seems likely that Cohen was confusing that with their opposition to Douglas as chairman of the commission twenty months later.

115 **Seeking to catch** "Washington Letter: Liberal Senators in Role of Bill Collectors in Cuba?" *The Wall Street Journal,* 8/31/35, p. 2.

116 **But, in fact** See "Bond Committee Got Salvador Ties," *The New York Times,* 10/12/35, p. 25; "El Salvador Group Is Accused of Seizing Bondholders' Funds," New York *Herald Tribune,* 10/12/35, p. 23. Meanwhile, Kintner continued to be helpful. In the middle of October, when the Sabath Committee's parallel examination of real-estate reorganizations was threatening to cut into Douglas's turf, Kintner wrote that of the two, "the SEC scrutiny is . . . the better organized." Kintner, "Financial Washington," ibid., sec. 2, p. 11. See also "S.E.C. Charge Halts Air Trip of Witness," ibid., 10/11/35, p. 37; "Big Bankers Aid Foreign Bond Body," *The New York Times,* 10/31/35, p. 27; "Foreign Bond Council Shown Aided by Banks," New York *Herald Tribune,* ibid., p. 25; "Inside Move Told in Cuban Bond Case," *The New York Times,* 11/2/35, p. 27.

116 **In what the New York** "At the Turn of the Week," New York *Herald Tribune,* 11/17/35, sec. 2, p. 15. For more on the other aspects of the committee's work during this period, see: "S.E.C. Hits Speyer on Brazilian Bonds," *The New York Times,* 11/8/35, p. 33; "City Officials Up Before S.E.C. on Bonds Suit," New York *Herald Tribune,* 11/9/35, pp. 20, 21; "Fishers in Market for Baldwin Notes," *The New York Times,* ibid., p. 33; "Houston Denies Manipulation in Baldwin Act," New York *Herald Tribune,* ibid., p. 21; "Baldwin Locomotive Set-Up Examined by S.E.C.," *The Wall Street Journal,* ibid., p. 7; "Tells S.E.C. of Role in Peru Committee," *The New York Times,* 11/10/35, sec. 3, p. 1; "Trustee Bound by Indenture, Says Newhall," New York *Herald Tribune,* ibid., sec. 2, p. 13; "Data Lapse Told in Baldwin Inquiry," *The New York Times,* ibid., sec. 3, p. 4; "Lawyer Admits Improper Plan for S.E.C. Inquiry," *The Washington Post,* ibid., p. 14; "Houston Denies

S.E.C. Charge on Balance Sheets," New York *Herald Tribune*, 11/13/35, p. 27; "S.E.C. Delays Study of Haiti Bond Offerings," ibid., p. 28; "New Charges Made on Salvador Bonds," *The New York Times*, 11/13/35, p. 30; "Juggling of Books by Baldwin Denied," ibid., p. 33; "Congress Blamed in Peru Bonds Chaos," ibid., 11/15/35, p. 35; "S.E.C. Inquiry Bares Chilean Loan Data," ibid., 11/16/35, p. 21; "Unfair Policy Laid to Chile on Bonds," ibid., 11/17/35, sec. 3, p. 1; "Chase Bank's Aims in Cuba Case Told," ibid., 11/3/35, sec. 3, p. 1; "S.E.C. to Sift El Salvador Bond Default," New York *Herald Tribune*, 10/8/35, p. 29.

116 **While the commission** "Celler Attacks S.E.C. Study of Bond Defaults," New York *Herald Tribune*, 11/7/35, p. 30.

116 **By the time** William T. Raymond, "SEC Needs More Time," *Barron's*, 12/9/35, p. 24.

116 **Douglas was preoccupied** James Landis Oral History, COHC, p. 233; see also Seligman, *Transformation of Wall Street*, p. 154; Schwarz, *New Dealers*, p. 167; and Simon, *Independent Journey*, pp. 151–53. Though he knew the truth, Douglas loved to curry favor with others, such as Joseph Kennedy and Felix Frankfurter, by thanking them for the formative roles that he claimed they paid in his appointment. WOD to Kennedy, 2/4/36, in Urofsky, *Douglas Letters*, pp. 31–32; see also WOD to Felix Frankfurter, 1/22/36, cited in Simon, *Independent Journey*, p. 153. See below. Douglas would later claim that he had been escorted by Joseph Kennedy to the White House to receive the appointment personally. James Simon proves effectively, however, that the first meeting between Douglas and FDR did not in fact happen until six months later. Compare Douglas, *Go East*, p. 264, and Simon, *Independent Journey*, p. 153.

117 **The selection did little** Landis had introduced his personal nominee to the public by saying that he had "contributed more to the development of corporation law than anyone else in the country." ("Wall Street Takes Notice," Yakima *Daily Republic*, 1/29/36, Yakima *Herald-Republic* Archives, Yakima, Wash.) Robert Kintner, now fully captivated by Douglas's talents, described him as "one of the ablest examiners in the SEC lawyer personnel." "Financial Washington," New York *Herald Tribune*, 1/19/36, sec. 2, p. 11.

117 **The real news** "Vacancy on S.E.C. Goes to Douglas," *The New York Times*, 1/17/36, p. 27; Edward H. Collins, "The Week in Finance," New York *Herald Tribune*, 1/20/36, p. 27; WOD to A. Howard Meneely, 1/24/36, WODP, Box 10. See also *Newsweek*, 1/24/36, p. 46.

117 **To which *Business Week*** "New Man on S.E.C.," *Business Week*, 1/25/36, p. 46.

117 **"It is not every day"** "Wall Street Takes Notice," Yakima *Daily Republic*, 1/29/36, Yakima *Herald-Republic* Archives, Yakima, Wash.

117 **"He is traveling"** Ibid. Not even the description of Douglas as a liberal bothered this conservative community, as it was, to them, just "another of his numerous appellations." However, Douglas's work over the next twenty-one months would cause them to reconsider. See below.

117 **Bill Douglas would** "Assails Financing of Old Paramount," *The New York*

Times, 6/21/35, p. 34. See also Edson Blair, "Washington: Both Sides of the Curtain," *Barron's*, 9/27/37, pp. 4–5.

CHAPTER 12

118 **"In matters"** Oscar Wilde, *The Importance of Being Earnest* (1895).

118 **Once the Douglases moved** AI, Millie Douglas Read, 8/20/89, Lostine, Oreg.

118 **The commissioner now occasionally** This scene is recounted in a number of places: ibid.; AI, Walter Lowe (recounting his conversations with Millie Douglas Read and William Douglas, Jr., Seattle, 4/27/89 [phone]); interview with William O. Douglas, Jr., 2/13/88, Lowe Videos; and Robert Mull, interview with William O. Douglas, Jr., 1981 (in author's possession).

118 **As he spoke, always** Description of Douglas's appearance when speaking comes from AI, Millie Douglas Read, 8/20/89, Lostine, Oreg.; confirmed by AI, Charles Reich, 11/15/89, San Francisco. This can be seen in an interview of WOD by Eric Sevareid, "Mr. Justice Douglas," *CBS Reports,* CBS News, 9/6/72.

119 **Whenever Millie later** The same answer would be given to other friends who had the temerity to challenge one or another part of the legend. AI, Simon Rifkind, 8/4/89, New York; AI, Isabelle Lynn, 8/7/89, Goose Prairie, Wash.; AI, Kay Kershaw, 8/9/89, ibid.; and AI, Cragg Gilbert, 8/17/90, Yakima, Wash.

120 **"This remarkable young man"** "Walla Walla to Washington," *Time*, 1/27/36, p. 50.

120 **While his family remained** "College Friend Denies Douglas 'Rode the Rods,'" *The New York Times*, 3/21/39, p. 16.

120 **that eastern writers** Chester Maxey Oral History, 1/16/76, Whitman Archives.

120 **"The kids would beg"** See Robert Mull, interview with Chester Maxey, 9/22/81 (provided to author by Mull).

121 **"Douglas' 6 Cents"** "Letters," *Newsweek*, 4/10/39, pp. 2–3. The man in Portland who claimed to have loaned Douglas money was very likely Bill Wilson, who helped Douglas at the Columbia University Beta house and was in the 1970s living and practicing medicine in Portland. James F. Simon found him there for an interview for *Independent Journey.*

121 **"Douglas himself is"** Ibid.

121 **Despite the lack of accuracy** Chester Maxey Oral History, 1/16/76, Whitman Archives.

122 **"Doubtless due to his Scotch"** Creel, "Young Man Went East," pp. 9, 95ff. While *The New York Times* was not entirely convinced ("There are stories that early in his college days he lived in a tent, and that about 1921, deciding to go to New York to study law, he rode part of the way in box cars": "Douglas Is Named Chairman of SEC," *The New York Times*, 9/22/37, p. 41), Douglas began telling this tale to other reporters, and the tale was repeated frequently. Each time the story was recounted now, new details were added to the growing legend. *Time* chimed in with a variation

when it revealed in October 1937 that during his "freshman year [at Whitman] he lived in a barn-like dormitory which had no running water. The next three he lived in a tent. . . . He registered at Columbia Law School in Manhattan, expressed his trunk ahead, [and] set out himself as 'herder' for a shipment of sheep going to Chicago for slaughter. He eventually arrived in Chicago riding the rods of a freight. Having learned from hoboes that this was too risky a procedure from Chicago to New York, he bought a ticket [and] got to Manhattan with 6 c[ents] left." "Bill and Billy," *Time*, 10/11/37, pp. 61–62).

See also Max Lerner, "Wall Street's New Mentor," *The Nation*, 10/23/37, pp. 429–32.

122   **"Dear Comrade"** Arthur Douglas to WOD, 6/14/37, WODP, Box 5.

122   **"The truth is that Bill"** See Robert Mull, interview with Chester Maxey, 9/22/81. In a rare admission that the tale had two sides, Douglas added to his account of the tent story in *Go East* this line: "Next I moved into the Beta Theta fraternity house, sleeping on an open porch or in a tent in the fraternity backyard" (p. 100).

122   **Even more interesting** Chester Maxey Oral History, 1/16/76, Whitman Archives, tells essentially the same story as Robert Mull, interview with Chester Maxey, 9/22/81. Chester Maxey recalled that Douglas "didn't deny it," leading those present to believe that "there must be some truth to" the charge.

122   **Maxey understood** Chester Maxey Oral History, 1/16/76, Whitman Archives.

122   **For decades at Democratic party** Hugh Sidey, "The Greatest Eclipse," *Time*, 6/3/91, p. 24.

123   **"I knew Bill Douglas"** Robert Mull, interview with Chester Maxey, 9/22/81.

CHAPTER 13

124   **"The story of Bill Douglas's"** Oral History of Abe Fortas, in Louchheim, *Making of the New Deal*, p. 222. See also "S.E.C. Report Hits Ethics of Bond Groups," New York *Herald Tribune*, 5/5/36, p. 25, and later, George Wanders, "Bias Viewed in Municipal Bond Report," New York *Herald Tribune*, 5/25/36, p. 21.

124   **Early in June** "SEC Urges Curbing Reality Bond Field," *The New York Times*, 6/4/36, p. 35.

124   **An admiring *New York Times*** "S.E.C. Asks New Law to Guard Investor Under Trustees," *The New York Times*, 6/19/36, p. 1.

125   **A front-page article** Ibid.

125   **"the tenor of the corporate"** Robert E. Kintner, "S.E.C. Pleads for Right to Aid Investor," 6/19/36, New York *Herald Tribune*, p. 33.

125   **These reports made** "Comment in Wall Street," New York *Herald Tribune*, 6/20/36, p. 23.

125   **The recommended reforms** W. S. Lyon, "S.E.C. Attack on Trustees Upsets Banks," New York *Herald Tribune*, 6/21/36, sec. 2, pt. 1, pp. 1, 12.

125   **Robert Kintner, now serving** Robert E. Kintner, "Financial Washington," New York *Herald Tribune*, 7/12/36, sec. 2, pt. 1, p. 9.

125   **With his new visibility** John T. Flynn, "Other People's Money," *The New Republic,* 7/29/36, p. 353.

125   **While the audience shifted** "Douglas Defends U.S. Spending, High Margins, Stock Regulation," New York *Herald Tribune,* 7/12/36, sec. 2, pt. 1, p. 9.

125   **In setting himself apart** "Exchange Formally to Weigh Segregation This Week as SEC Gives It Copies of Report," *The New York Times,* 7/19/36, sec. 3, p. 1.

125   **Why were these people** Ibid.

126   **Seeking to solidify** Simon, *Independent Journey,* pp. 155–56, quoting WOD to FDR, 7/7/36, FDRL Papers.

126   **The day after** Ibid., p. 156, quoting WOD to Steve Early, 7/8/36, FDRL Papers.

126   **Roosevelt was so impressed** Ibid., citing FDR to M. H. McIntyre, 7/9/36, FDRL Papers.

126   **Having learned how** Frank S. Adams, "Davis Predicts End of 1935 Utility Act," *The New York Times,* 8/26/36, p. 13; "Douglas Asks S.E.C. Regulation of Municipal Bond Committees," New York *Herald Tribune,* 8/26/36, p. 27; "S.E.C. Renews Plea for Bond Unit Control," New York *Herald Tribune,* 8/31/36, pp. 19, 20.

126   **Finally, Douglas met** FDR, Presidential Diary and Itinerary, 9/16/36, FDRL Papers.

126   **Three days later** Robert E. Kintner, "Ross to Quit S.E.C. Board After Election," New York *Herald Tribune,* 9/19/36, p. 36.

126   **Kintner also trumpeted** Robert E. Kintner, "Financial Washington," New York *Herald Tribune,* 10/4/36, sec. 4, p. 1.

126   **Even though Congress** See Simon, *Independent Journey,* pp. 149–50. Congress put a provision in the revised bankruptcy act empowering the SEC to advise the courts on corporate reorganizations. This led to the passage of the Trust Indenture Act, which set fiduciary standards for trustees dealing with trusts created upon the issuance of securities.

126   **Knowing that the financial** Robert Sobel, *NYSE: A History of the New York Stock Exchange, 1935–1975* (New York: Weybright and Talley, 1975), p. 25.

127   **Seeking to reinforce** Ibid., pp. 25–26.

127   **Publicly, though, Douglas** *Vital Speeches of the Day* (New York: City News Co., 1936), 11/15/36, pp. 86–93.

127   **"Irresponsible, laissez-faire democracy"** Ibid., cited in Simon, *Independent Journey,* p. 156.

127   **Two weeks later** "Douglas Warns of Fee-Hungry Stock Salesman," New York *Herald Tribune,* 11/13/36, p. 35. James Allen, ed., *Democracy and Finance: The Addresses and Public Statements of William O. Douglas as Member and Chairman of the Securities and Exchange Commission* (New Haven: Yale University Press, 1940), p. 107.

127   **The future brokers** Quotes taken from Allen, *Democracy and Finance,* pp. 107–19; "Douglas Maps Duty of Customers' Men," *The New York Times,* 11/13/26, p. 33; and "Douglas Warns of Fee-Hungry Stock Salesman," New York *Herald Tribune,* 11/13/36, p. 35.

127 **Douglas's call** "Douglas Maps Duty of Customers' Men," *The New York Times,* 11/13/26, p. 33.

127 **But the reaction did** "Douglas Urges Curbs on City Fiscal Agents," *The New York Times,* 11/18/36, p. 29. In addressing the U.S. Conference of Mayors on November 18, Douglas outlined his suggestions for improving the municipal-default situation.

127 **Early in January 1937** Robert E. Kintner, "Financial Washington," New York *Herald Tribune,* 1/3/37, sec. 4, p. 1.

127 **When Landis** "Landis Quits S.E.C. Post in Summer," New York *Herald Tribune,* 1/5/37, p. 25; and "Harvard Names Landis as Dean of Law School," New York *Herald Tribune,* 1/10/37, p. 15.

128 **For its part** "Harvard Law School Has a New Dean," *The Nation,* 1/23/37, pp. 86–87.

128 **While the White House mulled** For an excellent account of the Court-packing incident, see William Leuchtenburg, "The Origins of Franklin D. Roosevelt's 'Court-Packing' Plan," *Supreme Court Review,* 1966, pp. 347ff.; William Leuchtenburg, "Franklin D. Roosevelt's Supreme Court 'Packing' Plan," in Harold Hollingsworth and William Holmes, eds., *Essays on the New Deal* (Austin: University of Texas Press, 1969); Joseph Alsop and Turner Catledge, *The 168 Days: The Story Behind the Story of the Supreme Court Fight* (Philadelphia: G. Graham, 1938); and Leonard Baker, *Back to Back: The Duel Between FDR and the Supreme Court* (New York: Macmillan, 1967).

128 **Such an open attack** Robert H. Jackson Oral History, COHC, copy from the University of Chicago Library Archives, Hyde Park, Ill.

128 **For his part** WOD to A. Howard Meneely, 3/13/37, WODP, Box 10.

128 **"Douglas . . . took on one"** Louchheim, *Making of the New Deal,* p. 128.

129 **To supplement this effort** Kalman, *Legal Realism,* p. 133.

129 **"Dean Charley Clark"** AI, Irene Hamilton, 5/16/90, Washington, D.C.

129 **By trimming his own** Douglas also claimed that Yale was three to one in favor of the proposal. See WOD to A. Howard Meneely, 3/13/37, WODP, Box 10.

129 **Despite all these** "Jackson Seen as S.E.C. Head After Landis," New York *Herald Tribune,* 3/11/37, p. 27.

129 **Knowing FDR's predilection** Robert E. Kintner, "Financial Washington," New York *Herald Tribune,* 3/28/37, sec. 4, p. 1.

129 **Unwittingly, the Bond Club** Allen, *Democracy and Finance,* p. 32. Also see "Douglas Asks Changes in Corporate Financing," *The Wall Street Journal,* 3/25/37, p. 1.

129 **As he stood to speak** "End of Banks' Rule in Industry Hinted," *The New York Times,* 3/25/37, pp. 37, 46.

129 **Then, peering through** "Cynic on Grumpsters," *Time,* 4/5/37, p. 71.

129 **"Today, as you well know"** "End of Banks' Rule in Industry Hinted," *The New York Times,* 3/25/37, p. 37.

129 **These "oppressive plans"** "Corporations Usurp Power, Says Douglas," New York *Herald Tribune,* 3/25/37, p. 31.

130 **"democratization in industrial"** Ibid.; "SEC's New Chairman," *Literary Digest,* 10/9/37, p. 33.

130 **"I understand he used"** Richard L. Neuberger, "Mr. Justice Douglas," *Harper's Magazine,* summer 1942, p. 313.

130 **"Do you suppose"** *The New York Times,* 3/24/37, pt. 8, p. 9.

130 **When the speech ended** "End of Bank's Rule in Industry Hinted," *The New York Times,* 3/25/37, p. 46.

130 **All around the room** "Business & Finance," *Time,* 4/5/37, p. 71.

130 **"a grumpy lot"** "Comment in Wall Street," New York *Herald Tribune,* 3/25/37, p. 31.

130 **"rather gloomy"** "At the Turn of the Week in Wall Street," New York *Herald Tribune,* 3/28/37, sec. 4, p. 3.

130 **"nothing less than"** "Business & Finance," *Time,* 4/5/37, p. 71.

130 **"left bankers gasping."** "At the Turn of the Week in Wall Street," New York *Herald Tribune,* 3/28/37, sec. 4, p. 3.

130 **Following this speech** Edson Blair, "Washington: Both Sides of the Curtain," *Barron's,* 9/27/37, pp. 4–5.

130 **Wall Street** Robert E. Kintner, "Financial Washington," New York *Herald Tribune,* 6/20/37, sec. 4, p. 1.

131 **"excessive regulation [that]"** "Gay Assails 'Artificial' Market Curbs," New York *Herald Tribune,* 8/18/37, p. 25.

131 **The vituperative nature** "Mr. Gay's Report," New York *Herald Tribune,* 8/18/37, p. 16.

131 **The commission deliberated** Robert E. Kintner, "Financial Washington," New York *Herald Tribune,* 8/22/37, sec. 4, p. 1. There is of course the possibility that Gay was attempting to head off further reform by the probable new chair of the SEC.

131 **While the decision turned** "SEC Failure to Answer Gay Irks New Deal," New York *Herald Tribune,* 9/8/37, p. 27.

131 **By September** *The Wall Street Journal,* 9/17/37, p. 31, on Douglas at Cape Cod.

131 **Frustration built as Landis** "Landis Hits Wall Street Self-Interest," New York *Herald Tribune,* 9/15/37, p. 31; "Landis Insists U.S. Rules Bring Market Stability," *The Wall Street Journal,* 9/15/37, p. 1.

131 **"It would be difficult"** "Mr. Landis's Valedictory," New York *Herald Tribune,* 9/16/37, p. 24.

131 **Landis's resignation now** "Landis Hits Wall Street Self-Interest," ibid., 9/15/37, p. 31.

132 **The betting** "San Francisco Exchange Head May Succeed Landis," ibid., 9/17/37, p. 31.

132 **Journalists now began** Robert E. Kintner, "Comment on Wall Street," ibid., 9/15/37, p. 31; and "San Francisco Exchange Head May Succeed Landis," ibid., 9/17/37, p. 31.

132 **Meanwhile, Landis was** "San Francisco Exchange Head," ibid. See also "Saperstein Quits Trading Division of SEC for Law," *The Wall Street Journal,* 9/14/37, p. 2; and "Trade Division Post Resigned by Saperstein," New York *Herald Tribune,* 9/14/37, p. 31.

132 **Behind the scenes** DeBedts, *The New Deal's SEC,* p. 155, citing Secretary Daniel C. Roper to FDR, 9/18/37, FDRL Papers.

132   **Knowing that any** Robert E. Kintner, "Comment on Wall Street," New
       York *Herald Tribune,* 9/17/37, p. 31. Perhaps Douglas himself, given his re-
       lationship to Kintner, also leaked this report.

132   **Douglas decided** Douglas loved to tell this story and told it first in Doug-
       las Conversations, cassette no. 6, 1/18/62, pp. 116–22. While all Douglas
       memoirs are generally inherently suspect, for a variety of reasons these
       conversations have proved to be much more accurate than the rest. From
       12/20/61 to 12/10/63, Douglas recorded his memoirs with Professor Wal-
       ter Murphy of Princeton University, no doubt anticipating the production
       of a biography, which was never written. Murphy, one of the preeminent
       constitutional-law scholars in the nation, submitted a list of questions to
       Douglas in advance. As the interviews later ensued, if a matter arose about
       which Douglas had no memory, they would stop the tape and go up to
       room 210, where the files were kept, to research the question. Thus many
       of the answers have a sort of contemporaneous feel to them as Douglas is
       commenting based on his refreshed recollection. Perhaps because of his
       respect for Murphy's ability to verify any of these facts, Douglas's ac-
       counts here check out far more frequently than do his other versions. AI,
       Walter Murphy, 7/16/89, Princeton, N.J. (phone).

           This account also appears in a Drew Pearson column, *The Washington
       Post,* 12/23/61, and it was picked up in Richard J. Whalen, *The Founding
       Father: The Story of Joseph P. Kennedy* (New York: New American Library,
       1964), p. 373. Finally, WOD told the same tale in his *Go East,* p. 281. The
       dates of this story check out with the accounts offered in the popular
       press, and the fact that the reversal of the appointment was made even be-
       fore the vacancy was filled confirms Douglas's tale. See "Douglas Named
       Head of SEC," New York *Herald Tribune,* 9/22/37, p. 37, and "Douglas
       Elected SEC Chairman to Succeed Landis," *The New York Times,* 9/22/37,
       p. 1.

132   **As soon as he arrived** The reliability of Douglas's tale here is suspect. In
       her very thorough history of Yale Law School, Laura Kalman makes no
       mention of the deanship being available at this time (see Kalman, *Legal
       Realism,* pp. 140–45). This position is bolstered by a search of the Walton
       Hamilton Papers in the University of Texas Library in Austin, Texas, and
       the Charles Clark Papers in Yale University's Sterling Library, neither of
       which indicates that the deanship was available then. As outlined in chap-
       ter 16 below, perhaps Douglas confused this with a genuine offer of the
       Yale Law School deanship that came to him in 1939, before his Court ap-
       pointment. Or perhaps Douglas, if he felt he would not get the chairman-
       ship, had been persuaded to return to the faculty, in anticipation that he
       would be elected dean when Clark did decide to leave.

133   **The story was not** Douglas and others have claimed that this meeting oc-
       curred on the evening of the fifteenth, but White House documents in-
       dicate that this conversation had to have taken place two days later
       (Franklin D. Roosevelt Presidential White House Diary and Itinerary and
       White House Usher Books for 9/14–18/37, FDRL Papers). There is no

record of Joe Kennedy visiting the president, but that conversation could have taken place over the phone, or the meeting could have been "off the books," or he could have squeezed the meeting between scheduled appointments.

But the tale masked the real truth. If Douglas was blocked in his quest for the chairmanship, he would indeed have had to make a decision as to whether to return to teaching, whether he did so at that moment or in the months to come. And he had every reason to expect that his future would indeed have included the deanship after Clark stepped down.

133 **One phone call later** White House documents make clear that Corcoran was in and out of the White House on September 15, 16 (twice), 17 (twice), and 18 (once). While he would have this many other issues to discuss, this easy access to the president would have made it very likely that Corcoran used some of his time to lobby for Douglas, as he later claimed. See ibid.

See also Joseph Alsop and Robert Kintner, "We Shall Make America Over" (part 2 of 3), *The Saturday Evening Post*, 11/12/38, p. 104.

133 **"You will not be leaving"** Once more, the date is not the same as that claimed by Douglas, the press, and others (who claim that it was the sixteenth). See Franklin D. Roosevelt Presidential White House Diary and Itinerary and White House Usher Books for 9/14–18/37, FDRL Papers, which show that the meeting took place at 11:00 A.M. on Saturday, 9/18.

See "Stocks Tend Higher with Turnover Off," New York *Herald Tribune*, 9/22/37, p. 37: "The new chairman saw Mr. Roosevelt last week." See also "Bill and Billy," *Time*, 10/11/37, p. 61: "Three weeks ago Douglas went to the White House for a conference with the President." Despite Douglas's later account that FDR offered him the job on the phone, it is far more likely, and more in keeping with the president's practice, that he offered the job in person. I rely on Douglas's basic tale in Douglas Conversations, cassette no. 6, 1/18/62, pp. 120–21. Other versions are substantially the same, but this is the earliest version, and the dialogue is much less definite and thus more believable.

133 **With the offer firmly** "Douglas Named Head of S.E.C., Vigorous Regulations Policy Seen," New York *Herald Tribune*, 9/22/37, p. 37; "Douglas Elected S.E.C. Chairman to Succeed Landis," *The New York Times*, 9/22/37, p. 1.

133 **Despite the fact** "Wall Street's Lip Approval," *The Nation*, 10/2/37, p. 334.

133 **on September 21** The president actually had no formal role in choosing a successor, since the SEC is an independent agency.

133 **Unlike the largely invisible** "Douglas Named Head of S.E.C., Vigorous Regulations Policy Seen," New York *Herald Tribune*, 9/22/37, p. 37.

133 **"Landis likes to be liked"** *Business Week*, 9/25/37, p. 60.

133 **"The Yakima school"** *Yakima Republic*, 8/10/37, *Yakima Herald-Republic* Archives, Yakima, Wash.

134 **While most people** AI, Dagmar Hamilton, 2/25/90, Austin, Tex.

134 **When the tattered clipping** Robert W. Lucas, "William O. Douglas, a Cham-

pion of Freedom," *Yakima Herald-Republic*, 11/6/78; and Lucas's comments in Robert W. Mull's revealing television documentary on WOD, *When Court Adjourned* (1982), KYVE, Yakima, Wash.

134   **"So far as I could see,"** Cuneo, "The Near-Presidency," p. 7.

134   **"Under Joe [Kennedy]"** "Bill and Billy," *Time*, 10/11/37, p. 61.

CHAPTER 14

136   **With the all-male** Douglas always claimed that he knew Justice Louis D. Brandeis well and received advice from him before coming to the Supreme Court, but it does not appear to be true. For these claims, see Sevareid, "Mr. Justice Douglas," 1972, and Douglas, *Go East*, pp. 182, 306–7, 463. However, Douglas's contemporaneous diary ("The Diary of William O. Douglas," a transcription of portions of which can be found in the personal papers of Marty Bagby Yopp, Moscow, Idaho) indicates in the 3/26/39 entry that he did not know the Justice well at all.

136   **Though he was ready** Ernie Cuneo, "The Story of the Non-Election of a President in 1944," Cuneo Papers, Box 18, FDRL.

136   **His tie, usually adorned** Cuneo, "Near-Presidency."

136   **Now, with the camera** "Douglas Plans Vigilant Rule in S.E.C. Post," New York *Herald Tribune*, 9/23/37, pp. 37, 39.

136   **"What is the proper role"** For the text of these statements, see "Bill and Billy," *Time*, 10/11/37, p. 61, and "Text of W. O. Douglas's Statements at Press Conference," *The New York Times*, 9/23/37, p. 45.

137   **The SEC, he said** "Review and Outlook: William O. Douglas," *The Wall Street Journal*, 9/23/37, p. 4: The news conference "was couched in different terms than some of his previous statements."

137   **The "statement to the press"** "The New S.E.C. Chairman," New York *Herald Tribune*, 9/23/37, p. 26.

137   **"[Douglas] acted as if"** Cuneo, "Near-Presidency."

137   **By 1937, the forty-nine-year-old** Edwin Palmer Hoyt, *The Tempering Years* (New York: Scribners, 1963), p. 4; John Brooks, *Once in Golconda: A True Drama of Wall Street, 1920–1938* (New York: Harper and Row, 1969), p. 61. Brooks's book is considered to be the best account of the Whitney story.

138   **After serving a brief** Hoyt, *Tempering Years*, pp. 4–5.

138   **Whitney's base of power** Joseph Alsop and Robert E. Kintner, "The Capital Parade," *The Atlanta Constitution*, 12/17/37; and Joseph Alsop and Robert Kintner, "The Battle of the Market Place: Richard Whitney Leads the Fight," *The Saturday Evening Post*, 6/11/38, p. 75.

138   **These men traded** Brooks, *Once in Golconda*, p. 199.

138   **Whitney's Wall Street legend** Hoyt, *Tempering Years*, p. 4.

138   **With financial panic** Oral History of Judge Gerhard Gesell, in Louchheim, *Making of the New Deal*, p. 131.

138   **"What is the current price"** Sobel, *NYSE*, p. 14.

138   **A week later** Brooks, *Once in Golconda*, p. 61, and Hoyt, *Tempering Years*, pp. 125–27.

138   **Just three months later** Hoyt, *Tempering Years*, p. 6.

138   **By the mid-1930s** Brooks, *Once in Golconda*, p. 200.

139   **In the hopes of** Alsop and Kintner, "Battle of the Market Place," p. 76.

139   **"You association people"** Ibid.

139   **And fry they would** Ibid.

139   **Finally, in the spring** Max Lerner, "Notes on Black Tuesday," *The Nation,* 10/30/37, p. 468.

139   **A graduate of Brooklyn's** Sobel, *NYSE,* pp. 10–11.

139   **Gay was "an"** Alsop and Kintner, "Battle of the Market Place," p. 78.

139   **However, this election** "Ex-Knight," *Time,* 3/21/38, p. 63.

139   **"What else can I do?"** Alsop and Kintner, "Battle of the Market Place," p. 78.

139   **Upon hearing this** Oral History of Milton Katz, in Louchheim, *Making of the New Deal,* p. 127. See also Sobel, *NYSE,* p. 53.

140   **"We think the management"** Joseph Alsop and Robert Kintner, "The Battle of the Market Place: Wall Street and Washington Make Peace," *The Saturday Evening Post,* 6/25/38, p. 10 (hereafter "Wall Street and Washington Make Peace").

140   **Within minutes** Ibid. That the meeting took place is confirmed in the New York *Herald Tribune,* 10/17/37, sec. 4, p. 1.

140   **"That is primarily"** "Statements of William O. Douglas, Chairman; Francis P. Brassor, Secretary; William F. Murphy, Chief, Budget and Accounting Section; and James J. Riordan, Assistant Chief, Budget and Accounting Section," House Appropriations Committee, *House Congressional Hearings,* Independent Offices Appropriation Bill, 75th Cong., 1st sess., 12/1/37, p. 723 (hereafter Douglas Congressional Hearings). See Alsop and Kintner, "Washington and Wall Street Make Peace," p. 10; and also their "Capital Parade," 11/30/37, p. 6.

140   **Despite this encouragement** "Stocks Sink to New Lows," New York *Herald Tribune,* 10/20/37, p. 11.

140   **Publicly, the Roosevelt** "Roosevelt Plans No Move to Halt Sharp Breaks in Stock Prices," New York *Herald Tribune,* 10/20/37, p. 1.

140   **Privately, though** Alsop and Kintner, "Washington and Wall Street Make Peace," p. 10.

140   **While the younger Roosevelt** Ibid., p. 11.

140   **"[I am]** —— —— —— ——" Ibid.

141   **But Shields had promised** Ibid.

141   **Shields was designated** Ibid., p. 73. That all of the principals were at Hyde Park on 10/26/37 is confirmed in the next day's accounts: "S.E.C. Soon May Make Statement on Stock Market, Says Douglas," *The Wall Street Journal,* p. 1; "SEC Prepares to Blame Break on Short Sales," New York *Herald Tribune,* p. 47; and "Roosevelt Holds to Budget Pledge," *The New York Times,* p. 12.

141   **On October 29** This is confirmed by "SEC Launches Further Studies of Markets," *The Wall Street Journal,* 10/30/37, pp. 1, 3.

141   **"The job of regulation's"** "S.E.C. Study to Seek Reasons for Rise and Fall of Market," New York *Herald Tribune,* 11/4/37, p. 35.

142   **The reaction surprised** George Britt, "Wall Street vs. Washington," *Literary Digest,* 1/29/38, p. 12.

142　**"ratty," "third-class quarters"** Douglas, *Go East,* p. 304.

142　**There, expecting to meet** See picture accompanying Britt, "Wall Street vs. Washington," p. 12; "Bill and Billy," *Time,* 10/11/37, pp. 61–64.

142　**A good deal more shouting** Alsop and Kintner, "Washington and Wall Street Make Peace," p. 78.

142　**Gay returned to his office** Ibid.

143　**"I'm sorry."** Memorandum, Milton Katz to WOD, 4/13/38 (reviewing the meetings retrospectively to say that no contemporaneous drafts or memos exist on them), WOD/SEC Files, Box 25, File UNL-Z, "When Issued" folder; and WOD to Richard B. Wigglesworth, 4/13/38, in ibid.

143　**"Bill, they've adopted"** Oral History of Milton Katz, in Louchheim, *Making of the New Deal,* pp. 126–27.

143　~~**Knowing that he**~~ ~~Katz then became the special counsel to the public-utility-~~ holdings section of the SEC. See also ibid., p. 127. Katz's change in jobs was reported in "Allen, Katz, Sheridan Promoted by Securities and Exchange Unit," New York *Herald Tribune,* 12/30/37, p. 23.

144　**While no one really** Alsop and Kintner, "Washington and Wall Street Make Peace," p. 78.

144　**When the group reconvened** Ibid., pp. 78, 80.

144　**By the time Jackson** Ibid., p. 80.

144　**"Have you read the last draft"** This is the version contained in DeBedts, *The New Deal's SEC,* pp. 162–63, which Douglas said "is substantially correct" in a letter to DeBedts, 3/11/60. See also Alsop and Kintner, "Battle of the Market Place," p. 8, and Douglas, *Go East,* pp. 290–91. Douglas's version is only slightly different but is wholly unreliable because, as the newspapers confirm, his meeting with Shields took place well before this verbal exchange.

144　**For the old guard** Douglas Congressional Hearings, 12/1/37, p. 70.

144　**After twice rejecting** "Ex-Knight," *Time,* 3/21/38, pp. 62, 63.

144　**Unknown to nearly everyone** Hoyt, *Tempering Years,* p. 5.

145　**Unfortunately, his** Oral History of Judge Gerhard Gesell, in Louchheim, *Making of the New Deal,* p. 133.

145　**In a matter of a few years** DeBedts, *The New Deal's SEC,* p. 165, citing SEC, *In the Matter of Richard Whitney, et al.,* vol. 2, pp. 48–49, 179.

145　**When this massive** Sobel, *NYSE,* pp. 45–46.

145　**The process might have** SEC, *In the Matter of Richard Whitney,* vol. 2, p. 193.

145　**On five occasions** Ibid., vol. 2, p. 205. Why didn't Lutes say something? he was asked. "Mr. Whitney was a more or less sharp person and I could not go up to Mr. Whitney and say, 'Here, Mr. Whitney, you send those bonds over to us,' or anything of that sort, because Mr. Whitney was my superior. I was under him as an employee of the Exchange and I am only a clerk." Ibid., vol. 2, p. 155; vol. 1, p. 106.

145　**The truth was** Ibid., vol. 2, pp. 180, 193.

145　**On November 22** Ibid., vol. 1, p. 108.

146　**The trustees were** Ibid., p. 105.

146　**"As a friend"** Ibid., p. 109.

146　**Events were spiraling** C. Norman Stabler, "Stock Break Blame Denied by

Exchange," New York *Herald Tribune*, 11/23/37, pp. 1:4, 34:5. Hoyt, *Tempering Years*, p. 38, reports that Gay had given the exclusive interview. However, this is not a position taken by anyone else.

146 **When the Dow Jones** Fred Rodell, "Douglas Over the Stock Exchange," *Fortune*, February 1938, p. 64.

146 **Now "enraged"** Alsop and Kintner, "Capital Parade," 11/30/37, p. 6:3; "Douglas Spurs Revision Plan by Exchange," New York *Herald Tribune*, 11/24/37, p. 29.

146 **While it "would be desirable"** Douglas Congressional Hearings, 12/1/37, pp. 718–22. See also the next day's accounts: "Text of Douglas Statement Issued by S.E.C.," New York *Herald Tribune*, 11/24/37, p. 33; "Full Text of the Statement by W. O. Douglas," *The New York Times*, p. 39; and "Text of SEC Chairman Douglas' Statement," *The Wall Street Journal*, p. 10.

146 **The chairman was so** Rodell, "Douglas Over the Stock Exchange," p. 116.

147 **As they entered** See picture in *The Atlanta Constitution*, 11/25/37, p. 1.

147 **"Bullshit!"** Fearing that public sensibilities would be offended, the press chose to report the next day that the chairman had instead said, "Hooey." See Rodell, "Douglas Over the Stock Exchange," p. 116. Simon confirmed with Rodell that the comment was actually "Bullshit" (*Independent Journey*, pp. 171, 468).

147 **But Richard Whitney** SEC, *In the Matter of Richard Whitney*, vol. 1, p. 133.

147 *How could you do* Ibid., vol. 2, p. 63.

147 **Since George Whitney** Ibid., vol. 1, p. 143.

147 **Later that day** Ibid., pp. 113–15, 146–47; see also Alsop and Kintner, "Washington and Wall Street Make Peace," p. 80, and SEC, *In the Matter of Richard Whitney*, vol. 2, pp. 532–34.

147 **The following week** Ibid., vol. 1, p. 116.

147 **Incredibly, through all** Alsop and Kintner, "Washington and Wall Street Make Peace," p. 80.

147 **With this authorization** "Comment in Wall Street," New York *Herald Tribune*, 11/30/37, p. 27.

148 **"My experience has convinced"** "Exchange President's Reply to SEC," *The New York Times*, 11/30/37, p. 12.

148 **As shocking as** Alsop and Kintner, "Capital Parade," 3/17/38, p. 8.

148 **Fortunately for the chairman** Alsop and Kintner, "Washington and Wall Street Make Peace," p. 81, and "Comment in Wall Street," New York *Herald Tribune*, 12/11/37, p. 23.

148 **The committee worked** "Group to Expedite Report on Survey of N.Y. Exchange," *The Wall Street Journal*, 12/31/37, p. 1; Seligman, *Transformation of Wall Street*, pp. 164–65. Ganson Purcell, the head of SEC's Trading and Exchange Division, even delivered an outline to the committee of the SEC's suggestions for reform.

148 **By the end of 1937** "Revision Plan for Exchange Seen by Spring," New York *Herald Tribune*, 12/31/37, p. 20.

149 **Whitney's opponents** SEC, *In the Matter of Richard Whitney*, vol. 2, pp. 824–25, 852.

149 **"He['s] broke and"** Ibid., p. 825.

149 **It was the first time** Ibid., vol. 1, p. 36. Gay categorically denied ever having been told that Whitney was broke (p. 82).

149 **Still totally unaware** "Douglas Asks Exchange to Sift Fiscal Status of Member Firms," New York *Herald Tribune,* 12/18/37, p. 23.

149 **In late December** "SEC Report Warns Exchanges to Reorganize," *The Wall Street Journal,* 12/31/37, p. 3.

149 **This report, proclaimed** "S.E.C. to Push Its 'Policing' of Exchanges," New York *Herald Tribune,* 12/31/37, p. 19; "S.E.C.'s Next Round," *Time,* 1/10/38, p. 59.

149 **Then on January 7** "Text of Speech by SEC Chairman Douglas at Hartford," *The Wall Street Journal,* 1/8/38, p. 5.

149 **For some time, he** See Douglas memo, "Short Selling," in "N.Y. Stock Exchange St. Market Crash Oct. 1937," in WOD/SEC, Box 19, File NAV through O. For more see also Sobel, *NYSE,* p. 39.

150 **By creating falling prices** John T. Flynn, "Washing Wall Street's Face," *Collier's,* 1/29/38, p. 13.

150 **For Bill Douglas** Ibid.; Hoyt; *Tempering Years,* p. 40. See also Douglas, *Go East,* p. 289.

150 **So, just over two** "S.E.C. Curbs Short Sales," New York *Herald Tribune,* 1/25/38, p. 1.

150 **For the first time** Ibid. See also "Businesslike Exchange Plan Envisages Peace with SEC," *Newsweek,* 2/7/38, p. 31.

150 **The regulation accomplished** "Exchange Committee Seeks Power to Rule on Specialists' Activity," *The Wall Street Journal,* 1/27/38, pp. 1, 2.

150 **The following day** Even more important than the specific reform suggestions was the tone of the cover letter to President Gay, which urged him to forge "[a] close working relationship between" the SEC and the NYSE. Finally, the committee concluded that "neither the Stock Exchange nor the S.E.C. can be held responsible for major fluctuations in the price of securities." In short, both parties were absolved of any responsibility for the market crash. "Text of Report on Reorganization of Exchange," *The Wall Street Journal,* 1/28/38, p. 8; "Text of Report to the New York Stock Exchange of the Committee on Reorganization," New York *Herald Tribune,* 1/28/38, pp. 29; and "Stock Exchange Has Plan for Reorganization That Gives Public Larger Voice," New York *Herald Tribune,* 1/28/38, p. 1.

150 **Bill Douglas hailed** "S.E.C. Approves Conway Report Upon Exchange," New York *Herald Tribune,* 1/28/38, p. 27; and "Committee Urges Exchange Board Be Cut to 32 from 50," *The Wall Street Journal,* 1/28/38, pp. 1, 8.

150 **Meanwhile, an exuberant** "S.E.C. Officials Won't Criticize Exchange Reorganization Plan," New York *Herald Tribune,* 1/30/38, secs. 2–4, p. 12.

150 **But just as the time** See memorandum, Allen Throop to Commission, 3/25/38, in WOD/SEC, Box 25, UNL-Z, "Miscellaneous Memoranda on Richard Whitney and Co." folder. See also SEC, *In the Matter of Richard Whitney,* vol. 1, pp. 33–35.

150 **Wellington in turn** Ibid., and see SEC, *In the Matter of Richard Whitney,* vol. 1, pp. 35–36.

151 **Now Davis's curiosity** Ibid., pp. 35–37.

151 **With disaster staring him** Alsop and Kintner, "Battle of the Market Place," p. 81.

151 **Then, in an event** Quoted in Sobel, *NYSE*, p. 44.

152 **Four days later** SEC, *In the Matter of Richard Whitney*, vol. 1, pp. 41–43.

152 **How much money** Memorandum, Allen Throop to the Commission, 3/25/38, in WOD/SEC, Box 25, UNL-Z, "Miscellaneous Memoranda on Richard Whitney and Co." folder.

152 **But he was not beyond** Ernest Cuneo autobiographical draft, "Douglas Nearing the Presidency," Cuneo Papers, Box 114, FDRL.

152 **"After all," he said** Alsop and Kintner, "Washington and Wall Street Make Peace," p. 82.

152 **Gay, however, knew** SEC, *In the Matter of Richard Whitney*, vol. 2., pp. 325–26.

152 **A somber Charles Gay** Hoyt, *Tempering Years*, p. 41; Seligman, *Transformation of Wall Street*, pp. 167–68.

152 **Both of them knew** WOD, *Memorandum Regarding Events of March 7 and 8, 1938*, and John Hanes, *Memorandum Regarding Events of March 7 & 8, 1938*, in WOD/SEC, Box 25, UNL-Z, "Miscellaneous memoranda on Richard Whitney and Co." folder.

153 **Douglas then dispatched** Ibid.

153 **Douglas became so concerned** Douglas, *Go East*, p. 289, on Dowd. See also Montana Podva Diaries, Willets, Calif. (with sincere thanks to Podva for providing this material). Here, Douglas talks about how he deliberately had to keep the Whitney material out of the hands of Dewey, whom he saw as politically ambitious.

153 **"Not Dick Whitney!"** Douglas, *Go East*, pp. 289–90.

153 **At a hearing before** SEC, *In the Matter of Richard Whitney*, vol. 1, pp. 49–51.

153 **As a result** Alsop and Kintner, "Washington and Wall Street Make Peace," p. 82.

153 **Rumors of Whitney's insolvency** "Comment at the Turn of the Week in the Field of Finance," New York *Herald Tribune*, 3/13/38, sec. 2, p. 15.

153 **So at 10:05** Alsop and Kintner, "Washington and Wall Street Make Peace," p. 82.

153 **The news of Whitney's** "Comment at the Turn," New York *Herald Tribune*, 3/13/38, sec. 2, p. 15; "Wall Street Comment," New York *Herald Tribune*, 3/9/38, p. 27.

153 **In the words of another** "Wall Street Comment," New York *Herald Tribune*, 3/10/38, p. 27.

154 **Bill Douglas now governed** Seligman, *Transformation of Wall Street*, pp. 159–70, quoting telegram, WOD to Thomas E. Dewey, 3/22/38, WOD/SEC, Box 19, File NAV through O.

154 **Though he was not** *Scholastic Magazine*, 10/30/37, p. 28.

CHAPTER 15

155 **"[Bill Douglas] found the"** Robert W. Kenny, "My First Forty Years in California Politics," pp. 206–7, Robert W. Kenny Papers, carton 6, Bancroft Library, University of California at Berkeley.

155   **Douglas's "total victory"** Douglas, *Go East,* p. 292.

155   **Douglas had launched** "SEC to O-T-C," *Time,* 1/31/38, p. 51.

155   **So little was known** Douglas, *Go East,* p. 271.

155   **Anyone with a phone** "SEC to O-T-C," *Time,* 1/31/38, p. 52.

155   **Consistent with his overall** "S.E.C. Chairman Keeps Promise to Provide 'Program of Action,'" New York *Herald Tribune,* 1/23/38, secs. 2–4, p. 12.

156   **So confident was Douglas** Joseph Alsop and Robert Kintner, "The Capital Parade," *The Atlanta Constitution,* 2/16/38, p. 6. For the fact that the bill had prior approval, see "Counter Dealers Ask Federal Aid," *The New York Times,* 12/21/37, p. 35; and "SEC to Meet Dealers On Over-Counter Rules," *The Wall Street Journal,* 12/18/37, p. 1.

156   **The bill, journalists** Alsop and Kintner, "Capital Parade," 2/16/38, p. 6.

156   **But that did not make** "Comment in Wall Street," New York *Herald Tribune,* 2/13/38, sec. 2, p. 12.

156   **Douglas turned** Seligman, *Transformation of Wall Street,* p. 190.

156   **Douglas's chances** Ibid., p. 188 (quoting Felix Frankfurter to WOD, 1/16/34, WODP, container no. 6; and p. 191, citing Abe Fortas to WOD, October 1935).

156   **But without** Ibid., p. 190. Seligman suggests here that the Lea bill served as an education for Douglas and was "a milestone in Douglas's evolution from academic theorist to political tactician."

156   **Douglas could only** "Investment Trust Regulatory Steps Likely This Year," *The Wall Street Journal,* 1/3/39, p. 19. See also Bernard Kilgore, "SEC to Sidetrack Lea Bill at Next Congress Session," *The Wall Street Journal,* 11/30/38, p. 1.

156   **This lesson was** Seligman, *Transformation of Wall Street,* p. 193. So effective was this law that it lasted for forty years before being replaced. For articles on this act, see "Senate Group Acts to Limit SEC's Revamping Power," *The Wall Street Journal,* 5/25/38, p. 1; "Chandler Bill Reported by Senate Committee," *The Wall Street Journal,* 5/26/38, p. 15; "Chandler Bill Passes Senate; Enactment Likely This Session," *The Wall Street Journal,* 6/11/38, p. 3.

156   **The third bill** Seligman, *Transformation of Wall Street,* pp. 193–97.

156   **After skillfully splitting** Ibid., pp. 193–96. For example, see "Douglas Urges S.E.C. Control of Indentures," New York *Herald Tribune,* 4/26/38, p. 25; "Would Curb Trust Indenture," *The New York Times,* 4/26/38, p. 35.

157   **"One way or another,"** Alsop and Kintner, "Capital Parade," 2/16/38, p. 6.

157   **And now "boiling"** Michael Parrish, *Securities Regulation and the New Deal* (New Haven: Yale University Press, 1988), p. 146.

157   **Having already focused** Parrish, *Securities Regulation,* pp. 156–59.

157   **As Bill Douglas later** "Statement of William O. Douglas, Chairman, Securities and Exchange Commission," Senate Committee on Finance, 75th Cong., 2d sess., 3/30/38, p. 71.

157   **No sooner did Roosevelt** See Oral History of Robert Jackson, COHC, vol. 3, p. 7.

158   **To no one's surprise** "Douglas Hails Court Ruling on Bond & Share," New

York *Herald Tribune,* 11/9/37, p. 7; "Decision Pleases Douglas," *The New York Times,* 11/9/37, p. 33; Seligman, *Transformation of Wall Street,* p. 179.

158   **This "welcome conciliatory attitude"** "Stocks Firm to End Week 3 Points Up," New York *Herald Tribune,* 11/14/37, secs. 2–4, p. 12.

158   **But inside this velvet** "Douglas Says Management Bars Utility Expansion," *The Wall Street Journal,* 2/3/38, p. 1; "Douglas Assails 'N.Y. Finance' for Stalling Utility Expansion," New York *Herald Tribune,* 2/3/38, p. 23.

158   **The New York *Herald Tribune*** "Stock Market Sinks Lower on Late Sales," New York *Herald Tribune,* 2/3/38, p. 23.

158   **"Mr. Douglas does not have horns"** Joseph Alsop and Robert Kintner, "The Capital Parade," *The Atlanta Constitution,* 2/6/38, p. 4K.

158   **And all of this lobbying** "Review and Outlook," *The Wall Street Journal,* 4/2/38, p. 4; Seligman, *Transformation of Wall Street,* p. 188. (Eventually, this law would lead to the creation of a self-policing agency for the over-the-counter markets known as the National Association of Securities Dealers—from which came the NASDAQ listings.)

158   **When the Supreme Court** *Electric Bond and Share v. SEC,* 303 U.S. 419 (1938). The Court held that the utilities did have to register, but a consti-tutional test of the "death sentence" was delayed for a later case. "Court Rules Utility Holding Concerns Must Register," *The Wall Street Journal,* 3/29/38, p. 8; "Registration Rule in Utility Act Is Upheld," New York *Herald Tribune,* 3/29/38, p. 1.

158   **Several large holding** "Utilities May Trade Units to Meet Holding Act; Registration Upheld," *The Wall Street Journal,* 3/29/38, p. 1; "4 Giant Util-ity Holding Firms Act to Register," New York *Herald Tribune,* 3/29/38, p. 23; "Utilities Register," *Newsweek,* 4/11/38, p. 37.

To encourage further compliance with the law, Douglas proposed to Congress that the tax burden of utilities that were forced to liquidate companies because of the "death sentence" be eased by a capital-gains ex-emption. "Holding Firms That Liquidate May Avoid Tax," New York *Her-ald Tribune,* 3/30/38, p. 1; "SEC to Urge Tax Change to Promote Utility Unit Trades," *The Wall Street Journal,* 3/30/38, p. 1; "Senators Approve Ex-emption from Capital Gains Levy Under 'Death Sentence' Shifts," *The New York Times,* 3/31/38, p. 1. However, Douglas would work on this through-out the next month. See "Douglas Is Called by Tax Conferees," *The New York Times,* 4/19/38, p. 37; "Conferees Deadlocked on Capital Gains and Surtax Issues," *The Wall Street Journal,* 4/19/38, p. 2; "Roosevelt Told Spend-ing Plan Can Be Passed," New York *Herald Tribune,* 4/19/38, p. 1.

On March 30, the Senate Finance Committee approved Douglas's sug-gestions, after listening to him testify for more than an hour on a subject for which he obviously had been well prepared before the Supreme Court's decision.

158   **but not all were** On April 26, Douglas had asked SEC Commissioner Healy to prepare the agency "for the onslaught" by supervising a geographical survey of utility integration. Quoted in Seligman, *Transformation of Wall Street,* p. 180, n. 61; "Statements of William O. Douglas, Chairman; Fran-

cis P. Brassor, Secretary; and James J. Riordan, Chief, Budget and Accounting Division," *Congressional Hearings on Second Deficiency Appropriation Bill, 1938*, 75th Cong., 2d sess., 5/17/38, p. 97; and "Douglas Sees SEC Integrating Utility Systems in 5 Years," *The Wall Street Journal*, 6/8/38, p. 1.

158 **C. E. Groesbeck, the head** Seligman, *Transformation of Wall Street*, pp. 180–81.

159 **Before declaring another** "Douglas Urges Cooperative Approach on Reorganization Plans," *The Wall Street Journal*, 6/8/38, p. 7.

159 **A two-hour conference** "SEC Asks Utility Industry to Name Cooperation Group," ibid., 6/1/38, p. 1.

159 **Having learned from** "Utilities Power Named for 'Death Sentence' Test," ibid., 7/20/38, p. 1. See also "SEC Guinea Pig," *Newsweek*, 8/1/38, pp. 36–37; "Utilities Directed to File Integration Plans by Dec. 1," *The Wall Street Journal*, 8/5/38, p. 1.

159 **Just as Douglas was about** "Douglas Hails Cooperation," *The New York Times*, 10/10/38, p. 45.

159 **A few days later** "E.B.&S to Offer Integration Plan to SEC Shortly," *The Wall Street Journal*, 10/14/38, p. 1. See also the story in Joseph Alsop and Robert Kintner, "The Capital Parade," *The Atlanta Constitution*, 10/17/38, p. 4.

159 **None of these activities** "W. McC.Martin, 31, Slated to Govern Stock Exchange," New York *Herald Tribune*, 4/12/38, p. 1.

159 **"a straight arrow"** Oral History of Judge Gerhard Gesell, in Louchheim, *Making of the New Deal*, p. 136.

160 **"a thoroughgoing reformer,"** John T. Flynn, "Other People's Money," *The New Republic*, 6/22/38, pp. 187–88. But also see John T. Flynn, "It's the Same Old Wall Street," *The New Republic*, 8/24/38, p. 62.

160 **Upon taking office** "New Administration of Stock Exchange Takes Office," *The Wall Street Journal*, 5/17/38, p. 2.

160 **Six weeks later** "Martin Becomes Exchange's First Paid President," *The Wall Street Journal*, 7/1/38, p. 1; Seligman, *Transformation of Wall Street*, p. 176. Few knew that Douglas had been actively campaigning behind the scenes for McC. Martin.

160 **"an armistice"** John T. Flynn, "Other People's Money," p. 187.

160 **While McC. Martin's** "SEC, Exchange Will Reappraise All Market Rules," *The Wall Street Journal*, 5/10/38, p. 1.

160 **For the first time** From Milton Freeman, in Douglas Remembrances, p. 24 (unpublished), pp. 107–9 (published).

160 **"Some will always look"** "Text of Address by Commissioner W. O. Douglas," *The Wall Street Journal*, 5/21/38, p. 5.

160 **Just how much** "Douglas to Confer Here with Exchange Officials," *The Wall Street Journal*, 6/3/38, p. 7; "Douglas Praises Joint Progress on SEC Problems," ibid., 6/4/38, p. 1.

160 **Once the roundtable** Louchheim, *Making of the New Deal*, pp. 146–47; "Exchange Asks Banks' Views on Establishing Central Depository Unit," *The Wall Street Journal*, 5/28/38, p. 1; "Dozen Candidates Still Left on List to Head Exchange," ibid., 6/2/38, p. 1; "Douglas to Confer Here with Exchange Officials," ibid., 6/3/38, p. 7; "Exchange Settlement on Semi-Weekly Basis

Studied by Committee," ibid., 6/16/38, p. 1; Seligman, *Transformation of Wall Street,* p. 177.

161 **Seeking to spur** Seligman, *Transformation of Wall Street,* p. 177; Louchheim, *Making of the New Deal,* p. 135.

161 **Douglas also convinced** Robert Maynard Hutchins to WOD, 9/23/38, RMHP; "Exchange Elects C. C. Conway, R. M. Hutchins, and R. E. Wood to Represent Public on Board," *The Wall Street Journal,* 9/29/38, p. 1.

161 **With the release** "SEC Report Commends Exchange Officials' Acts in Whitney Case," *The Wall Street Journal,* 10/28/38, p. 1.

161 **Four days later** Joseph Alsop and Robert Kintner, "The Capital Parade," *The Atlanta Constitution,* 11/11/38, p. 12.

161 **To ensure the support** Seligman, *Transformation of Wall Street,* pp. 177–78. These companies would be subject to yearly audits, their ratio of indebtedness to capital could not exceed 15:1, and member firms and their partners were restricted from trading on margin with their own firm. Exchange president McC. Martin also promised to continue studying Douglas's idea for the formation of a central brokers' depository to hold customers' securities. But the brokers' bank was never going to happen ("Exchange Drafts Program Increasing Investors' Safety," *The Wall Street Journal,* 11/1/38, p. 1; "Text of SEC and NYSE Programs for Organization Changes of Exchange," ibid., p. 10; "Exchange's Summary of 15-Point Plan," *The New York Times,* 11/1/38, p. 40; "Exchange Expands New Rules of SEC," ibid.). Even reform-oriented brokers such as E. A. Pierce now opposed this idea because of the disruptions it might cause in brokers' relationships with customers. In time, the exchange would propose instead the total separation of customers' accounts through the use of surprise exchange audits as an enforcement mechanism.

161 **"going to town"** "New Stock Exchange Plan Real Self-Rule, SEC Holds," *The Wall Street Journal,* 11/1/38, p. 11.

161 **"lax, archaic, and unbusinesslike,"** "SEC Reports Scores 'Old,' Praises 'New' Exchange Management," ibid., 11/2/38, p. 1.

161 **But sometimes maintaining** Seligman, *Transformation of Wall Street,* pp. 171–72.

161 **Robert Maynard Hutchins** The result was an "exciting, if lopsided dispute" (Joseph Alsop and Robert Kintner, "The Capital Parade," *The Atlanta Constitution,* 12/22/38, p. 12).

161 **The other governors** Robert Maynard Hutchins to WOD, 12/17/38, RMHP.

162 **Hutchins's withdrawal** "Hutchins Action Jars Wall Street," *The New York Times,* 12/25/38, sec. 4, p. 7.

162 **And their fear** "Possible alternative courses of action by SEC re: the Whitney case in light of the recent white-wash," memorandum, 12/18/38, WOD/SEC files, quoted in Seligman, *Transformation of Wall Street,* pp. 172–73. It seems very likely that Douglas himself was the source of this story. Alsop and Kintner, "Capital Parade," 12/22/38, p. 12.

162 **No New Dealer** *Fortune,* December 1938, p. 162, and January 1939, p. 122. Slightly better dressed for his January photo, the still tired Douglas now

sported a boyish grin that, as one would expect, contrasted sharply with the polite smiles of the defeated business executives.

162 **"In my own personal"** "Exchange Is Commended," *The New York Times,* 12/30/38, p. 3; "Douglas Lauds Exchange for Its Handling of Sisto Expulsion," ibid., p. 1.

163 **"Mr. McC. Martin and I"** "In the Nation," ibid., 12/27/38.

163 **"The latest reform era"** "Hutchins and Wall Street Reform," *The New Republic,* 12/28/38, pp. 213–14.

163 **"the readiness of Chairman"** "The Shape of Things," *The Nation,* 1/14/39, p. 49. See also I. F. Stone, "Questions on the Whitney Case," ibid., pp. 55–58.

163 **"ultra-red warning signal"** "Let's Investigate Insurance," *The New Republic,* 2/8/39, pp. 5–6.

163 **Even *The New York Times*** Burton Crane, "Along Wall Street, *The New York Times,* 3/19/39, sec. 6, p. 1.

163 **Douglas tried to rebuild** "Life Insurance Scope Is Revealed by Inquiry," ibid., 2/12/39, p. 8. See also "Douglas Says Monopoly Study Needs $400,000," *The Wall Street Journal,* 1/25/39; "Monopoly Group Seeks to Curtail Testimony on Insurance Ballots," ibid., 2/10/39, p. 3; "Douglas Hints Hearings on Insurance Ballots Might Be Extended," ibid., 2/11/39, p. 3; Louchheim, *Making of the New Deal,* p. 136.

163 **"the disappearance of"** "Big Business Trend Evil, Douglas Says," *The New York Times,* 2/10/39, p. 36.

CHAPTER 16

164 **"I had never had"** Douglas Conversations, cassette no. 1, 12/20/61, p. 1. Douglas repeated this claim in Sevareid, "Mr. Justice Douglas." Douglas was asked, "Why do you think [FDR] appointed you [to the Court]?" Douglas responded: "I have no idea. I was not a candidate. I had no ambition to come on the Court. I had no ambitions for any public office. As a matter of fact, I was elected Dean of the Yale Law School, and I was going back there in a few months." Only a small part of this answer was even remotely true (see below).

164 **Long-term financial security** Interview with Mercedes Douglas Eicholz, 5/28/88, Lowe Videos.

164 **The answer to this problem** On Douglas's status at Yale see WOD to President Charles Seymour, 4/13/39, and WOD to Dean Charles Clark, 4/13/39, in WOD/SEC, Box 14, File COR through CZ, "Chronological April 1939" folder.

164 **After being informally approached** Douglas Private Diary, 3/19/39. Douglas says there that he received the offer in mid-February.

164 **While Douglas had decided** Kalman, *Legal Realism,* pp. 140–41.

165 **So while the *Yale Daily News*** While Douglas recorded that he had been offered the deanship a few weeks before March 19 (Douglas Private Diary, 3/19/39), Kalman, *Legal Realism,* p. 140, confirms that Douglas was the leading candidate, indicating from the documentary evidence that the offer was not tendered until after March 15.

165 **When he finally spotted** This account draws from Arthur Krock, *Memoirs:*

Sixty Years on the Firing Line (New York: Funk and Wagnalls, 1968), pp. 176–77. This seems more reliable than Douglas's version, in which Krock proposes a toast at the same event. Douglas, *Go East,* pp. 460–61.

165   **"What vacancy?"** See *The New York Times,* 4/5/39, p. 17.

165   **"Brandeis retired today,"** Krock, *Memoirs,* pp. 176–77.

166   **No sooner did Krock** Ibid.

166   **And the appointment** "President Recovered, Set for Caribbean Trip; W. O. Douglas Hinted as Brandeis Successor," *The New York Times,* 2/15/39, p. 30.

166   **Fully understanding** FDR Presidential Diary and Itinerary, 2/14/39, FDRL. The account of the talk can be found in Douglas's Private Diary, 3/19/39. As outlined below, this contemporaneous account is similar to the account offered in Douglas, *Go East,* pp. 462–63, but with one very important difference.

167   **"prominent among those"** "President Recovered," *The New York Times,* 2/15/39, p. 1. (Though Krock is not listed as the author, the story was filed from his Washington bureau.)

167   **Douglas saw the story** See WOD to Alan Thompson, 3/17/39, WOD/SEC, Box 14, File COR through CZ, "Chronological, March 1939" folder; Art Douglas to Howard Manning, 2/16/39, WODP, Box 5; and Arthur Douglas to Thomas Graham, 2/16/39, WODP, Box 239. Understandably, none of the letters were to be sent to Senator Schwellenbach. Arthur Douglas to WOD, 2/23/39, WODP, Box 239.

167   **Meanwhile, Carrol Shanks** Arthur Douglas to WOD, 2/27/39, WODP, Box 239.

167   **Knowing that** Cull's name was clearly still a good one in the Douglas household. In asking for his help, neither Douglas brother mentioned their mother's charges in late 1925 and early 1926 that Cull had stolen all her money.

167   **But try as Cull** Arthur Douglas to WOD, 2/21/39 and 2/27/39, WODP, Box 239; see also "President Names Douglas Justice of High Tribunal," Yakima *Morning Herald,* 3/21/1939, *Yakima Herald-Republic* Archives, Yakima, Wash. This effort was in February. When the appointment was made the following month, Douglas was forty years and five months, making him the second youngest appointment to the Supreme Court, after Joseph Story.

167   **In any event, stacks** Ickes Diary, 2/28/39 and 3/5/39.

168   **While the two men pressed** Ibid., 3/12/39.

168   **As soon as the lunch** Douglas Conversations, 12/20/61, cassette no. 1, p. 4, and Ickes Diary, 3/12/39.

168   **With a new lease** This was done on 3/21/39. Max Lowenthal, "Thomas G. Corcoran's Relation to Wm. O. Douglas," Max Lowenthal Papers, Box 2, University of Minnesota Archives, Minneapolis (with thanks to historian Robert Ferrell for supplying this document).

168   **This the president agreed** Ickes Diary, 3/12/39; Bill Hutchinson to WOD, 3/8/52, WODP, Box 241.

169   **When Douglas learned** Kalman, *Legal Realism,* p. 140. Kalman says, seemingly relying on Douglas, in *Go East,* p. 441, that he was offered and ac-

cepted the deanship at Yale sometime after this March 15 letter and before his Court appointment on March 20. If true, however, Douglas made no mention of either fact in his subsequent resignation letters.

169   **With his safety net** "The Shape of Things to Come," *The Nation,* 3/11/39, pp. 277–78.

169   **As luck would have it** AI, Milton Freeman, 5/21/96, Washington, D.C., (phone).

169   **Indeed, the exchanges** See Milton Freeman Reminiscences, in Douglas Remembrances, p. 24 (unpublished version), pp. 107–9 (published version). See also "Exchanges Push Revision of Law," *The New York Times,* 3/4/39, p. 21. The early meetings between the two groups had been quite promising, revealing a common area of agreement.

169   **To them, the SEC's** "SEC Officials Favor Constructive Changes in Securities Acts," *The Wall Street Journal,* 3/10/39.

170   **"Unhappily, there is every"** Joseph Alsop and Robert Kintner, "The Capital Parade," *The Atlanta Constitution,* 3/13/39, p. 4.

170   **The fireworks** See Seligman, *Transformation of Wall Street,* p. 211; bolstered by "Exchanges Likely to Request Broad SEC Law Changes," *The Wall Street Journal,* 3/14/39, p. 1; "Federal Rules Dam Capital Flow, Exchanges Hold," *The Wall Street Journal,* 3/15/39, p. 1.

170   **"Stripped of its legal"** "SEC Hits Proposals to Loosen Trading," *The New York Times,* 3/16/39, p. 35; "SEC Turns Down Proposed Changes in Securities Acts," ibid., p. 1; "Text of Statement Issued by SEC," *The Wall Street Journal,* 3/16/39, p. 2.

170   **Then, mirroring Alsop and Kintner's** "SEC Hits Proposals," *The New York Times,* 3/16/39, p. 35.

170   **Never one to leave any** Senator Lynn J. Frazier, citing press accounts, *Congressional Record,* 76th Cong., 1st sess., 4/4/39, 84, pt. 4, p. 3775. There is no evidence to be *certain* as to Douglas's motivation for acting in this manner. One possibility is that Douglas had nothing to lose since he was leaving the job. Or, this could have been an example of Douglas's temper and a self-destructive act, like the departure from Columbia. The fact that Alsop and Kintner were able to preview this attack in their column makes it more likely that Douglas made a calculated move here.

170   **Speaking at a press conference** Crane, "Along Wall Street," 3/19/39, sec. 6, p. 6.

170   **When reporters asked** "SEC Hits Proposals," ibid., 3/16/39, p. 35; "SEC Turns Down Proposed Changes," ibid., p. 1; "SEC Head Named to High Court; Rebuffs Brokers," *Scholastic,* 4/1/39. See also "Exchanges Wonder About SEC," *Business Week,* 3/25/39, p. 17.

170   **"Everybody in the financial"** "Topics in Wall Street," *The New York Times,* 3/17/39, p. 31. See also Crane, "Along Wall Street," ibid., 3/19/39, sec. 6, p. 6, who reported that this attack was "more bitter on Wall Street New Deal than ever on the Old Guard."

171   **These proposals were** AI, Milton Freeman, 5/21/96, Washington, D.C. (phone).

171   **With the pot now sufficiently** "No SEC-Exchange Cooperation Break

Likely over the Differences on Report," *The Wall Street Journal,* 3/17/39, p. 1.

171 **Having discovered that western** Bill Hutchinson to William O. Douglas, 3/8/52, WODP, Box 241.

171 **As soon as Douglas's allies** Douglas Conversations, 12/20/61, cassette no. 1, pp. 7–10.

172 **Borah's response came** Ibid.

172 **A short while later** WOD obituary, *The New York Times,* 1/20/80, p. 28. In *Go East,* WOD telescoped this call and linked the toast to Krock's first comment at Pavenstadt's residence (p. 459).

172 **"I'm going to the Supreme Court"** Interview of Judge Gerhard Gesell, 5/15/88, Lowe Videos. Ironically, Gesell himself later became a federal district judge.

172 **"a lot of us felt"** Ibid.

172 **Bill Douglas's life changed** This account relies on Douglas Private Diary, 3/19/39 entry. This account differs from Douglas's more dramatic story in *Go East,* one that he liked to tell frequently, that he learned about the life-altering call from the White House from a "breathless caddy" on the "ninth hole" of the golf course (p. 462). Douglas's contemporaneous diary takes historical precedence here.

The appointment does not appear in the FDR Presidential Diary and Itinerary for 1939, FDRL, because none was recorded on Sundays.

173 **Upon his arrival** The dialogue is taken from Douglas, *Go East,* p. 463. While it is similar to the dialogue recorded in Douglas's diary, the location of the speech and Douglas's reaction to it was substantially different. This conversation did not take place in the Oval Office, as Douglas wrote in *Go East,* and his reaction was far from silence. He well knew that this offer was coming. See Douglas Private Diary, 3/19/39.

173 **"It's William O. Douglas"** "Douglas, Jurist," *Newsweek,* 3/27/39, p. 13. Douglas always claimed that he was Brandeis's personal choice for the position. This was true. See Douglas Private Diary, 3/19/39.

173 **Congratulatory messages** Marquis Childs, "The Next Member of the U.S. Supreme Court," *St. Louis Post-Dispatch,* 4/2/39, p. 1.

173 **Demonstrating the public-relations** See quotations from *The New Republic* cited in *The New Yorker*'s review of *Go East,* 7/8/74, pp. 74–79.

Later, Douglas wrote that his nomination was very controversial, claiming that "such liberals as Gilbert Harrison of *The New Republic* opposed him" (*Go East,* p. 463). In fact, Harrison was not on that magazine's staff at the time.

173 **Even the Yakima *Morning Herald*** "President Names Douglas Justice of High Tribunal," Yakima *Morning Herald,* 3/21/39, *Yakima Herald-Republic* Archives, Yakima.

174 **Of all the accolades** Douglas speech to Beta Theta Pi, New York Banquet, 6/7/39, WODY.

174 **Still, the unpredictable** Roy Mersky and J. Myron Jacobstein, eds., *The Supreme Court of the United States: Hearings and Reports on Successful and Unsuccessful Nominations of Supreme Court Justices by the Senate Judiciary Com-*

mittee, 1916–1972, vol. 4 (Buffalo: William S. Hein, 1975), including a corrected copy of Senate Committee on the Judiciary, *Hearings on Nomination of William O. Douglas,* 76th Cong., 1st sess., 3/24/39, Charles A. Brown, official reporter (with thanks to Roy Mersky for leading me to this material). This account (supported by the photo in the picture section) revises the oft-told tale that, during his confirmation proceeding, Douglas remained outside the Senate hearing room and was only allowed to send a message inside asking whether the senators had any questions for him. When they did not, it is said, he left the building. This story is so fully ingrained into the folklore of the Supreme Court that it was repeated by *The New York Times*'s incomparable Supreme Court reporter, Linda Greenhouse, in a story filed during the Clarence Thomas hearings. See Greenhouse, "A Rehearsed Thomas Is Set for Hearings," *The New York Times,* 9/9/91, A. 12.

174   **Nowadays, a spark** Douglas Conversations, cassette no. 1, 12/20/61, p. 15.
174   **Could there be any doubt** *Congressional Record,* 76th Cong., 1st sess., 4/4/39, 84, pt. 4, p. 3788.
175   **On April 17, 1939** Douglas Private Diary, 4/17/39.
175   **Too feeble after** Simon, *Independent Journey,* p. 25, undoubtedly relying here on his interview of Martha Douglas Bost. It is a memory that she repeated from time to time in letters to WOD.

CHAPTER 17

179   **"It seemed to me"** Douglas, *Court Years,* p. 3.
179   **Congressman John Elliott Rankin** "Douglas Is Named to Supreme Court," *The New York Times,* 3/21/39, p. 16.
179   ***American* magazine agreed** Beverly Smith, "Tamer of Bulls and Bears," *American,* May 1939, pp. 20–21.
179   **Douglas protested** WOD to A. Howard Meneely, 4/7/39, WODP, Box 10.
179   **In a Mother's Day card** Martha Douglas Bost to WOD, 5/11/38, WODP, Box 5.
179   **Meanwhile, Douglas tried** Interview with Judge Gerhard Gesell, 5/16/88, Lowe Videos.
180   **Others weren't sure** Neuberger, "Mr. Justice Douglas," pp. 315–16.
180   **The job was demanding** AI, C. David Ginsburg, 8/28/89, Washington, D.C.
180   **And Douglas's tasks** AI, Stanley Soderland, 6/12/90, Shaw Island, Wash. Jed King, who served with Douglas from 1941 to 1942, later recalled: "Douglas was young, and wasn't nearly as secure, I don't think, as he got to be later on. . . . If you got a word or two into one of his opinions, you were damn lucky. . . . Douglas would write his own opinion and you had to footnote the past cases, check the records to make sure that the facts were properly stated, and things of that sort. It wasn't very exciting." AI, Jed King, 6/10/90, Seattle.
181   **Among those members** Douglas Conversations, cassette no. 3, 12/20/61 and 12/27/61, p. 48.
181   **Two of those cases** Douglas Private Diary, 4/22/39. As soon as he got the call from the president putting him on the Supreme Court, for the first time in his life Bill Douglas began to feel the weight of history upon him.

So, he began for a brief time to keep a diary of his activities. (A transcript of the early entries exists because his later secretary Martha Bagby used it to learn his handwriting during her first few months on the job.) The diary provides a window into Douglas's first months on the Court, often the most critical in the development of a Justice. This was certainly the case for Bill Douglas. For unlike most newly appointed jurists of that era, who took a year or two to learn their duties, serving a sort of apprenticeship to the older members in order to learn the job (in what experts have called the "freshman effect"), Douglas exerted his independent influence in his first months on the Bench. For more on the "freshman effect" on the Supreme Court, see Saul Brenner and Timothy M. Hagle, "Opinion Writing and Acclimation Effect," *Political Behavior* 18, no. 3 (1996): 238–61; Timothy M. Hagle, " 'Freshmen Effects' for Supreme Court Justices," *American Journal of Political Science* 37, no. 4 (November 1993): 1142–57; and Edward V. Heck and Melinda Gann Hall, "Bloc Voting and the Freshman Effect Revisited," *Journal of Politics* 43 (1981): 853–60.

Case citations for these cases are *Coleman v. Miller,* 307 U.S. 433 (1939) and *Chandler v. Wise,* 307 U.S. 474 (1939).

181 **As the chief** This two-step voting process no longer exists. Now members of the Court explain their positions and vote at the same time, moving from the chief, to the most senior Justice, and down to the most junior. Scholars debate when the earlier process ended, but it was after Douglas left the Court. See Larry Berman and Bruce Allen Murphy, *Approaching Democracy,* 3d ed. (Upper Saddle River, N.J.: Prentice Hall, 2001), p. 241, citing letters from Robert Bradley, Chief Justice William Rehnquist, and Henry J. Abraham in American Political Science Association, *Law, Courts and Judicial Process Section Newsletter,* no. 4 (summer 1989): 2–3, 7, and no. 1 (fall 1989): 3.

181 **When the Justices split** Douglas Private Diary, 4/22/39. Legal standing is the means by which the Court determines whether a suit will be heard and decided on appeal. In seeking to ensure that litigation will be presented by litigants who are openly contesting each other's claims in order to reach a proper result, the litigants must have a current case (not moot in legal terms), must have something to lose if the decision does not go their way, and cannot be raising a "political question," which should be left to elected officials.

182 **Hughes, however, saw** Douglas Conversations, cassette no. 2, 12/20/61, p. 38. See *United States v. Morgan,* 307 U.S. 183 (1939); *Newark Fire Ins. Co. v. State Board of Tax Appeals,* 307 U.S. 313 (1939); and *United States v. Powers,* 305 U.S. 214 (1939).

182 **So Douglas was told** Douglas Conversations, cassette no. 2, 12/20/61, pp. 37–38, 43, and Douglas Private Diary, 4/22/39.

182 **Douglas labored on** Douglas Conversations, cassette no. 3, 12/20/61 and 12/27/61, p. 54.

182 **Douglas's draft opinion** Ibid., 12/20/61, p. 43, and Douglas Private Diary, 5/13/39.

183 **One of the first cases** See 307 U.S. 277 (1939). Such an exemption existed

to avoid violating the constitutional provision in article 3, section 1, guaranteeing judges "a compensation, which shall not be diminished during their continuance in office," which some argued would occur if the government raised the Justices' income-tax obligation.

183   **Since the Constitution bars** Douglas Private Diary, 4/29/39.

183   **Years later, he told** Sevareid, "Mr. Justice Douglas."

183   **And from that day** Ibid. Failure to have a life off the Court, he explained, creates even greater dangers for members of the Court: "We are all human. And the decisions we make are profoundly important to the people. . . . And I think that the person who goes there and stays ten, twenty, thirty years should be very active in life. Otherwise, he ends up a dried husk, unrelated to anything that is going on in the world."

183   **Douglas, however, was inclined** Douglas Private Diary, 6/3/39. The technique here is called "substantive due process," whereby the Court looks under the due-process clause of either the Fourteenth or Fifth Amendment, beyond the formal procedures of the action to the fairness or wisdom of a statute or governmental action. Many charge that in deciding this way, the Court is acting politically as a "super-legislature." (The case was *American Toll Bridge Co. v. Railroad Commission,* 307 U.S. 486 [1939].)

184   **Within six weeks** Ibid. This evidence indicates that the origins of the split between WOD and Frankfurter occurred half a year earlier than I have previously argued. For more, see Bruce Allen Murphy, *The Brandeis/Frankfurter Connection: The Secret Political Activities of Two Supreme Court Justices* (New York: Oxford University Press, 1982), pp. 265–67.

184   **"My earliest memories,"** Interview with William O. Douglas, Jr., 2/13/88, Lowe Videos.

184   **"I found the Court"** Douglas Conversations, cassette no. 2, 12/20/61, p. 36.

184   **"He was not fulfilled"** AI, C. David Ginsburg, 8/28/89, Washington, D.C.

184   **It was not long** Alexander, "Washington's Angry Scotsman," p. 108.

184   **"Having been so suddenly"** Arthur Krock, "As Chairman Douglas Sees the Future of the S.E.C.," *The New York Times,* 3/29/39, p. 22.

185   **"break a few eggs"** AI, Thomas Corcoran, 9/29/77, Washington, D.C.

185   **Trying to boost Douglas's** Ickes Diary, 3/22/39; see also Douglas, *Go East,* pp. 330–32.

185   **"Bill was a"** AI, Clark Clifford, 8/27/89, Washington, D.C.

185   **But blessed with** See Lowenthal, "Thomas G. Corcoran's Relation," Max Lowenthal Papers, Box 2. With thanks to Lois G. Hendrickson for searching this document out, and to Robert Ferrell for generously providing a copy from his own research. And see also Douglas, *Go East,* p. 330.

185   **In October 1939** Joseph Driscoll, "What It'll Cost Roosevelt to Lift the Embargo," New York *Herald Tribune,* 10/22/39.

186   **With Douglas also rumored** "Arthur and William Douglas," *National Biographic,* p. 7.

186   **"This will damage"** "A Political Prowler Which Should Be Liquidated," *The New York Times,* 10/26/39, p. 22.

186   **"Justice Douglas's boomlet"** Ibid.

186   **Unlike the SEC** At this point, Douglas was aligned in what judicial scholar

C. Herman Pritchett called "complete and unprecedented unanimity" with Felix Frankfurter and Hugo Black in a "new left-wing alignment." A center bloc was composed of Chief Justice Hughes, Stanley Reed, and Harlan Fiske Stone, with Owen Roberts just on the right fringe of this group and both McReynolds and Butler lying in the extreme right wing. See C. Herman Pritchett, *The Roosevelt Court: A Study in Judicial Politics and Values, 1937–1947* (New York: Macmillan, 1948), passim.

186   **Douglas assumed** This story was confirmed by three interviews. AI, Edward F. Prichard, Jr. (Frankfurter's law clerk that term), 6/25/79, Frankfort, Ky.; AI, Charles Wyzanski, Jr., 1/13/77, Richmond, Va.; and Joseph L. Rauh, Jr. (another Frankfurter clerk), 7/9/79, Washington, D.C.

186   **So he developed** 308 U.S. 343 (1939).

186   **When Felix Frankfurter** See Frankfurter's Scrapbook, 1939, cited in H. N. Hirsch, *The Enigma of Felix Frankfurter* (New York: Basic Books, 1981), p. 146.

187   **The same day** AI, Edward F. Prichard, Jr., 6/25/79, Frankfort, Ky.

187   **When asked why** See Frankfurter Scrapbook, 1939, cited in Hirsch, *Enigma of Felix Frankfurter,* p. 146.

187   **"Douglas *never* thereafter"** Ibid. (italics in original).

187   **As a result** AI, Edward F. Prichard, Jr., 6/25/79, Frankfort, Ky.

187   **By this time** Oral History of Robert H. Jackson, COHC, pt. 6, chap. 1.

187   **When the double appointment** Pritchett, *Roosevelt Court,* p. 251. As a result, Pritchett concluded, "1940 saw considerable disintegration on the left."

187   **When the issue came** Douglas Conversations, cassette no. 2, 12/20/61, p. 45.

187   **To him, this was just** See *Reynolds v. United States,* 98 U.S. 145 (1878).

187   **"Knowing of my"** Douglas Conversations, cassette no. 3, 12/20/61 and 12/27/61, p. 48.

188   **Douglas personally praised** Joseph L. Rauh, Jr., "An Unabashed Liberal Looks at a Half Century of the Supreme Court," *North Carolina Law Review* 69 (1990): 221.

188   **"The Constitution expresses"** *Minersville School Dist. v. Gobitis,* 310 U.S. 586 (1940), p. 606.

188   **Immediately after the opinion** See Alpheus Thomas Mason's masterful *Harlan Fiske Stone: Pillar of the Law* (New York: Viking, 1956), and Rauh, "Unabashed Liberal," passim.

188   **After discussing this reaction** Douglas Conversations, cassette no. 3, 12/20/61 and 12/27/61, pp. 48–49.

188   **"We were concerned"** Ibid., p. 49.

188   **But not all of his** Ickes Diary, 6/29/40.

189   **Nevertheless, a month later** Ickes Diary, 7/19/40 (recording Ickes's recollections after the convention); Farley saw it as Jackson, Hull, or Douglas. James Aloysius Farley, *Jim Farley's Story: The Roosevelt Years* (New York: Whittlesey House, 1948), p. 227.

189   **When FDR announced** Ickes Diary, 8/4/40. This recounts a story from FDR about the convention, during one of their luncheons. Farley, *Jim Farley's Story,* p. 253.

189 **"In spite of my persistent"** WOD to A. Howard Meneely, 2/14/40, WODP, Box 10.

189 **"I'm convinced that he wanted"** AI, C. David Ginsburg, 8/28/89, Washington, D.C.

189 **With Douglas out of touch** Douglas Conversations, cassette no. 14, 4/5/63, pp. 295–97; see also chapter 19, below. This is the story that Douglas tells about that convention as well, but the real origin is here.

189 **Thinking that Hugo Black** Ibid., pp. 295–96.

189 **"It will be an interesting"** WOD to A. Howard Meneely, 8/21/40, WODP, Box 10. Like Harold Ickes and others, his public choice for the office was Robert Jackson. Ickes Diary, 6/29/40, and WOD to A. Howard Meneely, 2/14/40, WODP, Box 10.

189 **Far from disappointed** Ickes Diary, 9/28/40.

190 **Just one day after** Ibid., 11/9/40. Douglas later claimed that the president, once he found out about the letters, had asked him how he could get rid of Wallace. Douglas Conversations, cassette no. 9, 5/23/62, p. 198.

190 **While the information** AI, Eliot Janeway, 5/19/90, New York.

190 **"Let's do it through"** Ibid.

190 **At lunches** Ickes Diary, 11/9/40, 8/4/40, and 7/19/40.

190 **So Douglas arranged** Ibid., 11/9/40.

190 **Wallace was nonetheless** Ibid., 12/1/40; AI, Eliot Janeway, 5/19/90, New York.

190 **Believing that Harlan** Ickes Diary, 6/8/41.

191 **Hughes himself "strongly"** Mason, *Harlan Fiske Stone,* p. 567.

191 **While the president** Ickes Diary, 6/15/41. With entrance into the European war imminent, heightening the need to unite the country, the chance to do so by appointing one of the two Republicans on the Court to the Chief Justiceship (Owen Roberts being the other one) seemed to be politically advantageous. And with seventeen cases deadlocked at four-to-four and held over to the following term because of the unfilled McReynolds seat, the appointments to that vacancy and the one that would be created by the elevation of Stone would be critical for the direction of the Court. Ickes Diary, 6/22/41, citing conversation with Hugo Black.

191 **He told Jackson** Reminiscences of Robert H. Jackson, COHC, vol. 7, pp. 1–3.

191 **Seeking to solidify** WOD to Hugo Black, 6/22/41, WODP, Box 308, cited also in Ball and Cooper, *Of Power and Right,* p. 80.

191 **"They have their straws"** WOD to A. Howard Meneely, 6/30/41, WODP, Box 10.

191 **What was needed** Ibid.

191 **After unsuccessfully trying** Ickes Diary, 9/27/39, 6/2/40, and 6/15/40.

191 **"Bill does not have"** Ibid., 6/8/41.

192 **As soon as he heard** Ibid., 6/15/41.

192 **In a matter of days** Ibid., 6/22/41. A few days later, when it appeared that Baruch himself would take the appointment, Ickes wrote the president that such an appointment would be even more acceptable. Ibid., 6/28/41.

192   **Meanwhile, Douglas himself** WOD to A. Howard Meneely, 6/30/41,
        WODP, Box 10.

192   **"The talk about me leaving"** Ibid.

192   **"Actually," he claimed** Ibid.

192   **With the end of another** Richard Neuberger, "Much-Discussed 'Bill' Doug-
        las," *The New York Times Magazine,* 4/19/42, p. 10; Alexander, "Washing-
        ton's Angry Scotsman," p. 108.

193   **Other than that** Yakima *Morning Herald,* 7/8/41, *Yakima Herald-Republic*
        Archives, Yakima, Wash.

193   **But there was one exception** WOD to A. Howard Meneely, 9/16/41,
        WODP, Box 10. In the Douglas Conversations, he is inconsistent as to his
        response, saying that he "reluctantly" agreed to take the job (cassette no. 14,
        4/5/63, p. 293). In his letter to Meneely, Douglas says that he asked for
        more time to consider the offer. In a contemporaneous letter to Hugo
        Black, though, he admits that he agreed to return to D.C. (7/23/41). Hugo
        Black Papers, Box 59, Manuscripts Division, Library of Congress, Wash-
        ington, D.C. (hereafter Hugo Black Papers). Only later would Douglas
        find out, no doubt from Ickes, that it was Baruch who had pressed him for
        the post. WOD to A. Howard Meneely, 10/31/41, WODP, Box 10.

193   **But as soon as he** WOD to Hugo Black, 7/23/[41], Hugo Black Papers.

194   **Douglas bought** As it turned out, the only man more concerned now with
        Douglas going to Defense was presidential adviser Harry Hopkins, who
        now was seeking to persuade FDR to hold off on the matter. Ickes Diary,
        6/28/42. Just why the second call never came from FDR, no one seemed to
        know for sure. The story floating around the Frankfurter camp, though,
        placed the blame on Tommy Corcoran. According to this tale, Max Lowen-
        thal, a longtime bitter enemy of both men, explained, Douglas had placed
        a call from Oregon consulting Corcoran as to whether he should he take
        the job. Corcoran is said to have responded that he should take the job
        only if he held out for another position as a reward: the vice presidency.
        Later, Lowenthal claimed, Roosevelt told friends that he did not give the
        position to Douglas because throughout the entire affair Douglas had
        been angling for the vice presidency and that he would not agree to the
        deal. Max Lowenthal, "Thomas G. Corcoran's Relation," Lowenthal Pa-
        pers, Box 2; cited also in Robert Ferrell, *Harry S Truman: A Life* (Columbia:
        University of Missouri Press, 1994), p. 122.

194   **By the first week** WOD to Hugo Black, 9/8/41, Hugo Black Papers, Box 59;
        see also Ickes Diary, 9/20/41.

194   **This new call** WOD to Hugo Black, 9/8/41, Hugo Black Papers, Box 59,
        also cited in Ball and Cooper, *Of Power and Right,* pp. 80–81.

194   **"there comes a time"** Ibid.

194   **At that very moment** In time, he and Hopkins settled on a weak but ac-
        ceptable candidate in Donald Nelson, and they now tried to put him over
        the top. See Murphy, *Brandeis/Frankfurter Connection,* pp. 236–45.

194   **"God, how I hate"** WOD to A. Howard Meneely, 9/16/41, WODP, Box 10.

194   **"That job has absolutely"** Ibid.

195   **Despite these denials** Douglas gives two extended recollections of this in Douglas Conversations, cassette no. 9, 5/23/62, pp. 190–92, and cassette no. 15, 4/5/63, pp. 292–94.

195   **When he saw in** Ickes Diary, 9/28/41; see also Douglas Conversations, cassette no. 9, 5/23/62, pp. 190–92, and cassette no. 14, 4/5/63, pp. 292–94 (though Douglas recalls incorrectly that this was the announcement of Nelson to the WPB, which did not come until the following year).

195   **Max Lowenthal, former** Max Lowenthal, "Thomas G. Corcoran's Relation," Lowenthal Papers, Box 2.

195   **"He definitely has in mind"** WOD to A. Howard Meneely, 10/31/41, WODP, Box 10.

195   **But it didn't** Ibid.

195   **"Once it had been"** Ibid.

195   **But he said** Ibid.

195   **Not until the morning** The meeting was from 10:00 to 10:45 A.M. in the Oval Office. See White House Usher Books in FDRL.

       On October 16, his forty-third birthday, Douglas had seen the president, but it was a late-afternoon reception with all the other members of the Court, so the issue of Douglas's future could not be discussed personally. White House Usher Books and Presidential Diaries and Itineraries, FDRL; see also Douglas Conversations, cassette no. 9, 5/23/62, p. 191.

195   **"Now that we are"** WOD to A. Howard Meneely, 12/13/41, WODP, Box 10.

196   **"It was Harry Hopkins"** Douglas Conversations, cassette no. 14, 4/2/63, p. 294.

196   **"You know WOD"** AI, Lucas A. "Scot" Powe, 4/17/89, Seattle.

CHAPTER 18

197   **"[Bill Douglas] was"** AI, Eliot Janeway, 5/19/90, New York.

197   **With the Court's annual** Ickes Diary, 6/28/42.

197   **"I would be in"** WOD to A. Howard Meneely, 9/29/42, WODP, Box 10.

197   **"Bill Douglas called me"** Marvin McIntyre, memo, 6/2/42, Presidential Official File, Section 41A, Container 50, FDRL. This is also discussed in Douglas Conversations, cassette no. 14, 4/5/63, p. 292; at this time, Douglas could find no record of this request and denied his interest in any job. A closer inspection of his files does reveal the nature of the president's request (p. 293).

197   **By the end** Ickes Diary, 11/28/42.

198   **"What with me still"** WOD to A. Howard Meneely, 4/18/43, WODP, Box 10.

198   **Douglas's private life** Laura Kalman, *Abe Fortas: A Biography* (New Haven: Yale University Press, 1990), pp. 195–96, and Robert Caro, *The Years of Lyndon Johnson*, vol. 1: *The Path to Power* (New York: Alfred A. Knopf, 1982), chap. 25.

198   **Tommy Corcoran liked** Joseph Lash, *Dealers and Dreamers: A New Look at the New Deal* (New York: Doubleday, 1988), pp. 445–47.

198   **Harold Ickes had** T. H. Watkins, *Righteous Pilgrim: The Life and Times of Harold L. Ickes, 1874–1952* (New York: Henry Holt, 1990), chaps. 28 and 42.

Other than two long affairs, Watkins argued that this legend for Ickes was more overblown than real (see pp. 364–65).

198 **Seeing all of this** AI, Eliot Janeway, 5/19/90, New York.

198 **"Douglas was a tomcat"** Ibid., 5/8/92, New York (phone).

198 **"That whole crowd"** AI, Millie Douglas Read, 8/20/89, Lostine, Oreg.

198 **But there was a price** Ibid., and interview with William O. Douglas, Jr., 2/13/88, Lowe Videos.

198 **"You would speak"** AI, Millie Douglas Read, 8/20/89, Lostine, Oreg.

199 **"I admired him"** Interview with Millie Douglas Read, 4/16/88, Lowe Videos.

199 **"I think he was afraid"** AI, Millie Douglas Read, 8/20/89, Lostine, Oreg.

199 **"At these parties"** Interview with Millie Douglas Read, 4/16/88, Lowe Videos.

199 **Even life for** AI, Millie Douglas Read, 8/20/89, Lostine, Oreg.; and Douglas, *Of Men and Mountains,* chap. 18.

200 **For Douglas, a vacation** WOD to A. Howard Meneely, 9/29/42, WODP, Box 10; WOD, *My Wilderness: The Pacific West* (New York: Doubleday, 1960), chap. 11.

201 **"I didn't think"** AI, Vern Countryman, 11/14/89, Moraga, Calif.

201 **"He worked me"** Ibid.

201 **Lucile Lomen** AI, Lucile Lomen, 9/9/90, Seattle. For more on Lomen's background and her clerkship with WOD, see David J. Danelski, "Lucile Lomen: The First Woman to Clerk at the Supreme Court," *Journal of Supreme Court History* 1 (1999): 43–49.

201 **"He was not a warm"** AI, Vern Countryman, 11/14/89, Moraga, Calif.

201 **"He was a lone ranger"** Ibid. This experience was typical of clerks in that period. AI, C. David Ginsburg, 8/28/89, Washington, D.C.; AI, Lucile Lomen, 9/9/90, Seattle; AI, Stanley Soderland, 6/12/90, Shaw Island, Wash.; and AI, Jed King, 6/10/90, Seattle.

202 **"Frankfurter had lost"** Douglas Conversations, cassette no. 3, 12/20/61 and 12/27/61, p. 51.

202 **"Hugo would now not go"** Joseph P. Lash, ed., *From the Diaries of Felix Frankfurter* (New York: W. W. Norton, 1975), 3/12/43, p. 209.

202 **The opportunity to signal** *Jones v. Opelika,* 316 U.S. 584 (1942).

202 **"The opinion"** Ibid., pp. 623–24.

203 **Meanwhile, Douglas** *Skinner v. Oklahoma,* 316 U.S. 535 (1942).

203 **Relying on a 1927** *Buck v. Bell,* 274 U.S. 200 (1927).

203 **"Marriage and procreation"** *Skinner v. Oklahoma,* p. 541.

203 **"The power to sterilize"** Ibid.

203 **"The hand distribution"** *Murdock v. Pennsylvania,* 319 U.S. 105 (1943), pp. 108–9.

204 **"This form of religious"** Ibid., p. 109.

204 **"to their high, constitutional"** Ibid., p. 117.

204 **"Freedom of press"** Ibid., p. 115.

204 **"Check with Jackson's clerk,"** AI, Vern Countryman, 11/14/89, Moraga, Calif.

204   **"The clerk for Frankfurter"** Ibid.

205   **Several other religion** *Martin v. Struthers,* 319 U.S. 141 (1943).

205   **And, fulfilling the promise** *West Virginia State Board of Education v. Barnette,* 319 U.S. 624 (1943).

205   **"Words uttered"** Ibid., p. 644.

206   **"It outraged me"** AI, Vern Countryman, 11/14/89, Moraga, Calif.

206   **By the time the case** WOD to Harlan Fiske Stone, 5/31/43, WODP, Box 92; Ball and Cooper, *Of Power and Right,* p. 110; and Peter Irons, *Justice at War: The Story of the Japanese American Internment Cases* (New York: Oxford University Press, 1983), p. 237.

206   **He was tempering** WOD to Hugo Black, 6/21/41, Hugo Black Papers, Box 59, cited in Ball and Cooper, *Of Power and Right,* p. 338.

206   **"You used to be"** AI, Vern Countryman, 11/14/89, Moraga, Calif.

206   **"Well, the generals"** The term before, Douglas had illustrated this view in the case of *United States v. Pink* (315 U.S. 203 [1942]), in which the American government was seeking to recover surplus funds from a Russian insurance company that were still in the hands of the New York State superintendent of insurance. When the company was nationalized in 1919, its assets were frozen by the new Communist government and then assigned in a later executive agreement to the U.S. government. The case turned on whether the national government had the power to recognize the Communist government of the Soviet Union in 1933 and thus dictate the disposition of the funds, even if in doing so it was superseding the wishes of the state government. Here Douglas's views of presidential power were unequivocal: "The powers of the President in the conduct of foreign relations included the power, without consent of the Senate, to determine the public policy of the United States with respect to the Russian nationalization decrees. . . . Objection to the underlying policy as well as objections to recognition are to be addressed to the political department and not to the courts." As such, the executive agreement dealing with these funds did not require the participation of New York, because "no State can rewrite our foreign policy to conform to its own domestic policies. Power over external affairs is not shared by the States; it is vested in the national government exclusively." Like Justice George Sutherland before him, then, Douglas saw the president as representing "the sole organ" of the government in dealing with foreign affairs, while the action of New York represented "a dangerous invasion of Federal authority" (pp. 229–33).

       Years later, Douglas expressed complete confidence in his controversial decision. "The *Pink* case was in the field that traditionally had been reserved for a large degree of freedom by the Chief Executive and I think that in the long stream of history that it will . . . stand up." Douglas Conversations, cassette no. 7a, 1/18/62, p. 129.

206   **"When Stone made up"** Ibid., cassette no. 8, 5/23/62, p. 164.

207   **"We are engaged"** Douglas draft concurrence, *Hirabayashi v. United States,* 6/2/43, WODP, Box 92, cited also in Irons, *Justice at War,* pp. 237–39, and Ball and Cooper, *Of Power and Right,* p. 111.

207 **Then, reaching beyond** Ibid.

207 **This opinion landed** Felix Frankfurter to Harlan Fiske Stone, 6/4/43, *Hirabayashi* file, WODP, Box 92, cited in Ball and Cooper, *Of Right and Power*, p. 111.

207 **To Murphy** Lash, *From the Diaries*, 6/5/43, p. 251.

207 **When Stone refused** Harlan Fiske Stone to WOD, 6/9/43, *Hirabayashi* file, WODP, Box 92, cited also in Ball and Cooper, *Of Power and Right*, p. 111.

207 **Frankfurter then persuaded** J. Woodford Howard, *Mr. Justice Murphy*, p. 308, and Murphy concurrence in *Hirabayashi v. United States*, 320 U.S. 81 (1943), pp. 109–14.

207 **With no one left** *Hirabayashi v. United States*, 320 U.S. 81 (1943), pp. 105–9.

207 **When the case** Douglas Conversations, cassette no. 8, 5/23/62, p. 169.

208 **He also wrote** Douglas, *Court Years*, p. 280.

208 **It was another case** *Johnson v. United States*, 318 U.S. 189 (1943), pp. 193–97.

208 **In conference, Felix** Lash, *From the Diaries*, 1/18/43, p. 161.

208 **For Frankfurter this** Ibid., 2/2/43, p. 177.

208 **But Douglas was unconvinced.** Ibid., 2/3/43, p. 178.

209 **"Black [clearly speaking]"** Ibid., p. 179.

209 **Frankfurter believed** Ibid., p. 180.

209 **For him, "the only"** Ibid.

209 **Frankfurter told Roberts** Ibid.

209 **"Roberts is just beyond"** Ibid., p. 181.

209 **"Black always was"** Ibid., 2/4/43, p. 182.

210 **As the Court's term** See *Schneiderman v. United States*, 320 U.S. 118 (1943), and Lash, *From the Diaries*, 6/15/43, p. 257.

210 **When Murphy refused** Lash, *From the Diaries*, 6/15/43, p. 258.

210 **In time, relations** *Federal Power Commission v. Hope Natural Gas Co.*, 320 U.S. 591 (1944) and *United States v. South-Eastern Underwriters Ass'n*, 322 U.S. 533 (1944); see Douglas Conversations, cassette no. 6, 1/18/62, pp. 107–10; and Eugene C. Gerhart, *America's Advocate: Robert H. Jackson* (Indianapolis: Bobbs-Merrill, 1958), p. 258.

210 **Since Douglas had written** Douglas's denial here is confirmed by the lack of any existing documentary evidence in Drew Pearson's papers in the LBJ Library, Austin, Tex.

210 **When Pearson made** Douglas Conversations, cassette no. 5, 12/27/61, pp. 96–97, and cassette no. 6, 1/18/62, pp. 107–10.

210 **But Roberts was not** Ibid., cassette no. 5, 12/27/61, pp. 96–97.

CHAPTER 19

212 **"I had two classmates"** AI, Simon Rifkind, 8/4/89, New York.

212 **On the line** The title of the chapter is taken from Teddy Hayes's memoirs, *With the Gloves Off: My Life in the Boxing and Political Arenas* (Houston: Lancha Books, 1977), pp. 140–47.

This account of the Democratic National Convention of 1944, which was the pivotal incident in WOD's life and professional career, will be necessarily different from all others in print.

Few events in twentieth-century American political history have been discussed more thoroughly by a more distinguished set of scholars and writers than those in the choice of a vice-presidential candidate by the Democratic party in 1944. This decision was, in the words of distinguished Truman scholar Robert H. Ferrell, "the most extraordinary political arrangement of the present century" (Ferrell, *Harry S Truman,* p. 162).

Accounts of this incident can also be found in, among many other volumes: David Robertson, *Sly and Able: A Political Biography of James F. Byrnes* (New York: W. W. Norton, 1994), pp. 332–64; Frank Freidel, *Franklin D. Roosevelt: A Rendezvous with Destiny* (Boston: Little, Brown, 1990), chap. 38; Ferrell, *Harry S Truman,* chap. 8; Alonzo Hamby, *Man of the People: A Life of Harry S Truman* (New York: Oxford University Press, 1995), chap. 17; and Doris Kearns Goodwin, *No Ordinary Time: Franklin and Eleanor Roosevelt: The Home Front in World War II* (New York: Simon and Schuster, 1994), pp. 525–29.

Among the many articles dealing with all or some of this incident, two stand out as particularly useful: Brenda L. Heaster, "Who's on Second?" *Missouri Historical Review* 80, no. 2 (January 1986): 156–75 (thanks to Elizabeth Safly of the Harry S Truman Presidential Library for bringing this to my attention), and John M. Partin, "Roosevelt, Byrnes, and the 1944 Vice-Presidential Nomination," *Historian* 42 (1979–1980): 85–100.

This incident continues to interest scholars, as seen in James L. Moses, " 'An Interesting Game of Poker': Roosevelt, Douglas, and the 1944 Vice Presidential Nomination," unpublished paper, copy in author's possession (with thanks to Moses for providing this copy).

Among the most widely read of the literally dozens of accounts of this incident is that by Pulitzer Prize winner David McCullough, *Truman* (New York: Simon and Schuster, 1992), pp. 292–324. Using the highly revealing Frank Walker Papers at the Archives of the Library at Notre Dame University (hereafter Notre Dame Archives), which contain materials on this incident collected at the behest of Truman, Robert H. Ferrell expanded on McCullough's work in the most definitive book to date on the 1944 convention in general: *Choosing Truman: The Democratic Convention of 1944* (Columbia: University of Missouri Press, 1994).

Understandably concerned with the general story, rather than the particular one of William O. Douglas, Ferrell was persuaded by the Justice's denials of any interest in the vice presidency. Thus, he repeats Douglas's familiar account of being so uninterested that he spent the convention period on a horseback trip in the mountains.

My account, based on new sources, offers a new slant on Douglas's involvement in this incident, which I believe helps to explain the rest of his life.

212   **The two men became** See various accounts of this episode drafted by Ernest Cuneo; in Cuneo, "The Story of the Non-Election," Ernest Cuneo Papers, Box 18, FDRL; Cuneo unpublished autobiography, "I Played the Game," Box 117, ibid.; and Cuneo, "The Near Presidency," Box 114, ibid.

212   **Flynn was calling** Hayes, *With the Gloves Off,* pp. 140–44.

212   **With the 1944 Democratic** Edwin Pauley, "Memorandum to Jonathan Daniels," Jonathan Daniels Papers, Harry S Truman Presidential Library, Independence, Mo.; and see Edwin Pauley with Richard English, "Why Truman Is President," White House Central Files, Confidential Files, Box 30, Truman Library.

212   **For many Democrats** For his part, the president seemed to be promising the vice presidency to everyone. FDR had promised Wallace a public letter of support upon his return from a state visit to China, while also leading his assistant president for domestic affairs, Jimmy Byrnes, to believe that he would be the nominee. See Robertson, *Sly and Able* (p. 348), and see Walter J. Brown, in *James Byrnes of South Carolina: A Remembrance,* cited by Ferrell, *Choosing Truman* (p. 99).

213   **"I kept telling Flynn"** Hayes, *With the Gloves Off,* p. 141; the rest of the account of Hayes's conversation with Flynn is taken from pp. 140–44.

213   **Just before eleven** Ibid., p. 141.

213   **Since the Democratic** For more on Hannegan, see Irving Dilliard, "Robert E. Hannegan," *Current Biography,* Vertical File, Truman Library.

213   **"The President wants"** Hayes, *With the Gloves Off,* pp. 141–42.

214   **"To this day I"** The account of all of the above scenes and quotes comes from ibid.

214   **While Hayes was making** The account of this meeting relies on Pauley, "Memorandum to Jonathan Daniels." This version is an updated and expanded version of Pauley and English, "Why Truman Is President," Box 30, Truman Library, and the transcripts of two recorded memoirs by Frank Walker, filed in Frank Walker Papers, Box 123, Notre Dame Archives.

215   **After dinner** Ed Kelly, "Tells Why Wallace Isn't Nation's Chief Executive," *Chicago Herald American,* 5/14/47, in Frank Walker Papers, Box 49, Folder 6, Notre Dame Archives.

216   **"I know that this makes"** This technique of postdating was initially suggested, ironically enough, by Jimmy Byrnes when Henry Wallace had insisted on getting the president's endorsement for the post.

216   **"Although Father did"** James Roosevelt and Sidney Shalett, *Affectionately, FDR: A Son's Story of a Lonely Man* (New York: Harcourt, Brace, 1959), p. 351, cited in McCullough, *Truman,* p. 323.

216   **"I've got it"** Walker's account is in Frank Walker Memoirs, "Assisting Roosevelt," in "1944 — the Note to Bob Hannegan," Walker Papers, vol. 4, Box 113, Notre Dame Archives, also cited in Ferrell, *Truman,* p. 14, n. 31.

216   **But Hannegan's mood** Edwin Pauley, "Memorandum to Jonathan Daniels."

216   **Without knowing what** Cuneo, "The Near-Presidency."

216   **Everyone who got such** Lash, *Dealers and Dreamers,* pp. 447–48. See Murphy, *Brandeis/Frankfurter Connection,* pp. 190–94, for the full story.

217   **Having placed Douglas** Lowenthal, "Thomas G. Corcoran's Relation," Max Lowenthal Papers. Though Lowenthal was a political enemy of both Corcoran and Douglas, his contacts with Felix Frankfurter would have provided him more than enough information for this memo.

217   **By this time, Corcoran** See Murphy, *Fortas,* passim, for more here.

217   **From behind the scenes** Lowenthal, "Thomas G. Corcoran's Relation."

Henry Wallace Diaries, "Report by C B Baldwin on Democratic National Convention, 1944" (COHC), pp. 2990, 3384. Wallace had become aware that Corcoran and Fortas, the men he called "the extreme left-wingers," were spreading the story that he would be a handicap to the ticket. But the constant barrage was indeed weakening the president's resolve to keep him as a running mate.

217   **As Corcoran reviewed** Neal Gabler, *Winchell: Gossip, Power, and the Culture of Celebrity* (New York: Vintage, 1994), pp. 284–89.

217   **That mission accomplished** AI, Eliot Janeway, 5/19/90, New York.

218   **"[Mildred] was going"** Ibid.

218   **"wanted the Presidency"** Thomas Corcoran, "Rendezvous with Destiny," Corcoran's Unpublished Memoirs, Thomas Corcoran Papers, Library of Congress, p. 22 ("The Truman Years").

218   **"He really wanted it"** AI, Eliot Janeway, 5/19/90, New York.

218   **And they knew** Ickes Diary, 7/16/44, and Friedel, *Franklin D. Roosevelt*, p. 533.

218   **Given all these** AI, Eliot Janeway, 5/19/90, New York.

219   **Kenny had only one** Kenny's draft speech made clear that this westerner was a man of the people:

> Brought up in poverty, living the life of ordinary folk day after day, eating the hard bread of struggle, he achieved an understanding of the common man in a way in which no books could have taught it. Who can communicate to another who hasn't experienced it, the pain of returning home to a hungry family and an empty pantry? Who, except one who himself has lived the struggle from the ground up, can understand the meaning behind such common phrases as "equal economic opportunity," or "the fellowship of all who labor," or "property rights and personal rights"?

It was a clever speech, appealing to New Deal liberals who loved what Henry Wallace stood for, while also attracting those now searching for a clone of FDR. See Robert Kenny, "Nominating Speech for Honorable William O. Douglas," July 1944, Robert Kenny Papers, Berkeley Archives. See also Robert Kenny Memoirs, "My First Forty Years in California Politics," chap. 24, pp. 206–8, Kenny Papers, Carton 6, Berkeley Archives. On Douglas's contact with Kenny, see Abe Fortas to Robert Kenny, 7/12/44, Robert Kenny Papers, Berkeley Archives.

219   **With all this activity** Cuneo, "I Played the Game," pp. 545–48.

219   **When informed of this** Cuneo, "Story of the Non-Election."

219   **Corcoran had conveyed** Lowenthal, "Thomas G. Corcoran's Relation."

219   **"Victory has a thousand friends,"** Cuneo, "Story of the Non-Election."

220   **"I now had a following"** Cuneo, "I Played the Game," pp. 545–65.

220   **Seeking some psychological** Ibid., and Cuneo, "Story of the Non-Election."

220   **Whatever the letter** Cuneo, "I Played the Game," p. 550.

220   **"Tom was absolutely"** Ibid., pp. 545–65.

221   **"You know who the President"** Ibid., p. 551.

221   **Meanwhile, back in Washington** What follows is a melding of two Cuneo accounts: "I Played the Game" and "Story of the Non-Election."

221   **While Corcoran and others** WOD to Harlan Fiske Stone, 7/12/44, Harlan Fiske Stone Papers, Box 74, Library of Congress, Washington, D.C., also quoted in Philip Cooper and Howard Ball, *The United States Supreme Court: From the Inside Out* (New York: Prentice Hall, 1996), p. 301.

221   **Two days later** WOD to Senator Frank Maloney, 7/14/44, WODP, Box 353.

221   **Knowing that Maloney** Ibid.

221   **While the handwritten** A copy of the handwritten letter is in WODP, Box 353, but the original typed draft with revisions (on which Douglas has attached a small note reading, "This is my file copy of the letter I wrote Maloney on the eve of the conventions") is in WODP, Box 537, "1944 Convention" folder. The date for the sending of the letter on July 15 is taken from a letter, Catherine Flynn to WOD, 5/17/45, WODP, Box 353.

Douglas's secretaries all agreed that WOD did not type (AI, Fay Aull Deusterman, 3/3/91, Orlando, Fla., and Marty Bagby Yopp, 6/6/90, Moscow, Idaho), so Mildred must have typed the letter from a handwritten draft that has either not survived or not yet surfaced.

Years later, Douglas was still trying to cover his tracks, claiming in his memoirs that this highly revealing letter had disappeared: "Later I tried to get a copy of the longhand note refusing the nomination which I had given Frank Maloney. He had died prematurely; his wife, Martha, shortly following. They left a son, Bobby, who had all of his father's papers in a trunk. But by the time I caught up with Bobby the trunk had been in flood and all the papers destroyed." The Justice failed to mention Maloney's daughter, Marilyn, who found the letter in her review of the senator's papers after his untimely death and had a copy of it sent to Douglas, who duly placed it in his own personal papers. See Douglas, *Court Years*, p. 283.

221   **"What do we do now?"** AI, Eliot Janeway, 5/19/90, New York.

222   **At around 1:30** Just who was in this meeting is a matter of some dispute. Edwin Pauley has the best account of this conversation in "Memorandum to Jonathan Daniels." Ed Kelly recounts the meeting in sketchy detail but does not mention Pauley's presence, in "Secret FDR Letter Put Truman In," *Chicago Herald American*, 5/15/47, Frank Walker Papers, Box 49, Folder 16, Notre Dame Archives. Hannegan's only account can be found in the notes of an interview by Robert Sherwood, 5/25/46, Robert Sherwood Papers, Houghton Library, Harvard University, Cambridge, Mass. The log of the visitors to the president's train shows that only Hannegan and Kelly arrived. See "Log of the President's Inspection Trip to the Pacific, July–August, 1944," Box 68, Official File, FDRL. However, Robert Ferrell, based on his detailed study of this incident, accepts that Pauley was there, a reasonable supposition given the complete nature of his later account. Ferrell surmises that the keeper of the log simply did not recognize Pauley. (See Ferrell, *Choosing Truman*, pp. 36–38 and 108–9, n.3.) Regardless of how many boarded the train, it seems clear that Hannegan was the only one permitted to discuss this matter with the president.

222   **Hannegan was there** First, Hannegan wanted some changes made in the president's endorsement letter for Henry Wallace to make it even more lukewarm and thus finish his chances. Then, he wanted to ask the president directly whether he still considered Jimmy Byrnes a viable candidate.

222   **He wanted to get** Ferrell, *Choosing Truman,* pp. 36–38 and 108–9, n. 3. After the visitors chatted briefly with Eleanor Roosevelt and Judge Samuel Rosenman in the dining compartment, FDR and Hannegan moved into another compartment to speak privately.

222   **The time had come** Pauley, "Memorandum to Jonathan Daniels," recalls that the president wrote the note in front of both of them. So Pauley could not have known that on Walker's instructions Hannegan had gotten the letter four days before and had been carrying it on the train solely to be typed. The president himself confirmed this fact to Jimmy Byrnes on July 18: "The only thing I told Bob was to show you a letter I wrote to Bob on that assumption—it was in reply to a question from Bob; he wanted confirmation of the fact that I would be entirely happy with Truman or Douglas. This was a week ago. It was in reply to a question from him." "Telephone Conversation with F.D.R. on Tuesday, July 18, 1944," James Byrnes Papers, Folder 74, Clemson University, Clemson, S.C. Also see Ferrell, *Choosing Truman,* p. 49. Thanks to Berneice Holt for assisting me in the location of this letter.

223   **Pauley grabbed** See "President Roosevelt's note to Robert E. Hannegan, July 19, 1944," Robert Hannegan, Subject File, 1943–92, Truman Library; a copy is also in the miscellaneous files of HST, having gotten it from FDRL, President's Secretary's Files. Information on this material comes from AI, Dennis Bilger (Truman Library archivist), 9/19/95, Independence, Mo. (phone).

        It is possible that part of Hannegan's shock came from his belief that, after the report was delivered to the president, Douglas's name would be released as a contender.

223   **"Here we were"** Pauley, "Memorandum to Jonathan Daniels."

223   **Totally unaware** Cuneo, "I Played the Game," pp. 445–65, and see Steven Fraser, *Labor Will Rule: Sidney Hillman and the Rise of American Labor* (New York: Free Press, 1991).

223   **Indeed, Senator Joe Guffey** Ickes Dairy, 7/16/44.

224   **"I hadn't had one nod"** Cuneo, "I Played the Game," p. 553.

224   **"the silence was ominous"** Ibid., pp. 445–65.

224   **By this time** Ibid., p. 556.

224   **In doing this** Ibid., pp. 445–65.

225   **"You *are* a son-of-a-bitch."** Ibid.

225   **What he did not** Ibid., pp. 551–52. Byrnes, "Telephone Conversation with F.D.R." This conversation provides third-party confirmation that the letter was in fact produced on July 11, as Frank Walker recalled, rather than on July 15, as Edwin Pauley argues. Since Pauley was on the train but very likely not in the private meeting with Hannegan and Roosevelt, he would have had no way of knowing that the handwritten letter already existed and only the typed version was being produced.

See also Lowenthal, "Thomas G. Corcoran's Relation," and see "Hannegan, Now Truman's Grand Vizier, Clings to 'Team' Politics Formula" (condensed from Rufus Jarman's sketch of Hannegan in *The Saturday Evening Post*), *St. Louis Post-Dispatch*, 3/4/46, Vertical File, Truman Library.

225 **With several of the party** Ickes Diary, 7/16/44; Henry Wallace diaries, COHC, "July 18–22, 1944," p. 3378.

225 **"I can't, Airnee,"** Cuneo, "I Played the Game," pp. 555–56.

225 **For all his efforts** Kenny, "My First Forty Years," pp. 206–7, supplemented by Cuneo, "I Played the Game," pp. 445–65, 555–65.

226 **"I give you my word"** Cuneo, "I Played the Game," pp. 557–58.

226 **"Hello, fellows"** Ibid., p. 558.

226 **"Goddamn it"** Ibid.

226 **But Hannegan knew exactly** Henry Wallace had already launched his own effort with a compelling seconding speech of the president's nomination. Then, one by one, members of a dozen state delegations nominated their favorite-son candidates. The excitement of the moment apparently got to Mayor Ed Kelly, who in nominating Senator Scott Lucas of Illinois as an alternative to the more intellectual Wallace said proudly that the senator was "not a thinking man and he represents no thinking people." Cuneo, "I Played the Game," pp. 555–65.

226 **There it was for all** Pauley, "Memorandum to Jonathan Daniels."

227 **"When did you get it?"** Ferrell, *Choosing Truman*, p. 82, citing James Hagerty, *Chicago Tribune*, 7/20/44.

227 **"Our throats were slit"** Cuneo, "I Played the Game," p. 560.

227 **"At long last"** Ibid.

227 **"The truth is that"** AI, Eliot Janeway, 5/19/90, New York.

227 **By Thursday night** Ferrell, *Choosing Truman*, pp. 78–80.

227 **"Fuck 'em,"** AI, Eliot Janeway, 5/19/90, New York; and AI, Millie Douglas Read, 8/20/89, Lostine, Oreg.

228 **"If I send you"** AI, Eliot Janeway, 5/19/90, New York.

228 **With the final vote** Ibid.

228 **Douglas's men were willing** Ibid., and AI, Thomas Corcoran, 9/29/77, Washington, D.C.

228 **Douglas's forces** Roosevelt and Shalett, *Affectionately, FDR*, p. 351. (Once again, Hannegan was merely stretching the truth, as the president was in fact suffering from chest pains so severe that he had to lie on the floor of the train from time to time.)

228 **With no way to confirm** Ferrell, *Choosing Truman*, p. 77; Freidel, *Franklin D. Roosevelt*, p. 537.

At every stop along the route, Roosevelt called Hannegan to find out whether Truman had accepted the offer. With Truman in the room when one of these calls arrived, Hannegan explained that the senator was not yet on board. Roosevelt barked into the receiver, "Well, tell the Senator that if he wants to break up the Democratic party by staying out, he can; but he knows as well as I what that might mean at this dangerous time in the world."

"Jesus Christ!" cried Truman. "But why the hell didn't he tell me in the first place?"

228 **"Never before has"** AI, Eliot Janeway, 5/19/90, New York.

229 **"We brought Douglas"** Ibid., 5/8/92, New York (phone).

229 **"Clausewitz (in his book)"** Ernest Cuneo to WOD, 7/1/68, WODP, Box 319.

229 **On Friday morning** Pauley, "Memorandum to Jonathan Daniels." Gambling that Wallace would not win on the first vote, the plan was to hold off the second ballot while vote switches were lined up and then have the states not voting for Truman agree to pass their position to others who were. This would make it look like a rolling bandwagon of support had developed for Hannegan's man.

229 **"The guillotine dropped"** Cuneo, "Story of the Non-Election."

229 **"It would have been"** Kenny, "My First Forty Years," p. 208.

230 **"Bob," said Cuneo** Cuneo, "Story of the Non-Election."

230 **But one thing still** Ibid.

230 **Always acting with** AI, Eliot Janeway, 5/19/90, New York.

230 **Striding confidently** Robert Mull, interview with Chester Maxey, 9/22/81.

230 **After the final vote** AI, Eliot Janeway, 5/19/90, New York.

230 **"He talked for quite"** Robert Mull, interview with Chester Maxey, 9/22/81.

230 **"You didn't get it"** AI, Eliot Janeway, 5/19/90, New York, and 5/8/92, New York (phone).

231 **"He got the word,"** Robert Mull, interview with Chester Maxey, 9/22/81.

231 **With the battle** WOD to FDR, 7/27/44, Box 143, President's Secretary's File, Democratic National Convention Folder, FDRL.

231 **Three weeks later** WOD to Harlan Fiske Stone, 8/21/44, Box 74, Harlan Fiske Stone Papers, also quoted in Cooper and Ball, *The United States Supreme Court,* p. 301.

231 **Neither man would ever** WOD to Fred Rodell, 6/10/44, Fred Rodell Papers, Quaker Room, Haverford College, Haverford, Pa.

231 **"All I needed to do"** AI, Eliot Janeway, 5/19/90, New York.

231 **"It certainly would take"** AI, Clark Clifford, 8/27/89, Washington, D.C.

232 **For this reason, friends** Hayes, *With the Gloves Off,* pp. 140–47.

232 **Still three months shy** Ferrell, *Choosing Truman,* pp. 83–85. Political analysts would have been the first to tell him that without FDR's active and visible support, the combination of Douglas's lack of extensive political organization and his own failure to appear at the convention likely doomed his nomination chances from the start. Furthermore, his political philosophy made devising a winning strategy for this convention much more difficult. "For Douglas supporters the principal problem was that as long as Wallace was in the race they had no place to go," argued Ferrell. "Douglas's candidacy appealed to the same individuals who already had lined up with Wallace. Any serious Douglas movement could not begin until Wallace was out. . . . But as long as Wallace could stay in the race Douglas was out of the race."

232 **"He told me once"** Mike Murphey, "Yakima Never Sure About Douglas," *Yakima Herald-Republic,* 1/20/80, p. 6, copies available on microfilm in the Yakima Public Library and the archives for the *Yakima Herald-Republic.* Simon Rifkind recalled Douglas telling him, "President Roosevelt through

Mr. Hannegan transmitted and requested that the Vice President should be (1) Douglas, and (2) Truman, and in that order of preference. But Hannegan transposed the names." AI, Simon Rifkind, 8/4/89, New York.

232   **Truman's name** Few scraps of paper have changed more political careers and a greater portion of this nation's political history before disappearing from view entirely. Speculation about the name-switching was fueled when Grace Tully, Roosevelt's private secretary, published in her memoirs in 1949 that in instructing her to type the letter on the train, Bob Hannegan had told her: "Grace, the President wants you to retype this letter and to switch these names so it will read 'Harry Truman or Bill Douglas'!" As the secretary concluded: "The reason for the switch was obvious. By naming Truman first it was plainly implied by the letter that he was the preferred choice of the President." But when she later searched the files for the carbon copy of the original letter, it could not be found. It would be fifty years before the truth surfaced in the long-hidden private papers of one of the story's principal characters. The note had not disappeared from view accidentally.

After taking the original and typed letters from the presidential train, Hannegan gave them to his wife, Irma, for safekeeping. She hid them in her purse during the course of the convention; at night, they were tucked under her mattress. But when the convention ended, and no one ever asked to see either the original or the copy, the Hannegans took them home.

Years later, Bob Hannegan's son, William, and his wife were visiting the Truman Presidential Library in Independence, Missouri, when the ex-president approached them. *Do you know if your mother has the handwritten note,* Truman asked Hannegan, *and if so would you mind asking her to look for it?* By then, this note was also troubling Mrs. Hannegan, who had written Frank C. Walker in 1950 that she was "very disappointed" by Grace Tully's claim.

In 1960, Mrs. Hannegan finally sent both the original Roosevelt handwritten note and its typed copy to Harry Truman, who placed them both in a family trust that was closed to researchers until 1985. By this time, so many requests had begun coming to the library about this note that a request was made to the Roosevelt Library in Hyde Park to search their collection for it. (No one seemed to be aware of what was in the family trust.) All that could be found, though, was a carbon of the typed version, a copy of which was forwarded to the Truman Library, where it was placed in the Miscellaneous Historical Documents Collection. In 1985, the original handwritten letter and its original typed version were deeded to the Truman Presidential Library. They were placed in a vault to preserve the original presidential handwriting.

When the Truman Library opened the Robert Hannegan Papers in 1993, it was possible to see, in President Roosevelt's shaky handwriting on a lined piece of unmarked light tan notepaper, that the original reads:

July 19

Dear Bob:

You have written me about Harry Truman and Bill Douglas. I should of course be very glad to run with either of them and believe that either one of them would bring real strength to the ticket.

Always sincerely,
FDR

Hon. Robert Hannegan

Thus, the names on the typed letter were not switched from the original.

For the initial story of the preparation of the letter, see: Grace Tully, *FDR: My Boss* (New York: Scribner's, 1949), p. 276. Tully confirmed this account in an interview with Walker (Frank Walker Papers, Notre Dame Archives), and Dorothy Brady confirmed this recollection in a 1993 interview by Bill Hannegan, cited by Ferrell in *Choosing Truman,* p. 120, n. 41.

I am indebted for the story of the journey of this note before its disappearance to Bob Ferrell, who interviewed Hannegan's wife and son, among others, while tracing the letter through all the available archives (Ferrell, *Choosing Truman,* pp. 82–84 and 120–21, nn. 39–41). However, according to Dennis Bilger (AI, 9/19/95, Independence, Mo. [phone]), this letter was not released until the rest of Hannegan's papers were opened, which was after the publication of Ferrell's book. So Ferrell was not able to cite or discuss the actual document, which seemingly solves the mystery.

On the connection of the letters to the Hannegans, see: Irma Hannegan to Samuel I. Rosenman, n.d., "Correspondence re Truman nomination (Hannegan & others)," Samuel I. Rosenman Papers, Box 18, FDRL. Cited also in Ferrell, *Choosing Truman,* pp. 82–84, 120–21. Truman says that it was Tuesday, July 18, when Hannegan actually showed him the copy of the letter, but Ferrell theorizes that it was likely on Monday, July 17. Sometime during the week of the convention, Hannegan also showed the president's original handwritten note to Truman. Ferrell, *Autobiography of Harry S Truman,* p. 89; and Harry S Truman to Samuel I. Rosenman, 1/25/50, "Political—Vice Presidential Nomination 1944," Box 321, President's Secretary's File, Truman Library, also cited in Ferrell, *Choosing Truman,* p. 120, n. 39.

See also Irma Hannegan to Frank Walker, 2/11/50, Robert Hannegan Papers, Box 6, Truman Library; Frank Walker to Irma Hannegan, 3/5/51, "Letters from Famous People, Book 1, 1943–1966," Robert Hannegan Papers, Box 1, Truman Library, both cited in Ferrell, *Choosing Truman,* pp. 120–21, n. 41; and see finding aid to Robert E. Hannegan Papers, Truman Library; and Heaster, "Who's on Second," p. 174, n. 51; confirmed by AI, Dennis Bilger, 9/19/95, Independence, Mo. (phone). The Truman Library finding aid indicates that it was in Miscellaneous Historical Documents Collection, Box 415. Alonzo Hamby cites these papers, but he apparently saw them when they were still in the possession of Robert Hannegan, Jr.

On the FDR note, see "President Roosevelt's Note to Robert E. Hannegan, July 19, 1944," Robert E. Hannegan Papers, Subject File, 1943–92, Truman Library. Also placed here was the typed version, which came from the Miscellaneous File, FDRL. AI, Dennis Bilger, 9/19/95, Independence, Mo. (phone).

How can we know that this is the president's actual handwritten letter? Besides the recollections cited above of Robert Hannegan and others, as well as the account by Jimmy Byrnes of his phone conversation about the letter with the president on July 18, confirming evidence comes from other sources.

Harry Truman himself, universally acknowledged as a man of scrupulous honesty and respect for historical accuracy, recalled in his autobiography the handwritten note that *he* had been shown by Hannegan: "On Tuesday evening [July 18, 1944] Bob Hannegan came to see me and told me that President Roosevelt wanted me to run with him on the ticket for vice president. This astonished me greatly. Hannegan showed me a longhand note in the president's handwriting which said, 'Bob, it's Truman. FDR.' It was written on a scratch pad from the president's desk." (Ferrell, *Autobiography of Harry S Truman*, p. 89; Truman to Samuel I. Rosenman, 1/25/50, "Political—Vice Presidential Nomination 1944," Box 321, President's Secretary's File, Truman Library, also cited in Ferrell, *Choosing Truman*, p. 120, n. 39.)

Truman later told speechwriter Samuel I. Rosenman that the Roosevelt note, surely one that would have been charged to his memory because of its importance, was "written on a piece of scratch paper about two inches by eight and it had only one name mentioned in it and that was mine" (ibid.). The copy of the actual note in the Hannegan Papers is indeed penned on a piece of memo paper that measures five inches by eight and a half. How, then, to explain Truman's seemingly faulty recollection that he saw only his name on the note? Frank C. Walker suggests, without any proof, that two such letters did exist. See Frank C. Walker to Irma Hannegan, 3/5/51, Robert Hannegan Papers, Box 1, Truman Library, also cited in Ferrell, *Choosing Truman*, p. 121, n. 41. William P. Hannegan speculates that his father might have actually held up the handwritten note containing both names for Truman's inspection while carefully placing his thumb over Douglas's name, thus removing it from the reader's view (Ferrell, *Choosing Truman*, p. 83). The position of Douglas's name, in the top right-hand corner of the note, would have made this possible.

While independent observers at the time confirm the authenticity of the note, the wording of the handwritten letter also matches in every detail the letter that was released to the press. Since the order of the names in the handwritten note is in the order that Hannegan wanted, believing that the names were switched by the secretary requires a much more tortured explanation: The president would have had to have written *another* note with Douglas's name coming first and then produced this one by personally copying it over exactly but reversing the names himself.

Grace Tully's published account that the two names on FDR's letter were switched, then, could have been a faulty recollection, a confusion with another letter, or possibly even an effort to discredit President Truman. There is still one other possible scenario, acknowledging Truman's recollection, the universal appreciation of the power of Grace Tully's memory, as well as Dorothy Brady's dependability and the view of Frank C. Walker, who was present at the fateful July 11 meeting (Heaster, "Who's on Second?" p. 166, n. 26.). There still could have been two notes written: a short one on July 11 containing only Truman's name, which was never retyped, and the longer one written some time thereafter (either when Hannegan returned to the White House on July 12 at 5:00 p.m. or on the train), which had both men's names and was subsequently typed by Dorothy Brady. Even in this scenario, the names were not switched because the longer handwritten version that survives has the Truman-Douglas order. With no other evidence to verify that two such notes were written and the fact that Robert Ferrell could not verify this view after lengthy study, the only likely scenario is that the Truman-Douglas letter was the only one produced. Whatever the reason, this story of the names being switched was created initially by Tommy Corcoran and Ernie Cuneo and certainly spread by them. Whenever and however it was written, the most important fact for this study is that Douglas lived the rest of his life *believing* that the names on this letter had been switched, and that for a week he had been the president's choice.

232 **That a Douglas administration** After Truman became president in April 1945, did it matter that Douglas had been supplanted? "Well, a lot of different things would have happened," he told a journalist years later. "There would have been no bomb dropped on Hiroshima." Indeed, given Douglas's love of people in foreign lands, even in the face of likely huge losses of American lives in any invasion of Japan, it would have been a much more difficult decision for him (Sevareid, "Mr. Justice Douglas").

And, had he been president, Douglas told another interviewer, there would have been a series of other changes. Among them, he would not have allowed the American military to become as strong as it did under Truman; he would not have extended the Marshall Plan foreign-aid program to what he called "the feudal regimes" in Africa, the Middle East, Asia, and Latin America without wholesale democratic reforms; his appointments to the Supreme Court would have been much different from the series of cronies placed there by Truman (which Douglas believed set back civil-rights progress by at least ten years); and he never would have hesitated to recognize Red China (Douglas Conversations, cassette no. 16, 6/5/63, pp. 349–50). As Washington attorney Joseph Rauh put it, William O. Douglas as president "would have continued the portrait of the New Deal a lot longer." AI, Joseph L. Rauh, 8/29/89, Washington, D.C.

232 **"Bill, we really did"** Douglas, *Court Years*, p. 284.

232 **"Bob," responded** AI, Eliot Janeway, 5/19/90, New York, confirming the account in Ibid.

232 **"We are beginning"** Ibid.

CHAPTER 20

233 **"The Supreme Court is like"** Bernard Schwartz, *Decision: How the Supreme Court Decides Cases* (New York: Oxford University Press, 1996), p. 37. This phrase is almost universally attributed to Oliver Wendell Holmes, but my informal survey of constitutional-law scholars, Holmes biographers and scholars, and constitutional-history literature turned up no confirming source. This makes sense, as the Court on which Holmes served was not as turbulent as this quotation implies, whereas Alexander Bickel would have been speaking about the turbulence caused by the fighting between Douglas and Frankfurter.

This quotation could be a perversion of one Justice's comment on Cass Gilbert's much-mocked design for the new Supreme Court building. "Chief Justice Harlan Fiske Stone called it 'almost bombastically pretentious' and 'wholly inappropriate for a quiet group of old boys such as the Supreme Court.' Another Justice said that the Court would be 'nine black beetles in the Temple of Karnak.' Another asked: 'What are we supposed to do, ride in on nine elephants?' " Elder Witt, ed., *Congressional Quarterly's Guide to the U.S. Supreme Court* (Washington, D.C.: Congressional Quarterly, 1979), p. 772.

233 ***Korematsu*** *Korematsu v. United States,* 323 U.S. 214 (1944), pp. 216–17.

233 **Endo took the argument** *Ex Parte Endo,* 323 U.S. 283 (1944), pp. 287–89.

234 **In *Ex Parte Endo*** *Endo* conference notes, WODP, Box 115, cited also in Ball and Cooper, *Of Power and Right,* p. 115.

234 **Still conceding the existence** *Korematsu* draft dissent, 12/1/44, WODP, Box 112, cited also in Ball and Cooper, *Of Power and Right,* p. 114.

234 **In short, to Douglas** *Korematsu* draft dissent, 12/1/44, WODP, Box 112, cited also in Irons, *Justice at War,* pp. 332–46.

234 **Douglas, however, signaled** WOD to Black, 12/6/44, *Korematsu* file, WODP, Box 112, cited also in Ball and Cooper, *Of Power and Right,* pp. 113–15, and Irons, *Justice at War,* pp. 332–46.

234 **"This exclusion of"** *Korematsu v. United States,* 323 U.S. 214 (1944), p. 234.

234 **"My vote to affirm"** Douglas, *Court Years,* pp. 39, 280.

234 **"Whatever power"** *Ex Parte Endo,* 323 U.S. 283 (1944), p. 297.

235 **"It seemed to me"** Douglas Conversations, cassette no. 8, 5/23/62, p. 172.

235 **Not until later** Irons, *Justice at War,* pp. 344–45.

235 **"The distinction is between"** *Davis v. United States,* 328 U.S. 582 (1946), p. 589.

235 **"Whatever may be"** Ibid., pp. 592–93.

235 **Here, Felix Frankfurter** Ibid., p. 596.

235 **"The approval given today"** Ibid., p. 597.

236 **"I am constrained"** Ibid., p. 615.

236 **"the search was justified"** Ibid., p. 623.

236 **"When petitioner"** *Zap v. United States,* 328 U.S. 624 (1946), p. 628.

236 **"To require reversal"** Ibid., p. 630.

236 **"The legality of a search"** Ibid., p. 632.

237 **To him, Douglas had also** Ickes Diary, 5/23/45.

237　**In conferences** Ickes Diary, 6/16/46.

237　**And Felix Frankfurter was driving** AI, Edward F. Prichard, Jr., 6/25/79, Frankfort, Ky.; AI, Philip Elman, 7/10/79, Washington, D.C.; AI, Joseph L. Rauh, 8/29/89, Washington, D.C.

237　**Sometimes during these performances** Ball and Cooper, *Of Power and Right*, pp. 92 and 90–93.

237　**"Well, Chief, it seems"** AI, Vern Countryman, 11/14/89, Moraga, Calif.

237　**By this time** Ickes Diary, 7/7/45, p. 9865.

237　**When Chief Justice Stone** Douglas Conversations, cassette no. 5, 12/27/61, p. 98; and Mason, *Harlan Fiske Stone*, pp. 765–69.

238　**"This strained relationship"** Douglas Conversations, cassette no. 5, 12/27/61, p. 99.

238　**Unable to secure unanimity** Mason, *Harlan Fiske Stone*, p. 769.

238　**Seeking to ensure** Ickes Diary, 12/23/45, p. 10213.

238　**Douglas was now** Ibid., 1/12/46, p. 10215.

239　**The political uproar** Watkins, *Righteous Pilgrim*, pp. 832–36, and Murphy, *Fortas*, pp. 68–71.

239　**The men would delight** AI, Clark Clifford, 8/27/89, Washington, D.C.

239　**Once Douglas even returned** AI, Millie Douglas Read, 8/20/89, Lostine, Oreg.

239　**Having heard from Douglas** Douglas, *Go East*, p. 68.

239　**"Every now and then"** AI, Clark Clifford, 8/27/89, Washington, D.C.

239　**Clifford drove over** Ibid.

240　**"Whether [you] consider"** Ickes Diary, 2/23/46.

240　**The secretary proposed** Ibid., 2/24/46.

240　**Six weeks after** Kai Bird and Max Holland, "The Tapping of 'Tommy the Cork,'" *The Nation*, 2/8/86, pp. 141–43.

241　**"I'm doing my"** Corcoran Transcripts, 5/1/46, 11:55 A.M. phone call to Douglas.

241　**He even went to** Bird and Holland, "Tapping of 'Tommy the Cork,'" p. 145.

241　**"I had about three"** Corcoran Transcripts, 2/15/46, 9:00 A.M.

241　**Early that evening** Ibid., 7:25 P.M.

241　**Not even three hours later** Ibid., 10:20 P.M.

242　**After more reflection** AI, Clark Clifford, 8/27/89, Washington, D.C.

242　**By February 17** Corcoran Transcripts, 2/17/46, 11:00 A.M.

242　**"When President Roosevelt appointed"** Douglas Conversations, cassette no. 9, 5/23/62, p. 183.

243　**Seeking to change** Ickes Diary, 5/19/46, p. 18.

243　**After he did** Eben A. Ayers Diary 4/9/48, Eben A. Ayers Papers, Truman Library.

243　**Finally, a week later** Harry S Truman, *Memoirs*, vol. 2, *Years of Trial and Hope* (Garden City, N.Y.: Doubleday, 1956), pp. 190–91.

243　**War was formally** Mason, *Harlan Fiske Stone*, p. 806.

243　**Stone's death five hours** The best accounts of the following episode can be found in Dennis J. Hutchinson, "The Black-Jackson Feud," *The Supreme Court Review* 1988, 203–45, and Edwin M. Yoder, Jr., *The Unmaking of a*

Whig: And Other Essays in Self-Definition (Washington, D.C.: Georgetown University Press, 1990), pp. 3–106.

243 **"Oh Lord, does the world"** Technical surveillance summaries, J. Edgar Hoover's Official and Confidential Files, 1945, cited in Alexander Charns's highly revealing work based on his extensive Freedom of Information Act requests for FBI files on the Supreme Court, *Cloak and Gavel: FBI Wiretaps, Bugs, Informers, and the Supreme Court* (Urbana: University of Illinois Press, 1992), p. 29.

244 **"Washington adores a funeral"** Hutchinson, "Black-Jackson Feud," p. 243. Jackson intended to use this to begin a review of a book on Hughes but struck it from the final version.

244 **Even before Harlan Fiske Stone** Ibid., p. 215.

244 **For his part, Tommy** Corcoran Transcripts, 4/28/46, cited in Charns, *Cloak and Gavel,* p. 27.

245 **"Tom, I've been trying"** Corcoran Transcripts, 5/4/46.

245 **While there is no evidence** Douglas Conversations, cassette no. 10, 6/9/62, p. 211; and Truman, *Memoirs,* vol. 2, pp. 190–91.

245 **"Is it lost for Bill?"** Corcoran Transcripts, 4/4/46, cited in Charns, *Cloak and Gavel,* p. 29.

245 **Over the next six** Charns, *Cloak and Gavel,* p. 30.

245 **On May 16** Ibid.

245 **By May 19** Ickes Diary, 5/19/46.

246 **"Any man who had been"** Margaret Truman, *Harry S Truman* (New York: Avon, 1993 [1973]), pp. 330–31; quoting her father.

246 **As soon as Douglas heard** Douglas Conversations, cassette no. 10, 6/9/62, pp. 207–8.

246 **Two days later** The case was *Jewell Ridge Coal Corp. v. Local No. 6167, United Mine Workers,* 325 U.S. 161 (1945); Hutchinson, "Black-Jackson Feud," pp. 203–45; and Yoder, *Unmaking of a Whig,* pp. 3–106.

246 **When Jackson sent a similar** Ibid.

246 **In November 1946** *Cleveland v. United States,* 329 U.S. 14 (1946).

246 **"The establishment or maintenance"** Ibid., p. 19.

247 **"It is also urged"** Ibid., p. 20.

247 **"results in the imprisonment"** Ibid., p. 25.

247 **Hans Max Haupt** *Haupt v. United States,* 330 U.S. 631 (1947), p. 645.

247 **On the other side** Ibid., passim.

247 **"Though [Murphy] and I"** Douglas, *Court Years,* p. 26.

247 **These initial steps** *Craig v. Harney,* 331 U.S. 367 (1947).

248 **"A trial is a public"** Ibid., p. 374.

248 **"The vehemence of the language"** Ibid., p. 376.

248 **Even with this protective** Ibid.

248 **"With due respect"** Ibid., pp. 396–97.

249 **"Is it conceivable"** Ibid., p. 393.

249 **Writing for the five-person** *Saia v. New York,* 334 U.S. 558 (1947), pp. 560–61.

249 **"the power of censorship"** Ibid., p. 562.

249 **"neither judicious nor sound"** Ibid., pp. 566–67.

CHAPTER 21

251 **I never was** "Douglas 'Ain't A-Runnin' and He Ain't Goin' Tuh,' " *The New York Times*, 7/11/48, p. 5.

251 **While the Court labored** Ickes Diary, 1/10/48.

251 **Seeking to develop** Ibid., 3/10/47; Murphy, *Fortas;* AI, Simon Rifkind, 8/4/89, New York.

251 **In time, Hill issued** Lowenthal, "Thomas G. Corcoran's Relation."

252 **"To err is Truman"** AI, Joseph L. Rauh, Jr., 8/29/89, Washington, D.C.

252 **It took Franklin D. Roosevelt, Jr.'s** Ibid.

252 **"Joe, I have a message"** Ibid.

253 **Most of those present** Ibid.

253 **Finally, as the clamor grew** Ibid.; see also Nelson Lichtenstein, *Walter Reuther: The Most Dangerous Man in Detroit* (Urbana: University of Illinois Press, 1997), and Beatrice Hansen, *A Political Biography of Walter Reuther: The Record of an Opportunist* (New York: Merit, 1969).

253 **"There is not the slightest"** AI, Joseph L. Rauh, Jr., 8/29/89, Washington, D.C.

253 **Just as Robert** Ibid.

253 **"Since no one knows"** AI, Joseph L. Rauh, Jr., 8/29/89, Washington, D.C., and see "William O. Douglas: The Man, His Life, His Views," Americans for Democratic Action campaign document, 1948, generously supplied to the author by Ed Mitchell, Malibu, Calif. (hereafter ADA Convention Brochure).

254 **In a matter of days** Description of memorabilia in the author's collection.

254 **The ADA also produced** ADA Convention Brochure.

254 **"William O. Douglas is a"** Ibid.

255 **"Bill, you don't want"** AI, Joseph L. Rauh, Jr., 8/29/89, Washington, D.C., and AI, Eliot Janeway, 5/19/90, New York. Others believe that this quote is "a number-two man to a number-two man." As will become clear below, the original phrase relied on the concept of "fiddles."

255 **So Jack Beale of *Time*** Corcoran Transcripts, 5/5/48, pp. 3–4.

255 **Within days, the transcript** Corcoran Transcripts, 5/5/48; see also Bird and Holland, "Tapping of 'Tommy the Cork,' " pp. 141–43.

255 **While Corcoran went on** Corcoran Transcripts, 5/29/48.

256 **"The men and women who"** "Remarks of Mr. Justice William O. Douglas at the grave of Franklin D. Roosevelt," Hyde Park, N.Y., 5/30/48, and "Address of Mr. Justice William O. Douglas at the unveiling of the plaque in memory of the late Franklin D. Roosevelt," Hyde Park, N.Y., 5/30/48, FDRL; see also "Douglas Bids U.S. Put an End to Fear," *The New York Times*, 5/31/48, p. 3.

256 **Taking this as a sign** Ickes Diary, 5/29/48.

256 **Through Mildred Douglas** AI, Millie Douglas Read, 8/20/89, Lostine, Oreg.

256 **Calling up an old friend** "Douglas Asks Boom for Him Be Dropped," *The New York Times*, 6/6/48, p. 1.

256   **Later, when a group** Robert Bendiner, "Politics and People," *The Nation,* 6/12/48.

256   **On July 9** James A. Hagerty, "Eisenhower Boom Ended as He Issues a Final Rejection," *The New York Times,* 7/10/48, p. 1.

256   **Upon hearing that** "Douglas Declares He Isn't a Candidate," ibid.

256   **By July, Harry** AI, Clark Clifford, 8/27/89, Washington, D.C.

257   **Assistant Secretary of the Treasury** Ickes Diary, 7/5/48.

257   **"Hannegan was all over me"** AI, Eliot Janeway, 8/14/90, New York.

258   **"How do you think"** Ibid.

258   **Maybe Douglas could** AI, Clark Clifford, 8/27/89, Washington, D.C., and interview of Clark Clifford, 3/16/88, Lowe Videos.

258   **Getting in touch** AI, Millie Douglas Read, 8/20/89, Lostine, Oreg.

259   **When Clifford finally mastered** AI, Clark Clifford, 8/27/89, Washington, D.C.; AI, Millie Douglas Read, 8/20/89, Lostine, Oreg.

259   **Despite Douglas's casual air** Ibid.

259   **As soon as Tommy Corcoran** Corcoran, "Rendezvous with Destiny," p. 22; on the trip, the guest book at the Double K ranch, Goose Prairie, Wash., shows that it occurred in June 1948; confirmed also by AI, Isabelle Lynn and Kay Kershaw, 8/6–8/23/89, Goose Prairie, Wash.

259   **"Don't be a number two"** A bitter Truman later attributed this comment to others, failing to tell them that he had learned of it from the transcripts of J. Edgar Hoover's illegal wiretaps on Tommy Corcoran's office. Robert H. Ferrell, *Off the Record: The Private Papers of Harry S Truman* (Columbia, Mo.: University of Missouri Press, 1997), pp. 141–42.

260   **Now caught between** Murphey, "Yakima Never Sure about Douglas," p. 6.

260   **"I just can't do it,"** AI, Clark Clifford, 8/27/89, Washington, D.C.; and interview with Clark Clifford, 3/16/88, Lowe Videos.

260   **The truth was that he** AI, Joseph L. Rauh, Jr., 8/29/89, Washington, D.C.

260   **"I am not a candidate"** "Douglas Declares He Isn't a Candidate," *The New York Times,* 7/10/48, p. 1.

260   **Tan paper fans** Item in author's collection.

260   **"I think the only thing"** AI, Joseph L. Rauh, Jr., 8/29/89, Washington, D.C.

261   **Meanwhile, back at** Truman, *Memoirs,* vol. 2, pp. 189–91.

261   **"I'm doing what FDR did"** Robert J. Donovan, *Conflict and Crisis: The Presidency of Harry S Truman, 1945–1948* (Columbia: University of Missouri Press, 1977), p. 405.

261   **"The president asked Dad"** AI, Millie Douglas Read, 8/20/89, Lostine, Oreg., and interview of Millie Douglas Read, 4/16/88, Lowe Videos.

261   **"Dad had to have"** AI, Millie Douglas Read, 8/20/89, Lostine, Oreg.

262   **"they were waiting for us"** Ibid.

262   **"You know, in those days"** Ibid.

262   **"I think he felt if"** Ibid.

262   **"I would like to"** Truman, *Memoirs,* vol. 2, p. 190.

262   **Tommy Corcoran urged** Ickes Diary, 7/16/48.

262   **When the two men** Ibid., p. 14.

263   **But no career** AI, Eliot Janeway, 8/14/90, New York.

263   **Kennedy's answer** Ickes Diary, 7/16/48.

263   **Joe Rauh and Leon Henderson** Ibid.

263   **"I am very sorry, but"** Truman, *Memoirs,* vol. 2, p. 190.

264   **"Four years ago,"** W. H. Lawrence, "Douglas Refuses 2d Place on Ticket," *The New York Times,* 7/13/48, p. 4.

264   **"I stuck my neck"** McCullough, *Truman,* p. 637, citing Eben A. Ayers Diary, 7/13/48.

264   **"[Douglas] belongs to that"** Donovan, *Conflict and Crisis,* p. 405; Margaret Truman, *Harry S Truman,* p. 8; and Roy Jenkins, *Truman* (New York: Perennial Library, 1987), p. 128.

264   **By the time he** Harry S Truman Diary, 7/12/48, cited in Ferrell, ed., *Off the Record* pp. 141–42. As upset as Truman was about this result, it did not surprise Harold Ickes at all: "Truman was sore about it. Why he should have been is beyond me. If he had wanted Bill as his running mate, he should have gotten him off of the court two or three years ago, by making such an attractive administrative job for him that Bill could not turn it down. His contribution to Douglas' political career has been to be the instrument by which Bill was euchred out of the nomination for vice-president four years ago." Ickes Diary, 7/16/48.

264   **"stand[ing] shoulder to shoulder"** WOD to Harry S Truman, 7/31/48, President's Secretary's File, Box 95, Truman Library, also partially cited in Simon, *Independent Journey,* pp. 273–74.

264   **"I was very sorry"** Harry S Truman to WOD, 8/9/48, President's Secretary's File, Box 95, Truman Library.

264   **"Unfair and vicious reports"** Truman, *Memoirs,* vol. 2, p. 191.

265   **"And even if he does"** AI, Eliot Janeway, 5/19/90, New York.

CHAPTER 22

266   **"You make your own happiness"** AI, Kay Kershaw, 8/12/89, Goose Prairie, Wash.

266   **With Harry Truman's** Ickes Diary, 11/6/48, p. 9.

266   **So, in the course** Ibid., pp. 5–6.

267   *Terminiello v. Chicago* 337 U.S. 1 (1949).

267   **After Douglas's announcement** See memorandum, "Question No. 115," *Terminiello v. Chicago,* n.d., WODP, Box 186.

267   **However, when he realized** Douglas Conversations, cassette no. 18, 12/10/63, p. 378. Douglas explained that he had switched because "the opinion was assigned to me to write, perhaps because I had expressed some doubts. The reason that I voted to affirm and then changed my mind was . . . on the question of whether the question was . . . properly presented and at the conference I didn't see how we could reach it. When I studied the case, I concluded that we could for the reasons stated in the opinion."

268   **As Douglas argued** *Terminiello v. Chicago,* pp. 4, 5.

268   **"as construed by the trial"** Ibid., p. 5.

268   **In a long and bitter** Ibid., p. 23.

268 **"This Court has gone"** Ibid., p. 37.

269 **After several years of increasing** AI, Millie Douglas Read, 8/20/89, Lostine, Oreg. The name of this woman has been withheld for privacy reasons.

269 **"She was the most beautiful"** AI, Isabelle Lynn and Kay Kershaw 8/6/89, 8/7/89, and 8/9/89, Goose Prairie, Wash.

269 **Goose Prairie had experienced** Ibid.

269 **Kershaw was a special breed** AI, Ed Kershaw (Kay Kershaw's nephew), 6/7/90, Yakima, Wash.

269 **Kershaw and Kane** AI, Kay Kershaw, 8/11/89.

270 **On June 19, 1948** Ibid., 8/12/89.

270 **The Double K was** AI, Kay Kershaw and Isabelle Lynn, 8/6–8/23/89, Goose Prairie, Wash.; my account of life at the Double K is based on interviews conducted over a two-week stay at the ranch. My thanks to Kershaw and Lynn for their unique contributions to this book.

270 **"We never knew"** AI, Millie Douglas Read, 8/20/89, Lostine, Oreg.

270 **"Bill was the biggest"** AI, Isabelle Lynn, 8/6/89, Goose Prairie, Wash.

270 **"Bill came here when"** AI, Kay Kershaw, 8/10/89, Goose Prairie, Wash.

271 **"Douglas would just see"** Ibid., 8/6/89.

271 **"I was always"** Ibid., 8/12/89.

271 **By now, he had become** AI, Isabelle Lynn, 8/15/89, Goose Prairie, Wash.

271 **Heartbroken over this** AI, Clark Clifford, 8/27/89, Washington, D.C.; confirmed by AI, Mary Weiler (Clifford's secretary), 3/26/91, Saint Louis (phone).

271 **Usually Kay Kershaw** AI, Kay Kershaw, 8/21/89, Goose Prairie, Wash.

272 **"He was a terrible rider,"** Ibid., 8/6/89.

272 **"the truth was that he"** AI, Millie Douglas Read, 8/20/89, Lostine, Oreg.

272 **So when Douglas** AI, Kay Kershaw, 8/9/89, Goose Prairie, Wash.

272 **It took three days** This account is drawn from the *Yakima Daily Republic*, 10/3–10/5/49, on microfilm in the Yakima Public Library. Because of its contemporaneous nature, it contains the best and most comprehensive account of the accident. See "Douglas Rallies from Injuries," 10/3/49, p. 1; "Douglas Tells How Horse Fell," 10/5/49, p. 1; "Friends of Justice Send Best Wishes," 10/4/49, p. 1; and "Mrs. Douglas Arrives Here," ibid., all in *Yakima Daily Republic*.

272 **So, at first light** Douglas later falsely claimed that he had ridden Kendall "hundreds of miles in the mountains and found him trustworthy on any terrain" before the accident (see Douglas, *Of Men and Mountains*, p. xiii). In fact, this was the first time that he had ever ridden Elon Gilbert's horse. AI, Cragg Gilbert, 8/17/90, Yakima, Wash. Description of clothing from *Yakima Valley Genealogical Society*, 25, Yakima Valley Genealogical Society Library, Yakima.

272 **Four hours later** AI, Cragg Gilbert, 8/17/90, Yakima, Wash.; AI, Isabelle Lynn, 8/9/89, Goose Prairie, Wash.; and Ira Spring and Harvey Manning, *1000 Hikes in the South Cascades and Olympics* (Seattle: Mountaineers, 1985), passim.

273 **Several hundred yards** Gilbert told newsmen that Kendall was a thorough-

bred stallion. Maybe the animal was spooked by a hornet or maybe "the animal's hot blood may have caused him to rear and fall backward [on him]." "Douglas Rallies from Injuries," *Yakima Daily Republic,* 10/3/49, p. 2.

273 **Fearing that his mount** "Douglas Tells How Horse Fell," *Yakima Daily Republic,* 10/5/49, p. 1. Douglas writes in *Of Men and Mountains,* p. xiii (based on a letter he wrote Fred Rodell on 10/22/49, Fred Rodell Papers), that the horse rolled over him only once, when he was hung up on the main trail, which he then fell off. The account here is based on the much more reliable contemporaneous interview. This account, which is even more incredible, was confirmed by the author walking the scene, which showed that if the horse had gone off the main trail it would surely have been killed instantly in the 100- to 150-foot straight drop to the road below.

273 **But the crisis was not** Douglas's account of this accident in *Of Men and Mountains,* p. xii–xiv, is a much less elaborate version of the story. However, his more immediate accounts in the newspaper and in letters to friends are more reliable accounts.

273 **"He rolled over me"** Fred Rodell, "As Justice Bill Douglas Completes His First Thirty Years on the Court," *UCLA Law Review* 16 (1969): p. 281; the source of Rodell's story is clearly WOD's letter to him, 10/22/49, Fred Rodell Papers: p. 704; Cited also in Simon, *Independent Journey.*

274 **Gilbert put his** Elon Gilbert later told the wire services, "I first feared his back was broken" (copy of wire-service tape, 10/2/49, Clark Clifford private papers).

274 **Remembering that McGuffie** The names of participants come from two letters: Elon Gilbert to WOD, 11/23/49 and 1/10/50, WODP, Box 1769.

276 **"Who are you?"** "Douglas Rallies from Injuries," *Yakima Daily Republic,* 10/3/49, p. 1.

276 **Moments later, the interview** Ibid.

276 **"A prayerful"** Ibid.

276 **As they drove along** AI, Irene Hamilton, 5/16/90, Washington, D.C.

276 **When the dire news** AI, James Marsh (law clerk to Robert Jackson that term), 8/15/2000, Philadelphia.

277 **This was somehow a better** "Mrs. Douglas Arrives Here," *Yakima Daily Republic,* 10/4/49, p. 1.

277 **In time, when he became** Douglas speech to the Yakima Chamber of Commerce, 4/12/50, WODY; see also Douglas, *Of Men and Mountains,* p. xii; AI, Kay Kershaw, 8/12/89, Goose Prairie, Wash.

277 **"I want you to know"** "Friends of Justice Send Best Wishes" and "Mrs. Douglas Arrives Here," *Yakima Daily Republic,* 10/4/49, p. 1.

277 **"I regret that [a] mere"** Ibid.

277 **"When you have fourteen"** It would be weeks before doctors could detect the actual count on the X rays. "Douglas Ribs His Luck: 14th Broken, Jinx at End," *The New York Times,* 10/11/49, p. 17.

277 DOUGLAS RALLIES *Yakima Daily Republic,* 10/3/49, p. 1.

277 **In the end, his doctors** WOD to Fred Rodell, 10/22/49, Fred Rodell Papers.

278 **"Suddenly the horse reared"** Rodell, "Douglas Completes First Thirty Years," cited in Simon, *Independent Journey,* p. 281.

278   **"Douglas rode on Elie's"** AI, Millie Douglas Read, 8/20/89, Lostine, Oreg., and AI, Isabelle Lynn and Kay Kershaw, 8/6/89, Goose Prairie, Wash. Others saw different reasons for Douglas's behavior here. Some believe that Douglas wanted to still prove that he was a vibrant, young man by taking risks (AI, Dagmar Hamilton, 5/16/90, Austin, Tex., and AI, Isabelle Lynn, 8/6/89, Goose Prairie, Wash.). Walter Lowe detected, based on his interviews, the risk-taking, almost suicidal tendency of a middle-aged man engaging in such behavior. AI, Walter Lowe, 4/27/89, Seattle (phone).

278   **But since he did** "Justice William Douglas on the Mend," *The New York Times,* 11/5/49, p. 5; "Justice Douglas Shows Progress," *Yakima Daily Republic,* 10/6/49, p. 1, *Yakima Herald-Republic* Archives, Yakima, Wash.

278   **As he lay in** See Simon, *Independent Journey,* pp 282–83.

278   **In mid-November** *The New York Times,* 11/15/49.

278   **Thinking that his** WOD to Clark Clifford, 11/26/49, Clark Clifford private papers.

278   **Tommy Corcoran found** Thomas Corcoran to WOD, 11/7/49, WODP, Box 1769.

278   **But when he arrived** Edith Allen (WOD's secretary) to Martha Douglas Bost, 12/5/49, WODP, Box 238; and Arthur Douglas to WOD, 12/5/49, WODP, Box 239.

279   **"Again he hemmed and hawed"** Truman Diary, 1/14/52, in Ferrell, *Off the Record,* pp. 232–33; and Truman to WOD, 9/13/51, in ibid., pp. 217–18.

279   **"The bones are mending"** WOD to Hugo Black, 12/23/49, cited in Simon, *Independent Journey,* pp. 283–84.

279   **The truth was that** AI, Simon Rifkind, 8/4/89, New York; AI, Clark Clifford, 8/27/89, Washington, D.C.; and AI, Abe Fortas, 8/7/81, Washington, D.C.; also see Clark Clifford to WOD, 12/5/49, 11/22/49, and WOD to Clark Clifford, 11/26/49, Clifford private papers. See also Murphy, *Fortas,* p. 67.

279   **But the Justice was unwilling** WOD to Clark Clifford, 3/1/50 and 3/14/50, Clifford private papers.

280   **Now he was ready** Year after year, Douglas would implore Teddy Hayes to follow his lead. "Dear Teddy," he wrote to his eighty-two-year-old friend who was vacationing in Arizona in 1972,

> I wish I was there to look at Baboquivari with you. Next to that, I wish that you would climb it. I went up the first time alone without any prior instructions and made it to the top all right. . . . When you get to the top you will thank me for encouraging you to go because it is probably the prettiest view in all of Arizona. . . . You will find there, as I think I told you before, a copper capsule with a screw top which I carried up. In it is a notebook and in the notebook you will find my name and the names of many others. I want you to add your own.

Later Hayes would write: "I only regret that I didn't climb his mountain." Hayes, *With the Gloves Off,* pp. 146–47.

CHAPTER 23

281   **"Autobiographers with"** Erikson, *Young Man Luther,* p. 16.
281   **Having once helped** Douglas, *Go East,* pp. 184–88.
281   **Draper was now** "Pat" to George Draper, 8/5/46, George Draper to WOD, 10/2/43, 5/22/47, 6/25/47, all in WODP, Box 324.
281   **"is quite good enough"** George Draper to WOD, 4/19/46, WODP, Box 324.
281   **"I always told you"** Ibid., 8/10/48; see also ibid., 11/30/48 and 10/2/43.
281   **"Very excited about"** Ibid., undated letter.
281   **Having helped** Francis W. Peabody, George Draper, and A. R. Dochez, *A Clinical Study of Acute Poliomyelitis,* Monograph of the Rockefeller Institute for Medical Research, no. 4, 6/1/12; Draper, *Acute Poliomyelitis;* George Draper, *Infantile Paralysis* (New York: D. Appleton–Century, 1935). For more on the nature of his symptoms and the treatment of Roosevelt's polio, see Kenneth Sydney Davis, *FDR: The Beckoning of Destiny, 1882–1928: A History* (New York: Random House, 1993), pp. 647–710. And see Ward, *A First-Class Temperament,* pp. 576–648. Dissatisfied with the diagnosis from their family physician and the exorbitant bill that came with it, Eleanor Roosevelt called in Dr. Robert W. Lovett, the nation's leading authority on poliomyelitis at the time, for a consultation. A short time later, Roosevelt was moved to Presbyterian Hospital in New York and placed under the care of Lovett's protégé, George Draper. Davis, *FDR,* pp. 658–60; and Ward, *First-Class Temperament,* pp. 576–99. Also see, more generally, Hugh Gallagher, *FDR's Splendid Deception: The Moving Story of Roosevelt's Massive Disability, and the Intense Efforts to Conceal It from the Public* (Arlington, Va.: Vandamere Press, 1999); and Kathryn Black, *In the Shadow of Polio: A Personal and Social History* (Reading, Mass.: Addison-Wesley, 1996).
282   **When no publisher** "I am still interested to get the information about the true status of infantile paralysis before the public," Draper wrote Douglas on 4/19/46 (WODP, Box 324). But Douglas was then advising him "to leave that subject alone." See also Valentine Havens to WOD, 12/10/45, WODP, Box 324.
282   **Draper asked Douglas** Draper to WOD, 11/20/46, and WOD to Draper, 11/21/46, both in WODP, Box 324.
282   **The Justice told him** Draper to WOD, 11/28/46, in ibid.
282   **But Young believed** Stanley Young to WOD, 12/11/46; WOD to Draper, 12/13/46; and Draper to WOD, 12/23/46; all in WODP, Box 324.
282   **Now in reviewing** Draper to WOD, 11/30/48, ibid.; see also Draper to WOD, 7/8/49, WODP, Box 1032. Copies of book drafts are in WODP, Boxes 1038–39.
282   **To fill out** The view of the literary merits of Thompson's work differed. Douglas writes of his ancestor: "He worked hard for his education, and his biographer has described him as an ardent fisherman who wandered through the Vermont mountains taking notes for the books he would write" (*Go East,* pp. 3–4).
            Literary experts, however, agreed that the chronicler of early Vermont

and the so-called Green Mountain Boys "never, indeed, had much reputation as a writer, being much better known in Montpelier as the town eccentric, the rawboned slovenly man who shuffled downtown in carpet slippers and went fishing with the children." See Stanley Kunitz, *American Authors, 1600–1900: A Biographical Dictionary of American Literature* (New York: H. W. Wilson, 1960), p. 742.

For an explanation of what Douglas did in his own book, see below.

282 **When Douglas sent** Douglas had also sent copies of the early draft chapters to his brother to review, but Arthur was too involved with business and other matters to give it a comprehensive reading. WOD to Arthur [Douglas], 5/17/48, and Arthur [Douglas] to WOD 6/2/48, both in WODP, Box 1041.

282 **The book was too long** Stanley Young to WOD, 6/1/48, WODP, Box 1037.

282 **"There was a driving force"** Douglas, *Of Men and Mountains*, p. 30; compare with draft revised 10/23/48, WODP, Box 1034. This draft of chapter 4 became chapter 3 of the finished book.

283 **"I had it when I"** Ibid., pp. 31–32.

283 **Had readers and reviewers** See the account in chapter 1, above.

284 **The stunning polio tale** See the back cover of Douglas, *Of Men and Mountains.*

284 **With one bold stroke** "William O. Douglas," *Current Biography, 1950,* pp. 125–28.

285 **In doing so** Douglas's tax records reveal that he had gotten $5,000 in advance in 1949, another $5,945 in 1950, and $22,022 in 1951. See the tax records in WODP, Boxes 1736 and 1737; on money from Arthur, see WOD to Arthur Douglas, 4/18/50, WODP, Box 1032.

285 **"I am about half way"** Draper to WOD, 4/26/50, WODP, Box 1030. Douglas had inserted in his files a note on a conversation between the two of them in mid-February 1950 on how to deal with the "state of shock" after the nearly fatal horse accident (WOD to E[dith] W[aters], 2/26/50, WODP, Box 324). "You must beware of letting the state of shock which follows such an experience as yours from focusing too intensively on any one part. Some days the muscles will ache & feel weak; some days appetite will be uninteresting; on another humor will sap; and each of these days will be the worst until you come to the spirit day."

285 **Draper, of course,** For more, see chapter 6, above.

285 **However, this new story** As will be outlined below in chapter 37, Douglas provides in *Go East* the crucial link between this episode, his earlier diagnosis by Draper, and his later respinning of the meaning of all of this information by explaining the link between the baked beans and his depiction of his childhood illness.

> I grew up with a phobia about intestinal pains. . . . The story of Milo and my liking for baked beans, my favorite dish to this day, were mysteriously and inextricably interwoven. When my polio fever broke, I craved baked beans. Baked beans became a symbol of my return to a haven of security, which of course was my

Mother. But in my association with Mother, I subtly became Milo, who also had been frail and weak. And the fate of Milo was all too plain [Douglas, *Go East,* p.184].

However, as has already been shown, Draper links the baked beans of his patient "Lawyer Aged 37" to the true nature of this illness, an intestinal colic. While he quite likely draws the same conclusion about Douglas's state of mind, he bases it on a very different understanding of the nature of his patient's early physical illness. See Draper, *Disease and the Man,* p. 156.

285   **What better evidence** Should Draper have set his patient straight on his literary depiction of his childhood illness? Even though Douglas had asked for the doctor's input on an early draft, Draper hadn't seen the later version containing the polio story. His comprehensive letter containing comments on each chapter makes no mention of the polio account (Draper to WOD, 7/8/49, WODP, Box 1032). But even if he had been given the chance to counsel Douglas on this story prior to publication, Draper would have gained nothing in discrediting the Justice. So Draper's silence on that subject was all that Douglas received, as the doctor confined his comments to the overall impact of the story. For more, see George Draper to WOD, 11/30/48, WODP, Box 324.

285   **"Arthur [Douglas] told me"** Robert Mull, interview of Chester Maxey, 9/22/81, Walla Walla.

285   **"Bill had so much interest"** Ibid. Mull noted in his documentary:

In addition to his poverty, Douglas also wrote about a childhood bout with polio and how it, too, set him apart from others. Polio, he wrote, "was a driving force that took me first to the foothills and then to the mountains." The point is, these stories go unsubstantiated and are difficult to separate from the Douglas myth. Many who knew the family well feel that the stories of abject poverty and the polio stories are misconceptions brought on by the media and by Douglas himself. His biographers made a great deal of the legend passing on theories as to how the childhood tragedy shaped the mind of the great libertarian.

285   **Many others close** The new polio tale came as a complete surprise to members of his family, who had heard all of his autobiographical tales. Said Millie Douglas Read, "He never showed any signs of any sort of physical weakness in his leg. I would think that if he did have polio that it wasn't a very severe case. . . . But I think it is just as likely that he didn't have anything and he was covering up the fact that he was a rather skinny young man and he didn't have the physique that maybe his classmates had" (AI, Millie Douglas Read, 8/20/89, Lostine, Oreg.). The skepticism about the story extended to one of Douglas's wives. "Douglas's second wife, Mercedes, told me that he never had polio," Walter Lowe reported. "She said that he was probably just a little anemic. If you think about it, it makes sense. How does a country doctor near Fergus Falls, Minnesota,

at the turn of the century diagnose and treat polio? . . . The story just doesn't add up." AI, Walter Lowe, 4/27/89, Seattle (phone).

285   **bear them out** The question remains: Could William O. Douglas in fact have had polio as a youngster? While no early public-health records, which might confirm or deny the story, are extant on this question from either Maine, Minnesota, or Yakima, Washington, the answer lies in a comparison of Douglas's autobiographical tales, the contemporaneous newspaper accounts of the crisis, George Draper's own writing on the illness and his treatment of Douglas, and the recollections of the only living witness of that incident who was old enough at the time to remember it clearly, Douglas's sister, Martha. First, there is the matter of the timing of the disease. Draper wrote in his seminal 1917 volume on infantile paralysis, "Until 1907 this country had felt but little the terror aroused by visitations of acute epidemic poliomyelitis." While it is not impossible that the first known case of the illness occurred in a farmhouse in Maine, Minnesota, in 1900, misdiagnosed by a long-forgotten country doctor, Draper's writings raise other doubts about such an occurrence. One of the terrors of the illness, he explained, is its sharply spiking fever that ranges in duration from a few hours to a few days, usually averaging two to three days. The six-week fever that Douglas described does not fit the pathology. This fever, Draper wrote, is followed by the onset of paralysis of the limbs, which may or may not later dissipate. Surely, the local newspaper correspondents from Maine, who dutifully reported every fever, illness, carbuncle, sniffle, and rumor in the area, would have mentioned the onset of any paralysis in the reverend's only son. But on this issue they were completely silent. Not even Martha remembered him being paralyzed but in fact being able to sit up in his father's arms, chewing his fists and crying to be fed, while he was ill.

Then there is the matter of the effect of a polio diagnosis on those around the afflicted patient. Draper wrote that the airborne nature of the polio infection causes a rapid spread of the epidemic, meaning that "isolation of the patient is the essential point from which to start an effective quarantine. The disease would be managed like every other acute contagious infection." This quarantine, he added, should exist for about ten days for not only the affected patient but everyone else in the house. The failure to do this would, at the very least, cause many more around the affected patient to become quite ill with fever and listlessness, even if paralysis did not result. This does not square with the newspaper accounts of the rotating groups of visitors in the Salome Fisk household at the time of Orville's illness, not one of whom became ill in any way. And since this disease occurs not in isolation but in a wavelike epidemic over a widespread area, the fact that not one single case of poliolike paralysis was reported by any of the various newspapers' town correspondents in the entire Otter Tail County region either at, before, or after, the time of Orville Douglas's illness is significant. Instead, all of the talk was of a typhoid epidemic.

If all of these discrepancies were not enough for Draper, Douglas's account of his mother's six-week saltwater massage treatments, done to prevent atrophy of the limbs by increasing blood flow, whether they were limited as he says to his legs or extended to all of his limbs as his sister recalls, would surely have sealed his retroactive diagnosis. As Draper well knew, one of the traumatic parts of the treatment of FDR was that his legs were "so sensitive to touch that even the weight of the bedclothes was often painful to him." "Even the movement of the breezes across his skin caused acute distress," noted FDR scholar Kenneth Davis. Consequently, the pain of those early massages from Louis Howe and Eleanor Roosevelt was so excruciating for Roosevelt, as it would be for any polio patient, that he would groan in agony. Ten days later, the massages had to be stopped or else risk muscular damage in addition to further pain. Later, physicians would learn that the only thing that helped alleviate the pain was a *soaking,* not a massage, in warm saltwater. Could the little boy have been able to withstand a single massage of his polio-afflicted limbs, let alone *six weeks of them for fifteen minutes every two hours,* as the Justice writes? Only if little Orville Douglas was either much more tolerant of pain than FDR or, in fact, did not have polio.

Beyond the evidence cited above, additional support for this argument can be found in the following: AI, State Department of Health, Olympia, Wash.; Department of Public Health, Yakima, Wash.; Centers for Disease Control, Atlanta; Bureau of Vital Records, Olympia, Wash.; National Institutes of Health, Washington, D.C., all 4/4/90 (phone), and Draper, *Acute Poliomyelitis,* p. vii, chap. 2, and p. 85. Also see Martha Douglas Bost to WOD, 2/12/73, WODP, Box 238; Peabody, Draper, and Dochez, *Clinical Study,* p. 115; and Davis, *FDR: The Beckoning of Destiny,* p. 655.

285   **Did anyone remember** Said John Gavin, "Many people here in town do not believe it. He never showed any evidence of the disease—he wasn't lame or lacking in vigor." AI, George M. Martin, 4/4/90, Yakima (phone); AI, Frances Hare, 4/4/90, Yakima (phone); AI, Homer Splawn, 6/5/90, Yakima; and AI, John Gavin, 2/10/92, Yakima (phone).

286   **Helen Williams** AI, Helen Williams, 4/20/89, Yakima. Indeed, in response to Douglas's request, Jack Nelson had written him long letters containing his favorite stories, which were included in the book almost verbatim. See Nelson to WOD, "Hazardous Trips" and "CCC's," 1949, WODP, Box 1032.

286   **But to Bill Douglas** Unlike the other "literary license" efforts, this polio tale raises an intriguing question about the Justice's state of mind when he wrote this first memoir. It is hard to believe that Draper would have published his case study and not apprised Douglas of it. In the unlikely event that Draper did not, it seems equally unlikely that Douglas, a man who prided himself on reading everything, would have missed the work of his own psychiatrist. If so, is it also possible that Douglas could have remembered all of the exotic details of his session with Draper and forgotten the crucial conclusion of this first illness? Could he have remembered it fully but in publishing a contrary version simply forgotten that Draper had published his account years earlier? Or did he publish this tale knowing that at any point it could be challenged by material in the public library?

If so, the fact that this never happened might have simply emboldened Douglas to the point that he felt he could say and do almost anything.

CHAPTER 24

287 **"The smallest worm"** *King Henry VI,* 3.2.2.17.

287 **Bill Douglas was named** "William O. Douglas," *Current Biography, 1950,* p. 128; see also "Named Father of the Year," *Publishers Weekly,* 5/27/50, p. 2297. Interview of Millie Douglas Read, 4/16/88, Lowe Videos.

287 **"My brother and I"** Ibid.

287 **Yakima native Fred Redmon** AI, Del Bice, 6/9/90, Yakima.

287 **"He was a chaser,"** AI, Ken McCormick, 5/25/90 and 6/16/90, New York (phone).

287 **"Douglas's greatest weakness"** Helen Strauss, *A Talent for Luck: An Autobiography* (New York: Random House, 1979), pp. 185–86.

287 **"He worked his way"** AI, Ken McCormick, 5/25/90, New York (phone).

288 **Art Douglas immediately** Arthur Douglas to WOD, 11/25/49, 11/1/49, 12/12/49, 10/10/50; Arthur Douglas to City Bank, 11/1/49; also see untitled note, 10/25/49, and WOD to Arthur Douglas, 10/18/50, all in WODP, Box 239. By October 1950, Douglas had made enough money from *Of Men and Mountains* to repay $1,100 of his debt to Arthur.

288 **"I sure descended fast."** WOD to Clark Clifford, 12/10/49, Clark Clifford private papers.

288 *Torschlusspanik* Many thanks to my dear friend on Penn State's faculty, Bob Harkavy of the political-science department, for suggesting this description of a midlife crisis.

288 **"There was no particular"** Interview with Millie Douglas Read, 4/16/88, Lowe Videos.

288 **"We visited him"** Ibid.; AI, Cragg Gilbert, 8/17/90, Yakima.

289 **When he got** Edith Allen to Grace George, 4/20/50, WODP, Box 239.

289 **But his health was** Anthony Leviero, "Intrepid Douglas Will Take It Easy," *The New York Times,* 6/14/50, p. 32.

289 **Two severe bouts** Douglas Corpron [Yakima doctor] to WOD, 10/3/50, WODP, Box 316.

289 **Still, the trip became** "High Court Opens, Douglas Is Tardy," *The New York Times,* 10/3/50, p. 27.

289 **Mercedes Davidson** Mercedes Davidson to Edith Allen, 3/23/51, and 3/13/50, both in WODP, Box 243.

289 **"It was almost a frightening"** Interview of Mercedes Douglas Eicholz, 5/28/88, Lowe Videos.

290 **"She was a sexy"** AI, Charles Reich, 11/15/89, San Francisco.

290 **"Mercedes is one of"** AI, Robert Hamilton, 6/22/89, Austin, Tex.

290 **After Mercedes had returned** Merci Davidson to WOD, 4/27/51, and WOD to Merci [Davidson], 10/11/51, WODP, Box 243; confirmed by Simon, *Independent Journey,* p. 286. Helen Gahagan Douglas had also been defeated for reelection in November 1950.

290 **"[Douglas] had a ploy"** Interview of Mercedes Douglas Eicholz, 5/28/88, Lowe Videos.

290   **"It was like walking"** Merci Douglas to Millie Read, 2/4/63, quoted in Simon, *Independent Journey,* p. 374.

290   **By late summer 1951** AI, Millie Douglas Read, 8/20/89, Lostine, Oreg.

290   **As soon as she arrived** Tommy Corcoran description in *Mildred Douglas v. William O. Douglas* divorce proceedings; Tommy Corcoran to Blaine Hallock, 5/6/53, WODP, Box 241; AI, Millie Douglas Read, 8/20/89, Lostine, Oreg.; and WOD to Clark Clifford, 8/29/51, Clark Clifford private papers.

290   **The Justice imagined** WOD to Clark Clifford, 8/29/51, Clark Clifford private papers.

291   **"You don't have to"** AI, Tommy Corcoran, 9/29/77, Washington, D.C.

291   **"I told Bill that"** Simon, *Independent Journey,* p. 286.

291   **Hoping to contain** AI, Eliot Janeway, 5/19/90, Washington, D.C.

291   **When her husband's decision** AI, Millie Douglas Read, 8/20/89, Lostine, Oreg.

291   **"You are the only man"** Mildred Douglas to WOD, n.d. [ca. 1952], WODP, Box 241.

291   **Unable to wait** AI, Charles Reich, 11/15/89, San Francisco.

291   **One of his love letters** Bill Hutchinson to WOD, 3/8/52, WODP, Box 241.

291   **"I hope it is possible"** Mildred Douglas to WOD, 3/8/52, cited in Simon, *Independent Journey,* p. 287.

292   **A headline appeared** Copy of clipping, 4/11/52, in WODP, Box 241.

292   **"Supreme Court Justice"** Ibid. When a similar article appeared on 4/21/52 in *Newsweek,* the nation knew of Douglas's plan.

292   **"I think many people"** Interview of Millie Douglas Read, 4/16/88, Lowe Videos.

292   **"My father was very"** AI, Millie Douglas Read, 8/20/89, Lostine, Oreg.

292   **Douglas even claimed** Ibid.

292   **Douglas was so anxious** Ibid., and AI, Clark Clifford, 8/27/89, Washington, D.C.

292   **"When my father decided"** AI, Millie Douglas Read, 8/20/89, Lostine, Oreg.

292   **Operating from both** Mildred [Douglas] to Blaine Hallock, 4/8/53, and Moe Tonkon to WOD, 6/11/[53], both in WODP, Box 241; and Clifford to WOD, 8/3/53, Clark Clifford private papers.

293   **"Mr. Corcoran cared"** AI, Millie Douglas Read, 8/20/89, Lostine, Oreg.

293   **"For [Tommy], there were"** AI, Eliot Janeway, 5/19/90, New York.

293   **Early on, Tommy** Mildred Douglas to WOD, n.d. [ca. 1952], WODP, Box 241.

293   **Then there was the matter** Tommy Corcoran to Blaine Hallock, 5/6/53, WODP, Box 241, confirmed by WOD income-tax accounts for 1957 and 1958, WODP, Boxes 1739 and 1740.

294   **Douglas reserved to himself** So Douglas took out the mortgage through May 1955 (WOD to Art Douglas, 2/5/55, WODP, Box 239). "Mildred R. Douglas hereby grants, conveys transfers and bargains and sells to William O. Douglas any right, title, or interest which she may have in any property of William O. Douglas not otherwise provided for in this agreement." Corcoran wrote the agreement in the arcane language of the law,

but he had done his job well, for there was no other "property . . . not otherwise provided for in this agreement"—she had it all. "Agreement Relating to Support and Maintenance and Property Settlement," 6/2/53, WODP, Box 241; copy also in Clark Clifford Legal Files, Douglas Divorce, Clark Clifford private papers.

294 **Since Mildred had no other** Ibid.

294 **It was in the next provision** Mildred Douglas to Thomas Corcoran, 6/3/53, WODP, Box 241.

294 **Corcoran's instinct that** WOD to Clark Clifford, 5/6/55, and William Dorsey to WOD, 6/21/55, both in WODP, Box 241.

294 **He had an escalator** According to the divorce agreement, there would be a moratorium on the escalator payments until 1963, except that he would have to pay the amounts due for income over sixty thousand dollars immediately. WODP, Box 241.

294 **Corcoran knew that this** Just as soon as the Justices' salaries increased, Corcoran negotiated a separate escalator agreement that exacted yet another pound of flesh. At Douglas's request, the breaks were adjusted to $35,000–50,000; $50,000–70,000, and $70,000 and up. See Sheldon Cohen to WOD, 4/16/62, and also WOD to Clark Clifford, 5/6/55, both in WODP, Box 241.

295 **"Without you I would"** WOD to Clark Clifford, 2/9/53, Clark Clifford private papers.

295 **Douglas was left** WOD to Merci Douglas, 2/22/63, WODP, Box 243.

295 **By mid-April** Arthur Douglas to WOD, 4/16/53, 1/28/54, and copy of note, 4/13/53, WODP, Box 239. By this time, the relationship with Mercedes had progressed to the point that Arthur was informing her, but not Mildred, of the transaction as well.

295 **Finally, he was free** WOD to Merci Douglas, 2/22/63, WODP, Box 243.

295 **The evidence of** [Congressman] Frank W. Boykin to J. Edgar Hoover, 6/23/53, "William O. Douglas" file, no. 94-33476, 1–56, FBI building, Washington, D.C. (hereafter FBI Files).

295 **A short time later** L. V. Boardman to A. H. Belmont, 6/1/54, FBI Files, vol. 2.

295 **Seeking to avoid** Mildred Douglas to Blaine Hallock, n.d. [ca. 1953], WODP, Box 241.

295 **In yet another** According to the plea, "The defendant left plaintiff abandoned and alone while engaging in his work and in travels to remote places in the world, leaving plaintiff to become bereft of the comfort and companionship of a husband." Portland *Journal*, 7/21/53, WODP, Box 241, and see WOD to Clark Clifford, 7/25/53, Clark Clifford private papers.

295 **After thirty years** *Washington Times Herald*, 7/21/53, and see Douglas divorce decree, Clark Clifford private papers.

296 **By mid-1954** WOD to Merci Douglas, 5/1/54 and 10/26/54, and WOD to Lillian Young, 6/19/54, all in WODP, Box 243.

296 **"For a long time, Mercedes"** AI, Charles Reich, 11/15/89, San Francisco.

296 **"I was invited"** Ibid.

296 **"I found out that Mike"** Ibid.

296 **The announcement of** AI, Irene Hamilton, 5/16/90, Washington, D.C.

297   **When these efforts** WOD to Arthur Douglas, 6/17/54, WODP, Box 239.

297   **Then Arthur himself bought** Arthur Douglas to Merci Davidson, 8/19/54,
       and Arthur Douglas to WOD, 8/20/54, WODP, Box 239. "Of course you
       have made a nice profit on the stock that you bought," Arthur wrote his
       brother, who was then traveling in Australia (see also WOD's income-tax
       forms, 1955, WODP, Box 1738). Even then, Douglas had held on to his
       Statler stocks too long and had to dump them on a flooded market at a
       much lower profit. He would have made ten thousand dollars if he had
       sold them immediately. WOD to Arthur Douglas, 1/29/55 and 2/5/55,
       WODP, Box 239.

297   **He had already turned** Florence Smith to WOD, 5/24/54, WODP, Box 372.

297   **Douglas sought to avoid** WOD to Clark Clifford, 6/19/54, 8/13/54,
       5/26/58, 4/2/58, and 9/26/57, and Florence Smith to WOD, 6/18/54, all in
       Clark Clifford private papers. For more on the nature of Clifford's rela-
       tionship to Douglas, well documented even without access to Clifford's
       revealing personal and legal-office papers, and his eventual appearances
       before the Supreme Court, see Douglas Frantz and David McKean, *Friends
       in High Places: The Rise and Fall of Clark Clifford* (Boston: Little, Brown,
       1995), pp. 3–8 and passim.

297   **"I cannot put"** WOD to Clark Clifford, 6/17/54, WODP, Box 54, also
       quoted in Frantz and McKean, *Friends in High Places,* p. 5

297   **But since Clifford** By early 1956, though, the money coming from his pub-
       lishing endeavors made it possible for Douglas to repay five thousand
       dollars of that loan, adding more payments later on. WOD to William H.
       Dorsey, Jr., 1/16/56, WODP, Box 372. See also WOD to William H. Dorsey,
       9/25/56, in ibid. See also Frantz and McKean, *Friends in High Places,* pp. 3–8.

298   **He tried to cancel** WOD, income-tax forms, 1956, WODP, Box 1739.

298   **But the Justice would not** WOD to Arthur Douglas, 3/4/55, WODP, Box 239.

298   **But he never got** Robert Mull, interview of Chester Maxey 9/22/81, Walla
       Walla; and see Arthur Douglas to WOD, 4/5/[55]; Martha Douglas Bost
       to WOD, n.d. [ca. March 1956], coincident with Arthur's death; Al La-
       porte to Martha Douglas Bost, 5/24/55; and Martha Douglas Bost to
       WOD, 8/30/54, all in WODP, Box 238.

298   **Distraught at the thought** Martha Douglas Bost to WOD, 3/27/56, WODP,
       Box 238.

298   **When he was having** WOD to Clark Clifford, 9/26/57 and 4/2/58, WODP,
       Box 372.

298   **Douglas failed to tell** On the Glenwood property, see WOD's income-tax
       files, 1957, WODP, Box 1739.

298   **While Douglas asked** WOD to Clark Clifford, 9/26/57 and 4/2/58, WODP,
       Box 372.

298   **Once the escalator** WOD to Florence Smith, 6/11/58, in ibid.

298   **It cost him his friendship** AI, Eliot Janeway, 5/19/90, New York.

298   **Douglas's public reputation** WODP, Box 241, Mildred Douglas file.

298   **"Black loved Douglas"** AI, Charles Reich 11/15/89, San Francisco.

299   **"Mother knew that"** AI, Millie Douglas Read, 8/20/89, Lostine, Oreg.

299   **"Taking the cabins"** AI, Dagmar Hamilton, 2/27/90, Austin, Tex.

CHAPTER 25

300 **"Douglas inspires fanatical"** Arthur M. Schlesinger, Jr., "The Supreme Court: 1947," *Fortune*, 1/47, p. 201.

300 **"The bitter, really frightful"** Reminiscences of Marquis Childs, COHC, pp. 81–82.

300 **Frankfurter wrote Harold** Sidney Fine, *Frank Murphy: The Washington Years* (Ann Arbor: University of Michigan Press, 1984), p. 253.

300 **Having already described** Lash, *From the Diaries*, 3/9/48, p. 343.

300 **"the most cynical,"** Murphy, *Brandeis/Frankfurter Connection*, p. 268, and Fine, *Frank Murphy*, pp. 253–54.

300 **The feelings were mutual** Fine, *Frank Murphy*, p. 254.

301 **Douglas had even suggested** Ibid.

301 **When the two men** AI, Fay Aull Deusterman, 3/3/91, Orlando, Fla.

301 **The two men also** WOD to Fred Rodell, 5/14/49, Fred Rodell Papers. See also WOD to Fred Rodell, 5/22/49 and 5/23/49, Fred Rodell papers.

301 **By this time, even** Douglas Conversations, cassette no. 11, 6/9/62, pp. 238–40; and Tom Clark Oral History, Fred Vinson Papers, University of Kentucky, Lexington, Ky., pp. 50–52.

301 **The first of the** *Feiner v. New York*, 340 U.S. 315 (1951), pp. 316–19.

302 **"Rather," the Court** Ibid., p. 320.

302 **"public assemblies"** Ibid., p. 330.

302 **Then he considered** See *Chaplinsky v. New Hampshire*, 315 U.S. 568 (1942).

302 **Here, he argued** *Feiner v. New York*, p. 331.

302 **A week after *Feiner*** Murphy, *Fortas*, pp. 82–85.

303 **Unable to express his views** *Joint Anti-Fascist Refugee Committee v. McGrath*, 341 U.S. 123 (1951).

303 **"one of the gravest"** Ibid., p. 174.

303 **"There is no doubt"** Ibid.

304 **When Douglas examined** Ibid., p. 176.

304 **"The technique is one of"** Ibid., pp. 178–79.

304 **The Smith Act criminalized** *Dennis v. United States*, 341 U.S. 494 (1951), pp. 495–98.

305 **"cannot mean that"** Ibid., p. 509.

305 **"the defendants were not"** See Craig R. Ducat, *Constitutional Interpretation* (Minneapolis: West, 1996), p. 938.

305 **"What I want to know"** AI, Hans Linde, 8/18/90, Salem, Oreg.

305 **As Linde quickly worked** Ibid.

306 **Douglas's attention to detail** See, e.g., G. Edward White, "The Anti-Judge: William O. Douglas and the Ambiguities of Individuality," *University of Virginia Law Review* 74 (1998): 17ff.

306 **"People don't think"** AI, Hans Linde, 8/18/90, Salem, Oreg.

306 **"The freedom to speak"** *Dennis v. United States*, p. 581.

306 **"The present case is not"** Ibid., p. 583.

306 **It was freedom of belief** Ibid., p. 589.

306 **"authority the best"** WOD to Harry S Truman, 8/23/51, President's Secretary's File, Box 118, Truman Library.

306   **As soon as he arrived** "U.S. Should Recognize Red China; 'Fool Statement,' Connally Snorts," *Los Angeles Times,* 9/1/51, p. 2; "Recognize Peiping, Justice Urges U.S.," *The New York Times,* 9/1/51, p. 1; WOD to Harry S Truman, 9/25/51, President's Secretary's File, Box 118, Truman Library; and WOD, "Losing Asia," *Look,* 8/14/51.

307   **"Does that mean recognition"** "Recognize Peiping," *The New York Times,* 9/1/51, p. 1. What was not reported was that Douglas added that the United States had already "recognized many, many governments whose policies and practices we could never approve." WOD to Harry S Truman, 9/25/51, President's Secretary's File, Box 118, Truman Library.

307   **Failing to sense** "U.S. Should Recognize Red China; 'Fool Statement,' Connally Snorts," *Los Angeles Times,* 9/1/51, p. 2.

307   **"A high Administration"** Ibid., p. 1.

307   **"We do not intend"** Ibid., p. 1.

307   **"[He] may have considered"** "Justice Douglas Urges China Recognition," *The Washington Post,* 9/1/51, p. 2.

307   **"a private citizen without"** Ibid.

308   **"I was somewhat embarrassed"** Harry S Truman to WOD, 9/13/51, President's Secretary's File, Box 95, Truman Library, also cited in Ferrell, *Off the Record,* pp. 217–18.

308   **"I hate Communism"** WOD to Harry S Truman, 9/25/51, President's Secretary's File, Box 95, Truman Library.

308   **"nothing to dilute"** Ibid., 10/3/51.

309   **Just after New Year's** *Adler v. Board of Education,* 342 U.S. 485 (1952).

309   **"the school authorities"** Ibid., p. 493.

309   **"the law inevitably turns"** Ibid., pp. 509–10.

309   **"There can be no real"** Ibid., p. 510.

309   **In arguing now** Ibid., p. 511.

309   **A New York City program** *Zorach v. Clauson,* 343 U.S. 306 (1952).

310   **"beyond any question"** *McCollum v. Board of Education,* 333 U.S. 203 (1948), p. 210.

310   **While the religious** Compare with *Everson v. Board of Education of Ewing Tp.,* 330 U.S. 1 (1947).

310   **This time, though** *Zorach v. Clauson.*

310   **"this 'released time' "** Ibid., pp. 308–9.

310   **"we are a religious"** Ibid., pp. 313–14.

310   **"statement that Americans"** Ibid., p. 318.

310   **"My evangelistic brethren"** Ibid., pp. 324–25.

310   **"Today's judgment will be"** Ibid., p. 325.

311   **That same term** *Beauharnais v. Illinois,* 343 U.S. 250 (1952).

311   **"The First Amendment"** Ibid., p. 285.

311   **"Today a white man"** Ibid., p. 286.

311   **"The Framers of the Constitution"** Ibid., p. 287.

311   **"For example, privacy"** Ibid., p. 285.

311   **The first case involved** *Public Utilities Commission v. Pollak,* 343 U.S. 451 (1952).

312   **"substantially limited"** Ibid., p. 464.

312   **Even Hugo Black** Ibid., p. 466. Felix Frankfurter did not participate in the decision.

312   **"This is a case of"** Ibid., p. 467.

312   **"The streetcar audience"** Ibid., pp. 468–69.

312   **Having made this** Dorothy J. Glancy, "Douglas's Right of Privacy: A Response to His Critics," in Stephen L. Wasby, ed. *"He Shall Not Pass This Way Again": The Legacy of Justice William O. Douglas* (Pittsburgh: University of Pittsburgh Press, 1990), pp. 155–79; *On Lee v. United States,* 343 U.S. 747 (1952).

312   *Goldman v. United States* 316 U.S. 129 (1942).

312   *Olmstead v. United States* 277 U.S. 438 (1928).

312   **"I now more fully"** *On Lee v. United States,* pp. 762–65.

313   **Coming as this did** *Zap v. United States,* 328 U.S. 624 (1946).

313   **Having had some time** Robert J. Donovan, *Tumultuous Years: The Presidency of Harry S Truman, 1949–1953* (New York: W. W. Norton, 1982), pp. 386–88. Indeed, he had also, in an extraordinary action, privately received assurances from his good friend Chief Justice Fred Vinson that the action was constitutional.

313   **"Today a kindly President"** *Youngstown Sheet and Tube Co. v. Sawyer,* 343 U.S. 579 (1952), pp. 633–34.

313   **"really surprised me"** Harry S Truman to Roger Tubby, in Donovan, *Tumultuous Years,* p. 389.

313   **"would gladly leave"** WOD to Harry S Truman, 7/1/52, President's Secretary's File, Box 95, Truman Library.

314   **"I am writing a monograph"** Harry S Truman to WOD, 7/9/52, in ibid.

314   **"A little reading of history"** Truman, *Memoirs,* vol. 2, p. 476.

314   **"I think he felt he"** Interview of Mercedes Eicholz, 5/28/88, Lowe Videos.

CHAPTER 26

315   **"[This] stunning decision"** "Espionage: The Last Appeal," *Time,* 6/29/53, p. 8.

315   **The personal hostilities** There is a very extensive body of literature on the highly controversial *Rosenberg* case. This chapter was aided by Ronald Radosh and Joyce Milton, *The Rosenberg File: A Search for the Truth* (New York: Holt, Rinehart, and Winston, 1983), and Joseph H. Sharlitt, *Fatal Error: The Miscarriage of Justice That Sealed the Rosenbergs' Fate* (New York: Scribners, 1983).

This chapter concentrates only on Douglas's and the Supreme Court's involvement in this case. It is informed by a very instructive debate: Michael E. Parrish, "Cold War Justice: The Supreme Court and the Rosenbergs," *American Historical Review* 82 (1977): 805–42; response by William Cohen, "Justice Douglas and the *Rosenberg* Case: Setting the Record Straight," *Cornell Law Review* 70 (November–March 1984–1985): 211–52; and Michael E. Parrish, "Justice Douglas and the *Rosenberg* Case: A Rejoinder," *Cornell Law Review* 70 (August 1985): 1048–57.

315   **On October 7, 1952** The first part of this section comes from Frankfurter, Rosenberg Memo, pp. 1–2, discussed in detail in Parrish, "Cold War Justice."

316   **"I charge your conscience,"** Ibid., p. 4.

317   **"I cannot imagine,"** Frankfurter Rosenberg Memo, pp. 5–6.

317   **"I have done further"** Ibid., appendix 4, 5/22/53; Douglas, "Memorandum to the Conference: Re Rosenberg v. United States, Sobell v. United States," 5/22/53, WODP, Box 1144.

317   **"[To grant *certiorari*]"** William Rehnquist to Robert Jackson, n.d., Robert Jackson Papers, Box 6, Manuscripts Division, Library of Congress, Washington, D.C., quoted in Ball and Cooper, *Of Power and Right,* p. 120.

317   **"Don't worry"** Frankfurter Rosenberg Memo, pp. 6–7.

318   **Years later, Douglas** WOD to Michael E. Parrish, 12/13/74, WODP, Box 1070, cited in Ball and Cooper, *Of Power and Right,* p. 120.

318   **"That S.O.B.'s bluff"** Frankfurter Rosenberg Memo, pp. 7–9. Just why Douglas changed his mind at such a late date, having already passed on so many other chances to take this position, and then backed away from having a genuine impact on the appeal, became a matter of considerable debate. Robert Jackson and Felix Frankfurter saw it as being much like the *Zorach* case, with Douglas voting based on what appeared to them to be the political aspects of a case, seeking to improve his own public image. Others more sympathetic to Douglas's patterns of behavior saw this as just another example of him making late reversals of opinions either out of his unpredictable nature or out of the casual nature of his earlier decision-making that he later chose to review. Indeed, both interpretations have merit, for while his sudden reversals indeed dated back to his days on the SEC, Douglas was never oblivious to their political benefits. See Parrish, "Cold War Justice"; Cohen, "Justice Douglas and the *Rosenberg* Case"; and Parrish, "Justice Douglas and the *Rosenberg* Case," passim. See also Frankfurter Rosenberg Memo, passim.

318   **"it was becoming evident"** Frankfurter Rosenberg Memo, p. 9.

319   **Whether Douglas was saying** See Parrish, "Cold War Justice," and Cohen, "Justice Douglas and the *Rosenberg* Case."

319   **In sitting for its final** The following section relies on the Frankfurter Rosenberg Addendum.

319   **When the issue came** Simon, *Independent Journey,* p. 305.

319   **But Douglas voted** Ball and Cooper, *Of Power and Right,* p. 121.

319   **"petition presents substantial"** Douglas, "Memorandum to the Conference," 6/13/53, WODP, Box 1144.

319   **To a puzzled Felix** Frankfurter Rosenberg Memo, passim, esp. p. 9.

319   **After Chief Justice Vinson** Ibid., passim.

320   **"We know that we"** Frankfurter Rosenberg Addendum, p. 2 and passim, and Douglas Conversations, cassette no. 15, 4/5/63, pp. 317–28.

320   **"ran along rather broad"** Frankfurter Rosenberg Addendum, p. 2.

320   **But, he added** Ibid., passim.

320   **"It is to me questionable"** Written, typed, and printed drafts of opinion, "Julius Rosenberg and Ethel Rosenberg, Petitioners, v. The United States

of America: Application for a Stay," 6/16/53, WODP, Box 1144 (printed version) and Box 233 (dated 6/15/53).

321 **"the record makes"** Ibid.

321 **After reviewing** Ibid.

321 **But after all of this** Frankfurter Rosenberg Addendum, passim.

321 **While the two Justices** "Espionage," *Time,* 6/29/53, p. 8.

321 **While District Court** Ibid.

322 **"the offense was committed"** Douglas Conversations, cassette no. 15, 4/5/63, pp. 317–28, and Frankfurter Rosenberg Addendum.

322 **This new position** Robert Jackson, "Memorandum for Mr. Justice Douglas," 6/17/53, WODP, Box 1144.

322 **Since Douglas's law clerk** Douglas Conversations, cassette no. 15, 4/5/63, pp. 317–28.

322 **"this point has never"** *Rosenberg v. United States,* 346 U.S. 273 (6/17/53), p. 318. See also Douglas, "Julius Rosenberg and Ethel Rosenberg," 6/16/53.

323 **"I do not decide"** *Rosenberg v. United States,* pp. 320–21. An official copy of the Supreme Court's stay order for the *Rosenberg* case is in WODP, Box 1144.

323 **Washington was afire** "Espionage," *Time,* 6/29/53, pp. 7–10.

323 **After Vinson and Douglas** Douglas Conversations, cassette no. 15, 4/5/63, pp. 317–28.

323 **"The more that he talked"** Ibid., p. 321.

323 **"What do you think?"** Frankfurter Rosenberg Addendum, p. 6.

324 **"Bill: I think"** Hugo Black to WOD, on back of printed 6/17/53 opinion, WODP, Box 1144.

324 **As soon as Douglas left** AI, Fay Aull Deusterman, 3/3/91, Orlando, Fla.

324 **"instruc[ted] the Justice Department"** Herbert Brownell, *Advising Ike: The Memoirs of Attorney General Herbert Brownell* (Lawrence: University of Kansas Press, 1993), p. 244.

324 **By dusk, Douglas** WOD tells this story in his contemporaneous letter to Fred Rodell, 6/25/53, Fred Rodell Papers; Douglas Conversations, cassette no. 15, 4/5/63, pp. 317–29, esp. pp. 324–25; and Douglas, *Court Years,* p. 81.

324 **"The plan was to"** WOD to Fred Rodell, 6/25/53, Fred Rodell Papers.

324 **That accomplished** The next morning, to the amazement of Penn State University professor Robert Sholten, the man who had cast Douglas's only presidential nomination vote in the 1952 Democratic convention and who was staying in the same hotel, just as he was reading about the *Rosenberg* case during breakfast, whom should he see dashing across the hotel lobby in response to a page but his former candidate. Robert Sholten memoir, copy in author's possession.

324 **As soon as Fred Vinson** Douglas Conversations, cassette no. 15, 4/5/63, pp. 417–28.

325 **"before an audience"** Douglas, *Court Years,* p. 81.

325 **"If you lift the stay"** The account of the arguments before the Court are taken from "Espionage," *Time,* 6/29/53, p. 8.

325 **"Probably a fifth vote"** Douglas, *Court Years,* p. 237, and WOD to Fred Rodell, 6/25/53, Fred Rodell Papers.

325   **"a grandstand play,"** Rauh, "Unabashed Liberal," p. 225.

325   **"A conspiracy was charged"** "Espionage," *Time*, 6/29/53, p. 8.

326   **"Where two penal statutes"** Ibid.

326   **But six of his colleagues** Sam Roberts, *The Brother* (New York: Random House, 2001), p. 20.

326   **"Did the Rosenbergs"** WOD to Fred Rodell, 6/25/53, Fred Rodell Papers.

326   **A special five-man** Washington *Star*, 6/19/53. A copy of the full transcript for House Committee on the Judiciary, *Hearings to Impeach Justice William O. Douglas, H. Res. 290*, 83rd Cong., 1st sess., 6/30/53, can be found in Emanuel Celler Files, Manuscripts Division, Library of Congress, Washington, D.C.

326   **By the time** William D. Rogers to Edith Allen, 6/30/53, containing memo from Rogers to Abe Fortas, "Douglas Impeachment Resolution," 6/30/53, WODP, Box 1144.

326   **"When the motion"** *Rosenberg v. United States*, pp. 310–11.

327   **"No man or woman"** Ibid., pp. 312–13.

327   **Frequently in talks** AI, Charles Reich, 11/15/89, San Francisco.

327   **"The country was out"** Douglas Conversations, cassette no. 15, 4/5/63, p. 327.

327   **"This is the first solid"** Rauh, "Unabashed Liberal," p. 228.

327   **As a result of** Henry J. Abraham, *Justices, Presidents, and Senators: A History of the U.S. Supreme Court Appointments from Washington to Clinton* (Lanham, Md.: Rowman and Littlefield, 1999), pp. 191–92.

CHAPTER 27

328   **"I suspect that [Douglas]"** Hugo L. Black, "William Orville Douglas," *Yale Law Journal* 73 (1964): 915.

328   **"has been convicted"** *Barsky v. Board of Regents*, 347 U.S. 442 (1954).

329   **"It is equally clear"** Ibid., p. 451.

329   **Since that list** See *Joint Anti-Fascist Refugee Committee v. McGrath*, 341 U.S. 123 (1951).

329   **Speaking in dissent** *Barsky v. Board of Regents*, p. 459.

329   **Thus, he argued** Ibid.

329   **"The right to work,"** Ibid., p. 472.

329   **Douglas saw the danger** Ibid., pp. 473–74.

329   **"Bill was a genius"** AI, Charles Reich, 11/15/89, San Francisco.

330   **"Douglas wrote the first"** Ibid.

330   **Douglas sent a letter** WOD, "Potomac Sanctuary," *The Washington Post*, 1/19/54.

331   **"We are pleased"** "We Accept," ibid., 1/21/54.

331   **The plan, according to** Ibid., 3/7/54, p. 3.

332   **While the hike** Ibid.; and "Beef, Oratory Rare at Pre-Canal Hike Banquet," in ibid., 3/20/54, p. 13.

332   **Douglas surveyed** Ibid.

332   **"our eyes were focused"** Aubrey Graves, "More Recreation Spaces Needed for City People," ibid., 5/8/55.

332   **Each time they reached** Merlo Pusey, "Canal Hike," ibid., 3/22/54, quoted

in Jack Durham, "The C & O Canal Hike," *The Living Wilderness* 19, no. 48 (spring 1954): 7–8.

332 **"It is good to renew"** Ibid., p. 18.

333 **By the end** Aubrey Graves, "9 Stalwarts Stick Out Canal Hike," *The Washington Post*, 3/28/54, p. 1.

333 **But for Douglas** Ibid.

334 **"roaring welcome"** Ibid.

334 **"We also believe"** Editorial, ibid., 3/31/54, quoted in Durham, "C & O Canal," p. 24.

334 **"Shortly after 9 P.M."** Graves, "More Recreation Spaces," *The Washington Post*, 5/8/55, p. C1.

334 **Thereafter, each year** Ibid.; Aubrey Graves, "Douglas' Foot-Sloggers Flexing for Reunion Hike," ibid., 4/15/56, p. C7.

335 **"Hey Charlie"** Charles Reich, luncheon address, William O. Douglas Commemorative Symposium, 1939–1989, 4/16/89, Seattle.

335 **"He had to have"** AI, Charles Reich, 11/15/89, San Francisco.

335 **"When he walked"** Charles Reich, luncheon address, William O. Douglas Commemorative Symposium, 1939–1989, 4/16/89, Seattle.

335 **"Almost all that time"** Ibid.

335 **One time a pair** Ibid.

336 **Given the considerable** Strauss, *Talent for Luck*, pp. 188–89.

337 **With the money** Douglas, *Court Years*, p. 306.

337 **"Joe was convinced"** AI, Eliot Janeway, 5/19/90, New York.

337 **"He had big plans"** Douglas, *Court Years*, p. 306.

337 **"Kennedy was rude"** See the KGB files quoted in Aleksandr Fursenko and Timothy Naftali, *"One Hell of a Gamble": Khrushchev, Castro, Kennedy and the Cuban Missile Crisis, 1958–1964*, rev. ed. (London: Pimlico, 1999), p. 115.

337 **"Douglas told me"** AI, Eliot Janeway, 5/19/90, New York.

337 **Kennedy also tried** Fursenko and Naftali, *"One Hell of a Gamble,"* p. 115.

338 **"I told Bobby"** William O. Douglas Oral History, Robert F. Kennedy Oral History Collection, John F. Kennedy Presidential Library, Boston, p. 3 (hereafter Douglas Oral History).

338 **Soviet intelligence reported** Fursenko and Naftali, *"One Hell of a Gamble,"* p. 115.

338 **Still, he boasted** WOD to Clark Clifford, 8/22/[55], Clark Clifford private papers.

338 **The behavior of both** AI, Eliot Janeway, 5/19/90, New York.

338 **"I think Bobby and I"** Douglas Oral History, p. 4.

338 **But Douglas learned** WOD to Clark Clifford, 9/20/55, Clark Clifford private papers.

338 **"Have you seen the new"** Strauss, *Talent for Luck*, p. 189.

339 **When Strauss phoned** Ibid.

339 **Such was the case** *Ullmann v. United States*, 350 U.S. 422 (1955), p. 431.

339 **Relying on a precedent** *Brown v. Walker*, 161 U.S. 591 (1896).

339 **"real and dread uncertainties"** *Ullmann v. United States*, p. 445.

340 **"the privilege of silence"** Ibid.

340   **Having argued that** Ibid., p. 454.

340   **"Finally it is said"** Ibid., p. 455.

340   **"the decisions of yesterday"** WOD, address to the Association of the Bar of the City of New York, 4/12/49, WODY.

340   **"I would rather create"** Douglas, *Court Years*, p. 179, citing ibid.

340   **"I don't follow precedents"** AI, Simon Rifkind, 8/4/89, New York.

340   **the so-called** *Hicklin* **rule** *Regina v. Hicklin* [1868] LR 3 QB 360. See the explanation in C. Herman Pritchett, *Constitutional Civil Liberties* (Englewood Cliffs, N.J.: Prentice-Hall, 1984), p. 87.

340   **"whether to the average"** *Roth v. United States,* 354 U.S. 476 (1957), p. 489.

341   **"utterly without redeeming"** *Memoirs v. Massachusetts,* 383 U.S. 413 (1966), p. 418.

341   **"The test of obscenity"** *Roth v. United States,* p. 509.

341   **"Any test that turns"** Ibid., p. 512.

341   **"gives the State the paralyzing"** *Kingsley Books v. Brown,* 354 U.S. 436 (1957), p. 447.

342   **Convicted California murderer** *Chessman v. Teets,* 354 U.S. 156 (1957).

342   **But Douglas** in *Zap v. United States,* 328 U.S. 624 (1946).

342   **"that in substance"** *Chessman v. Teets,* p. 167.

342   **"it is impossible"** Ibid., pp. 167–68.

342   **"The conclusion is irresistible"** Ibid., p. 168.

342   **"A passport not only"** *Kent v. Dulles,* 357 U.S. 116 (1958), pp. 121–22.

343   **"The right to travel"** Ibid., pp. 125–26.

343   **Justice Harold Burton** *Beilan v. Board of Education,* 357 U.S. 399 (1958).

343   **"no requirement in"** Ibid., p. 406.

343   **"doubt created as to"** *Lerner v. Casey,* 357 U.S. 468 (1958), p. 475.

343   **"the right to believe"** Ibid., pp. 412–13.

344   **"The fitness of a subway"** Ibid., pp. 415–16.

344   **No better example** *Robert Cushman Murphy v. Lloyd Butler,* 4 L. Ed. 2d (1960), pp. 747–50. Rarely, if a Justice feels especially aggrieved by not being able to persuade his colleagues to accept a case, he may file a dissent to the announcement of the denial of the writ of *certiorari.* This is often done in cases where a jurist is angered by the control of the Court by philosophical opponents. It should be no surprise, then, that this practice became more common on the fractious Vinson Court. After more than two decades of Court silence on denied petitions, in 1946 a frustrated Frank Murphy and Wiley Rutledge issued a dissent to a writ of *certiorari* in the war-crimes-trial case of a captured Japanese army commander, *Homma v. Patterson* (327 U.S. 759). It was four years before Douglas, allied with Hugo Black, adopted the same form of protest. When the Court refused to hear the case of *Agoston v. Pennsylvania* in 1950, in which the defendant had not been promptly brought before a magistrate for processing, even the repository of etiquette on the Supreme Court, Felix Frankfurter, was moved to dissent (340 U.S. 844). For Douglas and Black, this case was much like an earlier one from Pennsylvania in which this strategy of dragging one's feet in order to secure a confession was deemed to be a denial of due process. Douglas used his chance here to take a swipe

at the police, arguing that they "may not be allowed to substitute their system of inquisition or protective custody for the safeguards of a hearing before a magistrate. My conviction is that only by consistent application of that principle can we uproot in this country the third-degree methods of the police" (p. 845).

Three years later, Douglas and Black dissented to the denial of a case coming from the *Corona Daily Independent* newspaper in California. The issue was whether the newspaper could avoid paying the city's license tax on businesses, claiming that it would infringe its freedom of the press under the First Amendment. Douglas argued that following their holding in the 1943 *Murdock v. Pennsylvania* case, banning a license tax that infringed on the freedom of religion, he was willing to ban this fee. The Justices, he argued, should not "shut our eyes to the nature of the tax and its destructive influence. The power to impose a license tax on the exercise of these freedoms is indeed as potent as the power of censorship which this Court has repeatedly struck down" *Corona Daily Independent v. Corona,* 346 U.S. 833 (1953).

After remaining silent on such occasions for the next half-dozen years, Douglas began using this technique sparingly over the next seven. Only seven times did he point out what he believed to be errors by his colleagues in their choice of cases to consider. See *Public Service Commission of New York v. Federal Power Commission* and *United Gas Improvement Co. v. Federal Power Commission,* 361 U.S. 195 (1959); *Murphy v. Butler,* 362 U.S. 929 (1960); *Scott v. California,* 364 U.S. 471 (1960); *Southern Ry. Co. v. Jackson,* 375 U.S. 837 (1963); *Ng Kam Fook v. Esperdy,* 375 U.S. 955 (1963); *Beck v. United States,* 375 U.S. 972 (1964); and *Stassen for President Citizens Committee v. Jordan,* 377 U.S. 927 (1964).

344   **While Douglas "express[ed]"** 4 L. Ed. 2d, pp. 749–50.
345   **"the death of the robins"** Ibid.

CHAPTER 28

346   **"I've never wanted"** Sevareid, "Mr. Justice Douglas."
346   **On June 27** WOD to Fred Rodell, 6/27/60, Fred Rodell Papers.
346   **What Douglas carefully** AI, Harry Datcher, 5/5/90, Washington, D.C.; AI, Fay Aull Deusterman, 3/3/91, Orlando, Fla; AI, anonymous, 4/15/89, Seattle.
346   **After finding a quiet** WOD to LBJ, 3/6/64, White House Famous Names File, Box 1, Douglas Folder, Lyndon Baines Johnson Library, Austin, Tex.
347   **"Has [LBJ] ever thought"** Sam Smith to WOD, 4/14/60, Box 3, ibid.
347   **"from a Republican friend"** WOD to LBJ, 4/16/60, ibid.
347   **To which Johnson** LBJ to WOD, 4/25/60, ibid.
347   **After a lifetime** AI, Harry Datcher, 5/5/90, Washington, D.C.; AI, Fay Aull Deusterman, 3/3/91, Orlando, Fla.; AI, anonymous, 4/15/89, Seattle.
347   **"He went to *every*"** AI, anonymous, 4/15/89, Seattle.
347   **This time there were** Ibid., supplemented by AI, Dagmar Hamilton and Lucas A. Powe, 6/20/89, Austin, Tex.
348   **They were headed** This account is based on AI, Isabelle Lynn and Kay Ker-

shaw, 8/16/89, Goose Prairie, Wash.; AI, Cragg Gilbert, 8/17/90, Yakima; AI, Del Bice, 6/9/90, Yakima. Bice recalled how shocked two friends, Walt Lewis and Bob Strauss, were to see the number of liquor bottles Douglas brought with him on a short camping trip to Goat Rocks in the late 1960s.

348 **But as the pack train** AI, Walter Lowe, 4/27/89, Seattle (phone).

350 **"Happy Hour was"** The guest log at the Double K ranch, Goose Prairie, Wash.

350 **"When Bill found"** Mike Murphey, "Yakima Friends Remember 'A Man You Could Count On,'" *Yakima Herald-Republic*, 1/20/80, p. 6. Cragg Gilbert remembers in this article and later accounts that the trip was on the eve of the convention, which would have been July 10, but the Double K guest log shows that in fact the trip took place in late August.

350 **"I think he would"** AI, Fay Aull Deusterman, 3/3/91, Orlando, Fla. For quotations after Aull's Court service, I have used her married name. She was unmarried in her early years of service for Douglas.

351 **"he found an adulation"** Interview with Mercedes Eicholz, 5/28/88, Lowe Videos. For quotations from later years, I have used Eicholz's name from her marriage after the one to Douglas.

351 **"I always got the impression"** AI, Peter Kay Westen, 9/26/90, Ann Arbor, Mich.

351 **Sensing this, Dellinger** AI, Walter Dellinger, 11/1/91, Durham, N.C.

CHAPTER 29

352 **"They were almost snarling"** Nat Hentoff, "Profiles: The Constitutionalist," *The New Yorker*, 3/12/90, p. 58.

352 **"I'm going to be"** AI, Fay Aull Deusterman, 3/3/91, Orlando, Fla.; confirmed by AI, Dagmar Hamilton and Lucas A. Powe, 6/20/89, Austin, Tex.

352 **"Bobby Kennedy liked"** AI, Dagmar Hamilton, 6/20/89, Austin, Tex.

352 **"He was a mushhead"** AI, Lucas A. Powe, 6/23/89, Austin, Tex.

353 **And by this time** Felix Frankfurter to Court, 9/29/60, cited in Urofsky, *Douglas Letters*, p. 89, n. 1.

353 **"I vote against"** WOD to Felix Frankfurter, 10/13/60, in ibid.

353 **"We are not first-year"** WOD to the Conference, 10/23/60, in ibid., p. 90.

353 **"I defend the right"** Ibid.

353 **"The continuous violent"** WOD to Earl Warren, 11/21/60, in ibid.

354 **"We had become"** Douglas Conversations, cassette no. 3, 12/20/61 and 12/27/61, pp. 52–53.

354 **Arthur M. McPhaul** *McPhaul v. United States*, 364 U.S. 372 (1960).

354 **"today's decision marks"** Ibid., p. 383.

354 **While the law** Ibid., p. 387.

355 **"permits conviction without"** Ibid., p. 384.

355 **"Today we take a step"** Ibid., p. 387.

355 **"Can there be"** *Uphaus v. Wyman*, 364 U.S. 388 (1960), pp. 407–8. Douglas is referring here to the Court's earlier protective ruling for the NAACP, *N.A.A.C.P. v. Alabama*, 357 U.S. 449 (1958).

356 **The Court's review** See *McGowan v. Maryland*, 366 U.S. 420 (1961); *Gal-*

lagher v. Crown Kosher Market, 366 U.S. 617 (1961); *Two Guys v. McGinley,* 366 U.S. 582 (1961); and *Braunfeld v. Brown,* 366 U.S. 599 (1961).

356   **Was this practice** *McGowan v. Maryland,* pp. 450, 452.

356   **If Douglas were still** Ibid., p. 563, citing *Zorach v. Clauson,* p. 313. See also the discussion of Douglas's view of the religion area in *Cleveland v. United States,* 329 U.S. 14 (1946) in chap. 20, above.

356   **"The question is not"** *McGowan v. Maryland,* p. 561.

356   **"The First Amendment commands"** Ibid., p. 564.

357   **This was made clear** *Engel v. Vitale,* 370 U.S. 421 (1962).

357   **"whether New York oversteps"** Ibid., p. 439.

357   **Here, Douglas abandoned** *Everson v. Board of Education of Ewing Tp.,* 330 U.S. 1 (1947).

357   **The disallowance** *Engel v. Vitale,* p. 443.

357   **"It is wholly speculative"** *Communist Party v. Subversive Activities Control Board,* 367 U.S. 1 (1961), p. 79.

358   **After conceding the government** Ibid., pp. 172–73.

358   **"My conclusion is that"** Ibid., p. 190.

358   **"our Constitution protects"** Ibid.

358   **While the conservative** *Scales v. United States,* 367 U.S. 203 (1961), p. 223, n. 15.

358   **Writing in dissent** Ibid., p. 263.

359   **For him, Scales's conviction** Ibid., p. 265.

359   **"When belief in an idea"** Ibid., p. 274.

359   **The Court ruled that three** See *Poe v. Ullman, Doe v. Ullman,* and *Buxton v. Ullman,* 367 U.S. 497 (1961).

359   **"What are these people"** *Poe v. Ullman,* p. 513.

359   **"this Connecticut law"** Ibid., pp. 515–16.

360   **"The regulation"** Ibid., pp. 519–20.

360   **"an invasion of the privacy"** Ibid., p. 521.

360   **Even though the majority** For more on the importance of *Poe v. Ullman* in Douglas's career, see Glancy, "Douglas's Right of Privacy," pp. 155–79. Also see David J. Garrow, *Liberty and Sexuality: The Right to Privacy and the Making of* Roe v. Wade (New York: Macmillan, 1994), pp. 168–89.

360   **The pressure of work** Whittaker even, as Douglas had claimed for years, allowed Douglas to write his majority opinion for him, in a tax case in which he had already dissented. Thus, the same Justice wrote both the majority and dissenting opinions in this case (*Meyer v. United States,* 364 U.S. 410 [1960]). AI, Fay Aull Deusterman, 3/3/91, Orlando, Fla., confirming Douglas's account in *Court Years,* pp. 173–74.

360   **The first vacancy** Douglas Conversations, cassette no. 7b, 1/18/62, p. 152.

360   **To the liberal Kennedy's** Abraham, *Justices, Presidents, and Senators,* pp. 276–78.

360   **"The conferences are *not*"** WOD to Felix Frankfurter, 10/19/62, Fred Rodell Papers.

360   **When Frankfurter finally retired** WOD Oral History, and Abraham, *Justices, Presidents, and Senators,* pp. 276–83.

CHAPTER 30

362 **"Douglas knew how"** AI, Harry Datcher, 5/5/90, Washington, D.C.

362 **"I was extremely happy"** Interview with Mercedes Eicholz, 5/28/88, Lowe Videos.

362 **"I always knew"** AI, Harry Datcher, 5/5/90, Washington, D.C.

362 **"If you got to"** Ibid.

363 **"If Douglas saw"** AI, Walter Dellinger, 11/1/91, Durham, N.C.

363 **"They would stand"** AI, Bob Ford, 6/3/90, Goose Prairie, Wash.

363 **"You could tell that"** AI, Cragg Gilbert, 8/17/90, Yakima.

363 **At one point** AI, Harry Datcher, 5/5/90, Washington, D.C.

363 **"Mercedes had a real"** Ibid.

363 **In the middle of** Joan Martin to WOD, 7/14/61, WODP, Box 240.

363 **The attractive** AI, anonymous Allegheny College official, 5/22/90 (phone), confirming a story told by an Allegheny political-science professor to Henry J. Abraham (AI, 5/21/90 [phone]).

364 **Over a hundred miles** AI, Thomas Magner, the Pennsylvania State University Liberal Arts College research dean, 5/20/90, State College, Pa., and AI, anonymous Allegheny College official, 5/22/90 (phone).

364 **Douglas was deeply** AI, anonymous Allegheny College professor, Allegheny College, 5/22/90 (phone).

364 **"[Joan] had drawn a"** AI, Dagmar Hamilton, 2/24/90, Austin, Tex.

364 **"I don't think"** AI, Fay Aull Deusterman, 3/3/91, Orlando, Fla.

364 **"He wasn't the sweetest"** AI, Harry Datcher, 5/5/90, Washington, D.C.

364 **Could they get** Joan Martin to WOD, 10/20/61, and WOD to Joan Martin, 2/10/62, both in WODP, Box 240.

364 **Would she like copies** For more on this and another account of this courtship, see Simon, *Independent Journey*, pp. 370–82.

364 **Would she accept** WOD to Mrs. John H. Martin, 6/11/62, WODP, Box 240.

364 **Would she like a summer** WOD to Joan [Martin], 4/10/62, ibid.

365 **His problems only began** See internal office memorandum, 12/15/55, Clark Clifford Douglas Legal Files, Clark Clifford private papers. The precise support figures were: 1961 and 1963, $10,950; 1962, $15,650; 1964, $16,700; and 1965, $19,150.

365 **In 1961 alone** WOD income-tax records, 1959, 1960, 1961, WODP, Boxes 1740 and 1741.

365 **And he used** Ibid., 1961, 1962, 1963, 1964, 1965, 1966, WODP, Boxes 1741, 1742, and 1743.

365 **After completing** John Weber of Doubleday to Sheldon Cohen, 2/6/63, WODP, Box 243.

365 **"I'm just an ordinary"** AI, Charles Reich, 11/15/89, San Francisco.

365 **In the spring of 1962** AI, Dagmar Hamilton, 2/23–3/2/90, Austin, Tex.

366 **When his lecture** WOD, income-tax records, 1959, 1960, and 1961, WODP, Boxes 1740 and 1741.

366 **The solution was** Peter Grant, " 'America Challenged' Has $3 Million Answer," *Los Angeles Times*, 11/8/64, p. H2; WOD income-tax returns, 1961, 1962, 1963, Boxes 1741 and 1742.

366   **The original plan** Harry S. Ashmore press release, 10/17/66, Earl Warren Papers, Box 352, Manuscript Division, Library of Congress, Washington, D.C. A year later, UN Secretary General Dag Hammarskjöld was selected as the foundation's first prizewinner. After his death in a plane crash, the prize funded a legal-education chair in the Congo.

366   **Parvin had built** See Grant, " 'America Challenged' "; and Ronald J. Ostrow, "Vegas-Linked Fund Pays Justice Douglas," ibid., 10/16/66, pp. 1, 4, copies in Earl Warren Papers, Box 352, Library of Congress. In addition, no one realized that Parvin himself had interests in three Las Vegas casinos.

367   **Unknown to the press** Ibid.

367   **But such niceties** Indeed, it was not clear whether this income for Douglas would be covered by the divorce and support agreement.

367   **In 1963, he took** WOD, income-tax records, 1963, WODP, Box 1742.

367   **the following year** Ibid., 1964, WODP, Boxes 1742 and 1743.

367   **In 1965, more Court** Ibid., 1965, WODP, Box 1743.

367   **Donations in 1966** Ibid., 1966, WODP, Boxes 1743 and 1744.

367   **"I did all of"** AI, Dagmar Hamilton, 2/26/90, Austin, Tex.

367   **"[Joan] never worked"** AI, Fay Aull Deusterman, 3/3/91, Orlando, Fla.

367   **Planning a trip** AI, Dagmar Hamilton, 2/26/90, Austin, Tex.

367   **"He was looking"** AI, Jared Carter, 8/30/90, Ukiah, Calif.

367   **"I think the Court"** AI, Fay Aull Deusterman, 3/3/91, Orlando, Fla.

368   **"He wanted somebody"** AI, Cragg Gilbert, 8/17/90, Yakima.

368   **"Other Justices at the time"** AI, Harry Datcher, 5/16/90, Washington, D.C.

368   **Court personnel watched** Ibid.

368   **That answer first** Ibid.

369   **"[Datcher's] either the dumbest"** Ibid.

369   **"Datch, the Chief"** Ibid.

370   **"She thought Dag"** AI, Robert Hamilton, 6/22/89, Austin, Tex.

370   **No one was very fond** AI, Jared Carter, 8/30/90, Ukiah, Calif.

370   **One day, Douglas** AI, Harry Datcher, 5/16/90, Washington, D.C.

371   **"Shots!" she screamed** AI, anonymous source from WOD's office staff during that period who personally observed the incident.

371   **"I suppose you know"** AI, Dagmar Hamilton, 2/24/90, Austin, Tex.

372   **"It took a long time"** Ibid.

372   **"You know what"** Ibid.

372   **Throughout the entire** Ibid.

372   **"I feel sorry for him"** Mercedes Douglas to Millie Douglas Read, 1/12/63, quoted in Simon, *Independent Journey,* p. 373.

372   **"Douglas could get away"** AI, Charles Reich, 11/15/89, San Francisco.

373   **"Don't worry—I won't"** Ibid., 2/4/63, quoted in Simon, *Independent Journey,* pp. 373–74.

373   **"The fates dealt me"** WOD to Clark Clifford, 3/28/63, Clark Clifford private papers.

373   **"You have been chosen,"** Sheldon Cohen to Joseph L. Rauh, 4/15/63, and copy of WOD–Mercedes Douglas separation agreement, 4/10/63, Clark Clifford private papers.

373   **Between his alimony** WOD to Mercedes Douglas, 2/22/63, WODP, Box 243.

373   **So it was arranged** WOD, income-tax records, 1963, WODP, Box 1743, and separation agreement, 4/10/63, Clark Clifford private papers.

374   **In addition to insisting** Separation agreement, 4/10/63, Clark Clifford private papers. Since Mercedes was already preparing to remarry, this meant only another three thousand dollars. Also see income-tax records, 1963, WODP, Box 1743.

374   **An Abercrombie** AI, Joseph L. Rauh, Jr., 8/29/89, Washington, D.C.; WOD to Ganson Purcell, 6/5/64, WODP, Box 243.

374   **"I remember the horse"** AI, Joseph L. Rauh, Jr., 8/29/89, Washington, D.C.

374   **Hardly willing to let** AI, Clark Clifford, 8/27/89, Washington, D.C.

374   **Five days later** "Justice Douglas, at 64, Marries Upstate New York Woman, 23," *The New York Times,* 8/6/63, and "Justice Douglas's Ex-Wife Wed to Lawyer on Coast," ibid., 8/7/63.

374   **"It was almost as if"** AI, Dagmar Hamilton, 2/26/90, Austin, Tex. "There was a race to the courthouse," added Joseph L. Rauh. AI, Joseph L. Rauh, Jr., 8/29/89, Washington, D.C.

374   **Ironically, the Eicholz** According to a WOD will drafted on 6/13/65, in the Douglas files at Clark Clifford's law office, Douglas still owed Mercedes the twenty thousand dollars. Two years later, Clifford negotiated the release of that obligation. See WOD to Clifford, 7/12/67 and 6/19/67, Clark Clifford private papers.

374   **"I remember taking"** AI, Jared Carter, 8/30/90, Ukiah, Calif.

375   **"You could see"** AI, Fay Aull Deusterman, 3/3/91, Orlando, Fla.

375   **"She was completely"** AI, Cragg Gilbert, 8/17/90, Yakima, Wash. Fay Aull Deusterman recalled that Joan once told her that Douglas had such "buyer's remorse" about the marriage that he actually asked her for a divorce en route to Goose Prairie. AI, Fay Aull Deusterman, 3/3/91, Orlando, Fla.

375   **"I think that she"** AI, Fay Aull Deusterman, 3/3/91, Orlando, Fla.

375   **"He was divorce-broke"** Ibid.; and AI, Harry Datcher, 5/5/90 and 5/16/90, Washington, D.C.

375   **First, Clark Clifford** Goose Prairie plot plan owned by Betty Ford Gallant; AI, Betty Ford Gallant, 8/20/89, Yakima. Also, AI, Del Bice, 6/9/90, Yakima; AI, Bob Ford, 6/3/90, Goose Prairie, Wash.; AI, Dagmar Hamilton, 2/26/90, Austin, Tex. See also Clark Clifford to WOD, 7/21/64; WOD to Clark Clifford, 7/14/65 and 6/21/65; and WOD to Bob Ford, 7/22/64 and 7/27/64, all in Clark Clifford private papers.

375   **To the disgust of** WOD to Mrs. Bruce (Florence) Smith, 4/27/65, 1/14/66, 3/31/66, 11/23/66, 12/2/66, 12/12/66, 4/15/67, 6/8/67, 7/18/67, 11/13/68, 4/8/69, 6/6/69, 12/6/69, 6/6/72, 4/5/73, and 5/29/73; and Mrs. Bruce Smith to WOD, 6/12/67, all in WODP, Box 372.

375   **But that mattered** AI, Doug Williams, 4/19/89, Cliffdell, Wash.; AI, Homer Splawn, 6/5/90, Yakima; AI, Del Bice, 6/9/90, Yakima, Wash.

376   **Now that the house** AI, Dagmar Hamilton, 2/26/90, Austin, Tex.

376   **It was not long** AI, Doug Williams, 4/19/89, Cliffdell, Wash.

376   **"He used 'em"** AI, Bob Ford, 6/3/90, Goose Prairie, Wash.

376   **"[Joan] called me"** AI, Jared Carter, 8/30/90, Ukiah, Calif.

376 **"After one tiff"** Jack Anderson, "Was Wife Whacked?" *The Washington Post,* 12/29/65, *The Washington Post* office morgue files, Washington, D.C.

377 **Later, Mrs. Douglas** Ibid.

377 **"When Bill made up"** AI, Ira Ford, 8/20/89, Goose Prairie, Wash.

CHAPTER 31

378 **"Once speech"** WOD, "The Bill of Rights Is Not Enough," *New York University Law Journal* 38 (April 1963): 242.

378 **Offered the chance** Ibid., p. 207. This speech was, in the words of one longtime Douglas scholar, Phillip J. Cooper, the work of "a man with a developing agenda [with respect to the Bill of Rights] and a growing intensity about the need to complete it." It became "the sounding of an alarm and a call to action." This speech is discussed in great detail in Phillip J. Cooper, "William O. Douglas: 'The Bill of Rights Is Not Enough,' " paper presented at the American Political Science Association meeting, Atlanta, 8/89.

378 **"People long submerged"** Douglas, "Bill of Rights," pp. 207, 209.

378 **Then, referring to** Ibid., p. 210.

378 **"When ideas become"** Ibid.

378 **"It is becoming more"** Ibid., p. 224.

379 **"a renaissance in liberty"** Ibid., p. 242.

379 **"The task of any"** Ibid., p. 240.

379 **The clearest signal** *Douglas v. California,* 372 U.S. 353 (1963); the Court paired this case with *Gideon v. Wainwright* (372 U.S. 335 [1963]), which ruled that states must provide counsel for indigent defendants in serious state felony cases. In *Douglas v. California,* the question became whether counsel must also be provided at the appeals level.

379 **"Here the issue"** *Douglas v. California,* p. 355.

380 **"Where the merits"** Ibid., p. 357.

380 **A year later** See Charles Reich, "The New Property," *Yale Law Journal* 73 (1964): 733ff.

380 **"To permit legislative"** *Gibson v. Florida Legislative Committee,* 372 U.S. 539 (1963), p. 558.

380 **"a Free Society"** Ibid., pp. 562–63.

381 **"In my view, government"** Ibid., p. 565.

381 **For Douglas, only in limiting** Ibid., p. 570.

381 **"One man's privacy"** Ibid., p. 572.

381 **This case involved** *Sherbert v. Verner,* 374 U.S. 398 (1963), p. 404.

382 **"Many people hold"** Ibid., p. 411.

382 **"The harm is the interference"** Ibid., p. 412.

382 **"no question preoccupies"** *Bell v. Maryland,* 378 U.S. 226 (1964), pp. 244–45.

382 **"We deal here with"** Ibid., p. 247.

383 **"There is no specific"** Ibid., p. 254.

383 **"The right of any person"** Ibid., p. 255.

383 **Five members of the Court** *Aptheker v. Secretary of State,* 378 U.S. 500 (1964), p. 505.

383 **"The prohibition against"** Ibid., p. 514.

384   **"Freedom of movement, at home"** Ibid., pp. 519–21.
384   **Still, when the Chief** AI, Fay Aull Deusterman, 3/3/91, Orlando, Fla.
384   **"The association of husband"** WOD draft opinion, *Griswold v. Connecticut*, in Bernard Schwartz, *The Unpublished Opinions of the Warren Court* (New York: Oxford University Press, 1985), p. 233. The discussion of this case was aided by a fine study by Garrow, *Liberty and Sexuality*, pp. 225–55.
385   **"Marriage does not fit"** Ibid., p. 235.
385   **"The prospects of police"** Ibid., p. 236.
385   **Before he circulated** Ibid., p. 237.
385   **"He had an uncanny"** Justice William Brennan, address via teleconference from Supreme Court building, William O. Douglas Commemorative Symposium, 1939–1989, 4/17/89, Seattle.
386   **"It always amazed me"** Ibid.
386   **"[Douglas's] last ten years"** Nat Hentoff, "The Justice Breaks His Silence," *Playboy*, 7/91, p. 122.
386   **"While I agree"** S. Paul Posner to Justice William Brennan, quoted in Garrow, *Liberty and Sexuality*, p. 246.
386   **For him, the absence** Ibid., p. 247.
386   **Brennan liked these** Brennan to WOD, 4/24/65, WODP, Box 1346, *Griswold* file, quoted in ibid.
387   **"specific guarantees"** Draft of WOD opinion circulated to all chambers, 4/28/65, quoted in Schwartz, *Unpublished Opinions of the Warren Court*, p. 238.
387   **In this way** *Griswold v. Connecticut*, 381 U.S. 479 (1965), p. 484.
387   **"a right of privacy older"** Ibid., p. 486.
387   **"The law is every"** Ibid., p. 507.
387   **"I like my privacy"** Ibid., p. 510.
387   **"Connecticut's law as applied"** Ibid., p. 527.
388   **"In the course"** Ibid., pp. 527–28.
388   **So for him, like** Ibid., p. 531.
388   **It was this opinion** Court of Appeals Judge Robert Bork made this clear in his confirmation-hearing testimony before the Senate Judiciary Committee in 1987. See Ethan Bronner, *Battle for Justice: How the Bork Nomination Shook America* (New York: Anchor, 1989).
388   **"The information being sought"** *DeGregory v. Attorney General of New Hampshire*, 383 U.S. 825 (1966), p. 829.
388   **"no showing whatsoever"** Ibid., pp. 829–30.
389   **In *Elfbrandt v. Russell*** See *Scales v. United States*, 367 U.S. 203 (1961) and *Aptheker v. Secretary of State*, 378 U.S. 500 (1964).
389   **"Those who join"** *Elfbrandt v. Russell*, 384 U.S. 11 (1966), pp. 17–18.
389   **"Wealth or fee paying"** *Harper v. Virginia Board of Elections*, 383 U.S. 663 (1966), p. 670.
389   **It bothered Douglas** *Breedlove v. Suttles*, 302 U.S. 277 (1937).
390   **"*Breedlove v. Suttles* sanctioned"** *Harper v. Virginia Board of Elections*, p. 669.
390   **The state has the power** Ibid., p. 666.
390   **"We say the same"** Ibid., p. 668.
390   **"Wealth, like race"** Ibid.

390   **"In *Breedlove v. Suttles*"** Ibid., pp. 670–72.

391   **"Although I join"** Ibid., p. 675.

CHAPTER 32

392   **"We went over"** Elizabeth Black, *Mr. Justice and Mrs. Black: The Memoirs of Hugo L. Black and Elizabeth Black* (New York: Random House, 1986), 10/16/66 entry, p. 152.

392   **No sooner had** AI, Elena Leonardo, 8/21/89, Sunnyside, Wash.

392   **After a while, they** Ibid., and AI, Elena Leonardo, 6/9/90, Seattle, confirmed by Isabelle Lynn to Charlotte Mayerson, 7/3/[n.d.], Random House office files, in author's possession.

392   **Life for him** This led him to send a series of letters to Leonardo in later years, enclosing articles on the problems caused by excessive bathing. AI, Elena Leonardo, 8/21/89, Sunnyside, Wash., and WOD to Elena Leonardo, 9/16/65, Elena Leonardo private papers, Sunnyside, Wash.

393   **By the end of** AI, Elena Leonardo, 8/21/89, Sunnyside, Wash., confirmed by AI, Jerry Cundiff, Jr., 5/31/90, Walla Walla, Wash.

393   **"absolutely wild"** WOD to Elena Leonardo, 9/16/65, Elena Leonardo private papers, Sunnyside, Wash.

393   **The two men generally** Simon, *Independent Journey*, p. 280.

393   **"I think she can"** Carla Hall, "Cathy Douglas—The Woman Beside the Man," *The Washington Post*, 12/9/79, p. K11. There is a disagreement whether Damon Trout or the owner of the restaurant first introduced them. Sandie North, "Justice Douglas' 23-Year-Old Bride Talks About Her Marriage," *Ladies' Home Journal*, November 1966, pp. 92–94, 172–73, and Simon, *Independent Journey*, pp. 380–81.

394   **"I loved her"** North, "Justice Douglas' 23-Year-Old," p. 171.

394   **"One day, four giggling"** AI, Cragg Gilbert, 8/17/90, Yakima.

394   **"Weekends are interminable"** WOD to Elena Leonardo, 10/16/65, in Elena Leonardo private papers, Sunnyside, Wash.

394   **Time and again** Ibid., 10/14/65 and 10/4/65.

394   **Eventually the relationship** AI, Elena Leonardo, 8/21/89, Sunnyside, Wash.

395   **"She just got kind"** Hall, "Cathy Douglas," p. K11.

395   **As carefully as** WOD to Elena Leonardo, 1/28/66, Elena Leonardo private papers, Sunnyside, Wash.

395   **"Cathy was a real"** AI, Cragg Gilbert, 8/17/90, Yakima, Wash.

395   **The temporary separation** Separation agreement, Joan Martin Douglas and WOD, 12/7/65, WODP, Box 24; and divorce decree between WOD and Joan Douglas, 6/24/66, Yakima County Courthouse, Yakima, Wash.

395   **Douglas was hurt** WOD to Elena Leonardo, 2/21/66, Elena Leonardo private papers, Sunnyside, Wash.

395   **"I think he felt"** AI, Elena Leonardo, 8/21/89, Sunnyside, Wash.

396   **Nonetheless, Douglas wanted** WOD, income-tax records, 1966, WODP, Boxes 1743 and 1744.

396   **The only good news** This action caused problems when he remarried and then made no clear provisions for the property in his final will. WOD to Joan Martin, 6/9/66, WODP, Box 240; "Last Will and Testament of Wil-

liam O. Douglas," 2/6/80, microfilm roll 1921182; separation agreement, Joan Martin Douglas and WOD, 12/7/65; and WODP, Box 240, Joan Martin Douglas Divorce File.

396   **Things were so bad** WOD to Clark Clifford, 6/8/66, 7/20/66, 1/18/67, 7/12/67, and 8/12/67, all in Clark Clifford private papers; also see Frantz and McKean, *Friends in High Places,* p. 196.

396   **Thanks to the escalator** WOD to Clark Clifford, 6/4/66, Clark Clifford private papers.

396   **Realizing this** Ibid.

396   **When Corcoran turned** Sheldon Cohen to WOD, 4/16/62; and WOD to Clark Clifford, 3/4/66; "Memorandum for T.G.C.[orcoran]," 6/7/55; Nan Burgess to City Bank, 1/13/60; WOD to Clark Clifford, 5/6/55; and William H. Dorsey to WOD, 6/21/55, all in WODP, Box 241; WOD to Sid Davis, 6/6/66, Clark Clifford private papers.

396   **Just to bury** WOD to Sid Davis, 6/6/66, Clark Clifford private papers.

397   **He had a Ninth Circuit** North, "Justice Douglas' 23-Year-Old," pp. 92–94, 172–73.

397   **"We might get married"** Ibid.

397   **"We hadn't really talked"** Ibid.

397   **"I don't want to marry"** Ibid.

398   **When he and Cathy** AI, John Gavin, 2/10/92, Yakima, Wash. (phone).

398   **Elena Leonardo, who** AI, Elena Leonardo, 8/21/89, Sunnyside, Wash.

399   **"the most wonderful thing"** WOD to Clark Clifford, 7/22/66, Clark Clifford private papers; also, AI, Clark Clifford, 8/27/89, Washington, D.C.

399   **"arrange for Cathy"** Clark Clifford to WOD, 7/25/66, Clark Clifford private papers.

399   **"Bill always liked"** AI, Clark Clifford, 8/27/89, Washington, D.C.

399   **"Bill was always happy"** Simon, *Independent Journey,* p. 374.

399   **He had made** AI, Elena Leonardo, 8/21/89, Sunnyside, Wash.

399   **Then Douglas started** Ibid.

399   **"In the back"** Ibid.

399   **"That's the very thing"** Black, *Mr. Justice and Mrs. Black,* p. 149.

399   **"That was a terrible"** AI, Dagmar Hamilton, 2/25/90, Austin, Tex.

400   **"Sorry Chief,"** Hall, "Cathy Douglas."

400   **The Justice was summarily** Black, *Mr. Justice and Mrs. Black,* 10/3/66 entry, p. 152, and North, "Justice Douglas' 23-Year-Old."

400   **It was a slight** Black, *Mr. Justice and Mrs. Black,* 10/3/66 entry, p. 152.

400   **"My father was certainly"** Interview of William Douglas, Jr., 2/13/88, Lowe Videos.

400   **"By the 1960s Douglas"** AI, John Gavin, 2/10/92, Yakima, Wash. (phone).

400   **On July 18, 1966** AI, Simon Rifkind, 8/4/89, New York.

400   **VEGAS-LINKED FUND** Ronald J. Ostrow, "Vegas-Linked Fund Pays $12,000 to Justice Douglas," *Los Angeles Times,* 10/16/66, pp. 1, 4; copies in Earl Warren Papers, Box 352.

400   **"largely as an expense"** Of course, Douglas said this knowing full well that the reporter could not gain access to his tax returns for 1961, which showed that just the opposite was true (WODP, Box 1741).

400 **While there was no** Ostrow, "Vegas-Linked Fund," pp. 1, 4.

401 **"in a trust fund"** Harry Ashmore press release, 10/17/66, Earl Warren Papers, Box 352.

401 **Douglas sent** WOD to Earl Warren, 10/18/66, ibid.

401 **"the recent regrettable"** Judge William Campbell to Harry Ashmore, 10/20/66, ibid.

401 **The *Los Angeles Times* editorialized** Ostrow, "Vegas-Linked Fund," pp. 1, 4.

401 **"there is a grave"** Senator John J. Williams to Earl Warren, 10/17/66, Earl Warren Papers, Box 352.

401 **"there has been no conflict"** WOD to Earl Warren, 10/31/66, and Harry Ashmore to Earl Warren, 10/24/66, both in Earl Warren Papers, Box 352.

401 **"a matter personal"** Here he chose to strike out language from an earlier draft that distanced him from the dispute by saying that he "had no knowledge of it." Earl Warren to Senator John J. Williams, 10/31/66, and two earlier drafts, Earl Warren Papers, Box 352.

401 **"not sure how much longer"** Ibid., and see Douglas income-tax records, 1967 and 1968, WODP, Boxes 1744 and 1745.

CHAPTER 33

402 **"The Court is really"** Sevareid, "Mr. Justice Douglas."

402 **In the fall of 1966** Research on WOD's Court career was greatly aided by the complete list of his cases and opinions listed in Douglas Impeachment Hearings. In the 1966–1967 term, Douglas wrote twelve majority opinions and twenty dissents; in 1967–1968 he wrote twelve majority opinions and twenty-five dissents; in 1968–1969 he wrote twelve majority opinions and sixteen dissents; and in 1969–1970 he wrote thirteen majority opinions and twenty-four dissents.

402 **As part of a body** More precisely, members of the Court dissent an average of 21 percent of the time, while Douglas dissented 41.8 percent of the time. By way of comparison, Oliver Wendell Holmes and John Marshall Harlan I, both nicknamed "the Great Dissenters," opposed the Court's rulings only 7.5 percent and 13.6 percent of the time, respectively. Over the next four terms, Douglas would dissent eighty-five times, nearly twice as many times as he would write for the majority. On the overall rate of Supreme Court dissents, see Gregory A. Caldeira and Christopher J. W. Zorn, "Of Time and Consensual Norms in the Supreme Court," *American Journal of Political Science* 42, no. 3 (1998): 874–902.

402 **Speaking alone** AI, Fay Aull Deusterman, 3/3/91, Orlando, Fla. This view is confirmed by interviews by the author and others with Douglas's later law clerks.

402 **And the results showed** No other Justice from 1953 to 1991 was within the 128 solo dissents of Douglas. See Lee Epstein, Jeffrey A. Segal, Harold J. Spaeth, and Thomas G. Walker, *The Supreme Court Compendium: Data, Decisions, and Developments,* 2d ed. (Washington, D.C.: Congressional Quarterly, 1996), p. 520.

402 **More than just** Figures for 1953–1991 terms are taken from ibid., pp. 514–20. Douglas spoke alone in 45.2 percent of his dissents. For 1939

to 1952, see the case list in Douglas Impeachment Hearings, and Linda Blandford and Patricia Russell Evans, *Supreme Court of the United States, 1789–1980: An Index to Opinions Arranged by Justice* (Millwood, N.Y.: Kraus International, 1981), pp. 801–51.

402 **But the question** See Walter Reed Army Hospital memo on WOD's medical condition, 7/5/68, WODP, Box 1769.

403 **"Traditionally, state capitol"** *Adderley v. Florida,* 385 U.S. 39 (1966), p. 41, citing *Edwards v. South Carolina,* 372 U.S. 229 (1963).

403 **"The Court errs"** Ibid., p. 49.

403 **"Conventional methods"** Ibid., pp. 50–51.

404 **"by allowing these orderly"** Ibid., p. 56.

404 **"To most, 'every person' "** *Pierson v. Ray,* 386 U.S. 547 (1967), p. 559.

404 **"What about the judge"** Ibid., pp. 566–67.

405 **The 1967–1968 term** *Levy v. Louisiana,* 391 U.S. 68 (1968).

405 **Douglas began his short** Ibid., p. 70.

405 **"Why should the illegitimate"** Ibid., p. 71.

405 **The Louisiana law** Ibid., p. 72.

405 **Douglas had a chance** *Board of Education v. Allen,* 392 U.S. 236 (1968).

406 **"Underlying these cases,"** Ibid., pp. 247–48.

406 **"Whatever may be said"** Ibid., p. 257.

406 **"Can there be"** Ibid., p. 256.

407 **Every staff member was** AI, Fay Aull Deusterman, 3/3/91, Orlando, Fla.

407 **"Mornings were the worst"** AI, Harry Datcher, 5/5/90, Washington, D.C.

407 **Office training was never** AI, Fay Aull Deusterman, 3/3/91, Orlando, Fla.

407 **Douglas's secretaries would watch** Ibid.

407 **"Where was everyone"** Ibid.

407 **On days when they** Ibid.

408 **The worst nights** Ibid.

408 **"He wasn't the sweetest"** AI, Harry Datcher, 5/16/90, Washington, D.C.

408 **"Law clerks are the lowest"** Justice Harry Blackmun, Address at William O. Douglas Commemorative Symposium, 1939–1989, 4/16/89, Seattle.

408 **"It is common knowledge"** From Reminiscences of Richard L. Jacobson, in unpublished Douglas Remembrances, pp. 34–37.

408 **"Ten thousand dollars"** AI, Fay Aull Deusterman, 3/3/91, Orlando, Fla.

408 **For all of these people** George Rutherglen [Douglas law clerk], unpublished Douglas Remembrances, p. 54.

409 **But since they had not** This account was informed by interviews done by the author or Walter Lowe with twenty-six Douglas law clerks, three members of his office staff, and his research/writing assistant. Additional reminiscences from fourteen clerks are drawn from the published and unpublished Douglas Remembrances. See also Melvin I. Urofsky, "Getting the Job Done: William O. Douglas and Collegiality in the Supreme Court," in Wasby, *"He Shall Not Pass,"* pp. 33–51; a version of this article was presented to the William O. Douglas Commemorative Symposium, 1939–1989, 4/16/89, Seattle, and included more information on the law clerks' experience.

409 **Just thirty-two** WOD to Lucas A. Powe, 8/3/70, Lucas A. Powe personal

papers, Austin, Tex. While Powe bases his account on his service during the 1970–1971 term, this treatment was standard. Now an internationally known expert on the First Amendment and on the law faculty of the University of Texas, Powe keeps this first letter from Douglas framed on his office wall as a reminder of his year in Douglas's boot camp.

409 **"What kind of clerks"** AI, Harry Datcher, 5/5/90, Washington, D.C.

409 **Finally, everyone** AI, Lucas A. Powe, 6/22/89, Austin, Tex.

409 **Speed in answering** AI, Fay Aull Deusterman, 3/3/91, Orlando, Fla.

409 **"After that first buzz"** AI, Harry Datcher, 5/5/90, Washington, D.C.

410 **"The buzzer would come"** AI, Lucas A. Powe, 6/22/89, Austin, Tex.

410 **"Find out the name"** Reminiscences of Charles Miller, unpublished Douglas Remembrances, pp. 44–45.

410 **In the days before** This, of course, changed when the list in the Douglas Impeachment Hearings was released. After Douglas had been teased by Justice Tom Clark that he had never upheld a patent, all law clerk Jerome Falk could do was trace the problem volume by volume in Douglas's collected opinions, a process that took weeks. When he could not find the case that the Justice recalled, Douglas simply said, "Perhaps there was a lower court decision upholding a patent and I voted against reviewing it." Reminiscences of Jerome Falk, unpublished Douglas Remembrances, pp. 21–23.

410 **"If you have time"** Reminiscences of Thomas J. Klitgaard, ibid., pp. 41–42.

411 **"Douglas clerks had"** Reminiscences of Charles E. Ares, ibid., pp. 10–11.

411 **In performing their duties** AI, William Reppy, 11/1/91, Durham, N.C.

411 **At one point, Reppy** Ibid.; see also Rauh, "Unabashed Liberal."

412 **"Don't worry,"** AI, Fay Aull Deusterman, 3/3/91, Orlando, Fla. When the opinion was later released, and *The Washington Post* criticized the result, taking special care to attack the argument in this one footnote, Douglas chose not to lord this small victory over his clerk. AI, William Reppy, 11/1/91, Durham, N.C. See also William Reppy, "Justice Douglas and His Brethren: A Personal Recollection," *North Carolina Central Law Review* 12 (1980–1981): 424–25; and Reminiscences of William Reppy, unpublished Douglas Remembrances, pp. 49–50.

412 **"Did you write"** Reminiscences of Jerome Falk, unpublished Douglas Remembrances, pp. 21–23.

413 **For some clerks** This story is based on Reminiscences of Richard Jacobson, in ibid., pp. 34–37.

413 **"My law clerk's"** AI, Harry Datcher, 5/5/90, Washington, D.C.

414 **"He was an enigma,"** AI, Fay Aull Deusterman, 3/3/91, Orlando, Fla.

414 **"He had a hard time"** AI, Cragg Gilbert, 8/17/90, Yakima.

414 **Still others argue** See Urofsky, "Getting the Job Done," passim.

414 **Or perhaps this** AI, Walter Lowe, 4/27/89, Seattle (phone).

415 **"When you left"** AI, Harry Datcher, 5/5/90, Washington, D.C.

415 **The cases dealt** *NAACP v. Overstreet,* 384 U.S. 118 (1966); *Thomas v. United States,* 386 U.S. 975 (1967); *Williams v. Shaffer,* 385 U.S. 1037 (1967); *Sandoval v. California,* 386 U.S. 948 (1967); *Granello v. United States,* 386 U.S. 1019 (1967); and *Mitchell v. United States,* 386 U.S. 972 (1967).

415 **"the larger problem"** *Williams v. Shaffer,* 385 U.S. 1037 (1967).

415   **"The effect is"** Ibid., p. 1038.

415   **One other failed** *Mitchell v. United States,* 386 U.S. 972 (1967).

415   **David Henry Mitchell III** Ibid., 973–74.

416   **Douglas's use of dissents** He would do it ten times the following term, and seven the term thereafter, the closing year of the Warren Court.

416   **Beyond that** This count is from a Lexis-Nexis search of Douglas's opinions. The most famous of these cases was *DeFunis v. Odegaard,* 416 U.S. 312 (1974), in which Douglas commented on the new "affirmative action" programs. For more, see chap. 36, below.

416   **Three times** In ruling this way, the Court overlooked the fact that the actual purpose of the law was to prevent people from protesting in this manner, a motive that was clearly unconstitutional. See Dean Alfange, Jr., "Free Speech and Symbolic Conduct: The Draft-Card Burning Case," *Supreme Court Review 1968,* pp. 1–52.

417   **Here the Court found** *United States v. O'Brien,* 391 U.S. 367 (1968), p. 377.

417   **"The underlying and basic"** Ibid., pp. 389–90.

417   **Albert H. Holmes** *Holmes v. United States,* 20 L. Ed 2d (1968), p. 856; and *Hart v. United States,* 20 L. Ed. 2d (1968), p. 871.

417   **"in the absence"** *Holmes v. United States,* p. 857.

417   **"while some decisions"** Ibid., p. 861.

417   **"There is a weighty"** Ibid., p. 863.

418   **"I think we owe"** Ibid., p. 864.

418   **While his colleagues** On that same day, he also dissented to the denials for *certiorari* in two other Selective Service challenges. Reuben Joel Shiffman (20 L. Ed. 2d [1968], p. 849) and Michel J. Zigmond (20 L. Ed. 2d [1968], p. 851), both twenty-six years old and thus seemingly free from call-up until other, younger registrants had been drafted, were both declared "delinquent" by their local draft boards, reclassified as 1-A, and made subject to immediate draft. Believing that this was punishment because both men had protested by turning in their draft materials to the government, Douglas argued: "I would grant the stays as I am unable to see any place in our constitutional system for Selective Service delinquency regulations employed to penalize or deter exercise of First Amendment rights" (ibid., pp. 851–52). Then, to underscore his point, he added: "The First Amendment means that whatever speech or protest a person makes, he may not, I submit, be taken by the neck by the Government and subjected to punishment, penalties, or inconveniences for making it" (p. 852).

418   **"No one outside"** Douglas, *Court Years,* p. 311; confirmed by AI, Dagmar Hamilton, 2/27/90, Austin, Tex.

418   **When more and more** In dissenting to the denial of *certiorari* handed William S. Johnson, Douglas displayed anger when he learned that these petitioners had already been shipped to Vietnam, meaning that the "hurried calculated change in military plans has deprived petitioners of the full hearing to which they are entitled" (*Johnson v. Powell,* 21 L. Ed. 2d [1968], p. 255). When the government argued that these men were not in the "militia," and thus covered by the Constitution, but were instead members of the Ready Reserves, Douglas was unpersuaded:

That contention might in time prevail, but it is not free of doubt; and I am not yet persuaded that either the Army or the Solicitor General can play loosely with the concept of "militia" as used in the Constitution and thus create a credibility gap at the constitutional level. It is, after all, the Constitution that creates in our people the faith that no one—not even the Department of Justice nor the military—is above the law [ibid.].

At the same time, Douglas dissented to the denial of a stay of deployment for Bradish G. Morse and others, who had been recalled from the Ready Reserve for service in Vietnam despite their contention that their unit had already fulfilled part of its active-service requirement. For Douglas, the question became whether this was the kind of "war" emergency that allowed for a call-up of the reserves: "Where the Secretary [of the Army] purportedly has no power to recall reservists whom he promised to activate only in war or national emergency, we have jurisdiction to prevent him from doing so, at least where Congress has not precluded such jurisdiction." *Morse et al. v. Boswell,* 21 L. Ed. 2d (1968), p. 434.

418   **When the Court chose** *Oestereich v. Selective Service Board No. 11,* 21 L. Ed. 2d (1968), p. 406. This was a position that Douglas had threatened to take in an earlier case: *Clark v. Gabriel,* 21 L. Ed. 2d (1968), p. 418.

418   **"There should not be"** Ibid., p. 406.

419   **"I feel precluded"** *Drifka v. Brainard,* 21 L. Ed. 2d (1968), p. 429.

419   **"a change in the"** Ibid.

419   **"The spectre of executive"** *McArthur v. Clifford,* 21 L. Ed. 2d (1968), p. 467.

CHAPTER 34

420   **In the middle** Stuart Auerbach, "Heart Device Enables Him to Lead Active Life, Justice Douglas Says," *The Washington Post,* 11/4/68, p. A1.

420   **Once they got him** Douglas, *Go East,* pp. 35–36. When they explained to him that the cause of this disease was an earlier virus infection, Douglas immediately seized on his bout with "polio" as the source.

420   **That same day** "A Heart Pacemaker Implanted in Body of Justice Douglas," *The New York Times,* 6/11/68, and Walter Reed General Hospital memo, "To Whom It May Concern," 7/5/68, p. 49, WODP, Box 1769.

421   **One night in the hospital** "To Whom It May Concern," 7/5/68, WODP, Box 1769.

421   **"I do think Dad"** AI, Millie Douglas Read, 8/20/89, Lostine, Oreg.

421   **"He had a black"** AI, Harry Datcher, 5/5/90, Washington, D.C.

421   **Douglas had justifiable** "To Whom It May Concern," 7/5/68, WODP, Box 1769.

421   **He was unable** AI, Doug Williams, 4/19/89, Cliffdell, Wash., and AI, Helen Williams, 4/20/89, Yakima.

422   **Douglas began pleading** WOD to Colonel Robert J. Hall, 7/18/69, WODP, Box 1769.

422   **But this did not** Colonel Robert J. Hall to WOD, 7/23/68, in ibid.

422   **He watched in sadness** Murphy, *Fortas,* pp. 528–30. Douglas complained to Fred Rodell that Fortas "threw off" on him during the hearings.

422   **Finally at 9:30** AI, Walter Dellinger, 11/1/91, Durham, N.C.

423   **One day, after he** AI, Clark Clifford, 8/27/89, Washington, D.C.; and AI, Walter Dellinger, 11/1/91, Durham, N.C.

423   **"What is interesting"** AI, Walter Dellinger, 11/1/91, Durham, N.C.

423   **Black Panther** *Cleaver v. Frank M. Jordan,* 393 U.S. 810 (1968).

424   **Douglas asked Peter** AI, Peter Kay Westen, 9/26/90, Ann Arbor, Mich.

424   *Braaackkk!! Braaackkk!!* Ibid.

424   **But the young law clerk** AI, Peter Kay Westen, 9/26/90, Ann Arbor, Mich. In the end, Thurgood Marshall did deny the appeal, and Cleaver did skip out on the bail.

424   **"By the way"** Ibid.

424   **Though informed** Ibid., and AI, Fay Aull Deusterman, 3/3/91, Orlando, Fla.

425   **The secretaries were not** AI, Fay Aull Deusterman, 3/3/91, Orlando, Fla.

425   **Douglas wrote Clark Clifford** WOD to Clark Clifford, 1/2/69, Clark Clifford private papers.

425   **"Cathy . . . had all"** AI, Cragg Gilbert, 8/17/90, Yakima.

425   **Then Douglas was reminded** WOD to Martha Douglas Bost, 2/24/69, WODP, Box 238.

425   **"Neither my brother"** AI, Millie Douglas Read, 8/20/89, Lostine, Oreg.

426   **Spurred by his sense** AI, Dagmar Hamilton, 2/26/90, Austin, Tex. For more on WOD's beliefs that the Supreme Court building was bugged, see Bob Woodward and Scott Armstrong, *The Brethren* (New York: Avon Books, 1979), p. 78, and Douglas, *Court Years,* p. 311.

427   **In May 1969** Douglas, *Court Years,* p. 358. Previously, relying on the account of Fortas himself, I have said that this conversation took place after the Justice had decided to resign (Murphy, *Fortas,* pp. 571–72). However, I was informed by Cathy Douglas Stone, in a conversation at the William O. Douglas Commemorative Symposium, 1939–1989, 4/16/89, Seattle, that her husband's account is correct.

427   **"Blood will taste good"** Robert Mull, interview of William O. Douglas, Jr., 1981.

427   **Douglas wrote his sister** WOD to Martha Douglas Bost, 5/24/69, cited in Urofsky, *Douglas Letters,* p. 391.

427   **"Impeachment proceedings"** WOD to Fred Rodell, 6/16/69, Fred Rodell Papers.

427   **On July 15** WOD to Clark Clifford, 7/15/69, Clifford private papers.

427   **To Clifford, it was** AI, Clark Clifford, 8/27/89, Washington, D.C.

427   **It was well-known** AI, Lucas A. Powe, 6/22/89, Austin, Tex.

427   **Once, a clerk** AI, Walter Dellinger, 11/1/91, Durham, N.C.

427   **One day, Douglas had boarded** AI, Harry Datcher, 5/5/90, Washington, D.C.; and AI, anonymous law clerk.

428   **One story making** AI, anonymous law clerk.

428   **"Hugo can't keep up"** Ibid. These are just two of a vast number of similar stories of Douglas groping women. Not until after Douglas did his own television interview with Eric Sevareid in 1972, after Black had died, did

he finally put the television issue behind him. Even then, his staff was worried about what he might say. AI, Thomas Armitage, 6/10/90, Seattle.

429 **Ten days after** WOD to Clark Clifford, 7/25/69, Clark Clifford private papers.

429 **"[Cathy] was determined"** AI, Harry Datcher, 5/16/90 and 5/5/90, both in Washington, D.C.

429 **"[Cathy just kept]"** AI, Dagmar Hamilton, 2/25/90, Austin, Tex.

429 **Still, determined to show** Isabelle Lynn to Charlotte Mayerson, 7/30/[n.d.], Random House office files, copy in author's possession.

429 **"Cathy says she doesn't"** AI, Elena Leonardo, 6/9/90, Seattle.

429 **"From the beginning"** John Ehrlichman, *Witness to Power: The Nixon Years* (New York: Pocket, 1982), p. 95.

429 **A presidential request** AI, Will Wilson, 2/26/90, Austin, Tex.

429 **While the file** Ibid., and Ehrlichman, *Witness to Power*, p. 95. Also, AI, Will Wilson, 2/26/90, Austin, Tex., confirmed by review of "William O. Douglas" FBI file, in author's possession.

429 **The Nixon administration's** Richard Harris, *Decision* (New York: Ballantine, 1982), passim.

429 **Nixon was told** Ehrlichman, *Witness to Power*, p. 98, and Ehrlichman Presidential Notes, 10/1/69.

430 **The president called** Ehrlichman Presidential Notes, 10/9/69.

430 **Seeking to light** Ehrlichman, *Witness to Power*, p. 102.

430 **A story in the** WOD to Clark Clifford, 10/23/69, Clark Clifford private papers. Also in Urofsky, *Douglas Letters*, p. 392.

430 **While publicly the Justice** Phone messages from Carolyn Lewis and Jean Heller, 11/7/69, WODP, Box 591.

430 **Later that month** WOD to Clark Clifford, 11/17/69, Clark Clifford private papers.

430 **Once the groundwork** Ehrlichman, *Witness to Power*, p. 102.

431 **Depressed by the unrelenting** WOD to Charles Horowitz, 4/15/70, referring to letter written 2/6/70, in Urofsky, *Douglas Letters*, p. 393.

431 **This was no idle** Black, *Mr. Justice and Mrs. Black*, 2/17/69 entry, p. 239. "Bill Douglas told Hugo for the first time he is thinking of retiring," Elizabeth Black wrote.

431 **Shortly thereafter** AI, Fay Aull Deusterman, 3/3/91, Orlando, Fla.

431 **"on February 6"** WOD to Charles Horowitz, 4/15/70, in Urofsky, *Douglas Letters*, p. 393.

431 **"No way, I'm not"** AI, Fay Aull Deusterman, 3/3/91, Orlando, Fla.

431 **"Fortas thought he could"** AI, Peter Kay Westen, 9/26/90, Ann Arbor, Mich.

431 **Attorney General John** AI, Simon Rifkind, 8/4/89, New York.

432 **After his call** William O. Douglas FBI files, copy released via a Freedom of Information Act request; in author's possession.

432 **"He was the supervising"** AI, Will Wilson, 2/26/90, Austin, Tex.

432 **While the department** Ibid.

432 **"I recall how incensed"** Ibid.

432 **"there was a connection"** Ibid.

433   **"The appearance"** Ibid.

433   **"It was very raw"** Ibid.

433   **And, on April 15** Gerald R. Ford, speech to Congress on William O. Douglas, 4/15/70, Emanuel Celler Papers, Manuscripts Division, Library of
Congress, Washington, D.C.

433   **Douglas had just published** WOD, *Points of Rebellion* (New York: Random
House, 1970), p. 95. Douglas wrote that "we must realize that today's establishment is the new George III. Whether it will continue to adhere to
his tactics, we do not know. If it does, the redress, honored in tradition, is
also revolution."

433   **"Where grievances pile"** Ibid., pp. 88–89.

433   **Did this not prove** Ford, speech to Congress, 4/15/70, Emanuel Celler Papers. In making this charge, it made little difference to Ford that he was
ignoring the final paragraph of the book, in which Douglas made clear
that such a revolution "need not be a repetition of 1776" but instead
could be "an explosive political regeneration" or a voting realignment of
party control of government. Douglas, *Points of Rebellion,* p. 97.

434   **All in all** Ford, speech to Congress, 4/15/70, Emanuel Celler Papers.

434   **Just as Ford** James T. Stoval to Clark Clifford, 4/16/70, Clark Clifford private papers.

434   **"Ford blew it,"** AI, Will Wilson, 2/26/90, Austin, Tex.

435   **"He was scared stiff,"** AI, Robert Hamilton, 2/23/90, ibid.

435   **By this time** Fred Rodell to Hugo Black, 5/6/70, and Hugo Black to Fred
Rodell, 5/13/70, quoted in Ball and Cooper, *Of Power and Right,* p. 307.

435   **"I have known Bill"** Quoted in ibid., p. 308.

435   **With his total savings** Douglas's total net worth, including property, was
$101,822. WOD to Gerald Stern, 6/3/70, and enclosure, WODP, Box 591,
and in Urofsky, *Douglas Letters,* p. 406. See also WOD to Ramsey Clark,
4/27/70, WODP, Box 587.

435   **Clark Clifford had appointed** Clifford memo, 4/22/70; WOD to Clark Clifford, 4/24/70 and 4/27/70, all in Clark Clifford private papers.

436   **"When Douglas came in"** AI, Simon Rifkind, 8/4/89, New York.

436   **Rifkind was both meticulous** Ibid.

436   **"the back of envelopes"** AI, Fay Aull Deusterman, 3/3/91, Orlando, Fla.

436   **"He was a real"** AI, Simon Rifkind, 8/4/89, New York.

436   **They would answer** Gerald Stern to Emanuel Celler, 9/11/70, WODP, Box
590.

436   **When Douglas was accused** WOD to Ramsey Clark, 4/28/70, 5/5/70, and
5/7/70 in WODP, Box 589, and in Urofsky, *Douglas Letters,* pp. 396–404.

437   **When questions were raised** WOD to Ramsey Clark, 5/22/70, WODP, Box
589, and in Urofsky, *Douglas Letters,* pp. 404–5. Douglas also promised
that he would recuse himself from these cases if they came to the Court.

437   **A question about** Memo, "1969," n.d., WODP, Box 589.

437   **"The House said"** Podva Diary, 4/9/79, p. 5 (with thanks to Podva for providing access to this valuable resource).

437   **Fearing that eighteen** Ehrlichman Presidential Notes, 3/13/70.

437   **The president predicted** Ibid.

437   **On Monday, April 13** Haldeman Diaries, 4/13/70.

437   **Several days later** Ibid., 4/17/70.

437   **After being informed** This he could do either in the Judiciary Committee or later in the Rules Committee, which determines whether an issue comes to the floor for debate and a vote. Ehrlichman Presidential Notes, 4/16/70.

438   **Four days later** Haldeman Presidential Notes, 4/20/70, Richard M. Nixon Presidential Papers; and Haldeman Diaries, 4/20/70.

438   **By acting in this manner** Haldeman Diaries, 4/20/70.

438   **Nixon now instructed** The voting bill eventually passed, 224–183, on 6/17/70. Ehrlichman Presidential Notes, 4/28/70.

438   **"it was not a bad idea"** Ehrlichman, *Witness to Power,* p. 110.

438   **Still believing that** Emanuel Celler to Richard M. Nixon, 4/29/70, Richard M. Nixon Presidential Papers, Confidential Files, Box 22.

438   **More than anything** Ehrlichman Presidential Notes, 5/8/70.

438   **Hoping that the Democrats** Ibid. A proposed executive order, "Inspection of Tax Returns by the Committee on the Judiciary, House of Representatives," a companion letter to the secretary of the treasury ordering him to release the tax files, and an explanatory press release were quickly generated. William Rehnquist to Richard Nixon, 6/11/70, and attachments, Richard M. Nixon Papers, Executive Files, FE 14-1; Bryce Harlow to William Timmons, 6/2/70, ibid., Ex 14-1; William Timmons to Richard M. Nixon, 6/3/70, and attachments, ibid.

438   **By the summer of 1970** Simon Rifkind to WOD, 5/15/70 and 5/21/70, WODP, Box 587.

438   **Douglas even suggested** WOD to Simon Rifkind, 5/23/70, WODP, Box 589.

438   **He would ask** AI, Harry Datcher, 5/5/90, Washington, D.C.

439   **As a result, he wrote** WOD to Fred Rodell, 7/18/70, Fred Rodell Papers.

439   **When his former** C. David Ginsburg to WOD, 5/23/70, WODP, Box 589.

439   **"[He was] unusually"** AI, Dagmar Hamilton, 2/27/90, Austin, Tex.; AI, Kay Kershaw, 8/10/89, Goose Prairie, Wash.; AI, Homer Splawn, 6/5/90, Yakima; and AI, Helen Williams, 4/20/89, Yakima.

439   **The first play** WOD, "The Devil and the Lord: Not Guilty," unpublished ms., WODP, Boxes 1095, 1096, and 1097.

439   **Created originally** See *Illinois v. Allen,* 397 U.S. 337 (1970).

440   **In its latest revision** Two years later, Douglas encouraged his son and the head of the Berkeley Repertory Theatre to produce this work. It appears never to have been staged. See WOD to William O. Douglas, Jr., 11/28/72, WODP, Box 1097.

440   **The other play** WOD, "The Couch," unpublished ms., WODP, Boxes 1094 and 1095. Timing of the drafting of the play can be dated by WOD to Nan Burgess, 8/22/70, and WOD to Owen Laster, 11/25/70, WODP, Box 1097. In what Douglas intended to be a theatrical version of his *Points of Rebellion,* he explores the psychological motivations of political figures. See collections of papers on Berrigan, 7/15/70, and on Dubcek, 11/25/70, WODP, Box 1094.

440 **Here, the action** A comparison of the description of the doctor's office in the play and Draper's office in *Go East* (chap. 12, esp. pp. 177–78) makes it very clear that the two offices are the same.

441 **In the end** See the files on "The Couch," WODP, Boxes 1094 and 1095.

441 **"A move might boomerang"** Memo, "Notes by Corcoran and Clifford of a Luncheon with Bill Douglas," 10/1/70, Clark Clifford private papers.

441 **Ten weeks later** See Douglas Impeachment Hearings. The investigators had uncovered information that Douglas had tried to borrow money from Parvin to buy his land in Goose Prairie (but Parvin had advised that this might prove embarrassing); that Douglas had accepted a great many gifts from Parvin, including the furniture that he had bought from him at cost for the summer home; and that Douglas, as president of the Parvin Foundation, had approved a loan of its funds to Parvin himself. See also Fred Graham, "Douglas Announces Intention to Remain on Court," *The New York Times*, 12/17/70, p. 43.

442 **"Manny Celler is"** AI, Vern Countryman, 11/14/89, Moraga, Calif. Douglas let nearly a year pass before sending a note to Celler "not of thanks . . . [but] of great admiration and respect." WOD to Celler, 12/1/71, WODP, Box 589; also in Urofsky, *Douglas Letters,* p. 413.

442 **With the attack over** Graham, "Douglas Announces Intention," p. 43; also in WODP, Box 591.

CHAPTER 35

443 **"He was 'the only' "** AI, Robert Mull, 4/6/90, Seattle (phone). Another account appears in Peter Menzies, "KYVE Presents Documentary on Justice Douglas," *Yakima Daily-Herald Republic,* n.d., *Yakima Herald-Republic* Archives, Yakima. The end of the documentary contains an appeal for assistance in cataloging the marvelous Douglas files in the Yakima Valley Museum. Douglas scholars are indebted to archivist Frances Hare for organizing this mountain of material, and to Yakima Valley Community College professor James Newbill for cataloging the material, among which are 364 prepared texts for speeches of the more than nine hundred that Douglas gave, and making it more accessible.

443 **As he pulled his truck** AI, Cragg Gilbert, 8/17/90, Yakima.

444 **"the man in the"** AI, Robert Mull, 4/6/90, Seattle (phone); confirmed by description of Douglas from AI, Lex Maxwell, 6/9/90, Yakima.

444 **"He used to come"** Robert Mull, interview with Maurice Helland.

444 **"Some of his former"** "William O. Douglas," *Yakima Daily Herald-Republic,* [1974], *Yakima Herald-Republic* Archives, Yakima.

444 **"Douglas had a love"** AI, George M. Martin, 6/5/90, Yakima.

444 **"I call it the love-hate"** Murphey, "Yakima Never Sure," p. 6A.

444 **"You would listen"** AI, Robert Hamilton, 3/2/90, Austin, Tex.

444 **"Douglas was one"** AI, Harry Datcher, 5/5/90, Washington, D.C.

444 **"I wrote you last fall"** WOD to Kay Kershaw and Isabelle Lynn, 5/12/70, in Urofsky, *Douglas Letters,* pp. 403–4.

445 **"Hip-Pocket Harry"** To be complete and fair, Justice Blackmun's votes began to change significantly toward the liberal side by the end of the

1970s. By the end of his tenure in the early 1990s, he was considered to be the most liberal vote on the Court.

445   **Among the many issues** "William O. Douglas: The Bill of Rights Is Not Enough" offers counts of WOD's dissents of twenty-four in 1970 and thirty in 1971. Revealing dissent numbers for WOD can also be drawn from Blandford and Evans, *Supreme Court of the United States*, pp. 801–51. Even more revealing was the geometric increase in the number of all kinds of dissents that Douglas issued during this period, both full opinions and to denials of writs of *certiorari*. The full number of dissents in the calendar year of 1970 — twenty-seven — doubled the following year, and more than tripled to eighty-six in 1972. That number increased again to eighty-nine the following year, before dropping to a still astonishing seventy-five dissents in 1974.

445   **In the middle of** *Wyman v. James,* 400 U.S. 309 (1971).

446   **"We are living in"** Ibid., p. 326.

446   **"Our concern here"** Ibid., p.327.

446   **"the central question"** Ibid., pp. 327–28.

446   **"If . . . [Barbara James]"** Ibid., p. 330.

446   **"Given the basic"** *Boddie v. Connecticut,* 401 U.S. 371 (1971), p. 374.

446   **"Here Connecticut has provided"** Ibid., p. 384.

447   **"The Court today puts"** Ibid., pp. 384–85.

447   **"The power of the States"** Ibid., pp. 385–86.

447   **By the spring of 1971** AI, Marty Bagby Yopp, 6/6/90, Moscow, Idaho. For quotations from her later years, after Bagby's Court service, I have used her married name.

447   **Faced with the question** AI, Lucas A. Powe, 6/22/89, Austin, Tex.

448   **"It was clear to me"** Ibid.

448   **When the procedure** WOD to William O. Douglas, Jr., 5/15/71, WODP, Box 242.

448   **Hazel Palmer and others** *Palmer v. Thompson,* 403 U.S. 217 (1971).

448   **"Probably few persons,"** Ibid., p. 227.

449   **"Is there anything"** Ibid., p. 233.

449   **"the enumeration in"** Ibid.

449   **"There is, of course,"** Ibid., p. 234.

449   **"Though a State may"** Ibid., p. 239.

449   **When the Court turned** *Lemon v. Kurtzman, Earley v. DiCenso,* and *Robinson v. DiCenso,* 403 U.S. 602 (1971).

450   **"First, the statute"** Ibid., pp. 612–13.

450   **"Sectarian education"** Ibid., p. 635.

450   **"breed division"** Ibid., p. 636.

450   **In writing this way** Ibid., p. 641.

450   **The 1970–1971 term** *New York Times Co. v. United States* and *United States v. Washington Post Co.,* 403 U.S. 713 (1971).

450   **By the time the cases** The other two times that Douglas was willing to, or actually did, return to Washington during the summer were during the War Production Board appointment discussion and the Court's extended conference in the *Rosenberg* case. See chaps. 17 and 26, above.

450 **Taking very seriously** Woodward and Armstrong, *Brethren,* pp. 142, 145; confirmed by AI, Lucas A. Powe, 6/22/89, Austin, Tex.

451 **The Court voted** *New York Times Co. v. United States* and *United States v. Washington Post Co.,* p. 714.

451 **"disclosure of any"** Ibid., p. 730.

451 **"only government allegation"** Ibid., pp. 726–27.

451 **"no room for governmental"** Ibid., p. 720.

451 **"The war power stems"** Ibid., p. 722.

451 **"The dominant purpose"** Ibid., pp. 723–24.

452 **"Secrecy in government"** Ibid., p. 724.

452 **"The Government's power"** Ibid., p. 717.

452 **"To find that the President"** Ibid., p. 719. But despite this passion and eloquence from the Court's two senior members, a careful reading of all of these opinions indicates that even though they were on the winning side, Douglas and Black risked one day losing the battle to protect the press. For hidden in the majority vote were five, and possibly even six, members who appeared to be willing to vote for the government if it decided to use laws barring the release of secret documents in order to punish the press *subsequent* to its publication of material deemed harmful to the government and the people. See the separate opinions of Burger, Harlan, Blackmun, Marshall, and White (which Stewart signed).

CHAPTER 36

453 **"Douglas had the best"** AI, Charles Reich, 11/15/89, San Francisco.

453 **Eight people** *Papachristou v. City of Jacksonville,* 405 U.S. 156 (1972), p. 164.

453 **On the other hand** Ibid., p. 169.

454 **"A presumption that people"** Ibid., p. 171.

454 **Writing for a unanimous** *Alexander v. Louisiana,* 405 U.S. 625 (1972).

454 **"I believe that the time"** Ibid., p. 635.

454 **"reasonably reflec[t]"** Ibid., p. 636.

454 **"If the shoe"** Ibid., pp. 637–38.

454 **"The absolute exemption"** Ibid., pp. 639–40. Since this case turned on Alexander's own due-process claims, rather than the equal-protection claims of the excluded women, Douglas left unanswered just what level of scrutiny—the legislatively deferential "rational basis" test or the more individual rights-protective "strict scrutiny" test—he would use to resolve the issues here. Not until four years later, after Douglas had retired, did the Supreme Court again consider the issue of gender discrimination in an Oklahoma case argued by Ruth Bader Ginsburg (*Craig v. Boren,* 429 U.S. 190 [1976]). The Court rejected both tests in favor of a midlevel "important governmental interests" test.

454 **Douglas also searched** See the discussion *infra* re *Murphy v. Butler,* 362 U.S. 929 (1960). In his seminal 1963 address, "The Bill of Rights Is Not Enough," Douglas had said: "If the Bill of Rights were being written today, it certainly would provide people with protection against poisoning by insecticides—one of America's acute problems, as Rachel Carson shows in her book, *Silent Spring*" (p. 235).

454   **Finally, in 1972** *Sierra Club v. Morton,* 405 U.S. 727 (1972).

455   **"special interest in the"** Ibid., p. 735.

455   **Fay Aull Deusterman recalled** AI, Fay Aull Deusterman, 3/3/91, Orlando, Fla.

455   **"When I ventured"** AI, Red Schwartz, 1/27/93, Syracuse University Law School, Syracuse, N.Y.

455   **The great naturalist** Ibid., p. 748.

455   **The conservative Burger Court** Ibid., p. 753.

455   **"The critical question"** Ibid., pp. 741–42; see also Christopher Stone, "Should Trees Have Standing?—Toward Legal Rights for Natural Objects," *Southern California Law Review* 45 (1972): 450ff.

456   **"those people who have"** Ibid., p. 744.

456   **"be assurances that all"** Ibid., p. 752.

456   **"the highest-placed advocate"** Introduction to a speech presented by WOD, "Nature and Value of Diversity," in Ann Gilliam, ed., *Voices for the Earth: A Treasury of the Sierra Club Bulletin, 1893–1977* (San Francisco, Sierra Club Books, 1979), pp. 538–39.

456   **The Sierra Club Legal** See Carr Clifton and Tom Turner, *Wild by Law* (San Francisco: Sierra Club Books, 1990). After their inability to persuade the Court to hear their case, members of the fund's legal team noticed in Justice Stewart's majority opinion the following footnote: "Our decision does not, of course, bar the Sierra Club from seeking in the District Court to amend its complaint." Taking the hint, the group marched back into federal district court and amended their complaint to refile their suit, adding nine people who visited Mineral King frequently to demonstrate the connection of the club to the potential loss of this natural resource, thus establishing the harm in the case. Eventually, the Mineral King development was stopped.

456   **After five years** Ibid., pp. 21–22.

456   **In March 1972** *Laird v. Tatum,* 408 U.S. 1 (1972).

457   **"Our tradition reflects"** Ibid., p. 19.

457   **"The act of turning"** Ibid., p. 24.

457   **"This case involves"** Ibid., p. 28.

457   **In the summer of 1972** AI, Harry Datcher, 5/5/90, Washington, D.C.; AI, Marty Bagby Yopp, 6/6/90, Moscow, Idaho; AI, Fay Aull Deusterman, 3/3/91, Orlando, Fla.; and Reminiscences of Marty Bagby Yopp, in unpublished Douglas Remembrances, pp. 65–66.

457   **Upon being told** Deusterman never suspected Douglas's feelings as he autographed a picture of them at her retirement party, "For Fay Aull, the indispensable lady in memory of a sentimental occasion. William O. Douglas." AI, Fay Aull Deusterman, 3/3/91, Orlando, Fla.

458   **He celebrated** *Aero Mayflower Transit Co. v. United States* and *Hutter v. Korzen,* 34 L. Ed. 2d 166; *United States v. Interstate Commerce Commission,* 34 L. Ed. 2d 169; *Ohio AFL-CIO v. Insurance Rating Board,* 34 L. Ed. 2d 180; *Chongris v. Corrigan,* 34 L. Ed. 2d 181; *Nebraska Board of Education v. School District of Hartington,* 34 L. Ed. 2d 182; *Felts v. Seaboard,* and *Adkins v. Kelly's Creek Railroad Company,* 34 L. Ed. 2d 184; *Sarnoff v. Schults,* 34 L. Ed. 2d

186; *Achtenberg v. United States,* 34 L. Ed. 2d 187; *Kresse v. Butz, Rasmussen v. Butz, Marcovich v. United States, Wallace v. Warner, Wetteroff v. Grand, Dorado v. Kerr, De Moulin v. Denver, Veterans and Reservists for Peace in Vietnam v. Regional Commissioner of Customs, Region II,* and *Noland v. Desobry,* all 34 L. Ed. 2d 188; *Hunter v. United States, Morton International, Inc. v. Southern Pacific Transportation Co.,* and *McLamore v. South Carolina,* all 34 L. Ed. 2d 189; *Hadley v. Alabama,* 34 L. Ed. 2d 190; and *Francis v. United States, Memphis Light, Gas and Water Division v. Federal Power Commission,* 34 L. Ed. 2d 192; *Solomon v. Seaboard Coast Line Railroad Company,* 34 L. Ed. 2d 193 (all in 1972).

458 **Douglas was objecting** See *Henderson v. Favre,* 34 L. Ed. 2d 193 (1972). By now he had made this technique so accepted within the Court that he was being customarily joined in dissent by the other two liberals—William Brennan and Thurgood Marshall—while new members, such as Harry Blackmun, were objecting to other denials of appeals on their own.

458 **By this time, Douglas** *Markle v. Abele,* 409 U.S. 902 (1972).

458 **Douglas had an opportunity** *Doe v. Bolton,* 410 U.S. 179 (1973), and *Roe v. Wade,* 410 U.S. 113 (1973).

458 **While promising to add** Ibid., p. 218.

458 **"at war with the clear"** Ibid., p. 214.

459 **"The Ninth Amendment"** Ibid., pp. 210–11.

459 **Using the instruction** Ibid., p. 211.

459 **"freedom of choice"** Ibid.

459 **"the freedom to care"** Ibid., p. 213.

459 **Citing precedent** Ibid., p. 211.

459 **Douglas's now annual** *Sigler v. Berrigan,* 410 U.S. 902 (1973).

459 **"To the contrary"** Ibid., pp. 902–3.

460 **"The ability to understand"** Ibid., p. 903. When the Court denied standing three months later for an association of current and former antiwar members of the armed-forces reserves who were suing to challenge the reserve membership of several members of Congress, Douglas was ready to offer his dissent once more. As Douglas argued: "The interest of citizens is obvious. The complaint alleges injuries to the ability of the average citizen to make his political advocacy effective whenever it touches on the vast interests of the Pentagon. It is said that all who oppose the expansion of military influence in our national affairs find they are met with a powerful lobby—the Reserve Officers Association—which has strong congressional allies."

460 **With his hiring** AI, Harry Datcher, 5/5/90, Washington, D.C.

460 **After a few weeks** AI, Fay Aull Deusterman, 3/3/91, Orlando, Fla.

460 **The incident had started** AI, Doug Williams, 4/19/89, Cliffdell, Wash.

461 **"You still have a"** Ibid.

462 **On August 1** *Schlesinger v. Holtzman,* 414 U.S. 1321 (1973).

462 **The hour-long hearing** Ron Kaye, "Douglas Ponders Bombing Verdict," *Yakima Herald-Republic,* 8/4/73, in *Yakima Herald-Republic* Archives, Yakima.

462 **He walked around** AI, Marty Bagby Yopp, 6/6/90, Moscow, Idaho.

463 **Just when they were beginning** Ibid.

463 **"The classic capital case"** *Holtzman v. Schlesinger,* 414 U.S. 1316 (1973), p. 1317.

464 **"It has become popular"** Ibid.

464 **"I do not sit"** Ibid., pp. 1319–20.

464 **"The merits of the present"** Ibid., p. 1320.

464 **The order was issued** *Schlesinger v. Holtzman,* 414 U.S. 1321 (1973).

464 **"I expected to be overturned"** AI, Marty Bagby Yopp, 6/6/90, Moscow, Idaho.

465 **"I do not speak"** *Schlesinger v. Holtzman,* p. 1324.

465 **The more he thought** AI, John Gavin, 2/10/92, Yakima (phone), and John N. Rupp, "The Douglas-Fortas Connection," *Washington State Bar News,* July 1993, pp. 39–40. My sincere thanks to Diane Polscer for drawing my attention to this piece.

465 **Fortas, who remained** Rupp, "Douglas-Fortas Connection," pp. 39–40.

466 **Seeing the wisdom** AI, John Gavin, 2/10/92, Yakima (phone).

466 **But Douglas had** Author's observation of WOD's re-created office at the Yakima Valley Museum, Yakima.

466 **Marco DeFunis, Jr.** *DeFunis v. Odegaard,* 416 U.S. 312 (1974).

467 **"there really was some kind"** This quotation and the account that follows comes from Nicholas Lemann, "Taking Affirmative Action Apart," *The New York Times Magazine,* 6/11/95, p. 52.

467 **"I don't know about"** Ibid.

467 **First, he vigorously attacked** As Douglas put it: "The Equal Protection Clause did not enact a requirement that Law Schools employ as the sole criterion for admissions a formula based upon the LSAT and undergraduate grades, nor does it prohibit law schools from evaluating an applicant's prior achievements in light of the barriers that he had to overcome." *DeFunis v. Odegaard,* p. 331.

467 **"the consideration of each"** Ibid., p. 333.

467 **"I do know, coming"** Ibid., pp. 334–35.

468 **"The reservation of a proportion"** Ibid., p. 338.

468 **"The purpose of the University"** Ibid., pp. 342–43.

468 **"All races can compete"** Ibid., pp. 343–44.

468 **In fact, his argument** Lemann, "Taking Affirmative Action Apart," p. 52. See *Regents of the University of California v. Bakke,* 438 U.S. 265 (1978).

469 **Douglas's four-page majority** See Woodward and Armstrong, *Brethren,* p. 63.

469 **"There can be no dispute"** *Kahn v. Shevin,* 416 U.S. 351 (1974), pp. 353–54.

469 **"We deal here with"** Ibid., p. 355.

469 **"I've known a lot"** Reminiscences of Richard W. Benka, in Douglas Remembrances, p. 12.

469 **"Perhaps he was thinking"** Ibid.

470 **"Not as long as"** AI, Prof. James Souls, University of Delaware, 10/7/97, Newark, Del.

470 **His initial thirty-page** Reminiscences of Jay Kelly Wright, unpublished Douglas Remembrances, pp. 63–64.

470   **"to allow [Nixon]"** WOD, Memo to Conference, 7/5/74, WODP, Box 1659, as quoted in Howard Ball, *"We Have a Duty": The Supreme Court and the Watergate Tapes Litigation* (Westport, Conn.: Greenwood Press, 1990), p. 102.

470   **"every citizen, high or low"** Ibid., 7/20/74. WODP, Box 1659, quoted in Ball, *"We Have A Duty,"* p. 102.

470   **As soon as he walked** Reminiscences of Jay Kelly Wright, unpublished 470 Remembrances, p. 63. The era of good feeling would end that fall when the notebook with *certiorari* petitions somehow got out of order and Douglas wrote them from the conference room, "Perhaps I should ask Datcher to do the certs [*certiorari* petition reviews] from now on."

471   **As soon as the Court's** Ibid.

471   **In the end, Douglas** Ball, *"We Have A Duty,"* p. 114ff.

471   **"the United States has"** *Secretary of the Navy v. Avrech,* 418 U.S. 676 (1974), p. 679.

471   **"Talk is of course"** Ibid., p. 680.

472   **"Soldiers, lounging around,"** Ibid.

CHAPTER 37

473   **"The Douglas I knew"** AI, Simon Rifkind, 8/4/89, New York.

474   **When Douglas rose** This scene and the quotation are from "Sovern Presents Medals for Excellence to William Douglas and Simon Rifkind," *The Columbia Law Alumni Observer,* 5/5/73, p. 2, Columbia Law School Archives, New York (with thanks to Whitney Bagnall of the Alumni Office, Columbia Law School, for helping to locate this document).

474   **"Not only can I assure"** AI, Herman Benjamin, 11/10/91, Palm Beach, Fla. I am indebted to Dean Arthur Kimball of the Columbia Law School (AI, 8/21/91 [phone]) and Herman Benjamin (AI, 8/21/91 [phone]), for explaining these class rankings. While no general listing of the three-year class averages and ranking survive from that era, Kimball says that, for him, the only man from the class of '25 who could be considered authoritative on any question relating to this class was Benjamin.

Milton Handler, who followed these events very closely as a member of the same Law Review, confirms Benjamin's recollection: "The fact of the matter is that [Douglas] was not in the same league with a half dozen of his classmates on the Law Review. . . . For Douglas to have suggested that he was the outstanding member of that '25 Class and that he was the first choice of the faculty [for the law clerkship], is stretching hyperbole beyond its limits" (Milton Handler to author, 7/10/91). Indeed a review of the Columbia Law School bulletins for Douglas's years there confirms that he never was named a James Kent Scholar, considered the usual barometer of academic success there. Rather, it was Carrol Shanks, Herman Benjamin, Arthur Kramer, Irvine Schubert, Andrew Sheridan, and Alfred McCormack who were thus rewarded in the third-year class. See copies of the *Columbia Law Bulletin* 1926–1927 (p. 20), 1925–1926 (p. 20), and 1924–1925 (p. 19).

Since Arthur Kramer was a Kent Scholar in all three of his law-school years, and Carrol Shanks and Alfred McCormack were honored for two years each, they were clearly among the leaders of the class. The other leaders would have come from among the seven other students who were named Kent Scholars in individual years: Dean Alfange, Solomon Sklar, William Gilbert, Harold Schwarzberg, Benjamin, Schubert, and Sheridan.

474 **"I've often wondered"** AI, Herman Benjamin, 11/10/91, Palm Beach, Fla.

474 **So it was then** Ibid.

475 **"so continually arresting"** Nat Hentoff, *The New York Times Book Review,* 4/14/74, p. 1.

475 **"This volume"** *Time,* 5/20/74, p. 88.

476 **became "barely sixteen"** Douglas, *Go East,* pp. 3–4.

476 **"lift me high"** Ibid., p. 12.

476 **The rest of the "characters"** Ibid., pp. 17–18, and "Arthur and William Douglas," *National Biographic,* p. 2. As seen by the earlier account here, in all of the times that the Justice told this story of his childhood, Douglas never mentioned Cull's name until after he was dead.

Relying on Douglas's account, to this day others in Yakima who knew Cull's history still believe that he chose to sell Julia, in 1904 rather than 1910, worthless stock in a frivolous irrigation canal rather than the productive two pieces of property that supported the family. AI, Fred Velikanje, 12/23/91, Yakima (phone); AI, George M. Martin, 6/5/90, Yakima; and AI, John Gavin, 2/10/92, Yakima (phone).

After Cull died a pauper in 1958, his last remaining local asset was disposed of by the bank; it was a piece of property, Lot 44 in Goose Prairie, which, after being considered and rejected for purchase by Douglas, was transferred to the local Boy Scout Council to become a wilderness camp. George M. Martin interview of Bruce Mallard, 9/16/91; AI, George M. Martin, 6/5/90 and 6/8/90, Yakima; and AI, Doug Williams, 4/19/89, Cliffdell, Wash.; WOD to Martha [Douglas Bost], 9/28/56, WODP, Box 238. See also James B. Cull obituary, *Yakima Herald-Republic,* 4/30/58.

476 **He also added** Douglas, *Of Men and Mountains,* p. 30.

476 **Here he revealed** Douglas, *Go East,* chap. 12, and pp. 182, 183–84. In recounting the story of Draper's analysis of the career-threatening stomach pains, Douglas revealed the psychological importance of the baked beans he sought after all of his illnesses: "When my polio fever broke, I craved baked beans. Baked beans became a symbol of my return to a haven of security." See chap. 6, above, and also Draper, *Disease and the Man,* pp. 155–57, esp. p. 156.

476 **According to the Justice's** Douglas, *Go East,* p. 180.

476 **"I never did"** Ibid.

476 **Douglas also now wrote** Ibid., pp. 103 and 102–4.

476 **As the developing young** Ibid., pp. 103–4.

477 **But Frances Penrose Owen** "I know the truth about those years, and it is so different from what people believe that I'm glad to finally set the record straight," Frances Owen said. Seeking to dispel the notion that she might not have remembered those events clearly or that she might have a certain bias, she checked an old composition book and a stack of pictures. "Those are my daily journals, which were written at that time.... And just

to be sure, I checked with [her sister] Mary, who was also at Whitman at that time. Her recollections are the same as mine." Owen provides unmistakable evidence that for a man who claimed to have gone "through college at a dead run" and worked "on the outside too many hours a day to get involved in many collegiate activities," William Douglas was somehow in every picture of a school event. These photos showed him being seated with his friends on the back of a truck going to a picnic, dressed as Daniel Webster in the Dramatic Club's play about Marcus Whitman, and thrown into the pond during a frolic. Here was a young man enjoying college to the fullest. AI, Frances Penrose Owen, 9/9/90, Seattle.

477   **"You see," said Frances Penrose Owen** Ibid. For more on Penrose's considerable contributions to Whitman College, see Robert Mull, interview of Chester Maxey, 9/22/81, and Chester Maxey Oral History, 1/16/76, Whitman Archives.

477   **Douglas exercised** Douglas, *Of Men and Mountains,* pp. 159–61; and Douglas, *Go East,* pp. 87–95.

477   **"mother was dependent"** Douglas, *Go East,* p. 91; confirmed by phrase "just about enlisted" in WOD School Diary, 4/9/17.

477   **Douglas wrote of** Douglas, *Go East,* pp. 91–92. It was true that "color confusion" was a reason for rejecting a candidate for the flying corps. See "Physical Examination for Flying," Special Regulations no. 65C, prepared in the office of the director of air services (Washington, D.C.: Government Printing Office, 1919).

477   **Only the armistice** Douglas, *Go East,* p. 93.

477   **But color blindness** See "Physical Standards for the Reserve Officers' Training Corps," Special Regulations no. 65B, prepared in the office of the surgeon general of the army (Washington, D.C.: Government Printing Office, 1919), p. 7; and "Physical Examination for Entrance into the Army of the United States by Voluntary Enlistment or by Induction Under the Selective Service Law," Special Regulations no. 65 (Washington, D.C.: U.S. Government Printing Office, 1918), pp. 4–7.

477   **"They had to get people"** AI, Hallam Mendenhall, 2/27/92, Ocean City, N.J. (phone). Douglas's tale of learning for the first time during these years that he was color-blind was not entirely untrue. One of Douglas's closest friends from this period, Jerry Cundiff of Walla Walla, liked to recall that when they worked together in Falkenberg's jewelry store, Orville [Douglas] waited on a woman who wanted a red umbrella:

> He reached down and picked out the brightest green we had. She said, "Young man, I said red." He looked again and gave her a blue umbrella. She said, "Young man, you certainly don't know your colors!" The young man then turned to another clerk named Ben Cowan for help, but it turned out he too was color-blind. So the lady selected her own umbrella.

Cundiff's son, Jerry Jr., now the owner of Falkenberg's, completes the tale with a chuckle,

Not being able to tell the difference between red and green is a fatal flaw in a jewelry business. Dad and his friends loved to play tricks on Douglas, asking him to pick out the best ruby and handing him a fistful of emeralds. So, Dad used to love to tell how Douglas would spend hours working with a box of men's ties trying to teach himself how to tell the difference between the two colors. Then he tried to work with hunks of yarn. But it never helped very much.

Likely Douglas learned of his color blindness not from a medical test for induction but from an embarrassing episode in a jewelry store. AI, Jerry Cundiff, Jr., 5/31/90, Walla Walla.

477 **The truth was that** See Woodrow Wilson Presidential Proclamation, 8/31/18, pp. 1840–42. For more, see Senate Committee on Military Affairs, *Amending the Draft Law,* 65th Cong., 2d sess., 8/6–8/9/18, p. 2.

478 **The fact, of course** This conclusion that Douglas was not a private in the regular army is drawn from Douglas's Military Record as well as other sources. For more on how WOD's service record was constructed, see the Epilogue, below. Douglas is listed here as a "Pvt. S.A.T.C.," and it is noted that on October 10, 1918, he rose to the position of "Acting Sergeant." Thanks to W. G. Seibert for helping to locate these materials.

Had Douglas been inducted in the regular army, his record would indicate whether his discharge was honorable or otherwise. Contrary to Douglas's later claim that he had been "honorably" discharged, the truth was that he had been discharged simply because of the "expiration [of] term service per tel[ephonic]. instructions A[djutant]. G[eneral's]. O[ffice]., dated November 26, 1918." In short, since the SATC was disbanded on that date, Douglas and all of the unit members were simply released.

Louise Arnold-Friend, reference librarian for the Carlisle Army Barracks at the U.S. Army Military History Institute in Carlisle, Pa., explained that this type of service and release indicates very clearly the nonactive-duty nature of Douglas's military time: "The SATC was a branch of dedicated civic-minded individuals who play soldier. They are like a cadet private or a military school. Douglas should not have a military record. Nowhere in the true sense of the word was William O. Douglas a private in the real army."

"The ranks given [in the SATC] are more an indication of your status in class, like freshman, sophomore, and so forth. So you are never a private but a 'cadet private'" (AI, Louise Arnold-Friend, 2/10/92, Carlisle, Pa. [phone]).

Dennis Vetock, also of the Military History Institute, concurred:

Members of the SATC were not in the military so much as they were *preparing* for military service. Students were there to get the skills necessary to later enter the military.... The only way to formally join the military would be to complete the training at school, take and sign an oath, and receive your commission.

> Once that is done, a person is inducted into the military. [AI,
> Dennis Vetock, 2/10/92, Carlisle, Pa. (phone)]

Indeed, the army was very explicit at the time about the differences between the real military and these training units. In the memorandums creating the SATC, the adjutant general of the army made clear that after graduation students in the training units would become "members of the Army of the United States" and "will become thereby subject to active service at the call of the President." Until that time, they "will be on furlough status until called to the colors." When was this call likely to come, making the young men full-fledged members of the military? "It will be the policy of the Government not to call members of the Students' Army Training Corps units to active duty until they reach draft age." In its various memos, the army was careful to differentiate the two groups, calling members of the SATC "student-soldiers." And members of these training units received only thirty dollars a month, while privates in the regular army got $870 in pay and allowances.

In the end, it was left to Congress after the war to decide whether participation in these training groups constituted military service. In 1924, after years of wrangling over the size of the bonus to be paid to war veterans, Congress passed the World War Adjusted Compensation Act. Every veteran was awarded money for each day of active duty after the sixtieth, in the form of an endowment insurance certificate, which would mature in twenty years. Seeking to reward the true veterans, Congress created long lists of groups that did not have creditable military service for such a payment. Exclusion C reads:

> In computing the adjusted service credit no allowance shall be
> made to . . . any civilian officer or employee of any branch of the
> military or naval forces, contract surgeon, cadet of the United
> States Military Academy, midshipman, cadet or cadet engineer
> of the Coast Guard, member of the Reserve Officers' Training
> Corps, [or] member of the Students' Army Training Corps (ex-
> cept an enlisted man detailed thereto).

By lumping the SATC with all of these other noncombatant groups, Congress indicated clearly that the training phase was to be treated differently from the active-duty phase of the service. *An Act to Provide Adjusted Compensation for Veterans of World War, and for Other Purposes*, 68th Cong., sess. 1, H.R. 7959, *U.S. Statutes at Large* 43, p. 121 (5/19/24).

Whitman College acknowledged this difference when *The Whitman Alumnus* 2, no. 3 (December 1918): 4–6, offered a list of graduates and nongraduates who served in various branches of the armed forces, but Orville Douglas's name was not among them. Instead, Douglas's name appeared at the end of the list as a member of the SATC.

478   **"We all knew"** AI, Hallam Mendenhall, 2/27/92, Ocean City, N.J. (phone).
478   **"We all *had*"** Ibid.

478   **Indeed, when the draft** See Wilson Presidential Proclamation, 8/31/18, pp. 1840–42.

478   **As one of only four** Count done from *Catalogue of Whitman College,* 1919 and 1920, Whitman Archives.

478   **"Through my tutoring"** Douglas, *Go East,* p. 144.

478   **However, the Douglases'** See Affidavit for Marriage License; Marriage Certificate; and Medical Certificate for Marriage License, all 8/15/23, Union County Clerk's office, La Grande, Oreg. For more, see chap. 4, above.

479   **Rifkind knew** AI, Simon Rifkind, 8/4/89, New York.

479   **"Douglas's memory seems"** Shaw, "Justice Douglas Once Lived Here," p. 1. Mercedes Douglas Eicholz could not help but notice her predecessor's fate in the book. After complaining to Douglas about this treatment of the woman who had played such a role in his life, she jokingly added, "When you get to the second volume, you had better do better by me." (He repaid her the way he had so many others: The second volume contains absolutely *no* mention of his second wife.) Interview of Mercedes Douglas Eicholz, 5/28/88, Lowe Videos.

479   **By burying** Douglas, *Go East,* pp. 3–4. See Kunitz, *American Authors, 1600–1900,* p. 742.

479   **As soon as the book** See Douglas, *Go East,* pp. 156–58, for the account of this period in WOD's life. See also chaps. 5–7, ibid.

479   **"Fred," said the Justice** AI, Fred Velikanje, 12/23/91, Yakima, Wash. (phone).

CHAPTER 38

481   **You see me here** William Shakespeare, *King Lear,* II, iv, 273–74.

481   **Christmas was fast** AI, Fay Aull Deusterman, 3/3/91, Orlando, Fla.

481   **What seemed most** AI, Marty Bagby Yopp, 6/6/90, Moscow, Idaho; AI, Harry Datcher, 5/5/90, Washington, D.C.; AI, Dagmar Hamilton, 2/26/90, Austin, Tex.; and see Woodward and Armstrong, *Brethren,* pp. 422ff.

481   **Once she and Douglas** AI, Marty Bagby Yopp, 6/6/90, Moscow, Idaho; AI, Harry Datcher, 5/5/90, Washington, D.C.; AI, Dagmar Hamilton, 2/26/90, Austin, Tex.

482   **"My God," he mumbled** Woodward and Armstrong, *Brethren,* p. 423.

482   **Once he arrived** AI, Harry Datcher, 5/5/90, Washington, D.C.; and see North, "Justice Douglas' 23-Year-Old," pp. 92–94, 172–73.

482   **An IQ test** Hall, "Cathy Douglas," p. K11.

482   **But with doctors disagreeing** AI, Dagmar Hamilton, 2/26/90, Austin, Tex.

482   **While Douglas had never** This account is taken from Douglas's manuscript draft, vol. 2, "Torture," Rider 72A, WODP, Box 1770. This appeared to be intended for use in the next part of Douglas's memoirs.

482   **A young nurse** Ibid., and Marty Bagby, "Torture and Non Compos Mentis memorandum," 5/6/80, WODP, Box 1770.

482   **What month was it?** AI, Marty Bagby Yopp, 6/6/90, Moscow, Idaho.

482   **Ever the feisty soul** This account is informed by the following: WOD "Torture" manuscript, and Bagby "Torture and Non Compos Mentis," WODP,

Box 1770. See also WOD manuscript drafts: "Vol. II, Ch. 6 Torture" and "Vol. II, GEYM [Go East Young Man], Non Compos Mentis," memorandums, WODP, Box 1770.

482 **A while later** Ibid.

483 **"Justice Douglas spent"** "Condition of Justice William O. Douglas," 1/3/75, WODP, Box 1769.

483 **"Where's Bagby?"** AI, Marty Bagby Yopp, 6/6/90. Moscow, Idaho.

483 **"It was like spinning"** AI, Dagmar Hamilton, 2/27/90, Austin, Tex.

483 **As bad as things** From time to time they would tighten and loosen the straps attached to his body; eventually, they damaged his lower torso so severely that he complained of pains there for the rest of his life.

483 **Now victimized** Based on a later account of this period, Bagby, "Torture and Non Compos Mentis," 5/6/80; and WOD, "Torture," WODP, Box 1770.

484 **When Marty Bagby returned** AI, Marty Bagby Yopp, 6/6/90, Moscow, Idaho; WOD, "Torture," WODP, Box 1770.

484 **So, seated with** WOD, "Torture," ibid.; and Bagby, "Torture and Non Compos Mentis," 5/6/80, ibid. See also, WOD, "Vol. II, Ch. 6 Torture," and "Vol. II, GEYM, Non Compos Mentis," ibid.

484 **"The door became"** Woodward and Armstrong, *Brethren,* pp. 426–27; and Glen Elsasser, "Justice Douglas: Whispers Grow," *Chicago Tribune,* 4/28/75, p. 1; see also Warren Weaver, "Douglas and the Court," *The New York Times,* 4/25/75, WODP, Box 1769.

485 **"He was screaming"** "Douglas Illness Raises Issues of High Court Secrecy," *The Washington Post,* 5/11/75, in WODP, Box 1769.

485 **When the rumors** Woodward and Armstrong, *Brethren,* pp. 427–28.

485 **"Have you thought"** Transcript of WOD news conference, 3/25/75, Clark Clifford private papers; Elsasser, "Justice Douglas." See also Weaver, "Douglas and the Court."

485 **Reports of this shaky** W. Dale Nelson, "Douglas Fit for Bench?" *Yakima Herald-Republic,* 10/12/75, p. 2A, *Yakima Herald-Republic* Archives, Yakima.

486 **Even the simplest aspects** Isabelle Lynn to Charlotte Mayerson, 8/17/[75], Random House files, copy in author's possession.

486 **"He couldn't use"** Interview of William O. Douglas, Jr., 2/13/88, Lowe Videos.

486 **Despite these problems** Personal observation, 4/21/75.

486 **The next day, Douglas** AI, Harry Datcher, 5/5/90, Washington, D.C.; and AI, Marty Bagby Yopp, 6/6/90, Moscow, Idaho.

487 **"We didn't want"** AI, Elena Leonardo, 7/17/2002, Toppenish, Wash. (phone).

487 **The challenge** Elsasser, "Justice Douglas."

487 **On the Justice's orders** AI, Harry Datcher, 5/5/90, Washington, D.C.

487 **Nonetheless, the Brethren** AI, Marty Bagby Yopp, 6/6/90, Moscow, Idaho.

487 **Unaware of this action** Alan Austin to WOD, 4/22/75, WODP, Box 1705.

487 **Douglas's process of writing** Handwritten WOD version for No. 73-7031, *Fowler v. North Carolina,* n.d., WODP, Box 1705, Death Penalty Case file.

487 **When they received** Ibid., attached to typed version.

487 **When Alan Austin** Alan Austin to WOD, 5/8/75, WODP, Box 1705.

488 **Which quotations** *Furman v. Georgia,* 408 U.S. 238 (1972).

488 **By the middle of May** First draft, "RE: NORTH CAROLINA CAPITAL CASES BEFORE THE COURT—OCTOBER 1974 TERM," WODP, Box 1705, Death Penalty Case file.

488 **When Douglas demanded** Memo, Alan Austin to WOD, 5/15/75, ibid.

488 **But he was still** *Warth v. Seldin,* 422 U.S. 490 (1975).

488 **"A clean, safe"** Ibid., p. 518.

488 **"Cases such as this"** Ibid., p. 519.

489 **"In all frankness"** Ibid.

489 **In June 1975** "William O. Douglas: '25 (1898–1980) Remembered," *The Columbia Law Alumni Observer,* 3/21/80, p. 6, Columbia Law School Archives, New York.

489 **"Constitutionalist, Environmentalist"** "Chair Endowed," *The Columbia Law Alumni Observer,* 7/15/75, pp. 1–2, ibid.

489 **Douglas's incapacitated** Warren Weaver, "Douglas's Future on Court Assayed: Physical Ability to Return in October Held in Doubt," *The New York Times,* 7/7/75, WODP, Box 1769.

489 **"He didn't go easily"** AI, Kay Kershaw and Isabelle Lynn, 8/7/90, Goose Prairie, Wash.

489 **"I'll be goddamned"** AI, Dagmar Hamilton, 2/27/90, Austin, Tex., and interview of William O. Douglas, Jr., 2/13/88, Lowe Videos.

489 **But later that summer** Ibid.

489 **"I thought his mind"** Interview of William O. Douglas, Jr., 2/13/88, Lowe Videos.

490 **Isabelle Lynn and others** AI, Isabelle Lynn, 4/19/89, Goose Prairie, Wash.

490 **But when his son** Robert Mull, interview of William O. Douglas, Jr., and interview of William O. Douglas, Jr., 2/13/88, Lowe Videos.

490 **Determined to quash** The district court and Ninth Circuit Court of Appeals had allowed the San Diego district attorney's office to gain access to secret federal grand-jury evidence that had led to indictments for conspiracy, mishandling of funds, and lying to bank examiners in conducting their own investigation. Speed was necessary for the state authorities, who were investigating Smith and one of his associates because the three-year statute of limitations on possible state offenses was running out. Rob Tucker, "Douglas Bars Use of 'Jury' Evidence," "Use of Jury Evidence Blocked," "Douglas Hears Case in Yakima Court," and "Douglas Brings Court to Valley," *Yakima Herald-Republic,* 9/12/75, p. 1, *Yakima Herald-Republic* Archives, Yakima, Wash.

490 **"I am returning"** AI, Elena Leonardo, 8/21/89, Sunnyside, Wash., and 6/9/90, Seattle.

490 **By this time** Isabelle Lynn to Charlotte Mayerson, 8/14/[75], Random House files, copy in author's possession.

490 **"Within a week or so"** When Smith's attorney tried to raise the specter of a double-jeopardy issue if his client was tried again for the same crimes as a result of this investigation, the Justice responded quickly, "That's a state law question."

491 **After the break** Nelson, "Douglas Fit for Bench?" p. 2A.

491 **"Friends of mine"** AI, John Gavin, 2/10/92, Yakima (phone).

491 **"It is a very beautiful"** Tucker, "Douglas Bars Use," "Use of Jury Evidence Blocked," "Douglas Hears Case," and "Douglas Brings Court," p. 1; and "Douglas Fit for Bench?" p. 2A.

491 **Sensing a problem** Ibid. Perhaps it was most appropriate that even this final ruling from the Yakima bench was overturned by the full Court when they returned to session.

491 **"What are we"** AI, Charles Reich, 11/15/89, San Francisco; and AI, Isabelle Lynn, 4/20/89, Goose Prairie, Wash., confirmed by Isabelle Lynn to Charlotte Mayerson, 9/30/[75], Random House files, copy in author's possession.

492 **"You're in no shape"** AI, Charles Reich, 11/15/89, San Francisco.

492 **"I didn't feel"** Ibid.

492 **For three days** Isabelle Lynn to Charlotte Mayerson, 9/30/[75], Random House files, copy in author's possession.

493 **Every time the Justice** AI, Charles Reich, 11/15/89, San Francisco.

493 **For just a moment** See WOD, "Torture"; and Bagby, "Torture and Non Compos Mentis," 5/6/80, both in WODP, Box 1770. See also WOD, "Vol. II, Ch. 6 Torture," and "Vol. II, GEYM, Non Compos Mentis," in ibid.

493 **The debate, Reich** AI, Charles Reich, 11/15/89, San Francisco; visit dated by Reich's entry in the guest log of the Double K Ranch, Goose Prairie, Wash., 9/28/75.

493 **By the time Reich** Isabelle Lynn to Charlotte Mayerson, 9/30/[75], Random House files, in author's possession.

493 **Only when the Double K** Ibid.; and AI, Isabelle Lynn and Kay Kershaw, 4/19/89, Goose Prairie, Wash.

493 **But Charles Reich** Memo, n.d., Clark Clifford private papers.

493 **Despite his condition** *Northern Indiana Public Service Co. v. Walton League,* 423 U.S. 12 (1975).

494 **"A certain danger"** Ibid., pp. 16–17. The Sierra Club, which had recently voted Douglas its prestigious John Muir Award and would later elect him an honorary vice president, termed this opinion "remarkable as a final expression of the views which made him a champion not only of conservationists, but of all citizens, against the excessive self-righteousness of governmental bureaucracy." John D. Hoffman, "Mr. Justice Douglas' Last Environmental Opinion," *Sierra Club Bulletin* 61, no. 5 (May 1976): 8.

494 **"Dear Mr. President"** Weekly Compilation of Presidential Documents, 11/12/75 (Washington, D.C.: Office of the Federal Register, 1975).

494 **When Marty Bagby received** AI, Marty Bagby Yopp, 6/6/90, Moscow, Idaho; and Reminiscences of Marty Bagby Yopp in unpublished Douglas Remembrances, pp. 65–66.

495 **"Bill wants me"** Woodward and Armstrong, *Brethren,* p. 467.

495 **Old battles were forgotten** Ball and Cooper, *Of Power and Right,* p. 316.

495 **After they heard** Ibid.

495 **With Douglas's record-making** On the number of cases, see Blandford and Evans, *Supreme Court of the United States,* pp. 801–51. On the number of articles, see the extended bibliographies in James C. Duram, *Justice Wil-*

liam O. Douglas (Boston: Twayne, 1981); Charles R. Bolger, "William O. Douglas: A Bibliography," in Robert H. Keller, Jr., *In Honor of Justice Douglas: A Symposium on Individual Freedom and the Government* (Westport, Conn.: Greenwood, 1977), pp. 182–220; and Haig A. Bosmajian, *Justice Douglas and Freedom of Speech* (Metuchen, N.J.: Scarecrow Press, 1980). On the number of speeches, see Dorris Norris, "Massive Undertaking," *Yakima Herald-Republic*, 3/18/86, p. 4.

Harry Blackmun returned to his chamber to set down on paper, with characteristic eloquence, what the old New Dealer had meant to him: "He was in a nice sense, a lone eagle but strong and soaring one. . . . Decisional life was never dull when William O. Douglas was participating. His like probably will not appear again for a long, long while." Years later, when asked about an upcoming abortion case on the Court, Blackmun said with a look of sadness, "It's times like this case that I miss Douglas the most" (Justice Harry Blackmun's address on William O. Douglas, William O. Douglas Commemorative Symposium, 1939–1989, 4/16/89, Seattle, and author conversation with Blackmun on that occasion).

But there were limits to Douglas's goodwill even on this historic occasion. The irascible old New Dealer could not bring himself to observe the custom of personally delivering his retirement letter into the hands of the president. Instead, he phoned Deputy Attorney General Harold Tyler at the Justice Department and told him that his wife, Cathy, would be delivering his letter at 3:15 P.M. that day. David O'Brien, relying on an interview with Tyler in "The Politics of Professionalism: President Gerald R. Ford's Appointment of Justice John Paul Stevens," *Presidential Studies Quarterly* 21, no. 1 (winter 1991): 106.

CHAPTER 39

496 **"He didn't have"** AI, C. David Ginsburg, 8/28/89, Washington, D.C.

496 **In the days following** Supreme Court Justices to WOD, 11/14/75, in Urofsky, *Douglas Letters*, pp. 418–19.

496 **"Where are the clerks?"** Woodward and Armstrong, *Brethren*, pp. 470–71; confirmed by AI, Marty Bagby Yopp, 6/6/90, Moscow, Idaho.

496 **One of his first** "Memorandum to the Conference," 12/17/75, WODP, Box 1705, Death Penalty Cases file.

496 **He needed the help** Ibid. Douglas was not even well enough during this period to sign his own initials correctly in an uneven scrawl to the letter, instead signing "W O W."

497 **"Good to see you"** Woodward and Armstrong, *Brethren*, p. 477. Neither man could know that the new jurist would prove to be just as independent as Douglas, and thus a disappointment to Ford.

497 **With the completion** AI, Marty Bagby Yopp, 6/6/90, Moscow, Idaho.

497 **When Burger ignored** As for the case itself, Douglas argued that the campaign-contribution and spending limits were constitutionally suspect. For him, the prospect was that the party in power would not be able to be ousted, because "history shows that financial power and political power eventually merge and unite to do their work together." Woodward

and Armstrong, *Brethren,* pp. 472–74, confirmed by WOD, draft of *Buckley v. Valeo,* WODP, Box 1705, Death Penalty Cases file.

497   **"Bill is like an old"** Woodward and Armstrong, *Brethren,* pp. 473–74.

497   **The Chief responded** Douglas's "Memorandum to the Conference," 12/17/75, is in WODP, Box 1705, Death Penalty Cases file, and is reproduced along with the Court's responding memo of 12/22/75 in Urofsky, *Douglas Letters,* p. 421. See also WOD to Chief Justice Warren Burger, 12/20/75, WODP, Box 1705. WOD amplified these views on his perceived role as a retired Justice in a later "Memorandum to the Conference: *In Re Capital Cases,*" 3/27/76, WODP, Box 1705, Death Penalty Cases file.

497   **And no such request** Woodward and Armstrong, *Brethren,* p. 474.

497   **"You are a traitor,"** Ibid.

497   **But Douglas was not deterred.** Memorandum to the Conference, n.d., and "Memorandum to the Conference: *In Re Capital Cases,*" 3/27/76, both in WODP, Box 1705, Death Penalty Cases file.

498   **The promise, though** "Memorandum to the Conference: *In Re Capital Cases,*" 3/30/76, and WOD original handwritten and typed versions, both in ibid.

498   **"The former justice"** Hall, "Cathy Douglas," p. K10.

498   **But those closest** AI, Dagmar Hamilton, 2/27/90, Austin, Tex.

498   **All too frequently** This portrait is based on a complete reading of the three years of journal entries contained in the Podva Diary.

498   **It was in this condition** Hall, "Cathy Douglas," pp. K1, K10. Eventually, Douglas told the press through Marty Bagby, "He has one statement about the book—he feels the Chief Justice has grown significantly during the last 10 years on the Court."

499   **"They never should"** AI, Abe Fortas, 8/7/81, Washington, D.C.

499   **In making his revisions** Memo, Charlotte Mayerson to Bob Bernstein, 6/22/78, Random House files, copy in author's possession. The advance in the two-book contract had been $250,000 and had earned out only $84,000 in royalties.

499   **Since serious writing** Podva Diary, 11/15/77.

499   **As he got older** AI, Millie Douglas Read, 8/20/89, Lostine, Oreg.; and AI, Montana Podva, 8/28/90, Willits, Calif.

499   **All he really wanted** AI, Dagmar Hamilton, 2/22/90, Austin, Tex.

499   **Douglas told his assistant** AI, Harry Datcher, 5/5/90, Washington, D.C.; and AI, Montana Podva, 8/28/90, Willits, Calif.

500   **"He was a folk hero"** AI, Harry Datcher, 5/5/90, Washington, D.C.

500   **His son, William** Bill Douglas, Jr., appeared in the movies *PT 109* and *Peyton Place.* (See WOD to Bill Jr., 10/12/75; Sandra Phillips to Bill Jr., 5/30/75; and WOD to Bill Jr., 1/15/75, all in WODP, Boxes 242 and 244.)

500   **"The fact is that neither"** AI, Cragg Gilbert, 8/17/90, Yakima.

500   **"We finally quit"** Murphey, "Yakima Friends," p. 6A.

500   **Knowing that he needed** AI, Harry Datcher, 5/5/90, Washington, D.C.

500   **Her fears were not** Martha Douglas Bost to WOD, 11/5/75, WODP, Box 239.

500   **"Where's Cathy?" he would say** AI, Harry Datcher, 5/5/90, Washington, D.C.

500 **A high point** AI, Montana Podva, 8/28/90, Willits, Calif.

500 **"He became obsessed"** AI, Dagmar Hamilton, 2/24/90, Austin, Tex.

501 **"It was as though"** Ibid.

501 **"To the man from"** Ibid.

501 **"The sense of weakness"** AI, C. David Ginsburg, 8/28/89, Washington, D.C.

501 **"Cathy loved him"** AI, Harry Datcher, 5/5/90, Washington, D.C.

501 **Friends point out** AI, Dagmar Hamilton, 2/24/90, Austin, Tex.

501 **And she insisted** AI, Marty Bagby Yopp, 6/6/90, Moscow, Idaho.

501 **"Some people thought"** Ibid.

502 **"It was so painful,"** AI, C. David Ginsburg, 8/28/89, Washington, D.C.

502 **"In his last years,"** AI, Dagmar Hamilton, 2/23/90, Austin, Tex.

502 **"By God, that is the face"** AI, Wendy M. Ross, 3/24/2001, Rockville, Md., phone, and University of Texas website for Martin Luther King memorial competition, www.utexas.edu/general/mlksculpture, last checked on 4/4/2002.

502 **"He sat in [the] shade"** Richard Cohen, "The Man Who Saved the C & O Canal," *The Washington Post*, 5/22/77, p. B8.

502 **"There are seven"** Karen De Witt, "A Tribute to Douglas on the C & O Canal," *The Washington Post*, 5/18/77, p. B3.

503 **"What I've been trying"** Cohen, "Man Who Saved the Canal," p. B8.

503 **When Douglas finished** When the canal was wrecked two decades later by successive spring floods and left unrepaired by the Interior Department, one could only wonder how long this condition would have continued if William O. Douglas were still around to shame the bureaucrats into action by wheeling down his beloved towpath. Angus Phillips, "Delays Leave Part of C & O Canal Dry," *The Washington Post*, 7/14/97, p. 1.

503 **"Being a judge"** Podva Diary, 11/15/78.

503 **Even at this late date** Douglas was also mad at Corcoran for trying to intercede with the Court on behalf of the El Paso Natural Gas Company in the early 1970s (Podva Diary, 11/16/78). For more on the incident, see Woodward and Armstrong, *Brethren*, pp. 88–95.

504 **"Tommy, I guess"** AI, Eliot Janeway, 5/19/90; confirmed by Podva Diary, 11/16/78.

504 **"I suppose the next thing"** Podva Diary, 12/6/79.

504 **One hundred and fifty people** AI, Marty Bagby Yopp, 6/6/90, Moscow, Idaho.

504 **"The lessons he has taught"** "William O. Douglas '25 Receives Special LL.D.," *The Columbia Law Alumni Observer*, 1/24/80, Columbia Law School Archives, Columbia University, New York.

505 **"By this time, his strength"** "William O. Douglas '25 (1898–1980) Remembered," ibid., 3/21/80.

505 **When Cathy Douglas brought** Interview of Cathy Douglas Stone, 5/17/88, Lowe Videos. Also, AI, Millie Douglas Read, 8/20/89, Lostine, Oreg.

505 **They were the last words** AI, Marty Bagby Yopp, 6/6/90, Moscow, Idaho. To bolster her interpretation, she could turn to Douglas's final unpublished manuscript, entitled "Forever," which was bequeathed to her in his

will. According to Marty Bagby Yopp, who typed it up, it was "several narrative pages which were more like a love poem."

505 **"It was clear to me"** AI, Millie Douglas Read, 8/20/89, Lostine, Oreg.

505 **"Cathy just didn't get it"** AI, Walter Lowe, 4/27/89, Seattle (phone). Indeed, Douglas had made very clear in "The Couch," with its hostile attack on motherhood, that this comment was not likely intended as praise. Neither side in this dispute knew the real Julia Douglas. But the Julia Douglas that Bill had discovered in her letters during the mid-1920s was the woman who had forced all of his life choices. She was the woman who had been so overbearing in every facet of his life, even to the point of saddling him with a destiny and dream of the presidency that was unreachable.

505 **"The gauges"** AI, Marty Bagby Yopp, 6/6/90, Moscow, Idaho.

506 **"He still scared us"** AI, Harry Datcher, 5/5/90, Washington, D.C.

506 **"Hey, he looks better"** AI, Montana Podva, 8/28/90, Willits, Calif. It was now clear to Podva what Fortas was saying—that he felt bad about not putting up that fight and preventing the subsequent impeachment battle. "It just wore him thin," explained Podva. "Abe always felt like he let his mentor down by not holding his ground."

506 **"Yep," said Fortas** Ibid. Indeed, the feeling of remorse may have weighed heavily on Fortas as well, who, though in fine health and twelve years younger than Douglas, would be dead just over two years later.

506 **By this time, Cathy** AI, Dagmar Hamilton, 6/20/89, Austin, Tex.

507 **"I saw Douglas"** Fortas, "In Memoriam," pp. 8–9.

507 **"This often amused me,"** AI, Fay Aull Deusterman, 3/3/91, Orlando, Fla.

EPILOGUE

508 **"Things are seldom"** *HMS Pinafore* (1878).

508 **The dark-clad figures** This account is based partly on "Funeral Service, William O. Douglas, Associate Justice of the Supreme Court (Retired) 23 January 1980," copy in Historian's Office, Arlington National Cemetery (with thanks to Kathy Shenkle for supplying this document). See also Kenneth Bredemeier, "Throngs Pay Tribute to Justice Douglas," 1/24/80, p. 1. Also see Lyle Denniston, "Douglas, Friend of Nature, Buried in Arlington," Washington *Star*, 1/24/80, Washington *Star* Archives, Martin Luther King, Jr., Library, Washington, D.C.; WOD to Edward L. R. Elson, 12/7/77, in Urofsky, *Douglas Letters*, p. 426.

508 **"William Orville Douglas"** Jim Mann, "Douglas Buried Near Oliver Wendell Holmes," *Los Angeles Times*, 1/24/80, sec. 1, p. 4.

508 *The New York Times* Karen De Witt, "Douglas Buried in Arlington Rites," *The New York Times*, 1/24/80, sec. 4, p. 23.

508 **But no one realized** WOD to Edward L. R. Elson, 11/28/77, and WOD to Cathy Douglas, 3/23/77, both in Urofsky, *Douglas Letters*, pp. 424–25.

509 **"I've remembered that"** WOD to Cathy [Douglas], 6/28/77, in ibid.

509 **No one would deny** "Interment in Arlington National Cemetery," prepared by the Casualty and Memorial Affairs Directorate, Adjutant General's Office, Department of the Army, November 1982. And see "Fact Sheet: Bur-

ial in Arlington National Cemetery," Public Affairs Office, U.S. Army Military District of Washington, Fort McNair, Washington, D.C.

509 **Burial for a nonmilitary** It is on this basis that prominent civilians are buried. According to AI (by research assistant Laura Gordon-Murnane) Kathy Shenkle, 2/18/92, these are the conditions under which a nonmilitary individual could be buried in Arlington: if someone died as a result of a terrorist attack; if the family of an individual made a humanitarian contribution to the nation; or by presidential exception.

509 **"If you want to pursue"** WOD to Cathy [Douglas], 6/28/77, in Urofsky, *Douglas Letters,* p. 425.

509 **After receiving the request** AI, W. G. Seibert, 3/2/92, Saint Louis (phone); and see W. G. Seibert to Laura Gordon-Murnane, 2/20/92, in author's possession. And see below re Douglas Military Record.

509 **The performance of** For information on how the record is created, see AI, Louise Arnold-Friend, 2/10/92, Carlisle, Pa. (phone); AI, source wishing to be identified only as "Loretta," 2/18/92, Interment Services, Arlington National Cemetery (phone); AI, W. G. Seibert, 3/2/92, Saint Louis (phone); and see W. G. Seibert to Laura Gordon-Murnane, 2/20/92, in author's possession. See also "William O. Douglas," *Who's Who in America,* 1975– (New Providence, N.J.: Marquis, 1975), copy in Yakima Valley Genealogical Society Office, Yakima, Wash.

510 **A Douglas newspaper** J. Y. Smith, "Douglas—Civil Liberties Champion—Dies," *The Washington Post,* 1/20/80, p. 1.

510 **And finally** Douglas, *Of Men and Mountains,* pp. 158–61, and Douglas, *Go East,* pp. 87–97. Douglas claims in both places that he attended ROTC training at the Presidio in San Francisco, and, according to the college-newspaper record at Whitman, this did happen (see "College Men Go to the Presidio," *Whitman College Pioneer,* 5/31/18, Whitman Archives). As explained in chap. 37, though, this did not mean that he was a private first class in the army as he was now claiming. See Douglas Military Record.

Had anyone checked his claims further, other "confirming" evidence could be found. The 1919 Yakima City Directory listed a flag next to Orville Douglas's name, commemorating his service as a war veteran. Herman Benjamin and the other members of the class of '25 at Columbia Law School still believed that he had been in the army for the two years, delaying his legal education (AI, Herman Benjamin, 11/10/91, Palm Beach, Fla.; and AI, Simon Rifkind, 8/4/89, New York). And members of Americans for Democratic Action in 1948 were told of presidential candidate Douglas: "In 1918 he enlisted in the army. He was sent to San Francisco and later to Camp Taylor, Kentucky, where he was demobilized—still a private" (ADA Convention Brochure).

510 **When a check** According to W. G. Seibert to Laura Gordon-Murnane, 2/20/92, in author's possession. "A search of records on file at this Center for the Special Collegiate Training Camp, S.A.T.C., Presidio of San Francisco, July 16–October 7, 1918, produced no entries for William O. Douglas. . . . Justice Douglas' military service record was reconstructed using

alternate record sources, specifically Government Accounting Office Pay Vouchers. Reports of changes from the S.A.T.C. at Whitman College, Walla Walla, Washington also document Mr. Douglas's service."

510   **Thus, the cemetery's records** AI, "Loretta," consulting Douglas's records at that time, 2/18/92, Interment Services, Arlington National Cemetery. "Douglas was buried in Arlington National Cemetery because he was an Associate Justice of the Supreme Court and that he had military service. . . . Justice William O. Douglas served three months in the army as a private during World War I." It is worth mentioning that others argue that this decision was made on the basis of WOD's reconstructed war record. According to this source, Douglas could not have been buried in Arlington without military service, but his ashes could have been entombed in the cemetery's Columbarium.

See also AI (by Laura Gordon-Murnane), Kathy Shenkle, 2/18/92, Arlington National Cemetery. According to James Edward Peters, *Arlington National Cemetery: Shrine to America's Heroes* (Kensington, Md.: Woodbine House, 1986), p. 81: "Refusing to allow his polio to keep him from fighting for his nation during World War I, Douglas enlisted in the United States Army and fought in Europe." The cemetery's Historian's Office also cites a document by Michael Stone, "Justices of the Supreme Court Who Have Served in the Military," commissioned by the secretary of the army, which states that William O. Douglas was a "Private, U.S. Army, 1917–1919."

Recently, this kind of exaggeration of claims resulting in burials in Arlington National Cemetery has caused problems. In 1997, former ambassador M. Larry Lawrence was removed from his burial plot in Arlington National Cemetery when it was discovered that he never actually served in the Merchant Marine but rather had been attending Wilbur Wright Junior College in Chicago at the time. See Margaret Carlson, "Lies My Ambassador Told Me," *Time,* 12/22/97, p. 31.

510   **Even in death** Harold Heifer, "Far More Than a Private," *Ford Times,* March 1983, indicates the power of this part of the Douglas legend. My thanks to Marty Bagby Yopp, who pulled this article from her own files and handed it to me, saying, "I have always thought that this piece captured the real Douglas better than any other." In doing so, she almost certainly had no idea about the true nature of Justice Douglas's "service." AI, Marty Bagby Yopp, 6/6/90, Moscow, Idaho.

510   **Even still** AI, Charles Reich, 11/15/89, San Francisco.

SELECTED BIBLIOGRAPHY

UNPUBLISHED PRIMARY SOURCES

PAPERS AND ARCHIVAL COLLECTIONS

Joseph Alsop Papers, Manuscript Division, Library of Congress, Washington, D.C.

James Rowland Angell Presidential Papers, Sterling Library, Yale University, New Haven.

Robert Angell Papers, Gerald R. Ford Presidential Library, Ann Arbor, Mich.

Eben A. Ayers Papers, Harry S Truman Library, Independence, Mo.

Hugo L. Black Papers, Manuscript Division, Library of Congress, Washington, D.C.

Louis D. Brandeis Papers, Harvard Law School, Cambridge, Mass.

Louis D. Brandeis Papers, Manuscript Division, Library of Congress, Washington, D.C.

Irving Brant Papers, Manuscript Division, Library of Congress, Washington, D.C.

William Brennan Papers, Manuscript Division, Library of Congress, Washington, D.C.

Eleanor Bumgardner Papers, Gerald R. Ford Presidential Library, Ann Arbor, Mich.

Harold Burton Papers, Manuscript Division, Library of Congress, Washington, D.C.

James F. Byrnes Papers, Clemson University, Clemson, S.C.

Emanuel Celler Papers, Manuscript Division, Library of Congress, Washington, D.C.

Charles E. Clark Papers, Sterling Library, Yale University, New Haven.

Tom Clark Papers, Harry S Truman Library, Independence, Mo.

Tom Clark Papers, Tarlton Law Library, University of Texas, Austin.

Clark Clifford Papers, Clifford and Warnke law firm, Washington, D.C.

Clark Clifford Papers, Harry S Truman Library, Independence, Mo.

Benjamin Cohen Papers, Manuscript Division, Library of Congress, Washington, D.C.

Matthew Connelly Files, Harry S Truman Library, Independence, Mo.

Thomas Corcoran FBI wiretap files, Harry S Truman Library, Independence, Mo.

Thomas Corcoran Papers, Manuscript Division, Library of Congress, Washington, D.C.

Oscar Cox Papers, Franklin D. Roosevelt Presidential Library, Hyde Park, N.Y.

Ernest Cuneo Papers, Franklin D. Roosevelt Presidential Library, Hyde Park, N.Y.

Jonathan Daniels Papers, Harry S Truman Library, Independence, Mo.

Democratic National Committee files, Harry S Truman Library, Independence, Mo.

William O. Douglas Conversations, transcriptions available in Firestone Library, Princeton University, Princeton, N.J., and at libweb.princeton.edu/libraries/firestone/rbsc/finding_aids/douglas.

William O. Douglas file, FBI Reading Room, FBI Headquarters, Washington, D.C.

William O. Douglas impeachment files, Gerald R. Ford Presidential Library, Ann Arbor, Mich.

William O. Douglas 1952 Presidential Campaign Papers, Oregon Historical Society, Portland, Oreg.

William O. Douglas Papers, Manuscript Division, Library of Congress, Washington, D.C.

Commissioner William O. Douglas Papers, Securities and Exchange Commission, Washington, D.C.

William O. Douglas Random House files, in author's possession.

William O. Douglas speech file, Yakima Valley Museum and Historical Association, Yakima, Wash.

Edward Foley Files, Harry S Truman Library, Independence, Mo.

Gerald R. Ford Congressional and Vice-presidential Papers, Gerald R. Ford Presidential Library, Ann Arbor, Mich.

Abe Fortas Papers, Sterling Library, Yale University, New Haven.

Jerome Frank Papers, Sterling Library, Yale University, New Haven.

Felix Frankfurter Papers, Harvard Law School, Cambridge, Mass.

Felix Frankfurter Papers, Manuscript Division, Library of Congress, Washington, D.C.

Eugene Gressman Papers, Michigan Historical Collections, Bentley Historical Library, University of Michigan, Ann Arbor.

Robert Hannegan Papers, Harry S Truman Library, Independence, Mo.

Walton Hamilton Papers, Tarlton Law Library, University of Texas, Austin.

Harlan Hatcher, Gerald R. Ford Presidential Library, Ann Arbor, Mich.

Ken Heckler Papers, Harry S Truman Library, Independence, Mo.

Harry Hopkins Papers, Franklin D. Roosevelt Presidential Library, Hyde Park, N.Y.

Robert Maynard Hutchins Papers, University of Chicago Library, Chicago.

Edward Hutchinson Papers, Gerald R. Ford Presidential Library, Ann Arbor, Mich.

Harold M. Ickes Papers and Unpublished Diary (on microfilm), Manuscript Division, Library of Congress, Washington, D.C.

Robert Jackson Papers, Manuscript Division, Library of Congress, Washington, D.C.

Walter Jenkins Papers, Lyndon B. Johnson Presidential Library, Austin, Texas.

Lyndon B. Johnson Presidential Papers, Senate Papers, and Vice-presidential Papers, Lyndon B. Johnson Presidential Library, Austin, Texas.

John F. Kennedy Presidential Papers, John F. Kennedy Library, Boston.

Robert Walker Kenny Papers, University of California, Berkeley.

James Landis Papers, Harvard Law School, Cambridge, Mass.

Elena Leonardo private papers, Granger, Wash.

Max Lowenthal Papers, University of Minnesota, Minneapolis.

Thurgood Marshall Papers, Manuscript Division, Library of Congress, Washington, D.C.

J. Howard McGrath Files, Harry S Truman Library, Independence, Mo.

Sherman Minton Papers, Harry S Truman Library, Independence, Mo.

Henry Morgenthau Papers, Franklin D. Roosevelt Presidential Library, Hyde Park, N.Y.

Frank Murphy Papers, Michigan Historical Collections, Bentley Historical Library, University of Michigan, Ann Arbor.

George Murphy Papers, Gerald R. Ford Presidential Library, Ann Arbor, Mich.

Richard M. Nixon Presidential Papers, National Archives, College Park, Md.

Frances Penrose Owen private papers, Seattle.

Anthony J. Panuch Papers, Harry S Truman Library, Independence, Mo.

Drew Pearson Papers, Lyndon B. Johnson Presidential Library, Austin, Texas.

Westbrook Pegler Papers, Herbert Hoover Presidential Library, West Branch, Iowa.

Montana Podva private papers, Willits, Calif.

Stanley Reed Papers, University of Kentucky Library, Lexington.

Fred Rodell Papers, Quaker Room, Haverford College, Haverford, Pa.

Franklin D. Roosevelt Presidential Papers, Franklin D. Roosevelt Presidential Library, Hyde Park, N.Y.

Charles Seymour Papers, Sterling Library, Yale University, New Haven.

Robert Sherwood Papers, Houghton Library, Harvard University, Cambridge, Mass.

Simon Soboloff Papers, Manuscript Division, Library of Congress, Washington, D.C.

Harlan F. Stone Papers, Manuscript Division, Library of Congress, Washington, D.C.

Harry S Truman Presidential and Senatorial Papers, Harry S Truman Library, Independence, Mo.

U.S. Supreme Court FBI file, Reading Room, FBI Headquarters, Washington, D.C.

Fred Vinson Papers, University of Kentucky Library, Lexington.

Frank Walker Papers, Notre Dame University, South Bend, Ind.

Henry Wallace Papers, Franklin D. Roosevelt Presidential Library, Hyde Park, N.Y.

Earl Warren Papers, Manuscript Division, Library of Congress, Washington, D.C.

INTERVIEWS, CONVERSATIONS, AND ORAL HISTORIES

INVERVIEWS AND CONVERSATIONS CONDUCTED BY THE AUTHOR

Martin Agronsky, 2/10/91, Washington, D.C.

Thomas Armitage, 4/14/89, 6/10/90, Seattle

Louise Arnold-Friend, 2/10/92, Carlisle, Pa. (phone)

Herman Benjamin, 11/10/90 (Palm Beach, Fla.), 8/21/91 (phone)

Raoul Berger, 7/20/88, Valley Forge, Pa.

Del Bice, 6/9/90, Yakima, Wash.

Harry Blackmun, 4/17/89, Seattle

Jean Boyd, 8/20/89, Yakima, Wash.

Jo Brown, 2/27/92, Portland, Oreg. (phone)
Jared Carter, 8/30/90, Ukiah, Calif.
Clark Clifford, 8/27/89, Washington, D.C.
Elaine Cohen, 8/10/90, Goose Prairie, Wash.
Sheldon Cohen, 5/13/93, Washington, D.C.
Betty Lou Cokum, 12/13/91, Shandon, Calif. (phone)
Thomas Corcoran, 9/29/77, Washington, D.C.
Vern Countryman, 11/14/89, Moraga, Calif.
Jerry Cundiff, Jr., 5/31/90, Walla Walla, Wash.
Harry Datcher, 5/5/90, 5/16/90, Washington, D.C.
Walter Dellinger, 11/1/91, Durham, N.C.
Fay Aull Deusterman, 3/3/91, Orlando, Fla.
Larry Dodd, 3/2/95, Walla Walla, Wash. (phone)
Steven Duke, 4/15/89, Seattle
Philip Elman, 7/10/79, Washington, D.C.
John Evans, 10/19/91, La Grande, Oreg.
Judge Betty Fletcher, 8/22/89, Seattle
Donna Fleming, 1/18/92, New Haven (phone)
Bob Ford, 6/3/90, Goose Prairie, Wash.
Ira Ford, 8/20/89 (Yakima, Wash.), 6/3/90 (Goose Prairie, Wash.)
Sharon Ford, 6/3/90, Goose Prairie, Wash.
Abe Fortas, 8/7/81, Washington, D.C.
Milton Freeman, 5/21/96, Washington, D.C. (phone)
Betty Ford Gallant, 8/20/89, Yakima, Wash.
John Gavin, 2/2/92 (Yakima, Wash.), 2/10/92, Yakima, Wash. (phone)
Cragg Gilbert, 8/17/90, Yakima, Wash.
C. David Ginsburg, 8/28/89, Washington, D.C.
Dagmar Hamilton, 6/20/89, 2/23–3/2/90, 5/16/90, Austin, Tex.
Irene Hamilton, 5/16/90, Washington, D.C.
Robert Hamilton, 6/22/89, 2/23/90, 3/2/90, Austin, Tex.
Frances Hare, 4/4/90 (phone), 6/8/90 (Yakima, Wash.)
Maurice Helland, 4/17/90, Yakima, Wash.
Gary L. Jackson, 4/15/90, Yakima, Wash. (phone)
Eliot Janeway, 5/19/90, 8/14/90, 5/8/92, New York
June Kennedy, 7/30/2002, Bernards Township, N.J. (phone)
Marion Kennedy, 10/24/91, 7/30/2002, Bernardsville, N.J. (phone)
Ed Kershaw, 4/20/89, 6/7/90, Yakima, Wash.
Kay Kershaw, 4/19/89, 8/6–8/23/89, Goose Prairie, Wash.
Arthur Kimball, 8/21/91, New York (phone)
Jed King, 6/10/90, Seattle
John LaCoCo, 11/20/91, San Jose
Elena Leonardo, 8/21/89 (Sunnyside, Wash.), 6/9/90 (Seattle), 7/17/02 (Toppen-
    ish, Wash. [phone])
Hans Linde, 8/18/90, Salem, Oreg.
Lucile Lomen, 9/9/90, Seattle
Walter Lowe, 4/27/89, Seattle (phone)

Isabelle Lynn, 4/19/89, 8/6–8/23/89, Goose Prairie, Wash.

Thomas Magner, 5/20/90, State College, Pa.

James Marsh, 8/15/2000, Philadelphia

George M. Martin, 4/4/90 (phone), 6/5/90, 6/8/90, 9/17/91 (Yakima, Wash.)

Rev. Herbert Matsen, 4/18/91, Cleveland, Wash. (phone)

Lex Maxwell, 6/9/90, Yakima, Wash.

Charlotte Mayerson, 12/11/90, New York (phone)

Kenneth McCormick, 5/25/90, 6/16/90, New York (phone)

Alta McMillan, 12/13/91, 12/14/91, Shandon, Calif. (phone)

Eben McMillan, 12/13/91, Shandon, Calif. (phone)

Ross McMillan, 12/13/91, Santa Cruz, Calif. (phone)

Hallam Mendenhall, 2/27/92, Ocean City, N.J. (phone)

Wesley (Jack) Mendenhall, 3/4/92, Portolla Valley, Calif. (phone)

James Milholland, 4/16/90, State College, Pa.

Robert Mull, 4/6/90, Seattle (phone)

Walter Murphy, 7/16/89, Princeton, N.J. (phone)

Frances Penrose Owen, 9/9/90, Seattle

Mike Passage, 8/17/90, Goose Prairie, Wash.

Penny Passage, 8/17/90, Goose Prairie, Wash.

Montana James Podva, 8/28/90, Willits, Calif.

Lucas A. "Scot" Powe, 4/17/89 (Seattle), 6/20/89, 6/22/89, 6/23/89 (Austin, Tex.)

Edward F. Prichard, Jr., 6/25/79, Frankfort, Ky.

William Pugh, 2/27/92, Yakima, Wash.

Joseph L. Rauh, Jr., 7/9/79, 8/29/89, Washington, D.C.

Millie Douglas Read, 8/20/89, La Grande, Oreg.

Charles Reich, 11/15/89, San Francisco

William Reppy, 11/1/91, Durham, N.C.

Simon Rifkind, 8/4/89, New York

Wendy M. Ross, 3/24/2001, Rockville, Md. (phone)

Eileen Ryan, 8/10/90, Goose Prairie, Wash.

Evan L. Schwab, 8/22/89, Seattle (phone)

Red Schwartz, 1/27/93, Syracuse, N.Y.

W. G. Seibert, 3/2/92, Saint Louis (phone)

Stanley Soderland, 6/12/90, Shaw Island, Wash.

James Souls, 10/7/97, Newark, Del.

Marilyn Sparks, 5/31/90, Walla Walla, Wash.

Pearl Sparrow, 10/14/91, New York (phone)

Stanley Sparrowe, 4/17/89, Seattle

Homer Splawn, 6/5/90, Yakima, Wash.

Cathy Douglas Stone, 4/16/89, Seattle

Larry Temple, 6/22/89, Austin, Tex.

Fred Velikanje, 12/23/91, Yakima, Wash. (phone)

Dennis Vetock, 2/10/92, Carlisle, Pa. (phone)

Denny Walsh, 3/23/90, Washington, D.C.

Chalmer Walter, 12/23/91, Yakima, Wash. (phone)

Mary Weiler, 3/26/91, Saint Louis (phone)

Peter Kay Westen, 9/26/90, Ann Arbor, Mich.
Judge Roy Wilkinson, 7/5/91, State College, Pa.
Doug Williams, 4/19/89, Cliffdell, Wash.
Helen Williams, 4/20/89, Yakima, Wash.
Will Wilson, 2/26/90, Austin, Tex.
Judge Charles E. Wyzanski, Jr., 1/13/77, Richmond, Va.
Marty Bagby Yopp, 6/6/90, Moscow, Idaho

INTERVIEWS CONDUCTED BY WALTER LOWE

Lowe, Walter. *William O. Douglas: A Life on the High Court.* KYVE-TV, Yakima, 1988.

William Alsup, 5/23/88, 5/24/88
Thomas Armitage (n.d.)
Alan Austin, 5/23/88
Justice Harry Blackmun, 5/12/88
Justice William Brennan, 5/13/88
David Brower, 5/26/88
Carol Bruch, 5/24/88
Walter Chaffee, 6/2/88
Warren Christopher, 5/31/88
Clark Clifford, 3/16/88, 5/16/88
William Cohen, 5/23/88
Vern Countryman, 5/25/88
Harry Datcher, 5/12/88
William O. Douglas, Jr., 2/13/88
Mercedes Douglas Eicholz, 5/28/88
Judge Betty Fletcher (n.d.)
Milton Freeman, 5/11/88
Judge Gerhard Gesell, 5/16/88
Claude Gilbert, 7/7/88
C. David Ginsburg 5/17/88
Harold M. Grossman, 6/3/88
Judge Irving Hill, 5/31/88
Donald Kelley, 5/24/88
William Norris (n.d.)
Montana James Podva, 5/26/88
Joseph L. Rauh, 5/11/88
Millie Douglas Read, 4/16/88
Chief Justice William Rehnquist, 5/13/88
Charles Rickershauser, 6/1/88
Marshall Small, 5/24/88
Cathy Douglas Stone, 5/17/88
1971 KIMA-TV interview with William O. Douglas

INTERVIEWS CONDUCTED BY ROBERT W. MULL

Mull, Robert. *When Court Adjourned: A Retrospective Look at Yakima's Most Famous Native Son, William O. Douglas.* KYVE-TV, Yakima, 1981.

William O. Douglas, Jr. [1981]
Chester Maxey, 9/22/81, Walla Walla, Wash.

INTERVIEW CONDUCTED BY GEORGE M. MARTIN

Bruce Mallard, 9/16/91, Yakima, Wash.

INTERVIEW CONDUCTED BY ERIC SEVAREID

"Mr. Justice Douglas." *CBS Reports.* Airdate: 9/6/72 (video).

ORAL HISTORIES

ORAL HISTORIES LOCATED IN THE COLUMBIA ORAL HISTORY
COLLECTION, BUTLER LIBRARY, COLUMBIA UNIVERSITY, NEW YORK, N.Y.

Adolf Berle; Max Bernays; Roger Blough; Leonard Boudin; Chester Bowles; Herbert Brownell; Marquis Childs; William H. Davis; Thomas I. Emerson; Felix Frankfurter; Max Friedman; Edward Greenbaum; Robert H. Jackson; Philip Jessup; Arthur Krock; James Landis; Charles T. Lane; Kenneth McCormick; Harold R. Medina; William Moran; James L. O'Brien; Ferdinand Pecora; Frances Perkins; Lee Pressman; Samuel Rosenman; Benno Schmidt; Bill Shields; Henry Wallace

ORAL HISTORIES LOCATED IN THE HARRY S TRUMAN PRESIDENTIAL
LIBRARY, INDEPENDENCE, MO.

John Abbott; George Allen; Eben Ayers; Lewis Barringer; Louis H. Bean; David Bell; Jack Bell; Andrew Biemiller; Raymond Brandt; Samuel Brightman; David K. E. Bruce; J. F. Carter; Oliver Carter; Tom Clark; Clark Clifford; Matthew J. Connelly; Josephus Daniels; C. Girard Davidson; William K. Divers; M. L. Dryden; Harry Easley; India Edwards; Thomas L. Evans; Oscar R. Ewing; Thomas Finletter; Edward Folliard; Judge Monroe Friedman; Roswell Gilpatric; Lincoln Gould; Charles Greene; Ruby Jane Hall; Edgar Hinde; Marvin Jones; Walter Judd; John A. Kennedy; W. John Kenny; Carleton Kent; Leon Keyserling; Milton Kronheim; James I. Loeb; Katie Louchheim; Max Lowenthal; McNeil Lowry; Lowell B. Mason; John McErney; Howard McGrath; Edward McKim; George Meader; Robert G. Nixon; Frank Pace; Paul Porter; Leonard Reinsch; Louis Renfrow; Robert L. Riggs; Arthur Ringwalt; Neele Roache; Samuel Rosenman; James L. Rowe; Harold Slater; John Snyder; John L. Sullivan; J. William Theis; Walter Trohan; Harry Vaughan; Robert K. Walsh; Earl Warren; Eugene M. Zuckert

ORAL HISTORIES LOCATED IN THE JOHN F. KENNEDY PRESIDENTIAL
LIBRARY, BOSTON, MASS.

William O. Douglas; Robert F. Kennedy

ORAL HISTORY LOCATED IN THE WHITMAN ARCHIVES

Chester Maxey

PUBLISHED SOURCES

SELECTED BOOKS

Abraham, Henry J. *Justices, Presidents, and Senators: A History of the U.S. Supreme Court Appointments from Washington to Clinton.* Lanham, Md.: Rowman and Littlefield, 1999.

Allen, James, ed. *Democracy and Finance: The Addresses and Public Statements of William O. Douglas as Member and Chairman of the Securities and Exchange Commission.* New Haven: Yale University Press, 1940.

Alsop, Joseph, and Turner Catledge. *The 168 Days: The Story Behind the Story of the Supreme Court Fight.* Philadelphia: G. Graham, 1938.

Asch, Sidney. *The Supreme Court and Its Great Justices.* New York: Arco, 1971.

Ashmore, Harry S. *Unseasonable Truths: The Life of Robert Maynard Hutchins.* Boston: Little, Brown, 1989.

Baker, Leonard. *Back to Back: The Duel Between FDR and the Supreme Court.* New York: Macmillan, 1967.

Ball, Howard. *Hugo L. Black: Cold Steel Warrior.* New York: Oxford University Press, 1996.

―――. *"We Have a Duty": The Supreme Court and the Watergate Tapes Litigation.* Westport, Conn.: Greenwood Press, 1990.

Ball, Howard, and Philip Cooper. *Of Power and Right: Hugo Black, William O. Douglas, and America's Constitutional Revolution.* New York: Oxford University Press, 1992.

Benedict, G. G. *Vermont in the Civil War: A History of the Part Taken by the Vermont Soldiers and Sailors in the War for the Union, 1861–65.* Vol. 1. Burlington, Vt.: Free Press Associates, 1886.

Black, Elizabeth. *Mr. Justice and Mrs. Black: The Memoirs of Hugo L. Black and Elizabeth Black.* New York: Random House, 1986.

Black, Kathryn. *In the Shadow of Polio: A Personal and Social History.* Reading, Mass.: Addison-Wesley, 1996.

Blandford, Linda, and Patricia Russell Evans. *Supreme Court of the United States, 1789–1980: An Index to Opinions Arranged by Justice.* Millwood, N.Y.: Kraus International, 1981.

Bosmajian, Haig A. *Justice Douglas and Freedom of Speech.* Metuchen, N.J.: Scarecrow Press, 1980.

Brackenridge, R. Douglas, and Lois A. Boyd. *Presbyterians and Pensions: 1917–1988.* Atlanta: John Knox, 1988.

Bronner, Ethan. *Battle for Justice: How the Bork Nomination Shook America*. New York: Anchor, 1989.

Brooks, John. *Once in Golconda: A True Drama of Wall Street, 1920–1938*. New York: Harper and Row, 1969.

Brownell, Herbert. *Advising Ike: The Memoirs of Attorney General Herbert Brownell*. Lawrence: University of Kansas Press, 1993.

Brownfeld, Allan C. *Dossier on Douglas, Impeach or Acquit: The Case Against Justice William O. Douglas*. Washington, D.C.: New Majority Book Club, 1970.

Butterfield, Frank G. *Revised Roster of Vermont Volunteers and Lists of Vermonters Who Served in the Army and Navy of the United States During the War of the Rebellion, 1861–1866*. Carlisle, Pa.: Military History Institute Collection, 1892.

Caro, Robert. *The Years of Lyndon Johnson*. Vol. 1: *The Path to Power*. New York, Alfred A. Knopf, 1982.

Carson, Rachel. *Silent Spring*. Boston: Houghton Mifflin, 1962.

Charns, Alexander. *Cloak and Gavel: FBI Wiretaps, Bugs, Informers, and the Supreme Court*. Urbana: University of Illinois Press, 1992.

Clifford, Clark, with Richard Holbrooke. *Counsel to the President: A Memoir*. New York: Random House, 1991.

Clifton, Carr, and Tom Turner. *Wild by Law*. San Francisco: Sierra Club Books, 1990.

Cooper, Philip, and Howard Ball. *The United States Supreme Court: From the Inside Out*. New York: Prentice-Hall, 1996.

Countryman, Vern. *Douglas of the Supreme Court: A Selection of His Opinions*. Garden City, N.Y.: Doubleday, 1959.

———. *The Douglas Opinions*. New York: Random House, 1977.

———. *The Judicial Record of Justice William O. Douglas*. Cambridge, Mass.: Harvard University Press, 1974.

Crawford, Jeanne R., ed. *As the Valley Was: A Pictorial View*. Yakima: Yakima Federal Savings and Loan Association, 1968.

Damasio, Antonio R. *Descartes' Error: Emotion, Reason, and the Human Brain*. New York: Avon, 1994.

Davis, Kenneth S. *FDR*. Vol. 2: *The New York Years, 1928–1933*. New York: Random House, 1985.

———. *FDR*. Vol. 3: *The New Deal Years, 1933–1937*. New York: Random House, 1986.

DeBedts, Ralph F. *The New Deal's SEC: The Formative Years*. New York: Columbia University Press, 1964.

Donovan, Robert J. *Conflict and Crisis: The Presidency of Harry S Truman, 1945–1948*. Columbia: University of Missouri Press, 1977.

———. *Tumultuous Years: The Presidency of Harry S Truman, 1949–1953*. Boston: W. W. Norton, 1982.

Douglas, Helen Gahagan. *A Full Life*. Garden City, N.Y.: Doubleday, 1982.

Douglas, William O. *An Almanac of Liberty*. Garden City, N.Y.: Doubleday, 1951.

———. *America Challenged*. Princeton: Princeton University Press, 1960.

———. *The Anatomy of Liberty: The Rights of Man Without Force*. New York: Simon and Schuster, 1963.

———. *Beyond the High Himalayas*. Garden City, N.Y.: Doubleday, 1952.

————. *The Bible and the Schools*. Boston: Little, Brown, 1966.

————. *The Court Years, 1939–1975: The Autobiography of William O. Douglas*. New York: Random House, 1980.

————. *Democracy's Manifesto*. Garden City, N.Y.: Doubleday, 1962.

————. *Exploring the Himalaya*. New York: Random House, 1958.

————. *Farewell to Texas: A Vanishing Wilderness*. New York: McGraw-Hill, 1967.

————. *Freedom of the Mind*. Garden City, N.Y.: Doubleday, 1962.

————. *Go East, Young Man: The Early Years: The Autobiography of William O. Douglas*. New York: Random House, 1974.

————. *Holocaust or Hemispheric Co-Op: Crosscurrents in Latin America*. New York: Random House, 1971.

————. *International Dissent: Six Steps Toward World Peace*. New York: Random House, 1971.

————. *Mr. Lincoln and the Negroes: The Long Road to Equality*. New York: Atheneum, 1963.

————. *My Wilderness: East to Katahdin*. Garden City, N.Y.: Doubleday, 1961.

————. *My Wilderness: The Pacific West*. New York: Doubleday, 1960.

————. *North from Malaya: Adventure on Five Fronts*. Garden City, N.Y.: Doubleday, 1953.

————. *Of Men and Mountains*. New York: Harper and Brothers, 1950.

————. *Points of Rebellion*. New York: Random House, 1970.

————. *The Right of the People*. Garden City, N.Y.: Doubleday, 1958.

————. *The Right to Be Let Alone*. Garden City, N.Y.: Doubleday, 1958.

————. *Russian Journey*. Garden City, N.Y.: Doubleday, 1954.

————. *The Three Hundred Year War: A Chronicle of Ecological Disaster*. New York: Random House, 1972.

————. *West of the Indus*. Garden City, N.Y.: Doubleday, 1958.

————. *We the Judges: Studies in American and Indian Constitutional Law from Marshall to Mukherjea*. Garden City, N.Y.: Doubleday, 1956.

————. *A Wilderness Bill of Rights*. Boston: Little, Brown, 1965.

Douglas, William O., with Charles E. Clark. *Cases on the Law of Partnership, Joint Stock Associations, Business Trusts, and Other Non-corporate Business Organizations*. Saint Paul: West, 1932.

Douglas, William O., with Carrol M. Shanks. *Cases and Materials on Business Units, Losses, Liabilities, and Assets*. Chicago: Callaghan, 1931.

————. *Cases and Materials on the Law of Corporate Reorganizations*. Saint Paul: West, 1931.

————. *Cases and Materials on the Law of Financing of Business Units*. Chicago: Callaghan, 1931.

————. *Cases and Materials on the Law of Management of Business Units*. Chicago: Callaghan, 1931.

Draper, George. *Disease and the Man*. New York: Macmillan, 1930.

————. *Human Constitution: A Consideration of Its Relationship to Disease*. Philadelphia: W. B. Saunders, 1924.

Ducat, Craig R. *Constitutional Interpretation*. Minneapolis: West, 1996.

Duram, James C. *Justice William O. Douglas*. Boston: Twayne, 1981.

Dzuback, Mary Ann. *Robert Maynard Hutchins: Portrait of an Educator.* Chicago: University of Chicago Press, 1991.

Ehrlichman, John. *Witness to Power: The Nixon Years.* New York: Pocket, 1982.

Epstein, Lee, Jeffrey A. Segal, Harold J. Spaeth, and Thomas G. Walker. *The Supreme Court Compendium: Data, Decisions, and Developments.* 2d ed. Washington, D.C.: Congressional Quarterly, 1996.

Erikson, Erik H. *Young Man Luther: A Study in Psychoanalysis and History.* New York: W. W. Norton, 1958.

Farley, James Aloysius. *Jim Farley's Story: The Roosevelt Years.* New York: Whittlesey House, 1948.

Ferrell, Robert H. *Choosing Truman: The Democratic Convention of 1944.* Columbia: University of Missouri Press, 1994.

———. *Harry S Truman: A Life.* Columbia: University of Missouri Press, 1994.

Ferrell, Robert H., ed. *Off the Record: The Private Papers of Harry S Truman.* Columbia: University of Missouri Press, 1997.

Fine, Sidney. *Frank Murphy: The Washington Years.* Ann Arbor: University of Michigan Press, 1984.

Frantz, Douglas, and David McKean. *Friends in High Places: The Rise and Fall of Clark Clifford.* Boston: Little, Brown, 1995.

Fraser, Steven. *Labor Will Rule: Sidney Hillman and the Rise of American Labor.* New York: Free Press, 1991.

Freidel, Frank. *Franklin D. Roosevelt: A Rendezvous with Destiny.* Boston: Little, Brown, 1990.

Fursenko, Aleksandr, and Timothy Naftali. *"One Hell of a Gamble": Khrushchev, Castro, Kennedy, and the Cuban Missile Crisis, 1958–1964.* London: Pimlico Press, 1999.

Gabler, Neal. *Winchell: Gossip, Power, and the Culture of Celebrity.* New York: Vintage, 1994.

Garrow, David J. *Liberty and Sexuality: The Right of Privacy and the Making of Roe v. Wade.* New York: Macmillan, 1994.

Gerhart, Eugene C. *America's Advocate: Robert H. Jackson.* Indianapolis: Bobbs-Merrill, 1958.

Getz, Gene A. *MBI: The Story of the Moody Bible Institute.* Chicago: Moody Press, 1969.

Gillon, Steven M. *Politics and Vision: The ADA and American Liberalism, 1947–1985.* New York: Oxford University Press, 1987.

Goebel, Julius, Jr. *A History of the School of Law, Columbia University.* New York: Columbia University Press, 1955.

Goodwin, Doris Kearns. *No Ordinary Time: Franklin and Eleanor Roosevelt: The Home Front in World War II.* New York: Simon and Schuster, 1994.

Hamby, Alonzo. *Man of the People: A Life of Harry S Truman.* New York: Oxford University Press, 1995.

Hansen, Beatrice. *A Political Biography of Walter Reuther: The Record of an Opportunist.* New York: Merit, 1969.

Harris, Richard. *Decision.* New York: Ballantine, 1982.

Hayes, Teddy. *With the Gloves Off: My Life in the Boxing and Political Arenas.* Houston: Lancha Books, 1977.

Helland, Maurice. *Tent to Tower, 1885–1985.* Yakima: Yakima Presbyterian Church, 1984.

Hentoff, Nat. *Living the Bill of Rights: How to Be an Authentic American.* New York: HarperCollins, 1998.

Hirsch, H. N. *The Enigma of Felix Frankfurter.* New York: Basic Books, 1981.

Hollingsworth, Harold, and William Holmes, eds. *Essays on the New Deal.* Austin: University of Texas Press, 1969.

Hoyt, Edwin Palmer. *The Tempering Years.* New York: Scribners, 1963.

———. *William O. Douglas: A Biography.* Middlebury, Vt.: Erikson, 1978.

Irons, Peter H. *Justice at War: The Story of the Japanese American Internment Cases.* New York: Oxford University Press, 1983.

———. *The New Deal Lawyers.* Princeton: Princeton University Press, 1982.

Jackson, Gary L. *Remembering Yakima: By Those Who Were There.* Yakima: Golden West, 1975.

Jenkins, Roy. *Truman.* New York: Perennial Library, 1987.

Kalman, Laura. *Abe Fortas: A Biography.* New Haven: Yale University Press, 1990.

———. *Legal Realism at Yale, 1927–1960.* Chapel Hill: University of North Carolina Press, 1986.

Keller, Robert H., Jr., ed. *In Honor of Justice Douglas: A Symposium on Individual Freedom and the Government.* Westport, Conn.: Greenwood, 1979.

Krock, Arthur. *Memoirs: Sixty Years on the Firing Line.* New York: Funk and Wagnalls, 1968.

Kunitz, Stanley. *American Authors, 1600–1900: A Biographical Dictionary of American Literature.* New York: H. W. Wilson, 1960.

Lash, Joseph. *Dealers and Dreamers: A New Look at the New Deal.* New York: Doubleday, 1988.

Lash, Joseph P., ed. *From the Diaries of Felix Frankfurter.* New York: W. W. Norton, 1975.

Levinson, Daniel. *Seasons of a Man's Life.* New York: Ballantine, 1978.

Lichtenstein, Nelson. *Walter Reuther: The Most Dangerous Man in Detroit.* Urbana: University of Illinois Press, 1997.

Lisagor, Nancy. *A Law unto Itself: The Untold Story of the Law Firm Sullivan and Cromwell.* New York: Paragon House, 1989.

Loetscher, Lefferts A. *The Broadening Church: A Study of Theological Issues in the Presbyterian Church Since 1869.* Philadelphia: University of Pennsylvania Press, 1954.

Longfield, Bradley J. *The Presbyterian Controversy.* New York: Oxford University Press, 1991.

Lonn, Ella. *Desertion During the Civil War.* New York: Century, 1928.

Louchheim, Katie. *The Making of the New Deal: The Insiders Speak.* Cambridge, Mass.: Harvard University Press, 1983.

Lyman, W. D. *History of the Yakima Valley, Washington.* Chicago: S. J. Clarke, 1919.

Martin, George M., Paul Schafer, and William E. Scofield. *Yakima: A Centennial Reflection, 1885–1985.* Yakima: Shields Bag and Printing, 1985.

Mason, Alpheus Thomas. *Harlan Fiske Stone: Pillar of the Law.* New York: Viking, 1956.

Mason, John W., ed. *The History of Ottertail County, Minnesota.* Indianapolis: B. F. Bowen, 1916.

McCullough, David. *Truman*. New York: Simon and Schuster, 1992.

McNeill, William H. *Hutchins' University: A Memoir of the University of Chicago, 1929–1950*. Chicago: University of Chicago Press, 1991.

Mosley, Leonard. *Dulles: A Biography of Eleanor, Allen, and John Foster Dulles and Their Family Network*. New York: Dial Press, 1978.

Murphy, Bruce Allen. *The Brandeis/Frankfurter Connection: The Secret Political Activities of Two Supreme Court Justices*. New York: Oxford University Press, 1982.

———. *Fortas: The Rise and Ruin of a Supreme Court Justice*. New York: William Morrow, 1988.

Nelson, Jack. *We Never Got Away*. Yakima: Franklin Press, 1965.

Newman, Roger. *Hugo Black: A Biography*. New York: Pantheon, 1994.

O'Fallon, James M. *Nature's Justice: Writings of William O. Douglas*. Corvallis: Oregon State University Press, 2000.

Orchard, Vance. *The Walla Walla Story: Washington Centennial Edition* [1953]. Walla Walla: General Printing, 1988.

Palmer, Jan. *The Vinson Court Era: The Supreme Court's Conference Votes*. New York: AMS, 1990.

Parrish, Michael. *Securities Regulation and the New Deal*. New Haven: Yale University Press, 1988.

Peters, James Edward. *Arlington National Cemetery: Shrine to America's Heroes*. Kensington, Md.: Woodbine House, 1986.

Pierson, George Wilson. *Yale: College and University, 1871–1937*. 2 vols. New Haven: Yale University Press, 1952.

Pritchett, C. Herman. *Civil Liberties and the Vinson Court*. Chicago: University of Chicago Press, 1954.

———. *Constitutional Civil Liberties*. Englewood Cliffs, N.J.: Prentice-Hall, 1984.

———. *The Roosevelt Court: A Study in Judicial Politics and Values, 1937–1947*. New York: Macmillan, 1948.

Radosh, Ronald, and Joyce Milton. *The Rosenberg File: A Search for the Truth*. New York: Holt, Rinehart, and Winston, 1983.

Relander, Click, and George M. Martin. *Yakima Washington Jubilee, 1885–1960*. Yakima: Franklin Press, 1960.

Renz, Louis T. *The Construction of the Northern Pacific Railroad Main Line During the Years 1870 to 1888*. Walla Walla: privately printed, 1973.

Robertson, David. *Sly and Able: A Political Biography of James F. Byrnes*. New York: W. W. Norton, 1994.

Roosevelt, James, and Sidney Shalett. *Affectionately, FDR: A Son's Story of a Lonely Man*. New York: Harcourt, Brace, 1959.

Rosenblatt, Emil, and Ruth Rosenblatt. *Hard Marching Every Day: The Civil War Letters of Private Wilbur Fisk, 1861–1865*. Lawrence: University Press of Kansas, 1992.

Schwartz, Bernard. *The Ascent of Pragmatism: The Burger Court in Action*. Reading, Mass.: Addison-Wesley, 1990.

———. *Decision: How the Supreme Court Decides Cases*. New York: Oxford University Press, 1996.

———. *Super Chief: Earl Warren and His Supreme Court—A Judicial Biography*. New York: New York University Press, 1983.

————. *The Unpublished Opinions of the Warren Court.* New York: Oxford University Press, 1985.

Schwarz, Jordan A. *The New Dealers: Power Politics in the Age of Roosevelt.* New York: Alfred A. Knopf, 1993.

Seligman, Joel. *The Transformation of Wall Street: A History of the Securities and Exchange Commission and Modern Corporate Finance.* Boston: Houghton Mifflin, 1982.

Shapiro, Fred. *The Oxford Dictionary of American Legal Quotations.* New York: Oxford University Press, 1993.

Sharlitt, Joseph H. *Fatal Error: The Miscarriage of Justice That Sealed the Rosenbergs' Fate.* New York: Scribners, 1983.

Simon, James F. *Independent Journey: The Life of William O. Douglas.* New York: Harper and Row, 1980.

Sobel, Robert. *NYSE: A History of the New York Stock Exchange, 1935–1975.* New York: Weybright and Talley, 1975.

Spring, Ira, and Harvey Manning. *1000 Hikes in the South Cascades and Olympics.* Seattle: Mountaineers, 1985.

Stevens, Robert. *Law School: Legal Education in America from the 1850s to the 1980s.* Chapel Hill: University of North Carolina Press, 1983.

Strauss, Helen. *A Talent for Luck: An Autobiography.* New York: Random House, 1979.

Swaine, Robert T. *The Cravath Firm and Its Predecessors, 1819–1948.* Vol. 2. New York: privately printed, 1948.

Truman, Harry S. *Memoirs.* Vol. 1: *Year of Decisions.* Garden City, N.Y.: Doubleday, 1955.

————. *Memoirs.* Vol. 2: *Years of Trial and Hope.* Garden City, N.Y.: Doubleday, 1956.

Truman, Margaret. *Harry S Truman.* New York: Avon, 1993.

Tully, Grace. *FDR: My Boss.* New York: Scribners, 1949.

Urofsky, Melvin. *Division and Discord: The Supreme Court Under Stone and Vinson, 1941–1953.* Columbia: University of South Carolina Press, 1997.

Urofsky, Melvin, ed. *The Douglas Letters: Selections from the Private Papers of Justice William O. Douglas.* Bethesda: Adler and Adler, 1987.

Ward, Geoffrey. *A First-Class Temperament: The Emergence of Franklin Roosevelt.* New York: Harper and Row, 1989.

Wasby, Stephen L., ed. *"He Shall Not Pass This Way Again": The Legacy of Justice William O. Douglas.* Pittsburgh: University of Pittsburgh Press, 1990.

Watkins, T. H. *Righteous Pilgrim: The Life and Times of Harold L. Ickes, 1874–1952.* New York: Henry Holt, 1990.

Whalen, Richard J. *The Founding Father: The Story of Joseph P. Kennedy.* New York: New American Library, 1964.

Wolfman, Bernard, et al. *Dissent Without Opinion: The Behavior of Justice William O. Douglas in the Federal Tax Cases.* Philadelphia: University of Pennsylvania Press, 1975.

Woodward, Bob, and Scott Armstrong. *The Brethren: Inside the Supreme Court.* New York: Avon, 1979.

Yoder, Edwin M., Jr. *The Unmaking of a Whig: And Other Essays in Self-Definition.* Washington, D.C.: Georgetown University Press, 1990.

————. *Whitman: An Unfinished Story.* Walla Walla: Whitman, 1935.

SELECTED ARTICLES

Alexander, Jack. "Washington's Angry Scotsman." *The Saturday Evening Post,* 10/17/47.

Alfange, Dean, Jr. "Free Speech and Symbolic Conduct: The Draft-Card Burning Case." *Supreme Court Review* 1968.

Alsop, Joseph, and Robert Kintner. "The Battle of the Market Place: Richard Whitney Leads the Fight." *The Saturday Evening Post,* 6/11/38.

———. "The Capital Parade." *The Atlanta Constitution,* 12/17/37.

———. "We Shall Make America Over" (part 2 of 3). *The Saturday Evening Post,* 11/12/38.

"Arthur and William Douglas." *National Biographic* 1:8 (May 1954).

Bendiner, Robert. "Politics and People." *The Nation,* 6/12/48.

Bird, Kai, and Max Holland. "The Tapping of 'Tommy the Cork.' " *The Nation,* 2/8/86.

Black, Hugo L. "William Orville Douglas." *Yale Law Journal* 73 (1964).

Brenner, Saul, and Timothy M. Hagle. "Opinion Writing and Acclimation Effect." *Political Behavior* 18:3 (1996).

Britt, George. "Wall Street vs. Washington." *Literary Digest,* 1/29/38.

Caldeira, Gregory A., and Christopher J. W. Zorn. "Of Time and Consensual Norms in the Supreme Court." *American Journal of Political Science* 42:3 (1998).

Childs, Marquis. "The Supreme Court To-day." *Harper's,* 5/38.

Clark, William, William O. Douglas, and Dorothy S. Thomas. "The Business Failures Project—A Problem in Methodology." *Yale Law Journal* 39 (May 1930).

Cohen, William. "Justice Douglas and the *Rosenberg* Case: Setting the Record Straight." *Cornell Law Review* 70 (November–March 1984–1985).

Conroy, Frank. "Think About It." In *The Best American Essays, 1989.* Ed. Robert Atwain. New York: Ticknor and Fields, 1989.

Coulter, Calvin B. "The Victory of National Irrigation in the Yakima Valley, 1902–1906." *Pacific Northwest Quarterly* 42 (1951).

Creel, George. "The Young Man Went East." *Collier's,* 5/9/36.

Danelski, David J. "Lucile Lomen: The First Woman to Clerk at the Supreme Court." *Journal of Supreme Court History* 1 (1999).

———. "The Origins of William O. Douglas's Jurisprudence." *Whitman: The Quarterly Magazine of Whitman College* 13:3 (summer 1991).

Douglas, William O. "The Bill of Rights Is Not Enough." *New York University Law Journal* 38 (April 1963).

———. "Directors Who Do Not Direct." *Harvard Law Review* 47 (June 1934).

———. "Functional Approach to the Law of Business Associations." *Illinois Law Review* 26 (March 1929).

———. "Protecting the Investor." *Yale Review* 23 (March 1934).

———. "Protective Committee in Railroad Reorganizations." *Harvard Law Review* 47 (February 1934).

———. "Some Functional Aspects of Bankruptcy." *Yale Law Journal* 41:3 (January 1932).

———. "Vicarious Liability and Administration of Risk II." *Yale Law Journal* 38 (April 1929).

Douglas, William O., and G. E. Bates, "Federal Securities Act of 1933." *Yale Law Journal* 43 (December 1933).

———. "Some Effects of the Securities Act upon Investment Banking." *University of Chicago Law Review* 1 (November 1933).

———. "Stock 'Brokers' as Agents and Dealers." *Yale Law Journal* 43 (November 1933).

Douglas, William O., and T. H. Marshall. "A Factual Study of Bankruptcy Administration and Some Suggestions." *Columbia Law Review* 32 (1932).

Douglas, William O., and Carrol M. Shanks. "Insulation from Liability Through Subsidiary Corporations." *Yale Law Journal* 39 (December 1929).

Douglas, William O., and Dorothy S. Thomas. "The Business Failures Project—II: An Analysis of Methods of Investigation." *Yale Law Journal* 40 (1931).

Douglas, William O., and J. H. Weir. "Equity Receiverships in the United States District Court for Connecticut: 1920–1929." *Connecticut Bar Journal* 4 (1930).

Durham, Jack. "The C & O Canal Hike." *The Living Wilderness* 19:48 (spring 1954).

Findlay, James. "Moody, 'Gapmen,' and the Gospel: The Early Days of the Moody Bible Institute." *Church History* 31 (September 1962).

Flynn, John T. "Other People's Money." *The New Republic,* 6/22/38.

———. "Washing Wall Street's Face." *Collier's,* 1/29/38.

Fortas, Abe. "In Memoriam." *American University Law Review* 29 (1979).

Hagle, Timothy M. " 'Freshmen Effects' for Supreme Court Justices." *American Journal of Political Science* 37:4 (November 1993).

Heaster, Brenda L. "Who's on Second?" *Missouri Historical Review* 80:2 (January 1986).

Heck, Edward V., and Melinda Gann Hall. "Bloc Voting and the Freshman Effect Revisited." *Journal of Politics* 43 (1981).

Hentoff, Nat. "The Justice Breaks His Silence." *Playboy,* 7/91.

———. "On Brennan." *The New Yorker,* 3/12/90.

———. "Profiles: The Constitutionalist." *The New Yorker,* 3/12/90.

Hockett, Jeffrey D. "Justice Robert H. Jackson, the Supreme Court, and the Nuremberg Trial." *Supreme Court Review* 1990.

Hoffman, John D. "Mr. Justice Douglas' Last Environmental Opinion." *Sierra Club Bulletin* 61:5 (May 1976).

Hopkirk, John W. "William O. Douglas—His Work in Policing Bankruptcy Proceedings." *Vanderbilt Law Review* 18 (1965).

Hutchinson, Dennis J. "The Black-Jackson Feud." *Supreme Court Review* 1988.

———. "Unanimity and Desegregation: Decision-Making in the Supreme Court, 1948–1958." *Georgetown Law Journal* 68 (1979).

Jennings, Richard W. "Mr. Justice Douglas: His Influence on Corporate and Securities Regulation." *Yale Law Journal* 73 (1964).

Kelsey, Mary. "A Home Missionary Wife." *Rocky Mountain Presbyterian* 6:4 (April 1877).

Lemann, Nicholas. "Taking Affirmative Action Apart," *The New York Times Magazine,* 6/11/95.

Lerner, Max. "Notes on Black Tuesday." *The Nation,* 10/30/37.

———. "Wall Street's New Mentor," *The Nation,* 10/23/37.

Leuchtenburg, William. "The Origins of Franklin D. Roosevelt's 'Court-Packing' Plan." *Supreme Court Review* 1966.

Linde, Hans. "Constitutional Rights in the Public Sector." *Washington Law Review* 40 (April 1965).

———. "Justice Douglas on Freedom in the Welfare State." *Washington Law Review* 39 (spring 1964).

Nesbit, Robert C., and Charles M. Gates. "Agriculture in Eastern Washington, 1890–1910." *Pacific Northwest Quarterly* 37 (October 1946).

Neuberger, Richard. "Mr. Justice Douglas." *Harper's Magazine,* summer 1942.

———. "Much-Discussed 'Bill' Douglas." *The New York Times Magazine,* 4/19/42.

Parrish, Michael E. "Cold War Justice: The Supreme Court and the Rosenbergs." *American Historical Review* 82 (1977).

———. "Justice Douglas and the *Rosenberg* Case: A Rejoinder." *Cornell Law Review* 70 (August 1985).

Partin, John M. "Roosevelt, Byrnes, and the 1944 Vice-Presidential Nomination." *Historian* 42 (1979–1980).

Penrose, Stephen B. L. "S.A.T.C.: A Comedy." *Outlook,* 2/19.

Perry, Ralph Barton. "Students' Army Training Corps." *National Service* 6 (1919).

Powe, L. A., Jr. "Evolution to Absolutism: Justice Douglas and the First Amendment." *Columbia Law Review* 74 (1974).

———. "Justice Douglas After Fifty Years: The First Amendment, McCarthyism, and Rights." *Constitutional Commentary* 6:2 (summer 1989).

Pratt, Reverend E. F. "Self Sacrifice of Home Missionaries—Personal Reminiscence." *Rocky Mountain Presbyterian* 4:2 (February 1875).

Rauh, Joseph L., Jr. "An Unabashed Liberal Looks at a Half Century of the Supreme Court." *North Carolina Law Review* 69 (1990).

Raymond, William T. "New SEC Rules in the Making." *Barron's,* 2/18/35.

———. "SEC Needs More Time." *Barron's,* 12/9/35.

———. "SEC Not Affected by NRA Defeat?" *Barron's,* 6/3/35.

———. "SEC Probes Paramount Reorganization." *Barron's,* 6/24/35.

Reich, Charles. "The New Property." *Yale Law Journal* 73 (1964).

"Remembrances of William O. Douglas on the Fiftieth Anniversary of His Appointment to the Supreme Court." *Journal of Supreme Court History* 1990: Yearbook of the Supreme Court Historical Society.

Reppy, William. "Justice Douglas and His Brethren: A Personal Recollection." *North Carolina Central Law Review* 12 (1980–1981).

Rodell, Fred. "As Justice Bill Douglas Completes His First Thirty Years on the Court." *UCLA Law Review* 16 (1969).

———. "Douglas Over the Stock Exchange." *Fortune,* 2/38.

Schlegel, John Henry. "American Legal Realism and Empirical Social Science: From the Yale Experience." *Buffalo Law Review* 28 (1979).

———. "American Legal Realism and Empirical Social Science: The Singular Case of Underhill Moore." *Buffalo Law Review* 29 (1980).

Schlesinger, Arthur M., Jr. "The Supreme Court: 1947." *Fortune,* 1/47.

Smith, Beverly. "Tamer of Bulls and Bears." *American Magazine,* 5/39.

Stone, Christopher. "Should Trees Have Standing?—Toward Legal Rights for Natural Objects." *Southern California Law Review* 45 (1972).

Strong, Frank R. "Reminiscences of Yale Law School of Fifty Years Ago." *Yale Law Report* 28:3 (spring-summer 1982).

Urofsky, Melvin. "Conflict Among the Brethren: Felix Frankfurter, William O. Douglas, and the Clash of Personalities and Philosophies on the United States Supreme Court." *Duke Law Journal* 71 (February 1988).

———. "William O. Douglas and His Clerks." *Western Legal History* 3 (1990).

Viorst, Milton. "Bill Douglas Has Never Stopped Fighting the Bullies of Yakima." *The New York Times Magazine*, 6/14/70.

White, G. Edward. "The Anti-Judge: William O. Douglas and the Ambiguities of Individuality." *University of Virginia Law Review* 74 (1988).

"William O. Douglas." In *Current Biography, 1941.* New York: H. W. Wilson, 1941.

"William O. Douglas." In *Current Biography, 1950.* New York: H. W. Wilson, 1950.

"William O. Douglas." *Yakima Valley Genealogical Society* 11:1 (January 1979).

GOVERNMENT HEARINGS AND DOCUMENTS

An Act to Provide Adjusted Compensation for Veterans of World War, and for Other Purposes, 68th Cong., sess. 1, H.R. 7959, Ch. 157, 1924. In *U.S. Statutes at Large* 43, 5/19/24, p. 121, Public, no. 120.

The Special Subcommittee on H. Res. 920 of the Committee on the Judiciary, *Associate Justice William O. Douglas: Final Report,* 91st Cong., 2d sess., 9/17/70, pp. 484–552.

Stone, Michael. "Justices of the Supreme Court Who Have Served in the Military." Commissioned by the secretary of the Army. Arlington National Cemetery Historian's office.

Supreme Court of the United States: Hearings and Reports on Successful and Unsuccessful Nominations of Supreme Court Justices by the Senate Judiciary Committee, 1916–1972. Vol. 4. Ed. Roy Mersky and J. Myron Jacobstein. Buffalo: William S. Hein, 1975.

Tributes to Honorable William O. Douglas, Associate Justice of the Supreme Court, to Commemorate the Occasion of His Retirement from the Supreme Court, 11/11/75. Washington, D.C.: U.S. GPO, 1976.

Woodrow Wilson Presidential Proclamation, 8/31/18. In *Congressional Record,* 66th Cong., 11/14–19/19, vol. 58, pt. 9, pp. 1840–42. Washington, D.C.: U.S. GPO, 1919.

OTHER SOURCES

UNPUBLISHED THESES AND DISSERTATIONS

Atkinson, David Neal. "Mr. Justice Minton and the Supreme Court, 1949–1956." Ph.D. diss. University of Iowa, 1969.

Cooper, Philip J. "Justice Douglas and Administrative Law." Ph.D. diss. Syracuse University, 1978.

Davenport, Deborah. "The Vinson Court, 1946–1949: Continued Tensions and Shifts." M.A. thesis. Penn State University, 1994.

Hopkirk, John William. "William O. Douglas—Individualist: A Study in the Development and Application of a Judge's Attitudes." Ph.D. diss. Princeton University, 1958.

Hull, Elizabeth Anne. "Sherman Minton and the Cold War Court." Ph.D. diss. New School for Social Research, 1977.

James, Dorothy Buckton. "Judicial Philosophy and Accession to the Court: The Cases of Justices Jackson and Douglas." Ph.D. diss. Columbia University, 1966.

Kennedy, Harry L. "Justice William O. Douglas on Freedom of the Press." Ph.D. diss. Ohio University, 1980.

Kraus, Richard James. "Free Individual in a Free Society: The Philosophy of Justice William O. Douglas." Ph.D. diss. Fordham University, 1971.

Meek, Roy L. "Justices Douglas and Black: Political Liberalism and Judicial Activism." Ph.D. diss. University of Oregon, 1964.

Pollock, Paul K. "Judicial Libertarianism and Judicial Responsibilities: The Case of Justice William O. Douglas." Ph.D. diss. Cornell University, 1968.

Resnick, Solomon. "Black and Douglas: Variations in Dissent." Ph.D. diss. New School for Social Research, 1970.

UNPUBLISHED PAPERS

Ball, Howard. "The Bill of Rights Is Enough: Justice Hugo L. Black on Constitutional Rights." Paper delivered at the annual meeting of the American Political Science Association, Atlanta, 8/89.

————. "Justices Hugo L. Black and William O. Douglas on the Limits of the Fourteenth Amendment's 'Equal Protection' Clause: Some Fundamental Differences Among Friends." Paper delivered at the annual meeting of the Western Political Science Association, Salt Lake City, 1989.

————. "Justice William O. Douglas's 'Spread-Eagle Speech[es]': One Justice's Style and Substance During a Time of National Crisis."

Ball, Howard, and Philip Cooper. "Fighting Justices: Hugo L. Black and William O. Douglas in Supreme Court Conflict." Paper delivered at the meeting of the Southern Political Science Association, Tampa, 1991.

Cooper, Philip J. "William O. Douglas: The Bill of Rights Is Not Enough." Paper delivered at the annual meeting of the American Political Science Association, Atlanta, 8/89.

Eveland, Joel T. "The Evolution of the Privacy Views of Justice Douglas Prior to *Griswold*." Penn State University, 1991.

Finkel, Robert. "Justice William O. Douglas's Wartime Civil Liberties Record." Stanford University Law School, 1990.

Mash, Kenneth. "William O. Douglas: Religion, Ideology, and Opinion." Penn State University, 1996.

Moses, James L. " 'An Interesting Game of Poker': Roosevelt, Douglas, and the 1944 Vice Presidential Nomination."

————. "Property Rights and Civil Rights: William O. Douglas, Hugo Black, and the Sit-Ins."

————. "William O. Douglas and the Vietnam War: Civil Liberties, Presidential Authority, and the 'Political Question.' "

Murphy, Walter F. "The Constitution and the Legacy of Justice William O. Douglas." Paper delivered at Franklin and Marshall College, Lancaster, Pa., 2/18/88.

"Remembrances of William O. Douglas by His Friends and Associates: In Celebration of the Fiftieth Anniversary of His Appointment as Associate Justice of the Supreme Court of the United States of America, 1939–1989." Ed. William Tod Cowan and Catherine Constantinou. Washington, D.C.: Supreme Court Historical Society.

Urofsky, Melvin. "Getting the Job Done: William O. Douglas and Collegiality in the Supreme Court." Paper delivered at the William O. Douglas Commemorative Symposium, 1939–1989, William O. Douglas Institute, Seattle, 4/89.

MISCELLANEOUS

Haldeman, H. R. *The Haldeman Diaries: Inside the Nixon White House.* Multimedia CD-ROM. Sony, 1994.

Scott, Douglas. *Mountain.* New York: Dramatists Play Service, 1990.

INDEX

CASE INDEX

ABOUT THE AUTHOR

BRUCE ALLEN MURPHY is the Fred Morgan Kirby Professor of Civil Rights at Lafayette College in Easton, Pennsylvania. He is the author of the nationally acclaimed and bestselling *The Brandeis/Frankfurter Connection: The Secret Political Activities of Two Supreme Court Justices* (1982) and the Pulitzer Prize–nominated *Fortas: The Rise and Ruin of a Supreme Court Justice* (1988), as well as other books and articles in the field of American government and constitutional law.

A native of Abington, Massachusetts, he is an avid fan of the Boston Red Sox, the New England Patriots, and the Penn State Nittany Lions. He and his wife, Carol L. Wright, live in Center Valley, Pennsylvania, and are the proud parents of two children, Emily and Geoffrey.

ABOUT THE TYPE

This book is set in Läckö, a typeface named after a seventeenth-century Baroque castle, now a museum, situated near Lidköping, Sweden. Designer Bo Berndal, asked to provide a typeface appropriate for the museum's exhibition signs and printed matter, drew inspiration from typefaces used in early-eighteenth-century French and Swedish books in the Rococo style; the present face, with its clean lines and prominent weight, shows a mixture of influences and the designer's own touches.